The Jossey-Bass Nonprofit & Public Management Series also includes:

Financial and Strategic Management
for Nonprofit Organizations

Financial and Strategic Management for Nonprofit Organizations

A Comprehensive Reference to Legal, Financial, Management, and Operations Rules and Guidelines for Nonprofits

THIRD EDITION

Herrington J. Bryce

JOSSEY-BASS
A Wiley Company
San Francisco

The previous two editions of this book were published by Prentice Hall and
were distributed by Simon & Schuster.

Manufactured in the United States of America.

Library of Congress Cataloging-in-Publication Data

Bryce, Herrington J.
Financial and strategic management for nonprofit organizations: a compre-
hensive reference to legal, financial, management, and operations rules and
guidelines for nonprofits/
Herrington J. Bryce.—3rd ed.
p. cm.—(The Jossey-Bass nonprofit & public management series)
Includes bibliographical references and index.
ISBN 0-7879-5026-2 (alk. paper)
1. Nonprofit organizations—Management. I. Title. II. Series:
Jossey-Bass nonprofit and public management series.

HD62.6.B78 2000   99-41581
658′.048—dc21   CIP

HB Printing   10 9 8 7 6 5 4 3   THIRD EDITION

The Jossey-Bass
Nonprofit & Public Management Series

CONTENTS

APPENDIXES

LIST OF TABLES, FIGURES, AND EXHIBITS

TABLES

FIGURES

EXHIBITS

LIST OF SIDEBARS

To Simon J. Bryce, Myra Bryce Laporte, Mable Goddard Laporte,
all the children to whom they gave so abundantly of themselves,
and their wishes for a healthier world

PREFACE

This book is intended to increase the efficiency by which the financial and the strategic management of nonprofit organizations are conducted. For top management, the two perspectives must be seen as a cohesive whole. Finance is simply a necessary tool to meet the organization's strategic goals. The challenge before all top managers, therefore, is how to develop and use financial and other tools successfully in a coordinated strategy to meet the responsibilities of the organization as these responsibilities fall on the managers themselves and on the trustees.

This book has a distinct managerial orientation. The core questions at every turn are the following: What should all managers and trustees of all nonprofit organizations and associations know in order to be very successful in moving their organizations forward? What are their legal responsibilities and barriers? What are the penalties on these managers and trustees and on their organizations when they fail?

This book presumes that active managers, as well as persons aspiring to be managers, are closer to Rodin's *Thinker* than to short-order cooks. Therefore, it first undertakes to explore fully the factual bases that undergird key topics, and only after that is satisfactorily done, does it proceed to recommend specific steps that managers should consider in altering their operations for the better. As a result, the readers of this book will get not only the technical, often legal facts, but will learn how to think about them and how they may continuously support his or her own managerial imagination and ambition.

It will be obvious to the reader that this book is firmly grounded in the following principles:

1. That managerial success in the nonprofit sector comes from a commitment to a core range of unique competencies grounded in the legal, financial, and environmental constraints in which nonprofit organizations are required to operate.

2. That the successful manager can more easily move from one organization to another and within an organization due to his or her mastery of these core competencies.

3. That success can continue if that manager has the wisdom to refer to and to consult these competencies whenever his or her organization or managerial command is confronted by a strategic challenge or crisis.

4. That being a successful manager is like being a successful coach. There is nothing but trouble from running a play that does not work or is not permitted by the rules of the game. A good coach checks the core competence of the team and the rules of the game before trying a new play. Just as the team and the coach can be hurt by penalties, so too can the organization and its managers and trustees.

To enhance its completeness as a reference and guide, the book provides a comprehensive reference to all types of nonprofits, from charities to associations. Chapters are self-contained, but readers are pointed to related topics covered in the book. Therefore, readers get a gestalt—a rounded, interconnected picture of subjects as they impact readers' own and other organizations. Occurrences tend to have ramifications throughout and across organizations. A successful manager never misses the bigger picture, even as he or she masters the details.

The book continues what the author introduced in the second edition as the *4Ms of nonprofit management*. These are *mission, money, management,* and *marketing*. It begins by firmly establishing in the very first chapter that mission, money, marketing, and management are the fundamental pillars of every nonprofit operation. It is the role of management and the trustees to create the environment and to instill the practices that make these 4Ms fully realized ethically, legally, and efficiently. This book builds on this core competency.

Because this third edition is intended to relate extensively to associations, it adds a fifth M. This M is *membership*. Associations exist first to serve their members. It is the willingness of members to participate that gives associations value. The types of associations discussed in this third edition range from professional and business associations to religious congregations and social clubs.

A discussion of the duties, responsibilities, and liabilities of membership is added to this text.

Although organized differently from the first editions, this edition retains many of the popular features of the first two editions, including the many models and forms developed by the author—many of which have become standard. But there are a significant number of new technical features and a new underlying theme.

AN UNDERLYING THEME

Every observer of the nonprofit sector over the past decade and a half is familiar with the long list of crass ethical breaches the sector has suffered and the resulting organizational setbacks. As young people are wont to say, some of them were really gross. I strongly believe that gross ethical violations are often made possible by faulty management. As a consequence, this book has adopted an underlying subtext to its extensive technical discussions. It begins with a presentation of barriers for blocking ethical assaults on the organization. Throughout the book, there are specific references to ethical codes and laws that should guide the manager.

These codes are mostly professional rules of conduct that deal with the specific issues discussed. The first chapter features a discussion of the centrality of ethics and money to the successful management of a nonprofit organization. A later chapter discusses the need to imbue ethics in strategic planning. As this book tries to advance the core technical competence of managers, it thus reminds them that the application of techniques unbounded by ethics is an open invitation to disaster and the undoing of all of their efforts.

WHAT'S NEW ABOUT THE THIRD EDITION

The first two editions of this book were published by Prentice Hall and distributed by Simon & Schuster. Part One of this new edition is virtually new. Its purpose is to lay out the technical and legal fundamentals. These are necessary not only for forming a nonprofit, but also for operating them in their various organizational forms, and consequently with varying legal limitations and powers. A sensible manager, whether in sports, the nonprofit world, or in the corporate world, needs to know the basic rules of the game. Plays, like strategies, are built to be effective within the rules.

Hence, Part One begins by laying out the core challenges that any manager in a nonprofit organization faces. These challenges stem from rules that managers cannot escape and relate to how nonprofit organizations must be formed and operated at all times. When operating within these rules, certain significant powers are given to the management of nonprofit organizations. These powers, when shrewdly used, transform managerial imagination into successful action.

The law answers several questions about a nonprofit corporation. How it is to be organized and operated? What are the tests that it must continuously meet to maintain its status? What are the responsibilities and penalties that confront the organization and its management when these rules are violated? What privileges come from compliance? How are these privileges gotten? How are they lost? What are the penalties on management for failure to comply? Managerial imagination is about obeying rules, but it is also about being creative within them. An enriched competence unlocks many doors.

The redesigned Part One has a broad scope. A chapter dealing with various types of associations, authorities, holding companies, affiliations, and political organizations is added. Unlike the previous editions, public (the charities, education, health, housing, the arts, and culture) organizations and private foundations are discussed in two separate chapters, and a section on soliciting private foundations is added. Further, since the second edition, a type of nonprofit, called a *supporting* or *affiliate organization,* has gotten very popular among the wealthy. Therefore, this edition gives this type of organization a more thorough treatment.

Each discussion of a substantive topic in this book makes reference to the impact of that topic on different types of nonprofit organizations. The intent is to be both descriptive and comparative. The powers of these other organizational forms differ. Associations are empowered to undertake actions that are prohibited in other organizations. Charities and other publicly supported organizations have privileges that others do not. Privileges always come with a price in the form of prohibited transactions.

Part One has a new section to assist managers in the development of ethical procedures to reduces outright fraud. Moreover, the discussion on the legal duties of trustees has been expanded to include the subject of conflict of interest from the perspective of state and federal laws and the legal obligations of each manager and trustee for enforcing these laws on each other. The IRS model conflict of interest policy is presented. As in the second edition, specific duties of trustees are highlighted with reference to where further elaboration on these specifics may be found in this book.

Finally, Part One has a new discussion of factors that can cause the loss of tax-exempt status and the penalties on management and the organization attendant to such losses. At the end of Part One, the reader should be well informed about the basic legal tenets controlling the formation and management of the major types of nonprofit organizations, the fundamental legal context in which these are managed, and the personal and organizational consequences of going astray. It also has two new sections that summarize some of the salient issues as they are resolved in Canadian law, thereby providing a basis for comparison between U.S. and Canadian laws on central issues. Maintaining the international flavor, Chapter Five has a discussion of associations in South Australia. All these international discussions provide a basis for broadening perspectives and for providing examples to countries in which this sector is emerging.

Part Two is strictly about money—raising revenues to finance the organization's mission. Every mission, no matter how charitable or fraternal, must be financed. The opening chapter is about increasing gifts and contributions. This edition expands the discussion about why corporations do not make certain contributions and why certain gifts should not be accepted by nonprofits.

The competition for gifts and contributions has increased not only because of the decline in government support, but also because of the growth in number of nonprofits that qualify for these gifts, increasing needs, and because many associations have created foundations within their corporate structures. Therefore, this chapter has become as important to charities as it is to tax-exempt subsidiaries of associations. Dues are the principal sources for financing associations, and these are discussed in Part One as part of the new discussion of membership responsibilities, powers, duties, and liabilities.

Part Two also has discussions of strategies and issues concerning the soliciting, giving, and receiving of certain types of assets. These include insurance policies, annuities, stocks, and real estates. As in previous editions, all these are discussed. But the discussion on stocks has been expanded because this asset has become more valuable. Changes in remainder trusts have led to the introduction of a discussion on advanced considerations in the use of trusts. A new form of giving, donor designated trusts, is added.

Since all funds raised must be invested, even in the short term, Part Two develops the concept of an endowment. A new feature is a discussion of the laws on management of trusts. In Part Three, the concept of endowment management is presented strictly from the investing side.

Part Two recognizes that business activities by nonprofits still remain controversial and misunderstood. Therefore, it begins by giving the manager the legal, intellectual, and practical reasons for undertaking this kind of activity. Then it proceeds to describe, not only the consequences of undertaking a business, but also lists seventeen questions that management should raise before making such a decision. These questions go to the heart of the practical aspects of business transactions.

Several other new discussions on business revenues appear in this edition. In particular, unrelated business income is described not only in general, as in previous editions, but also in the specific terms of the transactions that successful nonprofits are likely to contemplate. These discussions cover dues, leasing of mailing lists, advertising and corporate sponsorships, mortgages, securities transactions, portfolio and endowment management, and the use of subsidiaries or agencies for the conduct of these and other transactions. How must these be structured? What are the rules? The book offers a ten-part test for estimating the probability that a transaction would be deemed unrelated.

Keeping faith with its intent, the book shows the manager the arguments, the formulation of the transactions, and their consequences. It also offers the manager a list of questions that should be asked in determining whether a transaction is likely to trigger a tax consequence, in addition to similar questions for each specific type of transaction. The reader is given a list of activities that, on their face, are exempt from taxation.

Revenue raising revolves around marketing, soliciting, and often lobbying. Some nonprofits solicit for tax-deductible contributions, and some do not because they cannot. Some do extensive lobbying; others do not. All solicit in one form or another for membership dues or for donations. All these activities involve sending a message. Only the methods (marketing, soliciting, or lobbying) and their consequences differ. But in all cases state and federal laws stipulate what may be done, how, by whom, and when. Therefore, Part Two contains a new and extensive discussion of laws on marketing, lobbying, and solicitation. In addition, it has a discussion of contractual considerations when contemplating the use of a commercial fund-raiser.

As in previous editions, different sources of resources are discussed. A discussion has been added about preparing an organization for borrowing. Information about several aspects of federal government contracting—including cost allowability, auditing, and a glossary of financial terms—have also been added to this edition.

Part Three has to do with strategies for controlling costs and risks. The text distinguishes among different types of costs and how they can be controlled. The principal instrument for controlling operating and capital costs is the budget. Accordingly, Part Three begins with budgeting, but it contains new discussions on joint cost allocations—allocating costs where fund-raising is done along with some program or educational activity of the nonprofit. For example, how is cost treated when a fund-raising letter is accompanied by literature about one of the programs of the organization? This simple act has very important implications for reporting and treating costs and for budgeting and packaging solicitation campaigns.

A discussion of outsourcing as a method of cost control has also been added. The discussion of cash and accrued methods of budgeting has been revised to reinforce the concept of budgeting as a tool for dealing with planned expenditures and revenues as well as for controlling current cash flows.

The chapter on controlling compensation costs has several new discussions. There is a new discussion on excess compensation (intermediate sanctions), tax-favored medical accounts, a variety of retirement plans, and modifications in managed care. All of these are expressions of new laws and developments in the field. As in the previous editions, compensation is the one cost that is elaborated upon because it is the most important "controllable" cost in a typical nonprofit operation. Employee salaries and benefits can amount to 75 percent or more of the costs of running many nonprofits. This edition contains an expanded itemization of nontaxable fringe benefits that should be considered for the employees of nonprofits.

Part Three also deals with risk management. Risk management deals with contingent costs or liabilities that are due to the probability that an event that could be costly could occur, with profound economic consequences to the organization. As in previous editions, this one discusses various types of risks facing nonprofit organizations and possible strategies for identifying and managing these risks. However, new discussions on volunteer immunity and volunteer legal rights and the right to sue the organization are added. Also added is a discussion of the vulnerability of organizations and policies for protecting organizations from liability for sexual harassment by supervisors.

After reading Part Three, a manager should have the information necessary to control the immediate, long-term, and prospective costs the organization is likely to face. Moreover, the manager will convert budget making from a numbers game—often fictitious—into a mechanism for controlling the future of the organization and guiding it into new directions. The budget will also become a benchmark for evaluating actual with planned performance.

Part Four is about managing the finances of the organization. It begins with a discussion on the use of financial statements in support of managerial direction and to uncover concerns for which the manager is responsible—if not personally liable. Understanding this chapter does not require one to be an accountant or to be skillful with accounting rules. The reader learns by participating in a board meeting in which the financial performance of an organization is being discussed. Thus, a real-world flavor of the use and flow of financial information can be gotten. Principal concepts emerge from the discussion.

With regard to financial information, new discussions have been added on a manager's preparation for an audit, the distinction between managerial and accounting conventions on financial restrictions, and the accounting for gifts and contributions.

Once the financial status of the organization is assessed and the scope of discretionary actions that can be taken is revealed from the financial statements, management can prudently set the organization's course. Therefore, a second chapter in Part Four deals with setting new financial targets once the evaluation of the financial status of the organization is known. It also discusses the investment and spending (withdrawal) strategies to meet these targets—especially if the resources of an endowment are to be used.

These new goals may involve changes such as rebalancing a portfolio. A discussion on that topic is added, along with state rules on the management of endowment or common funds and a discussion of asset volatility. Strategies should not be separate from statutory strictures and organizational purpose. Accordingly, a new discussion centers on the creation of portfolios according to spending objectives dictated by the nature of the mission.

Part Five focuses on the managerial task of growing the organization and ensuring its vitality by always searching for new and exciting strategic opportunities and alliances. This begins with a strategic plan based in part on the evaluation of what the organization is, what it has accomplished, and the options before it.

The first chapter in Part Five retains many of the nonprofit-specific models on life cycles about making four-dimensional choices where mission, desirability, feasibility, and benefit-cost ratios are involved and about cooperative or competitive situations. But it also presents a new discussion on program evaluation.

A second chapter in Part Five is about the search for opportunities for new and exciting niches. It is also about strategic alliances and the search of the environment for alliances and opportunities that are consistent with the nearly 350 legal choices a nonprofit may make. At least three of these must appear in its letter of application for exemption to the U.S. Internal Revenue Service.

Part Five continues to argue, as in other editions, that partnerships and other strategic alliances are effective ways of expanding the organization's resources and reach. This third edition goes even further. Its discussion of partnership and other alliances is significantly expanded. How must they be structured to meet the tests of the IRS and the states? Strategic alliances have the very strong potential of surrendering control of the organization or subverting or diverting its assets as these are legally defined. This consequence has provoked the prosecutorial powers of some attorneys general, who have sued nonprofit organizations and their management.

The final chapter of the book is about restructuring the organization—changing the structure and configuration of the organization. These are serious legal actions that bring into play the dissolution plan discussed in Part One and the scrutiny of the IRS, the state attorney general, and the Justice Department or Federal Trade Commission. It is about the marriages, divorces, adoptions, conversion, death, and rebirth of an organization.

The chapter contains new discussions on anti-trust concerns and procedures that confront these activities. It demonstrates the use of private foundations (also discussed in Part One) to facilitate conversions. It also discusses the role of the dissolution plan and the contents of a plan and agreement to merge, and it gives graphic illustrations of various forms of mergers. The chapter also discusses new state laws that govern these transactions and the potential personal risk exposure of managers and trustees, who are bound by duty to protect the assets of the organization with loyalty, care, and prudence and to get a fair price for the assets transferred.

In this book, as in reality, the final chapter provides connection to the first chapter. Once an organization has reorganized (Part Five), in effect, dissolved (Part One) and has a new charter and birth. In short, Part Five is the beginning of a legal rebirth, or the reincarnation of the old into a new corporate body. This process is something about which the law is very vigilant because it implies a shift from the original mission and a misappropriation or misuse of public property.

THE MOVEMENT TOWARD INTERNATIONALIZATION

Let us share our best practices. Major lenders to foreign countries, international organizations, and U.S. foundations have generated a deep interest in the development of a third or nongovernmental sector (nongovernmental organizations; NGOs) in developing countries and in the countries that formerly constituted the Soviet Union. The author's stays in some of these countries (for example, Russia, Georgia, and Estonia) for purposes of providing technical assistance to public administrators through the auspices of the National Academy for Public Administration (NAPA) have brought a very deep appreciation for the need for a strong nonprofit sector.

There is little question that the absence of a vital nonprofit sector has contributed to the depth of economic problems in many of these countries. Where a for-profit sector is nascent and a nonprofit sector is nonexistent, the full weight of economic activities falls on the public sector. There is no buffer, no independent sector to substitute or reinforce governmental social programs, and no third sector to nurture and cradle new ideas or to which certain costs of research and development can be shifted until they become commercially viable and therefore able to attract investors.

There is no viable capital market. There are no nonprofits to assist the poor, carry on educating the population, assist the aged, heal the sick, comfort the weary, or guide the wayward, as there are no private pensions. In many of these countries, *nonprofit* meant cooperatives, the central purpose of which was to ensure production.

In the public sector, decisions become politicized, as they are everywhere, and needs that could be satisfied by the third sector, if it existed, compete (often unsuccessfully) with other needs. The loss of priority in the public sector budget is total because there is no strong, native, private foundation to finance these activities off the public sector budget.

TO THE PROFESSOR

From the very first edition of this book, a goal was to provide a comprehensive reference for senior officers and trustees of nonprofit organizations. This book may also serve as a teaching text. I have used it for years in teaching MBA students and students in our in-service executive program. Its breadth allows me to design a course, the content of which may change as my audience and my own interests change. I have even been able to use this text to teach doctoral students in education and law students jointly enrolled in the MBA program.

The text is much too large to be completed in one semester, as one professor in a leading national university in California has called to my attention. But because the chapters are reasonably independent and not cumulative, the professor can carve out a quarter or a semester or a year's course as she or he prefers. The economy of this strategy is that students can buy a book that will serve them beyond a single course and that may well be used in the course of employment.

As does every author, I hope these objectives are well served.

January 2000   Herrington J. Bryce
Williamsburg, Virginia

ACKNOWLEDGMENTS

A book reaches its third edition because it is well received by those whose interest and knowledge run deep. Principal among these readers are those who, after scrutinizing the book to their satisfaction, are willing to say to others that the book is worthy. In this regard, I begin by thanking Professors Regina Herzlinger and Carolyn Lett, both of Harvard University, Larry Lynn of the University of Chicago, Gregory Dees of Stanford University, and Raymond Horton of Columbia University, whose endorsements appear on this edition's back cover.

But there would have been no third edition without the scrutiny of those who endorsed the second and who saw it fit for their reviews. These include Jacqueline Dienemann of Johns Hopkins University, Alan "Scotty" Campbell, dean of the Maxwell School, chair of the U.S. Civil Service Commission, vice-chair of the ARA corporation, and executive professor of the Wharton School, and Caroline Lueloff Williams, an investment banker. The list also includes Brigadier General, U.S. Army, retired, Hazel W. Johnson-Brown, director of the Center for Health Policy at George Mason University, Jill Muehrcke, editor of *Nonprofit World*, Peter D. Bell, chairman of CARE, and Bonnie R. Plunkett of Meridian Asset Management.

I personally did the research for this and the previous editions and think that my years of being a research assistant to Professor S. M. Miller, with all his patience, made me addicted to grunt work; and to him, I am grateful. I am also grateful for the years of experience in practical administration in both the for-profit and nonprofit worlds, the years spent in insurance and finance, and the years of teaching—especially at the College of William and Mary and the University of Maryland, where my interest in this subject blossomed, building on a foundation established at Syracuse and Minnesota State Universities.

I thank Professor Ronald Sims for his continuous warning to control my obsession and for his writings, which I have quoted. I also thank Beverly Bryce for calling certain cases to my attention and for the years dedicated to raising three lawyers—Marisa, Simon, and Shauna—in her footsteps. And I thank R. Scott Fosler and Dr. Carole Neves for the international experiences.

I am also grateful to Sidney Bernstein and Julie Philipsen of Harcourt Brace for the privilege of developing some ideas in *Not-for-Profit Financial Strategies,* published by Harcourt Brace Professional Publishers.

Charlotte Brown of the Professional Resource Center and Virginia Woodward, Phyllis Viands, Patricia Whisnant, and Kathy Williams of the College of William and Mary as well as Maxine Johnson and Louise Murray at the college print shop were always helpful when I ran into trouble. Needless to say, this book would not have been possible without the excellence of Jossey-Bass. Alan Shrader, senior editor, persuaded me to let Jossey-Bass have this third edition; and so it has. Johanna Vondeling guided the initial production of the manuscript into text, Suzanne Copenhagen did the copyediting, Susan Bennett was the proofreader, Brittney Corrigan-McElroy of Interactive Composition Corporation managed the paging process, Virginia Woodward completed the index, and Rachel Anderson of Satellite Publishing Services supervised the production. To them, I extend my thanks for their competence and tolerance.

H.J.B.

THE AUTHOR

Herrington J. Bryce is Life of Virginia Professor of Business at the College of William and Mary. Previously he served as a member of the Treasury Board of the State of Virginia, which issues tax-exempt bonds and oversees cash management and custodial policies for state depositories. He also served as president of the National Policy Institute, president of the Carlogh Corporation, vice president of the National Academy for State and Local Governments, director of Research for the Joint Center for Political and Economic Studies, and senior economist at the Urban Institute.

He was a fellow at the Institute of Politics at Harvard University, an economic policy fellow at the Brookings Institution, and a NATO fellow in Belgium. He has taught at the Massachusetts Institute of Technology, the University of Maryland, and Clark University in Worcester, Massachusetts.

Bryce holds a Ph.D. in economics from the Maxwell School, Syracuse University, a B.A. degree from Minnesota State University, and the CLU and ChFC designations in the insurance and financial planning and services profession.

He is the author or editor of several books and articles, including op-ed pieces for the *Washington Post,* the *Wall Street Journal*, the *New York Times,* and the *National Employment Weekly*. He was the writer-editor of the *Not-for-Profit Financial Strategies,* a newsletter for CFOs, CEOs, J.D.s, and CPAs published by Harcourt Brace. Bryce teaches corporate financial strategy, corporate cost and profit-planning, and nonprofit finance and management.

PART ONE

TYPES OF ORGANIZATIONS AND THEIR OPERATING RULES

Four concepts form the foundation for the successful management of all nonprofit organizations. Absent a mastery of these, a misguided ego will manage an organization into extinction.

CHAPTER ONE

The Fundamental Pillars
of Nonprofit Management

To manage any nonprofit organization successfully, a person must master four fundamental concepts that we labeled, in the second edition of this book, the *4Ms*. These are

1. *Mission:* The adherence to its mission as required by law

2. *Money:* The financial resources to discharge the mission

3. *Marketing:* The ability to persuade others to support and benefit from the mission

4. *Management:* The ability to marshal and make the best use of all resources tangible and intangible, human and nonhuman, in an efficient and ethical manner.

In the case of associations or cooperatives, there is a fifth and very critical M:

5. *Membership:* The entities or persons the organization exists to serve

These Ms form the core of a unique managerial challenge.

THE UNIQUE CHALLENGE

Without money, no mission can be met or advanced in a market economy no matter how charitable or benevolent the mission may be. Incompetent management will destroy an organization's ability to discharge its mission and, left unchecked, will eventually destroy the organization itself. As Sims and Veres write: "the ever-increasing complexity of the challenges facing organizations and the pace of change both signal the escalating pressure that will be . . . and currently is brought to bear on employees to either be proactive initiators of their own success or be left behind as marginal and unsuccessful contributors."[1]

To be a proactive agent of change for his or her own success, a manager must fully appreciate the nature of the organization, master the tools available to it, and understand both its external and internal threats and opportunities.

Managing a nonprofit organization is different from managing a firm or a government agency. As developed in the first edition of this book, there are unique challenges to managing a nonprofit organization. Governments are financed by compulsion, the legally enforceable requirements that people pay taxes regardless of their preferences. Nonprofits are financed by an ever-increasing open competition for public support—all of which is completely voluntary and subject to the discretion of the donor. Nonprofits are also subject to open competition for business revenues and the alternative use that persons have for money used to pay membership fees and dues. The range of financial knowledge needed to finance and operate an organization under compulsion is different from that needed in an environment of keen competition and voluntary choices.

Nonprofit financing is also different from those of a for-profit corporation, even though the latter also operates in an environment of choice and competition. To get long-term financing, a for-profit corporation relies on stocks and bonds (debt). Nonprofits cannot issue capital stocks (unless they are cooperatives), but they are empowered to issue short-term and long-term debt in the form of bonds. Hence, the manager of a nonprofit must learn not only about debt management, but also about the techniques and instruments of gifts and contributions. The latter is not relevant to the corporate manager. The nonprofit manager must also learn techniques of managing a productive enterprise efficiently even though the end product of that enterprise is public good, not private profits.

The incentives are different. A person provides long-term money to a firm through the purchase of its stocks or bonds. The clear motive for doing this is personal financial gain. Moreover, the person's control over the corporation is proportionate to the amount of its voting stocks he or she controls. With the nonprofit, the manager's task is to induce people to give without even the hint of personal gain to themselves or their associates or families. And the more the donor gives, the more the manager must exercise scrutiny to deny the donor control over the assets of the organization.

A government justifies its incumbency every two to four years. The management of a nonprofit, like the management of a firm, must continuously justify its existence. There is a market test that knows no time constraint. People can stop buying products any time. They can also stop their memberships and their contributions any time. Therefore, market relevance is as important to nonprofits as to firms. Both feel the public's displeasure by an almost immediate decline in their revenues or clientele. They are financed by competition, not compulsion (taxation). They can pass no law to compensate for financial failure.

It is not particularly productive to argue which sector is the most difficult sector to manage. Each presents a unique cornucopia of challenges in which knowledge rather than folklore or fiction is the tool upon which management must rely. This book is about contributing to that core competency. It covers all types of tax-exempt organizations—from charities to associations. The guiding question at every turn in this book is, What should management know to be more efficient and to be truly successful?

THE FINANCIAL BENEFITS AND DISADVANTAGES OF BEING A NONPROFIT

Aside from a commitment to its social or public purpose, every nonprofit organization or association must operate within certain financial constraints. Organizers form nonprofits not merely because they believe in a mission but because they believe that that mission can probably be advanced and promoted more effectively through the nonprofit rather than the for-profit form of organization.

To conduct and advance a mission requires financing. What are the financial merits and demerits to the nonprofit form? I summarize these in Tables 1.1 and 1.2. Much of this book is about exploiting the benefits and converting the disadvantages into advantages. For example, a nonprofit may not issue stocks in itself. But it may own or form an enterprise that has the capability of issuing stocks or other capital (ownership) interests, such as a for-profit partnership. These are all subject to rules, and a smart manager learns the rules of the game—as explored in this and other books—before committing to a strategy.

THE BASES FOR EFFECTIVE MANAGEMENT

This third edition of *Financial and Strategic Management for Nonprofit Organizations,* as its predecessors, is written under the premise that managers of nonprofits should see their duty as managing an economic institution with a

Table 1.1. Financial Benefits of a Nonprofit Organization.

1. Exemption from certain taxes: In general income that is related to their mission is tax exempt.
2. Lower prices: Anti-trust laws allow vendor to sell items to a charity at lower price, as long as the item purchased is for use of charity.
3. Lower postage rates: Nonprofits pay lower postage rates provided that the envelope does not advertise a for-profit firm.
4. Lower labor costs: Nonprofits have lower labor costs because of volunteers.
5. Lower fees: Federal, state, and local governments may reduce or exempt nonprofits from certain fees charged firms in the same line of activity pay.
6. No quid pro quo: Donations or fees do not require the production of a service or product of at least equivalent value.
7. Building and equipment: These may be obtained by donation or, in some cases, from government surplus.
8. Limited liability: The liability exposure may be limited or partial (as compared to the liability of a firm).
9. Tax-exempt borrowing: The cost of borrowing is lowered by the amount of tax exemption of interest earned by the lender and the exemption from registration.
10. Contract bids: Some government contracts either set aside or give special considerations to nonprofits.

Note: All of these benefits apply to all exempt organizations. The donor in items 6 and 7 gets a deduction for the donation only if the recipient organization qualifies.

charitable or public welfare mission. Adjectives such as *economic, effective,* and *efficient* describe the organization, whereas words such as *welfare, community, public,* and *interest* describe the mission. This is true whether the organization is an association of highly trained professionals or a soup kitchen.

The Value of Nonprofits

An economic institution creates something of value. The assumption of this book is that nonprofits have measurable economic value—even if the measure is imperfect. The gross measure of the value created by firms is the price and quantity of their products and services that society uses. A gross measure of the value of a nonprofit that is not an association must be the public support it receives both financially and in the active participation of the public in promulgating and supporting its affairs; that is, their investing both sweat and financial capital *sin fines de lucro* (without the motive of personal gain) and also in their use of what the organization does.

Along similar lines, the gross value of an association may be measured by the fees people are willing to pay to be members of the association because of

Table 1.2. Financial Disadvantages of a Nonprofit Organization.

1. Limited access to capital markets: Nonprofits cannot raise capital through the sale of stocks.
2. Limitation on personal inurement: Nonprofits, except certain cooperatives and associations, cannot attract capital by promising or distributing the assets of the organization to individuals as if they were owners or investors.
3. Limited profits: While there are no dollar limitations on profits, profits cannot be the principal or overriding aim of a nonprofit organization.
4. Revenue balance: While profits are not limited, the support test for certain nonprofits requires that revenues remain in balance and the test for associations usually requires that a substantial part of their revenues comes from membership dues.
5. Limited financial reward for managers: The financial rewards as a fixed salary are not the issue. Both for-profit and nonprofit managers are limited by the concept of reasonable reward. The issue is largely that the nonprofit manager cannot be paid in stocks and options. These two have the potential of appreciating in value and can constitute the major part of the total earnings of for-profit managers.
6. Limitations on investments: For legal, moral, and sound investment reasons, a nonprofit is generally barred from undertaking highly risky investments unless its mission is to do so.
7. Limitations imposed by donors: A creditor can impose restrictions on both the nonprofit and the firm. A common stockholder of a minority share cannot tell the corporation how its money can be spent. But any individual donor can restrict how a nonprofit spends the money the individual or entity donates. Members, acting as a class, can limit the way an association uses their dues.
8. Limited creditworthiness: A firm's financial strength or credit worthiness is due in part to its ability to pledge assets to back a loan. It is also due to its ability to require, in the case of small corporations, that the borrower pledge personal assets in addition to the corporate assets. Furthermore, it can force an involuntary bankruptcy. None of this is as easily (and occasionally not at all feasible) with a nonprofit corporation.
9. Public expectations: The misunderstanding and expectations of the public place severe and often times irrational demands on the nonprofit corporation.
10. Tolerance of bad management: The tolerance of bad management and the willingness to substitute good intentions for efficient operation are eventually expressed in ruinous financial health of the organization.

Note: All of these benefits apply to all exempt organizations. The donor in items 6 and 7 gets a deduction for the donation only if the recipient is a 501(c)(3) organization. But any organization may be the recipient of such gifts.

what the association does for them and the amount of active participation by members in the affairs of the association. The gross value of a cooperative may be seen as similar to the association, except that unlike associations and charities, some cooperatives may and do pay a dividend. Therefore, in addition to what has been said about an association, a cooperative's value also contains the element of pecuniary gain to its members who are the owners of the cooperative and its assets.

When an organization loses its value, it has no purpose for being. The successful management of every nonprofit, regardless of type, must rest on a belief that it has a value that is worthy of being preserved and expanded.

The Costs of Running Nonprofits

In a similar vein, nonprofits are economic institutions because they have costs that must be managed. These costs require that revenues be raised. Expanding the value means raising more and more revenues, moderated only by the ability to control costs. An element in cost control is making choices about how to use these revenues among competing demands. No mission can be so tightly crafted to be devoid of options that management must choose. The question is, How sound are the choices? Are all of the options fully perceived? Choices, options, are useless if they cannot be financed, and they will be perilous to the organization if, once chosen, their costs cannot be effectively controlled.

Therefore, every manager needs effective tools by which

1. Costs can be measured and controlled.
2. Money can be raised to finance the programs.
3. Money can be invested with adequate risks and returns.
4. Money can be allocated.
5. Money can be accounted for and tracked.
6. Financial targets can be set based on experience and objectives.

A nonprofit is not a money machine. It is propelled by a mission in which there are public interests as well as interests by the members and clients of the organization. These have both legal and moral claims on the assets of the organization. Unlike firms, the assets of a nonprofit, tax-exempt organization are not at the disposal of private persons.

Therefore, every manager needs to develop tools by which

1. Both the legal and moral accountability of the organization are discharged.
2. The governance of the organization is effectively conducted.
3. The legal responsibilities of the trustees to the organization and of the organization to the trustees are clearly established.

4. There is appropriate understanding of the legal characteristics of a mission.

The mission of a nonprofit, unlike that of a firm, is not a planning document. It is a lasting commitment. Therefore, unlike a firm, which can change its mission to meet new opportunities and to avoid threats, a nonprofit's flexibility comes from its ability to explore and exploit its existing mission. The notion of the nonprofit as chameleon is an oxymoron.

Therefore, every manager needs to develop tools by which

1. Choices consistent with the mission of the organization can be plucked from the environment in which the organization operates.

2. These choices can be evaluated.

3. A rational basis for making these choices can be determined and communicated.

4. The choices lead to meeting the criteria of (a) feasibility, (b) effectiveness, (c) consistency with mission, (d) desirability.

Every nonprofit hires people. They must be compensated and should be compensated adequately. Compensation is a major cost. In recent years, the compensation of executives has become a major legal issue. The answer to this problem is not to keep compensation down. It is to keep it reasonable and competitive.

Therefore, every nonprofit manager and trustee needs to know about

1. What constitutes reasonable compensation

2. How compensation packages should be designed

3. What kinds of benefits are readily available and how they should be managed to the advantage of both the employee and the organization

4. When compensation becomes excessive and creates a legal problem

The nonprofit organization is a legal organization. There is a specified legal framework in which the organization must be created and operated. There are other rules by which the organization must operate by virtue of its exemption. Management that fails to understand these two principles—the legal organization, and tax exemption—will soon destroy or severely limit the usefulness of the organization.

Therefore, every nonprofit manager needs to know

1. The specific character of the nonprofit as a legal institution

2. The specific meaning of tax exemption

3. The varieties of categories of tax exemption and where the institution falls within this web

4. The specific operating rules in the category in which the organization is placed by the U.S. Internal Revenue Service

5. How state governments affect the management and performance of the organization

ELEMENTS OF STRATEGIC EFFICIENCY IN NONPROFIT MANAGEMENT

We use the term *elements of strategic efficiency* to acknowledge that it is impossible for a manager to know everything. Smart managers make strategic choices about what they will watch based on the weight of those elements in determining their overall success. A corporate CEO needs to know what a corporation is, how it operates by law and convention, and how the corporation is constrained by law and direction of the stakeholders. So, too, must the CEO of a nonprofit have a working knowledge of the scope of powers, responsibilities, risks, and reach that his or her organization is given by law and the reality of the environment.

The concept of *ultra vires* is as applicable to nonprofit as it is to for-profit corporations. It holds that an organization cannot void a commitment merely by arguing that it had no power to undertake that to which it has committed itself. Accordingly, Part One is about the commitments, responsibilities, and risks attendant to the way a nonprofit is organized and the basic operating rules that follow from such a form. What are the rules? What are the personal risk exposures? What are the penalties?

Unlike the for-profit corporation, the nonprofit has tax exemption. But all nonprofits are not tax exempt in the same way. Whether and how a nonprofit is tax exempt depends upon two very important concepts: (1) its purpose or its mission, and (2) the structure of its revenues and financial support.

These core concepts used in determining the nature of the tax exemption of a nonprofit corporation in turn determine the operating rules of the organizations and are strategic elements of managerial efficiency. An organization that is classified as a charity or an association is so classified precisely because it was able to meet certain operating standards required by law. Once it satisfies these standards, being classified as a charity or an association requires it to obey certain operating rules.

It is the management's legal duty to know these rules and to keep the organization within them. Protection does not imply stagnation. All organizations change voluntarily or involuntarily in some dimension or direction over time. Size may remain the same, but management cannot run the same game in exactly the same way forever. How does one make rational decisions when one is publicly accountable for choices that may imperil the organization?

Managed change is an excursion through options and probabilities. This is especially true for nonprofits with scarce resources and growing demand for their services. Therefore, part of this book is about making rational choices in growing or moving the organization forward. An assessment of the organization's competitive environment is an element of strategic efficiency.

So, too, is money. Every organization needs money, no matter how charitable or benevolent its purpose. Managers of organizations that qualify for receiving tax-exempt contributions need to be acquainted with advanced techniques of raising money through donations. But they will discover that the more astute the donor pool from which they draw, the more important it will be to know how to make the deal attractive from the perspective of the cost and tax consequences to the donor. Closing the deal successfully often relies on the ability to put a cost-effective package before the donor.

But which deals place the organization at risk? When does solicitation become a violation of law for charities or associations? When does business revenue make sense? What are the legal considerations in pursuing various types of revenues? When is it wise to walk away—say no? What types of solicitation are likely to elicit resistance, even a "no" response from corporations? Money raising in all its forms is strategically important in effective nonprofit management.

Knowing what to do with the money raised is a compound strategic element of effective management. This element comes in several parts: first, recording and reporting; then investing or spending. The law speaks of certain types of expenditures as taxable because they are prohibited and can lead to personal fines, loss of exemption, or disqualification. Other types of expenditures are mandatory. The law also gives nonprofits a flexible and powerful vehicle for saving and generating funds called an *endowment*. But the law also places limits on all of these—saving, investing, and spending. Knowing what the law disallows and how to use (if not maximize the benefits from) what the law does allow are all strategically important elements of nonprofit management.

It is obviously important to his or her success for the manager to garner control. When the manager loses control, the future of the organization is at stake. But before it crumbles, the attorney general of every state has the power to step in and order the nonprofit to adopt financial controls or shut down. In New York State, the attorney general stepped in and forced an agreement with a prominent foundation to do the following:

1. Create a three-person audit committee, two members of which must be new directors.

2. Hire a new financial officer, who will report to the foundation president and the audit committee.

3. Institute financial controls, including an annual budget and quarterly report that must go through an independent audit and be submitted to the attorney general for each of five years.

4. Institute an audit of the foundation's books for the past three years.

A reason for the above actions was that the foundation was believed to have been understating its assets to avoid making legally required annual distributions. The assets of every nonprofit organization are subject to the protection of the state.

Budgets, financial statements, compensation packages are all ways of controlling the direction of the organization and the performance of the people who make it work. But so, too, is the ability to recognize, anticipate, and avoid certain risks that are potentially very costly.

Nonprofits are not immune from suits and may very well be sued by their volunteers, trustees, members, clients, and the attorney general. The management cannot always indemnify itself for costs attendant to these suits. For personal as well as organizational reasons, risk management and cost control are strategic elements of effective management. Effective management anticipates as well as reacts to costs. An effective manager has foresight and the intellectual preparation to act wisely in the best interest of the organization.

> If an officer has discretionary authority with respect to any duties, an officer's duties shall be discharged . . . in good faith . . . with the care an ordinarily prudent person in a like position would exercise under similar circumstances . . . in a manner the officer reasonably believes to be in the best interest of the corporation. In discharging duties, an officer is entitled to rely on information, opinions, reports or statements, including financial statements . . . and other financial data [Section 10–3842, Standards of Conduct for Officers, Arizona Nonprofit Law].

THE CENTRALITY OF MISSION AND FINANCE

In nonprofits of all types—cooperatives, associations, and charities—the mission is the basis upon which both the charter and tax exemption are granted. Both state and federal laws are precise about what types of missions qualify for nonprofit and also tax-exempt status. The mission is a social contract among the nonprofit, the state and federal governments, members (in the case of associations), and the community in the case of 501(c)(3) organizations. These are the churches, the museums, the zoos, agencies for the needy, the hospitals, universities, and research centers. The mission is the foundation of all nonprofit organizations. For this reason, throughout this book, a concept of mission is treated as an ever-present operating constraint.

Given the need for money to operate, the structure of revenues as a determinant of corporate and tax-exempt classification, and the classification as a determinant of certain operating rules, finance is at the center of every nonprofit organization, no matter how benevolent or charitable it may be. A mission is dead—at least dormant—if not financed.

Given these facts and the quotation from Arizona law above, what type of financial information or data helps the manager perform these discretionary duties to which the law refers? How is financial information useful?

The Utility of Financial Information

In today's highly specialized world, all managers, chief executives, and members of the board of directors of nonprofit organizations are not expected to be financial wizards. What is important is that management has a working knowledge of the financial management function as it applies specifically to strategic elements in the nonprofit organization. As the quotation from Arizona law on nonprofits cited earlier notes, managers under the duty of prudence are expected to use financial information in the exercise of their roles. Here is a list of what this necessitates.

1. The management has to broaden its perspective about what it means to be a nonprofit from a philosophical to a financial perspective. The mission has to be translated into terms such as, How do we raise the money, manage it, and spend it? Recall that the financial management function does not debate the philosophical merits of a mission. It takes that as a given by the trustees and tries to solve how the mission will be financed. This means talking about money that is measurable. Hence, management's performance can and should be measured.

2. Management has to view its organization as a competitor for scarce dollars. To be financially successful, nonprofits must compete not only among themselves but among the alternative ways that potential donors have to use their money. Giving away money or paying dues are not the only, and frequently are the least attractive, alternatives that a person or corporation has for using money. Competition is also involved in recruiting good staff persons and chief executive officers and in being able to retain them by providing good but affordable benefits.

3. Management has to engage in the planning and the setting of attainable goals and strategies to carry out a mission successfully, including the mission of raising money. From a financial perspective, programs must compete for a limited supply of money. The most profitable program may not always be chosen, but the questions of how much money a certain program can bring the organization or how much the program will cost should never be treated trivially. Except in the cases of mercy and emergency, which are rarities for most

nonprofits, a program is not simply an exercise in benevolence. It is a vehicle, directly (through sales) or indirectly (through goodwill), to raise money so that even more clients may be served by the organization. Admittedly, money making should not always be the most persuasive reason for choosing one program over the other. Indeed, some money losers may be properly chosen, but the financial impact of such choices on the organization should be known in advance, monitored, and controlled.

4. Management has to understand the major streams of revenues to most nonprofit organizations: gifts and contributions. What are they? From where do they come? When is a gift not a gift? When is a gift likely to be a disguised financial disaster? How are gifts valued and recorded? How do they determine tax-exempt status? When might they lead to taxation and reporting requirements?

5. Management has to have a working knowledge of sophisticated tools for raising funds. How can a gift be arranged to provide income for the life of a potential donor or some other person and at the same time provide a handsome contribution to the nonprofit? How can a nonprofit get an annual income from a trust?

6. Management has to understand the legal boundaries placed on the organization and the hidden opportunities available to the imaginative leader. Often, the conclusion that "we can't do it because of our nonprofit status" is incorrect.

7. It is incumbent on management to explore the opportunities to earn the most cherished form of revenues, those self-generating revenues over which the nonprofit management has full discretion. These opportunities lie in making good short- and long-term investments, including the acquisition of profit-making enterprises.

8. Management has to be able to think through an investment decision. This can be done without being trapped by details or formulas that few managers will ever retain or calculate themselves. Yet every manager should be able to understand the thinking and solution to basic investment questions such as how do we know it is a good investment for our organization.

9. Management has to use the budget and the budgetary process as financial planning tools, as tools to coordinate or allocate resources among various programs, and as tools to control spending and the overall direction of the organization.

10. Management has to be able to use certain financial statements. These are the balance sheet, the statement of revenues and expenses, and the statement of changes in the financial conditions or of cash flows. It is the ability to interpret these statements that will give early warning of financial disasters, as well as the financial capacity to grow.

This book deals with all of these topics. It does not presume that the reader has prior knowledge of financial planning. The book tries to make the reader a competent and contributing member of the management staff of a nonprofit organization and its board of trustees. Such members know their potential liability and are capable of contributing to the growth and financial well-being of the organization. Why? Because such readers will have acquired a firm understanding of the basic blocks of knowledge of the nonprofit financial world and can proceed to institute imaginative and productive programs.

The Financial Function in the Organization Chart

Figure 1.1 shows one of many ways in which the financial function may be represented in the organizational chart of a nonprofit. Note that at the top of the organizational chart is the public. Nonprofits exist to advance public welfare and are fiduciaries of the public or of their members (as in the case of associations). Unlike a for-profit corporation, they are not owned by stockholders.

The board answers to the public or community, and much of the law that governs nonprofit corporations is intended to assure that decisions made by the board of trustees are aimed at advancing public welfare or the welfare of the members (in the case of associations). The board may be divided into

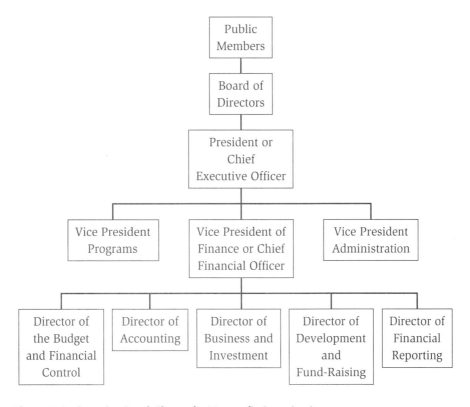

Figure 1.1. Organizational Chart of a Nonprofit Organization.

several committees, each having a responsibility to oversee a financial aspect of the organization; for example, there might be a budget committee, an investment committee, an audit committee, and a development committee, each possibly having several subcommittees. Committee members can be held personally liable for certain financial misdeeds of the organization. We shall say more about the board in Chapter Five.

The chief financial officer may carry the rank of a vice-president or senior vice-president and report directly to the president or chief executive officer of the organization. At the same rank as the chief financial officer may be vice-presidents for administration, including personnel and purchasing, and a vice-president for programs, who may be responsible for a number of operating programs.

Directly under the chief financial officer may be the office of budgeting and financial control, which is responsible for preparing the budget for the organization and setting up all financial controls, such as procedures for recording receipts and expenditures, scheduling of payments, regularly computing and comparing differences between actual and projected receipts and expenditures, preparing estimates of program costs and revenues for bidding on the contracts, and so on. This office may also keep track of various costs, such as employee benefits, equipment, and rental costs, and compare the products of various benefits and equipment providers.

Also directly under the chief financial officer may be an accounting operation. These people will systematically classify and record the actual income and expenditures of the organization. They keep systematic records of each type of expense, such as payroll, supplies, transportation, and entertainment, as well as records of receipts from fees, gifts and contributions, contracts, and so on. Moreover, this group must keep certain expenditures and receipts segregated from the general accounting of the organization. Certain funds are restricted by covenant, agreement, or contract to specific uses and may not become part of the general funds of the organization. Each building fund and scholarship fund, for example, must be accounted for separately. This is called *fund accounting.*

Also directly reporting to the chief financial officer may be a director of investments. Some nonprofits have sizable portfolios and businesses that they own and operate. The person who heads this function may not necessarily be the one who makes investment decisions. Investment decisions may be made by the board of directors or through contract with an outside investment advisor. Similarly, each business operated by the organization may have its own manager. All these may, however, report to one person who is responsible for coordinating and overseeing the entire spectrum of investment.

Fund-raising is another function that may report directly to the chief financial officer, although it need not. Organizations may have a vice-president for development to whom fund-raising is assigned. Even when this is the case, a chief financial officer has some direct responsibility for specific aspects of the fund-raising activity because so much of what is done here requires technical aspects of finance and goes beyond making and perpetuating financial contracts. Fund-raising involves conducting contribution campaigns; working with individual, corporate, or foundation donors; working with alumni; and using technical instruments such as wills, trusts, insurance, endowments, and noncash property.

Also reporting to the chief financial officer may be a director of financial reporting. This function covers preparing annual reports on financial matters of the organization and its donors and supporters, filing income tax forms, and preparing and making available to the public reports as required by law. The law requires public access to tax, financial, and annual reports and tax-exempt determination letters.

The nature of the configuration that any single organization may take will depend on the organization's complexity, the level of development, the mission (a hospital compared to a day-care center, for instance), the size of the organization, and the management style of its leadership. In some organizations, administrative and financial functions may be combined. Some small organizations may have only one vice-president, and the financial officer may also oversee purchasing and acquisitions. In others, the chief executive officer may carry on the function of chief financial officer. Organizations change structure when confronting new challenges; therefore, it is important to go beyond organizational structure and focus on the content of certain central financial functions.

Although certain configurations and assignments may change, the vice-presidents are always responsible to a president or chief executive officer who is, in turn, responsible to the board. The board is responsible to the public on whose behalf the legal system acts. To reiterate, in the nonprofit world the financial function is conducted within a set of legal rules that is different from those in the public or for-profit sector. Violation of these rules jeopardizes the organization's existence. The management, including the board of directors, may be held personally liable. Hence, in the nonprofit organization the financial function involves more than the art of investing. It is a specialized aspect of the overall strategic management of the organization.

To summarize, the financial management function is a staff function. It assists management in setting realistic financial and performance targets. How much can reasonably be raised and, therefore, how much can reasonably be done? It makes recommendations about ways to increase the inflow of funds into the organization, and it can improve the use of short-term investment techniques to turn idle cash balances into assets that earn interest. It can also assist the organization in making long-term investments in assets such as bonds, land, equipment, and buildings and in acquiring and managing its own business.

All these involve comparisons of income streams expected from alternative uses of the organization's money and the risks associated with investments, including that of losing the tax-exempt status of the organization.

Financial management also assists in the assessment of the financial standing of the organization. This is accomplished by interpreting the financial statements prepared by the accountants. Good management must know how to read the three principal financial statements: the balance sheet, the statement of revenues and expense, and the statement of changes in the financial position or of cash flows. Not being accountants, it is not necessary for managers to master the details of fund accounting, which is the accounting method used by nonprofits. However, the financial management function does require the ability to interpret the accounting data in light of the organization's objectives and to work out the alternatives available to management. Stated otherwise, the financial management function converts accounting data into a financial policy consistent with the organization's well-being and its mission.

MANAGERIAL ETHICS AND THE INTEGRITY OF THE ORGANIZATION

Every organization has a set of core values, even if unwritten. The shared values hold the organization together, discipline individual and collective behaviors, and provide a basis for evaluating performance. Ethics permeates every sphere of a nonprofit organization. To honor this fact, ethical questions are treated in two ways in this book. First, ethics is discussed as a core concept in strategic planning. Second, in various parts of the book, ethical dilemmas are raised. All of these are not-too-easy questions that a specific nonprofit has had to deal with, and each was reported in the national media.

Most ethical lapses can be traced to an opportunity created by the way an institution is managed. This does not imply that management is always responsible, but it does imply that a duty of management is to reduce those opportunities. In what follows we look at various perspectives of that duty.

Professor Regina Herzlinger of Harvard Business School views these ethical infractions as related to excessive risk taking by management, ineffective management procedures and practices, a desire for personal gain (called inurement), and operational inefficiencies. She argues that greater disclosures of operational information, better analysis of sector performance and accounting data, more dissemination of information, and the imposition of sanctions on those who persist in unethical behavior would be good antidotes and would restore confidence and contributions.[2]

Ethics, Disclosure, and the Nonprofit Manager

Today's managers of nonprofit organizations find themselves under constant scrutiny. They are watched by

1. Watchdog agencies, including the Better Business Bureau and the National Charities Information Bureau (whose standards for convenience of the reader appears in Appendix 1.1)

2. The IRS, not only through 990 forms, but also through tax forms and tax audits

3. The public as a result of federal laws that require public disclosure upon request by any person seeking documents such as 990s and tax forms for a three-year period if such persons are willing to pay the cost of reproduction and mailing or by visiting the principal offices of the organization during business hours

4. Access and availability of such information on the Internet, not only by the voluntary act of the organizations themselves, but also by organizations such as Guidestar

5. The growing community of scholarly researchers

6. State and local governments that require disclosure and registration

7. Their own members who by state law must be given such information on request

8. Clients

9. Foundations, corporations, and individual donors as a precursor to contributions

10. A federation if the organization is a member of one

11. Employee pressure, since many professional fund-raising associations urge disclosure

12. Combined Federal Campaign, which requires full disclosure as a condition for participating

13. A vigilant and inquisitive press

14. A board of trustees if it is doing its work well

15. Auditors

Therefore, every top executive has a duty and an incentive to create and to institutionalize an ethical working environment.

Managerial Inefficiency and the Fostering of Fraud

The *Audit Risk and Materiality* of the Auditing Standards Board provides guidance to auditors about detecting conditions where fraud is most likely to occur. Some of those standards lend themselves to providing guidance to management—not just to auditors. These conditions are paraphrased below:[3]

1. A lackadaisical, disinterested, or undisciplined attitude toward financial reporting and internal controls by senior management

2. Compensation that is based on performance measures that are hard to track or that promote unusual and unmonitored aggressive behavior in order to meet goals

3. The involvement of nonaccounting professionals in setting procedures and the unwillingness of the management or board to yield to professional standards for whatever purpose

4. Populating the audit committee of the organization with individuals who have no clue about financial statements, finance, or financial management

5. An unusually cozy relationship between the staff accountants and the auditors or between management and the auditors

6. Poor cash flow or unusually large cash on hand or large cash accounts or multiple cash accounts

7. Discontent among employees having access to valuable or portable organizational assets that are marketable

8. An unnecessarily complex administrative and reporting structure or one in which the flow of financial information is impeded or unnecessarily delayed, and the failure of top management to make timely response to reports indicating that the reports have been seriously considered

9. Inadequate documentation of transactions, including ordering, receiving, storing, and disposing of inventory and other assets

10. Improper training, retention, and assignment of employees and the lack of pre-employment screening

By the time the auditors discover and report fraudulent transactions, the damage has already been done, and often it is not easily overcome. Donors are discouraged from giving, additional audits are usually required, the assets of the organization are lost and even if recovered their use may be compromised through damage, alteration, and interests earnings foregone. Insurance premiums may rise; unrecoverable costs of prosecuting the employee(s) may be incurred. Employees and clients are demoralized or become cynical. All this said, it would pay each organization to take inventory at least of the ten factors stated above. The very act of taking inventory is a warning to those who may be disposed to commit fraud.

Some employees are at greater risk than others. Employees with access to marketable, portable, and valuable assets who have personal financial problems are always identified as high-risk. Beware. Employees with access or at high-risk can also be the most dedicated employees and the least prone to perpetrate a fraud. Further, focusing on the person rather than the working environment may create lasting resentment.

Elements of an Ethical Code

Fraud is merely the tip of the iceberg. An iceberg, we are reminded, has most of its mass below water where it cannot be seen. A function of a code of ethics is to permeate the behavior of all in the organization and provide a reference to ward off questionable behavior. Professor Ronald Sims of the College of William and Mary, who has written extensively on issues of ethics in organizations, writes that a code of ethics should[4]

1. Include an effective date, general statement of policy, and scope of coverage
2. Be consistent with the reality of the workplace
3. Be based on shared values
4. Not be arbitrarily imposed
5. Be periodically updated to reflect developments, learning, and experiences
6. Be written in lay terms
7. Clearly state what is expected of each person
8. Clearly describe a mode of implementation
9. Clearly describe a mode of reporting infractions and administrative procedures
10. Be enforced

Professor Sims offers two cautions: that ethical codes should be institutionalized behaviors and that they should not be so general and broad as to become "motherhood statements."

To meet his challenge, the reader will find ethical codes and statements throughout this book. These range from the responsibility of the trustees to oversee and encourage ethical management (not just efficient management), through setting of procedures for meeting this responsibility, to actual ethical codes that guide members of the profession and ways to ensure ethical guidance in strategic planning. Ethics and efficiency are not incompatible elements in managerial success.[5] The reader may refer to the standards of the National Charities Information Bureau that appear in Appendix 1.1.

SUMMARY AND PREVIEW

The bedrock of every nonprofit organization is its mission. We shall see in the next chapters the elements of a mission. A mission is more than a statement. The mission of a nonprofit is a binding social contract between it and various levels of government; between it and the community; and between it and its members. Managers cannot extricate themselves from this constraint. It has legal force.

Without money, the mission cannot be discharged or developed. Managers cannot extricate themselves from this responsibility either. The issue is how to discharge these responsibilities efficiently and ethically. This begins with an understanding of the legal powers and prohibitions that are inherent in the way the organization is organized for operating purposes.

CHAPTER TWO

Protecting
the Tax-Exempt Status

How does a nonprofit acquire and maintain its tax-exempt status? What should every top manager know about the key legal powers and prohibitions in managing a nonprofit corporation? What are the central characteristics of a legally qualifying mission? How can managerial ineptitude lead to the loss of tax-exempt status, and what are the personal financial penalties to which the law may subject the errant manager?

THE NONPROFIT CORPORATION

Although it is technically possible for a nonprofit to operate without being incorporated or being a trust, only the uninformed (unless a religious organization) would take that risk. Most state laws parallel that of Virginia in holding that all individuals acting on behalf of a nonprofit prior to its being incorporated are personally liable to any third party unless that party knew that the organization was not incorporated. This liability extends to personal property—house, car, jewelry, and the like.

Why would any sensible person take that risk? Certainly not in the name of charity when incorporating is so simple. As the statutes of the State of Florida state, "lack of a legal organization or capacity is no defense."

Not to be organized as a corporation or as a trust also limits the revenue-raising powers of the organization. Neither individuals nor corporations could make tax-deductible contributions to such a nonprofit (unless it is a religious organization) because it would not be legally qualified to receive them. Private foundations do not give grants to unincorporated organizations.

To operate without being a corporation would mean that the nonprofit would have limited ability to enter into contracts—including the contracts to set up a centralized management system that hires people to run the organization and that itself has the power to enter into financial contracts in the name of the organization. This would be the case because the organization would have no legal standing on its own.

Having no identity separate from its founders means that the life of the organization would be coterminous with the life of its founders. A corporation has a perpetual life unrelated to the existence of its founders.

Not having a separate identity means that the nonprofit could not get tax exemption, which can only be conferred on a legal entity that is separate from the founders, operators of the organization, and their relatives and associates. The nonprofit corporation is a legal entity—what lawyers call a person. As a person, the nonprofit corporation has its own powers, responsibilities, and identity distinct from those of its organizers, members, officers, trustees, or affiliates.

THE PROCESS OF BECOMING A NONPROFIT CORPORATION

The process of creating a nonprofit corporation is simple. One or more organizers or founders select a name not already chosen by a nonprofit in that state, but which is allowed by the laws of that state. Some states, such as New York, specifically prohibit the use of certain names or words in the name of a nonprofit.

A charter such as that shown below is then completed. Note that this is a prototype of the charter with the minimum requirements for exemption from the IRS. Most states use a similar charter for incorporation, except that they add a provision prohibiting the issue of capital stocks.

Draft A

Articles of incorporation of the undersigned, a majority of whom are citizens of the United States, desiring to form a Non-Profit Corporation under the Non-Profit Corporation Law of _____, do hereby certify:

First: The name of the Corporation shall be _____.

Second: The place in this state where the principal office of the Corporation is to be located is the City of _____, _____ County.

Third: Said corporation is organized exclusively for charitable, religious, educational, and scientific purposes, including, for such purposes, the making of distributions to organizations that qualify as exempt organizations under section

501(c)(3) of the *Internal Revenue Code,* or the corresponding section of any future federal tax code.

Fourth: The names and addresses of the persons who are the initial trustees of the corporation are as follows:

Name _____   Address _____

Fifth: No part of the net earnings of the corporation shall inure to the benefit of, or be distributable to its members, trustees, officers, or other private persons, except that the corporation shall be authorized and empowered to pay reasonable compensation for services rendered and to make payments and distributions in furtherance of the purposes set forth in Article Third hereof. No substantial part of the activities of the corporation shall be the carrying on of propaganda, or otherwise attempting to influence legislation, and the corporation shall not participate in, or intervene in (including the publishing or distribution of statements) any political campaign on behalf of or in opposition to any candidate for public office. Notwithstanding any other provision of these articles, the corporation shall not carry on any other activities not permitted to be carried on (a) by a corporation exempt from federal income tax under section 501(c)(3) of the *Internal Revenue Code,* or the corresponding section of any future federal tax code, or (b) by a corporation, contributions to which are deductible under section 170(c)(2) of the *Internal Revenue Code,* or the corresponding section of any future federal tax code.

If reference to federal law in articles of incorporation imposes a limitation that is invalid in your state, you may wish to substitute the following for the last sentence of the preceding paragraph: "Notwithstanding any other provision of these articles, this corporation shall not, except to an insubstantial degree, engage in any activities or exercise any powers that are not in furtherance of the purposes of this corporation."

Sixth: Upon the dissolution of the corporation, assets shall be distributed for one or more exempt purposes within the meaning of section 501(c)(3) of the *Internal Revenue Code,* or the corresponding section of any future federal tax code, or shall be distributed to the federal government, or to a state or local government, for a public purpose. Any such assets not so disposed of shall be disposed of by a Court of Competent Jurisdiction of the county in which the principal office of the corporation is then located, exclusively for such purposes or to such organization or organizations, as said Court shall determine, which are organized and operated exclusively for such purposes.

In witness whereof, we have hereunto subscribed our names this _____ day of _____ 19_____.

The bylaws are written, an organizing meeting to name the trustees and to adopt the charter and bylaws is held, and the papers are filed with the state along with requisite filing fees.

This procedure need not be done by an attorney. Any citizen or group of citizens can carry out this organizing function. It is wise, however, to get an attorney to do it. After the papers are reviewed by the state corporate secretary, the charter is returned with the state seal and becomes the birth certificate of a new person—the newly created nonprofit corporation. The founders or organizers become the parents of this newly created organization, which has its own identity, purpose (mission), powers, and prohibitions.

RESOLVING DIFFERENCES BETWEEN STATE CHARTERS AND THE IRS PROTOTYPE

The model charter of a state may differ from that of the IRS model charter shown earlier. Compare the articles of incorporation for a nonstock corporation for the State of Maryland with that of the IRS. Observe that it is technically possible to form a nonstock (nonprofit) corporation in Maryland without a precise commitment to the rules of 501(c)(3) or a disposition plan and without the promise to avoid personal inurement as in articles three, five, and six of the IRS's. Also observe the sentence under the IRS's article five: There is an alternative language assuming that there is a conflict between federal and state laws. This alternative language does not concede IRS exclusive power for awarding federal tax exemption.

Why is it not unusual to run into such differences? Because state law is the basis upon which the nonprofit corporation is born but the federal law enforced by the IRS is the basis upon which federal exemption is conferred. Incorporation and exemption are not one and the same and one does not automatically follow the other.

The exemption conferred by the IRS is dependent upon the nonprofit's charter having certain specific requirements—articles two, three, and six in Exhibit 2.1. The states may add to this, or they may simply wait, as most do, until the federal exemption is awarded and then honor it.

SPECIFIC POWERS OF THE NONPROFIT CORPORATION

The nonprofit corporation is given certain powers to enable it to carry out its mission. These powers are assigned by state law. Why are these powers important to the management? Because they define the legal parameters within which the management must operate. Borrowing from the District of Columbia, Section 29.505, we see that these powers may include

1. To sue and be sued

2. To purchase, take, receive, lease, take by gifts, devise or bequest, or otherwise acquire, own, hold, improve, use, and otherwise deal in and with, real or personal property, or any interest therein, wherever the situation

Exhibit 2.1. Articles of Incorporation for a *Nonstock* Corporation.

FIRST: The undersigned _____
whose address is _____
being at least eighteen years of age, do(es) hereby form a corporation under the laws
of the State of Maryland.

SECOND: The name of the corporation is _____
_____
_____

THIRD: The purposes for which the corporation is formed are as follows: _____
_____
_____
_____

FOURTH: The street address of the principal office of the corporation in Maryland
is _____
_____

FIFTH: The name of the resident agent of the corporation in Maryland is _____
_____
whose address is _____
_____

SIXTH: The corporation has no authority to issue capital stock.

SEVENTH: The number of directors of the corporation shall be _____which
number may be increased or decreased pursuant to the bylaws of the corporation.
The name(s) of the director(s) who shall act until the first meeting or until their successors are duly chosen and qualified is/are _____
_____

EIGHTH: _____

IN WITNESS WHEREOF, I have	I hereby consent to my designation
signed these articles and acknowledge the	in this document as resident agent
same to be my act.	for this corporation.

SIGNATURE(S) OF INCORPORATOR(S):   **SIGNATURE OF RESIDENT AGENT LISTED IN FIFTH:**

_____   _____

_____

_____

RETURN TO:

_____

_____

_____

3. To sell, convey, mortgage, pledge, lease, exchange, transfer, and otherwise dispose of all or any part of its property and assets

4. To purchase, take, receive, subscribe for, or otherwise acquire, own, hold, vote, use, employ, sell, mortgage, loan, pledge, or otherwise dispose of, and otherwise use and deal in and with, shares or other interests in, or obligations of, other domestic or foreign corporations, whether for profit or not for profit, associations, partnerships, or individuals, or direct or indirect obligations of the United States, or of any other government, state, territory, governmental district, or municipality or of any instrumentality thereof

5. To make contracts and incur liabilities, borrow money at such rates of interest as the corporation may determine, issue its notes, bonds, and other obligations, and secure any of its obligations by mortgage or pledge of all or any of its property, franchises and income

6. To lend money for its corporate purposes, invest and reinvest its funds, and take and hold real and personal property as security for the payment of funds so loaned or invested

7. To conduct its affairs, carry on its operations, hold property, and have offices and exercise the powers granted by this chapter in any part of the world

8. To elect and appoint officers and agents of the corporation, and define their duties and fix their compensation

9. To make and alter bylaws not inconsistent with its articles of incorporation or with the laws of the District of Columbia, for the administration and regulation of the affairs of the corporation

10. Unless otherwise provided in the articles of incorporation, to make donations for the public welfare or for religious, charitable, scientific research, or educational purposes, or for other purposes for which the corporation is organized

11. To indemnify any director or officer or former director or officer of the corporation, or any person who may have served at its request as a director or officer of another corporation, whether for profit or not for profit, against expenses actually and necessarily incurred by him or her in connection with the defense of any action, suit, or proceeding in which he or she is made a party by reason of being or having been such director or officer, except in relation to matters as to which he or she shall be adjudged in such action, suit, or proceeding to be liable for negligence or misconduct in the performance of a duty

12. To determine the voting powers of members and procedures for voting by proxy

13. To determine the manner of providing notice about meetings

14. To determine what constitutes a quorum

15. To dissolve

Note that these powers give the nonprofit a wide range of financing and operating authority, including the making of loans, issuing of bonds, and selling of goods and services, tangible and intangible, and finally the right to die—to dissolve.

Note also that the general powers include indemnification. Yet trustees and managers may be held personally liable for the misconduct of their nonprofits. Hence, their interests in books such as this transcend the corporate interest to the personal.

SPECIFIC PROHIBITIONS

Just as state laws assign powers to nonprofit corporations, they specifically deny certain powers. Why does management have to be familiar with these prohibitions? Because their violations invariably lead to the loss of nonprofit status and probably to personal penalties on management. These prohibitions are so important that states require nonprofits to include them in their charters and bylaws. The three most universal prohibitions are

1. A provision prohibiting the issuing of capital stock; that is, common stock for raising funds

2. A provision prohibiting the use of the assets of the organization for personal benefits (called personal inurement)

3. A provision prohibiting profit-making as a principal purpose

4. A provision prohibiting the use of the organization's assets for political purposes—except where the mission of the organization is political (We shall discuss these in Chapter Five.)

But beyond these universal prohibitions, states may have certain other prohibitions, and this is why organizers carefully choose the place of birth of their nonprofit incorporation. Some states have different requirements about board composition and size; others have specific requirements about mergers and procedures for dissolving the nonprofit. All have provisions about how many persons it takes to form a nonprofit organization. In many states, it takes only one person. Some states limit the number of offices that one person can fill. Some states prohibit the same person from serving as both president and the sole vice-president. Obviously, a deceased or incapacitated person cannot substitute for him- or herself.

Prohibited Names

States also limit the names that can be used by the organizers of a nonprofit. For example, New York (Section 301) lists twenty-four names, mostly connoting financial, legal, or insurance, that cannot be used in naming a nonprofit organization chartered in that state. These include terms such as *mortgage* and *investment, state trooper* or *lawyer, surety* and *bond.* Wyoming law 17–16–401 prohibits the use of words such as *banco, banca, banquer, banque, bancorp, bank,* or any other such name unless the organization meets the banking requirements of the state and federal governments or if the name does not connote a financial institution. Therefore, the Wyoming Blood Bank is acceptable. Maryland requires the organization to include the words *incorporated, corporation,* or *Inc.* in the name of the organization if it is organized as a corporation. Utah prohibits the use of any name that does not relate to the mission of the organization. All states prohibit the use of a name that is not distinguishable from a name already being used, and they permit a group of organizers to reserve a name as they proceed in the process of organizing.

Prohibition on Foreign Corporations

A *foreign* nonprofit corporation is one that was chartered in another state. The Gill foundation, chartered in Rhode Island, is foreign to South Dakota. An *alien* corporation is one that was chartered in another country. Every state requires foreign nonprofit corporations to obtain authority to operate in it. But this authority is not necessary for certain types of transactions. Utah 7–135–101 describes the usual exceptions:

1. For settling disputes in its own behalf
2. For holding meetings of its board and for conducting internal corporate affairs
3. Maintaining a bank account
4. Maintaining offices or agencies for the transfer of securities or registration of membership or depositories
5. Selling through independent contractors
6. Soliciting and obtaining orders—if the orders are accepted outside of the state
7. Obtaining security interest (as lender or borrower) in real or personal property
8. Collecting debt in its own behalf
9. Owning real or personal property
10. Conducting isolated transactions and within days

11. Conducting affairs in interstate commerce

12. Grant-making

13. Distributing information to members

Of course, a foreign corporation may always apply for *domestication*. This is like a naturalization process in which the organization changes its charter (citizenship) from one state (country) to another.

THE PURPOSE OR MISSION OF THE CORPORATION

The principal purpose or mission of every nonprofit corporation is to carry out an agreed upon mission without the objective of making a profit and with the promise not to distribute the organization's assets to benefit individuals other than the clients the nonprofit was formed to serve. All nonprofits, even associations, have a binding legal commitment to this overall principle.

All nonprofit missions have five characteristics. These are important to the management of the nonprofit organization because they describe the questions that the IRS and state governments use annually to evaluate the performance of every nonprofit. These five characteristics, developed by the author in the first edition, are

1. *Social contract:* The mission is a promise made to all members and to the society that for their support the organization will do certain things deemed by the society or members to be worthy of tax-exempt status. The attorney general of every state and the members of an organization can sue if the organization fails by diverting its resources to activities other than its mission. The organization's tax-exempt status can also be rescinded.

2. *Permanence:* A mission is adopted with a spirit of permanence even though it can be amended. Amendments to the mission require a vote of the board of trustees and must be reported in most states and to the federal government. An amendment could jeopardize the tax-exempt status of the organization if it causes the organization to veer from its mission.

3. *Clarity:* A mission should be stated clearly to communicate purpose, yet broadly to give options and to permit the organization to meet new challenges consistent with its mission.

4. *Approval:* The mission must be approved by the members, the trustees, the state corporate secretary, and the Internal Revenue Service. It must be consistent with existing permissible missions defined in state and federal laws.

5. *Proof:* A mission should be demonstrable. The key test is finance and resources. How did the organization use its assets? Where did they come from? What has the organization done? It must also be proven by the numerical and descriptive statements of accomplishments filed annually in the Form 990, which I describe later.

TAX CONSEQUENCES OF SPECIFIC MISSIONS

The statements made above apply to all nonprofit corporations regardless of mission. But the specific mission chosen by the organizers does matter. Other than binding how the nonprofit operates, the specific mission has tax consequences.

Table 2.1 shows twenty-seven types of nonprofit corporations. Each type is defined by a section of the IRS code. Note that the missions of these organizations are different. Table 2.1 also indicates that only seven categories of nonprofits qualify to receive tax-deductible contributions. These include cemeteries, veterans' organizations, nonprofit corporations organized or chartered by Congress, fraternal and beneficiary associations, organizations of past and present members of the armed forces, and a group-denominated 501(c)(3)s. An alternative to the classifications shown in Table 2.1. is given in Appendix 2.2., matched with the National Taxonomy of Tax-Exempt Entities used by researchers.

PURPOSES AND PRIVILEGES OF 501(c)(3) STATUS

Section 501(c)(3) includes the largest number of tax-exempt organizations. It is the most sought-after category because donors can make tax-deductible contributions to them, the net revenues derived by these organizations from activities related to their mission are not taxed, these organizations qualify for grants from private foundations, and on the state and local levels these organizations may be exempt from franchise, *ad valorem* taxes, and certain other fees.

Why would a group of organizations be given such privileges? First, because in the United States, they are expressions of the First Amendment to the U.S. Constitution concerning freedom of association. Second, these organizations are exclusively intended to promote public or community welfare directly—not private welfare, as in the case of firms, or the welfare of a definable subgroup, as in the case of associations. Put another way, firms advance society by advancing individuals (investors). Associations promote public welfare indirectly through operating for the benefit of their members.

Table 2.1. Organization Reference Chart.

Section of 1996 Code	Description of Organization	General Nature of Activities	Application Form No.	Annual Return Required to be Filed	Contributions Allowable	Numbers of ORG's
501(c)(1)	Corporations Organized Under Act of Congress (Including Federal Credit Unions)	Instrumentalities of the United States	No Form	None	Yes, if made for exclusively public purposes	27
501(c)(2)	Title Holding Corporation for Exempt Organization	Holding title to property of an exempt organization	1024	990[1] or 990EZ[4]	No[1]	7113
501(c)(3)	Religious, Educational, Charitable, Scientific, Literary. Testing for Public Safety, to Foster National or International Amateur Sports Competition, or Prevention of Cruelty to Children or Animals Organizations	Activities of nature implied by description of class of organization	1023	990[1] or 990EZ[4] 990-PF	Yes, generally	692524
501(c)(4)	Civic Leagues, Social Welfare Organizations, and Local Associations of Employees	Promotion of community welfare; charitable, educational or recreational	1024	990[1] or 990EZ[4]	No, generally[2,3]	141776

(continued)

Table 2.1. (*continued*).

Section of 1996 Code	Description of Organization	General Nature of Activities	Application Form No.	Annual Return Required to be Filed	Contributions Allowable	Numbers of ORG's
501(c)(5)	Labor, Agricultural, and Horticultural Organizations	Educational or instructive, the purpose being to improve conditions of work, and to improve products and efficiency	1024	990[1] or 990EZ[4]	No[2]	64902
501(c)(6)	Business Leagues, Chambers of Commerce, Real Estate Boards, Etc.	Improvement of business conditions of one or more lines of business	1024	990[1] or 990EZ[4]	No[2]	76406
501(c)(7)	Social and Recreation Clubs	Pleasure, recreation, social activities	1024	990[1] or 990EZ[4]	No[2]	66367
501(c)(8)	Fraternal Beneficiary Societies and Associations	Lodge providing for payment of life, sickness, accident, or other benefits to members	1024	990[1] or 990EZ[4]	Yes, if for certain Sec. 501(c)(3) purposes	67990
501(c)(9)	Voluntary Employees' Beneficiary Associations	Providing for payment of life, sickness, accident, or other benefits to members	1024	990[1] or 990EZ[4]	No[2]	14464

Section	Description of organization	Application Form Number	Annual Return Required	Contributions Allowable	
501(c)(10)	Domestic Fraternal Societies and Associations	Lodge devoting its net earnings to charitable, fraternal, and other specified purposes. No life, sickness, or accident benefits to members	1024	990[1] or 990EZ[4]	Yes, if for certain Sec. 501(c)(3) purposes	20954
501(c)(11)	Teachers' Retirement Fund Associations	Teachers' association for payment of retirement benefits	No Form[5]	990[1] or 990EZ[4]	No[2]	13
501(c)(12)	Benevolent Life Insurance Associations, Mutual Ditch or Irrigation Companies, Mutual or Cooperative Telephone Companies, Etc.	Activities of a mutually beneficial nature similar to those implied by the description of class of organization	1024	990[1] or 990EZ[4]	No[2]	6368
501(c)(13)	Cemetery Companies	Burials and incidental activities	1024	990[1] or 990EZ[4]	Yes, generally	9646
501(c)(14)	State Chartered Credit Unions, Mutual Reserve Funds	Loans to members	No Form[5]	990[1] or 990EZ[4]	No[2]	4959
501(c)(15)	Mutual Insurance Companies or Associations	Providing insurance to members substantially at cost	1024	990[1] or 990EZ[4]	No[2]	1206

(continued)

Table 2.1. (*continued*).

Section of 1996 Code	Description of Organization	General Nature of Activities	Application Form No.	Annual Return Required to be Filed	Contributions Allowable	Numbers of ORG's
501(c)(16)	Cooperative Organizations to Finance Crop Operations	Financing crop operations in conjunction with activities of a marketing or purchasing association	No Form[5]	990[1] or 990EZ[4]	No[2]	25
501(c)(17)	Supplemental Unemployment Benefit Trusts	Provides for payment of supplemental unemployment compensation benefits	1024	990[1] or 990EZ[4]	No[2]	542
501(c)(18)	Employee Funded Pension Trust (created before June 25, 1959)	Payment of benefits under a pension plan funded by employees	No Form[5]	990[1] or 990EZ[4]	No[2]	1
501(c)(19)	Post or Organization of Past or Present Members of the Armed Forces	Activities implied by nature of organization	1024	990[1] or 990EZ[4]	No, generally	31961

501(c)(21)	Black Lung Benefit Trusts	Funded by coal mine operators to satisfy their liability for disability or death due to black lung diseases	No Form[4]	990-BL	No[4]	27
501(c)(22)	Withdrawal Liability Payment Fund	To provide funds to meet the liability of employers withdrawing from a multi-employer pension fund	No Form[4]	990 or 990EZ[4]	No[4]	0
501(c)(23)	Veterans Organization (created before 1880)	To provide insurance and other benefits to veterans	No Form[4]	990 or 990EZ[4]	No, generally	2
501(c)(25)	Title Holding Corporations of Trusts with Multiple Parents	Holding title and paying over income from property to 35 or lower parents of beneficiaries	1024	990 of 990EZ	No	908
501(c)(26)	State-Sponsored Organization Providing Health Coverage for High-Risk Individuals	Provides health care coverage to high-risk individuals	No Form[4]	990[1] of 990EZ[4]	No	N/A

(continued)

Table 2.1. (*continued*).

Section of 1996 Code	Description of Organization	General Nature of Activities	Application Form No.	Annual Return Required to be Filed	Contributions Allowable	Numbers of ORG's
501(c)(27)	State-Sponsored Workers' Compensation Reinsurance Organization	Reimburses members for losses under workers' compensation acts	No Form[2]	990[1] or 990EZ[4]	No	N/A
501(d)	Religious and Apostolic Associations	Regular business activities. Communal religious community	No Form	1065[2]	No[3]	115
501(e)	Cooperative Hospital Service Organizations	Performs cooperative services for hospitals	1023	990[1] or 990EZ[4]	Yes	50
501(f)	Cooperative Service Organizations of Operating Educational Organizations	Performs collective investment services for educational organizations	1023	990[1] or 990EZ[4]	Yes	1
501(k)	Child Care Organization	Provides care for children	1023	990 or 990EZ[4]	Yes	N/A

Section of 1986 Code	Description of organization	General nature of activities	Application Form No.	Annual return required to be filed	Contributions allowable	Number of 1993 Returns
501(n)	Charitable Risk Pools	Pools certain insurance risks of 501(c)(3) organizations	1023	990[2] or 990EZ[4]	Yes	N/A
521(a)	Farmers' Cooperative Associations	Cooperative marketing and purchasing for agricultural producers	1028	900-C	No	1754

[1] For exceptions to the filing requirement, see chapter 2 and the Form instructions.

[2] An organization exempt under a subsection of Code Sec. 501 other than (c)(3) may establish a charitable fund, contributions to which are deductible. Such a fund must itself meet the requirements of section 501(c)(3) and the related notice requirements of section 508(a).

[3] Contributions to volunteer fire companies and similar organizations are deductible, but only if made for exclusively public purposes.

[4] Deductible as a business expense to the extent allowed by Code section 192.

[5] Deductible as a business expense to the extent allowed by Code section 194A.

Sources: Adapted from *Tax Exempt Status of Organizations*, Publication 557 (Washington, D.C., U.S. Government Printing Office, Rev. May 1997), p. 5. Numbers taken from U.S. Revenue Service, *Databook*, 1997, p. 23.

Third, 501(c)(3)s promote public welfare (1) in a manner that is beyond government such as religion, or (2) in a manner substituting for government such as housing and health. Therefore, fourth, the tax foregone by making them exempt is seen as equivalent to or less than the expenditure the local, state, and federal government would have made if either or all had undertaken the same activity (the organization's mission) to promote or to defend the public well-being. Fifth, since these organizations must conduct their missions in a charitable way, they are not normally expected to finance them exclusively through profits. *Charitable* does not mean necessarily zero price, free, or eleemosynary. It means to promote community rather than individual welfare.

ACQUIRING SECTION 501(c)(3) TAX-EXEMPT STATUS

To acquire and maintain 501(c)(3) status, the nonprofit corporation with a charter as described in the above paragraphs, must pass the organizational, political, and asset tests.

The Organizational Test

The organizational test states that a nonprofit corporation may be organized for any lawful purpose or purposes including one or more of the following: benevolent; charitable; religious; missionary; educational; scientific; research; literary; musical; social; athletic; patriotic; political; civic; professional, commercial, industrial, business, or trade association; mutual improvement. However, 501(c)(3)s, those with exemptions from income tax as well as deductibility of contributions, can only be organized for the following eight, specific purposes or missions:

Educational

Religious

Charitable

Scientific

Literary

Testing for public safety

Fostering certain national or international amateur sports competitions

Preventing of cruelty to children or animals

Because these eight functions could easily be conducted with a motive of making money for the organizers or the managers of the nonprofit organization, the IRS requires that the motive for conducting the mission not be one of advancing the private welfare of individuals. The motive must be *charitable,* which means that the motive cannot be to make a profit or to benefit individuals as owners or managers. The beneficiaries must be the community or the public. Therefore, 501(c)(3)s are often called *charitable* or *community welfare organizations*.

One condition that is common to all eight of these missions is that an organization formed exclusively for one or more of these reasons is not considered tax exempt unless the intent is to serve a public purpose—to improve public welfare. In the words of the IRS:

> (ii) An organization is not organized or operated exclusively for one or more of the purposes specified in subdivision (i) of this subparagraph unless it serves a public rather than a private interest. Thus, to meet the requirement of this subdivision, it is necessary for an organization to establish that it is not organized or operated for the benefit of private interests such as designated individuals, the founder or his or her family, shareholders of the organization, or persons controlled, directly or indirectly, by such private interests. [*Treasury Regulations*, Section 1.50(c)(3)–1, (d)(1)(ii), 1980]

The serving of a public purpose is equated to a community or welfare purpose. Hence, when the IRS writes of the conditions that would qualify an educational institution for tax exemption, it states:

> *(3) Educational defined—(i) In general.* The term "educational," as used in section 501(c)(3), relates to—
>> (a) The instruction or training of the individual for the purpose of improving or developing his capabilities; or
>> (b) The instruction of the public on subjects useful to the individual and beneficial to the community. [*Treasury Regulations*, Section 1.50(c)(3)–1(d)(3)(I) 1980]

Hence, in *Church of the Chosen People* v. *U.S.*,[1] a group that teaches the single tenet that pairings between persons of the same sex (men with men and women with women) are acceptable in the eyes of God was denied exemption because the court held, among other reasons, that this group existed for the benefit of individuals, not the community.

Each of the eight missions that qualify under the organizational test for 501(c)(3) status is specifically defined in Section 501(c)(3) of the IRS Code. Therefore, the mission chosen by the organizers must conform with the definition in the Code. Further, the management must operate in conformity with that definition.

An organization defined within the eight broad terms, such as educational, cultural, and health, can vary widely in what they want to do. Therefore, the IRS requires that the organizers be more specific. Within the broad definition as accepted within the Code, the organizers must elect three of the specific purposes shown in Table 2.2. (Religious organizations and their affiliates and organizations with gross annual receipts of less than $5,000 do not have to make these choices.)

Table 2.2. Specifically Authorized Missions of Exempt Organizations.

Activity Code Numbers of Exempt Organizations (Select up to three codes that best describe or most accurately identify your organization's purposes, activities, operations or type of organization and enter in block 6, page 1, of the application. Enter first the code that most accurately identifies the organization.)

Code		Code		Code		Code	
Religious Activities		**Schools, Colleges, and Related Activities**		038	School or college athletic association	---	Student travel (use 299)
001	Church, synagogue, etc.	030	School, college, trade school, etc.	039	Scholarships for children of employees	---	Scientific research (see Scientific Research Activities)
002	Association or convention of churches	031	Special school for the blind, handicapped, etc.	040	Scholarships (other)	046	Private school
003	Religious order	032	Nursery school	041	Student loans	059	Other school related activities
004	Church auxiliary	---	Day care center (use 574)	042	Student housing activities		
005	Mission	033	Faculty group	043	Other student aid	**Cultural, Historical or Other Educational Activities**	
006	Missionary activities	034	Alumni association or group	044	Student exchange with foreign country	060	Museum, zoo, planetarium, etc.
007	Evangelism	035	Parent or parent-teachers association	045	Student operated business	061	Library
008	Religious publishing activities	036	Fraternity or sorority	---	Financial support of schools, colleges, etc. (use 602)	062	Historical site, records, or reenactment
---	Bookstore (use 918)	---	Key club (use 323)	---	Achievement prizes or awards (use 914)	063	Monument
---	Genealogical activities (use 094)	037	Other student society or group	---	Student bookstore (use 918)	064	Commemorative event (centennial, festival, pageant, etc.)
029	Other religious activities					065	Fair

088 Community theatrical group
089 Singing society or group
090 Cultural performances
091 Art exhibit
092 Literary activities
093 Cultural exchanges with foreign country
094 Genealogical activities
--- Achievement prizes or awards (use 914)
--- Gifts or grants to individuals (use 561)
--- Financial support of cultural organizations (use 602)
119 Other cultural or historical activities

Other Instruction and Training Activities

120 Publishing activities
121 Radio or television broadcasting
122 Producing films
123 Discussion groups, forums, panels, lectures, etc.
124 Study and research (nonscientific)
125 Giving information or opinion (see also Advocacy)
126 Apprentice training
--- Travel tours (use 299)
149 Other instruction and training

Health Services and Related Activities

150 Hospital
151 Hospital auxiliary
152 Nursing or convalescent home
153 Care and housing for the aged (see also 382)
154 Health clinic
155 Rural medical facility
156 Blood bank
157 Cooperative hospital service organization
158 Rescue and emergency service
159 Nurses register or bureau
160 Aid to the handicapped (see also 031)
161 Scientific research (diseases)
162 Other medical research
163 Health insurance (medical, dental, optical, etc.)
164 Prepared group health plan
165 Community health planning
166 Mental health care
167 Group medical practice association
168 In-faculty group practice association
169 Hospital pharmacy, parking facility, food services, etc.
179 Other health services

Scientific Research Activities

180 Contract or sponsored scientific research for industry
181 Scientific research for government
--- Scientific research (diseases) (use 161)
199 Other scientific research activities

Business and Professional Organizations

200 Business promotion (chamber of commerce, business league, etc.)
201 Real estate association
202 Board of trade
203 Regulating business
204 Promotion of fair business practices
205 Professional association
206 Professional association auxiliary
207 Industry trade shows

(continued)

Table 2.2. *(continued).*

Code		Code		Code	
208	Convention displays	**Farming and Related Activities**		**Employee or Membership Benefit Organizations**	
—	Testing products for public safety (use 905)	230	Farming	260	Fraternal beneficiary society, order, or association
209	Research, development, and testing	231	Farm bureau	261	Improvement of conditions of workers
210	Professional athletic league	232	Agricultural group	262	Association of municipal employees
—	Attracting new industry (use 403)	233	Horticultural group	263	Association of employees
—	Publishing activities (use 120)	234	Farmers cooperative marketing or purchasing	264	Employee or member welfare association
—	Insurance or other benefits for members (see Employee or Membership Benefit Organizations)	235	Financing crop operations	265	Sick, accident, death, or similar benefits
211	Underwriting municipal insurance	—	FFA, FHA, 4-H club, etc. (use 322)	266	Strike benefits
212	Assigned risk insurance activities	—	Fair (use 065)	267	Unemployment benefits
213	Tourist bureau	236	Dairy herd improvement association	268	Pension or retirement benefits
229	Other business or professional group	237	Breeders association	269	Vacation benefits
		249	Other farming and related activities		
		Mutual Organizations			
		250	Mutual ditch, irrigation, telephone, electric company, or like organization		
		251	Credit union		
		252	Reserve funds or insurance for domestic building and loan association, cooperative bank, or mutual savings bank		
		253	Mutual insurance company		
		254	Corporation organized under an Act of Congress (see also 904)		
		—	Farmers cooperative marketing or purchasing (use 234)		
		—	Cooperative hospital service organization (use 157)		
		259	Other mutual organization		

279 Other services or benefits to members or employees

Sports, Athletic, Recreational, and Social Activities
280 Country club
281 Hobby club
282 Dinner club
283 Variety club
284 Dog club
285 Women's club
--- Garden club (use 356)
286 Hunting or fishing club
287 Swimming or tennis club
288 Other sports club
--- Boys Club, Little League, etc. (use 321)
296 Community center
297 Community recreational facilities (park, playground, etc.)
298 Training in sports
299 Travel tours
300 Amateur athletic association

--- School or college athletic association (use 038)
301 Fundraising athletic or sports event
317 Other sports or athletic activities
318 Other recreational activities
319 Other social activities

Youth Activities
320 Boy Scouts, Girl Scouts, etc.
321 Boys Club, Little League, etc.
322 FFA, FHA, 4-H club, etc.
323 Key club
324 YMCA, YWCA, YMHA, etc.
325 Camp
326 Care and housing of children (orphanage, etc.)
327 Prevention of cruelty to children

328 Combat juvenile delinquency
349 Other youth organization or activities

Conservation, Environmental, and Beautification Activities
350 Preservation of natural resources (conservation)
351 Combating or preventing pollution (air, water, etc.)
352 Land acquisition for preservation
353 Soil or water conservation
354 Preservation of scenic beauty
--- Litigation (see Litigation and Legal Aid Activities)
--- Combat community deterioration (use 402)

355 Wildlife sanctuary or refuge
356 Garden club
379 Other conservation, environmental, or beautification activities

Housing Activities
380 Low-income housing
381 Low and moderate income housing
382 Housing for the aged (see also 153)
--- Nursing or convalescent home (use 152)
--- Student housing (use 042)
--- Orphanage (use 326)
398 Instruction and guidance on housing
399 Other housing activities

Inner City or Community Activities
400 Area development, redevelopment, or renewal

(continued)

Table 2.2. (*continued*).

Code		Code		Code		Code	
---	Housing (see Housing Activities)	---	Referral service (social agencies) (use 569)	449	Other civil rights activities	484	Provide facilities or services for political campaign activities
401	Homeowners association	---	Legal aid to indigents (use 462)		**Litigation and Legal Aid Activities**	509	Other legislative and political activities
402	Other activity aimed at combating community deterioration	406	Crime prevention	460	Public interest litigation activities		**Advocacy**
403	Attracting new industry or retaining industry in an area	407	Voluntary firemen's organization or auxiliary	461	Other litigation or support of litigation		Attempt to influence public opinion concerning:
404	Community promotion	---	Rescue squad (use 158)	462	Legal aid to indigents	510	Firearms control
---	Community recreational facility (use 297)	408	Community service organization	463	Providing bail	511	Selective Service System
---	Community center (use 296)	429	Other inner city or community benefit activities		**Legislative and Political Activities**	512	National defense policy
405	Loans or grants for minority businesses		**Civil Rights Activities**	480	Propose, support, or oppose legislation	513	Weapons systems
---	Job training, counseling, or assistance (use 566)	430	Defense of human and civil rights	481	Voter information on issues or candidates	514	Government spending
		431	Elimination of prejudice and discrimination (race, religion, sex, national origin, etc.)	482	Voter education (mechanics of registering, voting, etc.)	515	Taxes or tax exemption
						516	Separation of church and state
---	Day care center (use 574)	432	Lessen neighborhood tensions	483	Support, oppose, or rate political candidates	517	Government aid to parochial schools
						518	U.S. foreign policy
						519	U.S. military involvement
						520	Pacifism and peace

521 Economic-political system of U.S.
522 Anti-communism
523 Right to work
524 Zoning or rezoning
525 Location of highway or transportation system
526 Rights of criminal defendants
527 Capital punishment
528 Stricter law enforcement
529 Ecology or conservation
530 Protection of consumer interests
531 Medical care service
532 Welfare system
533 Urban renewal
534 Busing students to achieve racial balance
535 Racial integration
536 Use of intoxicating beverages
537 Use of drugs or narcotics
538 Use of tobacco
539 Prohibition of erotica
540 Sex education in public schools
541 Population control
542 Birth control methods
543 Legalized abortion
559 Other matters

Other Activities Directed to Individuals

560 Supplying money, goods, or services to the poor
561 Gifts or grants to individuals (other than scholarships)
––– Scholarships for children of employees (use 039)
––– Scholarships (other) (use 040)
––– Student loans (use 041)
562 Other loans to individuals
563 Marriage counseling
564 Family planning
565 Credit counseling and assistance
566 Job training, counseling, or assistance
567 Draft counseling
568 Vocational counseling
569 Referral service (social agencies)
572 Rehabilitating convicts or ex-convicts
573 Rehabilitating alcoholics, drug abusers, compulsive gamblers, etc.
574 Day care center
575 Services for the aged (see also 153 and 382)
––– Training of or aid to the handicapped (see 031 and 160)

Activities Directed to Other Organizations

600 Community Chest, United Way, etc.
601 Booster club
602 Gifts, grants, or loans to other organizations
603 Nonfinancial services or facilities to other organizations

Other Purposes and Activities

900 Cemetery or burial activities
901 Perpetual care fund (cemetery, columbarium, etc.)
902 Emergency or disaster aid fund
903 Community trust or component
904 Government instrumentality or agency (see also 254)
905 Testing products for public safety
906 Consumer interest group
907 Veterans activities
908 Patriotic activities
909 4947(a)(1) trust

(continued)

Table **2.2.** (*continued*).

Code		Code		Code	
910	Domestic organization with activities outside U.S.	915	Erection or maintenance of public building or works	925	Section 501(c)(1) with 50% deductibility
911	Foreign organization	916	Cafeteria, restaurant, snack bar, food services, etc.	926	Government instrumentality other than section 501(c)
912	Title holding corporation	917	Thrift shop, retail outlet, etc.	927	Fundraising
913	Prevention of cruelty to animals	918	Book, gift, or supply store	928	4947(a)(2) trust
914	Achievement prizes or awards	919	Advertising	931	Withdrawal liability payment fund
		920	Association of employees	990	Section 501(k) child care organization
		921	Loans or credit reporting		
		922	Endowment fund or financial services		
		923	Indians (tribes, cultures, etc.)		
		924	Traffic or tariff bureau		

Source: U.S. Government Printing Office, Form 1023. Revised April 1996.

For instance, a religious organization is defined within Section 501(c)(3). But is it a church or synagogue? Is it a religious order? Is it Evangelism? See Codes 001–029. Similarly, a health organization is recognized as a 501(c)(3). But is it a hospital? Is it a blood bank? Is it a rescue squad? Is it a nursing or convalescent home? See Codes 150–179.

The organizational test requires clarity and specificity. It must be defined within the law. The IRS has developed tests to determine whether the way the organization functions is consistent with the intent of the definitions. It may look at such factors as the existence of a doctrine, a clergy, and a binding religious belief to determine whether an organization that calls itself a religion is within the terms and spirit of the law for purposes of extending tax exemption. Go back to *The Church of the Chosen People* v. *the U.S.* The IRS did not question whether it is a religion, for religion is protected by the First Amendment. As far as religion is concerned, the IRS will focus on whether the members are bound by a closely held belief that is not contrary to law or public policy. The status was denied because of personal inurement, which is contrary to law for a 501(c)(3). Would such a case stand today? Public policy changes over time.

The Political Test

To qualify under Section 501(c)(3), the nonprofit corporation must pass a political test. The organizing document must forbid the nonprofit from participating in any political campaign on behalf of a candidate. Participation is meant to include the preparation and distribution of campaign literature. Tax-exempt organizations are prohibited from making expenditures for political purposes, defined as spending to affect positively or negatively a candidate for political office. In *Campaign Academy* v. *Commissioner,* the organization was thus denied 501(c)(3) status because it was training candidates—all of whom turned out to be Republicans.

The Association of the Bar of the City of New York was denied status because its rating of judicial appointees was considered to be political and a substantial part of its activities. The Fund for the Study of Economic Growth and Tax Reform was denied tax-exempt status because, according to the IRS and the decision of Judge Ricardo Urbina, the reports of the organization "were intended to confer substantial private benefit to the Republican Party."

Nonprofits are also prohibited from making substantial expenditures for lobbying; because *substantial* is an elastic concept, a nonprofit may elect a more objective test of whether it is violating the lobbying law. This test distinguishes between two types of lobbying. One is to influence a proposed legislation. The other, called *grassroots lobbying,* is to influence people. Testifying on issues or sending information to members on issues or bills related to the mission of the organization is not lobbying. Telling them how to vote and how to influence their legislators is grassroots lobbying. Lobbying limited to approximately

20 percent of annual expenditure is permitted, but politicking is absolutely prohibited. I shall say more about lobbying later in this chapter.

The Asset Test

To be tax exempt as a 501(c)(3), it is also necessary for the nonprofit corporation to pass what is known as the asset test. To pass, the organizing charter must prohibit the nonprofit from distributing any of its assets or income to individuals as owners or as managers except for fair compensation for services rendered. Further, the nonprofit may not be used for the personal benefits of the founders, supporters, managers, their relatives, or personal or business associates.

The Plan of Dissolution

The dissolution plan is really an extension of the asset test. Each nonprofit, including associations, must have a dissolution plan. A dissolution plan is required to qualify as a Section 501(c)(3) corporation. The dissolution plan declares that in life as in death, the assets of a public welfare organization will not be distributed for the personal benefit of individuals.

The dissolution plan is like a living will. It tells how the assets of the corporation will be distributed if the corporation is dissolved. The dissolution plan needed for tax exemption by the IRS may be exactly the same as accepted by the state in the organizing document, be it a corporate charter or a deed of trust.

If the 501(c)(3) status is to be awarded, the federal requirement must be met even if it conflicts with the state's. Because states will often accept the classification of the federal government, and not necessarily the reverse, most dissolution plans follow the federal model. See the sixth stipulation in the IRS model charter above in the section, The Process of Becoming a Nonprofit Corporation.

A State's Dissolution Plan

In the state of Maryland, a typical case, a dissolution plan must provide that

1. The assets must first be used to meet the outstanding liabilities of the organization; that is, pay off its creditors.

2. The remaining assets must be distributed as is required by the contractual arrangements. For example, some assets are donated with the expressed agreement that the organization will, if necessary, dispose of them in a certain way, such as to offer them to a specific other but similar or related group.

3. The remaining assets not affected by the two previous conditions may be transferred to other charitable organizations (whether in or out of state) that are connected to the dissolving organization or that have a similar purpose for being.

4. Other assets may be distributed to members as provided for by law.

5. The remainder, if any, may be transferred to other persons as provided in the bylaws.

An actual dissolution plan may be as simple as that shown in the model charter. It may be more involved, depending upon the relationship of the organization to others or the intent of the organizers or founders. For example, the dissolving nonprofit may be part of a larger system, such as a hospital or religious order. Therefore, the concept *members,* in point four of the Maryland code stated above, refers invariably to another 501(c)(3) that is part of the system—not to an individual.

To dissolve an organization is to wind down its business and to terminate it at some precise date and hour that may or may not have been foreseen on the date of birth of the nonprofit corporation. As a living will, the dissolution plan must anticipate that at the time of dissolution a specifically named organization may no longer be in existence. Therefore, dissolution plans, like wills, carry concepts such as "successors" or "other 501(c)(3)s qualifying under state laws." State laws may be more (but not less) restrictive than the federal on how these assets may be distributed to these unanticipated "others." See point four in the Maryland law.

Changes in the dissolution plan have to be reported annually on Form 990 to the IRS and to the state. Clearly, these changes or amendments must be consistent with the provision that assets cannot be distributed to individuals or inure to their benefit, so the only qualified distributees are other 501(c)(3)s with a purpose similar to the one in termination, the state itself, or to organizations designated by the state.

Voluntary and Involuntary Dissolution

Dissolution may be voluntary or involuntary. Voluntary termination can take place either by a vote of trustees, a vote of members, or a combination of the two. Again, the individual state law dictates. In the state of Massachusetts, Section 11A says that the only way one of its nonprofits can dissolve voluntarily is by a majority vote of the board of trustees petitioning the court to dissolve the organization. The court then decides how the assets will be distributed. In Nevada and New Hampshire the members may elect to dissolve; but in the latter only 25 percent of votes is necessary whereas two-thirds is necessary in the former.

Involuntary dissolution can occur for many reasons. In Wisconsin, for example, these include (1) a fraudulent incorporation, (2) the abuse of authority and privileges, (3) the failure to appoint a registered agent for ninety days, (4) fraudulent acceptance of money or property or the use of them in ways unintended by their donors, (5) the failure to comply with court order for records, or if (6) the corporation by its own act or failure to act surrenders its charter, rights, and privileges. Missouri adds another condition, which is a finding by the court that the trustees are deadlocked and unable to act expeditiously on behalf of the organization. Minnesota adds to Wisconsin's reasons by allowing involuntary dissolution by discretion of the attorney general when the liabilities and obligations of the organization exceed its assets. In Missouri, the attorney general dissolved a nonprofit because it operated bingo without a license.

Whether dissolution is voluntary or involuntary, the distribution of the assets of the organization must be in accordance with the dissolution plan. In Minnesota, as long as the organization has substantial assets, such dissolution must also be supervised by the court.

Mergers, Sale, and Other Disposition of Assets as Dissolutions

In recent years, several states, including California, Oregon, and Michigan, have become very vigilant in cases of sale or changes in the control over assets of nonprofit corporations as forms of dissolution or dilution of control. In Chapter Nineteen we shall go further into this topic. The effect of these state initiatives is to attract greater attention to dissolution plans beyond fulfilling a requirement to gain 501(c)(3) status. The plan governs how assets are to be disposed of when such status is given up voluntarily or involuntarily, or when control over the assets of an organization is shared (joint ventures) or surrendered (sale or divestiture of assets) or contracted out through the organization's signing contracts (other than security or investment contracts) for firms to manage assets of the organization. The federal government requires the nonprofit to report annually the disposition of assets on Form 990. Some states have instituted more stringent rules. We shall discuss these in Chapter Nineteen. It is a fascinating topic.

Bankruptcy

Unlike the creditors of business firms, creditors of nonprofits cannot initiate an act of involuntary bankruptcy against the nonprofit and proceed to seize its assets. There is no involuntary bankruptcy by creditors. The attorney general of the state may petition the court. The organization's trustees may voluntarily declare bankruptcy. This means that the creditors cannot simply seize and liquidate the assets of a nonprofit to satisfy a debt, as they can with a firm or individual. This could be tantamount to seizing a public asset for personal gain.

ENACTMENT OF DISSOLUTION

States such as Tennessee and Alabama distinguish between involuntary dissolution due to administrative action and those due to judicial action and voluntary dissolution. Arizona 10–11420 specifies that a judicial dissolution can be based on the failure of the nonprofit to pay fees and penalties, to submit its annual report, or to have a resident agent or on the expiration of the corporation's duration as stated in its charter. In these cases the dissolution occurs by administrative action. These types of dissolution occur almost automatically by state administrative rules known at the time of incorporation.

Judicial dissolution occurs through actions of the court. It may be based on the organization's acquiring its charter deceitfully, or its continuous abuse of its legal authority, or by vote of fifty members holding at least 25 percent of the vote, or by a director petitioning the court for a dissolution. The directors or members may do this when (1) the directors are in such a deadlock that the continued functioning of the organization is in doubt, (2) the directors are about to or have engaged in illegal actions, (3) the corporate assets are being misused, (4) the members after at least two meetings cannot agree on who shall be on the board, and (5) the corporation is insolvent and either it or the attorney general has declared it unable to pay its debts. This type of dissolution occurs by the attorney general petitioning the court on his or her own initiative or on the behalf of a vote of the members themselves or their trustees.

A voluntary dissolution occurs by first a vote of the directors or members or founders (if the nonprofit has not yet started to operate). Then notice must be sent to the attorney general. The purpose is to give the attorney general an opportunity to request and receive an inventory of assets and financial statements and to assure accountability and the proper disposition of the assets. Dissolution can be done by vote of the directors or members—if it is an association. State law tells what the vote count must be.

What happens after dissolution? In the case of a judicial action in which it is determined that the nonprofit is incapable of winding down, the court may appoint a receiver. A receiver's job is to protect the assets of the organization and to make sure that the creditors are paid and that the best interests of the members are served if it is an association. This receiver is appointed by and given operating powers by the court. A receiver is usually given exclusive power over the assets of the organization. A receiver carries out the enactment of winding down, which is described below.

A dissolved organization continues as a corporation for the purposes of winding down. This means that it must continue to preserve and protect its assets, and continue to or make provisions for discharging its obligations and its liabilities and for disposing of its properties. Disposition of property may include returning properties, transferring properties, and other distribution consistent with law and the bylaws. Dissolution does not prevent the commencement of legal actions against the corporation in its own name. Neither does it terminate any legal actions already started, or discharge the registered agent from receiving legal papers against the organization—an act called *service*.

A dissolved organization must announce in the local media that it is dissolving and give those with unknown claims a deadline and the conditions for filing such claims. It need not honor claims made after the deadline. In Alabama, for example, the window is five days.

If a claimant did not receive the notice, or did not respond in time and in the form requested but the organization did not act upon the claim, or if the claim occurred after the dissolution, such claims must be honored. They can be honored to the extent of the assets of the organization. An entity or person (other than a creditor) to whom that organization distributed its assets during the wind-down will be responsible up to his or her pro rata share of the claim and the amount distributed.

The dissolution occurs when the attorney general or other designated agency of the state government extends certification that it is occurring. Finally, reorganizations, such as a merger or a sale of the entire assets of a nonprofit corporation, constitute a dissolution. A dissolution does not necessarily mean that the organization has no net assets. Whatever the source of the dissolution, the paragraphs above pertain.

EXEMPTION UNDER 501(c)(3) DOES NOT MEAN NO TAXES

A nonprofit corporation with tax-exempt status even under the most generous of these, 501(c)(3), may be liable for taxes. Tax exemption does not necessarily mean no taxes. Every nonprofit must have a Federal Employer Identification Number (EIN) for reporting, taxation, and other identification purposes. The Canadian equivalent of the EIN—the Business Number (BN)—is also required.

Nonprofit pays federal payroll tax. Exemption under 501(c)(3) means (1) that the organization does not pay taxes on gifts and donations, or on net business income as long as such is derived from an activity related to its mission, and (2) that gifts and donations to such an organization by individuals and corporations are tax deductible as long as they meet the criteria in Chapter Seven. Exemption for organizations in Table 2.2 that are outside the 501(c)(3) class does not cover the deductibility of gifts and contribution.

A 501(c)(3) and any other exempt organization may be subject to both federal and state income taxes on net earnings from business transactions unrelated to its mission. This is discussed in Chapter Ten. The organization may also be subject to state sales and local taxes, depending upon the specific state law. Hence, Virginia localities can tax gross business receipts of hospitals. In addition, states and localities may have special rules for determining whether a nonprofit is exempt from sales or real estate taxes or taxes on other property. In California, for example, only nonprofits that distribute food are exempt from sales tax.

In *Jimmy Swaggart Ministries* v. *Board of Equalization of California*, the Supreme Court, through the opinion of Justice Sandra Day O'Connor, affirmed the right of California to impose a 6 percent sales tax on the mail-order and crusade sales of religious items, noting that the tax was so incidental that it did not infringe on First Amendment rights of freedom of religion. In Pennsylvania, localities have worked out an agreement so that some prominent nonprofits, including universities, may negotiate a payment in lieu of paying taxes.

One reason the 501(c)(3) status does not automatically mean no taxes is that states (and provinces in Canada) are free to impose their own requirements for awarding state-level exemptions. Most states award exempt status to a nonprofit only after it is first awarded by the IRS. A few states—notably, Texas, Indiana, and California—require (Massachusetts recommends) that hospitals demonstrate that they provide specific community benefits as a condition for maintaining their tax-exempt status.

Pennsylvania goes beyond the IRS requirements for all nonprofit organizations. In Pennsylvania, to preserve its exemption at the state level, the nonprofit must be an organization (1) that advances a charitable purpose, (2) donates or renders gratuitously a substantial portion of its services, (3) benefits a substantial and indefinite class of people who are legitimate subjects of charity, (4) relieves the government of some of its burden, or (5) operates entirely free from private profit motive. In Pennsylvania, it is possible for a nonprofit to do all these things, be tax exempt, and yet end up making "a payment in lieu of taxes." This is a negotiated payment to cover the costs of services and benefits, including police services that the organization derives by virtue of its location in a specific Pennsylvania locality, such as Allegheny County.

STATES AND BLANKET EXEMPTIONS

State-level exemptions might be given for a class of organizations (typically hospitals, universities, or religious organizations), or all "charitable organizations," or in the form of private legislation (this simply means for the benefit of one specific organization—most often a university). The exemption may also be for a specific tax or some taxes. Alabama 40–9–12 is a worthy example of a blanket tax exemption. After naming many individual organizations with varying charitable missions by their proper names, it gives a broad and all-inclusive exemption. Accordingly, it states:

> a nonprofit corporation and . . . any branch or department of any of same heretofore or hereafter organized and existing in good faith in the State of Alabama, for other than pecuniary gain and not for individual profit, when such real or personal property shall be used by such associations or nonprofit corporations, their branches or departments in and about the conducting, maintaining, operating and carrying out of the program, work, principles, objectives, and policies of such associations or nonprofit corporations, their

branches or departments, in any city or county of the State of Alabama, are exempt from the payment of any and all state, county, and municipal taxes, licensers, fees, and charges of any nature whatsoever, including any privilege or excise tax heretofore or hereafter levied by the State of Alabama or any county or municipality thereof. The receipt, assessment, or collection of any fee, admission, service charge, rent, dues, or any other item or charge by any such association or nonprofit corporation for any services rendered by any such association or nonprofit corporation, its branches or departments or for the use or occupancy of any real or personal property of any such association or nonprofit corporation, its branches or departments in or about the conducting, maintaining, operating, and carrying out of the program, work, principles, objectives, and policies of any such association or nonprofit corporation, its branches or departments shall not be held or construed by any court, agency, officer, or commission of the State of Alabama, or any county or municipality thereof, to constitute pecuniary gain or individual profit by any such association or nonprofit corporation, its branches or departments, or the doing of business in such a manner as to prejudice or defeat, in any manner, the right and privilege of any such association or nonprofit corporation, its branches or departments, to claim or rely upon or receive the exemption of such association or nonprofit corporation, its branches or departments, and of all real and personal property thereof from taxation, as herein provided.

(b) With respect to gasoline, tobacco, playing card tax, or any other tax required by law to be prepaid by the retailer, the associations, nonprofit corporations, or organizations exempt under this section shall pay the appropriate tax at the time purchases are made, and the amount of such tax shall be refunded to such associations, nonprofit corporations, or organizations by the Department of Revenue pursuant to the procedures for refunds provided in Chapter 2A of this title. [Section 40–9–12 of the *Code of Alabama*]

States: Sales Tax Exemption

A church has among its members several craftsmen, builders, plumbers, laborers, and contractors—all of whom have volunteered their time and skill to build a new structure for the church. The church agreed to purchase the supplies by allowing these skilled workers to use its exempt certificate. This was disallowed by New Mexico tax ruling 407–72–1. States do not allow certificates to be used other than by agents or employees of the organization and only for the organization's charitable purposes. A parishioner cannot use the certificate even to purchase a donation for the church.

The vendor has interest in such laws granting exemptions to nonprofits. Another New Mexico ruling, 407–96–1, concluded that a vendor selling meals on a contract basis to nonprofits was selling a tangible personal property. And under the law, the receipts from such sales were deductible in calculating the vendor's gross receipts for tax purposes. In another part of the ruling, a hotel's receipts for meals, lodging, and similar services were deductible in calculating gross receipts because of the presentation of the nontaxable certificate by the nonprofit. But gratuities voluntarily given must be included.

In yet another case the use of the certificate to purchase construction materials without paying the New Mexico sales tax was denied because the tax applies only to the purchase of tangible personal property—not real estate or services. Therefore, its use to purchase construction material that would become part of an edifice (real estate) was denied. Again, even when the law may offer an exemption, the specific transaction may deny the availability of the exemption, and the nonprofit tax-exempt organization is taxed.

States: Income Tax Exemption

In general, states that have an income tax exempt nonprofits on the basis of their exemption from the federal income tax. But this is not always a sure thing. Basically, it is that an income stream may be defined both in its description and how it was acquired differently in the federal and state levels and thus cause an exception on the federal but not on the state level.

State and Local Property Tax

The property tax or *ad valorem* tax is principally a local tax. We are saved from going through local statutes for describing this tax because the permissible scope of these taxes is defined in state law. Therefore, if the state exempts the organization from local property tax, so does the local government. (See the Alabama case presented above.) This does not mean, however, that there are not instances (quite a number) in which the state offers no protection from local *ad valorem* taxes and therefore the organization pays it or makes a payment in lieu of taxes to the local government. This is true in several states, notably, Pennsylvania.

FACTORS THAT THREATEN THE LOSS OF TAX-EXEMPT STATUS UNDER 501(c)(3)

The 501(c)(3) status is an enviable one. How is it jeopardized and lost? What are the consequences on the managers?

The five principal reasons for the loss of tax-exempt (not the corporate) status are

1. Significant departure from the mission

2. Subversion of the assets to personal benefits

3. Excessive lobbying

4. Politicking

5. Persistent failure to obey reporting requirements

Note that the loss of exemption is not equivalent to a dissolution. In a dissolution, the corporation disappears. In the loss of an exemption, the corporation continues to exist and operate but without the benefit of whatever level of exemption it carried.

Departure from Mission

Earlier in this chapter we dealt with the character of the mission and the basic principle that a nonprofit, tax-exempt organization under 501(c)(3) operates in a noncommercial manner to fulfill a public purpose defined under the IRS code. The substantial breaking of this covenant will lead to the loss of exemption. The manager can be exposed to civil or even a state-level suit for transgressing a fiduciary responsibility by substantially diverting the assets of the organization. This is especially true when the organization is a membership organization or when it holds significant assets of public interest; that is, a hospital or an endowment.

Personal Inurement, Self-Dealing

Subversion of the assets of the organization for personal use results in self-dealing and personal inurement. Whether the organization loses its tax-exempt status will depend upon how systemic this breach is. If it is not endemic to the organization but relates to specific transactions, managers, other individuals associated with the organization, and the organization itself will risk severe penalties.

The reader may revisit *Chosen People* v. *the U.S.* The personal benefits disqualified the organization. For most operating nonprofits, however, the issue boils down to specific transactions that are of two types: (1) self-dealing in terms of excessive compensation in a sale or as compensation for work, and (2) self-dealing in terms of diversion of the assets of the organization for personal benefit or gain. This may range from loans to the use of facilities for personal benefits at a lease rate that is unreasonable. In all of these cases, the organization, management, and individuals are subject to stiff fines.

Federal and state laws prohibit self-dealing.

Excessive Lobbying

Lobbying is divided into two categories: *Grassroots lobbying* is the attempt to influence legislation through influencing the public, whereas *direct lobbying* is an attempt to influence legislation through influencing any member or employee of a legislative body or an employee of government who may participate in the formulation of a legislation.

Certain actions common among nonprofits are not considered to be lobbying. These include

1. Sharing the results of nonpartisan research
2. Studying or discussing social and economic problems

3. Providing technical assistance to a jurisdiction or governmental body when that assistance was requested in writing

4. Communicating or appearing before a legislative body on themes that may influence the organization, its mission, and its tax-exempt status

5. Communicating between the organization and its members on a proposed legislation unless the members are urged to take specific action or to encourage others to act

6. A communication with a government or legislative official when that is not intended to influence legislation

An organization may elect one of two limits on its lobbying expenditures. It may promise that no substantial part of its assets will be used in lobbying or related activities. Generally, the organization may satisfy this if some amount less than 20 percent of its annual expenditures is for such purposes. Organizations that plan on doing more than this may elect the mathematical limit on lobbying expenditures. See Appendix 2.1. for a step-by-step description of this mathematical procedure. Alternatively, the organization may seek classification as a 501(c)(4), (5), or (6) with unlimited lobbying privileges. We discuss these in Chapter Five.

For an affiliated group of 501(c)(3) organizations, the election of the mathematical procedure by any one member of the group will affect all. The excess lobbying by one will be divided proportionately among all members of the group. For these purposes, an affiliated group exists when there is a common governing instrument requiring members to be bound on legislative issues or where they share executives, officers, trustees, and staff members and these individuals have sufficient voting power among them to determine the action of the controlled organization on legislative issues. Notice that the "group" for lobbying purposes is not synonymous to the "group" for exempt purposes, as discussed in Chapter Three.

The tax on excess expenditures on lobbying is 25 percent of the excess amount that year. The excess may be defined in terms of either grassroots or direct lobbying expenditures. To determine this amount, the organization would calculate its actual or planned expenditures in each category that would be nontaxable because they fall within the acceptable range, and then calculate 25 percent of the excess.

What a manager has to keep in mind is that flagrant or continuous excess lobbying could lead to loss of exempt status. When this occurs, both the organization and the managers responsible are subject to a penalty. The manager will be subject to a tax equaling 5 percent of the excess amount if it can be argued that the manager agreed to this expenditure knowing that it could lead to revocation of exempt status. The manager is spared if he or she can demonstrate that the action was due to reasonable cause and was not willful.

The organization is also subject to a tax on excess lobbying expenditures that is 5 percent of the excess amount—if the excess leads to loss of exemption. This does not apply to churches, or church-related organizations, or to those who have elected the mathematical lobbying limits under Sec. 501(h). Lobbying is further discussed in Chapters Three and Five of this book.

Politicking

Expenditures for political purposes are prohibited for all 501(c)(3) organizations. Political expenditures include those intended to promote or oppose a candidate, the control of such an organization by a candidate, the dissemination or propagation of a political philosophy or position with the aim of promoting a party or influencing a campaign. When these occur, in any amount, the organization and the managers are taxed. This tax can be avoided if the amount spent and the materials distributed are recovered and if safeguards are implemented to protect against political actions in the future.

The tax on the management (defined as trustees, officers, or any employee having authority over these expenditures) is 2.5 percent of these expenditures if the responsible persons agree to correcting the situation. It rises to 50 percent if they do not agree. No tax is imposed on those who did not act willingly and knowingly and if their actions were due to reasonable cause.

The organization is subject to an initial tax of 10 percent of the expenditure. If it fails to correct the situation satisfactorily within a specified period, its tax rises to 100 percent of the expenditure. The ultimate penalty for the organization is the loss of status and the inability to re-qualify specifically for exemption under 501(c)(4) as a civic or social welfare organization (discussed in Chapter Five).

How does the IRS know that there are political expenditures or lobbying to be taxed? Every tax-exempt organization that files a 990, 990EZ, or 990PF has to report political and lobbying expenditures on those forms. Furthermore, every tax-exempt organization has to file Form 1120–L, which discloses lobbying expenditures for any organization with such expenditures and that also has net investment income. A bank money market account or certificate (CD) may be enough to meet the second condition.

The Lobbying Disclosure Act of 1995, as amended in 1998, requires certain organizations to register semiannually as lobbyists with the Secretary of the Senate and the Clerk of the U.S. House of Representatives. Any organization with lobbying expenditures at the federal level of $20,500 or more semiannually that makes contacts to influence high executive branch employees or Congress may also be required to register. The key areas covered by this registration are the subject matters of the lobbying activities, the expenses, the persons lobbied, and the role of foreign entities.

In calculating lobbying expenditures, an organization has to include the amount it expends on hiring an outside lobbyist. The outside lobbyists of churches and church affiliates that are normally not required to register, may have to include them among their reported clients. Whether an outside lobbyist includes the nonprofit organization among its clients depends upon two facts: It receives at least $5000 semiannually from the organization, and its lobbying effort is at least 20 percent of the effort it expends for the organization.

To calculate its own lobbying expenses, the organization must include that which it expends on outside lobbyists. To calculate its internal lobbying expenses, it may take the percentage of time spent by each worker involved in lobbying and multiply that by the average salary to get the worker costs. But supplies, communications, support staff, and overhead should also be added. Alternatively, if the organization has a Washington, D.C. office that has lobbying as its principal function, it might use the entire cost of that operation. Further, if there is a central organization that controls the lobbying of a number of its units, it can file a consolidated report. Finally, if a 501(c)(3) has to report lobbying expenses to the IRS it may use that amount in reporting its disclosure.

Often organizations form coalitions for lobbying purposes. The coalition must report any organization that donated $10,000 or more to its efforts. It must also report any foreign participant and its contribution.

All new lobbying arrangements must be reported forty-five days after the first contact is made or the lobbyist is employed or retained. If an organization hires an outside firm and pays that firm at least $5,000 semiannually and at least 20 percent of the work it does for that organization is lobbying, it must file a report indicating that that organization is its client. Therefore, using an outside firm may not obviate the need to register.

Section 18 of the Lobbying Disclosure Act makes 501(c)(4) organizations that lobby ineligible for federal grants, awards, or contracts. The False Statement Accountability Act of 1996 makes it unlawful for any person or organization to file false statements knowingly. Failure to comply with the Lobbying Disclosure Act is subject to civil action and a fine of no more than $50,000.

Failure to File: Form 990

Form 990 (or its short version 990–EZ) is the annual report that public organizations must file. Private foundations file 990–PF. Though it is submitted to the IRS, it is not a tax form, the latter being the 990–T. The 990 is similar to the 10Ks that public for-profit corporations file. Certain groups are exempted from filing. They are churches and church affiliates, organizations chartered by the U.S. Congress, state institutions, or corporations that are an instrumentality of the United States, some apostolic organizations that are required to file as partnerships, and 501(c)(3)s that have gross receipts of less than $25,000. In the case of a group exemption, both the central organization and each of the affiliates must submit a 990.

What does a Form 990 show? The Form 990 is the key to public disclosure and the key to the IRS monitoring of the organization—proof that it is fulfilling its mission and the terms of the social contract upon which the tax exemption was granted. It details debt, revenues and expenses, changes in fund balances, program accomplishments, and the amounts derived by various activities and whether they are taxable; it requires the organization to show how these activities relate to tax-exempt purposes and accomplishments, and it requires reporting on the percentage of ownership of subsidiaries and the income derived from them. It also shows a listing of the directors, officers, and key employees, the amount of time they put into the organization and the amount they were paid in compensation and expenses. In addition, it shows lobbying and politicking activities and expenses, whether there was a change in control or disposition of assets or changes in the organizing documents such as the charter or deed, whether the organization complied with disclosure requirements in its solicitations, and whether the organization is part of a reporting group. It is unfortunate that many managers never read their own 990s. Most are prepared by accounting firms.

Failure to file the 990 or to do so correctly can result in fines up to the smaller of 5 percent of the organization's gross receipts or $10,000, and up to $5,000 on the managers responsible.

Failure to File: Payroll Tax

All nonprofits that pay wages to employees are required to withhold, deposit, pay, and report federal income, social security and Medicare (FICA), and federal unemployment taxes unless the taxes clearly do not apply. Payments for the service of ministers of churches or a member of a religious order are not subject to FICA or FUTA, and payments to persons working for 501(c)(3) are exempt from FUTA. An organization's failure to pay these taxes will lead to a 100 percent tax on the manager, officer, or employee responsible.

To be exempt from FICA, a church and church affiliates must seek the permission of the IRS. If it is granted, the employees would be subject to self-employment taxes—effectively shifting the tax burden from the organization to the employee. Certain religious employees, on the basis of conscience, such as Christian Scientists, may seek exemption from FICA while performing religious-related duties.

Persistent Failure to File: State and Federal Conformance

The failure to file proper forms on a timely basis offends both the state and the federal governments, and both may impose penalties. Indeed, the state-level penalties can be more severe because they often lead to involuntary dissolution. Some of these penalties, such as filing an annual registration, can lead to automatic dissolution, and dissolution often leads to fines and disqualification. The failure to register annually whether or not a fee is due signals to the state that the organization no longer exists—not that it is dormant.

THE CHARITABLE PURPOSE IN CANADA[2]

According to Revenue Canada—Canada's counterpart to the United States Internal Revenue Service—there are some 70,000 organizations registered in that country as charities. These are equivalent to the 501(c)(3) organizations described in this chapter. Thus, the Canadian sector is about 10 percent as large as the sector in the United States.

In Canada, as in the United States, these organizations cover a wide range of missions—all intended to advance community rather than private welfare. Indeed, in all of these organizations in both countries, personal inurement is forbidden. So, too, is politicking. The Canadian organizations have a lower threshold for lobbying—about 10 percent of revenues. United States' organizations can be reasonably safe below 20 percent and can go higher if they specifically opt to do so and are grated permission by the Internal Revenue Service.

In both countries this status is received through a legal process of becoming a corporation or trust and then proceeding to obtain a tax-exempt status. In both countries, tax exemption does not mean no taxes, although there are significant differences between the two countries in this regard. In both countries, an organization once having achieved that status can lose it by violating certain rules, including the violation of the organization's mission, which is a social contract intended to be a permanent commitment.

In the United States, when the Internal Revenue Service (IRS) revokes a tax-exempt status, it publishes that fact for the public to know. So, too, does Revenue Canada. But, while the IRS usual does so by collecting taxes from the period of violation and imposing certain penalties, Revenue Canada may go an additional step and slap a 100 percent penalty on the assets of the corporation. Such an action is usually left to the individual states in the United States. Moreover, Revenue Canada may require the organization to keep and to hold records for several years after revocation of its tax-exempt status.

There are several key differences between the two countries, and these will be highlighted in the chapters that follow. The reader is alerted to look at how (1) the two countries measure the public support that both require, (2) the limitations on business activities, (3) the tax treatment of gifts and contributions, (4) the meaning of exemption, especially at the provincial level, (5) the general concepts of charities, associations, and nonprofits, (6) the required annual disbursement levels, (7) the limitations on the composition of the board of directors or trustees, and (8) how associated organizations are treated.

SUMMARY AND PREVIEW

The nonprofit corporation has certain powers and responsibilities. When these conform to certain expectations, the corporation may be assigned a tax-exempt status. The most generous of these is the 501(c)(3). This precious status can be lost by errant managers who can, themselves, be exposed to penalties at state and federal levels.

The 501(c)(3) status is a broad umbrella for organizations promoting public welfare. The umbrella covers a number of organizations with varying missions. The law further subdivides these organizations into those which rely on public financial support and those which are privately financed. The next chapter turns to a description of those organizations that are publicly supported.

CHAPTER THREE

The Nonprofit
as a Public Corporation

All nonprofit organizations do not have the same privileges and basic legal operating rules. The publicly supported nonprofit is given the greatest amount of tax and other benefits. These organizations are exempt at two levels. Donors can deduct charitable contributions to them at the highest deduction rate available, and revenues from doing the organization's mission are exempt from taxes.

States give these organizations even greater benefits and privileges. These range from blanket exemptions from all taxes to special privileges such as, in Mississippi, the ability to hire prisoners in food services in exchange for credit toward time served. To obtain these privileges, the organization must be both organized and operated in a legally prescribed way. Failure to follow these rules could lead to heavy fines on the managers.

How must these organizations be operated and what must be their legal foundation? What are the unequivocal prohibitions? What are the penalties on the organization and its management if there are violations? Appendix 3.1 demonstrates why it is important to know these rules.

FORMING THE PUBLICLY SUPPORTED ORGANIZATION

Rules concerning the formation and operation of the publicly supported organization are contained in Section 501(c)(3) of the *Internal Revenue Code*. The organizations formed to fit these rules are called 501(c)(3)s. But Section 501(c)(3) also describes organizations formed not to be publicly supported and that do not operate in this fashion. In short, contrary to common parlance, a publicly supported organization is merely a subset of the organizations described under Section 501(c)(3) of the Code.

Since the publicly supported organization is a subset of the 501(c)(3) we must begin by understanding the umbrella requirements of 501(c)(3)s and then proceed to the specific requirements of this subset known as publicly supported organizations. As we get deeper into this subject, we shall use certain numbers representing sections of the *Internal Revenue Code*. At first blush, this may seem unnecessary. It is, however, necessary. When the IRS or the courts or legal authorities refer to nonprofits, they use these codes. The reason is that these code numbers define specific rules on the formation, operation, and the financing of these organizations.

THE BASIC REQUIREMENTS OF 501(c)(3)s

A nonprofit corporation becomes exempt from taxation when it is given a 501(c)(3) status by the Internal Revenue Service. See Figure 3.1.

To get this status, the nonprofit must

1. Be organized as a nonprofit corporation or trust.
2. Pass three tests: (a) the organizational, (b) the political, and (c) the asset test, which is expressed in its charter as well as in its dissolution plan. These tests are described in Chapter Two.

Based on the above, the nonprofit is awarded a tax-exempt status into the 501(c)(3) club, which is divided into two broad categories—public organizations and private foundations.

As shown in Figure 3.1, there are four categories of public nonprofit organizations. They are known by the section of the IRS Code under which they are described. They are the 509(a)(1)s, 509(a)(2)s, 509(a)(3)s, and the 509(a)(4)s. In addition, there are two types of private foundations—the operating and the nonoperating. The manager must obey the operating expectations imposed by law on each of these. This chapter focuses on the public organization. The next chapter will deal with private organizations.

PRIVILEGES OF PUBLIC ORGANIZATIONS

Once a nonprofit has won classification under Section 501(c)(3), it must, by law, be further classified as shown in Figure 3.1. It must either be classified as a private foundation or a public organization. Public organizations enjoy several

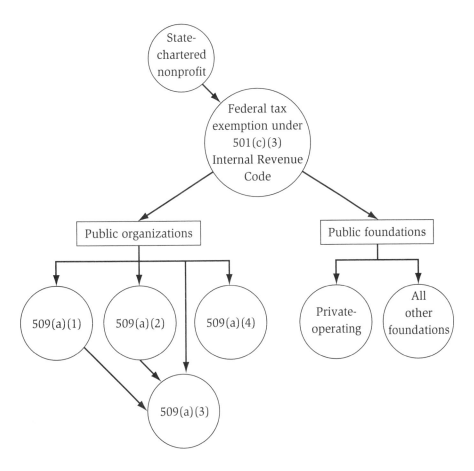

Figure 3.1. Transformation of Organization by Tax-Exempt Status under Section 501(c)(3).

privileges. Contributions to them receive the most favorable tax treatment in the sense that contributions are deductible by the donors. They do not have to pay an excise tax on their investment income. Unless they fall into the special category noted as 509(a)(3), they do not have to make annual distributions of their assets to other charities the way private foundations do. States recognize this status and confer additional exemptions to these organizations. This includes exemptions from income, sale, and real estate or property taxes.

The Public Charities: Section 509(a)(1) Organizations

Section 509(a)(1) organizations are nonprofits that are known as publicly supported organizations because their common characteristic is that they are supported by the general public. The characteristics required to be classified under this section are given in Section 170(b)(1)(A) of the *Internal Revenue Code.*

The types of organizations that are exempt under Section 170(b)(1)(A) are shown in Table 3.1. These are generally the public charities that provide direct services to the community, but also defined under Subtitle (v) are state and local government agencies. The Constitution of the United States is based on the principle that the federal government is the creation of the states and not vice versa. Therefore, the purpose of Subtitle (v) is not to create states; its principal purpose is to provide for gifts and contributions to be made to state and local government agencies, such as school boards, and be deductible by the donors. Therefore, we can make contributions to reduce the deficit of a jurisdiction, including the federal deficit, and deduct that amount.

Subtitle *vi* refers to public-supported charities—a broad category. This encompasses most of the organizations that we know as public charities and nonprofit organizations. Martha's Table is a public charity, a 501(c)(3) as defined under 509(a)(1) and 170(b)(1)(A)(vi). Martha's Table runs a soup kitchen, a thrift shop, and educational programs for poor children in the District of Columbia. But it also includes research institutions and a host of other organizations that would not consider themselves charities in the traditional sense. They are not eleemosynary. What they have in common is that they depend upon public support.

Proof of Public Support: 509(a)(1)

Since public support is key, how is it demonstrated? Proof of public support for 509(a)(1) organizations comes in the form of passing one of two tests: the one-third public financial support test, or the 10 percent financial support and facts and circumstances test. The facts and circumstances test shows that the organization operates in a public manner although it cannot demonstrate this by showing that at least one-third of its financial support is from the public.

To demonstrate that it "normally" has public support through the one-third test, a nonprofit must show that over the preceding four years, at least

Table 3.1. Nonprofits Described under Section 170 of the *Internal Revenue Code.*

Section 170(b)(1)(A)	Type of Nonprofit Described
i	Churches
ii	Educational institutions
iii	Hospitals and medical research
iv	Agencies that support government schools
v	Government units that receive gifts for public purposes
vi	Publicly supported charities
vii	Certain private foundations
viii	509(a)(2) and (a)(3) organizations

one-third of its financial support came from the government or the general public, foundations, corporations, or a combination of these. The words *support, normal,* and *public* are specifically defined.

Support includes gifts, contributions, membership fees (excluding the portion that is an assessment for special services), net income from unrelated businesses, gross investment income, revenues from taxes levied by the government for the benefit of the nonprofit, and the value of facilities furnished by the government free of charge if those facilities are usually rented or sold.

Note that 509(a)(1) support refers to income from unrelated business rather than to related business. This means that a nonprofit cannot include in its calculation of support any revenues it receives from an activity for which it is tax exempt if the payment benefits the payor. To illustrate, a nonprofit exempt as a day-care center cannot include as support fees from parents for caring for their children. These payments benefit the payors and are in conjunction with the tax-exempt purpose of the day-care center. If the day-care center owns a fast-food restaurant, an unrelated business catering to the general public, the net income from this business may be included in the calculation of support. If the parents made a contribution for assisting children (other than their own) who are members of the general public, this would be support. If the parents contributed anything such as services that are not deductible contributions, these contributions will not be included in the calculation of support. Do you see the rationale? It does not tempt the organization to penny-pinch poor people to show public support.

Also, membership dues qualify as support only after adjustment is made for the portion of the dues that is a payment for services, such as a magazine. It is only the portion that is for the general support of the organization that counts.

Facilities received by the organization from the government cannot be included as support unless the government usually charges for the use of these facilities or sells them.

By *public* is meant governmental units and the general population. A gift or contribution from a community trust, itself a tax-exempt nonprofit, is a contribution from the public if these trusts receive their funds primarily from contributions from the general public and are based on public participation. Earnings from an endowment created by public funds are also considered a public contribution. Obviously, contributions from foundations, persons, and firms are also public. It is the concentration of contributions from a few people that creates the problem.

The word *normally* also has a precise meaning. It spans the revenue-raising experience over the preceding four years. The classification of the nonprofit is determined for a current and the next year based on the performance of the organization over the four preceding years. It is publicly supported in years 2006 and 2007 if it passes the public support test in 2002 and 2005. It is publicly supported in 2007 and 2008 if it passes the test for the period 2003 to 2006, and so on. A nonprofit can have its classification changed depending on how it performed over the preceding four years. Since a classification is not given in perpetuity, a publicly supported organization will lose that favored status when it can no longer prove public support.

Calculation of Public Financial Support: 509(a)(1)

As I will explain further later in this chapter, public support in Canada is determined by limiting the percentage of revenues and trustees that can come from one source or from more than one related sources. In the United States, it is more complicated. For a nonprofit to be classified as a public organization under 509(a)(1) as defined in Section 170(b)(1)(A) by proving it has public support, it must demonstrate that a portion of its total support, as previously defined, is from the general public. How is this proved? One test requires that at least one-third of such support must come from the general public (government, foundations, firms, and people from the community at large). Alternatively, the nonprofit may show that at least 10 percent of its support comes from the general public, but that the facts and circumstances surrounding the operation of the organization prove that it encourages and involves public participation and that there is a continuous effort to attract public support, for example, through fund-raising drives.

A Deeper Look into the 10 Percent Test

One focus in applying the 10 percent facts and circumstances test is on the source of the other 90 percent. Is there some reasonable way to say that the amount came indirectly from the public? For example, is it from an endowment created by the public? If so, the nonprofit wins or maintains classification as a 509(a)(1) public organization.

If the interest and dividends are from the investment of funds in a publicly created endowment, the organization may be less likely to pass if the investment income is from a gift from a single individual. The circumstances are important.

But the IRS may focus on the 10 percent rather than on the 90 percent. If this came from one or two individuals, the lack of public support may be implied. Because the test is subjective, we cannot be sure how the given example will be interpreted. The nonprofit would probably be helped if a major source is a publicly supported community chest.

The IRS has five factors that it considers in its facts and circumstances test—which it now calls its "attraction of public support requirement":

1. Percentage of financial support: If the organization normally gets at least 10 percent of its financial support from the public, is this mostly from an endowment or investment created by the public rather than a few individuals?

2. Sources of financial support: Do the sources of the 10 percent represent government and a diversity of people rather than just a few?

3. Composition of the governing board and open membership: Is the board a cross section of the community, including elected or appointed public officials? Is membership in the organization open to the general public?

4. The availability of facilities or services factor: Does the nonprofit open its facilities to the public, and does it conduct or participate in programs for the general public?

5. Other factors representing broad community support: Does the organization appeal to people who have some broad but common interest? Are the dues of the organization for individuals set so high that a substantial part of the public cannot enroll?

The Effect of Large Contributions on Public Support

The nonprofit cannot meet either the one-third or 10 percent test by merely getting a few large contributions from individuals. Let us demonstrate what happens. Based on the definition of support given earlier, assume that a nonprofit we will call Doyle Charities has investment income (interest and dividends) of $100,000, contributions from its community chest of $40,000, and from Beverly for $50,000, Audrey for $10,000, and Anhela for $1,000. Its total support is $201,000. According to the rule, one-third ($67,000) of the total support must be from the general public. Note, however, that of the $101,000 coming from the public, about half came from one source, Beverly, who contributes $50,000. To defeat this ploy, the rules state that no individual's contribution may be included to an extent that it exceeds 2 percent of the total support (in this case, 2 percent of $201,000 or $4,020). Hence, the contributions of Beverly and Audrey are valued for calculation purposes at $4,020 each, or a total of $8,040. When this $8,040 is added to the $1,000 and the $40,000 from the community chest, the sum, $49,040, is less than the required $67,000, so the organization fails the one-third support test.

The nonprofit would have made the one-third support test if instead of two large individual contributions by Beverly and Audrey, it had at least fifteen small contributions of no more than $4,020 each. Again, the purpose is to avoid defeat of the intent of the law that public support be demonstrated.

Unusually Large Gifts and Grants

But a large gift or grant can cause a nonprofit to fail the one-third or 10 percent test of public support by increasing the denominator (total support) much more than the numerator (public support). How can such a gift be treated to reduce this negative impact?

The impact depends upon whether the gift is considered unusual. An *unusual grant* is one that the organization received because it is a publicly supported organization (as opposed to a private foundation), was unexpected, and would adversely affect the organization's ability to pass the public support test.

In addition to these three characteristics, an unusual grant is one made by a person who was not a founder or substantial donor to the organization prior to the gift, who receives no authority or power over the organization as a consequence of it, who makes no unusual demand of the organization as a condition of making the gift, and who makes the gift in the form of cash or an asset that represents the organization's tax-exempt purpose (art to an art museum) or marketable securities, and if the terms of the grant are limited to one year's operating (as opposed to capital) expenses. An unusually large grant is treated by removing the amount from the calculation of support and also from the calculation of "public." Being removed both from the numerator and the denominator, it has no impact on the organization's meeting the public support test.

Other factors may play a part in determining whether a gift is unusual. These include whether the organization would have made the public support hurdle without this grant, whether the organization has a representative board of trustees, whether the organization can reasonably be expected to meet the public support test in the future or whether it will become reliant on such unusual grants, whether the grant was the result of a fund-raising campaign and therefore a result of a public appeal rather than a private one or a private initiative, and whether it is from a living person or a dead one. The law assumes that a dead person cannot exert control over the organization. It aims at avoiding control of the organization by a single person or a small group via control of its purse strings.

But what if the grant or gift cannot be classified as unusual and it stops the organization from passing the public support test? Clearly, the classification could be changed to a private foundation. In such a case, the donor could become a disqualified person unless the contribution is less than 25 percent of the total support the organization received from all sources during the immediately preceding four years; or unless the person had received a notification from the IRS or from the management of the organization that such a large gift would not have had an adverse impact on its classification.

As a disqualified person, the donor now becomes exposed to self-dealing when engaged in economic transactions with the organization and in setting the compensation of others. See Chapters Four and Thirteen.

IRS Certification of Organization's Tax-Exempt Status

The letter finally awarding the status, a real prototype of which appears as Appendix 3.1., gives the following information:

1. The foundation status: in this case, a 509(a)(1) & 170(b)(1)(A)(vi)

2. When and if the organization has to file a 990 and the penalty for not filing

3. That the organization is described in section 501(c)(3) of the *Internal Revenue Code*

4. That it is not a private foundation

5. That it is liable for social security but not unemployment taxes

6. That there is a liability for excess benefit transactions

7. That the contributions to the organization are deductible by the donors

8. That donors and private foundations may rely on this letter until the status is lost and until that fact is published by the IRS and known by the public

9. That the value of benefits the organization gives the donor should be given to them by the organization for it is not deductible

10. That the organization must provide substantiation of the donation

11. That the organization is required to make its annual return available for public inspection for three years after the return is due and also make its letter of tax exemption available upon request

12. That the organization is not liable for federal income tax unless it earns unrelated business income

13. That the organization should use its employer identification in communicating with the IRS

In some cases, generally upon the request of the applicant for 501(c)(3), the IRS will award a provisional status of 501(c)(3) pending a final determination. Such a provisional letter will contain, in addition to the items listed above, the following:

1. A statement that because the organization is new, a provisional determination that it is a 501(c)(3) is being made based upon the information given and until further determination

2. That the organization is being treated as publicly supported

The reader should recall that the awarding of a status is not permanent. It may be lost. When it is, the IRS publishes that information and thus denies the organization certain cherished privileges and denies the donor the level of deduction to which they may otherwise have been entitled. The focus of this book is on the development of successful strategies that are consistent with the duties enumerated above.

Finally, while our example is a 509(a)(1) rather than an (a)(2), the letter for the latter is basically the same. The two have the same responsibilities and are exposed to the same risks of lost of status. There are differences in the way public support is calculated. We now turn to the determination of 509(a)(2).

FEE-FOR-SERVICE ORGANIZATIONS: 509(a)(2) ORGANIZATIONS

The 509(a)(1) and (a)(2) organizations are both publicly supported. But the (a)(2)s, unlike the 509(a)(1)s, have clients who can pay for services. Therefore, their mission-related business income is considered support. Universities (tuitions), museums (entrance fees), and hospital (charges) are examples.

A 509(a)(2) is subject to two tests: the one-third public financial support test, the denominator of which is different from that of the 509(a)(1); and "the not more than one-third support" test, which has no 509(a)(1) counterpart.

The 509(a)(2) organizations differ from 509(a)(1)s in what is included in the calculation of support (the denominator for calculating the one-third public support). Unlike 509(a)(1)s, they include not only unrelated business income but also related business income.

But their related business income from any one source can only be the greater of $5,000 or 1 percent of the organization's total support. The effect of this is to recognize that unlike the organizations under 509(a)(1), which tend to the needy who may not be able to pay, these organizations often function on the ability of their clients to pay a fee. But the rule limits the extent to which the charging of that fee to a few or a select class of people (clients) can substitute for the expression of the public that they are willing to support the organization financially; that is, that in the eyes of the public the organization does something of value for the community.

A similar rule for these organizations says that a source's gift (not just fees) can only be counted as public to the extent that it is not more than the greater of $5,000 or 1 percent of the organization's support. Therefore, the organization cannot escape by turning to single donors.

To pass the second test, the 509(a)(2) must demonstrate that the sum of their gross investment income and their after-tax profits from unrelated businesses does not exceed one-third of their total support. This latter test has the effect of forcing the search for public financial support even for organizations that could be self-supporting. As price is a measure of value in a commercial setting, public welfare is a measure of value with these types of nonprofits.

Gross investment income includes rents, royalties, interests, dividends but does not include any income that would be classified as unrelated. As we shall see in Chapter Ten, the effect of excluding unrelated business income in calculating gross investment income is that some investment incomes could be denominated by the IRS as unrelated and, therefore, be double-counted if not for this rule.

DIVERSIFICATION AND PRESERVATION OF TAX-EXEMPT STATUS

Section 509(a)(2) organizations are not conceptually different from 509(a)(1)s in the sense that both are publicly supported. But they are alternatives to each other based on the way their public support test is calculated. Many organizations that would satisfy one also would satisfy the other.

A comparison of the requirements of 509(a)(1) and (a)(2) classifications reveals that it is not simply the source of support that counts, but the composition or structure of support as well. Diversification of funding sources is always wise because it reduces the risk of financial failure. But as we shall see, diversification has an important implication for how a nonprofit is classified. Furthermore, because one classification tends to favor certain types of support while the other classification favors others, it does not necessarily follow that the favored combinations would lead predictably to either one or the other classification, a Section 509(a)(1) or (a)(2).

In referring to Figure 3.2, suppose nonprofit A expected to have a large investment income and a large unrelated business income (cell 1). Since both of these are included as support in the calculations for 509(a)(1) status, we may at first conclude that such a status is what nonprofit A would fit. The problem is that this combination only increases the size of support. The rule requires that one-third of the financial support be public. Thus, the larger the amount associated with cell 1, the greater the amount that has to be obtained from the general public through gifts and contributions in order for the nonprofit to meet either the one-third or the 10 percent support test.

If the organization's fund-raising strategy is represented by cell 1, being a 509(a)(2) may not be the answer either. This is so because the rules stated

		Type of business	
		Unrelated	Related
Other income	Investment income	1	2
	Gifts, grants contributions membership fees	3	4

Figure 3.2. Hypothetical Major Sources of Funding of Public Charities.

earlier limit that combination to no more than one-third of the total support. Therefore, the higher the amount represented in cell 1, the greater the amount of public support (the other two-thirds) that will be needed to meet the requirements to be a 509(a)(2). For (a)(2) organizations, this implies a larger amount from gifts and donations and from related business income; that is, income from conducting its mission. Both are derived from catering to the public, thus demonstrating greater public support. This is even more so because the amount of related business income from any one source that can be counted is limited by law.

Cell 2 is dangerous. Although many 509(a)(2)s may seem to fit because of their reliance on fees and the importance of investment income to them, the danger is that this revenue pattern is no different for a firm. A for-profit firm relies on sales of its products or services (a close resemblance to related income) and its earnings from marketable securities or other investments. Consequently, tax exemption is often denied an organization because it "looks" commercial. In short, the more an organization's income stream places it in cell 2, the more the need to demonstrate public support and a strong commitment to a defined tax-exempt mission, as explained in Chapters One and Two.

Cell 3 seems safe for a 509(a)(1) organization. The problem may arise from the relative weights of unrelated business income to gifts, grants contributions, membership fees, and the like. Obviously, if a nonprofit falls in cell 3 but with an overwhelming amount of its revenues being unrelated business, it must resort to providing evidence of a tax-exempt purpose like those in cell 2, because these organizations are also not easily distinguishable from a for-profit firm. They, too, rely heavily on sales.

Consider cell 4. The rules suggest that a nonprofit that emphasizes gifts and grants and related business as sources of income may be better off selecting Section 509(a)(2) because these two sources of funding are favorably treated. Indeed, the rules would be satisfied if all the funds came from this combination. Suppose, however, 60 percent of the funds fell in cell 4. Then the nonprofit may fail to qualify as 509(a)(2) if more than one-third of the remaining 40 percent falls in cell 1. This is so because a second rule, as described earlier, says that no more than one-third of the support may be a combination of unrelated business income and gross investment income. Again, it is the composition of support that counts.

The key. All the cells present problems of the same type. The lessons are two: (1) The classifications do not permit escape from the requirement of public support, and (2) it is the composition or structure of support rather than the individual source (unless all the funds come exclusively from public sources) that matters. Good management should pay attention to diversification to avoid risk of financial failure and also to meet and maintain the classification requirements.

COMPARISON OF 509(a)(1) AND (a)(2) ORGANIZATIONS

Both the 509(a)(1) and (a)(2) organizations must demonstrate public support, and in this sense they are both publicly supported nonprofits. Both must have a mission to advance public welfare and both may conduct related and unrelated businesses. The basic difference is that the (a)(2) organizations are financed more by business income, particularly related business income, than are the 509(a)(1) organizations. Museums are good examples because their support is heavily weighted in the direction of fees, subscription revenues for magazines, sales of related art products, and other business income and depends less on contributions by individuals or foundations. The backbone of 509(a)(2) organizations is that they are good businesses conducting a public service and generating a substantial amount of their support through sales.

In contrast, 509(a)(1) organizations cannot rely as heavily on the selling of their goods and services as a means of demonstrating public support. They rely more on gifts and contributions, including contributions from foundations, and may supplement these through conducting a business.

THE SUBSIDIARIES AND AFFILIATES: SECTION 509(a)(3) ORGANIZATIONS

Section 509(a)(3) organizations are nonprofits that exist to support and aid publicly supported nonprofits [Sections (509)(a)(1) and (a)(2)]. These organizations may be wholly owned subsidiaries of one or more 509(a)(1)s or 509(a)(2)s—publicly supported organizations. A fascinating aspect of these organizations is that even though they may be founded by one individual, they are not treated as private foundations because their entire being is defined in terms of and is solely in support of publicly supported nonprofits. They do not have to pass the public support test, but their tax-exempt status is completely dependent upon their relationship in furthering the mission of publicly supported organizations. The 509(a)(3) is a bridge between the public and the private 501(c)(3).

These organizations are excellent devices for conducting highly specialized functions for one or more organizations; when formed by more than one, they become an excellent means for joint ventures or cooperative arrangements among nonprofits. They are incorporated and have all the features of a corporation, including limited liability, central and independent management, and the ability to self-finance and issue debt. They may even have a strong profit motive in the sense that they may operate businesses as long as the proceeds go toward the furtherance of the mission of one or more publicly supported nonprofits.

Category One: Subordinate Corporations

The 509(a)(3) organizations fall into two categories. The first is composed of those organizations that are "operated, supervised, or controlled by a publicly supported organization," which means that they are controlled and directed by such organizations; or that are "supervised or controlled in connection with a publicly supported organization," which means that they have common boards and management. Stated otherwise, under this first category, the 509(a)(3) is controlled by its publicly supported parents by way of their naming and controlling its managers and trustees, or it is run by the same managers and trustees who run the parents. Either the management is separate but controlled, or it is identical.

Under this first category the mission of the 509(a)(3) organization is to operate exclusively to carry out the functions of and for the benefit of the parent corporations. This type of 509(a)(3) is a wholly or closely owned subsidiary. Its only function is to support its parents. It is subordinate to them. Its organizing document (charter) must meet an organizational test that reflects this subordination. It does so by the following:

1. It must state the specific organizations that the 509(a)(3) exists to support.

2. It must not undertake any activity that is not in furtherance of the mission of its parents.

3. It must limit its mission to carrying out the purpose, operating in benefit of, or carrying out the functions of the parents.

4. It must not work on behalf of any other organizations other than the ones specified in its charter.

In meeting the organizational test, the scope of the mission of the 509(a)(3) subsidiary cannot be any broader than the scope of the mission of the parents. It may be a subset of it, but not broader. The only cases in which the missions can and would be different is if the 509(a)(3) is formed by a trade, business, or civic league that is publicly supported. In that case, the 509(a)(3) must have an exclusive charitable mission consistent with the 501(c)(3) status. Hence, many business associations, civic leagues, and professional associations may have a foundation that carries out their charitable missions. The parent organizations cannot have such a public purpose mission because, as associations, they are focused on the narrow interests of their members—not the public.

In addition to the organizational test, category one 509(a)(3)s must also pass an operational test. This test has a beneficiary component and a permissible activity component. The beneficiary component simply says that the beneficiaries of the activities of the subsidiary must be the parents or the beneficiaries of the parents. This rule is cleverly written to provide that the subsidiary does not have to benefit the parent by, say, making payments to it but by making payments to those who are the clients of the parents. Therefore, a foundation that is a 509(a)(3) gives scholarships to students of the university—not to the university itself.

The permissible-activity component of the operational test for category one says that the subsidiary may carry out a specialized activity different from what the parents are doing but only on behalf of the parents. Hence, a 509(a)(3) can be a fund-raising corporation, an unrelated trade or business, and so on.

Category one rules specifically prohibit that the 509(a)(3) be controlled by disqualified persons. This rule buttresses the rule that the organization has to be controlled by its nonprofit parents. But it goes further than that. Many 509(a)(3)s are specialized in fund-raising, being foundations, or conducting businesses. Hence, it is important that there be no self-dealing or conflict of interests or that in its zeal the management does not co-mingle its interests with that of this subsidiary. Hence, the rule that it cannot be controlled by disqualified persons [except the foundation managers or managers of the publicly supported organizations associated with the 509(a)(3)]. Disqualified persons are

1. All substantial contributors to the foundation

2. All foundation managers

3. An owner of more than 20 percent of the voting shares of a corporation that is a substantial contributor, or 20 percent of the profit interests of partnership that is a substantial contributor, or the beneficiaries of a trust that is a substantial contributor

4. A member of the family of any of the above

5. A corporation in which the persons named above combined own 35 percent or more of the voting stocks, or a partnership in which they together own more than 35 percent of the profit interests, or a trust in which they together own more than 35 percent of the beneficial interests

One restriction that is placed on these nonprofits "operated, supervised, or controlled" by a parent 509(a)(1) or (a)(2) is that they cannot be under the influence of a disqualified person other than the manager. For instance, Carlos creates a foundation that gets 509(a)(3) status by being a subsidiary of Carlos's church. Carlos is a disqualified person with respect to the foundation he has created, which means that he is barred from having a business relationship with it. His church cannot circumvent this proscription by making him a member of the board of directors of the church with responsibility over the foundation he created.

"Control" by disqualified persons does not necessarily require these persons to be in a management or governance position. It may simply mean that these persons, by their combined vote, can determine decisions and directions of the 509(a)(3).

Being a disqualified person does not disqualify one from being in a governance or management position. The IRS will accept independent proof that such a person(s) is not directly or indirectly in control. Hence, substantial contributors sit on many of these boards—they just may not control directly or indirectly the decisions or activities.

Category Two: Closely Cooperating Affiliates

Whereas the category one 509(a)(3) organizations were controlled, supervised, or operated by or with the parents, the category two ones are "operated in connection with" other public organizations, specifically the 509(a)(1) or (a)(2). They work in tandem with them but are formed by them and are not their subordinates. This category of 509(a)(3)s are not necessarily formed by 509(a)(3)s or 509(a)(2)s. Many are formed by wealthy individuals who do not want to form private foundations.

These category two 509(a)(3) organizations must pass an organizational test that proves their affiliate connection and its strength. However, the charter does not have to name the public organization by name with which the affiliation is made. It may name a class or a historic connection.

A category two organization not under the control of 509(a), a(2), as parents must pass a responsiveness test. This means that it can prove that it is responsive to the needs of the public organization. It can do this by demonstrating in one of two ways that there is a continuous and close contact between the two. In the case of a 509(a)(3) foundation, that the foundation is responsive to the investment policies and the disbursement needs of the public organization; in the case of a trust, that the public organizations are not only named beneficiaries but that they can compel an accounting to them by the trust.

In addition, category two organizations must show that they are integral to the operation of the public organization, the 509(a)(1), or (a)(2). This means proving that the public organization is dependent upon the supporting organization and that the latter is involved in the former. This can be done by proving that the activities that the supporting organizations conduct are so essential to the ability of the public organizations to carry out their mission that without the supporting organization, the public organizations would have had to carry out these activities themselves in order to be successful.

An alternative proof is that the supporting organization gives its income to the public organization and that this amount is so large or so necessary that the latter's attention is gotten and maintained for want of more. For this reason, the integral test is sometimes called the *attentiveness test*.

Section 509(a)(4) Organizations

Section 509(a)(4) organizations are 501(c)(3)s that specialize in testing consumer products for safety. This section of the code simply exempts these organizations from being treated as private foundations—the subject of the next chapter.

CANADA'S CHARITABLE ORGANIZATIONS

As in the United States, a Canadian charity must be organized either as a corporation or as a trust. The organization can receive donations that are award-donor income-tax benefits. The organization is exempt from income taxes and is given a rebate of 50 percent of the goods and services taxes it pays at the provincial level. To get these benefits, the organization must be what is called a "registered charity." This is analogous to the Section 501(c)(3) in the United States.

To be registered, the organization—which must either be a corporation or a trust—must meet a public benefit test. This requires that the organization show that it (1) conducts a charitable purpose for the public's benefit, (2) does not function to benefit a restricted group such as a social club, and (3) does not conduct activities contrary to public policy.

The court has identified the following activities as consistent with advancing public benefits relief of poverty, advancement of religion, advancement of education, and certain other purposes that the courts have found to be consistent with advancing public welfare. The interpretation of these three principles by the Canadian courts admits to most of the functions defined under 501(c)(3), including certain sports organizations, in the United States.

In applying these principles, the courts determine if the mission of the organization (called its *object*) is consistent with those previously given registered status, if the object is an unequivocal commitment by the organization, and if there is private inurement for political expenditures.

The organization will not qualify if it does not pledge to the principle of no personal inurement and if one of its objects is political in the sense that it aims to affect elections or candidates, propagate political doctrine, or influence government policy or laws. The charity, however, may use up to 10 percent of its resources for activities such as workshops and other means of communicating ideas that are consistent with and advance the organization's mission. This is analogous to grassroots lobbying, providing information to government agencies, or nonpartisan voter education in the United States context.

Canadian registered charities fall into three groups:

1. Charitable organizations
2. Public foundations
3. Private foundations

A Canadian charitable organization is remotely comparable to a 509(a)(1) through (a)(3) organization in the United States. A Canadian charitable organization must not get more than one-half of its resources from a single source; one-half or more of its directors or trustees cannot be persons or parties related to each other; and it cannot change its mission so that more than one-half of its resources are used to finance other organizations rather than the operational conduct of its mission. Furthermore, it cannot indulge in businesses unrelated to its mission. At least 50 percent of its support must come from persons who are unrelated to each other either by blood or enterprise. Moreover, charitable organizations in Canada, unlike those in the United States, have a set level of disbursement requirements. These will be discussed in the next chapter.

A Canadian public foundation is required to give more than 50 percent of its annual income to qualified donees. These qualified donees are principally registered charitable organizations, but they may include federal, provincial, or local government, or the United Nations. Also, fewer than 50 percent of its trustees or directors can be related individuals. No more than 50 percent of its support can come from one or a related group of people. While a public foundation's principal purpose is to finance qualified donees, it may conduct its own charitable operation.

A Canadian private foundation is like a default mode. A registered charity that is neither a public foundation nor a charitable organization is classified as a "private foundation." Importantly, more than 50 percent of a private foundation's trustees may be related, and it may receive more than 50 percent of its support from one or more related persons. As in the case of the public foundation, it may choose to carry on its own mission in addition to funding others. But private foundations are not allowed to conduct any type of business. Public foundations and charitable organizations are allowed to carry on only related businesses.

All three categories of registered charities—charitable organizations, public foundations, and private foundations—must meet certain disbursement quotas as described in the next chapter. These are intended, among other objectives, to insure that registered charities spend on their purposes rather than accumulate wealth, help control costs, and force the organizations to meet their commitments to a charitable purpose.

Both public and private foundations are allowed to acquire no more than 50 percent control of any business. This limit can be exceeded if they owned 5 percent of the business prior to being given a 50 percent share in one block. Neither foundation is allowed to have debt except to facilitate current operational purposes and the purchase of investments, and in order to conduct their charitable missions. Comparisons with the United States on business holdings and income are made in Chapters Four, Nine, and Ten, where the importance and limitations on business revenues are discussed.

Registered charities can apply to become associated organizations analogous to the 509(a)(3) organizations that are affiliates. In this sense, they are allowed to donate their resources one to another as long as they have the same and common mission. An affiliate purpose also allows joint venturing. An affiliate purpose can be denied if the organizations have disparately different missions.

SUMMARY AND PREVIEW

The central distinction of publicly supported 501(c)(3)s is that they must be able to prove that they are financially supported by the public. This is done by showing that either one-third or at least 10 percent of their support is from the general public as defined. To demonstrate public support, managers need to operate according to a specific set of profiles on which this chapter centered.

When a 501(c)(3) organization cannot meet the hurdle of demonstrating public support, it is automatically classified as a private foundation. The operating rules surrounding these foundations are stricter. What are these rules? Why are they so strict? Why should every manager of any nonprofit know about private foundations?

CHAPTER FOUR

Private Foundations

Why is an understanding of the privately financed 501(c)(3) desirable? First, some of the rules that govern these organizations are good rules for all nonprofits to follow. Second, all publicly supported nonprofits are potential private foundations because this is the way they are classified when they fail the support test. Third, the private foundation is a principal source of financing publicly supported organizations. For this reason this chapter ends with a discussion of strategic information for soliciting foundations. Fourth, all endowments and charitable trusts, a major topic of this book, operate under the rules of private foundations. Fifth, the IRS presumes every organization that applies for exemption is a private foundation until proven otherwise.

THE PRIVATE FOUNDATION—WHAT IT IS

All private foundations are 501(c)(3)s that have not satisfied the public support test but have met the organization, asset, and political tests. Private foundations are

1. Created and financed by a corporation, individuals, or a small group with the sole intent of financing public organizations such as public charities and without the desire to demonstrate public support or a close alignment with a group of publicly supported organizations

2. Created by these same parties to discharge a mission that qualifies under 501(c)(3) but with the intent of having the organization be principally self-supporting and not dependent on public support

3. Organizations that fail to meet the public support test either at the time of application or during its operation

Private foundations are of two types. Under the first category, known as *private nonoperating foundations,* are endowments, corporate foundations, and many of the well-known foundations such as the Ford, the Pew, the Carnegie, and the Rockefeller. Unlike 509(a)(3)s, they are totally independent of any one or group of publicly supported organizations and they discharge no specialized mission (such as marketing or fund-raising) on behalf of such organizations. Unlike community foundations that also have as their principal purpose the financing of the sector, the private nonoperating foundation does not draw its financial support from the community or the public. It is privately funded.

Under the second category, known as *private operating foundations,* are the Getty, the Hughes, Russell Sage Foundation, Twentieth Century Fund, and the Kettering Foundation. These foundations are principally, although not necessarily exclusively, self-supporting. They can have one or a few major patrons as donors or clients. They can concentrate on the integrity of an operation and need not veer to demonstrate public support. Many operating foundations have a strong science background. Unlike nonoperating foundations, they can use their entire resources to carry out a mission. They do not have to distribute them, unless by election, to other 501(c)(3)s.

Consequently, private operating foundations are distinguishable from nonoperating foundations because they actively do things—not just finance them. Operating foundations tend to be very narrowly focused. For example, an interest may be art or health, but not art and health. Unlike other 501(c)(3)s that are publicly supported, they may elect (are not required) to demonstrate that they have public support.

The private foundation category is both a default and a penalty category. If an organization fails to demonstrate that it is publicly supported in the manner discussed in the previous chapter, it is by default a private foundation, and the only question is what type—an operating or a nonoperating foundation? If it is established as a public organization and then fails to demonstrate public support, the penalty is that it is categorized as a private foundation—one that is either nonoperating or operating.

A reclassification is said to be a *penalty* because the rules governing the private foundation are less lenient in terms of expenditure restrictions and requirements, investment income taxation, business holdings limitations, tax deductibility of contributions, and reporting requirements for private foundations than they are for publicly supported organizations. We shall discuss these shortly.

THE 501(c)(3) THAT IS NOT PRIVATE

Recall from the previous chapters that a 501(c)(3) is either publicly or privately supported, as evidenced primarily by its sources of support. There are two broad classes of tests to determine whether an organization is a private foundation. The first category is based on the ability of the organization to meet the public support formula after demonstrating its ability to meet the organization, asset, and political tests. The second broad category is different only because it places less weight on the formula and more on performance.

The Performance-Based Group

There are some organizations that are not classified as private based on their actual performance. But they must pass the organization, political, and asset tests. These organizations are treated as public without the requirement of satisfying the public support formula (one-third or 10 percent) tests:

1. Churches or a convention or association of churches defined as an organization in which a religious belief is truly and sincerely held and that practices rituals or beliefs that are not contrary to law.

2. Schools defined as an organization with a regular faculty and student body that carries out the primary function of presenting formal education and that does not discriminate.

3. Hospitals or medical research centers defined as organizations providing medical care (on an inpatient or outpatient basis), education, or research.

4. Governmental units (including educational institutions and authorities) of states or the local governments, territories, or the District of Columbia.

5. Organizations described in the previous chapters as 509(a)(3)s that are created by any of the above but that operate under the control, supervision, or in connection with the organization listed above.

6. Organizations, 509(a)(4)s, not associated with a manufacturer, that test for the safety of products.

7. Organizations operated for the benefit of universities and colleges that are owned or operated by a governmental unit.

Note that these seven categories are referred to in this book as *performance-based* because it is not just the statement of their missions that matters but how they perform that mission. Therefore, it is not simply that a hospital cares for the sick that matters (private for-profit hospitals do the same). What matters is that a substantial part of the output of 501(c)(3) hospitals must be charitable—benefiting the community—and this must be demonstrable. Another example: A private, for-profit school can discriminate by race or sex but not a 501(c)(3), unless, in the case of sex, this distinction is demonstrably inherent to the educational experience.

The Formula-Based Group

The formula-based organizations that are not private are those that can demonstrate public financial support as discussed extensively in the previous chapters. These are the 509(a)(1)s and the 509(a)(2)s. The 509(a)(1)s demonstrate that one-third or 10 percent (depending upon the facts and circumstances) of their support comes from the public or government and excludes related business income in that calculation. The 509(a)(2)s include all business incomes (related and unrelated) in their calculations, but in addition to satisfying the one-third test have a limit placed on their investment income and related business income, as discussed earlier.

With this understanding of what the category *private foundation* includes and excludes, let us turn to the operating rules of each of the two broad categories of private foundations.

PRIVATE NONOPERATING FOUNDATIONS

Over 90 percent of all private foundations are nonoperating foundations—they are the "financing arm" of the sector. They may finance the activities of either publicly supported 501(c)(3)s, such as the 509(a)(1)s, (2)s, and (3)s, or operating foundations. Over 90 percent of private operating foundations are active in grant-making. There are well over forty thousand nonoperating foundations in the United States supporting both domestic and international projects conducted by publicly supported organizations.

As we discuss private nonoperating and operating foundations, note the rules by which they must operate (see Table 4.1). These rules are intended to divorce the gifts that create and maintain them from their donors—a concern that is higher when an organization does not have to meet a public support test. They are also intended to force a minimum of annual expenditures on charitable

Table 4.1. Comparison of Foundations

	Types of 501(c)(3)s		
	Public Charities	Private Foundations (Nonoperating)	Private Operating Foundations
Charitable Mission	Conduct	Finance	Conduct and finance

missions, thus assuring that gifts that were made for charitable purposes are used for that purpose and not for political, private, or purely profitable purposes.

RESTRICTIONS ON EXPENDITURES, ECONOMIC TRANSACTIONS, AND INVESTMENT

The fundamental purpose of the prohibitions and requirements that follow is to force the private foundation to fulfill its mission of financing public welfare, to avoid its assets from being used for the personal benefits of its founders and relatives and associates of the founders or major contributors, to preserve and grow the assets, and to keep the organization out of politics.

Disqualified Persons

The key to understanding self-dealing from the perspective of a private foundation is the term *disqualified person*. A *disqualified person* is a person or entity who is barred from having a business relationship with a private foundation. One such person is a substantial contributor to the private foundation. A *substantial contributor* is a person or entity who gives a total of $5000 or more if this amounts to at least 2 percent of all the contributions received by the foundation since its beginning. But the law does not stop here.

The spouse, children, parents, and grandchildren of a substantial contributor are also substantial contributors, even if they did not contribute a penny. Based on the legal principle of attribution, the theory is that close relatives such as spouse and children are subject to the control and influence of the contributor. In the eyes of the law, they are all one. Oddly, brothers and sisters are excluded from the taint of attribution for private foundation purposes.

Attribution also extends to businesses in which the substantial contributor owns 20 percent or more of the voting stocks. And if the business is a substantial contributor, so is the owner or owners. Attribution runs both ways.

Management or anyone who has authority to set policies is also a disqualified person. The attribution rule also applies to the family of the managers of the nonprofit and their businesses and disqualifies them from engaging in certain business transactions with the organization. See Self-Dealing, which follows.

Government officials are also disqualified persons, including elected as well as appointed officials and at every level of government and in every branch, whether judicial, legislative, or executive. Again, the attribution rule is applied. Government officials are included among disqualified persons to preclude the use of the private foundation to influence these officials. The conditions under which government officials may receive benefits from private foundations are generally restricted to nonmonetary awards, annuities associated with employee programs during periods that the government official previously worked for the foundation, reimbursement for travel cost if the purpose of the travel was consistent with the tax-exempt purpose of the private foundation, and payment in anticipation of employing the government official if such payment is made within ninety days of termination from government service.

Self-Dealing

Direct or indirect business transactions between the private foundation and disqualified persons as defined above can lead to penalties imposed by the state and the IRS for self-dealing. What kinds of transactions lead to charges of self-dealing? Hiring, loans, the sale and purchase of assets, the paying of excessive compensation or reimbursement of expenses, the providing of facilities to disqualified persons, and the leasing of space by a disqualified person to the private foundation are all subject to charges of self-dealing.

There are some exceptions worth noting. A lease by a disqualified person to a private foundation is not self-dealing if no rental fees are involved. Self-dealing is not incurred if the transaction is for less than $5000 in one year or if the transaction is generally favorable to the organization. The basic way to avoid issues of self-dealing when a disqualified person must be engaged in a business transaction of any type is to be sure that the transaction is ordinary for such a private foundation and is necessary to discharge its duties, the good or service could not otherwise have been provided more favorably by dealing with a qualified person, and the private foundation was appreciably the net beneficiary of the transaction. We shall return to self-dealing in Chapter Six as it pertains to trustees and Chapter Thirteen as to compensation.

A penalty for self-dealing may be imposed on the self-dealer as well as the management if it can be shown that the management participated in the action or could reasonably be expected to have known about it, did not try to stop it, engaged in it, or remained silent. The penalty to the self-dealer can rise to 200 percent of the value of the transaction. For the manager, the penalty can rise to 50 percent of that amount.

While these penalties are imposed by the IRS, an individual may bring civil charges. Here is an example of a combination of terms we have used. About half the space of a building owned by a private foundation is occupied by a for-profit company owned by the foundation manager. The company was a disqualified person with respect to the foundation because of its ownership by the foundation manager. It did not matter that the leasing of the property was done by a property management company with which the manager had no association. The foundation had veto powers over leases, and guess who exercised that veto power on behalf of the foundation? The manager. This was declared self-dealing.[1]

Distribution of Income

Unlike public organizations, private foundations are required to distribute their income annually. Three types of distribution meet the qualification. The private foundation may distribute funds for paying expenses and for making grants to public organizations (509(a)(1), (a)(2), and (a)(3)) for conducting those activities for which the private foundation is tax exempt. These may be grants, but they can also be loans. These loans are called *program-related investments.*

A second type of distribution that qualifies is set aside to purchase assets to be used in the tax-exempt purpose if those set asides are absolutely necessary (as they are in a building program) and if the funds will be used within sixty months. Set asides or accumulations must be approved by the IRS. A third type of qualifying distribution is the amount spent to purchase assets to be used by the private foundation in its tax-exempt mission or other charitable purpose. These latter amounts, unlike the set asides, do not have to receive prior IRS approval.

The actual dollar amount that a private foundation must distribute is technically determined. Basically, it is substantially all (although 85 percent is acceptable) of the greater of either its minimum investment return or its adjusted net income. Its minimum investment return is the fair market value of its assets not used for tax-exempt purposes, minus the debt associated with those assets multiplied by 5 percent. Its adjusted net income is all income, including those from unrelated businesses, minus the expenses associated with producing that income.

The failure to distribute the correct amount can lead to stiff penalties, starting at 15 percent of the amount that should be distributed and rising to 100 percent if the distribution is not made in the time allotted for correction. Fortunately, unlike the self-dealing tax, this tax does not fall on the management but on the private foundation itself. When in doubt, a distribution is often preferable, since any such amounts may be carried over the next five years.

Jeopardy of Investments

Private foundations and their managers are prohibited from making investments that would jeopardize the financial well-being of the organization. Included among the prohibited actions are certain investment strategies, such as buying puts and calls, warrants, buying stocks on margin, selling short, and trading in commodity futures or in futures markets in general. This poses a problem of interpretation, since some of these actions, such as buying a put, are viewed in some investment quarters as defensive and conservative in the sense that they may put a limit on losses. Interpretation of the motives for certain transactions is subjective based on the investment intent and strategy, the frequency with which they are used, and so on. States may restrict the type of securities or the companies whose securities may be bought.

Certain investment risks are acceptable and encouraged if they are program related. Offering loans to individuals (or nonprofits) deemed to be among the least preferred risks by a commercial lender is acceptable as long as the making of such loans is within the tax-exempt mission of the nonprofit.

If this rule is violated, a 5 percent tax is imposed on the foundation and another 5 percent on the manager who is aware of or participates in the investment decision. In a case such as this, the finance or investment committee of the board of directors, the president, and the investment officers of the organization could all be held responsible.

Excess Business Holdings

There is a limit on the business holding of a private foundation. No more than 20 percent of the voting stock or interest of a single business may be owned by a private foundation and all its disqualified persons combined. Some types of businesses are unaffected by this rule. These are program-related businesses and businesses that make their income through dividends, royalties, rents, interest, or so-called passive income rather than by sale of goods and services. In addition, some foundations, such as the Kellogg and the Hershey, are exempt from this rule.

Where the nonprofit and its disqualified persons combined do not own (control) 20 percent of the voting stock, they may own unlimited amounts of nonvoting stocks. Their holding could exceed the 20 percent of voting stocks and move up to 35 percent if it is clear that someone other than the disqualified person effectively controls the corporation.

In the case of partnerships, the rules are exactly the same as they are for corporations. However, partnerships do not issue stocks. So the words *profit interest* are substituted for *voting stock* and the words *capital interests* are substituted for *nonvoting stocks*.

What does the foundation do if it receives a gift that causes an excess of business holdings? In general, it has five to twelve years (five plus an extension of seven if granted) to divest itself of such holdings. Private foundations have had to divest themselves of department stores, public utilities, aircraft manufacturers, automobile companies, golf courses and social clubs, newspapers, hotels, to name a few. This is not hard to understand. Many of their holdings came in the form of bequests of stocks by principal shareholders of these companies.

A private foundation cannot own a sole proprietorship unless obtained by bequest or prior to 1969. The reader should not confuse a sole proprietorship with sole ownership of a corporation or unrelated business as previously described. The term *sole proprietorship* simply means that the business is owned by a human and unincorporated. The nonprofit would be totally liable for any failures of the business. If sole proprietorships were allowed, all the assets of the foundation would be exposed to claims by creditors of the business. A large claim against the business that it could not meet by itself would lead to claims against the assets of the foundation.

Should the rule on excess business holding be broken, the penalty is 5 percent of the value of the excess holdings. This penalty is imposed on the foundation, not the management. The penalty could rise to 200 percent if left uncorrected in the time allotted.

Prohibited Expenditures

Some expenditures by private foundations, such as those aimed at influencing legislation, lead to tax penalties. Legislation includes any action by a legislative body at any level of government. School boards, commissions, and authorities such as housing or economic on any level are considered administrative rather than legislative bodies and therefore expenditures to influence them are not prohibited. In addition, expert testimony in response to a written request by a legislative body or nonpartisan studies made public are not construed to be attempts to influence legislation and are not prohibited.

Expenditures to influence the outcome of any election are prohibited. Such expenditures include producing or distributing supporting literature or paying campaign workers or providing facilities for campaigns. Critically, any expenditure such as voter registration is also prohibited if it is centered in a specific geographical area.

This prohibition is not violated

1. If the private foundation makes a contribution to an organization that is exempt under 501(c)(3)

2. If the activities of that receiving organization are nonpartisan and are conducted over more than one election period and in at least five states

3. If the organization spends most (at least 85 percent) of its income on the tax-exempt purposes for which it is organized

4. If 85 percent of its support is from the public (government units and the general public)

5. If the contributions from the private foundation are not used solely for a specific election or geographic area

The prohibition against political activities gave way to a strategy used in the presidential elections in the 1980s—a resurgence in the form of fund-raising by political action committees (to be discussed in the next chapter). Supporters of political candidates would form a nonprofit group under 501(c)(3)—not to support the candidate but to do research and disseminate information on subjects close to the heart of the potential candidate and even to support the potential candidate's travel to speak (not campaign) on these subjects. Some of these foundations even gave money to public charities. Under this guise, the organization did not become involved in politics because its activities were "educational."

There were several advantages to going this route:

1. The contributions to a nonprofit were deductible and did not suffer the same limitations on giving as contributions to a political campaign.
2. The nonprofit organization had several cost advantages, including the lower postal rate.
3. Gifts to foundations are not subject to public disclosure, as are contributions to political campaigns.
4. Many persons who may not otherwise contribute to a candidate may contribute to a foundation.
5. It gave an unannounced candidate a platform and a way of being identified with an issue in a nonpartisan light.
6. It was a source of information and dissemination of information with which the potential candidate could be identified.
7. The foundation can support foundation-related speaking engagements for the candidate that simultaneously coincide with the issues with which the candidate seeks identity and in the communities in which the candidate needs exposure.

Another category of prohibited expenditures is grants to individuals. Here the intent is to be certain that grants to individuals are intended to assist them in meeting some measurable objective, such as writing a book or earning a degree, are a bona fide prize or award, are nondiscriminatory (that is, not targeted as a payoff or bribe), or aim at improving skills. Many private foundations shy away from making grants to individuals due to this rule.

Expenditures to carry out missions that are not religious, scientific, or charitable, or to foster those activities that permit an organization to qualify under 501(c)(3) as discussed earlier are also prohibited.

Finally, private foundations may not make grants to organizations other than those 509(a)(1)s, (a)(2)s, and (a)(3)s previously discussed unless the foundation takes responsibility for how these funds are used by the donee. The rule means that private foundations must be sure the funds are used only for the purposes for which they are given, keep proper and thorough records, and report expenditures to the IRS.

Violation of these rules against prohibited expenditures leads to a 10 percent tax based on the amount involved on both the foundation and its management. An additional tax of 100 percent may be imposed on the foundation and 50 percent on the manager if they fail to correct the situation during the allotted time.

Investment Income

Finally, private foundations may pay a 2 percent tax on net investment income. Net investment income is the total of all income, including rents, royalties, dividends, interest, and business income, plus net capital gains. From this amount are subtracted all ordinary and necessary expenses for producing that income. These include management fees, depreciation, rents, supplies, and the like. Capital losses are deductible only to the extent of capital gains. For example, if the private foundation had $2000 in capital losses and $4000 in capital gains, its net capital gain is $2000 and that becomes part of its net investment income. If, however, it had $2000 in losses and no gains, it would not deduct anything as a capital loss in deriving its net investment income.

PRIVATE OPERATING FOUNDATIONS

The private operating foundation is a special type of private foundation. It is subject to modified versions of the rules governing private nonoperating foundations.

Operating foundations may receive contributions from private nonoperating foundations. An operating foundation may own up to 85 percent of the voting interests, not just a combined 20 percent of a single business, as in the case of a private nonoperating foundation. Operating foundations are not subject to the excise tax on undistributed income, for they are not required to make distributions to finance public organizations as do private nonoperating foundations (described in the previous section).

The major distinction between private nonoperating foundations and private operating foundations is that the first must conduct and implement programs and may elect to provide financial assistance to public organizations. The second conducts no program and must (not elect to) finance public organizations and may also financially assist operating foundations. Financing is an obligation, not an option for the private nonoperating foundation, and doing is an obligation, not an option for the operating foundation.

The Income Test

For a private foundation to qualify as an operating foundation, it must pass an income test. This test requires that the foundation spend at least 85 percent of its adjusted net income or minimum investment income, whichever is lower, on activities for which it received tax exemption and in which it is a direct participant.[2] Making a grant to a nonprofit that has a similar mission is not enough, but assigning its staff to work with that nonprofit or using its facilities is. Hence, many on the staff of the Howard Hughes Foundation do their research on university campuses. In short, the private operating foundation must do more than contribute money. It must directly participate through staff or facilities or a combination of the two.

Asset, Endowment, and Support Tests

In addition to the income test, a private operating foundation must meet one of three other tests: asset, endowment, or support. The *asset test* is designed to detect how much of the facilities or other assets of the organization are being used directly in activities for which it received exemption. At least 65 percent of the assets of the private foundation must be used directly in the meeting of its tax-exempt mission. If the organization chooses, it may satisfy this condition by running a program-related business using 65 percent of its assets to do so. Or it may control a for-profit corporation by owning 80 percent of all its voting stocks and 80 percent of all other types of stocks issued by the corporation—if all (or 85 percent) of the assets of the corporation are devoted to the same types of activities for which the organization received its exemption.

As an alternative to the asset test, the private operating foundation may elect to demonstrate that its grants are aimed at advancing its charitable cause. This is the essence of the *endowment test*. The basic requirement is that two-thirds of the minimum investment return be expended on qualifying distributions as defined earlier: expenses for conducting the tax-exempt mission, authorized set asides, and expenses for acquiring assets to conduct the mission.

Instead of the asset or endowment test, a private foundation seeking to be an operating foundation may elect to pass the *support test*. Notice that this test is elective, unlike for public organizations. This can be done by showing that 85 percent of the support of the foundation comes from the broad public and governmental units, or from more than five tax-exempt foundations, or that no more than 25 percent of its support is normally (as defined earlier) received from any one tax-exempt organization, or that not more than 50 percent of its support is normally received from gross investment income.

One of the problems public organizations that deal with private operating foundations have is that the latter constantly interfere. This, as we see, is because of legal requirements to be directly involved. Private nonoperating and public 509(a)(3) organizations (to the extent that the latter make grants) are not similarly constrained.

SOLICITING PRIVATE AND COMMUNITY FOUNDATIONS

The earlier parts of this chapter should give the reader a basic information that serves several purposes. First, it is the kind of information that a manager needs to know for increasing the efficiency of management. Second, it is the kind of information that persons who are contemplating the formation of a private foundation need to know. Not all foundations are alike. Put with the earlier chapters, such donors should also be aware now that alternatives to a foundation are supporting or affiliated organizations described as 509(a)(3) organizations. This section will show yet another, the community foundation.

But now, we take the perspective of the manager. It should be obvious that the private foundation rules are useful to know because they enhance managerial efficiency. An understanding of self-dealing, jeopardy of investment, political expenditures, and so on is useful no matter what type of organization one is running. But this information is useful in another way. It enhances the efficiency of solicitation of foundations. This is the perspective to which we now turn.

Private Foundations

The word *foundation* has become synonymous with the making of grants. We now know that all private foundations are not grant-making. In fact, a study for the IRS by Paul Arnsberger (see Suggested Readings) shows that 20 percent of all private foundations do not give grants. About half of all operating foundations and 95 percent of the nonoperating foundations make grants.

The earlier parts of this chapter should explain the legal requirements for giving and why the results are as they are. Hence, the first strategy in soliciting private foundations is to discover whether or not they are grant-making. We have seen that the fact that an operating foundation does not make grants does not mean that it will not provide other resources, such as experts, if that is consistent with its mission. Therefore, soliciting these foundations for human help or for co-venturing may be more successful than soliciting them solely for money.

A second step is determining the current interests of the foundations. All foundations, including corporate foundations, have areas of focus. This focus may be along several dimensions simultaneously. The foundation may be interested in religion, health, and culture. Within this area, it may be focusing on children or national and international aspects. The best way to detect this is by reading the president's message along with the history of the foundation and its current programs. Looking just at program interests is a mistake.

The letter of the president of the foundation gives a picture of the thinking behind the programs. Why are they interested? What is their angle? What is their philosophy? Being able to relate to that philosophy is important because the programs are merely a means of attaining the ends endorsed in the philosophical statement. That is what drives the programs that the foundation funds. Moreover, foundations tend to take long-term perspectives in fixing their basic programs and these are decided upon only after research to determine a niche, after consideration of the linkage between the inherent character of programs and the objectives of the principal founders and final endorsement by the board of trustees. The president's statement, an expression of all of these factors, can be relied upon as a long-term commitment and a basis of decision making about the programs that the foundation will fund. An innovative idea has a better chance of being accepted if it falls within the philosophical purpose of the foundation. The Kauffman foundation focuses on community self-sufficiency and on entrepreneurship, and it finances an array of programs connected to these concepts—including improving the management of nonprofit organizations and community innovation. All programs are connected by the same themes. A solicitation must fit these themes.

Community Foundations

Private foundations and individuals are not the only institutional sources of grants. Another major source is the community foundation. A community foundation is unlike a private foundation in that the first is formed usually by one person, corporation, or family—they are the angels. They, along with the earnings of their portfolios, are the only source of external funding of the private foundation, whether it is formed by a corporation or by individuals.

A community foundation, which is further described in Chapter Eight, is also a grant-maker. These foundations, like the private foundation, do not have to pass the public support test (they may elect to do so as in the case of the private operating foundation). Although such a foundation may be started in the same way as a private foundation, its sources are not only earnings, but also gifts from other individuals. A community foundation allows anyone to create a separate fund within it which finances programs that are separate from other funds in the overall foundation.

Moreover, a community foundation has assets not only from initial gifts, but also from annual giving by citizens and by constantly creating new funds to accommodate individual large donors and by the earnings on all of these.

The community foundation is an alternative to a private foundation. A major donor may make a gift to a community foundation and designate the way it is used and also be recognized perpetually by the naming and maintaining of his or her own fund within the foundation. A reason for going this way is to reduce the administrative costs of the private foundation. Another reason is that a community foundation focuses its efforts on a local community rather than on the nation or international scene that a private foundation is free to do. A community foundation is sometimes called a *common pool*. But all common pools are not necessarily community foundations. Common pools are discussed in the next chapter and in Chapter Sixteen.

A community foundation should probably be the first source a nonprofit with local interests should approach, because a community foundation, by law, designates a local area (which may be broadly defined) as its principal market. This means that the competition for funds may be less broad than that seen by decision makers in national foundations. Second, unlike private foundations, a community foundation is made up of several funds that donors have designated to be used only in specific ways. Only projects that meet the donor-intent of these funds can be financed through these individual funds. Therefore, an understanding of the intent behind these (as in the case of the private foundation) enlarges the probability of success. Third, because a community foundation is made up of several independent funds each potentially with a different funding purpose, its scope is potentially broader than that of a private foundation.

The Columbus Foundation and The Foundation Center are sources of information on community foundations and private foundations. See the Suggested Readings section.

The Affiliated or Supporting Organizations

A third source of grant-making are the support and affiliate organizations in Chapter Two—the 509(a)(3)s. These, too, are sometimes called foundations. These organizations, as in the case of private foundations, may also be created by one individual. They do not have to meet a 5 percent annual distribution requirement and, like community foundations or private foundations, do not have to meet the public support test. But unlike the private foundation or the community foundation, they have to be affiliated with or subservient to one or more public charities that are the sole or principal beneficiaries of their gifts.

The challenges for the manager in soliciting these organizations are different. First, the competition is restricted only to the specific or class of organizations that the donor stipulated as beneficiaries in creating the supporting or affiliated organization. Second, there can be competition among these nonprofit organizations that are designated beneficiaries. Third, the trustees of these affiliated or supporting organizations have a duty of loyalty to these organizations that may cause them to deny or seek denial from the attorney general of transfers of funds to the nonprofit organizations that are designated beneficiaries. This may be so even though the trustees of the affiliated or supporting organizations are the same persons as the trustees of the nonprofit beneficiaries. Their first duty is to protect the assets and be sure that they are not misused.

PRIVATE FOUNDATIONS, PUBLIC FOUNDATIONS, AND CHARITABLE ORGANIZATIONS IN CANADA[3]

Canadian law provides for a range of exempt organizations, such as those to be described in the next chapter. They also provide for a group of exempt organizations, the donations to which are tax deductible, as described in this and previous chapters.

Canada distinguishes among three types of charities: charitable organizations, private foundations, and public foundations. The *organizations* are similar to the 509(a)(1)s and (a)(2)s in the United States. They are basically the doers in the sector. They may be unincorporated, trusts, or incorporated. They are allowed to make a limited number of grants, but their key purpose is doing.

Both public and private *foundations* have financing charitable purposes as their primary mission. They must be organized either as trusts or as corporations. All three segments of the charity sector (the organizations and two classes of foundations) must be organized exclusively for charitable purposes— prohibiting personal inurement. A private foundation classification occurs automatically if more than 50 percent of the board or executives of the organization are related so that transactions among them do not occur at arm's length.

Any investment involving the private foundation and these significant others is valued at the greater of its cost or fair market value. A tax may be imposed on the difference between actual return on investments and the rate that should have occurred if the transaction were truly at arm's length.

A private foundation is restricted from carrying on any business at all. A foundation, public or private, that acquires (that is, by purchase) 50 percent or more of a business can have its exemption revoked. The foundation is allowed to purchase up to 5 percent of its holdings of that business without having its exemption pulled. This limitation refers only to control acquired by purchase by the organization—excluding control acquired by gifts. But a trust may hold these securities for the foundation.

All three—the charitable organizations, the public foundations, and the private foundations—are subject to a disbursement quota. For the charitable organization, this requires it to use exclusively for charitable purposes 80 percent of the donations it received in the preceding year for which the donor (individual or corporation) received a tax credit receipt (that is, substantiation) from the organization. This figure does not include other sources of revenues.

A charitable purpose does not include fund-raising and other administrative costs. Rather, it may include a transfer due to a reorganization of the organization and a transfer of funds to an endowment or other qualified organization. It also allows the organization to give up to 50 percent of its income to other qualified organizations. It may also give up to 100 percent of its income to an affiliate or associated charity. (See the discussion of 509(a)(3)s.)

The disbursement quota of the public foundation is based on several considerations. It includes the 80 percent figure for charitable organizations. But they must also disburse, unlike the charitable organizations, 80 percent of any unspecified gifts received from other registered charities in the preceding year. A specified gift is one that requires the organization to hold it for not less than ten years. To this they must also add, as part of their distribution quota, 4.5 percent of the value of their investment property in the preceding year.

The disbursement quota of the private foundation is the same as for the public foundation, with one exception. Instead of disbursing annually 80 percent of the unspecified gifts from other registered charities, 100 percent must be disbursed. All these disbursement rules are attempts to balance the ability of the organization to develop internal financial integrity and yet force it to comply with the duty of using "all" its resources for exclusively charitable purposes.

Two major sources of revenues—specified gifts, as defined earlier, and capital gifts by way of bequests and inheritance—are excluded from these disbursement quotas for all three types of organizations. For all three, excess disbursement can be carried forward for future use when actual disbursement falls short.

SUMMARY AND PREVIEW

Section 501(c)(3) organizations are divided into two broad categories—those that are privately funded and those that are publicly funded and supported in the manner in which they operate. These classifications and their subgroups are more than an academic typology. They are based on revenue structure, operational purpose, and operational results. They must conform to tax law.

Therefore, once the classification is established, it is the duty of the management and the trustees to keep the organization in conformity. Failure to do so may result in penalties to both the organization and the management.

But 501(c)(3)s are not the only important nonprofit corporations. There are others that deserve attention because they are important in numbers, often pay higher salaries than do the 501(c)(3)s, and represent powerful interests. What are the rules governing associations, authorities, affiliations, and groups? This is the subject of the next chapter.

CHAPTER FIVE

Associations and Other Forms of Organizations

In this chapter, we look at organizations that are aberrations of those discussed in previous chapters. They are empowered to do all the things the others cannot do, and as a consequence, they are exempt only on one level: Certain revenues from conducting their missions are not taxed. They are denied exemption on another level: Contributions to them cannot be deducted. The organizations in the previous chapters enjoy both levels of exemption. Unlike the organizations in the previous chapters, these are all membership organizations. Accordingly, this chapter also contains a discussion on the rights, duties, and liabilities of members.

REVENUES OF ASSOCIATIONS

Just as the organizations, other than foundations, in the previous chapters must demonstrate public support as an indicator of their value to society, associations must demonstrate membership support as an indicator of their value to their members. Membership support includes dues and fees from businesses related to the mission of the organization (for example, fees for providing a service or product to members).

Associations do not have a hard and fast test such as the one-third public support test or the 10 percent facts and circumstances test. However, they are expected to get about a third of their revenues from membership dues. Not surprisingly, a study by the American Society of Association Executives found that at the median, associations received 35.5 percent of their revenues from membership dues. This figure rose to 50.7 percent for associations with budgets below $500,000 and fell to 23.3 percent for organizations with budgets greater than $10,000,000.[1] Associations have all of the non-dues revenues available to 501(c)(3)s except that contributions to them are not tax deductible. Most of these other sources of income are described in Chapter Ten.

POWERS OF ASSOCIATIONS

The organizations to be described have a variety of powers denied those discussed in previous chapters—those organized and operated under the rules of Section 501(c)(3) of the *Internal Revenue Code*. There are common rules between these nonprofit organizations and those discussed earlier: They must be organized as nonprofits; there can be no personal inurement (benefit) from the organization's assets; and income related to the mission of the organization is not taxed, but income unrelated to the mission is taxed. These rules are true of both groups.

This new group contains organizations that can do one or more of the following:

1. Organize exclusively for the benefit of a small group of individuals—no public support necessary

2. Lobby without limit

3. Engage in politics exclusively

4. Organize specifically and exclusively for the recreation and entertainment of a select group of people

5. Issue capital stocks just as a firm does

6. Operate on behalf of government but purely for profit

7. Pay dividends

8. Do not have to yield to public requests for financial and other data

9. Serve the principal purpose of promoting profit-making

Yes, these, too, are nonprofit organizations. But if a nonprofit described in the previous two chapters did any one of these things it would lose its exemption, and both it and its management would be stiffly fined. The founders of nonprofit organizations often deliberately give up the right to charitable donations in order to get one or more of the privileges listed above.

A business or labor association may give up the right to charitable contributions, which it may not need, in order to focus exclusively on the interests of its members, to do unlimited lobbying, and to be able to form a political organization and engage in political activities. It may also want to avoid the scrutiny that applies to public organizations.

ASSOCIATIONS OF INDIVIDUALS

The word *association* merely means a voluntary grouping of two or more persons or entities. Therefore, by itself, the word does not distinguish between a for-profit and a nonprofit or one type of a nonprofit from another. Nonprofit associations are basically of four types: (1) an association of organizations, or (2) an association of individuals, or both of the two may be an association with (3) a public mission, or (4) a mission, the principal beneficiaries of which are a definable subset of the general population. In all cases except cooperatives, associations are formed without a profit motive, and there is no personal inurement allowed. These organizations are referred to as "nonprofit organizations" (NPOs) in Canadian law.

As an association, the organization may

1. Do unlimited lobbying as long as it furthers the cause of its members and the members are told what part of their dues is used for lobbying or politicking, for this part is not deductible. If substantially all of the dues are so used and if the members generally understand that this is the case, the association need not make an additional disclosure.

2. Focus exclusively on the causes and benefits of their members, thereby only indirectly benefiting the public.

3. Enjoy tax exemption only on incomes related to their carrying out their missions.

4. Minimize public disclosure of their finances.

They must, however, disclose to the public that contributions to them are not tax deductible if any portion of their membership dues is used for lobbying or politicking. Disclosures about contributions are required when the organization has gross receipts of $100,000 or more a year, or solicits more than ten persons in a year as part of a campaign and if the solicitation is made by telephone, in writing, or by radio or television. Violations are subject to limitless fines if wanton, and up to $10,000 per year otherwise.

Now a caution: The word *association* does not by itself tell whether the organization serves a specific group of people as opposed to the public or whether its members are individuals or entities. For this reason, organizations that are associations are assigned a number that derives from the section of the *Internal Revenue Code* that describes what they do and what their basic operating rules must be.

To illustrate, the American Medical Association is a 501(c)(3) because its mission is to advance medical education, including the certification of schools, and these activities benefit the larger community. Education is an authorized 501(c)(3) mission. It benefits society, the community, as a whole. At the same time, it is an association of individual persons as members.

However, the American Hospital Association (AHA) is a 501(c)(6) even though the individual hospitals making up its membership are 501(c)(3)s. This is so, not because the members are entities rather than individual persons, but because the mission is to serve the lobbying interests of these members. This is true even though the AHA also conducts educational activities. But these activities are for the direct benefit of its members.

Let's take two more examples and then derive some general rule. The American Movers Conference does not have the word *association* in its name but it is a 501(c)(6) association very much like the AHA. Its mission is to represent its members. The American Psychological Association is a 501(c)(3). It has individuals as members, but its local chapters are 501(c)(3)s or (c)(4)s. The League of Women is a 501(c)(6), but it operates a fund that is a 501(c)(3).

It is not the name that matters. It is not whether the members are individuals or entities that matters. What matters is what the organization is allowed to do by law. An association of entities has members that are entities, and these entities exercise the same rights as members that members of an association who are persons exercise.

An association does not have to contain the word *association* in its name; even if it does, it could still be one the organizations we described earlier. The U.S. Conference of Mayors is an association, but it is a 501(c)(3). Its mission is to advance the cause of municipalities—the community.

The key distinctions of an association are these:

1. It has members (whether individual or an entity does not matter), and

2. Its mission is narrowly defined to directly benefit a subgroup of the population and indirectly benefit the society as whole—rather than the reverse, which is true of the public organizations discussed in the two previous chapters, or

3. Its mission is not defined in Section 501(c)(3) of the tax code as public welfare

In a very famous case, *Gershinger Health Plan* v. *Commissioner,* Gershinger, a health maintenance organization (HMO) providing health care, which is clearly an identifiable 501(c)(3) mission, was denied such classification by the IRS and the courts. They argued that the beneficiaries were an identifiable group of people and there were no substantial services offered by the group to the public at large.

With this understanding, we shall look at different types of associations not classified as 501(c)(3)s, as are the organizations in our previous chapters. They are fascinating.

Civic Leagues and Welfare Organizations

These are associations such as the League of Women Voters, Common Cause, volunteer fire companies, homeowners associations, and recreational organizations as described in Section 501(c)(4) of the *Internal Revenue Code*. There are about 145,000 such organizations. Their common characteristic is that they advance the interest of the community as a whole by advancing the civic and social welfare interests of their members.

Gershinger, the HMO referred to above, was classified under this title because its principal purpose was construed to be serving its members and by doing this it was advancing public health.

A homeowners association, for example, is made up of people who own homes in a particular development, and its principal purpose may be to safeguard the value of the properties in the development by keeping common areas attractive and by setting standards for each home. To qualify for exemption under this title, however, it must also show that by carrying out this principal purpose, it is doing a public service.

In this vein, a volunteer fire department not only serves its members, but it does the civic duty of protecting the community as a whole. Fire departments are an exception because donations to them are deductible as charitable contributions as long as the donations are used for public purposes. This is not true of other 501(c)(4)s.

Labor and Agricultural Associations

Under this rubric falls the labor unions, professional associations, agricultural and horticultural organizations, of which there are some 73,000. Their central purposes are (1) to advance the cause of their members through representation, publicity, and lobbying, (2) to self-regulate and advance them through education and certification, and (3) advance the conditions of their members through providing certain welfare benefits.

Accordingly, labor unions provide accident, sickness, and death benefits to their members, and this use of the organization's assets is not considered personal inurement as long as eligibility, enrollment, and the distribution of benefits are available to the overwhelming majority of members—not just a few.

As in the case of other associations, contributions to them are not considered charitable and are not deductible as such. But they may be deductible as business expenses to the extent that they are not used for lobbying or political purposes. Unlike other nonprofits, except the business associations described below, these civic leagues or associations can form a political unit with the exclusive intent to engage in political activities. We address this point later in this chapter.

Business Associations

There are some 65,000 organizations classified as business associations under Section 501(c)(6). These are nonprofits that serve one or more lines of business. Their members are firms, proprietors, and business executives, most of whom represent their company's business interest. Virtually every U.S. firm belongs to one or more of these nonprofit associations.

Business associations serve the following functions: (a) They represent one or more segments of business in advertising, in public relations, and in lobbying on behalf of the industry at all levels of government; (b) they regulate members by setting educational, certification, and performance criteria and rules of conduct; and (c) they perform intra-industry functions that firms could not do without incurring greater risk of being charged with anti-trust violations.

For example, firms can form associations that create data banks and do research on prices, costs, and markets. While serving the industry, many of these also serve the public. This is the way we get data on real estate trends and prices, on business inventory and purchasing, and so on. In turn, this is the way the industry may obtain information on consumers—particularly in the insurance business.

Common Interest of Business Associations

Business associations must serve a common interest. What constitutes a common business interest?

The answer to this question can become murky. It is easy to see that a real estate association has a common business interest. But what about a national association to advance women in business, or a chamber of commerce comprising individuals or firms across several industry lines? The argument here is that these qualify as business associations because to the extent that the organization advances these members, it advances the industry in which they belong. This proposition required Revenue Ruling 76–400 to elucidate.

But classification as a business association is available if the objective is to improve general business conditions through activities such as advertising, lobbying, and the publication of statistics and other information.

The concept of a line of business means a trade or occupation that does not restrict membership to persons representing a particular brand name, trademark, or any concept that restricts the right to entry of persons engaged in the business. Accordingly, in *National Muffler Dealers Association* v. *U.S.,* the Supreme Court held that a restriction of membership to a group representing a particular brand denied the organization recognition as a business association. A similar judgment was rendered in the case of *Pepsi-Cola Bottlers' Association, Inc.* v. *United States.*

Nondeductibility of Business Lobbying Expenses

Like other associations, contributions are not deductible as charitable. Dues are not deductible as a business expense to the extent that they are used for lobbying. Business associations, like the labor and agricultural ones, can form organizations that have the exclusive mission of participating in politics.

A firm cannot deduct the portion of association dues that covers lobbying expenses either as a charitable donation or as a business expense. Lobbying expenses include all costs related to

1. Influencing legislation
2. Participating or intervening in any public political campaign
3. Attempting to influence the public about elections, legislative matters, or referenda
4. Communicating with the president of the United States, vice-president, a cabinet member or his or her deputy, or a top member of the federal executive civil service
5. Amounts paid or incurred for research, preparation, planning, or coordinating any of the above activities

Certain expenditures by a business are not treated as nondeductible lobbying expenses. These include expenditures to influence local legislative bodies (including Indian tribal governments), and the in-house cost for attempting to influence legislation by communicating with the executive or legislative officials covered by the law if the expenditure does not exceed $2,000 that tax year.

Examples of Missions of Business Associations

Here is an example of a mission statement of an association:

> The members of the XYZ association are the independent dealers in the WWW industry. The mission of XYZ association is to represent its members in the WWW industry before government agencies and in the public arena, and to conduct research and educational programs to improve the productivity and efficiency of its members.

The word *represent* in the above statement includes advocacy, lobbying, conducting advertising campaigns, and giving speeches that promote the causes of the members. These often take the form of public service messages, such as the campaign to promote safe and responsible drinking by the Beer Institute and the National Beer Wholesalers Association.

Note also that membership is restricted. ("The members are independent dealers in the XYZ industry.") They have a common interest to improve performance and profits within that industry—not just the performance of specific firms. Indeed, many of the activities of the association (such as improving public image or understanding of the industry) may benefit members of the industry who are not members of the association.

Nevertheless, the principal purpose of the association is to advance its members. Therefore, it might identify its members by certificates, names, or listing and allow them to use the association's logo. These give visibility and a halo of acceptability. Furthermore, a business association can run programs only for members and give access to certain information only to members.

Another form of a business association mission would substitute the word *industry* for words such as *the business environment* and the membership from a specific industry or portion of an industry such as independent dealers, wholesalers, and manufacturers to *forums* or *corporations*. This is the form that boards of trade, business roundtables, and chambers of commerce may take. They represent any business, and the common interest is the overall business environment, the improvement of which can benefit all members.

THE STRUCTURE OF THE ORGANIZATIONS

A common form of organizing a business association (and many labor and professional organizations) is depicted in Figure 5.1. The core body does administration in-house or by contract, lobbying, and carrying out of the basic mission of the organization. But the organization's educational and research functions are carried on by an educational foundation. This is a 501(c)(3) formed and operated by the association. This organization is financed largely from gifts

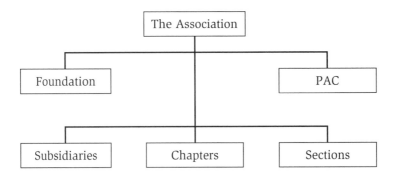

Figure 5.1. Structure of a Business Association.

and contributions from the membership, grants and contracts, conventions and seminars, and other program-related fees. Some associations use these 501(c)(3)s to make contributions to the publicly supported organizations discussed in Chapter Two.

The organization may also have a political action committee (PAC) that does all of the politicking for the organization. These PACs are funded by the membership and carry the name of the association as part of their name. The organization may also have a number of subsidiaries wholly owned by it or chapters affiliated with it. The accounting, even cost sharing, of all of these attached entities must be kept segregated. The walls erected to separate these organizations are more formal, firm, and impenetrable than those between the organization and subsections within it. These subsections are made of groups of members with specific interests; that is, those interested in finance voluntarily form a subsection and those in marketing another.

Political Action Committees

Labor, agricultural, and business associations, specifically if they are exempt under Sections 501(c)(4) and (c)(6), may form a separate entity, a PAC, for the purposes of supporting political candidates and activities, but the funds financing the PAC and management of the PAC must be separate from the remainder of the association. PACs may also be completely independent and free-standing.

PACs do not have to be incorporated or even formally organized. A bank account is sufficient evidence of the existence of a PAC. When a PAC is connected to a parent organization it carries the name of that organization and can only accept dues from the members of the parent organization. Such a PAC is easily recognized because it always bears the name of its parent. When a PAC is not the product of the formation of another organization, it is free to accept dues and contributions from a wider public and will not bear the name of another organization.

PACs, Section 527 organizations, are exempt from taxes on contributions, dues, and fund-raising income used to support their political mission. But contributions to them by their members are not deductible. Other incomes such as investment income are taxed. Chapter Eleven has a discussion of the rules regulating solicitations by PACs.

Significant Differences Between a PAC and All Other Exempt Organizations

The PAC is unlike all of the other organizations. First, the function for which it is exempt is to influence its political outcome. This is its principal and maybe its exclusive function. Second, it need not be incorporated, be a trust, or even be organized. A bank account set up to receive and expend funds for political purposes is enough. Its exemption, as stated, applies only to income it receives for political purposes; investment and other income are taxed. With the 501(c)(3)s, (4)s, and (6)s, an exemption may apply to investment income and other business income such as rents and royalties. Unlike all of the other exempt organizations, it doesn't have to apply for exemption from federal income tax and it doesn't have to file a Form 990. If it has taxable income, however, it must file Form 1120–POL, which is the sister form to the one associations and others file for lobbying. Like other tax-exempt organizations that are not qualified to receive tax-deductible contributions, PACs must make that clear in any solicitation. See Chapter Eleven on federal rules of solicitation by PACs.

Social Clubs

A social club is a nonprofit that exists solely for the pleasure, recreation, and entertainment of its members. A social club cannot win tax-exempt status if its membership is not restricted—it cannot be public in membership or in the regular (rather than incidental) availability of its facilities. Its principal source of money has to be its membership fees. All these facts make the social club just the opposite of the publicly supported organization.

Like the publicly supported organization, however, the social club cannot restrict its membership on the basis of race, color, or religion—except that religious organizations can exclude participation based on all of these differences. Like the publicly supported organizations, they cannot use their resources for personal inurement. Since they are membership organizations, an increase in the privileges of a few members without a corresponding increase in their membership fees or a charge, and without its being an incentive for actions in service of the social club, is considered personal inurement—the issue of discrimination aside.

A social club cannot offer corporate membership without jeopardizing its status because corporate membership is considered public. The membership of the social club is required to have a common set of values and fellowship among members. This does not require each member to have fellowship with each and every other. Thus, a social club can have locales and the fellowship within each locale is enough to satisfy the requirement of fellowship among members.

The social club, described under Section 501(c)(7) of the *Internal Revenue Code*, is required to show that approximately 35 percent of its gross revenues are from fees and dues from its members and that no more than 15 percent of its gross revenues came from the leasing of its facilities or selling of its services to the general public.

Fraternal Associations

Fraternal associations are of two types. One type of fraternal organization is a society, order, or association that, being fraternal, operates as part of a lodge system exclusively for the benefit of its members and provides these members or their families with payments of life, sickness, accident, or other benefits. These fraternal organizations, of which there are about 100,000, are described in Section 501(c)(8) of the Code.

A second type of fraternal association differs from the first in that it does not provide the insurance benefits of the first, but rather devotes its net earnings to religious, charitable, scientific, literary, educational, and fraternal purposes. It may, however, arrange with a third party to provide the insurance benefits of the first type of fraternal association. This second type of fraternal organization is described under Section 501(c)(10) of the Code.

In both of these groups, there is no need to serve the public and no need for public support. Indeed, if either extends these benefits to outsiders, it loses its tax exemption. This is contrary to the principles of the publicly supported organizations described as 501(1)(c)(3)s.

Unlike all of the other groups described above, contributions to fraternal groups are tax deductible as long as the group uses these funds to carry on a charitable purpose consistent with 501(c)(3).

The Association in Canada

The Canadian equivalents to many of the associations we have just discussed are known as "nonprofit organizations." These organizations are broken into three subgroups, each of which is defined in a paragraph of the Canadian Income Tax Act as follows:

1. Paragraph 149(1)(e): Agricultural organizations, boards of trade and chambers of commerce

2. Paragraph 149(1)(1): Social welfare, civic improvement, recreation and pleasure, and any purpose other than profits

3. Paragraph 149(1)(j): Scientific organizations involved in scientific work or that support such efforts by other organizations or associations and which itself conducts no business

As in the United States, these organizations exist principally to serve their members, and through this service, serve the society. Similarly, there can be no personal inurement other than that which is bestowed by membership or compensation for services rendered. Also, political expenditures to influence candidates or parties or to propagate philosophies are prohibited. Information and education are allowed.

As with their U.S. counterparts, donations to these organizations do not receive tax benefits, but their revenues are generally tax exempt. On the provincial and local levels, these nonprofit organizations (like charities) receive a rebate for part of the taxes they pay on goods and services bought on the provincial level. The percentage rebate varies by type of organization. In a few provinces where the goods and services taxes are said to be harmonized (combined), the organizations may receive a tax credit for the remaining percentage. This depends on their receiving at least 40 percent of their revenues from the government.

Unlike registered charities in Canada, these nonprofit organizations file a Canadian income tax information return and a corporate income tax return. Although the requirement to file is initially determined by size of assets and the amount of dividends, interests, rents, and royalties received, the law also requires these organizations to file annually once they have made an initial filing regardless of subsequent revenue performance.

Cooperatives

Not all cooperatives are tax exempt. Some cooperatives get favorable tax treatment on a state, but not on the federal level. The cooperative is significantly different from all of the groups we have visited both in this and in the previous two chapters. Cooperatives can issue capital stock and can pay dividends. Let's look at the farmers' cooperative, which is specifically exempt from federal and state income taxes. The cooperative must be organized to market the products of its members and then pay to them the proceeds minus costs, or for the purpose of buying equipment for them and turning the equipment over to them at actual costs plus expenses.

Cooperatives of this type may issue capital stocks—stocks intended not only as certificates of membership but to indicate a level of investment, the sum of which provides a capital base for the cooperative. The organization can pay dividends to these "investors" as long as the rate of dividend is not more than the legal rate of interest in the state of incorporation or 8 percent, whichever is greater. Only members can participate in the dividends, and only persons who are marketing their products or purchasing their equipment through these organizations can be members—participation by nonmembers in purchasing is limited to 15 percent of the dollar value of all purchases. And participation by nonmembers is limited to nonvoting stocks with fixed interest payments (preferred stocks).

Further, the cooperative may retain portions of its earnings in accordance with state law, which is normally concerned with not impairing the capital integrity of an organization—leaving it with empty pockets.

Religion

Religion is defined as a 501(c)(3), unlike the associations that we shall discuss in the next section. A church, temple, synagogue, any house of worship, any congregation, is an association of persons and is defined as such in law. Many states, including California, have a special section of their nonprofit laws that discuss religious organizations and make exceptions for how these associations are treated.

California, for example, states that every nonprofit described in the general form of a 501(c)(3) has a charitable and eleemosynary duty to the community; the duty to the community of religious organizations is religion. Religious groups are given other exceptions. Solicitation laws in many states do not cover them.

Religious groups are associations in that the local house of worship or congregation has members. But religious congregations also are parts of larger groupings—diocese, synods, and so forth, in which the association is made up of individual institutions. A special form of an association in which the members are organizations is called, for exemption purposes, a *group*. We shall now turn to associations in which the members are organizations.

ASSOCIATIONS OF ORGANIZATIONS

The next set of associations is distinguishable from the first because their members are not individuals, but organizations. This discussion will be followed by a discussion of the rights, liabilities, and powers of membership in both types of associations.

Federations

I shall define federations as being loosely or strongly bound. In a *loose federation,* the organizations are tied together for a single purpose. The United Way is an example of such a federation. The members are bound together for the purpose of efficiency in fund-raising. The federation may set standards for participation and try to increase the managerial capacity of its members so that they may more efficiently use the resources raised, but there is a single purpose that binds them.

In a *strong federation,* such as the Boys and Girls Clubs, Girl Scouts, Big Brothers and Sisters, Habitat International, and the like, the federation is made up of organizations that are independently incorporated and independently managed. However, they all subscribe to a similar dominant mission and a basic rule of performance and quality of what they do. In this kind of federation, the individual organization is called a chapter. A *chapter* is a local franchise in very much the same way that your local fast-food restaurant is.

Each chapter has its own organizing document or charter and its own officers and board, and it may offer its own special programs as long as they conform to the federation's rules of quality and conduct. The advantages of this kind of federation are constant quality, economy in advertising, name recognition, adaptability to local conditions and needs, localization of certain risks, and internationalization. Hence, like a fast food enterprise, members of these strong federations can be found throughout the world with a basic standard fare.

In this type of federation, the glue is the very common mission and a common basic method for meeting mission requirements. This agreement is formalized in a contract, a charter, or a covenant, as the agreement of common commitment may be called. Violation of this agreement by a member can result in disfranchisement of that member. Violation of it by the federation can result in suits either by an individual member or by members acting as a group. This latter action is called a *derivative suit,* as explained later in this chapter.

Affiliations

This term is so broadly used that it almost escapes being trapped into a neat definition. An *affiliation* implies that organizations are related but do not necessarily belong one to the other. As far as lobbying goes, however, an affiliation implies that one organization has the same or shares board members and that one is capable of committing the other. This is true even if the two are independently incorporated.

The nature of the interrelationship can be significantly stronger than it is in a federation. One way to distinguish between an affiliation and a federation is that an organization can voluntarily be part of and cease its connection with the federation and continue to operate. But it would drop "Boy Scout" because the name is copyrighted. Therefore, a Boy Scout troop can cease being a part of the federation, but it would have to change its name and cease using items that associate it with the Boy Scouts because that would be an infringement on copyright and a deception in solicitation—both illegal unless otherwise arranged.

In an affiliation this is not so easy because both groups share a common core. An affiliation is similar to what is called a brother-sister relationship among firms. Two organizations, though independent, are affiliated because they share a common core. (See the discussion of groups below.) Hence, for some purposes, such as payment of taxes or reporting on Form 990, they may report as one. Upon dissolution, the assets of one go to the other or to a common pool.

Therefore, it is not uncommon to find in the dissolution plan of a Catholic hospital that upon dissolution, the assets would pass to the order of nuns with which the hospital is affiliated. The nuns who run the hospitals are members of a large order that has other groups of nuns of the same order running other hospitals. Each hospital is a member of the affiliation.

Groups

The concept of a group is to be distinguished from the concept of an apostolic or religious association or community of individuals. The latter are not tax exempt in the sense that contributions to them cannot be deducted. However, a contribution to a 501(c)(3) created by them can be deducted.

Groups are associations of nonprofit organizations most common in religious organizations. A group is made up of organizations that share a common exemption certification. The organizations in a group are affiliates of the group. Hence, the group gets the exemption from the IRS, and every member, by being a part of the group, is exempt under the group umbrella. The members of a group are its affiliates.

For such a procedure to work, the tax laws require that there must be a central organization that has one or more subordinates under its general supervision or control. The subordinates may be chapters, posts, locals, or other such units, which may or may not be incorporated although each must have an organizing document. Each subordinate must also have its own employer identification number even if it does not have employees. A private foundation or a foreign charity does not qualify for being a subordinate organization.

Each subordinate must indicate that it is affiliated with the central organization and is subject to its control and general supervision. Each must qualify as a tax-exempt organization although not necessarily the same type; that is, one may qualify as a 501(c)(3) education and health organization, and another may even be one of the other organizations we have described in this chapter and in Table 2.1. If the subordinates are to be included in group tax returns or filings, they must all be using the same accounting period as the central organization's. There must also be a uniform governing document for the group to which each member of the group affirms commitment. The group can expand as long as each new recruit commits to these terms.

Three months before the end of its accounting period, the group is required to file notice about any changes in name, method of operation, or mission of any of the subordinates and to list the subordinates that have changed names, new subordinates, and those disaffiliated. Failure to supply these can cause loss of group exemption. So, too, can the failure to file 990s. The group exemption ends if the central organization fails to continue to qualify for whatever reason as a 501(c)(3).

The Lodge System

Many associations—such as fraternities, sororities, and veterans groups—are structured on the lodge system. A lodge system is one in which there is a hierarchy between a center organization and a number of branches (which may or may not be independent corporations). The arrangement is held together by a common belief and a ritualistic requirement for membership. An organization that is a certified member of a lodge system can support its quest for exemption on the basis of its certification.

Holding Companies

A nonprofit corporation can be a holding company. Tax law provides for two types of holding companies as nonprofits. Section 501(c)(2) provides for the type of holding company that has one parent. Here the sole purpose of the holding company is to acquire property, hold title to it, collect income from it, and distribute this income to the parent of the holding company. Contributions to this holding company are not tax deductible.

Moreover, income that passes from the holding company to its parents retains its character in the determination of the parent's classification, as we discussed in Chapter Three, and for tax purposes, as we shall discuss in Chapter Ten. Accordingly, if the holding company receives rental income it is treated as rental income when received by the parent.

What the parent receives in a distribution is always in a net form. Again, with rental income the holding company would deduct costs before making any distribution to the parent. As is often the case, the parent itself may occupy space.

A holding company could take another form. It could have multiple parents—up to 35 tax-exempt parents. These are stockholders. But they must all have the same class of stocks so that variation in voting power is based upon the number, not the type of stock held. In this form, described under Section 501(c)(25), all the shareholders have the same rights to terminate their participation in the holding company with ninety days of written notice. Their shares must be redeemed by the holding company. They cannot be traded in the sense of a corporate stock outside of the holding company family.

Again, contributions to holding companies are not deductible, and funds moved from them to their parents retain the character in which they were earned by the holding company. Holding companies provide an efficient way of managing assets outside of the corporate shell of the nonprofit organization and therefore allow the organization to focus on its mission.

Common Trusts or Charitable Risk Pools

Another form of association of organizations is a common trust. A *common trust* is an investment pool. These obtain their exemption under Section 501(n). Although these pools are exempt under federal tax law, contributions to them are not deductible and the investment strategies they employ are determined by state law. Here is New Hampshire's under its Section 292–19, entitled "Collective Investments":

> charitable corporation may combine money and property belonging to various trusts in its care for the purpose of facilitating investments, providing diversification and obtaining a reasonable income, provided, however, that the participating contributory interest of said trusts shall be properly evidenced by appropriate bookkeeping entries showing on an annual basis the capital contribution of and the profit and income allocable to each trust; and provided, further, that not more than 10 percent of the fund shall be invested in the obligations of any one corporation or organization, excepting deposits in savings banks, obligations of the United States and of the state of New Hampshire and its subdivisions, and provide, further, that nothing herein shall be construed to authorize the investment of funds of a trust in any manner not authorized by law.

MEMBERSHIP POWERS, DUTIES, AND LIABILITIES

Each of the associations we just discussed are by definition of being an association a membership group. Each of the organizations discussed in the previous chapters may also have members. Therefore, concerns about membership applies to 501(c)(3)s through (6). But it also applies to mutuals and cooperatives. They, too, have members. Following are some basic rules about membership.

An organization's membership policies are written in its bylaws. Bylaws must be framed to satisfy state law. When the bylaws are silent the state law will apply. Bylaws cannot contravene state law.

In general, a member is a person or entity that has the right to participate in the setting policy and in determining the leadership of an organization. For most associations, membership is determined by qualifications set in the bylaws. For professional organizations, particularly those requiring a professional license—called a *professional association* or *corporation*—membership may be restricted by law to those who are licensed to practice the profession or occupation. The concepts of *affiliate* or *associate* members have been used to accommodate persons who do not meet the qualifications.

All members of an association or a nonprofit organization generally have identical rights and obligations with respect to voting, dissolution, redemption, and transfer. The bylaws, however, may establish different classes of membership and assign to each a preferred right or voice in any of these transactions. For a particular transaction, a member may be disqualified because of a conflict of interest. Such a member has the same duty as a trustee to reveal that interest and to allow the others in keeping with the bylaws to decide on the extent of the member's participation on the issue at hand.

Among the voting powers members have is to remove trustees. In some states it is left up to the bylaws to define how such removal can be accomplished. Maine Title 13–b-Section 704 confers a statutory right to members. It states that a two-thirds vote is required, but that the bylaws can place a smaller percentage that cannot be less than a majority. Members can call a special meeting and remove a trustee with or without cause. Another vital power that members have, as discussed in Chapter Six, is to dissolve the organization. In religious organizations, the law defers to the religious canon on these matters of powers, duties, and hierarchies and obedience of members.

Members may also sue the organization. Arizona 10–3631 allows the lesser of fifty members or 25 percent of the votes the power to sue their organizations. A suit of an organization by its members or directors is called a *derivative suit* and must be done by members at the time of the infraction and in good faith on behalf of the organization.

The member may be made liable to the organization for dues, assessments, or fees but is not liable to the others for the actions of the association or the organization. Although a member, under certain circumstances (where a promise of the member commits a third party), may be liable for the act of the organization, membership, per se, does not expose one to liabilities of the organization even if the association is unincorporated.

Here is an example. Grace and Violet are members of an unincorporated association carrying free lunch to the elderly. Violet, acting in the name of the corporation, runs into a truck and destroys it. This does not make Grace liable, even though she was carrying out the mission of the association.

But as Mississippi Law 79–11–185 points out, a creditor, having tried to collect from the association or organization without success because of the insolvency of the latter, may seek a judgment to have members pay the amount they owe the nonprofit. This payment, presumably, can in turn be used to satisfy the creditor's claim against the nonprofit. The creditors can do this only after a court has rendered a judgment for payment by the organization. The creditors may act singularly or jointly.

Stocks as Evidence of Membership

State laws provide for certain cooperatives and associations that are nonprofit to issue stocks as certificate of membership. Some of these stocks can indeed pay dividends and make other distributions because they are carrying on an activity to further the consumer or commercial interests of their members. A fish marketing association in California is an example. These "dividends" are sometimes tricky. Sometimes they are nothing more than a return of capital because of a member's overpayment. With a 501(c)(3) and nonstock associations, a dividend is an illegal distribution of the organization's assets.

In these associations, as in California, the association may issue one type of stock, a common stock, but the transfer of that stock can only occur to people licensed to do business in that industry. It therefore does not have the transferability that a for-profit common stock has. Anyone, for example, can buy stocks in IBM, Microsoft, or Sears.

When the organization is a stock corporation, membership requires buying the stock. The organization may repurchase the stocks when its directors vote to do so. When a member is expelled from such a corporation, the board of trustees must assess his or her capital interest minus penalties and charges and return the difference to the ex-member.

The bylaws of a stock-issuing association must also provide for the eventuality that a stock is abandoned—that is, that it was issued to someone who fails to keep up membership. The issues with which the organization must be concerned are about the voting power of such a stock, its rights to accumulate

dividends, the period after which all of these rights are terminate̶
ability to restore these rights.

Termination of Membership

A member may resign his or her membership but remain liable to the organ̶
zation for any of the member's outstanding debt to it for charges, assessments, or fees incurred. Membership may be given for a fixed period and terminated at the end of it unless renewed.

In California, 5340–5342, a member cannot be suspended or expelled or membership rights terminated unless it is done in good faith and it is fair. This means it is done according to the bylaws, the member was given at least fifteen days to respond, and an appeal process is available.

NONPROFITS CREATED FOR STATE PURPOSES

A reason for tax exemption is that a nonprofit relieves government of a burden. Almost all of the nonprofit organizations that are so exempt are organized by individuals. We make reference to them throughout this book and they range from poverty and drug centers, through health and child-care centers, to centers of recreation and education. They even include organizations that promote a community's development. In South Dakota, an organization that does this is entitled to financial, even construction assistance from the government according to an attorney general ruling, 9–12–11.

In this section, we are concerned with a different type of nonprofit. These are organized by governments, not individuals, to take on big and expensive projects—running transportation systems, providing water and sewer, and building and operating athletic facilities. While creating these authorities, the government will neither manage nor take responsibility for financing them. This section describes an important type of nonprofit generally called an *authority* or *public service corporation*. The U.S. Bureau of the Census reports that there are 32,000 such organizations, not including those involved in education.

In Section 22–21–71 of its code, Alabama authorizes several of its counties to organize public corporations for the purposes of acquiring, owning, and operating public hospitals and other health care–related facilities. This allows the governments to fulfill their responsibilities to the community but off the public budget and outside of the public bureaucracy. With an authority, it accomplishes this goal in a charitable manner, meaning that no part of the net earnings of the authority can inure to the benefit of any individual or corporation or be paid as dividends to the state.

To effectuate this, Alabama municipalities can elect to transfer all or parts of its hospital and health-related assets to this corporation. These assets are both tangible and intangible, and they may well be assets that were to have been received in the future, such as government or patient payments. Hence, the initial capitalization of this authority is the pool of assets transferred from all of these hospitals—many of them on the brink of economic disaster.

FLORIDA INDUSTRIAL DEVELOPMENT FINANCE ACT

In Florida's Industrial Development Finance Act the state created a number of industrial development authorities and granted them powers because they "will be for the benefit of the people of the state, for the increase of their industry and prosperity, for improvement of their health and living conditions, and for the provision of gainful employment and will constitute the performance of essential functions." Notice that these organizations have the mission of improving public welfare.

The Act continues, "The . . . agency will not be required to pay any taxes on any project or any other." Further, "The bonds issued under the provisions of this part, their transfer, and the income therefrom (including any profit made on the sale thereof), and all notes, mortgages, security agreements, letters of credit, or other instruments which arise out of or are given to secure the repayment of bonds issued in connection with a project financed . . . shall at all times be free from taxation by the state or any local unit, political subdivision, or other instrumentality of the state." The earnings of the bonds (revenue bonds discussed in this book) issued by the authority are tax exempt by the state. Incidentally, they are tax-exempt by the federal government as long as the money raised from selling the bonds is used exclusively (not less than 95 percent) for public purposes or for purposes of the environment or pollution abatement.

The powers of the authority do not include the ability to tax. Authorities do not have taking powers. Florida 159.48 gives the board of commissioners (legislature) the power to levy an *ad valorem* tax for the purposes of helping their industrial development authority carry out their mission but specifies that no part of this tax may be used to pay off the indebtedness by these authorities. Notice that the authorities do not have the power to levy a tax. The municipal government does and may earmark these for the authority.

The authorities can "fix, charge, and collect rents, fees, and charges for the use of any project." It is these revenues that pay off the bonds. Therefore, the principal sources of financing an authority are the revenue bonds, fees, and charges.

ABAG FINANCE AUTHORITY FOR NONPROFIT CORPORATIONS

Authorities, which are government-created nonprofit corporations, run a number of services, ranging from cemeteries, airports, and ports to stadiums and hospitals, water and sewer systems, lotteries, and municipal transportation systems. But authorities may be created to raise money by selling bonds and using this money to finance nonprofits. That is what ABAG Finance Authority for Nonprofit Corporations does. It finances governments and nonprofits, specifically 501(c)(3) organizations, in the San Francisco Bay Area.

Among these, it has financed hospitals, the acquisition of primary care clinics, retirement facilities, and residential facilities for the treatment of women, the acquisition and renovation of substance abuse facilities, the construction of community clinics and refinancing of existing debt, the acquisition and renovation of multifamily complexes, and the construction of a new YMCA facility.

ABAG can sell revenue bonds and raise money for projects that are too small to be financed through borrowing by the organization or the jurisdiction. It can do so more inexpensively because of its experience, standard forms, and the size of its transactions. It does all of this for fees.

ABAG Finance Authority for Nonprofit Corporations conducts several financing programs through its nonprofit subsidiaries. Among these is a housing program specifically designed to provide low-cost financing of smaller urban projects. It has a credit pool for financing larger infrastructure projects. It runs a leasing program that allows organizations and jurisdictions to acquire equipment.

The ABAG raises funds through the issuing of revenue bonds. It also issues certificates of participation (COPs). Revenue bonds issued by the ABAG are likely to be tax exempt (1) because it is a tax-exempt nonprofit and (2) to the extent that the proceeds of the bonds are entirely used (no less than 95 percent) by tax-exempt organizations or government jurisdictions. The certificate of participation is used to finance leases. A COP is a security bought by an investor, such as banks, to participate in the earnings of a pool created to purchase equipment that the authority then leases to the nonprofit or the government agency. These COPs, like the revenue bonds, also earn tax-exempt interest.

LOBBYING AND SOLICITATION

Lobbying may be a principal purpose, sometimes the exclusive purpose, of an association. But associations have unlimited lobbying powers as long as they lobby on issues of common interest to their membership. Therefore, the formulas in Appendix 2.1. do not apply. The disclosure statement, however, does apply and the reader is referred to the discussion on disclosures on lobbying in

Chapter Eleven. Also, associations do become involved in solicitation. The rules on solicitation, including those for associations, are in Chapter Eleven.

THE ASSOCIATION IN SOUTH AUSTRALIA

The United States is different but not unique. In South Australia, the Associations Incorporation Act of 1985 provides for the incorporation of organizations for[2]

1. Promoting religious, educational, charitable, or benevolent purposes

2. Encouraging literature, science, or the arts

3. Providing medical treatment or attention or promoting the interest of persons who suffer from a particular physical, mental, or intellectual disability

4. Promoting sport, recreation, or amusement

5. Establishing, carrying on, or improving a community center or promoting the interests of a local community or a particular section of a local community

6. Conserving resources or preserving any part of the environmental, historical, or cultural heritage of the State

7. Promoting the interests of students or staff of an educational institution

8. Supporting political purposes

9. Administering any scheme or fund for the payment of superannuation or retiring benefits to the members of any organization or the employees of any body corporate, firm, or person

10. Promoting the common interests of persons who are engaged in, or interested in, a particular business, trade, or industry

11. Carrying on any purpose approved by the Minister as subject to this act

Under this act, organizations cannot have as a principal or "subsidiary object," the securing of a pecuniary profit for the members of the association or any of those members. It cannot have as a principal or subsidiary object, the engaging in (as opposed to protecting or advancing) a trade or commerce, unless authorized by the Minister.

The association is not said to be engaging principally in a trade or business if it buys or sells or deals in or provides goods or services in a manner ancillary to the principal objects of the association, and if with respect to transactions with nonmembers who are unrelated to members the transactions are (1) not substantial in number or value in relation to other activities of the association, (2) intended to provide financial support to the association in a manner that is directly related to the objects of the association, or are related to the charging of admission fees to functions that promote the objects of the association.

The membership in the association is determined by the rules of the association, and both the association and the members are bound by these rules. The rules must contain the following:

1. The name and purpose of the association
2. Any provision that is contrary to the standard rules in the Association of Incorporation Act of 1985
3. The conditions of membership
4. The powers and duties and manner of appointments to committees
5. The appointment of an auditor
6. The beginning and ending dates of the association's fiscal year
7. The calling and procedures of general meetings
8. Identification of the person controlling the assets of the association
9. The powers of the association, by whom and under what conditions they are exercised
10. How the rules of the association may be amended
11. Any other matter required by law

Among the powers of the association are the following:

1. To acquire, hold, deal with, and dispose of any real or personal property
2. To administer any property on trust
3. To open and operate bank accounts
4. To invest its money according to the rules of the association and that permitted by law
5. To borrow money
6. To give collateral in conjunction with the borrowing of the association
7. To appoint agents to conduct transactions on behalf of the association
8. To enter into contracts

Contracts must be in writing. Contracts between the association and a third party cannot be made invalid because the agent representing the association did not have the power to enter into such a contract. This is the rule of *ultra vires*. Members of the association, however, may stop the association and take action against it for entering into such contracts.

An association cannot invite nonmembers to invest or make deposits with it unless it gives full disclosure of its financial conditions to that person. It must also disclose the use and security of his or her deposits, the rates of return and terms of the deposits. In addition, the name and occupation of those overseeing the deposit must be disclosed.

The court may dissolve an association for the following reasons:

1. By request
2. If the organization has not commenced any activities or function after more than one year of its incorporation
3. The association is unable to pay its debt by judgment of the court
4. The members of the association have acted unfairly and in their self-interest rather than that of the association or the membership as a whole
5. The affairs of the organizations are being done in a discriminatory manner unfair to some or the entire organizational membership
6. A decision by the court that it is equitable and fair that the organization be terminated

The Commission (agency of government overseeing the sector) may terminate the association for the following reasons:

1. The failure to comply with conditions imposed by the Commission
2. The certificate of incorporation was obtained by fraud or deceit
3. The association is defunct

Of course, dissolution could be voluntary by the association board.

SUMMARY AND PREVIEW

This chapter is about an amazing constellation of nonprofits that are empowered to do one or more of the things that are denied public charities and educational, health, religious, and artistic organizations under Section 501(c)(3). These powers range from having a political mission to paying dividends, and from promoting profit-making firms to operating almost for the exclusive benefit, even recreational benefit, of a few. All these missions must be overseen by a board of trustees acting under the pain of prosecution for certain prohibited acts—the subject of the next chapter.

CHAPTER SIX

Legal Responsibilities of and to Trustees

This chapter concludes Part One. Previous chapters dealt with the fundamental requirements for organizing and operating nonprofits of various types within the constraints of law. This chapter turns to the responsibility for overseeing the operation and assuring conformance with law.

Both federal and state laws require that the nonprofit organization assign this responsibility to the board of trustees. Trustees have certain specific responsibilities and some broad legal responsibilities. Within the parameters set by law, the organization may choose to expand specific roles but only as allowed by state law. Every board is at risk for sanctions and stakeholder actions when it or one of its members crosses certain lines.

This chapter deals with the following types of questions:

1. What are the defined legal duties of trustees and what are the rights of the trustees in terms of their power to demand and to expect certain information and levels of performance?

2. How can economic efficiency reduce the management cost of the board of trustees?

3. What are the responsibilities of the organization to the board?

4. What is the legal definition of conflict of interest and how must it be avoided to meet both state and federal requirements?

5. What are the obligations of the trustee to stop or to sue other trustees, the organization, or the management?

6. When does the law prohibit the nonprofit from indemnifying its trustees when they are sued?

7. Why are trustees so important?

ULTRA VIRES AND THE DUTY OF TRUSTEES

The concept of *ultra vires* simply states that the corporation cannot defend itself by an act it takes by claiming that the act is void because it did not have the power to undertake it. An extension of this concept is that the trustees, managers, and members have a specific duty—to hire and oversee managers who understand the organization, its powers, and its mission. Indeed, state laws permit trustees, managers, and members to challenge whether an impending act is consistent with these powers and responsibilities. Once the act is taken, the ball game is over. The concept of *ultra vires* says that the act cannot be voided because the organization did not have the power.

THE IMPORTANCE OF TRUSTEES

Trustees or directors of for-profit corporations are charged with setting policies, selecting the chief officers, and monitoring the performance of the corporation so that the wealth of the stockholders who are the owners of the corporation is maximized. In short, in the for-profit world, the trustees represent the economic interests of the stockholders. Because corporate directors are also stockholders, they also represent themselves.

The trustees or directors of a nonprofit organization represent the interests of the public, not the private interests of stockholders. Their principal function is to set policies consistent with the public mission of the organization, select managers who can carry out the mission, and monitor the performance of the organization so that public welfare is maximized in a manner consistent with the specific mission of the organization. Their duty, therefore, is to maximize public, not private, welfare.

In between these two extremes is the role of trustees in associations. In these nonprofits, the trustees have a clear responsibility to set policies, select managers, and monitor performance so as to help members. But even here the welfare of the public is important. Professional certification, for example, does give value to practitioners, but it also protects the public against quacks. Similarly, in-service training helps members learn the most advanced techniques, but it also helps them serve the public better. Hence, even in a membership association that is nonprofit, trustees have substantial responsibility to the public.

PUBLIC INTEREST IN THE BOARDS OF NONPROFITS

Because the nonprofit is a creature of the state, states have laws telling how the trustees of a nonprofit organization should operate. In the accompanying insert (see sidebar), note how specific the state of Connecticut is in defining who, how many, and other aspects of the board of mental health nonprofit organizations. It should now be easy to understand why in the paragraphs that follow we shall continuously remind the readers to check their bylaws and statutes of the state. The board of trustees of a nonprofit organization is a legal agency created, as is the organization itself, by state law. Some states are more specific and extensive in their requirements than others, and the requirements may vary according to the mission of the organization.

Statute of the State of Connecticut
Sec. 33–179g. Management of health care center. Directors. (a) If the health care center is organized as a nonprofit, nonstock corporation, the care, control, and disposition of the property and funds of each such corporation and the general management of its affairs shall be vested in a board of directors. Each such corporation shall have the power to adopt bylaws for the governing of its affairs, which bylaws shall prescribe the number of directors, their term of office, and the manner of their election, subject to the provisions of this chapter. The bylaws may be adopted and repealed or amended by the affirmative vote of two-thirds of all the directors at any meeting of the board of directors duly held upon at least ten days' notice, provided notice of such meeting shall specify the proposed action concerning the bylaws to be taken at such meeting. The bylaws of the corporation shall provide that the board of directors shall include representation from persons engaged in the healing arts and from persons who are eligible to receive health care from the corporation, subject to the following provisions: (1) One-quarter of the board of directors shall be persons engaged in the different fields in the healing arts at least two of whom shall be a physician and a dentist; (2) one-quarter of the board of directors shall be elected directly at the annual meeting of members of the community, including subscribers who are eligible to receive health care from the health care center, but no such representatives need be elected until the first annual meeting following the approval by the insurance commissioner of the initial agreement or agreements to be offered by the corporation, and there shall be only one representative from any group covered by a group service agreement.

(b) If the health care center is not organized as a nonprofit, nonstock corporation, management of its affairs shall be in accordance with other applicable laws of the state, provided that the health care center shall establish and maintain a mechanism to afford its members an opportunity to participate in matters of policy and operation such as an advisory panel, advisory referenda on major policy decisions, or other similar mechanisms.

New Hampshire law on voluntary corporations and associations, which applies to secular organizations chartered after August 1996, says:

> In the interest of encouraging diversity of discussion, connection with the public, and public confidence, the board of directors of a charitable nonprofit corporation shall have at least five voting members, who are not of the same immediate family or related by blood or marriage. No employee of a charitable nonprofit corporation shall hold the position of chairperson or presiding officer of the board.

California Section 5220–5227 states that the term of directors of nonmember organizations can be a maximum of six years and member organizations a maximum of three years. In the absence of these limits, the limit is one year. Re-election is possible.

The bylaws can allow staggered terms, and the terms of each do not have to be the same. The trustees can be elected by class of membership or region of membership or some other category of this type. But only members of the stated class can vote for its trustee and remove its trustee.

Trustees serve until a qualified replacement occurs. But a trustee can be removed by other trustees if the trustee is found to be of unsound mind by final order of a court, is convicted of a felony, or if found by a court to have breached his or her fiduciary duties. A trustee or all trustees can be removed without cause by the members (the required size of the vote depending upon the size of the membership) or by a majority of trustees if there are no members.

When the board is deadlocked, it or the members can petition the attorney general or the court to intervene. An impartial board member is appointed by either the attorney general or the court. This impartial member cannot be a member of the organization or be related to any of the trustees by "consanguinity or affinity within the third degree according to the common law to any of the other directors of the corporation or to any judge of the court by which such provisional director is appointed." Such an impartial director serves with compensation until the deadlock is broken or removed by order of the court.

Public interest is also reflected in the reporting requirements of nonprofits. The federal government, some states, and some localities require nonprofits to report annually the names of their trustees and principal officers and whether serving on the board of another organization is a requirement for serving on the board of the reporting organization. We shall discuss interlocking directorates later in this chapter. The compensations, fees, benefits such as retirement and the use of an automobile, severance pay, and loans made by the organization to trustees must also be reported.

For each loan made to a trustee or manager, the name of the borrower, the original amount loaned, the balance, the date of the loan and of its maturity, the terms of repayment, interest rate, the security or collateral provided by the borrower, the purpose of the loan, and what was loaned (cash or property) along with its fair market value must be reported.

Any loan to a trustee, officer, or their personal or business associates should fall within the bylaw provisions for such loans if such loans are permitted by the state in the first place. See the discussion on prohibitions later. If permitted, the loan should occur on a businesslike basis. This means proper collateral, interest, and timely repayments. Loans should also not be repetitive and discriminatory in favor of trustees and officers as compared to other employees.

For the federal government, all the above information must be submitted on Form 990, which, when completed, is available to the public on request. Organizations that fail to provide this information are subject to penalty.

SIZE AND COMPOSITION OF THE BOARD

The charter and bylaws of the organization must state the number of trustees required. The law usually states a minimum and will permit the membership to increase the size in accordance with the bylaws of the organization. Several factors may influence the size of the board other than the state-required minimum.

One of these is costs. The larger the board, the more expensive it is to recruit and to operate because of mailing, lodging, transportation, telephone, insurance, printing costs, and honoraria, if paid.

Diversity by race, sex, geography, political party, and professional specialty can all be important considerations. Diversity enhances the public image and purpose of the organization and gives it a better chance to reflect its constituency accurately and therefore to meet its public mission. Many national nonprofits try to maintain a balance between Democrats and Republicans on their boards so as to give the appearance of nonpartisanship.

The board should be sufficiently large to involve persons with different skills. For example, the board may choose to have someone who knows about press relations or financial matters. It should always have people who understand the mission and are imaginative about how it may be carried out. Adding a well-known person to a board adds legitimacy.

The size and composition of the board should be determined by considerations of operational efficiency. Large boards can become unwieldy, and a quorum is mathematically more difficult to attain the larger the board is. A paralyzed board is a frustrating, costly, and debilitating experience for trustees, managers, and staff. One way to deal with this is to divide the board into committees. When this is done, there must be an executive committee that can act on behalf of the entire board on certain crucial matters. Another strategy is to permit voting by proxy or phone. Yet another arrangement is to permit some decisions to be made by the majority of those present and voting. In sum, the larger the board, the more it is necessary to create ways in which a smaller group can act on behalf of the entire board.

Finally, the size of the board should reflect convention and certifying requirements, whether these requirements are set by an association for all its members or by a certifying board. The National Charities Information Bureau, which is a watchdog of nonprofits, uses a minimum of five voting members as its standard for assessing the governance structure of a nonprofit.

Organization of the Board

The bylaws of the organization will state the way the board is to be organized. Clearly, the way the board is organized will depend on its size, but it should also depend on the complexity of the mission of the organization. There should almost always be at least one committee that is responsible for overseeing the fiscal integrity of the organization. Money is critical and fungible. The committee or its subcommittees may have responsibility for auditing, fundraising, budgeting, and investments. Other committees may oversee personnel and administrative policies; another may oversee membership and professional practices.

Some committees may be standing as opposed to ad hoc. The latter committees are created for a specific purpose and disband once that purpose is fulfilled. Standing committees are part of the permanent structure of the organization. They are created in the bylaws.

Term of Service

The term of service for each trustee is stated in the bylaws of the organization, which also state how and under what conditions the term of any member may be ended before its due date. In choosing the length of term, consideration ought to be given to the learning curve. How long does it take the average person to learn enough about the organization and its mission and environment in order to participate effectively?

Conversely, how long will it take the average person to become bored and useless? One way to handle this problem is to have staggered terms and also to permit persons to have more than one consecutive term. Hence, each member of a five-person board may have a three-year term, but the term of each may not end in the same year. By also permitting members to succeed themselves, the organization gets continuity, which is important.

The issue is always a trade-off between continuity and fresh blood. This is particularly true in membership organizations that are undergoing rapid change either in size or direction. Therefore, limiting the number of persons who may succeed themselves or the number of times a trustee may succeed himself or herself is always advisable. It replaces tired blood conveniently and also stimulates interest in board membership. Some organizations make the turnover palatable by asking replaced board members to serve on an advisory committee or by giving them emeritus status. Yet another strategy is to allow persons to requalify for board membership after "sitting out" for a couple of years.

QUALIFICATION AND REMOVAL OF TRUSTEES

The bylaws of the organization should state who is qualified to serve on the board. Qualification may cover years of membership, residence, sex, and the like. Qualification may also be determined by state law, as we saw above with the state of Connecticut. Within the broad parameters of law, organizations may exercise discretion.

Disqualified or Interested Persons

A disqualified or interested person may not necessarily be barred from serving on the board. Rather, the law intends to limit the voting power of these individuals so that they do not dominate the activities of the board. In the state of California, only 49 percent of the board may be made up of interested persons, defined as persons paid by the board in the past twelve months. More broadly, in many states an interested person is one who has a material financial relationship to the organization and includes the close relatives or business associates of such a person. They, too, will be classified as interested persons.

A trustee can also become an interested or disqualified person based on one transaction. Hence, a trustee who has the potential of a material financial gain resulting from a specific transaction becomes an interested person for purposes of that transaction and should be disqualified from influencing the organization on that specific or closely related transaction. The person's business and close relatives should also be disqualified.

Because all trustees who permit such a person to vote, knowing the nature of the relationship, can be held liable, disclosure of trustee interest is advisable.

Removal of Trustees

Generally, the board of trustees or the membership can vote to reduce the size of the board as long as in so doing they do not cause the removal of a trustee whose term is not expired. In addition, members, trustees, the court, and the attorney general of some states may act to have a board member removed.

There are several reasons for removing a board member. Section 224 of the code of Louisiana gives an example of commonly held reasons:

1. Death

2. Resignation

3. Incompetence

4. Bankruptcy

5. Incapacitation for at least six months

6. Failure to attend meetings

7. Failure to accept the board appointment in writing in sixty days.

Being an interested party where such interest does not violate state law is not in itself justification for removal unless disclosure is fraudulent. Being an interested person is more a restriction on participation. Obviously, at some point interest prohibits total participation. Hence, a major supplier of an organization, its landlord, or the spouse of its chief executive officer may be so intertwined as to prohibit their participation on the board. In sum, a board member does not have to be removed once he or she becomes an interested person.

INTERLOCKING DIRECTORATES

An interlocking directorate is one in which one or more persons serve on two or more boards, thus linking them. With a limited pool from which organizations choose, it is not uncommon to find individuals who serve on several boards. The issue of interlocking directorates is less concerned with these incidental occurrences than it is in the questions of control, loyalty, and taxation. The basic question is, Does the degree of interlocking imply that one organization is really controlled by the other?

Two organizations, though different in name and mission, may for purposes of policy, control, and taxation be considered related or essentially one entity if they have the same board members or if the majority of their trustees are the same people. In addition to causing possibilities of conflict of loyalty, there can be tax consequences. Therefore, the choice of an interlocking directorate should be strategic and purposeful.

In Chapter Three we saw that in a supporting organization, a 509(a)(3), an interlocking directorate may be very wise and legally encouraged. The subservience of one organization to the mission of the other is intended and may be effectively accomplished by interlocking the directorates.

In the case of two related nonprofits, each carrying out a different mission, an interlocking board of trustees would imply that one is controlled by the other. Hence, the receipt of income (especially interest and rental) from the controlled organization by the organization that is in control would expose that income to taxation. We shall make much of this point in Chapter Ten.

PROHIBITIONS ON TRUSTEES

Three basic principles describe the duties of trustees. Remembering these is important, and they are described in the next section. But first, let us look at some prohibited acts.

Personal Loans Prohibited by Some States

Many states bar trustees from using their organization's assets for guaranteeing or making loans to themselves other than as advances for expenses. Section 719 of the laws of the state of New York is an example. Not only do these statutes prohibit trustees from receiving loans, but they also go one step further by making a trustee who attends a meeting in which such a loan was approved personally liable for repayment even though he or she may have abstained in the vote.

To be free of such liability, the trustee must take one of the following steps: (1) record dissent in the minutes of the meeting, (2) submit a dissent to the secretary in writing before the adjournment of the meeting, or (3) if the trustee is absent, send a registered letter informing the secretary of the organization of the dissent to the loan shortly after the meeting. The trustee who obtained the loan can hold all abstaining trustees and those who voted in favor of the loan liable for repaying it.

In California, loans to directors and officers are strictly prohibited and directors can be made personally liable for such loans. If such loans are to be made, prior consent must be obtained from the attorney general of the state or from the courts.

The IRS and Loans to Officers and Directors of the Nonprofit

In some states, loans to officers and directors are expressly prohibited transactions. The IRS does not prohibit these loans, but it requires specific reporting of them on the Form 990. The organization must note the year-end balance of such loans outstanding, the borrower's name and title, the original amount of the loan, the balance due, the date of the note and its maturity date, the repayment terms, the interest rate, the security provided by the borrower, the purpose of the loan, and the fair market value of what was furnished by the lender—cash, securities, art object, and so on. For federal purposes, a loan could be a salary advance.

DEALING WITH POSSIBILITIES OF CONFLICTS OF INTERESTS

Every nonprofit organization needs to consider ways to avoid conflicts between the interests of the organization and those individuals in management, governance, and decision-making positions in the organization. The IRS has recommended that organizations consider adopting a conflict of interest policy that includes provisions to which these individuals should conform when considering transactions in which they have a potential, actual, direct, or indirect financial interest. The policy might require

1. Disclosures by interested persons of these financial interests and the facts that are material to them

2. Procedures for determining whether the financial interest could result in a conflict

3. Procedures such as abstaining from a vote or excusing one's self from the discussion on matters related to the transaction

4. Procedures for taking corrective action should such a conflict occur

5. Procedures for recording discussions and decisions, including votes

6. Procedures for being sure that each trustee has received, read, and understood the policy

Because this issue is so important, the Services sample conflicts of interest policy is reproduced in Appendix 6.1. See also Brauer and Kaiser (1996) in the Suggested Readings section. The reader should note that many of the specific transactions alluded to in this policy are covered extensively in this book. These include compensation and various strategic alliances such as joint ventures and mergers.

STATES AND TRUSTEE CONFLICT OF INTEREST

The federal government's interest in the conflict of interest among trustees is largely aimed at preventing a trustee from using the assets of the nonprofit corporation for the personal benefit of the director or his or her associates or relatives. This is only part of the state's interest. The state is also interested in whether the transaction is enforceable.

Mississippi 79–11–269 explains the position of many states. A trustee is said to have a conflict of interest when he or she directly or indirectly (through a relative or associate) has an economic interest in the decision to be taken. This fact alone does not make the decision subject to being voided by the nonprofit corporation or its members. The decision is enforceable if (1) the material facts of the conflict was made known to the other trustees or to the members, (2) the transaction was fair, and (3) the vote of the majority of qualified trustees—not including the trustee with the conflict—supported the decision.

Trustees and Derivative Suit

A derivative suit is the ultimate power that a trustee has against an organization and other trustees. A trustee may sue the organization on behalf of the members. Arizona 10–3631 allows that any director or 25 percent of the directors, whichever is greater, can sue the organization they serve. But the person or persons must have been a director of the organization at the time the act was committed, and the suit must be in the interest of the organization.

A FIVE-PART CONFLICT OF INTEREST POLICY

Borrowing from the law in the state of New Hampshire, any organization can come up with a reasonable policy to discourage a conflict of interest among its trustees and officers.

First, require commitment to the duties of trustees—for example, require commitment to the four ethical statements enumerated by the State of New Hampshire:

1. The *Duty to Undivided Loyalty* to the charity—meaning placing the interest of the organization before that of the trustees.

2. The *Duty of Care*—meaning reading financial statements, asking questions, keeping the organization current legally.

3. The *Prohibition Against Self-Dealing*—meaning disclosing and scrutinizing financial transactions between the trustees and the organization.

4. The *Need for Accountability and Stewardship*—"501(c)(3) charitable assets are public assets, held in trust . . . trustees are accountable to the public."

Second, as in the New Hampshire law, prohibit certain specific transactions with trustees, such as:

1. For the organization to make loans of money or property to a board member.

2. For the organization to sell or lease land to or from a board member without court approval, although the organization may accept these items as gifts from the member.

3. For the organization to do business with the member in a way that is unfair to the organization.

Third, put in place a dollar trigger. New Hampshire law states that if the total transaction with the member is less than $500 in a fiscal year, the transaction may be permitted if it is fair to the organization. But if the total of all transactions with that member exceeds $500, the following must occur:

1. The goods and services must be sold to the nonprofit only at the actual, reasonable, or discounted cost.

2. The details of the transaction must be disclosed to the board and the trustee involved cannot participate in the debates or vote.

3. Two-thirds of the board members who did not sell goods or services to the organization in the past fiscal year have to authorize the transaction, and minutes of the transactions must be kept.

4. The attorney general must receive notice of the transaction before it is consummated and the transaction must be published in the local media where the organization has its principal offices if the transaction exceeds $5,000.00.

Fourth, adopt a policy of transparency that

1. Requires disclosure by each trustee of possible points of conflict.

2. Prohibits the participation of a trustee involved and all other similarly situated trustees from participating or even having presence when such matters are discussed.

Fifth, as in the New Hampshire law, set sanctions and remediation rules:

1. Provide that transactions undertaken with a conflict of interest with a trustee can be voided by the director of the organization.

2. State that no charitable organization can lease for a term of more than five years, or sell or purchase real estate from a trustee or in which the trustee has an interest without a probate court finding that the transaction is fair to the organization.

When considering the adoption of a conflict of interest policy, the trustees may wish to extend their coverage to all principal managers. It would also be wise to consider extending these to principal donors who, in the case of public organizations and private foundations, can affect the tax-exempt status of the organization. Further, the bylaws should provide that an officer be substituted for a trustee when the conflict of interest situation leads to the inability to form a quorum.

Self-Dealing Prohibited

We visited self-dealing in Chapter Four and will revisit it in Chapter Thirteen.

California's Section 5233 clearly defines self-dealing as any transaction involving the organization and in which one or more trustees or officers have a material financial benefit, unless (1) the attorney general gave approval, (2) the organization entered into the transaction for its own benefit, (3) the transaction was fair and reasonable for the organization, (4) it was favorably voted for by the majority of the board, not including the affected members, and (5) the board had information that more reasonable terms were not available; (6) if the action was taken in an emergency, the board must approve it in its next meeting. The penalty for the infraction of self-dealing may include the return of the property with interest, payment of the amount by which the property appreciated, and a fee for the use of the property. It may also include a disciplinary penalty for the fraudulent use of the assets of the organization.

The following examples should remind us what self-dealing is all about:

The president of a college forms a partnership to lease land for ninety-nine years. The partnership constructs a building to the specification of the college and leases it to the college at fair market price. In the future, the college will purchase the building and the land at the fair market price. The IRS ruled that this was not self-dealing and the college did not lose its exemption.[1]

Again, self-dealing does not bar an honest, arm's length transaction that benefits the nonprofit and does not unduly favor the trustee or officer over others. These types of transactions should always be approached with very careful legal and ethical scrutiny and within the scope of a carefully crafted and existing policy. Here is an example of self-dealing:

A trustee of Kermit Fischer Foundation receives irregular compensation ranging from $200 to $8,300, sometimes days apart. The foundation purchased a truck used exclusively by him. It made investments with his brother. It never reported him to be an employee in its IRS report. The court ruled that irregularity was suspicious and, using a formula for trustee compensation of $4 to $5 per $1,000 of assets plus 50 percent of foundation earnings, that his payments were excessive and self-dealing. The 501(c)(3) status was revoked and an excise tax imposed on both the organization and the trustee.

Falsification of Data Prohibited

Both the federal government and states require that records be kept by the trustees, that they be made available to the public, and that they be accurate. Section 6215 of the California code, for example, holds all the trustees of an organization responsible for the accurate reporting of the following records: (1) membership roles, (2) financial statements, including major changes in the assets or liabilities of the organization or in the distribution of assets, (3) minutes of the board, and (4) any indemnification (actual or promised payments for legal expenses due to suits).

These reporting rules go beyond satisfying government needs and monitoring of the organization. The trustees are liable to any third party who uses falsified information for the purpose of making decisions, for example, a creditor. Therefore, many states, such as New York, require the organization not only to provide this information accurately to creditors, but they must also provide creditors with the names and addresses of the trustees when these are requested.

STANDARDS OF ACTION OF TRUSTEES

State laws require trustees to perform certain specific duties. These include approving a plan of dissolution (mentioned in Chapter Two), approving the compensation of officers, voting, and overseeing any merger or consolidation and any distribution of the assets of the organization. The YWCA reminds its trustees that they serve as (1) representatives of a membership, (2) trustees of a corporation, (3) stewards of an idea, and (4) leaders of a movement.

From a legal perspective, each trustee has three standards of action: loyalty, care, and obedience. A trustee who behaves in conformity with these standards escapes personal liability for his or her action on behalf of the organization even if the result is an error so serious as to cause the organization to lose its status. The standards guide actions; they do not judge their brilliance or consequences.

These standards recognize the possibility of error, so they judge only unintentional negligence—not whether the decision was fruitful or intelligent. The application of these principles in a court of law prohibits second guessing as long as the trustees made their decisions in good faith. This is called the *business judgment rule.*

Together, the terms *loyalty, care,* and *obedience* define the fiduciary responsibility of the trustees and the officers of the nonprofit, both of whom can be held personally liable for monetary damages for breaching these duties. Let us see what each of these principles means.

Duty of Loyalty

The duty of loyalty means that while acting in the capacity of a trustee or manager of a nonprofit, the person ought to be motivated not by personal, business, or private interest, but by what is good for the organization. The use of the assets or goodwill of the organization to promote a private interest at the expense of the nonprofit is an example of disloyalty; in such cases, an individual places the nonprofit in a subordinate position relative to his or her own interest. The nonprofit is being used. One purpose of the annual reporting referred to above is to check on self-dealing.

Self-dealing is a form of disloyalty. Again, self-dealing means using the organization to advance personal benefits when it is clear that the personal gains outweigh the benefits to the organization. Hence, a trustee is not prohibited from engaging in an economic or commercial activity with the organization; but such a transaction can be construed as self-dealing if it can be shown that the trustee gained at the expense of the nonprofit, that the trustee offered the nonprofit a deal inferior to what is offered to others or what the nonprofit could acquire on the open market, or that the nonprofit was put in a position of assuming risks on behalf of the trustee. A numerical amount, $5,000 or more, makes the self-dealing an illegal—not just an ethical—infraction.

Another form of self-dealing can occur when two or more nonprofits merge assets or transfer assets one to the other and they have the same trustees. Here the issue is whether a good purpose is being served. Therefore, before consummating a merger or any major transaction, it is wise to set a barrier against self-dealing. The State Board of Regency for the university system in California asked its members to make public their land holdings in California so as to avoid self-dealing, that is, voting to expand the university system in areas where, as a result of their decisions, the value of their landholdings would rise.

One common way in which the board of trustees must defend the nonprofit organization against self-dealing is not in cases of corporate officers abusing their trustee status for the benefit of their firms; rather, it is against the founders of these organizations. It is not unusual to find that after years of personal sacrifice in calling the public's attention to a good cause, founders of organizations confuse the assets of the nonprofit with their own, confuse the interest of the organization with their own, and begin to take dominion over these assets, or install themselves or relatives into highly favorable tenured positions. Operating under the burden of loyalty, boards must separate these persons from the organization.

Duty of Care

The duty of care requires trustees of nonprofits to act in a manner of someone who truly cares. This means that meetings must be attended, the trustees should be informed and take appropriate action, and the decisions must be prudent.

The test of prudence depends on state law. In many states, the trustees of nonprofits are held under the same rules that govern trustees of for-profit corporations. In these states, prudence can be construed to mean making decisions not unlike those expected of any other group of trustees faced with relatively the same "business" facts and circumstances. In other states, nonprofit trustees are held to a higher standard. Prudence means using the same wisdom and judgment that one would if his or her personal assets were at stake. The first is called the *corporate model,* and the second is called the *trust model.*

The duty of care can deny using ignorance as a defense. Therefore, it is inconsistent with this responsibility to allege that a trustee or manager does not hold any responsibility merely because he or she does not know. To know is the duty. It is this duty that makes many compassionate but busy people reluctant to serve on nonprofit boards. In a real sense, they can't care enough—not in the legal sense.

An example of the breach of this duty of care is a suit brought against a nonprofit organization by the state of Minnesota, allegedly because the nonprofit failed to exercise due care of neighborhood facilities for which it was trustee. It implies that the community has invested some confidence in the trustees. The betrayal of this confidence is both illegal and unacceptable.

Duty of Obedience

The duty of obedience holds the trustee responsible for keeping the organization on course. The organization must be made to stick to its mission. We are reminded throughout this book that the mission of a nonprofit is unlike the mission of a firm. The mission is the basis upon which the nonprofit and tax-exempt status are conferred. Unlike a firm, a nonprofit cannot simply change its mission without the threat of losing either its nonprofit or tax-exempt status or both.

An Alternative Statement of Duties of Trustees

In Ohio, the legal duties of the trustees are broken down into four categories. The *duty of care* requires familiarity with the affairs of the organization, evidenced by the reading of reports, attendance and participation in meetings, and the exercise of independent judgment in discharging the oversight responsibility of each member of the board. It is the exercise of diligence.

The *duty of loyalty* means that every attempt is to be taken by the trustees to avoid disloyalty or subordinating the interest or the assets of the organization to personal or other interests.

In Ohio, the *duty of obedience* is referred to as the duty of compliance. Three elements of that duty are (1) to be familiar with the organization's charter, bylaws, and other governing documents, (2) to be familiar with the laws that nonprofit entities must obey, and (3) to assure compliance with registration and other filing requirements.

In addition, the State sees trustees as having a *duty to manage accounts.* This duty involves setting budgetary targets, helping to raise funds and establishing investment policies, developing internal controls, helping to achieve cost-savings in the running of the organization and in its purchasing policies, and insisting on the maintenance of good records of transactions and minutes of meetings.

Duty of Trustees of Religious Organizations

In addition to all the duties specified earlier, state law recognizes another duty of trustees of religious organizations. That duty is to be obedient to the creed or discipline of the religion. So *prudence* becomes taking the religious creed or belief into account in addition to those other factors that trustees of other organizations must take into account. In addition, state law recognizes the hierarchy and other ecclesiastical authorities in addition to lawyers, consultants, and investment advisors as experts upon whom the board may rely in carrying out their duty of care. States and the IRS will not challenge decisions made by trustees within these doctrinal parameters.

SPECIFIC FUNCTIONS OF THE BOARD

Being on the board of directors of a nonprofit organization is a serious matter— even though legions of persons sitting on boards do not fully grasp this fact until trouble breaks out. The truth is that for many organizations, being on the board is a routine, pedestrian experience. This does not make it any less serious and the responsibilities any less onerous. Here are some specific responsibilities that virtually every board has. The chapters in this book where related discussions can be found are in parentheses.

1. Vote on executive and employee benefit packages (Chapter Thirteen)
2. Decide on budgets and broad program areas and on the strategic direction of the organization (Chapter Twelve)
3. Contract with auditors and lawyers and receive their reports in a deliberative forum (Chapters Fourteen, Fifteen, and Sixteen)
4. Decide on and participate in capital campaigns and in making certain gifts (Chapters Seven and Eight)
5. Vote on policies concerning loans, accumulations, and restricted accounts (Chapters Fifteen and Sixteen)
6. Vote on voluntary dissolution and reorganization plans (Chapter Two)
7. Contract with investment advisors and custodians of assets, and oversee their performance according to an investment policy set by the board (Chapters Eight, Nine, Fifteen, and Sixteen)
8. Vote on the sale of assets that are significant or on the use of such assets in significant ventures (Chapter Nineteen)
9. Establish bank accounts (Chapter Sixteen)
10. Hire the CEO, approve contracts of other senior officers, recruit and appoint or certify other members of the board (Chapter Thirteen)
11. Make sure the organization's mission is adhered to in every way including legal and ethical (Chapters Seventeen, Eighteen, and Nineteen)
12. Oversee the management of institutional and custodianship funds and other assets (Chapter Sixteen)

Obviously, these responsibilities vary in the amount of time and effort required of the board member. Most banks will not allow an organization to open a bank account unless the organization can show and file a resolution of the board for it to do so. The board will not oversee every program or every grant request, but it has to have a vote on the broad direction, and therefore, sometimes on the details of programs. How else can it carry out its principal purpose of having the organization stick to its mission?

It takes tremendous skill to manage a board of a complex organization—especially when that board is made up of diverse, intelligent people who have other professional or personal priorities.

EMERGENCY AND APPOINTIVE POWERS OF TRUSTEES

States give trustees of nonprofit organizations certain powers to be exercised during emergencies—such as a natural disaster—defined in terms of the inability of the trustees to meet and to serve adequate notice of a meeting. Arizona 10–3303 gives them the emergency powers to:

1. Modify lines of succession of directors or officers.

2. Relocate the principal officers of the organization.

3. Give notice of meetings only to those directors that can be reached, although radio or other mass media may be used to give such notice.

4. Achieve a quorum in these meetings by using an officer such as the president or vice-president to substitute for a member of the board. The choice of officer is to be based on rank or seniority.

5. Take actions under these conditions that bind the organization but cannot be used to sue the trustees as long as they acted in good faith.

Informal or Irregular Action by Trustees

Several states allow trustees to make decisions without a formal meeting even in a nonemergency situation. Maine Title 13–B-Section 708 describes this protocol. A decision made by a majority of trustees is binding if all of the trustees are aware of the decision and none objected to it in writing to the secretary of the organization. Otherwise, the trustees are bound by the decision. The Maine law requires "prompt" action. In other states, a period for action may be specified.

When the organization is an association, the Maine rules require that the members be notified and that they, too, may act promptly to challenge the decision. Rules such as these allow organizations to function every day without the requirement of 100 percent presence of board members. But these rules are crafted so as not to relieve the absent member of the duty of care. Absence or abstention does not relieve responsibility.

Appointment of Committees and Alternates

Not only does the board have the power to form committees, it may also designate the members of that committee and their alternates. This must be done in conformity with the bylaws. A common problem exists when there are more alternates than persons missing from a meeting or when the organization must choose among designated alternates to sit at a specific meeting. This problem is resolved in Maine because the law there requires that without a previous provision by the directors, the alternates must be chosen in the order of their appointment—even if they were appointed at the very same meeting.

Legal Limitations on the Executive Committee

States may specify the size and powers of the executive committee. For example, Maine Title 13–1 prohibits the executive committee from (1) amending the articles of incorporation, (2) adopting a plan of merger or consolidation, (3) recommending to the membership the sale of the organization's assets unless these sales are a normal part of the everyday business of the organization, and (4) amending the bylaws of the organization.

TRUSTEE OVERSIGHT AND ETHICS

Here are ten steps the board of trustees can take in its oversight role that can help promote and institutionalize ethics in a nonprofit organization:

1. The trustees must acknowledge, communicate, and accept custodial responsibilities for all of the assets of the organization.

2. The trustees must adopt an ethical code that is institutionalized in the organization's bylaws and communicated to all internally and externally.

3. In setting directives and targets, the trustees must evaluate how these affect ethical behavior.

4. The board of trustees should have an audit committee composed of informed and attentive persons who annually receive the audit done by an outside auditor whom they hire and from whom they get an oral as well as a written opinion.

5. In addition to a financial audit, the board should get an audit done of internal control at least every two years.

6. The board should require that top executives take leave of sufficient duration to cause subordinate officers to act in their stead.

7. The board should set term limits, not only on its membership, but for officers in specific positions. This term limit may be flexible; that is, it

may provide for re-appointment but only after a full evaluation. It should preclude dismissals without specific cause and due process.

8. In at least one of its meetings per year, the trustees should hear directly from senior executive officers about their responsibilities, including procedural matters.

9. The trustees should limit check-writing responsibilities and other powers to commit the resources of the organization without certain procedural actions. This limitation should fall on all, including the trustees.

10. Trustees and senior management must be trained and must care.

INSTITUTING PROCEDURES

Trustees do not and should not be involved in micromanagement of the organization. Yet they are ultimately responsible for what occurs. One way to meet this dilemma is to set up rules; that is, broad procedures for management. Here are some suggested ones:

1. Procedures for filing, receiving, and recording complaints of fraud and for protecting those filing such complaints, whether they be employees or clients.

2. Procedures to be followed when fraud is suspected by management and found to warrant an investigation.

3. Procedures for launching and conducting the investigation, such as the protocol that must be followed. This may include the individuals in management that must be notified and data they must collect.

4. Procedures and conditions that would trigger an audit or the calling in of an outside investigator or the local authorities.

5. Procedures for disposing of cases when fraud is found.

6. Procedures for disposition of cases when allegation or suspicion is found to be false—including the disposition of records, apologies, and restoration of the employee or manager.

7. Procedure to avoid employee retaliation in any form but certainly in the form of libel, defamation, harassment, or discrimination suit.

ILLUSTRATION: TRIALS AND TRIBULATIONS OF TRUSTEES

In recent years, the duties of a trustee have not been easy. The public relations and the liability questions have been tough. Nowhere in 1990 was this problem greater than in the arts and in religion, where the issue was the same—sex.

So much of what trustees in the arts continue to confront during the 1990s are conflicts of duties relating to freedom of speech, sex and obscenity. Indeed, the question that Kristol poses in the following box is legitimate. Is it art? What should trustees do?

We are reminded that the courts exonerated the trustees of the Cincinnati museum that displayed Mapplethorpe and that many in Congress reacted sharply and negatively to the Washington museum that showed his work. Indeed, the use of federal funds to finance this kind of work became a cause célèbre.

The University of the District of Columbia (UDC) had a similar well-publicized problem. Judy Chicago made it a gift of the *Dinner Party*. The piece is of thirty-nine female genitalia, each decorously placed in a seating arrangement on a dinner table. This, it is said, depicted the struggle of women. As is common, the artist-donor made some display stipulations, which required expensive renovation of a building, and the trustees voted $80,000 for moving and insuring the piece. The work was valued at $2 million. Previously, the piece had been shown and was well received in a number of prestigious

---

An Example of Trustees on the Hedge

It is very difficult to convey to people who do not follow the weird goings-on in our culture an appreciation of the animating agenda of the "arts community" today. An ordinary American reads about a woman "performing artist" who prances nude across the stage, with chocolate smeared over her body, and though he may lament the waste of chocolate or nudity, it does not occur to him that she is "making a statement," one that the "arts community" takes seriously indeed.

Even museum trustees in Washington, D.C., or Cincinnati—an elite, educated, and affluent group of arts philanthropists—had no idea what Mapplethorpe was up to in his photograph of a man with a bullwhip handle inserted into his rectum. All they knew is that Mapplethorpe was a very talented photographer (which he was), that no such talent could ever create an obscene work (which is false), and that any discriminating judgment on their part was a form of censorship that verged on the sacrilegious. Those trustees are there to raise money and watch the museum's balance sheet. They may or may not know what they like, but they would never presume to assert what is, or is not, "art." To qualify to become a museum trustee these days one must first suffer aesthetic castration.

To reach our current condition, it took a century of "permanent revolution" in the arts, made possible, ironically, by a capitalist economy which created affluent art collectors and entrepreneurial art dealers. "Patrons" of the arts were replaced by "consumers" of the arts, giving the artist an intoxicating freedom.

Source: Irving Kristol, "It's Obscene But Is It Art?" *Wall Street Journal*, August 7, 1990, p. A16. Reprinted by permission of author.

settings—some religious. The art promised badly needed revenues from displays as well as from sales of replicas. Moreover, it was argued by some trustees that as a university, UDC has a responsibility to respect freedom of speech and to recognize that art is frequently controversial. Nevertheless, the *Dinner Party* had to be returned because of Congressional outcry.

DUTY OF ORGANIZATION TO TRUSTEES

Trustees have the right to expect that the nonprofit has exactly the same duty to them as they have to the organization. They should expect obedience to their policies that are consistent with the mission of the organization. Trustees share liability for infractions; therefore, they should expect that their directions will be obeyed. It is they, rather than the employees, who represent the public interest.

Similarly, they should expect a duty of care directed toward them. As their duty of care toward the organization means that they need to be informed and to act prudently on behalf of the organization, so too they should expect that they will be kept informed about those things that matter. These include being kept up to date on major changes in the organization's direction or assets, annual budgets and financial statements, changes in key employees, new risks to which the organization is exposed, employee compensation packages, and an evaluation of the organization's performance.

The duty to the trustees also encompasses loyalty. This concept implies a protection of the trustees. Hence, trustees have a right to presume that the relationship between them and the organization is above board (so to speak), at reasonable arm's length, and that the organization does not expose any trustee to personal or professional risks—even if it forewarned him or her that such risks might be present. Put simply, they have a right to expect that they are not being used or "set up" and that the information given them to form the basis of their decisions is as clear, complete, correct, and relevant as possible, and that the organization will not act imprudently.

Consistent with the exercise of prudence, trustees may rely on information they obtain from appropriately assigned employees, accountants, lawyers, engineers, and other experts. Relying on the expertise of such persons is an act of prudence and not necessarily a skirting or shifting of responsibility.

RIGHTS OF TRUSTEES

The attorney general of New Hampshire brought suit against the board of trustees and president of a nonprofit organization for violation of the rights of trustees. Here is a list of specific rights of trustees that were involved:

1. To have a copy of the articles of organization (incorporation or deed), bylaws, and other documents that are necessary to understand the operations of the organization.

2. To inquire about an orientation session for board members and about a board manual containing the policies and procedures for the organization.

3. To have reasonable access to management and reasonable access to internal information about the organization.

4. To have reasonable access to the organization's principal advisors, including auditors and consultants on executive compensation.

5. To hire outside advisors at the organization's expense.

Observe that these rights are consistent with exercising the duty of care and with the law's protection of trustees and officers if they rely on the expert judgment of persons such as auditors and accountants, lawyers, and investment advisors. They are also consistent with the duties of the organization to the trustees.

VOLUNTEER VERSUS PAID BOARDS

Clearly, volunteer boards are less expensive from the point of view of compensation. Their responsibility, however, is no less serious, and they, too, must operate on the three standards given above. From the individual's point of view, there are no major tax benefits from volunteering, since the time worked and the lost income cannot be deducted. Only certain expenses can be deducted, such as transportation and specifically required clothing (for example, protective garments and uniforms).

From the point of view of a corporate officer or the corporation itself, volunteering is not only good citizenship and public relations, but it also reduces the nuisance of accounting for inconsequential pay. Furthermore, compensation increases the odds of being an interested person, as described above, and may even expose the person to personal liability (to be discussed later).

Most states that limit liability of trustees are more clear in doing so if the trustee is a volunteer than if compensated. This is an advantage of an all-volunteer board. Paid boards are more common with private foundations than with other nonprofits. The word *paid* includes benefits and other indirect compensation. These must be reasonable. The federal law, Volunteer Protection Act of 1997, discussed in Chapter Fourteen, defines one who gets less than $500 a year from the nonprofit as a volunteer and limits his or her liability for unintentional negligence.

CONTROLLING TRUSTEE MEETING COSTS

Accomplish as much as possible by e-mail, "snail mail," fax, or phone. Send out detailed agendas in advance. Avoid giving credit cards to trustees to cover their expenses. This is equivalent to giving each trustee the authority to decide individually, whenever or for whatever reason, personal or otherwise, to create a debt for the organization. Because credit cards allow cash advances, the trustee can use it just as if it were a personal checkbook.

This practice is of questionable legality, and is definitely a potential nightmare in an audit. Each expense of an organization ought to be traceable to a specific authority or mission-related action and ought to be reasonable. Once the debt has been incurred, the organization has a liability no matter how much it may protest. Avoid the problem. Take the following steps:

Step 1. If the trustees must have a credit card, have them pass a resolution authorizing the issue of the cards and a limit (my preference is $500), and prohibiting cash advances. Each trustee should know that it is possible to be personally liable if any other trustee uses these cards for personal reasons or to make loans to themselves unless they unequivocably prohibit it. Each person who gets a card also gets a copy of the resolution, which should, of course, be part of the organization's records if the chief executive officer is not to be personally liable. Have the monthly credit report sent to the organization's office.

Step 2. Do all billings for trustee meetings through a master account that the organization makes with a local hotel, restaurant, and travel agent. Eliminate the need for cash expenditures by the trustees for any reason other than ground transportation. Some trustees may prefer to use their personal credit cards for air travel so as to get the travel insurance or frequent traveler rights. You may be better off buying the insurance, but because of legitimate personal considerations such as these two, you may allow them to purchase their own tickets, but restrict the reimbursement to below first-class unless specifically approved. When the organization buys tickets, it can shop for the lowest price and take advantage of discounts.

Step 3. Require the trustees to submit all bills within fifteen to thirty days after the event. This is reasonable and will aid your accounting department.

Step 4. Have your auditor prepare an expense voucher that you can send to your trustees. This form should conform with the information needed for tax and reporting purposes. Keep a copy and return a copy to the trustee for his or her tax and business purposes.

Step 5. Make it clear that your policies do not permit paying entertainment expenses. These are the most abused and often the hardest to support as a legitimate organizational expense. Pick up the tab. Have a reception.

Step 6. Be grateful. Give a holiday present of moderate cost, say $25.00. A birthday card or anniversary present will go a long way—especially if it carries the organization's logo.

Step 7. When meetings are held far from a trustee's office or residence, there may be a concern for telephone billing. Avoid it. Most businesses will accept a collect call, and a business call is not an appropriate expense for you. Most certainly a personal call is not. Let them use your telephone or a pay phone.

There is no ethical imperative to be stingy. But trustee costs, as any other costs, must be controlled and accounted for because they have financial, legal, and tax implications. They may be considered self-dealing, taxable compensation to the trustee, and inappropriate expenses for the organization. In addition, they may lead an auditor to give less than a clean audit opinion of your organization's financial procedures. The use of the credit card to make a personal purchase that the organization pays for is taxable compensation to the trustee. The organization is legally bound to report all compensations, including these.

LIABILITY OF TRUSTEES

The board of trustees of a nonprofit organization may be sued by (1) the members in a so-called "derivative suit," whereby the members are suing the trustee on behalf of the greater good of the organization, (2) a third private party, (3) a government, and (4) one of its own members or employees.

Before proceeding, take a look at Table 6.1. Note the forty ways in which a trustee can be held liable. Even though this chart was prepared for corporate directors, it applies to nonprofits, too. Recall that many states use exactly the same rules for for-profit and nonprofit corporate governance, and many nonprofits own for-profit corporations. Either way, the rules apply.

Every trustee and every nonprofit organization has to be concerned with the extent to which trustees and officers can be held personally liable. Liability may arise either for actions taken or for the failure to act. Furthermore, in some instances liability may arise because of the actions of other trustees or officers. For example, a trustee can be held liable for failing to block an inappropriate action by other trustees or by management. Also, the duties of care and loyalty mean that a trustee cannot choose to look the other way when any other trustee or officer may be involved in actions that are wrong.

This liability threat would discourage many good people from serving nonprofits. If the trustee can be held personally liable, then he or she faces the possibility of being sued and having to pay monetary damages out of personal resources. Even if monetary damages are not assessed, the trustee faces the unpleasant possibility of having to spend time and resources in a personal defense. In addition, there are the emotional and social costs.

Recognizing this deterrent, many states have taken actions to limit a trustee's personal liability. Such limitations must be balanced to discourage failure to care, be loyal, and be obedient. In Oregon and Maryland, among other states, for example, the legislatures passed *expansive* laws, meaning that the legislatures

Table 6.1. Potential Claim Areas for Directors, Officers, or Trustees.

(1) Acquiescence in conduct of fellow directors engaged in improper self-dealing.

(2) Acts beyond organization powers.

(3) Acts of executive committee.

(4) Approval of organization acquisition with resulting loss of organization assets.

(5) Attendance at directors' meetings and committee meetings.

(6) Conflicts of interest.

(7) Continual absence from meetings.

(8) Disclosure of material facts.

(9) Dissemination of false or misleading information.

(10) Dissent from improper or wrongful acts by board of directors or committee.

(11) Examination of all reports and documents before signing.

(12) Extension of credit where not warranted.

(13) Failure to ascertain whether extension of credit would be warranted.

(14) Failure to detect and stop embezzlement of organization funds.

(15) Failure to file annual report.

(16) Failure to inspect organization books and records in order to keep abreast of its activities.

(17) Failure to require withholding in connection with social security and income tax.

(18) Failure to record dissent from wrongful acts by board of directors whether or not dissenting director attended the meeting at which such action was taken.

(19) Failure to supervise the activities of others in a proper manner.

(20) Failure to verify facts in official documents before signing and filing them.

(21) False or misleading reports.

(22) Fraudulent conduct.

(23) Fraudulent reports, financial statements, or certificates.

(24) Ignorance of organization books and records.

(25) Inducing organization to commit breach of contract.

(26) Inducing or abetting organization in commission of torts.

(27) Inefficient administration resulting in losses.

(28) Loans from officers, directors, or trustees.

(29) Permitting organization to engage in activities prohibited by statute.

(30) Permitting organization to make improper guarantees.

(31) Permitting organization to pay bribes or make other illegal payments.

(32) Preferences at the expense of organization creditors.

(33) Sale of organization assets for unreasonably low price.

(34) Shrinking responsibility.

(continued)

Table 6.1 *(continued)*.

(35) Transactions with other companies in which officers or directors are personally interested.

(36) Unreasonable accumulations.

(37) Violations of specific provisions of articles or bylaws.

(38) Violations of state statutes.

(39) Wasting of organization assets.

(40) Willful wrongdoing.

Source: Reprinted, with permission, from the *Journal of the American Society of CLU,* Vol. 39, No. 6 (November 1985). Copyright © 1985 by the American Society of CLU, 270 Bryn Mawr Avenue, Bryn Mawr, PA 19010.

gave the nonprofits considerable power and discretion to exempt or indemnify their trustees from personal liability.

The Maryland law says that a nonprofit corporation can specify in its bylaws or charter those actions or inactions for which a trustee or an officer of the nonprofit may be held personally liable and the extent of that liability. Therefore, at least in Maryland, the nonprofit can choose to impose no personal liability or liability for only certain actions or inactions—and, if so, the amount of personal liability.[2]

The Maryland law also says that the personal liability of the trustee or director cannot exceed the amount by which he or she is insured personally or by the organization. Some students of the law conclude that if the trustee has no insurance, then ipso facto no monetary damage can be assessed against that person. Furthermore, if the organization carries insurance, then the limits of any damages would be the amount available through the organization's insurance coverage. There would be no damage assessed personally on the trustee or director.[3]

Hence, trustees and officers of nonprofits in Maryland and in similar states are protected (1) by the exemption the nonprofit should declare in its bylaws or charter of incorporation, (2) by the insurance carried by the organization, and (3) by the personal insurance of the trustees and officers. Presumably, since there has been no test case, items 1 and 2 ought to be sufficient to protect a citizen who serves as a trustee of a Maryland nonprofit corporation—providing that the organization has taken steps to amend its bylaws. This demonstrates one reason that trustees should make sure that bylaws are periodically reviewed.

Before closing this discussion, let us note that even in an "expansionist" state like Maryland, the nonprofit cannot shield the trustees from liability for *willful* illegal acts and for acts that lead to improper personal gains or profits on the part of the trustee or director, or *willful* failure to carry out the duties (care, loyalty, and obedience) of the trustee.

Table 6.2 gives a listing of the different special provisions found in states' statutes across the country as far as the liability of trustees is concerned.

Table 6.2. Summary of State Laws Offering Liability Protection for Volunteers and Board Members.

| | For All Volunteers | | | | | | | | For Officers and Directors | | | | | | | |
| | Exceptions to Liability Protection | | | | | | | | | Exceptions to Liability Protection | | | | | | |
	No Protection	Bad Faith	Willful or Intentional Action	Recklessness	Gross Negligence	Fraud or Breach of Fiduciary Duty	Use of Motor Vehicle	Knowing Violation of Law	Covers Only Volunteer Officers	Bad Faith	Willful or Intentional Action	Recklessness	Gross Negligence	Fraud or Breach of Fiduciary Duty	Lawsuit by Organization	Knowing Violation of Law
Alabama	●										●		●	●		
Alaska	●												●		●	
Arizona	●									●	●		●		●	
Arkansas		●			●		●[2]				●					
California[1]	●								●	●	●	●		●		
Colorado	●										●			●		●
Connecticut	●								●	●	●	●				
Delaware			●		●		●[2]		●		●	●	●			
D.C.	●															
Florida	●									●	●	●		●		●
Georgia		●	●						●	●	●					
Hawaii	●								●				●			
Idaho	●									●	●			●		●
Illinois			●								●					
Indiana		●							●	●	○	○	○			
Iowa	●		●			●		●	●	●	●					
Kansas[1,2]			●						●		●			●	●	●

Kentucky	●	●		●							●[3]	●			●	●			●
Louisiana	●	●	●								●[3]	●			●	●			●
Maine				○	○						●	○	○	○	○		
Maryland[1,2]				●	●						●	●	●	●	●		●
Massachusetts	●															●[4]
Michigan	●							●			●					●
Minnesota	●	●	●	●	●	●		●			●	●	●	●	●	●
Mississippi	●	●	●	●	●						●		●		●
Missouri	●		○	○							●		●		●
Montana								●			●
Nebraska	●										●		●		●
Nevada											●		●		●
New Hampshire	●	●	●	●	●			●			●	●	○	●	●	●
New Jersey	●		●	●							●	●	●	●	●
New Mexico	●										●	●		●
New York	●										●
North Carolina[2]	●	●	●	●	●			●			●	●	○	●	●
North Dakota	●		●	●	●						●	●	●
Ohio											●		●
Oklahoma	●										●		●		●
Oregon	●										●
Pennsylvania	○	●	○	○				○			●		○	○	●	○
Rhode Island											●		●
South Carolina	●										●
South Dakota[2]	●		●	●	●						●		●		●
Tennessee	●										●		●		●

(continued)

Table 6.2. *(continued)*.

	For All Volunteers — Exceptions to Liability Protection									For Officers and Directors — Exceptions to Liability Protection						
	No Protection	Bad Faith	Willful or Intentional Action	Recklessness	Gross Negligence	Fraud or Breach of Fiduciary Duty	Use of Motor Vehicle	Knowing Violation of Law	Covers Only Volunteer Officers	Bad Faith	Willful or Intentional Action	Recklessness	Gross Negligence	Fraud or Breach of Fiduciary Duty	Lawsuit by Organization	Knowing Violation of Law
Texas		●	●	●			●[2]		●	●	●	●		●		
Utah[1]		●	●		●		●	●		●	●					
Vermont	●							●		●	●		●			
Virginia	●								●	●	●			●		●
Washington	●												●		●	
West Virginia	●								●		○	○	●			
Wisconsin			●			●	●	●		●	●			●		●
Wyoming	●										●					●

● Indicates that the exception applies in this state.

○ Indicates that the exception has been inferred from the wording of the legislation.

[1] For volunteers or officers to be protected, the nonprofit organization must carry specified insurance.

[2] Liability is limited to the amount covered by insurance.

[3] Paid directors and officers of nonprofit organizations defined by state law are protected. Directors of other charities are not.

[4] Pertains only to acts that result in harm to a person.

Source: Nonprofit Risk Management Center. Reprinted with permission. *For updated information by state, contact Nonprofit Risk Management Center, 1001 Connecticut Avenue N.W., Suite 900, Washington, D.C. 20036, (202) 785-3891.*

Liability Insurance

An organization can elect to cover its trustees and officers by purchasing D&O (directors and officers) insurance. This type of insurance is sold by property and casualty insurance agents. It can also be obtained through some insurance pools for nonprofits and through some associations. How does D&O work? Basically, for an annual fee called a *premium,* an insurance company promises to pay damages arising from certain acts of negligence on the part of the trustee or officer.

In assessing these insurance contracts, it is important to go beyond the premium. It is important to determine what is excluded from coverage. Companies will list specific exclusions for which they will not pay. These should be understood in determining whether the contract is suitable. Can the organization live with the stated exclusions? Some common exclusions include libel or slander, governmental penalties, bodily injury, claims covered by other insurance, active and deliberate dishonesty, and actions leading to personal or illegal profits or gains.

Companies pay either on a claims-made or an occurrence basis. These offer significantly different coverages. Strictly speaking, a claims-made policy pays only if the event occurs and is discovered during the contract period—the period up to the moment that the contract ends or lapses. Under an occurrence basis, the company will pay if the event occurred while the contract was valid, although the discovery and consequently the claim may have been made long after the contract terminated. Therefore, it is important to know how long after cancellation or termination of a contract the company will pay for an event (not necessarily the claim) that occurred during the life of the contract. Let us illustrate.

A nonprofit has a liability insurance contract that terminates in 2001. In 2002 its trustees are sued for an act taken in 2001. Under which one of these claim bases would you prefer your liability insurance coverage? If you said the occurrence basis, you are right. The act of negligence was discovered after the policy had terminated. Under a claims basis, the act, its discovery, and claim would have had to occur prior to January 1, 2002, because the policy terminated on December 31, 2001. (In actuality, there is some leeway even under the claims basis, but it might be very, very short.)

Other concerns in choosing D&O insurance are deductibility and co-insurance. Deductibility means that the company pays only after damages have reached a certain amount. Hence, the company may pay after the nonprofit has already paid the first $10,000 or some other amount agreed to in the contract. Co-insurance means that after a certain amount is reached the company will then ask the nonprofit to share the cost of the damage. To illustrate, the contract may read that if a suit is successful and a judgment, say of $100,000, is awarded, the nonprofit would pay the first $10,000 and 20 percent of any amount over the next $80,000. This would mean that the nonprofit would come up with a total of $12,000, whereas the insurance company would pay $88,000.

Another concern in choosing among D&O policies is to compare the amount that is covered per claim and the total cap for all claims combined during the policy period. Like all the other considerations above, there is no one good formula for all nonprofits. They must choose among alternatives.

In choosing an insurance policy it is also wise to check to see whether there is a right to defend clause.[4] This is important. It means that the insurance company assumes an obligation to defend the trustees or officers so that they would not have to expend personal or organizational funds in their own defense.

Umbrella Policy

It is possible to get extra coverage by buying an umbrella policy. This is an insurance policy that covers all liabilities, both property and personal, beyond the amount covered by each liability policy the organization has. Thus, an umbrella policy would provide protection beyond the automobile, property, and D&O policies. With this umbrella, the organization would have the capacity to spread dollars around when claims are made that are above the limits of the individual policies.

Indemnification

As we saw in Chapter Two, a nonprofit may indemnify its trustees or officers. This means that in the event of a suit the organization will repay the trustee or officer for expenses. In the state of Pennsylvania, under Section 7743, indemnification is obligatory. It is required if the trustee or other agent of the organization is successfully defended in a lawsuit. Virtually every state permits the organization to allow indemnification in its bylaws. What are the limits to indemnification?[5]

First, indemnification usually does not imply a right to defend. The trustee or officer must pay for his or her own defense and is reimbursed. Furthermore, it is not unusual that indemnification is made only if the trustee or director wins the case. In many states, if the damages are punitive, no indemnification can be made because punitive damages are intended to hurt. Out-of-pocket expenses could cause severe personal financial hardship. Even a successful defense could be socially and financially costly, taking a lot of valuable time and energy.

The organization may offer both indemnification and insurance. Under these arrangements, the insurance company pays for the amount in excess of the indemnification paid by the nonprofit. Alternatively, the nonprofit may offer indemnification by purchasing an insurance policy for the amount by which it promises to indemnify the person. This means that the money for the reimbursement does not come from the limited resources of the organization. Indemnification and insurance are thus composites of an overall strategy to limit the personal liability of the officers and trustees. Hence, when an organization chooses to indemnify its trustees and officers, it can reduce its own financial risk by purchasing an insurance policy to cover the amount by which it promises to indemnify.

There are ethical and legal limits on indemnification. This is particularly true when the cause of damage is the willful violation of appropriate trustee conduct. One way to reduce exposure to these worries is to choose trustees wisely, to educate and inform them, and to recognize the organization's duties to them.

LEGAL LIMITATIONS ON TRUSTEE INDEMNIFICATION

Although an officer or trustee may be indemnified by a nonprofit or held immune for certain acts as a director of the nonprofit, that immunity or indemnification does not necessarily cross over to the for-profit subsidiaries of that organization. In general, an officer or trustee is immune from civil suit for conducting the affairs of a nonprofit unless the action taken is willful or wanton misconduct or fraud, or gross negligence or that the person personally (or through a relative or associate) benefited from the action taken.

But a trustee is liable for unlawful distributions of the assets of the organization. An unlawful distribution can be one that is inconsistent with the mission of the organization, inconsistent with the bylaws and tax-exempt laws, outside of the powers of the organization, and for private gains of the trustee of associates. A loan to a trustee is just one type of unlawful distribution. Using the assets for political purposes is another, and so, too, is excessive executive compensation.

Not only are the trustees who voted in favor of the unlawful distribution liable, but so, too, are all other directors who failed to voice an objection. Arizona 10–3833 requires that objection to be noted in the minutes of the meeting when the act was taken, or by 5:00 P.M. the day after. It further states that "the right to dissent does not apply to a director who voted in favor of the action." Furthermore, any trustee found liable for the unlawful distribution can collect from all trustees who voted affirmatively, all trustees and members who shared in the distribution, and all who failed to assent in the manner proscribed by law.

Even though the nonprofit has the power to indemnify a trustee or officer, some states specify the conditions under which such indemnification can be offered. In Mississippi 79–11–281, indemnification can be offered only if the trustee (1) conducted him- or herself in good faith, and (2) believed that the conduct was in the best interest of the organization or at least not contrary to its best interest or those of its members.

The nonprofit may not indemnify the trustee or officer when he or she is judged to be liable to the nonprofit or in any situation where he or she benefited improperly. Indemnification may be limited to reasonable expenses incurred. Generally, reimbursement may occur only after the case is disposed of, but Mississippi, as an example, provides for payment in advance. However, the trustee must provide a written statement attesting to having undertaken the action in question in good faith, the trustee promises to repay the sum if the judgment is against him or her, and the act is not one that would otherwise preclude indemnification. A trustee that is entitled to indemnification may turn to the court to have such indemnification paid by the nonprofit.

If the proceeding is against the organization, rather than against the trustee, the trustee may be indemnified by the organization for his or her expenses. This is so if the trustee acted in good faith, a majority of the directors (not seated at the time of the action) votes in favor of the indemnification and a reasonable amount of compensation, or by the legal counsel selected by a majority of trustees not involved in the action or by members also not involved. When it is the corporation, not the trustees, that is being sued, the trustees can sue the organization for indemnification.

THREE Cs FOR SELECTING TRUSTEES

In congressionally chartered nonprofits, such as the United Service Organization (USO), it is customary to have the president of the United States or the first lady, as in the case of the John F. Kennedy Center and the Girl Scouts, as honorary chairpersons of the board of trustees in addition to having cabinet members on the board. In the case of the Kennedy Center, there is a forty-five member board, thirty of whom must be U.S. citizens from the general public and appointed by the president; nine trustees are ex-officio members from the executive branch of the federal government and six are from Congress. Each trustee serves for a period of ten years. Some organizations have almost no discretion over their boards because one is automatically a board member by being an officer of a constituent group. Here is another variation. The General Board of Church and Society of The United Methodist Church has ninety-two board members. Seventy-four are from the constituent missionary conference—one person from each. Twelve are chosen by the board itself, and six are nominated by the Council of Bishops.

A person may be named a trustee because of involvement in the organization and prominence. Steven Spielberg, an Eagle Scout, serves on the board of trustees of the Boy Scouts.

Sometime ago, a white scientist, Albert Barnes, was rebuffed by a number of top-rated Pennsylvania colleges and universities. Their faculties mocked his art collection and his theories about education. The president of a black college, Lincoln University, invited the scientist to speak, but he declined. Subsequently, the mocked scientist named Lincoln University as the trustee of his art collection and gave it the responsibility to name other trustees, except none could come from the schools that mocked him. Today, the collection is worth more than $1 billion and is one of the famous collections in the world.[6] This true story reminds us that trustees may be chosen for very strong personal reasons.

Whatever the personal or strategic reasons, we recommend that three Cs should always guide the selection of trustees:

Character: By this is meant integrity and all that it implies, including good judgment.

Contribution: A trustee should be able to contribute at least time and competence.

Constituency: The trustee should represent more than himself or herself. Trustees need to represent portions of the membership, the community, donors as a group, a philosophy, a region—something other than themselves or an individual donor or the management.

We are reminded by the university chancellor who said, "We need to show the consequences to the public of poor trustee selection."[7] Bad choices can paralyze if not destroy a good organization.

FIVE STEPS TO ATTRACTING GOOD TRUSTEES

Trustees can attract financial and technical resources and attention to an organization. Here are some steps that should be taken to attract good trustees once they have been selected according to the three Cs.

1. Sell the mission of the organization, for this is what the trustees must promulgate. Focus on getting an appropriate match among persons, purpose, and organizational mission.

2. Establish a good record of service, management, and finance. Prudent persons shy away from situations that put them at risk.

3. Make sure that your bylaws speak clearly to each of the following:
(a) the role of the trustee, (b) time and place of meetings, (c) liability and indemnification protection of the trustees, (d) qualifications necessary to serve on the board, (e) compensation and reimbursement procedures, (f) term of board members and method of removal, (g) disclosure requirements of the management, including trustees, and the organization, (h) commitment such as fund-raising, technical assistance, membership enhancement or donation that the organization requires from its board members, and (i) prohibited acts such as making of loans. State laws speak to each of these when the bylaws of the organization are silent.

Quick Tips to Corporate Executives on Being a Trustee

• *Be sure you understand the mission of the nonprofit.* While many nonprofit executives speak of multiple objectives and the complexity of their mission, the mission statement itself should always be simple and direct. Unlike your corporation, which may change its mission by decision of the board of directors acting on behalf of the stockholders, the mission of a nonprofit is a legal commitment. It is the basis upon which tax-exempt status is conferred. Violations of the mission may result in the loss of tax-exempt status.

• *Insist that the management of the institution view it as an economic institution.* Public welfare—not the organization's—is the mission. That means producing a product or service that meets a test of social acceptability and therefore warrants support. And concern for financial discipline must be engendered: Full costs have to be covered, no matter how charitable the mission.

• *Encourage the view that the tax-exempt organizations are fundamentally unlike government bureaucracies.* Government agencies are financed by compulsion (taxation), while charity is financed by competition for voluntary gifts, donations, and by earned income.

Further, tax-exempt organizations can go bankrupt and close down. This demands a discipline which makes the tax-exempt more like a business than like a government agency. But unlike a business, the tax-exempt's purpose is to promote public, not private welfare.

• *In a competitive environment, it is important for the management to develop planning skills.* Therefore, nonprofits must be concerned with product life cycles (e.g., the length of an exhibit), changes in technology (e.g., hospital equipment), and changes in production, marketing, and financing strategies.

• *If the nonprofit enters into a legally permitted business venture, always ascertain if the business activity is related to programs essential to the mission of the organization.* If it is unrelated, any net income may be taxed. Charges of unfair competition or impropriety may also arise. Therefore, subject every investment decision to tests of practicability, propriety, and profitability. An art museum can earn considerable revenues by selling art work. These revenues are considered to be related business income, and therefore those revenues are not taxed. If the same art museum earns unrelated business income by selling scientific pieces (e.g., compasses or magnifying glasses) such income is taxed, but it would not be taxed if earned by a science museum.

• *The trustee should avoid focusing on the budget at the expense of balance sheets, income statements, or statements of changes in financial position.* The budget is a plan, a tool for financial control and—perhaps most misunderstood—a marketing aid.

There is nothing in the law that says a nonprofit must show either a zero or negative fund balance. Often, negative balances are the result of sloppy management rather than deliberate policy. Moreover, a positive balance provides the institution with a source of discretionary funds, as opposed to restrictive funds which can be used only for specific purposes.

(continued)

(continued)

> The principal source of finance for many nonprofits is gifts and contributions.
>
> • *Not all states exempt officers and directors or volunteers from liability.* Trustees serve with the presumption of care and loyalty to the organization and in a fiduciary capacity. Understand the risks to which the organization is exposed and understand the board may carry the same exposure.
>
> ---
>
> *Source:* Abbreviated from Herrington J. Bryce. "Answering the President's Call to Public Service." *Wall Street Journal,* July 10, 1989, p. A10. Elaborations of these points can be found in the author's articles appearing in *The Corporate Board* and the *National Association of Corporate Directors.* See Recommended Readings.

4. Demonstrate a consciousness and commitment to the trustees as individuals and as a group.

5. Start with the strongest person. Good people attract other good people.

Let us close this chapter by noting that serving on a board of trustees is a good public service. The above insert summarizes much of this chapter and gives a few guidelines, especially to corporate officers who are candidates for service on boards of trustees of nonprofits.

SUMMARY AND PREVIEW

This chapter has reviewed the duties of trustees. The key is that the trustees have as their principal and overriding purpose the selfless care of the assets of the organization and the use of these assets to advance the organization's mission. Failure to abide by these strictures can result in legal sanctions. In later chapters we shall look more closely at some of the tools trustees can use for better financial management.

PART TWO

FINANCING
THE ORGANIZATION

A mission is meaningless without the means to finance it.
Success distinguishes between sophisticated persuasion and pleading
and it encourages the generating of revenues by establishing and
assigning a value to what the organization does.

CHAPTER SEVEN

Increasing Gifts and Contributions

Every nonprofit organization needs money, no matter how charitable its mission. The principal source of revenues for nonprofits that are 501(c)(3)s is the charitable donations made by individuals and firms with the expectations, although not necessarily the principal motivation, that these gifts can be deducted in calculating their federal and state income taxes. Therefore, in a highly competitive world for donation dollars, it behooves every manager to know something about the deductibility of gifts and contributions beyond the probable falsehood that "it can be written off." The fact is that there are many donations that cannot be deducted even though they may be given to a charitable organization. A manager who misleads a donor to think otherwise is culpable of something akin to fraud. Such an act is expressly illegal.

There are many organizations to which a donation cannot be deducted. These include associations 501(c)(4), (5), and (6). But charitable donations to the 501(c)(3) foundations of associations can be deducted. Because many of these associations, as do firms, have these foundations that qualify for charitable donations, this chapter is also pertinent to associations and to firms with their own foundations.

Why should all nonprofit managers, even those housed in firms and associations, profit from this chapter? Knowing the legal and tax aspects of giving allows the manager to (1) make an effective appeal, (2) avoid problematic gifts and transfers, (3) avoid ethical charges of improper inducement of a donor, and (4) in general, do the right thing. Part of making an effective appeal is appreciating why corporations, in particular, would say no to a charitable cause. Therefore, this chapter contains a discussion of these reasons; and, incidentally, why the nonprofit may also wish to say no given certain "opportunities" of receiving certain gifts.

THE IMPORTANCE OF CONTRIBUTIONS

As we stated in Chapter Two, the deductibility of contributions distinguishes 501(c)(3) organizations from other nonprofits. Even within this category, however, the 509(a)(1)s and the 509(a)(2)s are financed differently; the former have less business-related income and more contributions than the latter. Consequently, contributions, as a category, is a varying percentage of support and revenues among nonprofit organizations. Among 501(c)(4)s, (5)s, and (6)s there is no deductible contribution unless made to their 509(a)(3) subsidiary or to social clubs exclusively for charitable use.

Among nonprofits, even religious groups serving the needy, there is also considerable reliance on funding from governments. Yet gifts and contributions (in cash and in kind) are a significant part of their public support and revenues. Size also makes a difference. Among organizations with assets less than $1,000,000, over 50 percent of their revenues comes from contributions. Among larger institutions, it can be as little as 13 percent—not a negligible amount. Among nonprofit hospitals, contributions as a part of total support vary with size and whether the organization is secular or religious.

THE COMPETITION FOR GIFTS
AND CONTRIBUTIONS

Donors' dollars are not free-flowing. Yet as we have seen in Chapters Two and Three, contributions are essential to the 501(c)(3) public organizations' qualification for tax-exempt status. There is heavy competition among them for these dollars. A portion of income earned by a household or a corporation goes to pay current liabilities. These are legal obligations due to be paid within a year and most within thirty days. The obligations include the payment of rent, alimony, child support, food, tuition, credit-card balances, mortgage payments, payment of wages and salaries, current insurance premiums, estimated taxes, and notes and accounts payable. These dollars are not available for giving.

But both corporations and households have discretionary use of some of their dollars after putting away for their own futures. These include saving and planning for retirement and future obligations of the family, investment in new plants or equipment, buying of furniture, buying of automobiles, repayment of long-term debt, paying of dividends to stockholders, research and development, and so on.

Only after such needs are met is there a residual that can be donated. We may call this residual *donatable funds*. This residual is competed for by the approximately one million existing nonprofits. Hence, it is a marketing challenge to cause a corporation or household to view a specific nonprofit as more deserving than others, or to obtain a commitment, such as a tithe, so that giving becomes the moral equivalent of a legal obligation.

Foundations, too, have similar financial obligations that must be met even though their principal purpose is to give. They must pay for office space, equipment, and workers. Some foundations also have long-term commitments to support specific nonprofit organizations. Like individuals and corporations, they sometimes experience a decline in their income. It is only after they have met all obligations that donations can be made.

Annual surveys by the American Association of Fund-Raising Counsel published in *Giving, USA,* show that about half of all donations from all donors (individuals, corporations, and foundations) go to religious groups. Although the actual percentage varies from year to year, the most compelling story is that the remaining 50 percent of the contribution pool must be competed for by a variety of missions. Obviously there is competition for funds among and within these large groupings. With such keen competition, an understanding of the motives and methods of giving offers an important edge. What are some of these motives and methods?

INDIVIDUAL AND CORPORATE MOTIVES FOR GIVING

The evidence is very strong that the ability to deduct all or some portion of a gift is a strong impetus for giving.[1] This is so because the deduction means that the cost of the gift is shared by the government. For a person in the 30 percent bracket, a gift of $3,000 means that the gift only costs that person $2,100, since income tax liability is reduced by $900. A person in the 20 percent bracket who makes the same gift saves $600 from income tax so that the gift costs only $2,400. Hence, the higher the income tax bracket is, the greater the savings and the less the gift costs the donor. For this reason, economists agree that tax reform lowering the income tax rates dampens the tax motive for giving and, by the same token, any increase in the rate strengthens the motive.

The tax motive for giving occurs even when planning one's estate. Economists have found that the ability to deduct 100 percent of all charitable deductions at death is an important reason that wealthy donors pass on property and cash to nonprofits at the time of their death.[2]

There are also nontax reasons for giving that go beyond the emotional appeal. Some people give to express thanks. Hence, alumni make gifts to their alma mater. Gifts are also made to further a mission with which the donor agrees, such as donations to religious causes. Gifts are made in response to group pressures, objectives, and common goals and expectations—payroll deduction or office contribution campaigns in which the office sets or is given a target, for instance. People also give simply because they are asked—street corner collections. People give to honor and to memorialize others or special events. Giving sometimes brings attention, influence, and satisfaction. Giving is both altruistic and egotistic.

Sophisticated ways of appealing to a potential donor have been studied. There are many old standbys. Social psychologists have studied the effect of "foot-in-the-door" approaches.[3,4] These imply that there can be increased giving if an approach that begins with a plea for a small gift is followed by a plea for a large gift. The thinking here is that a smaller request provides an entry that can be used to get a larger gift once the organization has a foot in the door.

There is also some evidence to support the "door-in-the-face" approach.[5] This approach confronts the potential donor with a very large request, which one does not expect to receive, and then follows with a smaller request. Supposedly, the potential donor, after rejecting the larger amount, is more receptive to the smaller as a compromise. It appears that the efficacy of these approaches depends on the length of time that passes between the first and second appeal and the probability that the same person in a family or in a corporation receives both appeals.

It has also been shown by social psychologists that *modeling* can influence giving.[6] This means that a potential donor is more likely to make a gift when there is evidence that some other person who has significance to him or her has made a similar or larger gift.

Such phrases as "even a penny" or a "generous family donation" are also considered to be stimuli for giving.[7] The former legitimizes paltry or small gifts, and the latter implies a large gift reflecting well on the family rather than on a single individual. There is even reason to believe that seeking a check is preferred to cash because persons are more accustomed to dealing with larger numbers when writing checks. The gift is, therefore, likely to be larger.[8]

When these techniques are used within a framework that maximizes the tax benefits from giving and appreciates that most people who give have no legal, tax, or charitable advice on how to give for tax purposes,[9] and that most people give at the time a request is made rather than a long time after,[10] it is evident that a good education in the tax fundamentals of giving could enhance the productivity of fund-raising.

Before turning to the fundamentals of giving, however, there are preliminaries to be discussed. The evidence is clear that as do households, corporations are influenced by the ability to deduct their gifts.[11] There are also nontax reasons.[12] One is the belief of many corporate leaders that they have a social responsibility to respond to the need of the community and that this is a form of expressing corporate citizenship.[13] A second belief held by some corporate leaders is that giving is a form of prudent investment.[14] It stimulates goodwill with workers, clients, and the community and improves the corporate market. A third view is that giving represents "enlightened self-interest."[15] This view states that the motive for corporate giving is a combination of corporate citizenship, prudent investment, and the desire to take a leadership role in promoting an activity to encourage others to give, by permitting each donor to be identified with the success of the project to reap direct and indirect benefits from the gifts. A fourth motive is that giving is an extension of the corporate marketing, sales, and profitability.

These motives for corporate giving are buttressed by responses of corporate leaders about why they give to specific causes. It has been shown that the two most important reasons for corporate giving are to achieve a sense of corporate citizenship and to protect and improve the corporate business environment.[16]

As in the case of households, the method of appeal is as important as the motive. Some methods have been identified to stimulate corporate donations.[17] One method is to form a corporate group that pledges a certain percentage of their pretax net income (profits before taxes) and that challenges other corporations to do the same. A second is for the stockholders as a group to instruct the corporation to send perhaps $2 per share owned by the stockholders to a specific organization or to have it set aside for a specific nonprofit mission. A third method is to get the corporation to match employee contributions to qualified nonprofits.

All these methods must be incorporated into a good marketing scheme, whether the target is made up of individual donors or corporations or combinations of the two. The marketing scheme will be more successful as more is known about the primary motives for giving—one of which is the tax deductibility of gifts in the United States and the tax credit in Canada.

Just as individuals and corporations have motives for giving, so too do governments and foundations. Foundations give to certain causes because this is the purpose of their being. Although the government rarely gives, it contracts out government services as a means of promoting social welfare in a manner that is more efficient than if the government itself conducted the activity. As a matter of fact, foundations and governments are similar in the sense that most of what they "give" are contracts requiring specific performance. That is, they typically give with the understanding that only certain activities will be conducted with their funds. Some of these are highly restrictive and are really payments for services and should not be confused with gifts. A gift is an unrequited transfer in which nothing of equal value is given in return. I shall say more about this later.

DANGERS IN RECEIVING GIFTS

Some gifts are simply not worth taking. The management of most major non-profits has had the experience of turning a gift down, wishing they had turned one down, or wishing they had been sufficiently alert so as to have negotiated more favorable terms. Chicago Goodwill, for example, was given a sizable piece of property. Sometime after accepting the gift, but too late to protect themselves, they discovered that the land teemed with hazardous waste. This not only precluded their use of the land, but the value of the land fell, liabilities rose, and the cost of moving the waste became prohibitive. It was too late to return the gift or even have its donor share the liability for the waste removal or any damage that it may do.

Appendix 7.1 relates a case in which a gift was made by a firm to a nonprofit with restrictions on its sale. This is not an uncommon restriction. In this case it violated antitrust laws.

In recognition of these tragic events, I prepared the following guide to alert managers about some dangers in accepting different types of gifts. Following each is a chapter reference where reading in this book, in addition to this chapter, may be of help.

Type of Gift and Precaution

1. *Land:* Beware of easements, restrictions on how all or parts of the land may be used, outstanding debt, hazardous waste and environmental conditions, liabilities, liens held by creditors using the property as security, new restrictions imposed by donor and local zoning laws, unrelated business income tax depending on use, and the cost and risks of holding unimproved land (Chapter Ten).

2. *Appreciated property:* Beware of being a co-conspirator in a fraudulently inflated appraisal. Art, securities, jewelry, real estate, and historical artifacts are common types of appreciated property (Chapter Seven).

3. *Unappreciated or worthless property:* Accepting junk leads to disposal costs and potential liability if others are placed at risk (Chapter Seven).

4. *Real estate:* Beware of all considerations in 1 through 3 above. Determine costs of maintenance and improvements, income stream to support, feasible use and disposition (Chapter Seven).

5. *Cash:* Beware of the impact on the organization, such as changing its character to private foundation, changing its mission, or causing its image or 501(c)(3) status to be lost. Check out the source. Also beware of undue influence of the donor on the organization (Chapters Two through Four and Eleven).

6. *Short-term gifts:* The organization must comply with reporting requirements for gifts it disposes of within two years of acquisition (Chapter Seven).

7. *Long-term and future interest gifts:* Be sure that maintenance and operating costs are projected and can be met (Chapter Twelve) and that the item will be transferred without impediment and loss of value.

8. *Gifts subject to debt:* Who will pay off the debt? Beware of unrelated business income tax and valuation problems (Chapter Ten).

9. *Insurance:* Who owns the policy? Who will collect? Who will pay premiums? The beneficiary status is no assurance (Chapter Eight).

10. *Testamentary gifts:* Be prepared for delay if the will is challenged. Also, the person may change his or her mind prior to death (Chapter Eight).

11. *Stocks:* Is this a minority or controlling interest, and if a private foundation, does this represent excess business holdings? Should the stock be sold to protect against loss of value (Chapter Seven)?

12. *Large gifts:* Does this change the status of the organization? (Chapter Three)?

13. *Gifts subject to restrictions:* Can you meet the conditions? Are they legal (Chapter Fifteen and Appendix 7.1)?

Some gifts are dangerous because they cause division and controversy. Others create expenses. Some gifts come with restrictions on their use or display. Some are contingent upon matching funds. These *challenge grants,* as they are called, may push the organization in a specific direction. All of these factors must be taken into account by the trustees. Be cautious about accepting large gifts without a predetermined plan of their use and disposition or without thinking through how they might affect the organization's exempt status (see Chapter Two). How do they fit?

A sensible strategy is to sell properties immediately that are received as donations. This frees the organization of risks and expenses. The cash can be folded into on-going plans already approved by the trustees. Remember there is a reporting requirement. There is also a disclosure required by many corporations. Their deduction may be affected. See discussion later in this chapter.

WHY CORPORATIONS MAY SAY NO

What do corporations have to give and why may they resist? In short, what must the corporation consider before it makes a specific type of gift? This knowledge should enhance the fund-raising capacity of the nonprofit. Good fund-raisers, like good salespeople, anticipate points of resistance and prepare for them.

1. *Stocks:* More than a token gift by the corporation of its own stock could require shareholder approval as well as a costly reporting of the transaction. Forget it. A stockholder may make gifts of his or her shares of stock to the non-profit. This is how Macalester College became a major holder of *Readers Digest,* the Hershey Foundation of Hershey stocks, and the Kellogg Foundation of Kellogg breakfast stocks. Appeal to the individual as a stockholder—not to the corporation for its stocks.

To get the controlling shares of a privately held corporation is also to assume the company's liabilities and problems. One owns the company lock, stock, and barrel, so to speak. Check it out before accepting, or prepackage the deal with the understanding that the shares will be sold.

Stocks will have to be appraised if they are not publicly traded (that is, on the stock market) and have an estimated value in excess of $10,000. Officers and directors of corporations cannot give stock based on the anticipation that the price of the stock is about to decline so that they can maximize their deductions. This is insider trading, which is illegal. Moreover, some stocks acquired by the officers of a corporation are subject for a time to restrictions against their sale or transfer, even in the form of a charitable gift.

2. *Real property:* This is buildings and land. The corporation would have to consider tax implications, particularly the depreciation and investment tax credit it took on the property or its improvements. It would also have to consider easements—prohibitions about what it can and cannot do with the property, covenants or agreements with creditors who placed restrictions on the disposition of the property, its exposure to environmental hazard liability, future use of the land in corporate long-range plan, resale price, and the donee's use of the land or building, which affects the amount of deduction they can take.

Real property may also be given for conservation purposes. Many times what motivates the company or individual gift is that the value of the property has declined.

3. *Bonds:* When a corporation issues a bond, it does so to raise capital from creditors. Giving these away would most certainly create legal problems. Again, the best source is a holder of the bond.

4. *Equipment:* Often the corporation does not own the equipment. It is leased. When the property is owned, it may be possible that the tax benefits to be obtained from selling the equipment at a loss are greater than could be gained from a charitable deduction. Moreover, the equipment has trade-in value. The corporation may also be required to hold the equipment to meet the holding requirements for depreciation and investment tax credit. Also, the equipment may be subject to a lien.

5. *Inventory:* Except for small corporations, small donations, groceries, and restaurant food, gifts of inventory may have to be appraised and discounted for spoilage and obsolescence. They must also meet legal quality standards. For many nonperishables, selling at a discount may yield greater gains for the corporation than giving it away. Moreover, the inventory may not be owned by the corporation. Many retailers use trust receipts. This means that the inventory is actually owned by their wholesaler-distributor or by a financing company. Therefore, it is not the retailer's to give.

In addition, in calculating the value of inventory, the firm has to subtract any gain from the fair market value. This means that the amount the firm can deduct is its cost of that inventory. For public affairs purposes, however, firms announce their donations in the higher retail value.

Idaho Title 6–1301 states that a donor or a gleaner (one who harvests a donor's perishable crops for free distribution to a charity) cannot be liable for the perishable food as long as it was given in good faith and apparently fit for consumption by human beings. The exception to this occurs when an injury is due to the gross negligence, recklessness, or intentional misconduct of the donor or gleaner. Perishable foods include bakery products, fruits, vegetables, poultry, seafood, dairy products, and frozen or refrigerated products but does not include canned foods. They may be fit for human consumption even though their appearance, freshness, or grade does not make them marketable. It is important to remember, even when the gleaner or donor may not be held liable, the nonprofit can be so held.

Work-in-progress inventory, which means materials, supplies, and unfinished goods, is not available because it is to be used in the production activities of the firm. Even if such materials are flawed or damaged, it might be better to sell them at a discount or under some other brand name or no brand name at all, as is sometimes done with clothing and bad wine.

If the value of the inventory is already included by the corporation in its cost of goods sold, its charitable deduction for that inventory is zero.

6. *Employee:* Several companies assign employees to nonprofit organizations and encourage others to volunteer. The company gets no charitable deduction but continues to pay wages and benefits to these employees and deducts their salaries and benefits as normal business expenses. Hence, the deduction is not the issue. It is whether the company can afford the loss of services of an individual it continues to pay and whether that individual wishes to do the job.

7. *Cash:* This is the easiest for the company to give. The company considers alternative uses of cash, including paying off debt, the paying of dividends to stockholders, employee benefits and executive bonuses, stock repurchases, increasing cash balances, and reinvestment. Companies have missions to which they commit themselves. Some companies prefer giving in their local or corporate communities. Some prefer the arts, education, or health.

The above relates to why corporations may say no with respect to specific assets. Here are reasons that cover all assets even for the most benevolent of firms.

1. *Proposed use:* A United States corporation cannot take a charitable deduction for a donation that is to be used abroad. It will have to lower its deduction if a donated personal tangible asset (a tangible asset other than real estate) is used by the organization for activities unrelated to the tax-exempt purpose of the organization or if the asset is sold.

2. *Mission:* The request may fall outside of the purposes targeted by the directors of the corporation and may be inimical to the marketing strategy of the firm.

3. *Losses:* A corporation cannot take a charitable deduction on a donation that contributes to its having a loss for the year. The corporation must be profitable to take advantage of a charitable deduction.

4. *Limits:* A corporation may have reached its 10 percent net-income legal limit for charitable deductions or whatever limit it might have elected for charitable gifts that year. The corporation may not carry back or forward losses due to charitable contributions. Furthermore, there is a limit to which a corporation may utilize all of its different types of deductions before the corporation is required to pay the alternative minimum tax. When this happens, the value of charitable contributions—especially those made in the form of property—have to be reduced. These points are elaborated upon later in this chapter.

5. *Lobbying:* A corporation cannot take a business or a charitable deduction for contributions made to a nonprofit that lobbies on matters beneficial to the corporation.

6. *Partying:* A corporation may not take a charitable or business deduction for a contribution to any organization a principal purpose of which is the entertainment of its members.

7. *Disclosure and publicity:* The organization may not wish the publicity attendant to its gift.

8. *Disqualified persons:* The organization may be disqualified because of its previous gifts or because of the ownership of its shares by the organization or others associated with it. This by itself should not stop the corporation, but may condition its gift.

9. *Taint of improperness:* Corporations such as accounting firms need to protect against the taint that they have bought business with the organization.

10. *Opportunity cost:* Every dollar given to charity comes from some alternative corporate use of that dollar.

What do all these negatives say? Simply that corporate solicitation requires homework and skill. For example, the corporation may be able to exceed its 10 percent limit by considering the transaction a business expense. It can do so if the expense is ordinary, necessary, and likely to lead to greater profits; that is, the contribution of inventory as a marketing rather than a charitable strategy.

The bottom line is that the corporate assets belong to the shareholders of the corporation, not to the corporate officers. The U.S. Supreme Court gave weight to this when it refused to hear a case concerning a New York public utility. The utility made donations and charged it as an expense that its customers paid. The high court in New York held that this could not be done because the utility was actually giving a property of the shareholders (retained earnings) and that shareholder approval was needed. Utilities now separate donations in bills.

GOVERNMENT PROMOTION OF GIVING

It is estimated that the deductibility of donations costs the federal government $77 billion in lost revenues.[18] State and local governments also forego revenues in income, sales, and property taxes. Increasingly, states are requiring performance measures to justify these tax breaks. With hospitals, Texas requires demonstration of a community benefit. Pennsylvania requires all nonprofits to prove their charitable performance or one that reduces the burden of government.

States promote giving in many ways. Texas allowed hunters to deduct $15 in processing fees for the deer they donate to a program that provides meat for the poor. But there are basically two ways in which governments promote giving. One is through ongoing payroll deduction and the other is through the tax system.

Payroll Deduction

One principal way in which federal, state, and local governments assist giving is through payroll deduction. The largest of these is the Combined Federal Campaign (CFC). Through this mechanism, federal employees can have tax-deductible contributions made to charities. They may elect how much to give to each or may leave their contributions undesignated.

To qualify to be a recipient of any CFC fund, an organization must be a 501(c)(3) and certify that it is a human health and welfare organization. It must submit proof of activities and achievements in this mission. It must agree to public disclosure of its financing and governance structure. Additionally, it must promise not to release information on CFC contributors. These requirements reconfirm the ethical standards noted throughout this book and the need for engaging in good financial practices and reporting.

An organization has two avenues for joining the CFC, assuming that it qualifies. National organizations, those with at least three years of experience serving at least fifteen states, or those that are international may apply directly to the Office of Personnel Management or, if it is a member of a national federation, through that body. A local organization, one with a local office with regular office hours and providing services to local and adjoining communities, must apply through a local federation (for example, local United Ways).[19]

Tax Deduction and Credit

The federal government coordinates a giving campaign and allows a deduction for charitable contributions. States also allow such a deduction by permitting taxpayers to include the same contributions in computing their state income tax. In addition, in several states, there is a check-off system. This system allows the taxpayer to check off and to get a deduction for an amount that is to be forwarded by the state to a specific charity as designated by the taxpayer. The most common available check-off is for wildlife. In North Carolina, it is the only check-off option. Massachusetts offers checkoffs for AIDS, wildlife, and organ transplants. California, Colorado, Delaware, Idaho, Iowa, Kentucky, Rhode Island, and Virginia (see sidebar) used a check-off for the United States Olympics Committee. Check-offs are most often used when the taxpayer is expecting a refund, but may also be added to the tax liability.

A tax credit is more valuable than a deduction because, for each dollar of credit, the taxpayer reduces his or her tax liability by one dollar. With a deduction, the tax liability is reduced by only a fraction of a dollar, which varies with the tax category of the person. To illustrate, if my tax liability is $1,000 and I have a credit of $200, my tax bill is reduced to $800. All states give charitable

---

Authorized Deductions from Overpayment for Contributions

29 AUTHORIZED DEDUCTIONS FROM OVERPAYMENT
FOR CONTRIBUTIONS below. Add (a) through (f)
below 29

(a) VA Nongame Wildlife Program . . . . (a)
(b) $2 VA Democratic Party . . . . (b)   00 ▶
(c) $2 VA Republican Party . . . . (c)   00 ▶
(d) U.S. Olympic Committee . . . . (d)
(e) Open Space Recreation and Conservation
       Fund . . . . (e)
(f) Housing Program . . . . (f)

30 Amount to be **REFUNDED TO YOU** (subtract line
29 from line 28) 30

deductions. Among those that give credit, Michigan offered a 50 percent tax credit up to $200 a year for a joint return and up to $5,000 on a business return for gifts to community foundations. North Carolina gave a credit of 25 percent (but not exceeding $5,000) of property given for public access to a beach, wildlife, fishing, trails, and waterways.

THE IMPORTANCE OF TAX DEDUCTIBILITY OF CONTRIBUTIONS

The tax consequences are always taken into account by the large or small donor. It is said that the Howard Hughes Medical Institute was created by Howard Hughes to avoid cancellation of a profitable contract made by the Air Force to the Hughes Aircraft Company and to avoid paying taxes. The gift of the stocks of the aircraft company provided Hughes with a huge tax deduction, impressed his workers and lowered their discontent with him, and impressed the public and the Defense Department, which had threatened to cancel his contract. The defense work was now being done by a company that was owned by a nonprofit and the profits would go to serve public welfare. In 1986, the nonprofit sold the Hughes Aircraft Company to General Motors for $5.2 billion.

The tax benefit (whether a deduction or credit) reduces the cost of the gift to the donor. A person in the 30 percent bracket giving property worth $100,000 to a qualified nonprofit obtains a deduction worth $30,000 from the federal government. A person in the 20 percent bracket gets a deduction worth $20,000 for the same gift. With the first person, the gift of $100,000 only costs $70,000; for the second person it costs $80,000. The savings to the donor is higher as the income bracket of that donor increases. This basic relationship between taxing and giving remains though tax ates are changed. It is for this reason that the lower the tax rate, the less tax incentive there is to give; that is, the less that can be deducted and therefore the more the true cost of the gift to the donor.

Competent management must have a working knowledge of the tax laws as they apply to giving. The ability to work with these laws enhances the chances of getting large commitments. We shall deal deeper with them because all gifts and contributions are not deductible. Whether or not a gift is deductible and how much is deductible depends on the item given, to whom it is given, the form in which it is given, and by whom it is given. Gifts of free rent and gifts of labor (volunteering) are never deductible.

Certain gifts may lead to a deduction, but only at a point in the distant future. This is particularly true when the donor wishes to retain some rights or obtain some benefits from the property, or to have someone or entity other than a charity benefit from the good. An example of this is one who makes a gift of a large portfolio of securities but wants to share in the income from it. If a deal to satisfy the donor's conditions cannot be worked out, the potential gift may be lost. Such a deal to offer a present deduction can be arranged through the proper creation of a trust or a gift annuity. These strategies were successfully used by a number of North Carolina schools with the leverage buyout of RJR Nabisco.

TAX DEDUCTIBILITY: THREE CASES

Three court decisions highlight some key ingredients in the law to check abuses of the tax deductibility of a donation. In *Venni v. Commissioner*, taxpayers were denied a charitable tax deduction for donations made to a church and for property transferred to the local congregations of the church.[20] The donors could not show that the congregations qualified as a tax-exempt religious group; that the donations were not intended for the personal benefits of the donors, given that the donors maintained control over the gifts; or that the gifts were not made because the donors expected something in return. Similarly, in *Davis v. Commissioner*, the donation made by a couple to a church was not deductible because the wife maintained sole control over the accounts.[21] In *Magin v. Commissioner*, the court held that the contribution made by the taxpayer was not deductible because the recipient was not qualified and because the contribution inured to the private benefit of the donor.[22]

With these and other cases to be illustrated in mind, we can appreciate some of the constraints placed on the deduction of contributions. This knowledge helps in designing effective contribution campaigns. Let us begin with the definition of a gift. I first give a broad definition and then define each term.

Canada **v.** *Commissioner*
Petitioners seek to deduct as charitable contributions certain transfers of land and money to the Kneadmore Life Community Church (KLCC). The KLCC's members occupied the land as an "intentional community where [they] could pursue common values of living in harmony with nature." The KLCC provided its members, *inter alia,* with rent-free accommodations and farmland, use of farm equipment and seed, and food grown in community gardens and orchards. These benefits were not provided as compensation for services performed. *Held,* petitioners, deductions denied because the KLCC was operated for a substantial nonexempt purpose and because its net earnings inured to the benefit of its members. Sec. 170(c)(2), I.R.C. 1954.

Source: Canada v. *Commissioner*, 82 T.C., No. 73, June 1984, p. 973.

LEGAL CHARACTERISTICS OF A TAX-DEDUCTIBLE GIFT

A deductible gift is an irrevocable transfer of property or cash from a qualified donor to a qualified donee for less than full consideration. The property or cash must be accepted by the donee without any retained, remainder, or partial rights belonging to the donor. The donor must not maintain control or influence over the property and may not continue to receive economic benefits from it.

Cash or Property

Deductible gifts must be in the form of property or cash, not services or free rent. Although services are not gifts, expenses such as unreimbursed meals or transportation costs that are necessary and directly related to providing the service are deductible.

Likewise, free rent is not deductible. A donor would be better off to lease the space and then donate the earnings to the nonprofit. Alternatively, the building might be donated.

If the nonprofit sells a property that it received as a donation and that has a value of $500 or more within two years after it was received, it must report the sale on Form 8282. Exceptions are those properties sold for less than $500 and those that are distributed or consumed without charge and in conducting the nonprofit's mission such as thrift shops and soup kitchens.

Transfer

Deductible transfers must be voluntary, purposeful, and complete. A transfer of property under duress is not a gift. A transfer that is clearly the result of a misunderstanding is also not a gift; neither is a transfer a gift when the donor is not mentally or legally competent. A transfer made in expectation of death is not a gift if the person survives. There must be a clear donative motive.

Typically, a transfer that is partial or incomplete is not a gift. Technically speaking, writing a check in the name of a nonprofit is not a gift. To illustrate, Dorotea writes her personal check for $4,000 in the name of the Class of '55 to their school, LaBoca High. If she holds the check or destroys it, either action nullifies giving. The situation is only slightly better if she hands the check over to a responsible officer of the nonprofit or if she mails it. Neither of these constitutes a complete gift, for Dorotea could have insufficient funds in the bank, she could call and cancel the check, or the bank could refuse to honor the check. The gift actually takes place when the check is honored by the bank. In its leniency, tax law treats a check as a donation on the date it was mailed, providing that it is not postdated, which would then be the date, and that it does not bounce. If the check has a condition, the gift is not completed until the nonprofit has accepted the conditions.

A nonprofit needs to keep in mind that it does not have the same recourse as a for-profit when a check bounces. A check made out to a firm represents payment for a service or goods bought. It is a legal obligation. A promise of a gift constitutes no such legal obligation. The nonprofit cannot enforce payment unless the promise to give is contractual or the failure to keep the promise results in economic harm. This is true even though some large nonprofits have succeeded in bringing action against those who have reneged on their promises to give.

State and local laws specify how some properties are to be legally transferred. Suppose that instead of $400 in cash Celestina gave the nonprofit her automobile. This act by itself does not constitute a gift. She must also sign, date, and complete the information required on the car title and hand the title over to the nonprofit.

Real property, land and buildings, is transferred in a similar manner. A proper title must be completed, conveyed, and the transaction recorded. A person who holds stock certificates must endorse and deliver them to the nonprofit or its agents if the gift is to be complete. Gifts of U.S. Savings Bonds must follow rules prescribed by the federal government. These rules might require changes in registration. In some cases, the bond may have to be cashed. Gifts of creative work must be accompanied by gifts of their copyrights. Gifts to help low-income persons pay their energy bills are deductible, but the amount of the gift should be indicated as a specific part of the total paid the utility company: that is, it must be possible to distinguish the gift from the consumer's own bill.

Irrevocable

A transfer must be irrevocable to be a gift. There can be no way in which the donor may repossess the property other than by arm's-length purchase. Any transfer with the intent or with conditions to permit repossession even by purchase is not a gift.

To illustrate, suppose Jeanine makes a transfer of her car and attaches conditions to its use. Suppose she requires that the automobile be returned to her if it is abused. This is not a gift. The transfer provides conditions for revoking the "gift." In a similar vein, an option is not a gift of value until the option is exercised.[23]

Retained Rights

There are times when a potential donor wishes to make a gift of property but also wishes to retain certain rights over it. The rights might simply be to enjoy its use. Let us couple the concept of retained rights with that of irrevocability and see the results. Shauna makes an irrevocable gift of her horse to a riding academy with the stipulation that she has use of it on Saturdays. The gift is irrevocable if there are no conditions by which she may recapture ownership of the horse. However, she has retained rights over its use. The consequence is that the gift is partial from the point of view of the IRS and therefore there is no tax deduction. It is, however, legally irretrievable. The horse belongs to the academy.

Here is another case:

> United Artists gave old movie negatives to the Library of Congress in 1969 and took a $10 million charitable deduction. But the Claims Court has denied any deduction: Because United Artists kept all commercial rights, . . . the negatives had no value.[24]

Remainder Rights

Sometimes potential donors would consider making a transfer to a nonprofit with the condition that after some event or passage of time, all or some portion of the property be returned. These are *remainder rights*.

To illustrate, assume that the academy needs the horse to prepare for a show. Shauna might make a transfer with the condition that the horse be returned at the end of the show. This is not a gift. She has maintained remainder interests. No deduction is allowed and the nonprofit has no more than a loan. Furthermore, she cannot deduct the rental not charged the academy, since free rents are not deductible gifts.

Present Interests

A donor may choose to make a gift at some time in the future. This is a future-interest gift, which is not deductible. A gift has to be of present interest to be deductible. This means that the nonprofit must acquire immediate and full control and ownership of the property or cash without restrictions. By inference, a future-interest gift becomes deductible only at the time that full control becomes effective, that is, when the conditions of future interest no longer exist so that the future interest is now a present interest. Accordingly, an option to buy a property in five years is a future interest and not deductible until the five-year period has passed and the option is exercised.

There is an important exception to the present-interest rule when the gift is of real property, such as a building or a house. This exception will be discussed later in the chapter. What is to be remembered is that as far as tangible personal property (property other than real estate and intangibles) is concerned, future interests are not deductible until all the contingencies of control, either by the donor or someone related to the donor, are removed. Therefore, a gift that is to go from Beverly to her son H. Simon and then to a charity is not a deductible future-interest gift. But if after her son receives it he passes it on to an unrelated person, the gift at that point becomes deductible even though it has not yet reached its final destination—the nonprofit.[25]

Options

Gifts of options have no value until the option is exercised. The option is worthless whenever the market value of the property is lower than the purchase price allowed by the option.

Exceptions to Incomplete Transfers

In general, a transfer must be complete and of present interest to be deductible. This means that the donee must acquire complete and immediate control of the gift. The donor must maintain no retained, revocable, partial, or remainder rights.

There are notable exceptions to the general rule. One exception pertains to a situation in which the donor owns less than 100 percent of a property and is therefore unable to give the entire property. Under these conditions, the donor must give an undivided share of his or her total interest in a property if such a gift is to be deducted. To understand this exception, consider the following example. Shauna owns one-half of an interest in a property consisting of a stable and ten horses. Her undivided interest is one-half of the property as it is comprised. Therefore, the maximum she can give and take a deduction for is one-half of the property. One-half is 100 percent of what she owns of each horse. She may give less than 100 percent, but the amount she gives must be undivided; that is, the property, in this case, is the stable and horses together. She cannot divide the property such that she gives some of the horses and none of the stable.[26] The key is how the property is defined.

A second exception to the general rule refers specifically and only to personal (not necessarily a principal) residence or a farm. A personal residence may include a vacation home or condominium. A person may make a future-interest gift of either of these two types of properties to a qualified nonprofit and get an immediate tax deduction. Accordingly, Marisa could get an immediate tax deduction on a gift of her home to her favorite nonprofit while continuing to live in it.

A third exception to the complete transfer rule relates to gifts of real property for qualified conservation purposes. Qualified conservation purposes include preservation of land area, protection of natural habitat, preservation of open space, and preservation of a historic site for public benefit. The gift of the property must be accompanied by some easement that will permanently restrict the future use of the land for any purpose other than for conservation. The donor may continue to use the property until some date in the future when it passes to the qualified organization.[27]

The other exceptions to the requirement that gifts be complete and of present interest require the use of a trust. We shall postpone discussion of these other exceptions until Chapter Eight.

Qualified Donor

Gifts can only be made by qualified donors who must be of age and of sound mind and must own the property. Ownership occurs in various forms, some of which compromise or defeat the goal of giving.

The most straightforward form of ownership is called *fee simple*. In this case, the person owns all rights to the property by himself or herself and is free to do with it as desired. H. Simon buys a condominium for cash without a mortgage and is the sole owner. He owns it fee simple and may do with it as he wishes.

Some properties are owned in the form of *tenants in the entireties*. This is a form of ownership normally used only by spouses. It means that neither party may give the property without the express consent of the other. Many homes are owned in this form and therefore no single spouse may, under normal circumstances, give the property without an affirmative approval of the other.

Other properties may be owned as *tenants in common*. This means that either party may make a gift, but only of that share of the property that he or she owns. When a percentage of ownership is not specified, it is assumed that each cotenant has an equal share. This might be a little more tricky than tenants in the entirety, where one-half ownership by each spouse over the entire property is presumed. In the case of tenants in common, an unequal share or only a specified piece of the property may be owned by the donor.

Property may also be owned in the form of *joint tenants with the rights of survivorship*. Many properties are owned in this form. It is a popular form of ownership among people who are trying to avoid probate. The objective is to be sure that upon death the property is passed directly to a designated person. It is impossible to make gifts of property owned in this form at the time of death. Full ownership passes automatically on to the survivor.

In the states of Idaho, Washington, Nebraska, California, Arizona, Louisiana, Texas, and Nevada, there is a form of ownership called *community property*. It is presumed that any property bought during marriage is owned on an equal basis by both spouses. The laws on the transfer of community property differ by state, but in general a person is only free to give the one-half of the property owned.

A person may have ownership that terminated upon death, such as a life estate. This form of ownership is obviously temporary. The owner of the life estate can give only the earnings received during his or her life, but cannot give the property that yields those earnings. That property must be passed on to another beneficiary when the first dies. Furthermore, the person with the life estate is obligated to preserve the property so that it may be transferred.

For example, Marisa may own the earnings of a rental unit through bequest from her mother, who stipulated that the unit should belong to Marisa's sister. Marisa can donate the earnings, but not the property. However, she cannot donate the earnings if by doing so there are no funds to repair and maintain the unit to transfer it to her sister in good condition. In the same vein, Marisa's sister cannot give the rental unit while Marisa is still alive, particularly if her giving it means that Marisa's flow of income would be terminated.[28]

Ownership may be contingent or nonvested. In these cases, ownership takes place only after some condition is fulfilled. Until those conditions are recognized as being satisfied, the "owner" has no legal power to give. A common contingency is the passage of time. If, for example, ten years must pass before ownership of the amount in a pension account is vested, then prior to that time the person in whose name the account appears has no power to give those funds, even though they appear in his or her name.

Acceptance or Substantiation

If Enrique gives $250 or more to Doyle Center for the Handicapped, he cannot deduct it unless the gift is acknowledged by the donee organization, Doyle Center for the Handicapped. This acknowledgment is known as *substantiation*. The substantiation must be in writing and must be made contemporaneously with the gift. It must state the amount of the gift, and whether the organization gave the donor something in return for the gift. If so, what was given by the organization must also be described and it must give a good faith estimate of what it gave the donor. It does not have to give an estimate of what it received from the donor.

The organization does not have to make an estimate of what it gave in return if what it gave the donor is insubstantial in value, or if it pertained to certain membership privileges worth less than $75 per year, or if what it gave were certain privileges to the donor's employees or partners. If the organization received a gift of more than $75 and it gave something in return, then it must disclose certain information in its substantiation statement to the donor. In this case, the written substantiation must contain an estimate of the value of what the organization gave the donor and inform the donor that the charitable contribution is limited to an amount equaling the donor's contribution minus what the organization gave in return. The exceptions to this rule are intangible religious benefits given by the organization, goods and services of insubstantial value, or certain membership benefits.

What are examples of these "certain membership benefits"? In general, these are benefits that the donor can use frequently, such as free or discounted parking and free or discounted admissions to the organization's events or facilities. "Certain membership benefits" also include admissions to events that are not open to the public and the fees for which are on a per person basis (rather than group), and if the items are low-cost items such as jugs, pencils, pens, and so on.

The donor also has certain substantiation responsibilities. These involve obtaining a value for what was given to the organization, the donation, and obtaining a separate statement from each organization given $250 or more.

In the case of payroll deduction a check stub or pledge card showing that the organization gave nothing in return or even the employee's W2 form showing the same would do.

Substantiation, as stated above, must be contemporaneous. This means that it must occur on the earlier of the due date for filing the donor's tax returns for the year the gift was made, or the date the donor files the original (not amended) tax return for that year.

Failure to substantiate may result in a fine of $10 per contribution, not to exceed $5,000 per fund-raising event (including mailing campaign) on the organization unless it can prove that the omission was due to reasonable cause. The real cost may be the loss of potential donors who would be unable to take the tax deduction because of the organization's failure. The cost for falsifying a substantiation is the exposure to the criminal charge of aiding and abetting an understatement of tax liability.

Substantiation covers gifts of cash, benefits, privileges, property, or services.

Qualified Donee

Canadian citizens with incomes earned in the United States can get a tax credit on their Canadian income tax for donations to a qualified U.S. donee. Generally, foreign (except Canadian and some Mexican) charities are not qualified donees for U.S. tax deduction purposes, and therefore, donations to them cannot be deducted by U.S. taxpayers. Neither can donations to domestic charities if such charities are serving as conduits for a foreign charity or for American donors. For this reason, a domestic charity that wanted to assist foreigners arranged with a foreign charity to identify a group of several thousand potential recipients from which the domestic charity freely chose twenty-five for its assistance. American donors did not know the twenty-five foreign persons who were to be helped and had no part in choosing them. The "qualified donee" did not deposit or transfer money to the foreign charity. Consequently, the donations to the American charity were deductible.[29]

Also many organizations form *internationals.* These are U.S. nonprofit corporations operating abroad. The U.S. taxpayer can get deductions for donations to them; that is, World Vision (World Vision International), Salvation Army (Salvation Army World Service Office). The next time there is a disaster abroad check out the places to send money. The names are familiar and are legally separate U.S. corporations from their namesakes operating exclusively within the U.S.

Calling an organization charitable, even though religious, does not make it so in the eyes of the law, as we saw in Chapters Two through Four, and therefore does not make it qualified for tax-deductible donations. Nowhere is this issue more problematic than in religion, which is protected by the First Amendment. In *Davis, et ux* v. *U.S.,* the Supreme Court said that the parents of Mormon missionaries who sent them money, in keeping with their religious prescription and purpose, could not deduct it because their sons (not the church) were not qualified charities.

In *Davis*, as in many scholarship cases, the IRS is arguing that the organization is serving as a conduit.

The IRS has identified several characteristics that make a religious organization a qualified donee. These include a distinct legal existence, recognized creeds and form of worship, an ecclesiastical government, doctrine and discipline codes, religious history, a membership not associated with any other church or denomination, an organization of ordained ministers who have completed a prescribed course of religious studies, and an established place of worship and regular religious services. This was not at issue in *Davis*.

Qualified donees are domestic charities, such as the ones described in Chapters Three and Four. Also included are nonprofit cemetery companies, volunteer fire companies, war veteran organizations, states, territories, and possessions. We are reminded that all nonprofits are not tax exempt, and only tax-exempt nonprofits qualify for tax-deductible contributions.

An American donor can deduct a donation to a Canadian charity as long as the donor had income in Canada. An American donor can deduct a donation to a Mexican charity that meets the 501(c)(3) criteria and as long as the donor had income in Mexico.

Less than Full Consideration

A key concept in defining a gift is that the transfer must be for less than full consideration. Simply, this means that the donation must exceed the value of anything the nonprofit may give the donor as an inducement or in appreciation for the gift. By way of illustration, suppose that the fair market value for Shauna's horse is $4,000. That is, the most that she could get from someone who wants to buy her horse is $4,000. If she gives it to a nonprofit and receives a check for $4,000, this is a sale; it is not a gift.

Suppose, however, that instead of a check for $4,000, the nonprofit gave her a check for $2,000. The transaction has two parts: a gift of $2,000 and a sale of $2,000. The gift is the difference between the market price and the amount received by the donor in the transfer.

A gift also occurs when one pays more than the value of a service. Hence, a gift occurs when one buys a banquet or dinner ticket for more than either is worth. Paying $150 for a dinner when the dinner and entertainment are worth $50 results in a contribution of $100. The value of the service is declared by the nonprofit sponsor of the event.

Here is another illustration. A university accepted annual payments from individuals in the amount of $300 each for membership in the university's athletic scholarship program. For an additional $120, each member was permitted to purchase a season ticket to the university's home football games and to have preferred seating between the forty-yard lines. Nonmembers were not allowed to sit in this area. Some 2,000 persons were on the waiting list for membership. The IRS ruled that no part of the $300 was deductible because the right to preferred seating was of considerable monetary value to the donee. These were not gifts, but purchases of privileges for value.[30]

In a similar ruling, the IRS held that the $20 contributions obtained by a symphony from donors, to whom it gave season memberships, for the privilege of attending cocktail parties and a motion picture premiere and obtaining reserved seats at concerts that were not otherwise available were not deductible contributions. These were sales.[31]

The 1986 tax law allows full deductions for tickets bought for sporting events if the sponsors turn over the net receipts to the nonprofits and use volunteers. Many sports events, such as tennis and golf tournaments, fall in this category.

BORROWING TO MAKE A DONATION

One can borrow to make a donation and obtain a tax deduction. At least three conditions must be met. First, the loan should be from an independent lender; that is, an individual should not borrow from him- or herself or from a corporation that he or she controls. Second, the money should meet the conditions of a gift, as described earlier, and the donor should remain responsible for paying off the debt. Third, the charity must benefit from the receipt.[32] These conditions were met by Mr. and Mrs. Joel Goldstein, who purchased art partly through debt and made a gift of it to a nonprofit. Note that they did not borrow the art; rather, they bought it by borrowing the money and remaining responsible for the debt. Their deduction was the amount they paid in cash plus the present discounted value of the note they gave the seller of the art.[33] In short, they deducted the cash plus the value of the note—the fair market value.

When a donor borrows to make a gift, the value of the gift is the sum of any cash the donor puts up, plus the present discounted value of the note. This term, *present discounted value,* is easier to understand than it seems. Ask yourself: If I have to pay off a note, say, in five years, how much would I have to put in the bank today, given today's rate of interest, so that at the end of five years enough money would be in the bank to pay off the note? This single amount that I have to put in the bank is the present discounted value of the note.

PROBLEMS OF ACCEPTING GIFTS SUBJECT TO DEBT

Many properties are bought on credit. The purchaser borrows to acquire the property so that part of the dollar value of the property represents ownership or equity; the other part is debt. Raymond owns a home subject to a mortgage. The fair market value of the home is $50,000 and the home is subject to a $30,000 mortgage, meaning that Raymond's equity is $20,000 from his income-tax perspective. That is all he can deduct, even though the fair market value of the house is $50,000 and the nonprofit may carry such value on its books and even honor him for making a gift of that amount. But who is going to pay the bank the $30,000 that Raymond owes?

Raymond can only give that which he owns. He owns only $20,000, so the gift is worth $20,000. But who is going to pay the bank? Suppose that the nonprofit decides to assume the mortgage. In that case, Raymond has made a gift for which he gets a tax deduction, but he now has to report income. The relieving of his $30,000 debt is income to him even though he has not received a dime. If he agrees to pay the debt, then this payment is included as part of the deductible gift.[34]

Let us assume that the debt is not paid by Raymond. The nonprofit has obtained a piece of property worth $50,000 for which it has only to pay the $30,000 of outstanding debt over a period of years. In addition to assuming a debt, it must now pay operating costs. If it rents the house, it must pay taxes, since the property is subject to debt. If it tries to sell the building, it may be subject to tax, for the property is subject to debt. If the building has declined in value, the nonprofit must support an asset with a diminishing market value. Raymond may offer to pay the mortgage. If he defaults, the nonprofit pays the bill or loses the property.

BARGAIN SALES

Raymond may contemplate a different strategy. He may resort to a bargain sale. Assume that he paid $50,000 cash for the home and owns it fee simple. He has no debts and may do as he wishes with the property. Assume further that the property is in an attractive neighborhood so that rather than declining in price, it appreciated to $100,000. He may decide to give it to his favorite nonprofit through a bargain sale. Instead of the nonprofit paying $100,000, it pays $50,000. Since he receives less than full consideration, the difference between what he gets and the fair market value ($50,000) is a gift. A gift?

The bargain sale is part gift and part sale. Its effects on the unsuspecting donor can be devastating. In the above example, the gift amounts to $50,000, which is one-half of the fair market value. Therefore, Raymond gave away one-half of what he could have gotten had he sold the house. He must now reduce his cost by half. Hence, he is deemed to have paid only $25,000 for the house. Since he received $50,000 from the nonprofit, he is deemed to have made a gain of $25,000 on the deal and he must pay taxes on it. Bargain sales can be very cruel to donors because they can lead to taxes on gains never received and to a reduced deductible amount. In this case, Raymond reports a gain of $25,000 even though he sold the property for the amount he paid for it and $50,000 less than its true market value. He would have been better off selling the property, paying the tax, and taking a deduction for the contribution.

A bargain sale may also lead to loss of a deduction because a bargain sale is subject first to the regular rules of gifts and sales and then to the specific rules governing bargain sales. To illustrate, suppose H. Simon bought stocks a month ago for $4,000. The stocks rise to $10,000 in two months. The sale of these stocks, held for six months, under any circumstance would lead to an ordinary income tax on the $6,000 of gain. Suppose H. Simon decides to donate the stocks. He cannot deduct $10,000. Knowing this, he takes a check from the non-profit for $4,000 to cover his cost and then gives them the stocks. Will he be able to deduct the $6,000 difference as a gift? No.

The reasoning is that his cost was $4,000 for which he got a check from the nonprofit. The stocks, held for six months, are ordinary income property deductible at cost. The cost is $4,000, but he was paid that amount from the nonprofit so there is nothing to deduct. He has lost $10,000 worth of stocks.

A bargain sale is indicated and should be considered when the potential donor needs cash, when the asset is of value to the nonprofit and for some reason (that is, an extremely specialized equipment) the donor cannot dispose or sell the asset readily, and where the tax benefit from donating at fair market value exceeds the 10 percent of net income limit that a corporation is allowed to deduct. A firm operating at close to zero profits needs cash more than it needs a charitable deduction. Therefore, the fact that a bargain sale may reduce its charitable deduction may be less important than its ability to get cash and dispose of the asset. Similarly, a firm that has been experiencing losses for years and carrying them forward may have more than enough deductions that it can use. The charitable deduction may have little value to such a firm.

LOSSES

A loss realized by making a contribution cannot be deducted. Stocks or other assets that have fallen in price below the donor's cost may still be attractive to a nonprofit but foolish for a person to give. Losses experienced in giving cannot be deducted, but losses experienced in the sale of the property can be deducted. Hence, it is often wiser for the potential donor to sell the property, deduct the loss, give the proceeds to the nonprofit, and deduct the gift of cash.

VALUE OF GIFTS OF PRESENT INTERESTS

In general, the value of a gift for purposes of tax deduction is the fair market value of the property. The *fair market value* is the price a knowledgeable buyer would willingly pay and an equally knowledgeable seller would willingly accept for the property on a specific date, that is, its valuation date.

Determination of Fair Market Value

The fair market value of a property is the actual price for which it could be sold on the date it was donated. The market must not have changed radically between the date of sale and the date of the valuation. A donor cannot deduct $50,000 for a gift that has declined to $20,000 on the date it was given. The value is $20,000. Used clothing is valued at the price it may be sold for at a thrift shop. Some properties, like art and antique furniture, require a competent appraisal.

Valuation of Real Estate

Real estate may be valued at the price similar properties are being sold for in the same neighborhood at the time. Natural restriction on use such as the soil quality or legal restrictions such as easements must be taken into account. Commercial property may be valued according to the expected future income stream, or at replacement cost.

Valuation of Closely Held Stocks

A closely held corporation is one whose stocks are not publicly traded on the stock market but are held by a few (even one) person. These stocks may be valued through an appraisal of its assets, liabilities, and expected income stream, all of which can be discounted for risks, or through a formula agreed to by the owners at a much earlier date. Closely held stocks may be discounted because there is no public market for them, they are powerless minority shares, or the donor has such a large quantity that selling them depresses the price.

Valuation of Art

Appraising art is a challenge. The IRS uses a citizen commission to check on valuations because there are endless opportunities to be dishonest. One official of a famous museum was once accused of determining the value of an artwork based on the amount of deduction the potential donor needed. Value is in the eyes of the beholder. As one observer noted, the value of an art piece may be affected by the purpose for which it is being valued; that is, to determine an inheritance tax, charitable donation, insurance claim, sale as opposed to display or exchange, gift taxes, security, collateral, or resale royalties, which are payments to the seller in the form of a work of art rather than cash.[35]

There are many factors to be considered in determining the value of any single piece of art. These include the identity of the artist, the date or period of its creation, the physical condition of the piece, the amount of restoration it has undergone, the subject of the art, the medium in which it was done, its physical dimension and authenticity, its rarity, and its artistic and esthetic value.[36] In one very controversial case to decide on the value of a seventy-foot sculpture by Bufano called *Expanding Universe,* the weighted average of three separate methods (the replacement cost, cost of comparable pieces by Bufano's contemporaries, and an extrapolation of fair market value) called the *French grid system* was used. The IRS accepted it with the warning that it cannot always be used.[37] The valuation of art remains tricky but required.

Valuing a property 150 percent higher than its true value is penalized by the IRS on the donor if the tax liability of the donor is reduced by at least $1,000 and if the donor owned the property for at least five years (and therefore presumably knows the true value).[38] Participation in fraudulent appraisals by the nonprofit will result in legal consequences on it and its leadership.

Ordinary Income and Capital Gains Valuations

Some properties must be treated for valuation purposes as ordinary income property. An ordinary income property is one for which the proceeds from the sale are taxed as ordinary income, such as wages and salary, and not as a capital gain or loss. Examples of ordinary income property that may be given are (1) items from the inventory of a retailer or dealer, (2) a product in the hands of its producer, such as a piece of art in the hands of the artist or a machine in the hands of its manufacturer, (3) a piece of equipment or machinery used in a trade or business, such as a truck in the hands of a company that uses it in its business, (4) property held for investment purposes but for less than twelve months, such as stocks in the hands of an investor held for less than twelve months, and (5) some properties subject to depreciation recapture, such as a real estate, using a method of rapid depreciation.[39]

Ordinary income property, even if it has appreciated in price, is valued for purposes of deducting a contribution at cost rather than fair market value. The fair market value of the property is determined. From this, the amount of appreciation over cost that is ordinary income is subtracted. The remainder is the value of the property for tax-deduction purposes. Usually it equals cost.

Jeanine buys stocks for $1,000 and holds them for two months. The stocks appreciate to $10,000. The gain of $9,000 is short term and is subtracted from the fair market value of $10,000 in determining the amount that can be deducted as a gift. This is equal to $1,000 or the cost.

Capital gain properties are ones in which the proceeds from their sale would be taxed as capital gains. Examples are (1) properties held for investment purposes but for a period of greater than twelve months, and (2) coal and timber by special treatment of the tax law. Generally, capital gain property may be deducted at fair market value.

It would be useful to consider one probable consequence of treating a good as a capital gain or an ordinary income good. Robertino is a painter and has produced a masterpiece. The cost of supplies and equipment is $1,000. The market values the painting at $920,000. If he sold the property to Yvonne for $920,000 and its value rose to $1,600,000 while in her hands for a year, under the general rule she would be able to deduct its fair market value, which is now

$1,600,000, if she donates it. In her hands, held for more than six months, the property is a capital gain property.

Whether Robertino or Yvonne makes the contribution may be of consequence to the nonprofit if, for example, the property is subject to debt. If it sold the painting for $2,000,000 after receiving it from Yvonne, it will pay taxes on the appreciation of $1,080,000. This is the difference between its cost to Yvonne ($920,000) and the sale price ($2,000,000) to the nonprofit. If it sold it after receiving it from Robertino, it will pay taxes on $1,999,000 (the sale price of $2,000,000 and the cost to Robertino of $1,000). In this example, the tax base for the nonprofit will be nearly $900,000 greater if it received the property from Robertino. This is so because when a nonprofit accepts a gift, it simultaneously accepts the value of the gift when it was in the hands of the donor.[40]

In general, ordinary goods offer the donor a lower tax deduction and the organization a lower base than capital gains property. The basis for deduction in the former is cost. In the latter it is fair market value, which may be higher or lower than the original price paid by the donor.

Appreciated Property

Whereas ordinary income property is valued at cost regardless of the appreciation, capital gain property is usually valued at its fair market value—reflecting the appreciation, if any.[41] Accordingly, a property that has appreciated in value, called *appreciated property,* is not necessarily valued for contribution purposes at its new higher value. It depends. Is the property ordinary income property? Is it capital gains property? Together, the classification and the appreciation determine the amount of deduction.

Nonprofit Can Cause Donor to Lose Appreciated Value

If the property is *tangible personal property* (a property other than real estate or an intangible such as stocks) and if it is given to a public charity, private nonoperating, or private operating foundation to be used in any way that is not related to its tax-exempt purpose, then the deduction must be reduced to cost or basis.

Clive donates an appreciated tangible personal property (an antique car) to a medical school that runs an antique business. The business is unrelated to teaching medicine. Clive bought the car for $10,000 and it is now worth $40,000. He cannot deduct $40,000 but must deduct $10,000. A nonprofit that induces a donor to give property to be used in an unrelated way may be doing that donor a disservice.

Examples of Valuation Problems: Morgues and Cemeteries

An entertainment company gave a newspaper morgue to a nonprofit. The *morgue* is its file of articles, background materials, photographs, and the like. The entertainment company assumed that the value of these had risen over the years, so it took a level of deduction to reflect this appreciation. The IRS ruled that this was incorrect. This was property that probably did appreciate, but it was not a capital asset subject to treatment as a capital gains property. Rather, because it was produced for and by the newspaper, it was to be treated as an ordinary income property, thus justifying a lower deduction.[42]

Mr. and Mrs. Thornton bought cemetery lots some years ago for about $20,000. They gave the lots to the University of Nevada at Reno and took a deduction on the basis that the dilapidated cemetery is best used for real estate development, which makes its value over $500,000. The court ruled that such a prospect is so far and so remote that it is an improbable basis on which to calculate a charitable deduction.[43]

In another cemetery case, some donors made a gift of cemetery property and proceeded to take a fair market value deduction. The court ruled that there was no proof that the fair market value exceeded cost. The donor was unable to prove this claim.[44]

ALTERNATIVE MINIMUM TAX AND APPRECIATED PROPERTY: 1990

Many years ago, Congress decided that too many wealthy people were escaping taxation by exploiting deductions, including charitable deductions, and making investments in real estate, oil and gas, livestock, and farming that gave them huge paper losses.

To curb this practice, Congress instituted the *alternative minimum tax.* This law, as amended in 1982, requires taxpayers to compute their taxes two ways: with all the deductions they can legally take, and without some specified deductions. The second way, without certain deductions, often yields the higher of the two tax liabilities, which is the amount the taxpayer must pay. In computing the second alternative, charitable deduction cannot reflect the amount by which a property appreciated. This lowers the amount of the deduction. Gifts of appreciated property (art and securities), especially to universities and museums, plummeted. In 1990, Congress suspended this law, hoping to revive the giving of appreciated property.

GIFTS OF STOCKS: PERSPECTIVES OF DONOR AND DONEE

Why is a discussion on gifts of stocks so important? First, because stocks are the most commonly used asset for financing the creation of private foundations—both operating and nonoperating—and many community foundations. Their appreciated value does not have to be reduced when given to nonoperating foundations as long as the donor does not give more than 10 percent of the outstanding voting stocks.

Second, they are common assets given to charities, universities, museums, hospitals, and other public organizations. An appreciated stock that has been held for twelve months or more is deductible at fair market value when given to any of these qualified organizations. This means that the out-of-pocket cost to a donor is lower (by the amount of the appreciation) than giving the equivalent amount in cash. A stock bought by Matthew for $2,000, held by him for twelve months, and then given to his favorite charity when the stock's value is $4,000 is deductible at $4,000. Moreover, if Matthew is in the 30 percent tax bracket his tax saving is $1,200. The effective out-of-pocket cost of his $4,000 gift to him would be $800 ($2,000–1,200).

Alternatively, if he had sold the stock, he would have paid a capital gains tax at the federal level of 28 percent or $560, which is equal to 28 percent of the gain ($2,000) plus the brokerage fee for selling the stock, plus state and local taxes on the gain. Hence, the gift of $4,000 in cash after selling the stock would easily have cost him over $2,600 in out-of-pocket expenses minus the 30 percent savings from the deduction of the $4,000 or $1,200. When this is subtracted from the $2,600, the cost to him would be $1,400, or $600 more than if he had given the stock to the organization.

Another alternative would be for him to keep the stock and take the $4,000 out of his cash account at the bank. Being in the 30 percent tax bracket, the deduction would be $1,200 and so the cost to him of the gift would be $2,800. It is the most expensive way of making the gift, followed by selling the stock. The least expensive would be to give the stock away.

By donating the stock to a remainder trust, depending upon how it is constructed, it is possible that that stock cost $2,000 would not only yield a deduction, but would also provide a lifetime stream of income to him or his beneficiaries. If taxable, this income would first be taxed as ordinary, then as medium-term, then as long-term capital gain and then as return of capital. Even if it is taxable, there is a big advantage because the timing of when the income would be received by the donor or the donor's beneficiaries can be set as long as the term does not exceed twenty years. We shall discuss these trusts in the next chapter.

Whether or not the added advantage of a trust is used, the arithmetic works to the advantage of giving appreciated stocks. The tax outcome depends upon the amount of appreciation over cost to the donor (known as the *basis*), the tax bracket of the donor, the length of time the stock is held, the transfer costs and brokerage fees, and state and local taxes. The arithmetic is simple and all of the numbers are ascertainable.

What are some of the other considerations when stocks are used to make a donation? It makes a difference whether the stock is publicly or privately held. The first is traded on the stock market and the second is traded face-to-face and is often not traded at all. If your plumber, tailor, or dressmaker is incorporated, the stocks of their corporation are privately held. Some large companies, UPS, for example, are also privately held.

The value of the publicly traded stocks can be determined by taking the average of the high and low price on the date of the transfer. If the stock was not traded on the date of the transfer, the value is the weighted average of its price on the last day it was traded prior to the transfer and the first day after the transfer, the weights being the number of days between the two points. Thus, if the stock traded two days before the transfer and for a price of $5.00 and three days after the transfer for a price of $6.00, then, it is $3 \times 5.00 + 2 \times 6.00$ divided by 5, or $5.40. The weights are assigned inversely.

If, however, the stock is a privately held stock worth more than $10,000, a qualified appraisal must be made. Appraisal can have shocking results. One reason is that the administrator may have a strong incentive to have this value high or low so as to affect the size of the estate for tax purposes. If the stock is a minority share, it may have considerably less value than the same stock held by the majority shareholder because the value must be adjusted downward for lack of any control over how the corporation operates and also because minority shares are less marketable.

Another major problem with gifts of closely held stocks is that if the organization gets the majority shares it ends up owning the company lock, stock, and barrel and is liable to all other stockholders for not impairing the value of their investment. If it ends up with a minority share it is at the mercy of the majority holders. In that sense, it is in a position equivalent to being a silent partner. It has little or no formal power to direct the course of the company.

The frustration will heighten when the nonprofit discovers that the stock is not highly marketable. It cannot call up a broker on the stock exchange and sell it. A broker is needed to find a potential buyer and negotiate a price. But the sale can only occur without court intervention if the condition of the gift allows a sale. Second, the condition of the gift may allow a sale, but prior agreement between the company and other shareholders may specify both the price and to whom the sale must be made. This is very common in closed corporations as a method through which owners protect themselves against each other's deaths or incapacities.

What is the point? When receiving closely held stock find a competent attorney who, among other things, knows something about estate planning for corporations that are closely held.

The price that is used to determine deductible value depends upon the date of transfer and the removal or meeting of all contingencies. If the stock was put into the mail without any contingency and properly signed, the relevant date is the date of mailing. If the stock was delivered, it is the date of delivery. If the transfer had to be recorded, it is the date that that was done.

When receiving or bargaining for gifts of stocks, the organization needs to make sure that the stock is the donor's to give. Many stocks held by executives or employees are restricted stocks—meaning that there are legal constraints on their transfer and negotiability. In divorce cases, these stocks may be partly owned by the donor's partner. In other cases, the stocks may be jointly held and so owned by more than one person. In other cases, specifically where the stock was part of a person's compensation, the stock may not be vested or its disposal may be restricted.

For private foundations, the gift of a large block of stock also raises the question of excess business holding (discussed in Chapter Four). For all nonprofits, the gift of a large block of stocks means that sooner or later the trustees would have to make a decision (assuming that the donor did not restrict their discretion) as to whether to hold or to sell. With public charities, this question arises for purposes of diversifying the investment portfolio. It also occurs because of pressures of potential buyouts and from other investors doubtful of how the nonprofit would utilize its voting power. For whatever the reason, a large block of stocks cannot just sit unattended.

Reporting Requirements and IRS Vigilance

Under the new rules, donors who contribute property with a stated value of over $500 (the old rule was $5,000) must file Form IRS 8283. The form requires that the donor give the name of the charity and its addresses, a description of the donated property, the date of the contribution, the date the donor acquired the property, how it was acquired, the cost to the donor adjusted for any improvement, the fair market value of the property, and the method used to determine the fair market value.

If the value of the property exceeds $5,000, the donor must also provide an acknowledgment by the charity that it was received. Either the donor or the appraiser must provide information on the donated property, and the appraiser must certify the appraisal.

LIMITS ON GIVING

Tax deductions allowed for contributions to nonprofits are limited on a calendar year basis except for corporations using the accrual method of accounting. Such firms have three and a half months after the closing of their fiscal year to make such contributions if they were approved earlier by the directors. In this section, we discuss these limits as they apply federally, and in the next we discuss strategies that nonprofits may take for accepting large gifts. As discussed in Chapter Three, certain large gifts can cause a change in the nonprofit tax status.

Foundations

Unlike individuals and corporations, the law seeks to encourage giving on the part of foundations, primarily private nonoperating foundations. The law seeks to force these foundations to distribute their income. So, instead of having limits on giving, it has limits and penalties on the failure to give. These rules were discussed in Chapter Four. Public charities 509(a)(1) and (2) are often not grant-making and are not required to give, but 509(a)(3)s that are endowments are required to make distributions either to their parents or to the clients (beneficiaries) of their parents; that is, scholarships to the students attending the parent or affiliated university.

Individuals

However, there are limits to the amount of charitable gifts that an individual or corporation is permitted to deduct in any one calendar year. It is important, therefore, to establish the year that a gift is made. The limits are all annual, although excesses may be carried forward to other years.

Conrad signs the certificate of stocks he owns and is donating to a nonprofit. The certificate is to be delivered by an agent of the company or a bank to the nonprofit. The gift occurs when the change in name is recorded on the books of the agent or company. If Conrad makes the gift on December 31, it is unlikely that the recording of the transfer would occur in time for him to unchallengeably take a deduction in that year. The same kind of situation (recording ownership change) occurs in real estate, except there is no way to mail it. A better strategy is to mail the stock to the nonprofit, since, like cash, the date of the mailing would be used as the date of the gift.

Assuming that the date of the gift is properly established, the limits depend on whether the donor is a corporation or an individual, the type of foundation, the purpose of the gift, and whether the gift is appreciated property.

A person is permitted to deduct charitable contributions up to 50 percent of adjustable gross income per calendar year if the contribution is made *to* a public or a private operating foundation. A community foundation such as the Gainesville Community Foundation of Georgia qualifies as much as the soup kitchen and the church as a public charity.[45] If the charitable contribution is *to* a private nonoperating foundation, the annual limit is 30 percent of adjusted gross income. If the contribution exceeds the limits, the taxpayer can carry it forward for five years. These are the basic rules. They come into play once the total charitable contribution of the individual for the year is 20 percent of adjusted gross income. Hence, if the total contributions of Conrad are less than 20 percent of his adjusted gross income, he can deduct the entire thing regardless of whether the donee is a private operating foundation or a public charity or a private nonoperating.

Here are some variations from the basic rule. Notice the word *to* that is used above. It is deliberate. If the contribution is *for the use of* any one of the three—public charity, private operating, or nonoperating foundation, the limit is 30 percent. So, a contribution *to* and/or *for the use of* a private nonoperating foundation is limited to 30 percent of adjusted gross income. It is also 30 percent if it is *for the use of* a public charity or a private operating foundation. But if it is *to* the public charity or operating foundation, then, the limit is 50 percent. *For the use of* implies an indirect and delayed gift, that is, through a third party that holds the gift for the eventual use of the nonprofit in its mission. *To* implies an immediate and direct donation from donor to the nonprofit and therefore to its mission.

There are also reduction rules. Unlike the rules in preceding paragraphs, these do not limit a donor's deductibility based on adjustable gross income. Rather, they reduce the value of the property. Here are three. First, capital gains property must be reduced from its fair market value if it is tangible personal property (a truck, typewriter, computer, furniture) donated to be used in a way unrelated to the mission of the nonprofit. We met this rule before. Next, the value of the gift must be reduced if the taxpayer chooses, for example, to give in one of the ways described above that yields a 30 percent limit, but for tax planning purposes, the taxpayer would rather use a 50 percent limit. Finally, capital gains property given to a private nonoperating foundation must also be reduced unless the property given is a qualified exception. Probably, the most important of these exceptions are stocks that are traded on the stock market and where the donor does not give more than 10 percent of the outstanding shares. Hence, rich people who give publicly traded stocks to form private foundations usually are not subject to this reduction rule.

Trusts, Endowments, and Wills

One strategy for limitless giving that individuals may use is the creation of a trust, or an endowment (the subject of Chapter Eight). A charitable trust is permitted limitless charitable contributions as long as the trust does not engage in unrelated business, unreasonable accumulation of funds, distribution of funds for noncharitable purposes, or prohibited transactions, and its funds are not used against the best interest of the charitable beneficiaries. If it does any of these, it is subject to the same limitations imposed on individuals. Although trusts may have limitless power to give, only liquidating trusts do so because most trusts are intended to last into perpetuity.

Another strategy to avoid the limits on individuals is to make the gift through the individual's estate—contingent on the death of the donor as through a will. These types of gifts will also be discussed in Chapter Eight. Through a will, a gift can be made of limitless cash or property as long as there are sufficient assets in the estate to meet the legal obligations of the deceased.

There is a subtle but important difference between a death-time gift and a trust created and funded during life. The latter may make limitless gifts, but the contributions that create them are limited as described in this chapter and the next. In death-time gifts through the settlement of an estate, both the amount bequeathed by the donor in the estate and the transfer from the estate to the charity are limitless.

Corporations

Corporations are limited to 10 percent of their taxable net income regardless of the type of property and foundation to which they give. Any excess over the 10 percent limit for companies is deductible over five years. Corporations, on the average, do not exceed 2 percent of net income.

Corporations often are required to reduce the fair market value of property so that the most they can deduct is their cost (called their *basis*). In some cases, the deduction is below basis if the market value has declined. However, corporations are permitted to deduct cost plus up to 50 percent of the appreciation on the value of equipment used in their line of business or of their inventory if the nonprofit will use it solely for the caring of the ill, the needy, and infants. These gifts must meet quality tests of the Food, Drug and Cosmetic Act. Further, the 50 percent is not permitted if the nonprofit will sell the gift once it has been received. To assure compliance with these conditions, the corporation must receive a letter from the nonprofit promising that it will comply with the no-sell restriction and have records as to when the goods were received and dispensed by the organization.

Corporations are also allowed a deduction of cost plus up to half of the appreciation on certain research property that they contribute. The donation must be made to an educational institution.

PROBLEMS AND STRATEGIES OF LARGE GIFTS

Nonprofits do not normally see themselves as being limited to the amount that they may receive from any one source. But gifts and contributions are evidence of public support, and public charities must demonstrate a high level of public support. Intuitively, one may think that getting a large gift or contribution would be evidence of public support, but this is not necessarily so.[46]

First, in calculating the one-third or 10 percent of public support described in Chapter Three, no one contribution may be included at a level that is greater than 2 percent of the entire support level as consideration as being public. Therefore, if the support level is $200,000 and Anhela gave $88,000, her gift will be treated as though it were only $2,000 of the $200,000. If Emeline gave

$105,000, hers would be treated as $2,000. The effect of this is to cause the organization to fail the one-third support test because $4,000 (the 2 percent sum of the two gifts) is less than one-third of $200,000.

Second, large gifts and contributions risk making the nonprofit a private foundation and the donor a disqualified person—one who would be limited in his or her economic involvement in the organization and become exposed to certain restrictions discussed in Chapters Three and Four. The rules do, however, provide some protection against this eventuality. If the large donor is not a disqualified person and is not likely to be disqualified because of death, or if the donor is unable to place any conditions or exercise control over the organization, an unusually large gift that is in response to a public appeal may be omitted in calculating public support.

An individual who makes a large gift to a nonprofit may follow one of several strategies. The excess may be deducted over five years, or the individual may make the gift at the time of death because there is no limit on charitable deductions made at that point. The process is discussed in Chapter Eight. Or, the individual may form a private foundation or a public charity such as a 509(a)(3) and make it a subsidiary to or affiliate of a public 509(a)(1) or (a)(2). These are some of the possibilities described in the accompanying article, which first appeared in the *Washington Post* and then in a number of newspapers across the country.

Individuals who make large gifts should always be concerned with the possibility that the gift would be so large that it would convert the organization from a public charity to a private foundation and disqualify that individual. The way individuals may avoid such a taint is to obtain a letter from the organization assuring him or her that the gift would not have a disqualifying effect, or by making the gift as a response to a public appeal without stating any conditions of control over the gift, and by not being in a position to exercise any control over the organization. Being dead is an acceptable position for this purpose. At death, large gifts do not disqualify donors under the assumption that no control can be exercised.

Nonprofits, particularly public charities, since they are more vulnerable than private foundations, may take certain defensive measures when large gifts are expected:

1. The organization should be sure that the intent and honor of the donor are consistent with the mission of the organization and that there is no misunderstanding. Having to return a sizable gift may destabilize the organization not only in its operation but also because Financial Accounting Standards Board (FASB) rules require reporting these gifts and their return.

Michael Jackson Has a Tax Dilemma Like Joe Louis, the More He Gives Away to Charity the More He Has to Earn

Michael Jackson's decision to donate his estimated $5 million in proceeds from his multi-city "Victory" tour is an uncommon act of charity, but it could land him in deep trouble with the Internal Revenue Service.

Wealthy as his work has made him, Jackson would do well to review the bitter experience of heavyweight champion Joe Louis. Louis donated large portions of the proceeds from his fights to his country's war effort. But the matter of his giving left him with enormous tax liabilities that ruined him financially. It took a presidential directive to absolve him of his entanglements with the tax laws.

Commonly, when celebrities perform for charity, they do so by prior agreement not to be paid. They designate organizations or institutions to receive the proceeds, or a share of them. Since no pay is received, no tax liability is created and there is no deduction.

From everything that has been printed and stated about Jackson's financial arrangements, however, his contract calls for him to be paid. From a tax standpoint, this means that it may be too late for him to declare that he is performing without compensation and intends to donate his full share to charity. His services are not deductible. And the tax rules clearly state that income once earned cannot escape taxation by shifting it to another entity, even if it is a charity.

All this means that Jackson's performances will create a sizeable tax liability. At his level, 50 cents of every dollar earned is potentially payable as federal taxes. Hence, his $5 million will create a federal tax liability of approximately $2.5 million, on top of state and local levies.

For Jackson to deduct the full $5 million in the year he donates it, he will have to earn some $10–$16 million. This is because the IRS currently limits charitable deductions to 30 percent or 50 percent of income, depending on whether the recipient is a public or private charity. So the more Jackson gives, the more he must earn in order to get the full tax deduction from his contribution in one year. Yet the more he earns, the larger his total potential tax liability will be.

If he gives the full $5 million to a *public* charity such as his church (he is a Jehovah's Witness), he has to earn only $10 million. The tax laws allow deductions to such charities of up to half an individual's income. If he fails to earn $20 million, he can still apply unused portions of his deductions to public charities to his returns during the subsequent five years.

If he donates to a *private* charity, such as a family foundation, he would only be allowed to deduct up to 30 percent of his adjusted income and would have to earn some $16 million in order to deduct the full $5 million that he plans to donate.

(continued)

Because giving to a public charity has a substantial tax advantage over giving to a private charity, Jackson, faced with a huge tax liability and wanting to keep his commitment to donate his share to charity, may choose to sprinkle his gifts among a number of worthwhile public charities.

It may be too late for him to completely solve his immediate tax problem. But there is a step he could take to ease future difficulties, deal with other immediate concerns, and perpetuate his goodness for many years. This is the creation of a charitable foundation.

Dispensing charity through a foundation rather than by making random personal gifts would benefit Jackson as much as it has benefited other wealthy Americans.

Even the initial disadvantages, including the possibility that all $5 million might not be deductible in one year, can be overcome by distributing the gift over several years and by making the gift while seeking tax-sheltering investments to make up the difference.

Moreover, foundations help shield donors from the animosity of disappointed charity seekers. Not every applicant can be satisfied. Foundations deflect criticism and bad publicity.

Foundations can invest their resources and grow. Jackson's contributions would attract donations from others. Invested prudently, these funds could touch the lives of deserving persons for many years.

Foundations have the time and expertise to evaluate options for charity and to nurture causes to which Jackson is committed.

And a foundation must make sure that the assets and earnings are not used for purposes that do not qualify, such as the personal benefit of donors and their relatives.

Jackson won't be able to control the foundation once it is operating. But neither will he be able to control the use of his direct contributions after they are made. In setting up the foundation, he could stipulate its overall mission, choose the board of directors or trustees, and withdraw his support if he became dissatisfied with it.

This is an opportunity that should not be lost. Few blacks who have done well in entertainment or sports have been able to accumulate and preserve great wealth. Few persons white or black, in any walk of life, have created lasting philanthropic memorials to celebrate their struggle and achievement and to perpetuate their generosity. The $5 million Jackson has committed to charity gives him the rare opportunity to be an exception.

Source: Herrington J. Bryce, "Michael Jackson Has a Tax Dilemma," *Washington Post,* Sunday, August 5, 1984, p. C5.

2. The organization may increase the number of contributions from sources such as the government and the public that are considered public support and thereby offset the effects of the large gift.

3. The organization may petition the IRS to modify its computation period to include the year of the large gift plus the four preceding years. This tends to dampen the magnitude of the large gift.

4. The organization may shift from attempting to qualify under 509(a)(1) to (a)(2), or vice versa, depending upon the amount obtained from investment income, unrelated business, or related business sources. This is a judgment made by IRS.

5. The organization may exclude any extraordinary large contributions both from the calculation that gives the sum of all support and from the portion that is considered public support. This removes it from consideration in the calculation of the one-third or 10 percent test. Such exclusion is only possible, however, if the person is not disqualified and had no reason to believe that the effect of the contribution would have been to jeopardize the public charity classification of the organization and if the gift is deemed unusual. See Chapter Three.

GIFTS AND CONTRIBUTIONS IN CANADA[47]

In Canada, as in the United States, a tax benefit can only be received if the donation is to a qualified donee. In Canada, these are mostly registered charities, defined as charity organizations, private foundations, or public foundations (as explained in Chapters Two and Four). The organization is required to give the donor a receipt very much as in the United States, where this process is called "substantiation." In the United States, substantiation can be achieved in the form of a letter. In Canada, the donee must give an actual receipt with a number, and that number must appear in the letter of the substantiation. Such a receipt is not required in the United States. In Canada, records of these receipts must be kept by the organization for several years, even after its license to issue these receipts is revoked.

In both countries, the gift must be a voluntary and irrevocable one in the form of cash or property. Property may include annuities or insurance, and because these products are basically similar in the United States and Canada, both countries have the same considerations for both. Donors should be careful, however, about the rules concerning how these properties are valued for charitable purposes.

However, there are major differences in the treatment of charitable donations in the United States and Canada. In the United States, a donor gets a tax deduction of up to 50 percent of adjusted gross income, in the case of an individual, and of more than 10 percent, for a corporation. But in Canada, the donor gets a tax credit of up to 75 percent of his or her taxable income. The 75 percent limit holds even if the donation was made to a qualified U.S. organization.

Dollar for dollar, a tax credit is worth more than a deduction, because the credit is subtracted in full from the tax liability. Thus a person with a tax bill of $1,000 and a tax credit of $100 will owe only $900. A deduction of $100 reduces the tax bill by the person's tax rate. Thus, if a person is in the 20 percent tax bracket, a $100 deduction reduce his or her bill by only $20.

In Canada, unlike in the United States, a person who donates appreciated capital property—whether during his or her lifetime or at the time of death—must recognize part of the gain as income. In general, the amount recognized is 37.5 percent of the fair market value of the property. In the United States, this is true only if the gift is part of a bargain sale, as described earlier in this chapter. But in Canada, if the property is certified to be one of significant historical or cultural value to the Canadian society, the donor takes a tax credit for the full fair market value of the property as ascertained by a certifying board. The donor pays taxes on no part of the gain.

In the United States, one cannot deduct a loss. Canadian law allows a donor of a capital asset that has not been depreciated to take that loss into account when calculating that donor's income taxes.

For *ecologically sensitive property* (the term used in Canadian law to refer to property that has ecological value), the donor may take a tax credit for the fair market value or for the reduction in the value resulting from having made the gift. An easement or restriction must accompany such a gift in the United States and in Canada. This tends to cause the value of the property to decline. In Canada, a donor is not limited in the percentage of his or her income on which the tax credit awarded such gifts is based.

As in the United States, the donor may not use fair market value in calculating the tax benefit of donating certain goods. Specifically, the Canadian law refers to works produced and donated by artists and works from the collection of an art collector. Both are treated as inventory items—as in the United States.

Those who are interested in accounting would find a subtle difference in how capital gifts can be accounted for in the two countries. In Canada, a donor can be deemed to have transferred a property, received its fair market value, recorded that value as income for his or her income tax, and then taken a full tax credit for 63 percent of it up to 75 percent of his or her taxable income. In the United States, the assumption of income received on the transfer or disposition of the property is not necessary, unless it is a bargain sale.

ETHICAL GUIDANCE IN FUND-RAISING

Ethics in fund-raising can be broken down into two parts. First, the rights of the donors; second, the behavior of the fund-raiser. Donor's rights include the right to

1. Be informed of the organization's mission and how it intends to use the donation to advance its mission effectively

2. Be informed about the individuals in the leadership of the organization and expect them to perform stewardship with prudence

3. Be able to get the most recent financial statements of the organization

4. Be assured that their gifts will be used for the purposes given

5. Receive appropriate recognition and acknowledgment

6. Expect that their gifts will be treated with respect and confidentiality to the extent allowed by law

7. Expect that relationships with the organization will be professional

8. Be informed about the relationship of the fund-raiser to the organization

9. Have the opportunity to delete his or her name from mailing lists

10. Feel free to ask and expect prompt and forthright responses to questions

The above paraphrases a ten-point ethical code developed by the American Association of Fund Raising Counsel, Association for Healthcare Philanthropy, Council for Advancement and Support of Education, and the National Society for Fund Raising Executives. It was endorsed by the Independent Sector, the National Catholic Development Conference, National Committee on Planned Giving, National Council for Resource Development, and the United Way of America.

The National Society of Fund Raising Executives has its own code. It is divided into two parts: ethical principles, and standards of professional practices. The principles commit the fund-raiser to adhere to and promote ethical standards throughout the organization for which he or she works and "affirm through personal giving, a commitment to philanthropy and its role in society." Here are four examples of the nineteen standards of professional practice:

1. Members shall work for a salary or fee, not percentage-based compensation or a commission.

2. Members may accept performance-based compensation such as bonuses provided that such bonuses are in accord with prevailing practices within the members' own organizations and are not based on a percentage of philanthropic funds raised.

3. Members shall not pay, seek, or accept finders' fees, commissions, or percentage-based compensation for obtaining philanthropic funds and shall, to the best of their ability, discourage their organizations from making such payments.

4. In stating fund-raising results, members shall use accurate and consistent accounting methods that conform to the appropriate guidelines adopted by the American Institute of Certified Public Accountants (AICPA) for the type of institution. (In other countries, comparable guidelines should be used.)

A complete version of these documents can be obtained from any of the organizations mentioned above. Their reproduction and wide distribution are encouraged by the organizations. They probably should be prominently posted.

MIX STRATEGIES

In order to emphasize the basics of dealmaking, we have treated each strategy as discrete. Often they are discrete, but sophisticated fund-raising often requires the dealmakers to put a set of strategies together. A donor can make a contribution of appreciated stocks, get a deduction for it, and have the stocks placed in a remainder trust. The trustee could sell the stocks and purchase municipal bonds and provide the donor with a tax-free income for the term of the trust. A donor could sell a property that has declined in value, take a tax loss, and use the proceeds of that sale to purchase an insurance policy. Because of its multiple or leverage effect, this strategy would provide the organization with considerably higher potential proceeds than a straight gift of the proceeds of the sale. If a single premium policy is bought, and the organization is the owner, not only will the donor receive a deduction for the gift (roughly equaling the premium if no loans are taken or dividends received), but the organization will get more because the proceeds will exceed the premiums. Furthermore, the organization will not have to wait for the death of the donor to experience benefits.

Mix strategies are best undertaken with counsel of financial and legal advisors to both parties. But such counsel is of limited practicability unless the organization's officials understand the rudiments of this and the following chapter.

SUMMARY AND PREVIEW

Gifts and contributions are the two most common forms of support of nonprofit organizations. An underlying reason for giving is the tax deduction. Therefore, understanding the impact of taxes on donors increases the efficiency of the appeal. Many forms of giving expose the nonprofit to high risks once the gifts are received. Therefore, it is important that the nonprofit manager understand the pitfalls of giving and receiving.

Many appeals are likely to fail because the contribution works to the financial and tax detriment of the potential donor. Knowledge of these pitfalls avoids the resentment and waste of energy of and disservice to unwitting donors, and can be avoided by taking the steps to be discussed in the next chapter or the strategies of dealing with large contributions discussed in this chapter.

This chapter guides the reader through some pitfalls associated with the acceptance of certain properties such as gifts and delineates reasons that corporations may resist giving certain properties. The next chapter attends to the question, How does the organization attract and accommodate large, deferred gifts?

CHAPTER EIGHT

Trusts, Wills, Annuities, Life Insurance, and Endowments

A sophisticated money-raising campaign must do more than appeal for cash or property that the potential donor can immediately surrender. Many donors rightfully wish to make a gift of property that they are totally unwilling to surrender any time in the near future. Trusts, wills, insurance, and annuities are instruments that accommodate such desires. They permit the donor to defer the actual transfer of the gift until some future date while getting an immediate benefit in the form of tax savings, the continued use of the property, and the satisfaction of having made a charitable commitment. The nonprofit benefits because it does not take the risk that in the future the gift would not be available or that the donor might give it to some other group.

How does the organization structure deferred giving to reduce its risks of failure? What is an endowment and how is it organized? Why is insurance a good asset to give and to receive? How is the value of a deferred gift determined? What are the risks associated with gifts in a will?

Some donors wish to give larger sums than they can presently afford. An insurance policy is one way in which a small gift may multiply itself several times. It is one of the most intriguing gifts. The American Bar Association Endowment gets gifts from bar members by having them donate the dividends on their insurance policies.[1] This involves no out-of-pocket expense to the members because the dividends are paid by the insurance company.

This chapter is a discussion of techniques that can be used to increase the magnitude of giving. They all involve legal and tax technicalities. No person or manager should attempt to implement any of them without very competent legal and tax advice. The reason is that although the law is permissive and encouraging of the use of these techniques, it also requires that specific rules be obeyed. This chapter has been prepared so that the manager of the nonprofit will be in a position to (1) identify when one of these techniques may be appealing to a donor, (2) recognize the specific reasons that a donor may be attracted to a specific technique and what may be the reasons for being leery about it, and (3) identify the benefits to the organization and the constraints on the organization once a specific technique is adopted. In short, the chapter aims to put the manager in a position to negotiate large and difficult gifts.

THE USES OF TRUSTS: DEFERRED, EXTENDED BENEFITS, AND CASH FLOW

A trust is a legal entity created by one or more persons for the purposes of receiving, accumulating, managing, and distributing wealth according to an agreement between those who create the trust and the trustees who manage the trust. All this is done on behalf of one or more persons or institutions that are the beneficiaries named by those who created the trust.

The person who creates a trust is called the *grantor, creator,* or *donor.* The trust may have more than one grantor and may be created by the donation of property or cash. This initial contribution is called the *principal, corpus,* or *res* of the trust.

The creators select a trustee or trustees to manage the trust according to an agreement signed by the trustee and the creator. This agreement specifies the purpose of the trust, the beneficiaries, the term of the trust, and other conditions required by state law. The trust, like the corporate nonprofit, is created according to state law.

The trustees may be the nonprofit itself, individuals who may or may not be donors, a bank, or a combination of these. A bank may be the custodian or keeper of the corpus. The creator of the trust may serve as a trustee and, in some cases in which the beneficiary is some person other than the creator, the creator may be the sole trustee. This is often unwise, however, because any incidence of ownership or control by the creator over a trust could lead to income as well as estate taxes falling on the creator, thus nullifying any possibility of a deduction because the donor may be construed not to have made a gift.[2]

Like a corporation, a trust is an independent tax and legal entity. It pays its own taxes and is responsible for its own liabilities. As an independent legal entity, a trust has legal ownership over the property entrusted to it. Its relationship to the beneficiary is said to be one of a fiduciary. This means that the obligation of the trustees is to act in ways to promote the interest of the beneficiaries. Violations of this fiduciary relationship can result in civil and criminal charges.

A trust may be simple or complex. A *simple trust* is one that cannot make charitable contributions, cannot distribute its corpus, and must make annual distributions. Naturally, such a trust cannot be used as a vehicle to make gifts to nonprofits. A *complex trust*, however, may accumulate income, distribute its corpus, and make charitable donations. A simple trust is automatically converted to a complex trust once it makes a charitable donation, accumulates income, or distributes its corpus. For the purpose of giving, trusts ought to be initially designed as complex rather than simple. Arriving at this status by default or accident is poor planning.

Trusts may be revocable or irrevocable. A nonprofit that obtains a transfer in a revocable trust may have no gift at all because the transfer may be revoked. The donor will receive no tax deduction and indeed will have to pay taxes on the earnings of the trust if it is revocable. Recall from Chapter Seven that revocable transfers are not gifts. Therefore, from the vantage point of nonprofits, obtaining contributions by way of trusts means using an irrevocable, complex trust.

Trusts may be created to operate during the lifetime of an individual *(inter vivos)* or upon death *(testamentary)*. The rules and discussions are for the most part the same. Obviously, a revocable trust becomes irrevocable at death.[3]

Trusts as Charitable Organizations

A nonprofit can be organized as a trust rather than as a corporation. As a charitable organization, the trust must abide by the two central restrictions on corporations: The assets and income cannot be used for the benefit of individuals, and when the trust is dissolved, the assets and income must be distributed to a qualified tax-exempt nonprofit. At that point, the rules of control and attribution discussed in Chapters Two through Four apply.

Specifically, the governing document of a trust that is a nonprofit—as an alternative to a corporation—should contain the following if it is to qualify for tax exemption. Note that in point two, such a trust cannot have personal inurement. But other trusts to be discussed in this chapter will provide for personal gain. Also note in point two that when a trust other than a corporation is used to form the nonprofit, a gift by a firm cannot be used overseas.

1. The trustees will have the power to accept and dispose of property according to the terms of the trust, but may not accept property if it requires distribution of the income or principal to organizations that are not charitable.

2. The trustees may accept additional property and distribute such property at their discretion as long as they are for charitable purposes. These distributions may be made through a nonprofit, or the trustees may make such expenditures directly. But the donations of a U.S. corporation to a trust, as opposed to a nonprofit corporation, may not be used outside the United States. Further, no distribution shall inure to the benefit of individuals or may be used in political campaigns, and no substantial part may be used to influence legislation.

3. The trust will exist in perpetuity unless the trustees determine otherwise. The donor authorizes them to use the funds to create a nonprofit corporation if the trust is dissolved.

4. The trustees may amend the trust.

5. No fewer than two trustees are permitted.

6. The trustees have the power to invest, sell, hold, exchange, lease, or borrow any type security, and to execute contracts, vote, reorganize, employ a bank, and use investment advisors.

7. The powers of trustees are exercisable only in a fiduciary capacity.

8. Any person dealing with trustees may accept their actions as representing that of the trust and need not inquire further about the representation.

9. The declaration of trust is governed by the law of the state in which the trust is created.

This last provision is worthy of additional note because it affects the actual operation of the trust in the interpretation of some of the items previously enumerated. For example, the state may restrict the types of investments a trust may make. Generally, these restrictions are intended to prohibit risky investments or investments in the business of the trustees. A current law in Ontario, Canada, prohibits trustees from investing in mutual funds, because this would be a delegation of the duties of the trustees.

THE LAW AND THE MANAGEMENT OF TRUST FUNDS

Just as states have rules for trustees of nonprofit organizations, they have similar rules for trusts that hold assets for the benefit of such organizations. To appreciate these situations, visualize an account that contains assets not only for a charity or charities, but also for the benefit of noncharities, including the donors themselves and their families. Hence, the assets of charities are comingled with the assets that belong to individuals. In most of these trusts, the assets being held for the charities are not turned over to them until some considerable period of years has elapsed or some event such as death has occurred.

In these instances, the trustees who may be different from the trustees of the organization, have a tricky responsibility. They must manage these assets in such a way that the future interests of the organization are safe. Therefore, states have policies that are triggered to protect these assets between the time that a nonprofit has a vested and irrevocable interest in these accounts and the time the benefits are turned over to them.

Let us take a look at an example of these laws. Michigan 26.1200 is such a law. It applies to all trustees of these types of trusts, as long as the assets due the nonprofit are not "remote." Technically, this means that the amount due to the nonprofit is not less than 5 percent of the present value of the trust at the time the trust is created. The rule applies to all trustees (except for religious organizations, hospitals, and universities that are exempt from the law) even if the trustee is a bank or other institution.

Under the Michigan law, the attorney general may require annual reports on all aspects of these trusts. In addition, the attorney general may require that trustees who receive assets for the trust report an inventory of these assets. He or she may also require that after the close of a fiscal year, audited financial statements be filed by the trustees along with an inventory of securities held and how they are administered and any petition made to the courts about the disposition or handling of these assets.

In addition to these annual reports, the attorney general may also ask for periodic reports and may investigate transactions, represent the people's interest in any case relating to the trusts, and institute procedures for ensuring compliance with the law. Reports and appearances of the trustees may be done under oath, and the trustees may interpret the organizing documents, amending the trust or require that it be amended, and dissolve the trust in accordance with law.

A trust that is a charitable organization is bound by the rules that cover private foundations. This is so even if the trust becomes a public charity. This means that trusts are bound by rules of self-dealing, and they have to pay excise taxes and penalties as do private foundations. The purpose is to protect the assets and income of the trust against abuse and invasion for individual benefit. The trustees are thus bound not merely by the general rules of trusts and the particular stipulations of trust agreements, but by the rules of a private foundation as well.

Community Trust

A special example of a trust is the community trust. A *community trust,* unlike the community chest, is a trust normally started by one or two individuals. It may subsequently become a public trust by passing the one-third public support test, having an organizing document stipulating the conditions mentioned before, or passing the facts and circumstances test. A community trust may be one single entity, or it might be a composite of individual trusts. Unlike a community chest, it does not have to carry on a campaign to gain a large number of small contributions.

A trust as a nonprofit organization may be created by one or more persons. It may specifically designate one or more charitable beneficiaries, and it need not receive additional donations. The task of the trustee is primarily to manage the principal so that it grows and to distribute it prudently or according to the trust agreement among the stated beneficiaries. Again, once such a trust is created having only charitable beneficiaries, it immediately becomes a *charitable* trust and is subject to the rules governing private foundations.

Trusts for Future, Remainder, and Partial Interests

In another vein, trusts can be used to make partial, future, and split-interest gifts (gifts that are split between a charitable and noncharitable beneficiary). Specifically, the trusts to be discussed next provide for both personal and charitable gains from the same core assets. Only through a unitrust, annuity trust, or pooled trust can such gifts be deductible.[4] When a trust is used to split interests between a charity and a noncharity, it may operate as a regular trust that is not subject to the special tax-exempt rules of nonprofits until such time that the interests of the noncharity are exhausted. The trust is treated as a private foundation and is subject to all the stringent rules discussed in Chapter Four.

A basic characteristic of unitrusts, annuity trusts, and pooled trusts is that they distinguish between remainder interest (what is left after the occurrence of some event, usually the passage of twenty years or death) and the income interest, the annual earnings, and distribution. One of these interests is kept by the donor or given to someone other than a nonprofit, and the other interest is given to the nonprofit.

In those trust arrangements whereby the donor or a noncharity receives the income, leaving the remainder to the nonprofit, the trust is referred to as a *remainder trust*. In these cases, the charity is the remainderman; it gets what is left of the principal or corpus of the trust. The *charitable lead trust* is one in which the nonprofit gets the income and the donor or the designated noncharitable beneficiary gets the remainder of the principal or corpus.

Essentially, then, a trust permits a donor to give a property and still enjoy it or to give it to more than one beneficiary (only one of which is a charity) and in both cases get an immediate income-tax deduction. Obviously, the trust is a useful tool.

We discussed incomplete or partial transfers in Chapter Seven. With the exception of a primary residence or farm, transfers that are partial or of future interest do not qualify as gifts and are therefore not deductible. Without the possibility of a tax deduction, the person may prefer not to give the property. How can a tax benefit be arranged?

Moreover, there are times when the donor wishes to continue enjoying the property and would prefer to relinquish it at a time in the distant future. The nonprofit, on the other hand, is eager to obtain the property as a gift. How can a deal be arranged?

A trust can solve these types of problems. It can satisfy both the interests of the potential donor and the interests of the nonprofit. The trust can provide for a gift to be split between a beneficiary that is a charity and one that is not. It can provide for a property to be given but still enjoyed by the donor, and it can do this while getting the donor an immediate tax deduction for a property not fully relinquished. Since trust arrangements of this type make the gifts irrevocable, the nonprofit does not have to wait to own it. It does not risk a change of heart by the donor.

From a tax perspective, a trust does the following for the donor. It provides for an immediate deduction of the present value of the gift. It solves an estate tax problem by removing the property from the donor's estate. At the same time it allows the donor to receive some benefits from the property (even though it has been given away) or to assign some benefits to others, such as a relative or a friend.

To illustrate, Marian wishes to make a gift of $1 million to a nonprofit but knows the needs of her children. It is possible to arrange to have the money set aside to produce a steady stream of income for her children, and at the end of their lives the remainder could be donated to her favorite nonprofit.

Remainder Trusts

A remainder trust permits the donor to make a contribution to one or more charities, get an immediate tax deduction on that contribution, and still get an annual income from the gift or to provide an annual income for a spouse, children, or some other beneficiary that is not a charity for a period up to twenty years or for the remainder of their lives. Some or all of this income may be free from taxes.

New law requires that the income from a remainder trust be related to the length of time the trust has held the property. First it is considered short-term and subject to the highest tax rate, then mid-term, next long-term, and only after that as return of capital, which has zero tax rate. A tax-exempt security may have zero federal income tax. Hence, it is possible for the donor not only to get a tax deduction, but also a tax-free income for life or for the life of a beneficiary, including a spouse, children, or pet.

At the termination of the designated period, the remainder that is left in the trust will go to the charity. The donor may even be a trustee of the trust, but this is not advisable because the more influence she exercises, the more she is exposed to being taxed. The trust may carry the donor's name.

There are three types of remainder trusts: an *annuity trust,* a *unitrust,* and a *pooled income trust.* Let us see how each works.

A remainder trust that is in the form of an *annuity trust* is one that offers the donor or some other designated beneficiary or beneficiaries the income generated by the trust. Remember, the donor may designate himself or herself as a beneficiary. The donor receives the income for a term that cannot exceed twenty years or for the life or lives of the donor and/or one or more beneficiaries alive at the time the trust is made. Accordingly, the donor and the spouse may receive the income from the trust for their lives; or the donor may choose to give the income from the trust to a child for a period not to exceed twenty years or for the life of the child. In short, the donor has a choice of whom and how many beneficiaries. The gift can be made over the life or lives of the individual(s) or for a specific period of time called a *term.* The beneficiary cannot be unborn and obviously not dead; hence, the word *alive.*

All or part of the income received by the donor or beneficiaries might be tax free. This is so if the trust is funded by the use of securities such as municipal bonds that are tax exempt. It is also the case when part of the income is a return of the original investment of the donor. This part of the original investment is not taxed (see the accompanying insert).

Once the annuity trust is created, no further contributions can be made to it. And at least 5 percent of the value of the assets of the trust at the time it is created must be paid to the income beneficiaries at least once a year. This 5 percent annual distribution is used to reduce the value of the deduction as a charitable gift.

As long as the trust does not invest in an unrelated business, its income is not taxed. If it does so invest, all its income, not just the portion coming from the unrelated business, is taxed. In any period, when the income of the trust exceeds that which is necessary to make the payments to the beneficiaries, a donation can be made to clarity. Hence, it is possible for the charity to also be receiving annual donations from the trust (although this amount is not tax deductible by the donor). The trust deducts it. Moreover, part of this excess income could also go to the income beneficiaries as long as it is to cover a shortfall in the payment they received in a past year.

Because the income that the donor and other income beneficiaries receive is a fixed proportion of the value of the assets at the time the fund is created, they do not participate in the growth of the assets; conversely, if the value of the assets declines, they do not suffer. If the initial value of the assets is $1,000,000, 5 percent is $50,000, and $50,000 is received regardless of whether or not the value of the assets increases. If the assets decline, $50,000 is still owed and any shortfall can be made up in future years.

This brings us to an important point. No tax deduction of the gift is gotten by the donor unless there is a strong probability (at least 10 percent, as calculated by special IRS tables) that the assets in the charity will not be used up so that nothing will be left for the charity at the end of the term or the lives of the income beneficiaries.

In times past, donors would arrange the trust so that they or their relatives who held the income interests would exhaust both the income and the principal of the trust so that eventually there was nothing left for the charity. Today, this is less likely. For one, both the unitrust and annuity trust require that the amount or percentage to be paid be stated when the trust is created and that this amount be set so as not to deplete the trust. Second, unitrust agreements often provide that capital gains should not be distributed but added to the principal of the trust. Hence, if a trust included among its holdings a property that was worth $1 million at the time it was received, if that property is later sold for $1.2 million, the $200,000 gain is added to the principal of the trust and not distributed to the person or entities holding the income interests. Third, the fiduciary rules require that the remainder interest always be protected.

Despite this fact, however, the annuity trust does pose a risk for the charity. Because the income is based on the value of the assets at the opening of the trust, some trust assets may have to be sold to keep that promise in years when the earnings of the trust are not sufficient to meet its payments to the beneficiaries and if they are unwilling to wait to make up the difference. Because of this fact, annuity trusts tend to invest in securities that maintain their value or provide a steady stream of income, at least to cover the amount the trust must pay annually to the donor or other designated beneficiaries.

Recall that the income from the annuity trust was based on a predetermined percentage or amount of the value of the assets at the time the trust was created. The *unitrust* is different on this point. It, too, is a remainder trust with all the characteristics of an annuity trust except that the amount it pays is determined annually. That is, the trust is valued annually, and a fixed percentage of that value (as determined each year) is paid to the income beneficiaries. If the value goes up, the amount they receive goes up. If the value goes down, the amount they receive declines.

In addition, a unitrust provides that the donor may make annual contributions to the trust. Furthermore, unlike the annuity trust, the unitrust can protect the interest of the charity by having a clause written into the trust agreement that says that the donor or the beneficiaries are paid only from the income of the trust. This is not permitted with an annuity trust. This clause is important because it means that the assets of the trust do not have to be sold in order to meet the required annual payments to the beneficiaries.

A third type of remainder trust is a *pooled income trust*. These trusts are particularly useful when the potential donor does not have sufficient money to justify the cost of setting up and administering a separate trust and investment agreement. How does this work?

The donor makes a gift to the charity and gets a tax deduction for the gift. The donor can also be named or name some other person or persons as beneficiaries. Unlike an annuity or unitrust, this designation cannot be for a term or number of years; it must be for the life or lives of the individuals.

Also, unlike the unitrust or annuity trust, there is no separate identity. The trust cannot carry the name of the donor because the trust is a pool to which many donors have contributed. Their funds are all co-mingled into one trust. Furthermore, neither the donor nor any beneficiary may serve as a trustee of the trust, and the trust may not invest in tax-exempt securities. One disadvantage of this is that all the income that the donors or their designated beneficiaries get regularly from the trust is taxable.

The amount of income the donor or beneficiaries get annually is not based on the value of the assets of the trust but on their pro rata share of the trust. Hence, a donor whose contribution makes up 10 percent of the pooled income trust will get 10 percent of the earnings it distributes.

The pooled income trust can be a good tax shelter. To illustrate, a university recently used a pooled income trust to finance the construction of athletic facilities. Being a tax-exempt organization, some of the tax benefits could not be used by the university. The IRS ruled (GCM 30976) that the depreciation expense and the investment tax credit could be passed on to the contributors of the pool. Depreciation expenses, according to a later ruling, must be matched by reserves so that the pool would not depreciate its original value to zero. These "expenses," although they were not incurred by the donors, could nevertheless be used by them to reduce their taxable incomes. Hence, the donor to a properly structured pooled income trust can get a tax deduction on the original gift, a regular flow of income, and an "expense" to reduce taxable income.

Charitable Lead Trusts

With the remainder trust, the donor or a designated beneficiary got the annual income and the charity got the remainder that was left after the predesignated period. Is there a technique that might reverse this process so that the charity gets the annual income and the donor or beneficiary gets the remainder? Such an approach would provide a steady and regular annual flow of income into the coffers of the nonprofit. But what would it do for the donor? Why should he or she go along with the proposal?

The technique is called a *charitable lead trust*. Such a trust provides a steady flow of income to the nonprofit. This trust must also be either in an annuity form (the flow being based on a fixed amount or fixed percentage of the value of the initial assets) or the unitrust form (based on an annual appraisal of the value of the assets). In either case, unlike the remainder trust, the payments can be less than 5 percent.

As in the case of a remainder trust, the payments to the charity could cover the life of an individual or individuals (either conterminously or consecutively), but unlike the remainder trust there is no limit to the number of years if the donor prefers to make the payments for a term of years rather than for the life of some person or persons.

What is the appeal to the donor? The charitable lead trust offers four distinct approaches, each with its advantages and disadvantages to the donor. In one approach, the trust is set up and the donor can take a one-time deduction for the gift. The size of this deduction is based on calculations of what the present value of the amount the charity will receive over the years will be. The way the special IRS tables for calculating this deduction works, the deduction will generally be larger the greater the amount and frequency of payments to the charity (called the *payout rate*) and the longer the period over which this payment is to be made (designated either in terms of years or the lives of individuals).

If this first approach is taken, part of this deduction will be recalled (recaptured) if for some reason the donor should cease to honor the trust. However, every annual payment the charity gets counts against the 50 or 30 percent individual limit for charitable contributions discussed in Chapter Seven. Hence, the donor gets a large one-time deduction covering all of the years that the charity is expected to receive annual payments, but takes the risk of recapture and limits the amount of annual contributions thereafter. For most donors, the recapture possibilities are more serious than the annual limitations because few donors ever legitimately approach that annual limit.

A second approach to setting up a charitable lead trust is to forego the one-time large deduction for annual deductions. This will appeal to only a few potential donors because the law requires that if they take an annual deduction they must also report the earnings of the trust as theirs. For most potential donors, this will put them in an adverse position because it will increase their income and therefore their tax liability.

A third approach to a charitable lead trust is to set up a trust in which the donor does not by implication or otherwise act as the owner of the trust. In this case, the donor does not have to report the earnings of the trust as his or her own, but neither can the donor take the deduction.

A fourth alternative way of using the charitable lead trust, which is the most common, is to reduce transfer (estate and gift taxes). For example, a potential donor wishes to make a gift to a charity in the form of an annual payment. The donor can be persuaded to do so by pointing to the fact that a trust can be set up such that at the end of some period, payments to the charity are ended, and the remainder of the trust is turned over to a beneficiary. If the trust is well invested so that the annual income is very high and the payments to the charity are correspondingly high, these payments could constitute a deduction so large that they would wipe out the estate tax upon the death of the donor. The benefit of this is that more of the wealth of the donor would be passed on to his or her heirs rather than to the state and federal governments in the form of death, estate, or inheritance taxes.

To this point we have talked about the charitable lead trust as providing annual income to the charity. But it can simultaneously provide a flow of income to the donor or beneficiary. The price for doing this is that the deduction will be decreased by the amount that all noncharitable beneficiaries get. Furthermore, these latter beneficiaries can get paid only after the charity is paid, even if some of the assets of the trust must be sold to meet the obligations to the charity. The donor gets no deductions for the sale of assets to meet the obligations of the trust.

EXAMPLES OF THE APPLICATION OF TRUST CONCEPTS

We shall take a look at some illustrations of how some of the concepts concerning a trust may be applied. There are infinite variations; therefore, the wise financial officer learns to consult an expert. Always work with a lawyer, accountant, and financial planner—all specializing in estate planning and taxation.

Illustration 1

Myra, who turned 44 on April 1, 1991, transfers $100,000 to a pooled income fund and retains a life income interest in the property. The highest rate of return experienced by the fund in the immediately preceding three years is 9.2 percent. What amount of deductions did Myra take on her income tax?

Refer to Table 8.1. The factor in the cell referring to age 44 and 9.2 percent is .12167. By multiplying the fair market value of the gift, $100,000 by .12167, we get $12,167, the amount of her deduction. If she is in the 50 percent bracket, she saves $6,083 on her income tax (50 percent of $12,167). But she will get an annual income from the trust. Suppose the trust paid her $4,000 in income the following year.

To calculate the rate of return, her net investment would be $100,000 minus the $6,083 she saved in income taxes. This is $93,917 and the rate of return on her net investment is 4 percent. Hence, she would have made a gift, gotten a deduction, and continued to get a positive rate of return for as long as she lives and as long as the pool earns money. The advantage is even greater if one recognizes that often gifts are made of appreciated property. She might have made a gift with a market value of $100,000 for which she paid substantially less. Therefore, the true rate of return might well exceed 4 percent.

The effects of this transaction depend on the age of the donor; that is, the donor's life expectancy is the number of years the donor may expect to receive

Table 8.1. Single Life, Unisex, Showing the Present Worth of the Remainder Interest in Property Transferred to a Pooled Income Fund Having the Yearly Rate of Return Shown.

(1) Age	(2) Yearly Rate of Return					(1) Age	(2) Yearly Rate of Return				
	9.2 percent	9.4 percent	9.6 percent	9.8 percent	10.0 percent		9.2 percent	9.4 percent	9.6 percent	9.8 percent	10.0 percent
5	.01283	.01221	.01164	.01111	.01062	24	.03735	.03577	.03428	.03290	.03159
6	.01350	.01284	.01224	.01168	.01116	25	.03927	.03761	.03605	.03459	.03322
7	.01425	.01356	.01292	.01233	.01178	26	.04141	.03966	.03803	.03649	.03505
8	.01512	.01439	.01372	.01309	.01252	27	.04377	.04194	.04023	.03861	.03710
9	.01612	.01535	.01464	.01398	.01337	28	.04639	.04447	.04267	.04098	.03938
10	.01724	.01644	.01569	.01499	.01435	29	.04922	.04721	.04532	.04354	.04187
11	.01851	.01766	.01688	.01615	.01547	30	.05228	.05017	.04819	.04633	.04457
12	.01991	.01902	.01819	.01742	.01671	31	.05554	.05334	.05126	.04930	.04746
13	.02139	.02045	.01958	.01877	.01802	32	.05904	.05674	.05456	.05251	.05058
14	.02288	.02190	.02098	.02013	.01934	33	.06279	.06038	.05810	.05595	.05392
15	.02435	.02331	.02235	.02146	.02063	34	.06677	.06435	.06187	.05962	.05750
16	.02575	.02466	.02366	.02272	.02185	35	.07102	.06839	.06590	.06355	.06132
17	.02709	.02595	.02490	.02391	.02300	36	.07553	.07278	.07019	.06733	.06540
18	.02839	.02721	.02610	.02507	.02410	37	.08030	.07745	.07474	.07217	.06974
19	.02971	.02846	.02730	.02621	.02520	38	.08534	.08237	.07955	.07687	.07433
20	.03108	.02977	.02855	.02741	.02635	39	.09065	.08755	.08462	.08182	.07917
21	.03251	.03114	.02986	.02866	.02755	40	.09624	.09302	.08996	.08706	.08429
22	.03402	.03258	.03123	.02998	.02880	41	.10212	.09878	.09560	.09258	.08970
23	.03562	.03410	.03269	.03137	.03014	42	.10833	.10486	.10156	.09842	.09543

43	.11484	.11125	.10783	.10456	.10145
44	.12167	.11795	.11441	.11102	.10779
45	.12880	.12495	.12128	.11777	.11442
46	.13625	.13227	.12847	.12484	.12137
47	.14402	.13991	.13599	.13223	.12863
48	.15214	.14791	.14385	.13997	.13626
49	.16060	.15625	.15207	.14806	.14422
50	.16944	.16496	.16065	.15653	.15257
51	.17862	.17401	.16959	.16534	.16126
52	.18816	.18343	.17888	.17451	.17031
53	.19805	.19320	.18853	.18404	.17972
54	.20825	.20328	.19850	.19390	.18946
55	.21878	.21370	.20881	.20409	.19954
56	.22963	.22443	.21943	.21460	.20994
57	.24081	.23551	.23040	.22546	.22069
58	.25231	.24691	.24170	.23665	.23178
59	.26418	.25868	.25336	.24822	.24325
60	.27640	.27081	.26540	.26016	.25509
61	.28899	.28332	.27782	.27249	.26733
62	.30197	.29622	.29064	.28523	.27998
63	.31533	.30950	.30385	.29836	.29304
64	.32905	.32316	.31743	.31188	.30648
65	.34311	.33716	.33138	.32576	.32030
66	.35751	.35151	.34568	.34001	.33449
67	.37221	.36618	.36030	.35459	.34902

77	.53514	.52934	.52364	.51806	.51258
78	.55177	.54605	.54043	.53492	.52951
79	.56837	.56273	.55720	.55177	.54643
80	.58497	.57944	.57401	.56866	.56341
81	.60148	.59606	.59073	.58548	.58033
82	.61775	.61245	.60723	.60210	.59705
83	.63381	.62863	.62354	.61852	.61358
84	.64974	.64470	.63973	.63484	.63002
85	.66558	.66068	.65586	.65110	.64641
86	.68096	.67622	.67154	.66692	.66236
87	.69542	.69082	.68628	.68180	.67738
88	.70891	.70445	.70005	.69570	.69141
89	.72172	.71739	.71312	.70891	.70474
90	.73422	.73004	.72591	.72182	.71779
91	.74632	.74229	.73829	.73435	.73045
92	.75763	.75373	.74988	.74606	.74229
93	.76791	.76414	.76042	.75673	.75308
94	.77710	.77345	.76983	.76626	.76272
95	.78510	.78155	.77804	.77457	.77113
96	.79183	.78837	.78494	.78155	.77819
97	.79783	.79445	.79110	.78779	.78450
98	.80306	.79975	.79647	.79322	.79000
99	.80797	.80471	.80149	.79830	.79514
100	.81283	.80964	.80648	.80335	.80025
101	.81708	.81394	.81082	.80774	.80468

(continued)

Table 8.1. (continued).

(1) Age	(2) Yearly Rate of Return					(1) Age	(2) Yearly Rate of Return				
	9.2 percent	9.4 percent	9.6 percent	9.8 percent	10.0 percent		9.2 percent	9.4 percent	9.6 percent	9.8 percent	10.0 percent
68	.38723	.38116	.37526	.36950	.36390	102	.82165	.81856	.81550	.81247	.80946
69	.40257	.39649	.39056	.38478	.37914	103	.82754	.82452	.82153	.81857	.81563
70	.41826	.41217	.40623	.40043	.39478	104	.83312	.83017	.82723	.82433	.82144
71	.43435	.42827	.42233	.41652	.41086	105	.84165	.83880	.83597	.83316	.83038
72	.45084	.44478	.43885	.43305	.42739	106	.85562	.85297	.85034	.84772	.84512
73	.46765	.46161	.45571	.44994	.44429	107	.87523	.87288	.87054	.86822	.86591
74	.48460	.47861	.47274	.46700	.46138	108	.90652	.90471	.90291	.90111	.89932
75	.50155	.49561	.48979	.48409	.47851	109	.95788	.95704	.95620	.95537	.95455
76	.51841	.51253	.50677	.50112	.49559						

Source: Internal Revenue Service, Code of Federal Regulations, Vol. 26, Part I, Sec. 1.641 to 1.850, April 1, 1985, p. 40.

annual or monthly income. It also depends on the expected payout rate measured by the highest rate of return to the pool in the preceding three years. The higher the expected payout rate is, the lower the deduction, because the greater the income that a donor will receive. Also, the younger the donor is, the lower the deduction, because income may be flowing to him or her for a considerable period. The tax savings depend on the tax bracket of the donor; the higher the tax bracket, the greater the savings. As is shown by the following illustration, it also depends on the number of noncharitable beneficiaries and their ages regardless of sex.

Illustration 2

Let us add another complication to the pooled income trust. Assume that Simon decides he would like to make a contribution of $100,000 to a pooled income trust but that the income should go to his two daughters prior to the remainder being turned over to the charity. What will his deduction be?

Assume that his two daughters, Emeline and Celestina, are thirty-five and thirty years of age, respectively. Then we must take both of these ages into account because we are concerned not only with the life expectancy of one person, but of two persons jointly. Assume also that the highest rate of return experienced by the pooled trust in the preceding three years was 9.2 percent. Turn to Table 8.2, Part 4. The factor is .02043, so his deduction would be $2,043. But both of his children will receive annual incomes equaling their share of the earnings of the pooled trust for the remainder of their lives.

Note that in both of these cases the nonprofit gets $100,000 and its payments to the donor or his designees depend on the earnings of the investment made with the $100,000. In a pooled trust, the annuity to the donor or his designees is for life. Recall that the income that noncharitable beneficiaries get will be taxable as ordinary income.

Illustration 3

Let's assume that Roy decides to make a gift of $100,000 to a charitable remainder unitrust. The trust instrument requires that the trustee pay, at the end of each taxable year of the trust, 5 percent of the fair market value of the trust assets as of the beginning of the trust's taxable year to his son, Rene, for life, and then to his son, Robertino, for life. Robertino is thirty-five and Rene is thirty. What will the deduction be for Roy? The factor in Table 8.3, Part 2 (see page 231) is .09193, so the deduction will be $9,193. All the arguments stated above about Myra and Simon apply, except that the incomes flowing to the noncharitable beneficiaries Rene and Robertino are not necessarily treated as ordinary income. They may be totally or partially tax free.

Table E(2)—Part 4

Table 8.2. Two-Life Last to Die Pooled Income Trust.

		Yearly Rate of Return									
		8.2 percent	8.4 percent	8.6 percent	8.8 percent	9.0 percent	9.2 percent	9.4 percent	9.6 percent	9.8 percent	10.0 percent
O	Y										
34	5	.00890	.00812	.00742	.00679	.00622	.00570	.00523	.00481	.00443	.00408
34	6	.00936	.00855	.00782	.00715	.00656	.00602	.00552	.00508	.00468	.00431
34	7	.00985	.00900	.00824	.00754	.00692	.00635	.00583	.00537	.00494	.00456
34	8	.01037	.00948	.00868	.00796	.00730	.00670	.00616	.00567	.00523	.00482
34	9	.01092	.00999	.00915	.00839	.00771	.00708	.00651	.00600	.00553	.00510
34	10	.01150	.01053	.00965	.00886	.00814	.00748	.00689	.00635	.00585	.00540
34	11	.01210	.01109	.01017	.00934	.00859	.00790	.00728	.00671	.00620	.00572
34	12	.01274	.01168	.01072	.00985	.00907	.00835	.00769	.00710	.00656	.00606
34	13	.01339	.01229	.01129	.01039	.00956	.00881	.00813	.00750	.00693	.00641
34	14	.01407	.01293	.01188	.01094	.01007	.00929	.00857	.00792	.00732	.00678
34	15	.01477	.01358	.01249	.01150	.01060	.00978	.00903	.00835	.00772	.00715
34	16	.01548	.01424	.01311	.01208	.01114	.01028	.00950	.00879	.00813	.00753
34	17	.01622	.01492	.01375	.01268	.01170	.01080	.00999	.00924	.00856	.00793
34	18	.01697	.01563	.01440	.01329	.01227	.01134	.01049	.00971	.00899	.00834
34	19	.01775	.01635	.01508	.01392	.01286	.01189	.01100	.01019	.00945	.00876
34	20	.01855	.01711	.01579	.01458	.01348	.01247	.01154	.01070	.00992	.00921
34	21	.01938	.01789	.01652	.01527	.01412	.01307	.01211	.01122	.01041	.00967
34	22	.02025	.01869	.01728	.01598	.01478	.01369	.01269	.01177	.01093	.01015
34	23	.02114	.01953	.01806	.01671	.01548	.01434	.01330	.01235	.01147	.01066
34	24	.02206	.02040	.01888	.01748	.01620	.01502	.01394	.01294	.01203	.01119

34	25	.02302	.02130	.01972	.01827	.01695	.01572	.01460	.01357	.01262	.01174
34	26	.02401	.02223	.02060	.01910	.01773	.01646	.01530	.01422	.01323	.01232
34	27	.02503	.02320	.02151	.01996	.01854	.01723	.01602	.01490	.01388	.01293
34	28	.02609	.02419	.02245	.02085	.01938	.01802	.01677	.01561	.01455	.01357
34	29	.02717	.02522	.02342	.02177	.02024	.01884	.01754	.01635	.01524	.01422
34	30	.02828	.02627	.02442	.02271	.02114	.01969	.01834	.01711	.01596	.01491
34	31	.02942	.02735	.02544	.02368	.02205	.02055	.01917	.01789	.01670	.01561
34	32	.03057	.02844	.02648	.02467	.02299	.02144	.02001	.01869	.01747	.01633
34	33	.03175	.02956	.02754	.02568	.02395	.02236	.02088	.01952	.01825	.01708
34	34	.03295	.03070	.02863	.02671	.02493	.02329	.02177	.02036	.01906	.01785
35	0	.00871	.00803	.00741	.00685	.00634	.00588	.00546	.00508	.00473	.00442
35	1	.00752	.00686	.00627	.00574	.00526	.00482	.00443	.00407	.00375	.00346
35	2	.00785	.00716	.00654	.00599	.00548	.00503	.00462	.00425	.00391	.00360
35	3	.00823	.00751	.00686	.00628	.00575	.00528	.00485	.00446	.00410	.00378
35	4	.00864	.00789	.00722	.00660	.00605	.00555	.00510	.00469	.00432	.00398
35	5	.00909	.00831	.00760	.00696	.00638	.00585	.00538	.00495	.00456	.00420
35	6	.00957	.00875	.00801	.00733	.00673	.00618	.00568	.00523	.00482	.00444
35	7	.01007	.00921	.00844	.00774	.00710	.00652	.00600	.00552	.00509	.00470
35	8	.01061	.00971	.00890	.00816	.00749	.00689	.00634	.00584	.00539	.00497
35	9	.01117	.01023	.00938	.00861	.00791	.00728	.00670	.00618	.00570	.00527
35	10	.01177	.01079	.00990	.00909	.00836	.00769	.00709	.00654	.00603	.00558
35	11	.01239	.01137	.01044	.00959	.00883	.00813	.00749	.00692	.00639	.00591
35	12	.01305	.01198	.01101	.01012	.00932	.00859	.00792	.00732	.00676	.00626
35	13	.01373	.01261	.01160	.01067	.00983	.00907	.00837	.00774	.00715	.00662
35	14	.01443	.01327	.01221	.01124	.01037	.00957	.00884	.00817	.00756	.00700

(continued)

Table 8.2. (continued).

Table E(2)—Part 4

O	Y	8.2 percent	8.4 percent	8.6 percent	8.8 percent	9.0 percent	9.2 percent	9.4 percent	9.6 percent	9.8 percent	10.0 percent
						Yearly Rate of Return					
35	15	.01515	.01394	.01283	.01183	.01091	.01008	.00931	.00861	.00798	.00739
35	16	.01589	.01463	.01348	.01243	.01147	.01060	.00980	.00907	.00840	.00779
35	17	.01665	.01533	.01414	.01305	.01205	.01114	.01030	.00954	.00884	.00820
35	18	.01743	.01606	.01482	.01368	.01264	.01169	.01082	.01003	.00930	.00863
35	19	.01823	.01682	.01552	.01434	.01326	.01227	.01136	.01053	.00977	.00907
35	20	.01907	.01760	.01625	.01503	.01390	.01287	.01193	.01106	.01026	.00953
35	21	.01994	.01841	.01701	.01574	.01457	.01350	.01251	.01161	.01078	.01002
35	22	.02083	.01925	.01780	.01648	.01526	.01415	.01312	.01218	.01132	.01052
35	23	.02176	.02012	.01862	.01725	.01598	.01482	.01376	.01278	.01188	.01105
35	24	.02272	.02103	.01947	.01805	.01674	.01553	.01443	.01341	.01247	.01161
35	25	.02372	.02197	.02036	.01888	.01752	.01627	.01512	.01406	.01309	.01219
35	26	.02476	.02295	.02128	.01975	.01834	.01704	.01585	.01475	.01373	.01280
35	27	.02583	.02396	.02223	.02065	.01919	.01785	.01661	.01546	.01441	.01344
35	28	.02694	.02500	.02322	.02158	.02007	.01868	.01740	.01621	.01512	.01411
35	29	.02808	.02608	.02424	.02255	.02098	.01954	.01821	.01698	.01585	.01480
35	30	.02924	.02718	.02529	.02354	.02192	.02043	.01906	.01778	.01661	.01552
35	31	.03044	.02832	.02636	.02456	.00289	.02135	.01993	.01861	.01739	.01626
35	32	.03166	.02947	.02746	.02560	.02388	.02229	.02082	.01946	.01820	.01703
35	33	.03290	.03066	.02858	.02667	.02490	.02326	.02174	.02033	.01903	.01782
35	34	.03416	.03186	.02973	.02776	.02593	.02424	.02268	.02123	.01988	.01863

35	35	.03545	.03308	.03089	.02887	.02699	.02525	.02364	.02214	.02075	.01946
36	0	.00896	.00827	.00764	.00707	.00655	.00609	.00566	.00527	.00492	.00460
36	1	.00769	.00702	.00642	.00588	.00539	.00495	.00455	.00419	.00386	.00357
36	2	.00802	.00732	.00670	.00613	.00562	.00516	.00474	.00437	.00402	.00371
36	3	.00841	.00768	.00702	.00643	.00590	.00542	.00498	.00458	.00422	.00390
36	4	.00883	.00807	.00738	.00677	.00621	.00570	.00524	.00482	.00445	.00410
36	5	.00929	.00849	.00778	.00713	.00654	.00601	.00553	.00509	.00469	.00433
36	6	.00978	.00895	.00820	.00752	.00690	.00634	.00584	.00538	.00496	.00458
36	7	.01030	.00943	.00864	.00793	.00728	.00670	.00617	.00568	.00524	.00484
36	8	.01085	.00994	.00911	.00837	.00769	.00708	.00652	.00601	.00555	.00513
36	9	.01143	.01048	.00961	.00883	.00812	.00748	.00589	.00636	.00587	.00543
36	10	.01204	.01104	.01014	.00932	.00858	.00790	.00729	.00673	.00622	.00575
36	11	.01268	.01164	.01070	.00984	.00907	.00836	.00771	.00712	.00659	.00610
36	12	.01336	.01227	.01129	.01039	.00958	.00883	.00816	.00754	.00698	.00646
36	13	.01406	.01293	.01190	.01096	.01011	.00933	.00862	.00797	.00738	.00684
36	14	.01479	.01361	.01253	.01155	.01066	.00984	.00910	.00842	.00780	.00723
36	15	.01553	.01430	.01318	.01216	.01123	.01037	.00960	.00889	.00823	.00764
36	16	.01630	.01501	.01385	.01278	.01181	.01092	.01010	.00936	.00868	.00805
36	17	.01708	.01575	.01453	.01342	.01240	.01148	.01063	.00985	.00914	.00848
36	18	.01789	.01650	.01523	.01408	.01302	.01205	.01117	.01035	.00961	.00892
36	19	.01872	.01728	.01596	.01476	.01366	.01265	.01173	.01088	.01010	.00937
36	20	.01959	.01809	.01672	.01547	.01433	.01327	.01231	.01143	.01061	.00987
36	21	.02049	.01893	.01751	.01621	.01502	.01393	.01292	.01200	.01115	.01037
36	22	.02142	.01981	.01833	.01698	.01574	.01460	.01356	.01260	.01171	.01090
36	23	.02238	.02072	.01919	.01778	.01650	.01531	.01422	.01322	.01230	.01145

(continued)

Table E(2)—Part 4

Table 8.2. (*continued*).

Yearly Rate of Return

O	Y	8.2 percent	8.4 percent	8.6 percent	8.8 percent	9.0 percent	9.2 percent	9.4 percent	9.6 percent	9.8 percent	10.0 percent
36	24	.02339	.02166	.02007	.01862	.01728	.01605	.01492	.01388	.01292	.01203
36	25	.02443	.02264	.02100	.01949	.01810	.01682	.01565	.01456	.01356	.01264
36	26	.02551	.02366	.02196	.02040	.01896	.01763	.01641	.01528	.01424	.01328
36	27	.02663	.02472	.02296	.02134	.01985	.01847	.01720	.01603	.01495	.01395
36	28	.02779	.02582	.02400	.02232	.02077	.01935	.01803	.01682	.01569	.01468
36	29	.02899	.02695	.02507	.02333	.02173	.02026	.01889	.01763	.01647	.01539
36	30	.03021	.02811	.02617	.02437	.02272	.02119	.01978	.01847	.01726	.01615
36	31	.03147	.02930	.02729	.02545	.02374	.02216	.02070	.01934	.01809	.01693
36	32	.03275	.03052	.02845	.02655	.02478	.02315	.02164	.02024	.01894	.01774
36	33	.03406	.03176	.02964	.02767	.02585	.02417	.02261	.02116	.01982	.01857
36	34	.03539	.03303	.03085	.02882	.02695	.02521	.02360	.02211	.02072	.01943
36	35	.03675	.03432	.03208	.03000	.02807	.02628	.02462	.02308	.02165	.02032
36	36	.03813	.03564	.03333	.03119	.02921	.02737	.02566	.02407	.02259	.02122
37	0	.00922	.00852	.00788	.00730	.00678	.00630	.00587	.00547	.00511	.00478
37	1	.00785	.00718	.00657	.00602	.00553	.00508	.00468	.00431	.00398	.00368
37	2	.00819	.00749	.00685	.00628	.00576	.00530	.00487	.00449	.00414	.00382
37	3	.00858	.00785	.00719	.00659	.00605	.00556	.00511	.00471	.00434	.00401
37	4	.00902	.00825	.00755	.00693	.00636	.00585	.00538	.00496	.00457	.00422
37	5	.00949	.00868	.00796	.00730	.00670	.00616	.00568	.00523	.00483	.00446
37	6	.00999	.00915	.00839	.00770	.00707	.00651	.00599	.00553	.00510	.00472

37	7	.01052	.00964	.00884	.00812	.00747	.00687	.00633	.00584	.00540	.00499
37	8	.01108	.01016	.00933	.00857	.00789	.00726	.00670	.00618	.00571	.00528
37	9	.01168	.01072	.00984	.00905	.00833	.00768	.00708	.00654	.00605	.00560
37	10	.01231	.01130	.01039	.00956	.00881	.00812	.00749	.00693	.00641	.00593
37	11	.01297	.01192	.01097	.01010	.00931	.00859	.00793	.00733	.00679	.00629
37	12	.01367	.01257	.01157	.01066	.00983	.00908	.00839	.00776	.00719	.00666
37	13	.01440	.01325	.01220	.01125	.01038	.00959	.00887	.00821	.00761	.00706
37	14	.01514	.01395	.01286	.01186	.01095	.01013	.00937	.0868	.00805	.00747
37	15	.01591	.01466	.01353	.01249	.01154	.01067	.00988	.00916	.00850	.00789
37	16	.01670	.01540	.01421	.01313	.01214	.01124	.01041	.00965	.00896	.00832
37	17	.01751	.01616	.01492	.01379	.01276	.01182	.01095	.01016	.00943	.00876
37	18	.01835	.01694	.01565	.01448	.01340	.01241	.01151	.01068	.00992	.00922
37	19	.01921	.01775	.01641	.01518	.01406	.01303	.01209	.01123	.01043	.00970
37	20	.02011	.01859	.01720	.01592	.01475	.01368	.01270	.01180	.01097	.01020
37	21	.02104	.01946	.01802	.01669	.01548	.01436	.01333	.01239	.01153	.01073
37	22	.02201	.02037	.01887	.01749	.01623	.01507	.01400	.01302	.01211	.01128
37	23	.02301	.02131	.01975	.01832	.01701	.01580	.01469	.01367	.01273	.01186
37	24	.02405	.02229	.02068	.01919	.01783	.01657	.01542	.01435	.01337	.01246
37	25	.02514	.02332	.02164	.02010	.01868	.01738	.01618	.01507	.01405	.01310
37	26	.02627	.02438	.02265	.02105	.01958	.01822	.01697	.01582	.01476	.01377
37	27	.02744	.02549	.02369	.02204	.02051	.01911	.01781	.01661	.01550	.01448
37	28	.02865	.02664	.02478	.02306	.02148	.02002	.01868	.01743	.01628	.01522
37	29	.02990	.02782	.02590	.02412	.02249	.02098	.01958	.01829	.01709	.01598
37	30	.03119	.02904	.02705	.02522	.02353	.02196	.02051	.01917	.01793	.01678
37	31	.03250	.03029	.02824	.02635	.02460	.02298	.02148	.02009	.01880	.01761

(continued)

Table 8.2. (continued).

O	Y	8.2 percent	8.4 percent	8.6 percent	8.8 percent	9.0 percent	9.2 percent	9.4 percent	9.6 percent	9.8 percent	10.0 percent
						Yearly Rate of Return					
37	32	.03385	.03157	.02946	.02750	.02570	.02402	.02247	.02103	.01970	.01846
37	33	.03523	.03288	.03070	.02869	.02683	.02510	.02349	.02201	.02063	.01935
37	34	.03663	.03422	.03198	.02990	.02798	.02620	.02454	.02301	.02158	.02025
37	35	.03807	.03558	.03328	.03115	.02917	.02733	.02562	.02403	.02256	.02119
37	36	.03952	.03697	.03461	.03241	.03037	.02848	.02672	.02509	.02356	.02215
37	37	.04099	.03838	.03595	.03370	.03160	.02966	.02784	.02616	.02459	.02313
38	0	.00949	.00877	.00813	.00754	.00701	.00652	.00608	.00568	.00531	.00498
38	1	.00802	.00734	.00672	.00617	.00567	.00521	.00480	.00443	.00409	.00379
38	2	.00836	.00765	.00701	.00643	.00590	.00543	.00500	.00461	.00426	.00394
38	3	.00876	.00802	.00735	.00674	.00619	.00570	.00525	.00484	.00447	.00413
38	4	.00920	.00843	.00772	.00709	.00652	.00599	.00552	.00509	.00470	.00435
38	5	.00968	.00887	.00814	.00747	.00687	.00632	.00583	.00537	.00496	.00459
38	6	.01020	.00935	.00858	.00788	.00725	.00667	.00615	.00568	.00525	.00485
38	7	.01074	.00985	.00905	.00832	.00765	.00705	.00650	.00600	.00555	.00514
38	8	.01132	.01039	.00955	.00878	.00808	.00745	.00688	.00635	.00588	.00544

Source: Actuarial Values I: Valuation of Last Survivor Charitable Remainders, Part D: Two-Life Last to Die Pooled-Income Fund Factors, Internal Revenue Service, Publication 723D (9–84), p. 128.

Table E(2)—Part 2

Table 8.3. Two-Life Last to Die Unitrust.

		Adjusted Payout Rate									
O	Y	4.2 percent	4.4 percent	4.6 percent	4.8 percent	5.0 percent	5.2 percent	5.4 percent	5.6 percent	5.8 percent	6.0 percent
34	5	.06343	.05605	.04957	.04388	.03887	.03447	.03059	.02718	.02417	.02151
34	6	.06558	.05803	.05139	.04554	.04040	.03586	.03187	.02834	.02523	.02248
34	7	.06780	.06007	.05326	.04726	.04198	.03731	.03319	.02955	.02634	.02349
34	8	.07008	.06217	.05520	.04905	.04361	.03881	.03457	.03081	.02749	.02455
34	9	.07243	.06434	.05720	.05089	.04531	.04037	.03600	.03212	.02869	.02565
34	10	.07484	.06657	.05926	.05279	.04706	.04198	.03748	.03348	.02994	.02679
34	11	.07731	.06886	.06138	.05474	.04886	.04364	.03901	.03489	.03124	.02798
34	12	.07984	.07121	.06355	.05675	.05062	.04535	.04059	.03635	.03258	.02922
34	13	.08241	.07360	.06577	.05881	.05262	.04711	.04221	.03785	.03396	.03049
34	14	.08502	.07603	.06802	.06090	.05456	.04890	.04387	.03938	.03537	.03179
34	15	.08767	.07849	.07031	.06302	.05652	.05073	.04555	.04093	.03681	.03312
34	16	.09033	.08097	.07262	.06517	.05852	.05258	.04727	.04252	.03827	.03447
34	17	.09303	.08349	.07497	.06735	.06054	.05446	.04901	.04413	.03977	.03585
34	18	.09575	.08603	.07734	.06956	.06260	.05637	.05078	.04578	.04129	.03726
34	19	.09850	.08861	.07974	.07181	.06469	.05831	.05259	.04745	.04284	.03871
34	20	.10129	.09122	.08219	.07409	.06682	.06029	.05443	.04917	.04444	.04018
34	21	.10411	.09387	.08467	.07641	.06899	.06232	.05632	.05092	.04607	.04170
34	22	.10697	.09655	.08719	.07876	.07119	.06437	.05824	.05271	.04774	.04325
34	23	.10985	.09926	.08973	.08115	.07343	.06647	.06019	.05454	.04944	.04484

(continued)

Table 8.3. (*continued*).

Table E(2)—Part 2

O	Y	Adjusted Payout Rate									
		4.2 percent	4.4 percent	4.6 percent	4.8 percent	5.0 percent	5.2 percent	5.4 percent	5.6 percent	5.8 percent	6.0 percent
34	24	.11276	.10201	.09231	.08359	.07570	.06860	.06219	.05640	.05118	.04646
34	25	.11570	.10478	.09493	.08604	.07801	.07076	.06422	.05830	.05296	.04813
34	26	.11866	.10758	.09757	.08853	.08036	.07297	.06629	.06024	.05478	.04983
34	27	.12165	.11041	.10024	.09105	.08273	.07520	.06839	.06222	.05663	.05156
34	28	.12465	.11325	.10293	.09359	.08513	.07747	.07052	.06422	.05851	.05333
34	29	.12765	.11610	.10564	.09615	.08755	.07975	.07267	.06625	.06042	.05513
34	30	.13065	.11895	.10835	.09872	.08998	.08205	.07484	.06830	.06235	.05694
34	31	.13364	.12180	.11105	.10129	.09242	.08436	.07702	.07036	.06430	.05878
34	32	.13661	.12464	.11376	.10386	.09486	.08667	.07922	.07243	.06626	.06063
34	33	.13957	.12747	.11645	.10643	.09730	.08899	.08142	.07452	.06823	.06250
34	34	.14250	.13027	.11913	.10898	.09973	.09130	.08361	.07660	.07021	.06437
35	0	.05746	.05075	.04489	.03977	.03528	.03134	.02789	.02485	.02218	.01983
35	1	.05602	.04929	.04341	.03828	.03378	.02985	.02641	.02339	.02074	.01841
35	2	.05783	.05094	.04492	.03964	.03502	.03098	.02743	.02431	.02157	.01916
35	3	.05977	.05272	.04654	.04112	.03637	.03220	.02854	.02532	.02249	.01999
35	4	.06180	.05458	.04824	.04267	.03779	.03349	.02972	.02639	.02346	.02088
35	5	.06392	.05652	.05002	.04430	.03928	.03485	.03096	.02752	.02449	.02182
35	6	.06610	.05853	.05186	.04600	.04083	.03627	.03255	.02871	.02558	.02281
35	7	.06836	.06060	.05377	.04775	.04244	.03775	.03361	.02994	.02671	.02384
35	8	.07068	.06274	.05574	.04956	.04410	.03928	.03501	.03123	.02789	.02492

35	9	.07307	.06495	.05778	.05144	.04583	.04087	.03647	.03257	.02912	.02605
35	10	.07552	.06722	.05988	.05338	.04762	.04251	.03798	.03396	.03039	.02722
35	11	.07804	.06956	.06204	.05538	.04946	.04421	.03955	.03541	.03172	.02844
35	12	.08062	.07195	.06426	.05743	.05136	.04597	.04117	.03690	.03310	.02971
35	13	.08325	.07440	.06653	.05953	.05331	.04777	.04283	.03843	.03451	.03102
35	14	.08592	.07688	.06884	.06167	.05529	.04960	.04453	.04000	.03596	.03235
35	15	.08862	.07940	.07118	.06385	.05731	.05147	.04626	.04161	.03744	.03372
35	16	.09135	.08195	.07355	.06606	.05936	.05337	.04802	.04324	.03895	.03512
35	17	.09411	.08452	.07595	.06829	.06144	.05530	.04981	.04489	.04049	.03654
35	18	.09690	.08713	.07839	.07056	.06355	.05727	.05164	.04659	.04206	.03799
35	19	.09973	.08978	.08086	.07287	.06570	.05927	.05350	.04832	.04366	.03948
35	20	.10260	.09247	.08338	.07522	.06790	.06132	.05540	.05009	.04531	.04101
35	21	.10550	.09520	.08594	.07761	.07013	.06340	.05735	.05190	.04699	.04257
35	22	.10844	.09796	.08853	.08004	.07241	.06553	.05933	.05375	.04872	.04418
35	23	.11142	.10076	.09116	.08251	.07472	.06769	.06136	.05564	.05048	.04582
35	24	.11443	.10360	.09383	.08502	.07707	.06990	.06342	.05757	.05229	.04751
35	25	.11747	.10647	.09654	.08757	.07947	.07215	.06553	.05955	.05414	.04924
35	26	.12054	.10937	.09928	.09016	.08190	.07444	.06768	.06157	.05603	.05101
35	27	.12363	.11231	.10205	.09278	.08437	.07676	.06987	.06362	.05796	.05282
35	28	.12675	.11526	.10485	.09542	.08687	.07912	.07209	.06571	.05992	.05467
35	29	.12987	.11823	.10767	.09809	.08940	.08150	.07434	.06783	.06192	.05655
35	30	.13300	.12121	.11050	.10077	.09193	.08391	.07661	.06997	.06394	.05845
35	31	.13612	.12418	.11333	.10346	.09448	.08632	.07889	.07213	.06598	.06037
35	32	.13924	.12715	.11616	.10615	.09704	.08875	.08119	.07431	.06804	.06232
35	33	.14233	.13011	.11898	.10884	.09960	.09118	.08350	.07650	.07011	.06428

(continued)

Table 8.3. (*continued*).

Table E(2)—Part 2

| | | Adjusted Payout Rate | | | | | | | | | |
O	Y	4.2 percent	4.4 percent	4.6 percent	4.8 percent	5.0 percent	5.2 percent	5.4 percent	5.6 percent	5.8 percent	6.0 percent
35	34	.14541	.13306	.12179	.11152	.10216	.09361	.08581	.07869	.07219	.06625
35	35	.14846	.13598	.12459	.11420	.10471	.09604	.08812	.08089	.07428	.06823
36	0	.05797	.05125	.04537	.04023	.03572	.03177	.02829	.02524	.02256	.02019
36	1	.05640	.04966	.04376	.03861	.03411	.03016	.02670	.02367	.02100	.01866
36	2	.05823	.05133	.04528	.03999	.03536	.03129	.02773	.02460	.02184	.01942
36	3	.06020	.05312	.04692	.04149	.03672	.03253	.02886	.02562	.02277	.02062
36	4	.06225	.05501	.04865	.04307	.03816	.03385	.03005	.02671	.02377	.02117
36	5	.06439	.05697	.05045	.04472	.03967	.03523	.03132	.02786	.02482	.02213
36	6	.06661	.05901	.05233	.04644	.04125	.03667	.03264	.02907	.02592	.02313
36	7	.06890	.06112	.05427	.04822	.04289	.03818	.03401	.03033	.02707	.02419
36	8	.07126	.06330	.05627	.05007	.04458	.03974	.03544	.03164	.02828	.02529
36	9	.07369	.06554	.05835	.05198	.04635	.04136	.03693	.03301	.02953	.02644
36	10	.07618	.06786	.06049	.05386	.04817	.04303	.03848	.03443	.03084	.02765
36	11	.07875	.07024	.06269	.05599	.05005	.04477	.04008	.03591	.03220	.02890
36	12	.08138	.07268	.06496	.05809	.05199	.04657	.04174	.03744	.03361	.03020
36	13	.08406	.07518	.06727	.06024	.05398	.04841	.04344	.03901	.03506	.03154
36	14	.08679	.07771	.06963	.06243	.05601	.05029	.04518	.04062	.03655	.03291
36	15	.08955	.08029	.07203	.06466	.05808	.05221	.04696	.04227	.03807	.03432
36	16	.09234	.08290	.07446	.06692	.06018	.05416	.04877	.04394	.03962	.03575
36	17	.09517	.08553	.07692	.06921	.06231	.05614	.05060	.04565	.04120	.03721

36	18	.09803	.08821	.07942	.07154	.06448	.05815	.05248	.04739	.04281	.03871
36	19	.10093	.09092	.08196	.07391	.06669	.06021	.05439	.04917	.04447	.04024
36	20	.10387	.09369	.08454	.07633	.06895	.06232	.05635	.05099	.04616	.04182
36	21	.10686	.09649	.08717	.07879	.07125	.06447	.05836	.05286	.04790	.04344
36	22	.10988	.09934	.08984	.08130	.07360	.06666	.06041	.05477	.04969	.04510
36	23	.11295	.10222	.09256	.08385	.07599	.06890	.06250	.05673	.05151	.04680
36	24	.11605	.10515	.09532	.08644	.07842	.07118	.06464	.05873	.05338	.04855
36	25	.11919	.10812	.09812	.08908	.08090	.07351	.06683	.06078	.05530	.05035
36	26	.12237	.11113	.10096	.09176	.08343	.07589	.06906	.06287	.05727	.05219
36	27	.12558	.11417	.10383	.09447	.08599	.07830	.07133	.06501	.05928	.05407
36	28	.12881	.11724	.10674	.09723	.08859	.08076	.07365	.06719	.06133	.05600
36	29	.13206	.12032	.10967	.10000	.09122	.08324	.07599	.06940	.06341	.05796
36	30	.13531	.12342	.11262	.10280	.09387	.08575	.07836	.07164	.06552	.05995
36	31	.13857	.12653	.11557	.10560	.09653	.08827	.08075	.07390	.06765	.06196
36	32	.14182	.12963	.11853	.10842	.09920	.09081	.08315	.07617	.06981	.06400
36	33	.14506	.13272	.12148	.11123	.10188	.09336	.08557	.07847	.07198	.06606
36	34	.14827	.13581	.12443	.11405	.10457	.09591	.08800	.08077	.07417	.06813
36	35	.15147	.13887	.12736	.11685	.10724	.09846	.09043	.08308	.07637	.07022
36	36	.15464	.14191	.13028	.11964	.10991	.10101	.09286	.08540	.07857	.07231
37	0	.05848	.05175	.04585	.04069	.03616	.03219	.02870	.02564	.02294	.02055
37	1	.05678	.05002	.04411	.03894	.03442	.03046	.02699	.02394	.02126	.01891
37	2	.05862	.05170	.04564	.04034	.03569	.03161	.02803	.02488	.02211	.01968
37	3	.06061	.05352	.04730	.04185	.03707	.03286	.02917	.02592	.02306	.02053
37	4	.06269	.05542	.04905	.04345	.03853	.03420	.03038	.02703	.02406	.02145
37	5	.06486	.05742	.05088	.04512	.04006	.03560	.03167	.02820	.02513	.02243

(continued)

Table 8.3. (*continued*).

						Adjusted Payout Rate					
O	Y	4.2 percent	4.4 percent	4.6 percent	4.8 percent	5.0 percent	5.2 percent	5.4 percent	5.6 percent	5.8 percent	6.0 percent
37	6	.06711	.05949	.05278	.04687	.04166	.03707	.03301	.02943	.02626	.02345
37	7	.06942	.06163	.05475	.04868	.04333	.03859	.03441	.03071	.02743	.02453
37	8	.07182	.06384	.05679	.05056	.04505	.04018	.03587	.03205	.02866	.02566
37	9	.07429	.06612	.05890	.05251	.04685	.04183	.03739	.03345	.02994	.02683
37	10	.07683	.06847	.06109	.05452	.04870	.04355	.03897	.03490	.03128	.02806
37	11	.07944	.07090	.06332	.05660	.05063	.04532	.04060	.03641	.03267	.02935
37	12	.08212	.07339	.06563	.05874	.05261	.04715	.04230	.03797	.03412	.03068
37	13	.08485	.07593	.06800	.06093	.05464	.04904	.04404	.03958	.03560	.03205
37	14	.08763	.07852	.07041	.06317	.05672	.05096	.04582	.04123	.03713	.03346
37	15	.09045	.08115	.07286	.06545	.05884	.05293	.04764	.04292	.03869	.03490
37	16	.09331	.08382	.07534	.06776	.06099	.05492	.04949	.04463	.04028	.03637
37	17	.09619	.08652	.07786	.07011	.06317	.05695	.05138	.04638	.04190	.03788
37	18	.09912	.08926	.08042	.07250	.06539	.05902	.05331	.04817	.04356	.03942
37	19	.10209	.09205	.08302	.07493	.06766	.06114	.05527	.05000	.04526	.04099
37	20	.10511	.09487	.08568	.07741	.06998	.06330	.05729	.05188	.04701	.04262
37	21	.10817	.09775	.08838	.07994	.07235	.06551	.05936	.05381	.04880	.04429
37	22	.11128	.10068	.09113	.08252	.07477	.06778	.06147	.05578	.05064	.04600
37	23	.11443	.10365	.09392	.08515	.07723	.07008	.06363	.05780	.05253	.04777
37	24	.11763	.10667	.09677	.08783	.07975	.07244	.06584	.05987	.05447	.04958

37	25	.12087	.10973	.09966	.09055	.08231	.07485	.06810	.06199	.05646	.05144
37	26	.12416	.11284	.10260	.09332	.08492	.07731	.07042	.06417	.05850	.05335
37	27	.12748	.11599	.10558	.09614	.08758	.07982	.07278	.06639	.06058	.05531
37	28	.13083	.11917	.10860	.09900	.09028	.08237	.07518	.06865	.06271	.05732
37	29	.13420	.12238	.11164	.10188	.09301	.08495	.07762	.07095	.06488	.05936
37	30	.13758	.12560	.11470	.10479	.09577	.08756	.08009	.07329	.06709	.06144
37	31	.14097	.12883	.11778	.10772	.09855	.09020	.08258	.07565	.06932	.06355
37	32	.14436	.13207	.12087	.11065	.10134	.09285	.08510	.07803	.07157	.06568
37	33	.14774	.13530	.12395	.11360	.10415	.09552	.08763	.08043	.07385	.06784
37	34	.15110	.13852	.12704	.11654	.10695	.09819	.09018	.08285	.07615	.07001
37	35	.15445	.14174	.13011	.11948	.10976	.10087	.09273	.08528	.07845	.07221
37	36	.15777	.14492	.13317	.12241	.11256	.10354	.09528	.08771	.08077	.07441
37	37	.16105	.14809	.13621	.12533	.11535	.10621	.09783	.09014	.08309	.07662
38	0	.05899	.05224	.04633	.04115	.03661	.03262	.02912	.02603	.02332	.02092
38	1	.05714	.05037	.04445	.03927	.03473	.03076	.02727	.02421	.02152	.01916
38	2	.05900	.05207	.04599	.04067	.03601	.03192	.02832	.02516	.02238	.01993
38	3	.06101	.05390	.04767	.04220	.03740	.03319	.02948	.02621	.02334	.02080
38	4	.06311	.05583	.04944	.04382	.03888	.03454	.03071	.02734	.02436	.02173
38	5	.06531	.05785	.05129	.04552	.04044	.03596	.03201	.02853	.02545	.02273
38	6	.06758	.05995	.05322	.04729	.04207	.03745	.03338	.02978	.02659	.02377
38	7	.06993	.06212	.05522	.04913	.04376	.03900	.03480	.03108	.02779	.02487
38	8	.07236	.06436	.05729	.05104	.04551	.04062	.03629	.03245	.02904	.02602

Source: Actuarial Values I: Valuation of Last Survivor Charitable Remainders, Part C, Two-Life Last to Die Unitrust Factors, Publication 723C (9–84), Internal Revenue Service, p. 46.

Illustration 4

Henry decides to create a charitable remainder trust. The trust instrument requires that 10 percent of the market value of its assets on June 30 of each year be paid to Camila for a period of fifteen years. The adjusted payout rate is 10 percent. Refer to Table 8.4. The factor for 10 percent for fifteen years is .205891, so the deduction will be $20,589. Notice in this case the trust must pay a specific percentage and that the valuation date of the trust, once chosen, is fixed: In this case, June 30 of each year. The amount that is received thus depends on the value of the trust on that date. If the trust does exceedingly well, say its market value is $400,000 on that date, Camila would receive

Table 8.4. The Present Worth of a Remainder Interest Postponed for a Term of Years in a Charitable Remainder Unitrust Having the Adjusted Payout Rate Shown.

(1)	(2) Adjusted Payout Rate				
Years	9.2 percent	9.4 percent	9.6 percent	9.8 percent	10.0 percent
1	.908000	.906000	.904000	.902000	.900000
2	.824464	.820836	.817216	.813604	.810000
3	.748613	.743677	.738763	.733871	.729000
4	.679741	.673772	.667842	.661951	.656100
5	.617205	.610437	.603729	.597080	.590490
6	.560422	.553056	.545771	.538566	.531441
7	.508863	.501069	.493377	.485787	.478297
8	.462048	.453968	.446013	.438180	.430467
9	.419539	.411295	.403196	.395238	.387420
10	.380942	.372634	.364489	.356505	.348678
11	.345895	.337606	.329498	.321567	.313811
12	.314073	.305871	.297866	.290054	.282430
13	.285178	.277119	.269271	.261628	.254187
14	.258942	.251070	.243421	.235989	.228768
15	.235119	.227469	.220053	.212862	.205891
16	.213488	.206087	.198928	.192001	.185302
17	.193847	.186715	.179830	.173185	.166772
18	.176013	.169164	.162567	.156213	.150095
19	.159820	.153262	.146960	.140904	.135085
20	.145117	.138856	.132852	.127096	.121577

Source: Internal Revenue Service, *Code of Federal Regulations,* Vol. 26, Part I, Sec. 1.641 to 1.850, April 1, 1985, p. 119.

$40,000. Henry might only have put in a small fraction of the $400,000, which is based on his initial investment, plus the compound rate of growth in the value of the assets. Moreover, only part or possibly all of the $40,000 may be received untaxed.

It should be noted that in this example the income is to flow not for the life of an individual or individuals, but for a specific term. Remainder trusts, unlike pooled trusts, can be set up either for a life or for a specific term. Notice from Table 8.4 that the amount that can be deducted varies inversely both with the length of the term and the rate.

These are four simple examples. How a trust operates depends on the nature of the trust, whether it is a pooled, remainder unitrust, or remainder annuity trust, a guarantee trust, or a charitable lead trust, and the terms specified in the trust document. For example, a creator of a charitable lead trust could get either a one-time or an annual deduction. The latter will depend on the earnings of the trust and the amount transferred each year to the charity. But to do this, the donor has to report the income of the trust as his or her income. Therefore, the net effect of an improperly constructed trust agreement could be to raise the tax liability of the donor.

Furthermore, each trust has a different set of annuity tables and each annuity table differs according to the age and the number of noncharitable beneficiaries. What is important for the reader is to have a firm grasp of the descriptions and applications of each trust as described in this text. With a good tax and legal consultant specializing in estates and trusts, it is possible to construct trusts that yield a donor a higher rate of return on the gift than he or she was receiving prior to the gift.

Let us turn to two examples of advanced uses of these trusts now that we understand the basics.

AN ADVANCED APPLICATION OF A REMAINDER UNITRUST

Consider a remainder trust being set up and funded by a nonincome or low-income producing asset. The remainder trust is required to pay an annual sum to the noncharity; but its income from these types of assets is low or may even be nonexistent. A strategy is to set up the trust as a special type of unitrust, sometimes called a *net income* or *flip trust.* Under this arrangement, the trust would pay the donor the lower of the income actually realized by the trust or a fixed percentage of the trust's asset value as annually determined.

Let us say that the fixed percentage to be received by the noncharity is 8 percent of the value of the trust as assessed each year. The trust only earns 2 percent on its investment. The donor will get the 2 percent. And the trust will owe the donor the remaining 6 percent. This process continues until the trust actually earns a sufficient amount to pay the 8 percent of its value, at which time the payment formula will "flip" to the 8 percent. In the meantime, the difference accumulates and is a debt of the trust to the donor that can be made up in future years. Therefore, once the flip occurs, the donor would receive the 8 percent plus any make-up amount of the dollars not paid in the past.

Donors with high current income and expectations of lower income and lower taxes in the future can use this technique to postpone their annuities from the trust to sometime in the future when they expect to be in a lower tax bracket.

To do this four conditions must be met:

1. At least 90 percent of the assets funding the flip trust must be nonmarketable; that is, cannot be easily sold for fair market value at the time and, therefore, the donor cannot reasonably expect the fixed ratio either from earnings or from sales of the assets.

2. But the flip to the fixed percentage must automatically occur when the nonmarketable assets that funded the trust are sold or if the sale of any part of these assets means that less than 50 percent of the resulting value of the trust is attributable to the remaining nonmarketable assets.

3. The flip must occur in the very next fiscal year after any of these two previous events.

4. Once the flip has occurred to the fixed percentage, all future payments must be based on this percentage. There is only one flip allowed; that is, there is no flipping back.

AN ADVANCED APPLICATION OF A CHARITABLE LEAD TRUST

Enrique, a very wealthy donor, can afford to forego considerable annual earnings from an investment and wishes to help out his favorite charity, the Giselle Museum. He also wishes to pass on a considerable sum to his children upon his death but he is afraid that the tax on his estate would cut into this inheritance. In addition to helping his favorite charity and passing on a sizable inheritance to his children, he can reduce his current taxes, not by a charitable deduction, but by placing the assets into a charitable lead trust that donates the annual income to the charity. He neither claims this income nor deducts the contribution.

The tax advantage comes through the gift tax imposed upon his estate at the time of his death. How does this work? First, the present value of the annual flow of dollars from the trust to the charity is determined. Second, the fair market value of the gift he placed in the trust is determined. Third, the difference between the two is calculated. If the difference is zero, he pays no gift tax on passing that asset along to his heirs because the charitable contribution is equal to or greater than the amount he gives to his children.

Table 8.5 compares and summarizes some of the basic features of the trusts we have discussed. This summary may provide a quick reference to the advantages and disadvantages of these trusts. There are features they have in common. Each provides for a gift to the nonprofit that is deductible by the donor. Some provide for an annuity to the donor or beneficiaries while the remainder goes to the nonprofit. This remainder, depending on the financial and investment management of the gift, can be substantially larger than the initial gift. This is so because only a portion of the income in many cases will go to the donor. The remainder accumulates and grows with the investment experience of the fund, and the gift itself may appreciate several times in value by the time it is turned over to the nonprofit.

THE USES OF WILLS: GIFTS DEFERRED UNTIL DEATH

A gift through a will (a bequest) can be easily arranged. All that is basically necessary to make a gift in a will is a statement in the will to the effect that "I give, devise, and bequeath to . . . the . . . [amount of dollars or name of property]." It is the execution of the will at the time of death that can confound, and this can occur for several reasons. Let us start with the well-known case of Howard Hughes. At least 40 wills have turned up as being allegedly written by him. Most are declared forgeries. Hughes died in 1979, and in 1986, after the Supreme Court of the United States had appointed Wade McCree, former Solicitor General, as special master, settlements were being made but not yet complete.

There was even confusion about where Howard Hughes lived, and this had an impact on his will. Hence, the estate of Howard Hughes had to pay inheritance taxes to the states of Texas ($50 million in cash) and California ($119 million in cash and real estate), even though the lawyers for the estate had argued that his residence was in the state of Nevada, which had no inheritance taxes. Hughes had lived four of his last ten years in Nevada and forty years in California; he was born in Texas, but left when he was twenty years old and had not been in the state for 48 hours in the fifty years before he died. He had, in an attempt to escape California state taxes, frequently filed papers indicating that Texas was his state of residence.[5]

Table 8.5. Comparison of Advantages and Disadvantages of Trusts by Type.

	Type of Trust	Advantages	Disadvantages
Income Flow to Donor, Remainder to Charity	Pooled income	Small gifts can be placed in pool for more efficient investment management	Income must flow for life of one or more individuals, not for term; income usually is fully taxed
	Remainder unitrust	Income flows for life of one or more noncharity recipients or for a specified term; some or all of income may be untaxed; income keeps pace with growth of value	Because income is percentage of value year to year income declines if value declines
	Remainder annuity	Same as above except income is fixed percentage of initial value; income is protected against decline in value	Income does not keep pace with growth
Income Flow to Charity, Remainder to Donor	Guaranteed (Gift or Charitable) annuity	Income is assured	Assets of nonprofit exposed to need to pay donors guaranteed income
	Charitable lead unitrust	Flow of income to nonprofit keeps pace with growth of trust	Exposes recipient to tax liability if annual deduction chosen
	Charitable lead annuity	Flow of income to charity not jeopardized by slow growth	Same as above

In a case before the Chester County Courthouse in Westchester, Pennsylvania, the thirty-year-old widow of a millionaire was said to have spent her ninety-year-old deceased husband's $4 million fortune on personal expenses, travel, and gifts. His children and the charities that were named as beneficiaries in his will allegedly lost out because of her spending.[6]

Similarly, upon the death of Ron Hubbard, founder of the Church of Scientology, his will was challenged by a son who was disinherited because he had denounced his father and his church. The will provided a trust for his wife and four other children and a trust for the church.[7]

Football fans will remember the long delay in transferring funds from the estate of Jack Kent Cooke to the foundation he created because of the settlement of the sale of the Redskins. Which buyer was to be approved and at what price? The proceeds of the sale were to fund the foundation.

A will specifies how an individual's estate (all properties in which the decedent had an incidence of ownership) is to be distributed. A will must generally be written, signed, dated, and witnessed. Under some conditions, an oral will may have the force of law. Like a trust and a nonprofit corporation, a will must abide by the laws of the individual state. State laws also determine how property will be treated. For example, some properties are subject to taxation and valuation on the basis of their location (situs), whereas others are determined on the basis of the domicile of the deceased. State laws vary.

A will names an executor (male) or executrix (female) who is responsible for collecting all properties, paying all taxes and debt, preserving the value of the property, and distributing it according to the desires of the deceased. The executor or executrix, unlike the trustee, is nominated by the deceased but serves at the pleasure and approval of the court.

The court may or may not require that the executor or executrix be bonded. It is customary that the testator (the person to whom the will belongs) would not require bonding. Bonding is insurance to protect the creditors of the estate against the errors of the executor. Executors can be held liable for losses but cannot share in the gains made as a consequence of their actions. Therefore, the incentive for most executors is to do the minimum required to expeditiously settle an estate in a reasonable period.[8]

Estates comprise probate and nonprobate property. Probate property is distributed according to the terms of a will. Nonprobate property is distributed by the operation of the law or by contract or by agreement. If a property is owned through joint tenancy with the right of survivorship, or through tenancy in the entirety (as these terms are defined in Chapter Seven), or subject to claims of the government or creditors, or a spouse, such claims are honored without regard to the instructions in a will.

Wills can lead to disappointments. One source of disappointment is that the property supposedly given by bequest may not be probate property and may pass to another through the operation of the law, some previous agreement, or contract. It may not be the deceased's to give, for example, if the property is owned with rights of survivorship being held by another person.

Disappointment might occur for another reason. Promises in a will are not obligations of the testator. A person might change his or her will at will, so to speak. A nonprofit that was once a beneficiary can be dropped whenever the testator wishes.

Furthermore, the will may be too generous. James LaPorte, who is married, decided to leave all his property to his favorite nonprofit, but this will not work. A spouse, and often children, no matter how disliked, cannot be left with nothing. The spouse may go to court to "take against the will." The court may permit the spouse to take between one-third to one-half of the estate despite the will. The nonprofits might be left out, have a reduced share of the estate, and have to wait a long time as legal battles are fought.

Worse yet, the entire will could be invalid. This may result if the will or any codicil (amendment) does not conform with the law (or if the will was not signed, dated, or prepared by a person mentally competent and acting freely). There might be a later will. Any of these could cause the will to be invalidated. Even if the will is valid, it may be rescinded if written at the point of death and testator does not die. And even if death occurs, such a will may be rescinded if the cause of death is different than specified as a condition of the gift.

Still other problems could occur. If the amount being given is a residual after all other donees and legal and tax matters are taken care of, there might be nothing left. Here again state laws come into play. These laws, known as abatement laws, govern how an estate is distributed when it is not large enough to cover all distributees. When the amount going to a nonprofit is the residual rather than a specific amount taken off the top, there might be nothing for the nonprofit to receive.

Despite these uncertainties, wills are necessary if deathtime gifts are to be made. If a person dies intestate, without a will, no provision is made by state law for contributions to nonprofits. Distributions are made to a legally married spouse, children, parents, and the state. Brothers and sisters may, like nonprofits, get nothing.

Even if the nonprofit is named in the will, it makes a difference how it is named. Table 8.6 summarizes the risks of not getting anything when a nonprofit depends upon transfer of properties at the time of death even though there may be a will. These risks vary by the way the nonprofit is named by the donor. The weakest position is to be included among the residue, because the residue is what's left over after all other gifts and liabilities are paid. This may be zero or a very large number. At the other extreme, if one is the owner through

Table 8.6. Relative Risk of Bequests Through a Will.

Rank	Status of Nonprofit in Estate Settlement
1	Ownership, lifetime or by survivorship: automatic ownership
2	Irrevocable beneficiary: cannot be removed
3	Beneficiary: can be removed without warning
4	Specific bequest: gets only a specific amount or property if available
5	Residue: gets what's left over

Note: Number 1 is the strongest position, and 5 is weakest.

survivorship, the property gets passed automatically and is not determined by the will at all.

Also, gifts occurring at death are more favorably treated than gifts made during one's lifetime. The latter are subject to deductible limits as described in Chapter Seven, but there are no limits to how much one may give to a charity at time of death—once all legal claims are satisfied.

Hence, if the property has appreciated substantially, a deathtime rather than a lifetime gift may be advantageous to the donor, since there are no limits to the amount that can be given at death and still receive a tax deduction. But there are also advantages to the nonprofit. This is particularly true if the nonprofit would be subject to unrelated business income tax on the appreciated value of the property when sold because the property was subject to debt as described in Chapter Ten.[9] To illustrate, if James LaPorte purchases a property for $50,000 but paid only $25,000, so that the property is subject to debt, and the property appreciated to $200,000, and if he bequeathed the property to his favorite nonprofit, the nonprofit will receive it at the value at the time of his death.[10] This value would be $200,000. If, however, the gift were made just before his death, the appreciation on which the tax would be calculated would be $175,000 ($150,000 in appreciation plus the $25,000 owed).

Finally, death-time gifts give the donor a lifetime to decide among potential donees and to enjoy the property, secure in the knowledge that he or she will have no use for it after death. Little wonder that the largest single gifts take effect at death.

LIFE INSURANCE: MAGNIFYING THE VALUE OF SMALL GIFTS

Through life insurance policies, it is possible for persons of modest means to make gifts of hundreds of thousands of dollars. Therefore, anyone can give well above his or her means. When the person departs, the policy matures and death benefits received by the nonprofit are many times larger than premiums paid by the donor.

Insurance allows the donor to stretch out a gift. This is the case when the donor makes a gift of a policy that requires periodic premium payments. In this way, the organization gets a regular and long-lasting commitment for an annual donation—the premiums—and it maintains contact to facilitate additional giving.

If the policy is one that accumulates savings, called *cash value,* the organization also gets a valuable pool of funds that it can use within years, even though the donor is very much alive. Moreover, regular premium payments shift the burden of fund-raising to the insurance company, which sends the donor notices of when the premium is due. It replaces the telephone call and letter from the nonprofit asking for annual donations.

Death and the Collection of Gift

An insurance policy may be used to make a joint gift. Frequently, a husband and wife may want to make a joint gift to a nonprofit. If each bought an insurance policy separately, it would be more expensive than if they bought it jointly. In a joint policy, sometimes called *last to die,* both persons should agree to take out and to give the policy to the nonprofit. This strategy has some peculiarities that call for caution. One is that joint policies often pay only after the last of the two persons has died, hence its nicknames "last-to-die" and "survivor" policy. Some policies pay only a portion of the face value after the first has died; the balance is paid at the death of the second person.

Even though the death of the first spouse could yield no immediate benefit to the nonprofit, this does not make such a strategy useless. The nonprofit will get some or all of the proceeds eventually; both parties will die. In the meantime, the cash value (if it is provided in the contract) and collateral value of the policy are always available as long as the organization owns the policy.

Alternatively, a policy could be bought on the life of each person separately and the proceeds will be obtained by the nonprofit on each person's death rather than upon the eventual death of both. These policies are more expensive than joint policies.

Ownership

A gift of insurance must be carefully planned, for an insurance policy that is owned by the donor, even if it is being held by the nonprofit, is subject to the control of the donor. The owner can cancel the policy or permit it to lapse so that it no longer exists. Nothing bars an owner from dropping the name of the nonprofit as beneficiary. If any of these happens, the nonprofit will not collect, even though it may have the policy in its possession. Furthermore, if the policy is owned by the donor, he or she may borrow on it. Should that be done and the loan not be repaid prior to the death of the donor, the proceeds that will go to the nonprofit will be the face value minus the amount of indebtedness. In short, the nonprofit could end up with less than the face value if there is outstanding indebtedness.

The outcome could be worse if the owner used the policy as collateral for a loan. In that case, depending on state law, the creditor of the donor may have first claim. Not only will the amount obtained by the nonprofit be less than the face value, but the nonprofit could get nothing at all if in the process of getting the loan made a permanent assignment of the policy to the creditor. A permanent assignment cannot be reversed; the creditor owns the policy as long as the credit is outstanding and even then until it is formerly released.

Also, an insurance policy that is owned by the donor may be included in his or her estate even though it is in the physical possession of the nonprofit. This could mean that some or all the proceeds may be subject to estate (not income) tax, and some or all the proceeds could be subject to the claims of the creditors of the donor and to claims of the donor's spouse should the latter choose to take against the will. Insurance proceeds, while exempt from income tax, are not automatically exempt from estate tax. The donor must have either (1) named the nonprofit or any other qualified charity as a beneficiary of the policy, or (2) designated them as donees of the proceed as it goes through the estate.

These difficulties as the proceeds go through the estate may not be resolved in favor of the nonprofit even if it could prove that it paid the premiums. Ironically, one possible interpretation of paying the premiums is that the nonprofit in its charitable benevolence made a nondeductible gift to the insured. The point simply is that the nonprofit should own, not merely hold, the policy. It does this by being sure that its name appears on the policy not only as beneficiary but also as owner.

Ownership and possession of the policy give the nonprofit another benefit. The nonprofit does not have to wait for the donor to die; for, as owner, the nonprofit may assign the policy, use it as collateral for loans, or borrow the cash value of the policy. The nonprofit will also be able to avoid the creditors of the donor and legal fights over the instructions in the will. The policy will be nonprobate property, meaning that it will escape the legal hassle, delays, costs, and claims that are likely in the settlement of an estate.

The insert in the box on page 248 reviews ownership options and outcomes.

Form of Gift

The donor does not have to purchase insurance or use a paid-up policy in order to make a gift. It is possible to make a gift of insurance in the form of the face value in excess of $50,000 in a qualified employee insurance contract, as discussed in Chapter Thirteen. Such a gift is not likely to bring any deduction to the donor, but the excess premium is not taxable as income. The employer

Life Insurance Risks by Ownership Option

Risks to which the nonprofit is exposed under various ownership options:

Option 1. The donor owns the policy and names the nonprofit as a beneficiary on the policy. The donor may change beneficiary unless the nonprofit is named an *irrevocable* beneficiary. In either case, the risks are the use of the cash value by the donor, and cessation of payments by donor without knowledge of nonprofit but with nonownership precluding the nonprofit from picking up payments. This strategy avoids probate and lump-sum proceeds go directly to the nonprofit tax free.

Option 2. The donor owns the policy and makes his or her estate the beneficiary. The nonprofit can collect only if donor's will so specifies. As part of the estate, an additional risk is that the proceeds become exposed to creditors of both the decedent and the estate itself and may be used not only to satisfy such debt but also to pay taxes of the estate and to satisfy other beneficiaries, such as spouse and dependent children. Probate and settlement of estate may prolong receiving gift.

Option 3. The nonprofit owns the policy. Upon death, the proceeds go directly to the nonprofit without probate and without exposure to creditors of the decedent or the estate. IRS private ruling 9110016 reminds us to check state law to be sure that insurable interest, defined as at risk of economic loss if person dies, is satisfied. If not, a federal donation may be denied.

Key to all options: To reduce default of nonpayment of premiums, have donor make annual gift of at least premium amount directly to nonprofit, which uses it to pay premium.

who pays the excess may deduct it if it is customary for the firm to give in this fashion. Many corporations are offering a similar option to their officers and directors, who choose which charity they wish to be beneficiaries.

A gift of insurance can be made in the form of an outright gift of the contract itself; or the policy could be placed in a trust. The trust should be irrevocable, permitting an immediate tax deduction for the gift and immediate ownership by the nonprofit. The deduction of premiums can be lost, however, if the trust is not properly set up, because an insurance policy in a trust is a future interest, as discussed in Chapter Seven, since the gift cannot be obtained until the person dies. To qualify the premium payments for immediate tax deduction, the trust agreement should contain a promise to make the premium available to the nonprofit at the time premiums are paid. The nonprofit need not take the money; it must simply have the option to do so. Lawyers call this amendment a *Crummey clause*.

If the insurance policy is in a trust, there is a second concern; the policy could be considered to have been acquired by debt and, as discussed earlier, lead to unrelated business income tax. To avoid this, the trust agreement should not permit a person who is a noncharitable beneficiary to have an interest in the income of the trust that exceeds the person's lifetime. That is, all such interests should cease upon the person's death so that the remainder goes to the charitable beneficiary rather than being bequeathed by the person to some other beneficiary.

A gift of insurance may also be made through a will at the time of death. The will might provide for the formation of a trust or for outright gift of the insurance proceeds to the nonprofit. One disadvantage of giving at the time of death is that the proceeds must be included in the donor's estate, albeit that a 100 percent tax deduction is available for charitable donation. It precludes, however, any annual deduction for premiums paid.

As part of the estate, the insurance proceeds are also exposed to the claims of the creditors of the deceased. Also, if the gift is made by a trust that becomes irrevocable at the time of death, the charity is less protected, since there is some passage of time, generally after the federal taxes are paid, before the trust becomes a charitable trust and subject to the rules covering private foundations. These rules protect the corpus of a trust for charitable purposes.

There is no single best strategy for using life insurance as a gift. The "best" strategy depends first on the financial position of the donor and the needs of the organization. Each strategy that has been mentioned should be considered. Each strategy is implemented through an insurance policy, which is a contract. As we shall see next, there are several contract or policy options.

Types of Policies

The *universal-life* policies give the donor a considerable amount of flexibility. He or she may vary the amount and timing of premium payments or change the face value of the contract. For example, some years the donor may pay more than the minimum premium required. The excess is used to build up a side account called the *cash value,* which gains interest. In a year when the donor cannot afford to pay, the cash value may be used to pay the premiums. Alternatively, the donor may reduce the face value of the policy and pay the lower premium or increase the face value (called *death benefit*) by increasing the premium. A universal life's selling point is that it can be tailored to match the current circumstances of a donor and still provide a benefit during his or her lifetime and also at death.

Some universal plans provide for the policy to be paid up in a specific number of years, often seven. These are usually good for a nonprofit because it can receive a fully paid-up policy in seven rather than twenty or even ninety-five years. In addition, like the universal life, these policies provide cash value for the use of the nonprofit while the donor lives and the death benefit (decreased by the amount of cash value used) when the insured dies. In addition, the non-profit has a shorter period to worry about a default by a donor. The deal is completed in seven years. Because the annual payments in these policies are larger (so that they can be fully paid up in seven years), they are very expensive, but they offer a large tax deduction to the donor and a large cash value to the nonprofit.

Unlike universal-life policies, *whole-life* policies do not provide for variations in premiums or death benefits. Both premiums and benefits are fixed at the time the policy is bought. Now the nonprofit takes a greater risk. If the donor defaults, the policy lapses unless the nonprofit pays or there is enough cash value to pay the premium that is due. When a policy lapses, it terminates. Whole-life policies provide certainty of premiums and death benefits, as long as the circumstances of the donor do not change. With a universal life, the death benefit can be reduced to meet a lower ability to pay. With a whole life, that is not possible, although some companies would consider reissuing a completely new policy.

At the other extreme is *single-premium* life insurance. In this case, the donor pays off the policy in one single sum at the time the policy is bought. The paid premium qualifies for a tax deduction. In these policies, as in the case of universal life, the nonprofit has the cash value, which it can borrow. It also has the death benefit that will be paid when the donor dies. The advantages of a single-premium policy are that the nonprofit need not worry about default. There is no need to make continuous payments because the total required sum would have been paid at the outset. The nonprofit also gets the cash value while the insured lives if it owns the policy. It gets the death benefit when the donor dies.

Let me give a specific example: Clara Springer, forty-six years old, purchased a policy with a face value of $100,000 for $22,100 and gave it to a favorite charity, which is now the owner. She got to deduct $22,100; the church gets the $100,000 when she dies. In the meantime it gets to borrow on the account, which grows at, say, 9 percent tax deferred. In about eight years at 9 percent, this account would have in excess of $40,000 that would be available for use by the church.

A person may have a life insurance policy that has already been paid up. There will be no more annual premiums. Hence, a gift of these policies to a non-profit means that the donor gets a deduction without ever making an out-of-pocket transfer of cash now or in the future. Upon the death of the donor, the organization gets the face value of the insurance minus any outstanding debt, that is, unrepaid withdrawals made during the life of the donor. Prior to the death of the donor, the organization gets to use the cash value in the policy. For an older person who never took a loan or withdrawal, this could be very large, depending on how long ago the policy was taken out and the untaxed interest it earned.

Even *term* policies, those that do not accumulate cash values, are suitable gifts because they are inexpensive. In dealing with term policies, the organization would want to know the term; is it one, seven, ten, twenty, thirty, or a hundred years? Is it level or decreasing? A one-year term means that if the donor does not die within that year the institution gets nothing. The same principle corresponds to seven, ten, fifteen, twenty, thirty, a hundred, or any other term. Since most people will not live to be a hundred, such a term policy does assure some benefits to the organization.

The amount of benefits in any term policy depends on whether the face value of the contract is level, increasing, or decreasing. If the term is level, then the death benefit is constant throughout the term of the contract. It is the same whether the person dies in the first or last year of the contract. If it is a decreasing term, then the amount that the organization is due upon the death of the donor decreases the older the donor gets. A decreasing hundred-year term policy with an initial death benefit of $100,000 would be worth approximately $10,000 if the person dies at age sixty-five. Yet the person would only have paid about $7,000 in premiums during that time.

For this small difference, would it not be better to make a direct contribution to the nonprofit, giving it the advantage of having the money on hand to invest rather than waiting? Not necessarily. The advantage of insurance, even term, over regular donations is that it immediately magnifies the gift. In the above case, if the donor paid the annual premium of, say, $300 and then dies after the first, second, third, or even fifth year, the organization would get approximately $100,000. It would have cost the donor a total of $200, $600, $900, or $1,500 in premiums, depending on how long he or she lives, minus the charitable gift deduction. The organization would have foregone anywhere from $98,500 to $99,700 if instead of an insurance policy the donor had made a direct gift of cash. A selling attraction of term is that it is inexpensive.

Comparing Characteristics of Contracts

Life insurance, through the death benefits, magnifies a gift many times. This is leverage. All policies except term provide for a cash value, which is the money that accumulates with interest. This money can be borrowed, used as collateral, used to pay premiums, or even used to purchase additional insurance on the donor with the same company.[11]

The dollars that accumulate grow according to the interest being paid and the length of time it is permitted to remain undistributed. The amount borrowed *never* has to be repaid and neither does the interest on the loan, which is generally well below market rate and fixed in the contract at the time the insurance is bought. Any principal and interest owed at the time of death are subtracted from the face value. Hence, a $100,000 face value would lead to a death proceed going to the nonprofit of $90,000 if the sum of the interest and principal due as a result of the loan is $10,000.

It may be useful to compare all we have said in tabular form. How does one type of insurance match the other?

Table 8.7 summarizes four types of policies based on their generic nature. Term policies are the cheapest and single-premium policies are the most expensive; but the amount of leverage is just the reverse. That is, if the donor should die immediately or within a few years after the creation of the gift, the death benefit per dollar of premium paid is highest with a term policy and lowest with a single-premium; hence, the term gets you a lot more dollars per dollar invested.[12] However, term policies have no loan value and require the longest period of donor commitment, since the premiums must be paid every year until either the policy ends or the donor dies.

Universal life is the most flexible. Flexibility is not an issue with single premiums because the policy is fully paid up at the inception. Generally, there is no flexibility with whole-life or term policies, although some companies will sell term policies in which you may in the future elect a different premium or a face value. On the other extreme is the single premium. It is the most expensive, but it requires the least amount of donor commitment—only long enough to write the check. It also creates the biggest nest egg that can be used by the nonprofit.

Because insurance companies are imaginative in how they configure a policy, Table 8.7 should be considered a guide as to the fundamentals. When working with a potential donor, illustrations of specific and actual policies should be used. The companies will gladly supply them.

In recent years a whole-life policy called a *split-dollar policy* has become a popular policy for the wealthy to use in making a contribution. Such a policy

Table 8.7. Insurance Policies by Characteristics.

Type	Cost	Leverage[a]	Loan[b]	Flexibility	Length of Commitment Required
Term	1	4	1	2	4
Universal	2	3	2	4	2
Whole life	3	2	3	3	3
Single premium	4	1	4	1	1

Key: 1 = lowest.

[a]Death benefits relative to premium costs.

[b]Cash value.

splits the interest into a cash value amount and the proceeds available at death. One of these goes to the charity and the other to the nonprofit beneficiary.

ROLE OF INSURANCE IN FUND-RAISING STRATEGY

Insurance policies are morbid. When Boston University launched a campaign to have its alumni buy insurance policies and make it their beneficiary and owner, the announcement was met with cynicism. Yet it is said that when St. Louis University launched its insurance program, it was met with enthusiasm and success.[13]

Life insurance should be part of an overall fund-raising package. Instead of launching an insurance campaign, launch a campaign in which insurance is one possibility. This requires the organization to know how insurance can best fit into the ability and taste of potential donors. Then choose the right policy and always try to be the owner and be prepared to explain the benefits to the donor; insurance turns people of moderate income into philanthropists, and when the nonprofit owns the policy, probate and estate taxes are avoided, the nonprofit can make premium payments, and it can also use the cash value for loans and the policy for collateral.

Many nonprofits that have tried insurance policies have run into nonpayments of premiums by donors. This is to be expected as not all pledges are ever paid. This translates into a credit-management problem not unlike those faced by every pledge campaign and every business that extends credit. There are three actions the nonprofit can take to minimize the risk of unpaid premium. First, educate the donor. Second, choose policies that require few premium payments. Many policies can be paid up in one to seven years, thus matching short periods of donor enthusiasm and commitment.

Finally, the nonprofit should determine how much of its fund-raising budget it can spend each year to make unpaid premiums so that policies would not lapse. It should pay these premiums only if it owns the policy (otherwise, it would be making a loan or a gift to the owner, who may then change the beneficiary). The nonprofit can then collect at a later date from the donor, who will then get a tax deduction for his or her donated premiums. Even if the donor does not reimburse it, the nonprofit will collect if the donor dies. The donor cannot change the beneficiary if the nonprofit owns the policy. The risks of paying these premiums even if the nonprofit owns the policy are that the proceeds could be taxable and state laws could deny that the nonprofit has an insurable interest (that is, that the organization is at risk).

Mix Strategies

Life insurance can also be part of a mix strategy. For example, suppose an elderly person wishes to put a home in a remainder trust but she has relatives who would possibly be angered. Or suppose that the nonprofit is concerned about having to repair the home. It can get the donor to agree to purchase an annual term insurance policy on her life. The proceeds can be used to make the repairs or to pay off the relatives.[14]

Another example of mix strategy: Percy Pouff promises a gift of $1 million to be delivered in seven years. The nonprofit now has an insurable interest in him. It buys a policy to cover him during this period. When he delivers the million dollars the nonprofit may exchange the policy for it, discontinue its premium payments, or keep the policy alive.[15]

Sometimes a *replacement* strategy is used. It allows a donor to make a gift and then use an insurance policy to replace it in dollar terms.

Safety

Insurance policies are reasonably safe even when the company is shaky. Insurance companies are required to carry reserves to cover their potential claims, and most insurance companies also engage in reinsurance. This is a process through which companies try not to keep too many high-risk policies on their books. By prior agreement, through reinsurance they sell some of these to other companies. Moreover, in all but six states, the insurance companies guarantee payments through an insurance pool, thus protecting the citizens of that state against the bankruptcy of any company selling in that state. For added protection, make sure the insurance company is financially sound. Insurance companies are rated in several ways, including their ability to settle claims.

Insurance policies and premiums are also calculated and designed based on actuarial calculations (the probability that a person of a certain age, sex, and health condition will die within a given period). The insurance company is not taking a wild gamble when it insures someone; it is taking a calculated risk and protecting against it through the creation of reserves, its investment, and future sales policies.

Of course, risk can vary depending on whether the annuity or insurance policy is one with a fixed proceed or a proceed that varies with the performance of the stock market. But this risk is determined by the choice of the donor.

The Deductible Value

From the donor's point of view, when a policy is given makes a considerable amount of difference in the value for tax-deduction purposes and in the cost to the donor. The value of an insurance policy that has just been issued is the gross premium paid. If a policy has just been issued to the donor and the premium on it is $500, all that can be deducted is $500. But $500 can buy over a $100,000 in insurance for a person under thirty-five years of age. The benefit to the nonprofit is therefore $100,000. What leverage! In addition, regular contributions to the organization that can be used to pay annual premiums qualify as taxable deductions.

The tax-deductible value of a policy that is fully paid up is its replacement cost at the donor's age at the time the gift is made. Giving a paid-up policy might be a superior strategy for an older person rather than a younger one, particularly if the policy is one that was taken out many years before and is no longer needed. A newly paid-up policy, called a single premium, is expensive—ordinarily a minimum of $5,000.

In between these two extremes is a permanent policy that is presently being paid for, and the value of such a policy is roughly its cash value. It is the amount accumulated as savings up to the point the gift was made. This is the approximate (not the exact) amount that can be deducted. The cash value is shown in the policy. The value of a policy on which premiums are still being paid may involve the estimation of its permutated value—premiums minus dividends and withdrawals are all calculated on a present-value basis. No nonprofit would attempt calculating this.

ANNUITIES: PROVIDING INCOME FLOWS

Annuities are merely payments that must be made over a period of time. Unitrust, annuity trusts, and pooled trusts all pay annuities. Sometimes the annuity is paid to the donor or a noncharitable designated beneficiary and sometimes it is paid to a charity, as in charitable lead trusts.

In Chapter Thirteen, we discuss the possibilities of a worker giving his or her pension annuity to a nonprofit. Let us anticipate that discussion briefly. In the giving or receiving of annuities, care must be taken that the potential donor actually owns the annuity. Most pension annuities have a period that must lapse before the accounts are vested and fully owned by the future annuitant. Until that time has elapsed, the person does not own the balance in the account and is not legally able to donate it, even though the account may be in his or her name. Also, the surviving spouse may have a legal claim on the annuity.

The value of annuities for tax-deduction purposes is determined by finding its present value after discounting at a rate announced by the IRS quarterly. Basically, this value is the amount that would have to be invested today at a specific interest rate given by the IRS so that the annuity would be worth the amount promised at a time in the future. This formula is used in calculating an annuity provided by an employer. If there is a going market for the type of annuity to be donated, that is, if the annuity is a commercial one, then the value is its replacement cost.

Guaranteed or Charitable Gift Annuities

In the case of gift annuities, the donor gives the nonprofit a large amount of money or property with the understanding that the nonprofit will guarantee a specific annual payment to the donor or to some other person for life or for the joint lives of two or more persons. Gift annuities are not issued for a term less than life.

The payments may be immediate, meaning commencing one year after the gift was made, or they may be deferred to sometime after. The promise to make this payment is backed by all the assets of the nonprofit. Can you see what happens when the earnings of the pool of money given to the nonprofit are too small to make the payments promised? Yes, the assets have to be liquidated in order to meet the payments. This caused many of these annuities to go bankrupt during the Depression.

The way a modern financial planner for a nonprofit should use a gift annuity today is as follows. The donor wishes to make a gift but needs an income flow. Unlike the property that may create a remainder trust, the property in a gift annuity may be unable to do so; or even if it could, the nonprofit wants to protect against defaulting in payments because of a downturn in the cash being generated by the assets. What is the solution? The nonprofit takes the property and then turns to an insurance company and buys an annuity that will generate the income required to meet the guarantee payments to the donor. As an example, Calvin decides to give an art piece with a market value of $1 million. He needs an income. The Ellis Malcom Art Center accepts the gift. It then uses $487,000 to buy an annuity to pay Calvin at age fifty-nine an annual sum of $50,000 for the remainder of his life. Part of this payment to him may be tax free if it includes any part of the capital used to purchase the annuity by the nonprofit.

Notice that the risk of payment is shifted from the nonprofit to an insurance company. The nonprofit is no longer at risk. Calvin's deduction would roughly be $1 million minus the $487,000, which is the present value (the amount presently needed) to generate an income of $50,000 for the remainder of his life.

A gift of annuity is unlike a remainder or charitable lead trust because it is not necessarily the same property that passes from the donor to the trust and then to the nonprofit or back to the donor or some other noncharitable persons. Furthermore, in some states, gift annuities are regulated and therefore state law should be consulted. For federal tax purposes a gift annuity must either be in the form of a trust or an insurance contract.

Application of Charitable Gift Annuities

Gift annuities must also be concerned with the unrelated business income tax. Let us illustrate this with one of the most common uses of a gift annuity. Clive makes a gift to a university. It gives him an annuity and names one beneficiary and one alternative, who are his children. The life annuity (annual payments) may be used to pay the beneficiary's tuition at the school or to make other payments to another school or any other person. This is a common nontaxable use of gift annuities, and this specific case is based on Private Letter Ruling 9042043.

What conditions are necessary to avoid the unrelated business income tax?

1. The annuity should be the only thing—called *consideration*—the donor receives in exchange for the gift.
2. It must be less than 90 percent of the value of the donation.
3. Payment must be scheduled over the life of one or two individuals alive (not unborn) at the time the gift was made.
4. The issuing of annuities must not be a substantial part of the activities of the recipient organization.
5. The contract must not guarantee a minimum payment or maximum payments that vary with changing values of the original gift.[16]

STEPS FOR DETERMINING DEFERRED GIVING INSTRUMENTS

The settlement of the Barron Hilton estates is a good example of some of the principles we have reviewed. Hilton was chairman and president of the Hilton Hotels. It took nine years to settle a dispute over his will. The settlement created a charitable remainder trust in which was placed his sizable gift of Hilton Hotel stocks to the Conrad H. Hilton Foundation. The foundation supports Catholic nuns throughout the world. His son, Conrad, will be a trustee (if not the sole trustee of the trust). At the end of his life or after twenty years, whichever comes sooner, all of the assets of the trust will be turned over to the foundation. What should guide?

1. Be sure that the financial position, responsibilities, and intent of the prospective donor are understood and that they drive the choice. Sophisticated deferred giving is like making a business deal. It works well when both parties can claim satisfaction.
2. Be sure that you understand the basic properties of each type of trust, insurance, and the risk associated with testamentary gifts. Discuss the options.
3. Have your legal counsel meet with the potential donor and his or her counsel. Your counsel should be guided by what is best for the donor and what is consistent with the objectives of the organization. You cannot leave your lawyer alone to determine these facts. Exercise your opinion about the instrument as well as about its details. Your organization, not the lawyer, is at risk.
4. Think of mix strategies.
5. Be patient. These types of deals take time.

ENDOWMENTS: PERPETUATING A GIFT

Any of the mechanisms discussed in this chapter and in Chapter Seven may be used for funding an endowment. An endowment is an account that is established to have perpetual life and to finance a specified set of activities. The endowment may be a separate nonprofit corporation.

To fund an endowment is merely to put money or other property in it. An endowment can therefore be funded singularly or in combination with outright gifts and contributions, annuities, life insurance, and lifetime or testamentary gifts.

Use of Endowments

An endowment serves several important purposes. One purpose is to provide a pool of funds to which the organization can turn in an emergency. As such, it gives some financial stability and quick-response capability to the organization.

A closely related use occurs when the endowment is used to cover shortfalls between the expenditures and revenues of the organization. Continuous invasion of an endowment for this purpose, however, is not to be encouraged. This problem should be solved by better financial management. These types of "endowments" are usually set up as board-designated restricted funds. Sometimes the trustees will approve an interfund transfer from an endowment to operating funds. The Philadelphia Orchestra Association, for example, set up an income stabilization fund to offset operating deficits. The fund is financed by transfers from general operations.

Endowments provide a source of funds that the organization may use to finance activities that are important to it but for which it cannot readily obtain support from outside sources. Many organizations use endowments to finance activities that are innovative, experimental, and developmental. When used this way, the endowment serves to push the organization forward. It helps the organization carry out its mission without having to meet the constraints and demands of an outside funding agency.

An endowment might be used to separate out and finance specific charitable missions.

Endowments are sometimes required by funding sources to ensure the organization's financial stability and to reduce its decline.

Endowments provide for accumulating funds to finance long-term and major activities or acquisitions by the organization. In this vein are building funds, scholarships, and so on.

Spending from an Endowment

All these ideal uses of endowments can be defeated, however, if (1) the endowment is unintentionally exhausted, and (2) restrictions are violated.

Let's deal with these in turn. In practice, there is something called an *exhaustible* or *expendable endowment*. These are really restricted funds that may be treated as though they were endowments. So sometimes the term *quasi-endowment* is used. A true endowment is a perpetuity even though for some purposes, such as life annuities, it may be defined in terms of life expectancy.

A quasi-endowment connotes that the principal—not just the earnings—of the fund may be spent. This implies that the fund could be exhausted or totally expended. Even in these cases, however, unless the conditions specified in the gifts call for total exhaustion, management is wise to treat these funds as true endowments—perpetuities.

Structure of Endowment

An endowment should be organized around four functions or responsibility centers: (1) revenue-raising, (2) investment management, (3) disbursement, (4) guardian or stewardship. Figure 8.1 shows the structure of an endowment. Note that the investment advisor and custodian report to the committee of the trustees of the organization, even though they may do this through the CEO. They, like auditors, are accountable directly to the trustees.

The investment advisors make investment recommendations and invest the funds. In large endowments there may be several advisors competing with the funds assigned them. Advisors may specialize—oil, stock, bonds, real estate, and so on. The custodian's job is to hold the funds or securities. Custodians are often banks.

The revenue function is what fund-raising does. It feeds the endowment portfolio with seed money and a continuous flow of fresh funds. Natural lapse

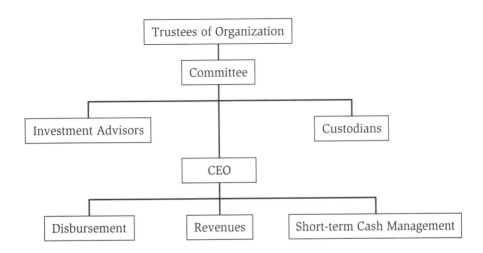

Figure 8.1. Organization of an Endowment.

of time means that these funds rarely go directly to the investment advisor. During the interim, they should be managed as short-term cash. From there the funds pass to the discretion of the investment advisor, who, given the limits placed on that discretion by the trustees, proceeds to invest.

Annually, the trustees review this performance and make decisions about whether to retain an advisor or change the amount under his or her guidance. They also decide how much to disburse from the endowment. Many endowments operate by simple, fixed rules set by the board of trustees. For example, it may disburse only a fixed percentage of the total endowment or a fixed percentage of its growth. Its growth may be calculated for the most recent year or for the most recent couple of years. For example, the board of trustees may decide that every year they will calculate the amount of earnings (dividends and appreciation) in the portfolio for the most recent five years and disburse only 5 percent of that amount.

One advantage of using a moving average (using the last five years) is that it smoothes out variations. If the organization used only the most recent year, if that is a good year the disbursement will be high; if it is a very poor year, the disbursement will be very low. The objective should always be to (1) develop a simple rule, and (2) enable the endowment principal or corpus to be preserved and grow so as to finance future needs.

Endowments as Community Foundations

Community foundations are public charities, most of which meet the 10 percent rather than the one-third public support test discussed in Chapter Four. A community foundation is, in reality, a consolidated endowment supporting, as a 509(a)(3), a group of local charities. It is an alternative to a private foundation. It is consolidated because it can consolidate a number of gifts and endowments into one by meeting four conditions: (1) being a legal entity with a name, (2) having one board of directors that oversees all gifts, (3) consolidating all reporting, and (4) having a common governing document over all gifts. In lieu of setting up a private foundation, a donor may make a named gift to a community foundation and designate the causes or specific local organizations that are to be funded in the name of the donor. All the fiduciary rules apply.

Endowments as Private Foundations

An endowment is subject to the rules of a private foundation. This means that the trustees must be concerned with transactions with disqualified persons, self-dealing, the distribution of income, jeopardy of investments, excess business holdings, prohibited expenditures, unrelated business income—all of which we have discussed in this book. In short, the endowment is a nonprofit organization in its own right. It can even be a 509(a)(3), subject to the strict fiduciary rules that we discussed under private foundations in our discussion of the role of trustees.

Donor-Designated Trusts as an Endowment Offered by Mutual Funds

A donor-designated trust is one in which the donor makes an irrevocable contribution to a fund (a mutual fund) and annual contributions thereafter. The donor may then designate the beneficiaries of that fund and provide for annual payments to be made to the beneficiaries. The donor may name the fund—and to some extent—is allowed to change beneficiaries. It is an alternative to a community foundation, which, in turn, is an alternative to private foundations. One advantage of a donor-designated fund is that the charitable beneficiary can be in any part of the country. Community foundations have the local area as their first priority, although some may fund projects outside that area to the extent that they have an impact on the area; for example, the funding of an evaluation project or demonstration project elsewhere as long as the results are relevant to similar situations in the local community. Donor-designed mutual funds are new and controversial entrants into the giving market. They are controversial partly because mutual funds are clearly for-profit enterprises competing with nonprofit foundations. Is this unfair?

THE LAW AND THE INVESTMENT OF ENDOWMENT AND OTHER INSTITUTIONAL FUNDS

Indiana's law on the Uniform Management of Institutional Funds applies to endowments, community trusts, nonprofit corporations, associations (whether incorporated or not), or any combination of these. Its only clear exceptions are religious organizations and when the gift instrument contains other restrictions by the donor who can restrict the use of all or any portions of any kind of income—rents, royalties, interest, dividends, capital gains in the fund at the time the gift was made.

The law gives the governing body, after it has adopted a resolution to incorporate the law in its bylaws, the power to expend any net appreciation, realized or unrealized, in the fair market value of the endowment over its historic value. This historic value is the value at the commencement of the endowment, its value after each contribution has been made, and its accumulation at the time. The law states that "the determination of historic dollar value made in good faith by the governing board is conclusive." Notice that this broad discretion applies only to net appreciation—not to the principal or the corpus.

Subject to law and subject to the restrictions in the gift instrument, the trustees may (and I quote):

1. Invest and reinvest an institutional fund in any real or personal property considered advisable by the governing board, whether or not the property produces a current return, including mortgages, stocks, bonds, debentures, and other securities of for profit or not-for-profit corporations, shares in or obligations of associations, limited liability companies, partnerships, or individuals, and obligations of any governmental entity, sub-division of that entity, or instrumentality of that entity.

2. Retain property contributed by a donor to an institutional fund as long as the governing board considers it advisable.

3. Include all or part of an institutional fund in a pooled or common fund maintained by the institution.

4. Invest all or part of an institutional fund in another pooled or common fund available for investment, including shares or interests in regulated investment companies, mutual funds, common trust funds, investment partnerships, real estate investment trusts, or similar organizations in which funds are commingled and investment determinations are made by persons other than the governing board.

The board may also

1. Delegate to committees, officer, agents (including investment counsel), or employees of the institution or the institutional fund the authority to act in place of the board in investment and reinvestment of institutional funds.

2. Contract with independent investment advisors, investment counsel or managers, banks or trust companies to act in place of the board in investment and reinvestment of institutional funds.

3. Authorize the payment of compensation for investment advisory or management services.

The trustees are expected to discharge these responsibilities in good faith and with prudence. Again, the law requires adherence first to the restrictions imposed by the donor. The trustees are empowered to seek release of such restrictions by agreement of the donor and by *cy pres* (by the courts). The conditions of that will favor a favorable *cy pres* decision are discussed in Chapter Fifteen. If released from restrictions, the funds must be used for some other purpose in the organization.

Many states, including New Hampshire and California, either give nonprofits the right to create investment pools, sometimes called *common funds,* or the state may create an agency that is such a pool for the benefit of the nonprofits.

In almost all states, there are rules concerning how the nonprofit will handle its own funds. Some states merely speak to the improper distribution of funds to trustees and officers. Some deal directly with investment.

California 5240–5241 makes a clear distinction between funds used for charitable programs and those that the organization uses for investment purposes. It requires that these investment dollars be invested in a way that will "avoid speculation, looking instead to the permanent disposition of the funds, considering the probable income, as well as the probable safety of the corporation's capital." An exception to this rule occurs when the donor places other restrictions or gives other permissions in the instrument transferring the gift to the organization.

The state of Alabama in Section 19–3–120 of its code, authorizes bonds of the U.S. government, of state governments, of the federal land bank, promissory notes and debt backed by mortgages, savings accounts and deposit accounts, bonds issued by the African Development Bank, and mortgages guaranteed by the Federal Housing Administrator and the Administrator of Veterans' Affairs of the United States as authorized investment when assets are held in a fiduciary capacity such as a charitable trust unless the organizing document authorizes otherwise. Note that revenue bonds issued by authorities, stocks or bonds issued by corporations, foreign securities, options, and derivatives are not on this list.

What does *prudence* mean? It means taking into account the attributes and needs of the organization that is the beneficiary of the trust. It means accessing the nature of the investment and the overall investment portfolio of the organization, the existing and expected economic environment, the risks, and other relevant factors and applying all the care and skill that can be reasonably acquired in making a decision. Then it calls for monitoring performance and making adjustments, taking the same factors into account. These are further addressed in Chapter Sixteen.

FOUR ESSENTIAL STEPS FOR AN ENDOWMENT

Every nonprofit organization should consider an endowment. To do this, the following steps are necessary:

1. The board of trustees should pass a resolution that an endowment be started. It should state (a) the purpose of the endowment and how it fits into the mission of the organization, (b) how it will be managed, (c) the investment objective and strategy (even as broadly as stating that it will only invest in stocks of blue-chip companies, government securities, and money market accounts), (d) how disbursements and transfers into and out of the endowment will be determined, and

(e) whether or not a subcommittee of the board will oversee the endowment, and if so, how many members will be on the subcommittee.

2. The board should also determine how performance will be measured. The most common formula is one that adds all dividends to the amount of appreciation in the value of the portfolio and divides this by the amount invested. This is called the total rate of return.

3. The board should also assess, each year, how each responsibility center (revenue generation, investment, custodial, and disbursement) has performed.

4. Finally, the board should review restrictions from time to time. Some may be dated, contrary to policy, and may not provide marketing flexibility to potential donors. Minimize donor-imposed restrictions.

VALUATION OF FUTURE GIFTS

The valuation of deferred gifts (as present gifts discussed in Chapter Seven) is of interest to the donor because it determines the amount that can be deducted from federal and state income taxes. It is of interest to the nonprofit financial manager because

1. It may have to be included among the organization's assets at value and among its in-kind contributions. As we shall see in Chapter Eighteen, contributions are assets appearing on the balance sheet of the organization.

2. It may lead to tax and liability consequences if the gift is subject to debt or if it has been so depreciated by the donor that its value in transfer is decreased. For example, a gift that has a market value of $400,000 would be less if the donor owes money on it and the nonprofit assumes the donor's debt. Being a debt-acquired property, it would lead to unrelated business income tax if the property generates income.

3. Its value, as discussed in Chapter Four and earlier in this chapter, may be used in the calculation of public support, which must be demonstrated in order to retain the tax-exempt status of the organization.

4. Since tax considerations are a major impetus for giving, the amount of deductibility that is directly determined by the value of the gift may be used by the nonprofit to encourage the potential donor to make the gift. In some cases (Chapter Nine), the IRS requires that value be known.

A financial manager of a nonprofit would be unwise to try to determine the value of a gift for a potential donor, except as required by law and for accounting purposes. Donations are often part of an overall tax strategy of a person or corporation, and the valuation of specific gifts is a special skill. It is important, however, that the manager understand the key variables that determine the values of gifts and how they interact to determine the level of deduction that a taxpayer may take. Knowing this will help the manager make a deal by appealing to the tax motive for making the gift. As a general rule, the dollar value of the gift in the hands of the donor is its dollar value to the nonprofit at the time of the transfer to the organization. For accounting and tax purposes, the good does not change values simply because it is now in the hands of a nonprofit, although it may change value later due to market appreciation and depreciation.

The basic rule is that the value of the gift is its fair market value. This is the amount that a knowledgeable buyer would voluntarily pay a knowledgeable seller for the property at the time and under the conditions that the property was transferred from the donor to the nonprofit organization. Note that you cannot presume an extraordinary past or future situation to inflate the value of the gift and you cannot assume *laissez faire* to mean that the property could be sold to an ignorant buyer or to a buyer acting under duress for more. If the property is one that is usually sold through classified ads, then the value is that appearing in such ads on the day of the transfer. If the property is normally subject to retail sale, then its value is the retail price on that date. Furthermore, the transfer between the nonprofit and the person must represent an arm's-length agreement. That is to say, they cannot conspire or use influence to set an artificially high value.

The simple term *fair market value* can be very complex when the gift is made in a form other than an outright and immediate transfer of cash from the donor to the nonprofit organization. A check written for $1,300 by Orvin to his church is a gift valued at $1,300. But what if the gift is in some form other than cash? What if the gift is to pass to the nonprofit at a time in the distant future? What if the nonprofit will be permitted to get the income from a gift and then pass the gift on to Orvin's children upon his death? How are deferred gifts valued?

Several factors would affect the answers to these questions: the age of the donor, the term of the gift, the kind of property being transferred, whether the gift is being transferred to the nonprofit first and then to a noncharity or whether the nonprofit gets the gift only after a noncharitable beneficiary has enjoyed it, the payout rate, and the discount or interest rate that is presumed and the kind of trust being used. Let us discuss some of these factors. Our discussion of trusts introduced their importance to us.

Age is a determinant of the value of the gift whenever the transfer of the gift to the nonprofit is keyed to life expectancy. This is so if the gift is to pass to the nonprofit at the death of the donor or some other person or persons before being transferred to the nonprofit, or if the gift must first be used by the nonprofit and then passed on to some other noncharitable entity or person upon the death of the donor. For example, Margaret may elect that a gift be passed on to her church only after her death and her husband's death. This gives both of them the opportunity to enjoy the property during their lifetimes. In this case, the life expectancy of both persons must be taken into account. However, she may elect to have the church enjoy the benefits of the gift during her lifetime, but require that it be passed on to her husband upon her death, since he would need it to sustain life. In this case, only her life expectancy is important.

Life expectancy affects valuation because the longer the noncharitable beneficiary is likely to live, the smaller the contribution that is being made to the charity. If Margaret's gift is to pass to her church at the time of her death and she is only twenty-five years old, she could live many more years, and the contribution to the church, barring a growth in the value of the property, could be very little at the time of her death. Similarly, if Margaret's gift is to pass to the church only after her death and the death of her daughter who is two years old, it could be another sixty years before the gift is passed. However, if she is eighty years old and the transfer of the property to the nonprofit will occur at the time of her death, it is conceivable that at her age the transfer could take place in a reasonably short time. Therefore, the value of the gift for purposes of deduction is closer to its current market value.

The term or the specific number of years that must pass before the gift is transferred works similarly to the age variable. Sometimes a donor will make the gift conditional on the passage of a number of years rather than upon death. The donor may require that five, ten, or twelve years must pass before the gift can be transferred to the nonprofit or that the nonprofit may have use of the gift for a specific number of years before it must pass it on to a noncharitable beneficiary. The longer the term that the nonprofit may possess the gift, or the shorter the term it has to wait to receive it, the closer is the present market value to its value for the purposes of deduction.

As in the case of present gifts, the kind of property affects value. Unimproved real property, land that does not have building and developments that increase its value, is valued at the price paid for it or at comparable sales price of similar geographically located and geologically constituted undeveloped land, subject to the same zoning limitations and development rights on the date of the transfer to the nonprofit. Stocks and bonds are valued at the midpoint between their highest and lowest selling price on the stock exchange on the date of the transfer. If the stock exchanges are closed on that date (weekends and holidays), the most recent last date of its opening is used. Unpaid dividends may also be included in the valuation of the security. If the security is a share of a mutual fund, then the valuation price is the redemption price on the date that the funds are transferred.

If the stock or interest in a business is not sold on the exchange, then the price is based on factors such as its book value (assets minus liabilities).

If the gift is an annuity regularly sold by a financial company, then the value of the annuity is the price that is usually sold for by the company. But often the value of an annuity, life estate, or remainder of reversionary interests must be calculated by special tables issued by the IRS. An annuity is merely a contract that agrees to pay an annual payment over a number of years. A remainder interest refers to the transfer of the property to the nonprofit after a passage of time expressed in either a specific number of years (term) or the lifetime of one or more persons. A life estate is an interest for payment during the life of an individual.

The way the good is transferred also affects its valuation for purposes of deduction. As stated earlier, a gift of a future interest, a gift that does not take effect until a time in the future, has no deductible value unless the gift is a conservation property or is transferred through a trust. In the case of an annuity, this is handled by an insurance company. But if a trust is used, the value also differs if the transfer is made through a pooled income, a unitrust, or an annuity trust and if it is a charitable lead or charitable remainder trust. The latter usually has very limited deductible value, since it often requires that the donor include the income of the trust in his or her own taxable income. These considerations were discussed earlier in this chapter.

Also, as stated earlier in this chapter, the payout rates have a considerable bearing on the value of future gifts. The higher, longer, and more frequent the payout to a noncharitable beneficiary is, the lower the deductible value of the gift. Payout must be at least once a year, but can be monthly, quarterly, or semiannually.

The interest rate or discount rate also affects the value of the property. It is a mathematical fact that the higher the discount rate is, the lower the present value of a gift because the value is being discounted by a greater number. The IRS announces the applicable rate quarterly.

To understand how these concepts work or interact to determine value, refer to Table 8.8. Note that the table is based on a 10 percent discount rate (a presumption that the rate of return on an investment is 10 percent). Note that the annuity factors (column 2) get smaller the older the age while the remainder values (column 4) increase. A person who is 109 years old is not expected to live very long; therefore, an annuity contract promising to pay such a person a specific sum for the remainder of his or her life has a small income (annuity) value but a large remainder value. Hence, a gift of an annuity of $100,000 payable annually over the lifetime of such a person would be valued at ($100,000 $\times$ .4545) or $45,540. However, a similar $100,000 annuity payable each year over the life of a twenty-five-year-old person would be valued at ($100,000 $\times$ 9.6678) or $966,780. Hence, an annuity may provide either a large or small deduction depending on the age of the donor or the person for whom it is designed.

Table 8.8. Table A—10 Percent.

1 Age	2 Annuity	3 Life Estate	4 Remainder	1 Age	2 Annuity	3 Life Estate	4 Remainder
0	9.7188	.97188	.02812	38	9.2567	.92567	.07433
1	9.8988	.98988	.01012	39	9.2083	.92083	.07917
2	9.9017	.99017	.00983	40	9.1571	.91571	.08429
3	9.9008	.99008	.00992	41	9.1030	.91030	.08970
4	9.8981	.98981	.01019	42	9.0457	.90457	.09543
5	9.8938	.98938	.01062	43	8.9855	.89855	.10145
6	9.8884	.98884	.01116	44	8.9221	.89221	.10779
7	9.8822	.98822	.01178	45	8.8558	.88558	.11442
8	9.8748	.98748	.01252	46	8.7863	.87863	.12137
9	9.8663	.98663	.01337	47	8.7137	.87137	.12863
10	9.8565	.98565	.01435	48	8.6374	.86374	.13626
11	9.8453	.98453	.01547	49	8.5578	.85578	.14422
12	9.8329	.98329	.01671	50	8.4743	.84743	.15257
13	9.8198	.98198	.01802	51	8.3874	.83874	.16126
14	9.8066	.98066	.01934	52	8.2969	.82969	.17031
15	9.7937	.97937	.02063	53	8.2028	.82028	.17972
16	9.7815	.97815	.02185	54	8.1054	.81054	.18946
17	9.7700	.97700	.02300	55	8.0046	.80046	.19954
18	9.7590	.97590	.02410	56	7.9006	.79006	.20994
19	9.7480	.97480	.02520	57	7.7931	.77931	.22069
20	9.7365	.97365	.02635	58	7.6822	.76822	.23178
21	9.7245	.97245	.02755	59	7.5675	.75675	.24325
22	9.7120	.97120	.02880	60	7.4491	.74491	.25509
23	9.6986	.96986	.03014	61	7.3267	.73267	.26733
24	9.6841	.96841	.03159	62	7.2002	.72002	.27998
25	9.6678	.96678	.03322	63	7.0696	.70696	.29304
26	9.6495	.96495	.03505	64	6.9352	.69352	.30648
27	9.6290	.96290	.03710	65	6.7970	.67970	.32030
28	9.6062	.96062	.03938	66	6.6551	.66551	.33449
29	9.5813	.95813	.04187	67	6.5098	.65098	.34902
30	9.5543	.95543	.04457	68	6.3610	.63610	.36390
31	9.5254	.95254	.04746	69	6.2086	.62086	.37914
32	9.4942	.94942	.05058	70	6.0522	.60522	.39478
33	9.4608	.94608	.05392	71	5.8914	.58914	.41086
34	9.4250	.94250	.05750	72	5.7261	.57261	.42739
35	9.3868	.93868	.06132	73	5.5571	.55571	.44429
36	9.3460	.93460	.06540	74	5.3862	.53862	.46138
37	9.3026	.93026	.06974	75	5.2149	.52149	.47851

(continued)

Table 8.8. *(continued)*.

1 Age	2 Annuity	3 Life Estate	4 Remainder	1 Age	2 Annuity	3 Life Estate	4 Remainder
76	5.0441	.50441	.49559	93	2.4692	.24692	.75308
77	4.8742	.48742	.51258	94	2.3728	.23728	.76272
78	4.7049	.47049	.52951	95	2.2887	.22887	.77113
79	4.5357	.45357	.54643	96	2.2181	.22181	.77819
80	4.3659	.43659	.56341	97	2.1550	.21550	.78450
81	4.1967	.41967	.58033	98	2.1000	.21000	.79000
82	4.0295	.40295	.59705	99	2.0486	.20486	.79514
83	3.8642	.38642	.61358	100	1.9975	.19975	.80025
84	3.6998	.36998	.63002	101	1.9532	.19532	.80468
85	3.5359	.35359	.64641	102	1.9054	.19054	.80946
86	3.3764	.33764	.66236	103	1.8437	.18437	.81563
87	3.2262	.32262	.67738	104	1.7856	.17856	.82144
88	3.0859	.30859	.69141	105	1.6962	.16962	.83038
89	2.9526	.29526	.70474	106	1.5488	.15488	.84512
90	2.8221	.28221	.71779	107	1.3409	.13409	.86591
91	2.6955	.26955	.73045	108	1.0068	.10068	.89932
92	2.5771	.25771	.74229	109	.4545	.04545	.95455

Source: Federal Estate and Gift Taxes, Publication 448, rev. Sept. 1984, Internal Revenue Service, p. 17.

A life estate given to a nonprofit through a charitable lead trust means that the donor gives the charity the earnings from the property for the duration of a lifetime with the property to revert to a noncharitable donor, such as an heir, at the time of the donor's death. A donor who is 109 years old is not expected to live much longer. Therefore, a gift of a life estate of $100,000 is worth ($100,000 × .04545) or $4,545.

The value of remainder interest (column 4 of Table 8.8) is also affected by age. Take a gift appraised at $100,000 that is to be enjoyed by a noncharitable beneficiary who is twenty-five years of age and then passed on to a charity upon the death of that beneficiary. The present value of that gift ($100,000 × .03322) is $3,322 for purposes of tax deduction. The same gift would be worth ($100,000 × .95455) $95,455 if the person is 109 years old. Being that old, the gift would be expected to pass on soon so the deduction and the value of the annuity are higher.

Let us assume that instead of using age, we use a specific term, that is, a number of years. Refer to Table 8.9. First, we see that the upper panel of the table presumes a 6 percent discount rate and the lower a 10 percent. We see the difference that a higher discount rate makes by comparing the same cells in both panels. We observe that with a 10 percent discount rate the value of the property is reduced.

Table 8.9. B—6 Percent, 10 Percent.

Table B—6 percent

1 Number of Years	2 Annuity	3 Term Certain	4 Remainder	1 Number of Years	2 Annuity	3 Term Certain	4 Remainder
1	0.9434	.056604	.943396	22	12.0416	.722495	.277505
2	1.8334	.110004	.889996	23	12.3034	.738203	.261797
3	2.6730	.160381	.839619	24	12.5504	.753021	.246979
4	3.4651	.207906	.792094	25	12.7834	.767011	.232999
5	4.2124	.252742	.747258	26	13.0032	.780190	.219810
6	4.9173	.295039	.704961	27	13.2105	.792632	.207368
7	5.5824	.334943	.665057	28	13.4062	.804370	.195630
8	6.2098	.372588	.627412	29	13.5907	.815443	.184557
9	6.8017	.408102	.591898	30	13.7648	.825890	.174110
10	7.3601	.441605	.558395	31	13.9291	.835745	.164255
11	7.8869	.473212	.526788	32	14.0840	.845043	.154957
12	8.3838	.503031	.496969	33	14.2302	.853814	.146186
13	8.8527	.531161	.468839	34	14.3681	.862088	.137912
14	9.2950	.557699	.442301	35	14.4982	.869895	.130105
15	9.7122	.582735	.417265	36	14.6210	.877259	.122741
16	10.1059	.606354	.393646	37	14.7368	.884207	.115793
17	10.4773	.628636	.371364	38	14.8460	.890761	.109239
18	10.8276	.649656	.350344	39	14.9491	.896944	.103056
19	11.1581	.669487	.330513	40	15.0463	.902778	.097222
20	11.4699	.688195	.311805	41	15.1380	.908281	.091719

.086527	.913473	15.2245	42	.294155	.705845	11.7641	21
.048316	.951684	15.8614	52	.081630	.918370	15.3062	43
.045582	.954418	15.9070	53	.077009	.922991	15.3832	44
.043001	.956999	15.9500	54	.072650	.927350	15.4558	45
.040567	.959433	15.9905	55	.068538	.931462	15.5244	46
.038271	.961729	16.0288	56	.064653	.935342	15.5890	47
.036105	.963895	16.0649	57	.060998	.939002	15.6500	48
.034061	.965939	16.0990	58	.057546	.942454	15.7076	49
.032133	.967867	16.1311	59	.054288	.945712	15.7619	50
.030314	.969686	16.1614	60	.051215	.948785	15.8131	51

Table B—10 percent

.385543	.614457	6.1446	10	.909091	.090909	.9091	1
.350494	.649506	6.4951	11	.826446	.173554	1.7355	2
.289664	.710336	7.1034	13	.751315	.248685	2.4869	3
.263331	.736669	7.3667	14	.683013	.316987	3.1699	4
.239392	.760608	7.6061	15	.620921	.379079	3.7908	5
.217629	.782371	7.8237	16	.564474	.435526	4.3553	6
.197845	.802155	8.0216	17	.513158	.486842	4.8684	7
.179859	.820141	8.2014	18	.466507	.533493	5.3349	8
.163508	.836492	8.3649	19	.424098	.575902	5.7590	9
.022095	.977905	9.7791	40	.148644	.851356	8.5136	20
.020086	.979914	9.7991	41	.135131	.864869	8.6487	21
.018260	.981740	9.8174	42	.122846	.877154	8.7715	22
.016600	.983400	9.8340	43	.111678	.888322	8.8832	23
.015091	.984909	9.8491	44	.101526	.898474	8.9847	24

(continued)

Table 8.9. (*continued*)

Table B—6 percent

1 Number of Years	2 Annuity	3 Term Certain	4 Remainder	1 Number of Years	2 Annuity	3 Term Certain	4 Remainder
25	9.0770	.907704	.092296	45	9.8628	.986281	.013719
26	9.1609	.916095	.083905	46	9.8753	.987528	.012472
27	9.2372	.923722	.076278	47	9.8866	.988662	.011338
28	9.3066	.930657	.069343	48	9.8969	.989693	.010307
28	9.3066	.930657	.069343	49	9.9063	.990630	.009370
29	9.3696	.936961	.063039	50	9.9148	.991481	.008519
30	9.4269	.942691	.057309	51	9.9226	.992256	.007744
31	9.4790	.947901	.052099	52	9.9296	.992960	.007040
32	9.5264	.952638	.047362	53	9.9360	.993600	.006400
33	9.5694	.956943	.043057	54	9.9418	.994182	.005818
34	9.6086	.960857	.039143	55	9.9471	.994711	.005289
35	9.6442	.964416	.035584	56	9.9519	.995191	.004809
36	9.6765	.967651	.032349	57	9.9563	.995629	.004371
37	9.7059	.970592	.029408	58	9.9603	.996026	.003974
38	9.7327	.973265	.026735	59	9.9639	.996387	.003613
39	9.7570	.975696	.024304	60	9.9672	.996716	.003284

See *Valuation* in both the *Estate Tax* and *Gift Tax* sections of this publication to determine whether you should use the 6 percent or 10 percent tables to value these items.

Source: Federal Estate and Gift Taxes, Publication 448, rev. Sept. 1984, Internal Revenue Service, p. 18.

Therefore, for a term of twenty years at 6 percent, the factor is 11.4699 for an annuity compared with 8.5136 for 10 percent, .688195 for a term certain period (a specific term rather than a lifetime which is an uncertain term) compared with .851356, and .311805 compared with .148644 for a remainder interest.

Also notice that the factors in the 10 percent panel are different from the factors in Table 8.8, which also assume a 10 percent rate of discount. One reason is that the latter has an element of uncertainty. To make a gift contingent on someone's death involves an uncertainty about how long the person may live. The estimates are based on actuarial tables, which are estimates of the life expectancy of persons at specific ages. When a specific term is used, the length of time is for a term certain or a period of time that is certain. A 109-year-old person may live one month, one year, one day. To make a gift after a specific period is to set a specific term regardless of whether or not the person lives.

Large gifts are often induced by applying the right combinations of factors to bring about a high valuation when a tax motive is important to the potential donor. Some simple rules may help:

Rules of Thumb When Using Deductible Value in Appeal for Deferred Gift

1. Age (life expectancy) works inversely with value when the charity gets a remainder interest and positively with value when the charity gets a life estate (an income interest).

2. The longer the time the nonprofit has the benefits of the property, the greater the deductible value.

3. The deductible value must be consistent with the fair market value of the property.

4. The higher the payout rate to the noncharitable beneficiary is, the lower the value of the property as a charitable deduction.

This last point suggests trade-offs. A high payout rate may attract a potential donor because it offers a good income to the donor or a loved beneficiary; but it is at the expense of a higher tax deduction. Hence, the tax problem is one of coming up with a trade-off between a present benefit (tax deduction) or a flow of income (the payout) that suits the donor's needs. The loss of an initial part of a tax deduction can be partly offset by investing in securities that lead to tax-free earnings. Always let the lawyers and accountants advise and the donor choose.

SUMMARY AND PREVIEW

This chapter has presented techniques and tools that every manager of a nonprofit organization should know if the organization is to be successful in raising big money. These techniques allow the donor to have a deduction on present income tax, avoid estate taxes on gifts made, have a current income from the earnings of the gift, or make a gift of that current income to someone such as a relative or friend. The techniques also allow the nonprofit to receive annual income from a property only temporarily in its possession or, in the reverse, to finally take possession of a property that was providing an annual income to the donor. Basically, these tools and techniques are ways to strike a deal.

The tools that were discussed were charitable remainder trusts of the unitrust, annuity trust, and pooled trust types. These permit the income interest to go to someone other than the nonprofit. The nonprofit gets the remainder or corpus. The other type of trust is the charitable lead trust, also of the unitrust or annuity trust types. These trusts permit the nonprofit to get an annual payment, with the principal eventually going to someone else.

Life insurance policies are also instruments for getting large gifts. Insurance policies can magnify the size of the gift thousands of times larger than the actual money outlay of the donor, and they shift the burden of periodic reminders of donations to the insurance companies in the form of premium notices. Annuities are yet another tool. These range from gifts of pension plans, including private plans such as individual retirement accounts (IRAs) to gift annuities.

The chapter closes with a discussion of the valuation of future gifts and endowments, a special fund set aside for financing a special program or set of programs. An endowment may be funded by any one or (where permitted by law) any combination of the techniques discussed here and in Chapters Seven and Ten. We say permitted by law because once a trust is established, sometimes no further contributions can be made and some trusts must be separate and independent. Indeed, one motive for a donor's setting up a trust or an endowment is to maintain identity. This is why trusts and endowments usually carry the names of persons or corporations. It is their memorial. Regardless of how it is funded, each endowment requires a separate set of financial records.

CHAPTER NINE

Business Revenues and Tax-Exempt Status

A principal source of revenues for nonprofits of all types is *business revenues*. Business revenues derive from charging a price. A formal business organization is not required. Business revenues are the opposites of pure charity, which means that no price is charged. Therefore, there are very few nonprofits in the United States and all but private foundations in Canada, including religious organizations and charities, that do not derive some level of business revenues. Bingo and other forms of gaming also are businesses—a price is charged with the aim of generating a profit. For this reason, gaming and gambling are addressed in this chapter.

A central concern of this chapter is the manager's ability to collect evidence and convey that business income is appropriate, complementary, and suitable when the conditions in fact do justify such income.

For a nonprofit the fact that an activity is profitable is insufficient reason for its pursuit. For management, the issue is more than ethics or the popular untruth, "profits are okay as long as they are plowed back into the mission." The source of profits and their impact on the composition of revenues are also important. See Chapters Three, Five, and Ten.

Therefore, this chapter begins by laying the foundation for business revenues and then discussing the seventeen questions management should answer before entering into a business. Why? Because these are the very same questions that would be raised to prove that the managerial decision was wrong and detrimental.

THE NONPROFIT AS AN ECONOMIC INSTITUTION

A proper way of viewing the issue is appreciating, as argued in all previous editions of this book, that adjectives such as *charity* and *benevolent* define the mission; *economic* defines the organization. Therefore, a nonprofit or an association is an economic institution with a charitable or a benevolent mission.

Reflecting this fact, a study of 160 health maintenance organizations (HMOs) in the United States found that the rates of profitability were not significantly different between nonprofit and for-profit HMOs. It explained that this is so because both depend on the same credit markets for funds to finance capital needs and the cost of debt in these markets is significantly determined by the ability of the organization to cover interest costs and profitability. The study explains that the way the market in which HMOs operate tends to force convergence of the rates of profitability—regardless of the absence of a profit motive by the nonprofit organization. This is so because the factors that determine costs and revenues are very much the same for both groups.[1]

Whatever the mission, the organization has to pay its bills. Nonprofits are economic institutions because nonprofits are productive units. These two statements are key.

To repeat, nonprofits are economic institutions because nonprofits are productive units. Such units acquire inputs of land, labor, and capital and transform them through a productive process into goods and services that have value to society. In the case of a business firm, these values are measured in terms of the market price for which the goods and services are sold. In the case of nonprofits, the value is imputed, a term used by economists to mean approximated. Imputation is required because all the goods and services produced by nonprofits are not sold for a price that truly reflects the value of the good or service or even its cost. Many nonprofits charge no price or charge one that is well below the true market price of the good or service they produce. For others, such as religion, their output is priceless.

Economists take the view of nonprofits as productive units so seriously that they annually impute the value of goods and services produced by nonprofits and include the imputations in their calculations of the gross national product (GNP) of the country. The gross national product is the sum of goods and services produced by the economy of the country in any given year. It is the most comprehensive indicator of economic production and the wealth of the nation.

Notice that what is central in the definition of the economic institution is the transformation of inputs into goods and services that have value. A school takes the input of teachers (labor) and capital (buildings and books) and land (the playground) and transforms these into something called an educated student who is valuable to society. Whether or not a price is charged for the good or service produced by the school is not what matters in the definition. The price serves to measure the value of the output of the institution rather than to determine whether the institution is an economic entity. What makes the institution an economic entity is that it uses society's scarce resources (land, labor, and capital) to produce a product or service of value. Translated, the nonprofit (1) has operating costs, (2) imposes a cost on the community to the extent that it wastes contributions and voluntary services that could be used by other nonprofits providing superior value to society, and (3) needs a reliable flow of revenues, as do all economic institutions.

The purpose for producing the good or service must be to finance the mission. As an economic institution, the nonprofit's purpose for producing the good or service must be to finance its mission. This is law.

It is commonly held that nonprofits cannot or should not make profits because they are supposed to be charitable. What does *charitable* mean? The courts have historically maintained a loose definition of the term. This has been done to accommodate the fact that, over time, the charitable needs of society change; that is, new needs are recognized.[2] In practice, the IRS and the courts use the following criteria to determine whether a motive is charitable:[3]

1. The motive of the organization must be to meet a recognized need of the community or some segment thereof in a manner and level that are significantly different to what a for-profit firm would do.

2. The means used to meet the charitable purpose must be integrally related to satisfying the needs that have been identified as charitable.

3. There must be a clear manifestation of providing the service without seeking personal gain for the providers or for the providing organization.

4. The charitable purpose must be consistent with public policy.

Using these principles, the IRS and the courts have awarded charitable status to nonprofits that specialize in otherwise commercial activities. The IRS has granted charitable status to an organization specializing in making loans to minority businesses that are located in a distressed area and that are unable to get loans from regular commercial sources.[4] Similarly, charitable status was awarded to an organization located in a rural area that made development loans to businesses unable to get loans from normal commercial sources and that were located in distressed parts of rural communities.[5]

And although manufacturing is a for-profit activity, the IRS awarded charitable status to a job-training organization that also ran a toy manufacturing business. The organization hired, trained, gave job counseling, and placed unskilled workers.[6]

Is It Charity?

(2) *Charitable defined.* The term "charitable" is used in section 501(c)(3) in its generally accepted legal sense and is, therefore, not to be construed as limited by the separate enumeration in section 501(c)(3) of other tax-exempt purposes which may fall within the broad outlines of "charity" as developed by judicial decisions. Such term includes: Relief of the poor and distressed or of the underprivileged; advancement of religion; advancement of education or science; erection or maintenance of public buildings, monuments, or works; lessening of the burdens of Government; and promotion of social welfare by organizations designed to accomplish any of the above purposes, or (i) to lessen neighborhood tensions; (ii) to eliminate prejudice and discrimination; (iii) to defend human and civil rights secured by law; or (iv) to combat community deterioration and juvenile delinquency.

Source: Treasury Regulations Section 1.501(c)(3)–1(d)(1)(2), 1980.

In addition, although barber and beauty shops are traditionally for-profit businesses, a beauty and barber shop was given charitable status even though it operated for a profit. The IRS concluded that the shop operated at the convenience of elderly citizens and serving these citizens was a charitable mission.[7]

In the same vein, a medical and dental referral service was designated a charity even though it charges a price and makes a profit. The court held, among other things, that both the profits and salaries were kept reasonably low and that the purpose of the referral system was to improve medical service to the community and not to benefit the medical practitioners. Their benefits were incidental to those of the community.[8]

From these examples it should be clear that a nonprofit is an economic institution with a charitable mission, even if it charges a price and makes a profit. Unfortunately, even when described by their most ardent supporters, nonprofits are too often viewed as purely charitable organizations. A pure charity is defined as an organization that functions to meet benevolent objectives and does not sell its goods or services.[9] What is important, the law does not restrict nonprofits to operating in this purely charitable or eleemosynary mode.

To view nonprofits in this purely charitable mode is to limit them to the detriment of the community. Notice this in the case of the loans mentioned above. These loans are business transactions normally carried out by a bank or other commercial lender. To bar the nonprofit from doing so in this case is to deprive individuals to whom commercial lenders would not lend. To deny them is not to improve social or public well-being.

What distinguishes nonprofits from other economic institutions is not that all nonprofits are pure charities. The fact is that most nonprofits, including churches, could not meet a stringent application of this test of not selling any good or service. Raffles, bargain sales, tuitions, and contributions related to the receipt of a specific good or service by the contributor involve a sale. It is not the inability to sell the good or service that is the distinguishing feature.

The distinguishing feature is that the organization must not have been *created* with the motive of selling its goods and services at a gain; absent this restriction, the organization would merely be a for-profit firm doing well or operating at a loss. Recall the discussion in Part One. The word *created* is emphasized because the exclusive motive for creating and operating the nonprofit must be for community welfare or charity, directly so in the case of 501(c)(3)s and indirectly so in the case of others, as measured by the four criteria previously stated. However, the nonprofit does not have to be a pure charity.

This point is well illustrated in a series of court cases. In *Fraternal Medical Specialist Services, Inc.* v. *Commissioner,* the court stated:[10]

> In determining whether petitioner is operated exclusively for exempt purposes, or whether instead, petitioner is operated in furtherance of a substantial commercial purpose our inquiry must focus upon the purpose or purposes furthered by petitioner's activities, and not on the activities themselves. The fact that an organization's activities may even constitute a trade or business does not, of itself, disqualify it from classification under section 501(c)(3). . . . The determination of whether petitioner is operated for a substantial commercial purpose is primarily a question of fact. . . . Factors such as the particular manner in which the organization's activities are conducted, the commercial hue of these activities, and the existence and amount of annual or accumulated profits are relevant evidence of a proscribed commercial purpose.

Similarly, the Supreme Court has held that having a trade or business does not disqualify the organization from tax exemption.[11] However, the existence of a single nonexempt (commercial) activity that is a substantial part of the purpose for the existence of the organization would destroy its qualification as tax exempt regardless of how many tax-exempt purposes it has.[12] In short, the trade or business cannot be a substantial reason for the creation of the organization.

To illustrate, the training or educating of people is a recognized tax-exempt purpose, one that is beneficial to public welfare. But the training of dogs is not a recognized public purpose (although the neutering of dogs is). Hence, in a well-known case, the courts ruled:

> By contrast, petitioner has not shown that actually training a dog is necessary for teaching an individual how to train a dog. While it is clear that an infant needs custodial care when he or she is learning, it is not plain that an individual cannot be taught to train animals without the animal being present for the entire class time. Essentially, unlike in *San Francisco Infant School,* there are no facts

in the administrative record regarding petitioner's curriculum, theories, or methods. While we know that the dogs receive degrees and awards, we do not know whether or how the individual's skills are evaluated.

We find, therefore, that since the training of dogs is a substantial, if not the primary, purpose of petitioner, petitioner is not operated exclusively for one or more exempt purposes specified in section 501(c)(3). [*Ann Arbor Dog Training Club, Inc. Petitioner* v. *Commissioner*, T.C., 174, pp. 207–212]

The existence of one substantial nonexempt purpose (the training of dogs) led to the denial of the tax-exempt status. Ironically, the status may have been awarded if the training of people were the substantial purpose for which this organization was formed, and the training of dogs only incidental to the training of people. This is what the court meant when it said, "By contrast, petitioner has not shown that actually training a dog is necessary for teaching an individual how to train a dog."

In further illustrating this point of a community welfare or charitable motive, it should be noted that if the organization was created with the motive of making a gain (a profit) on its activities, the failure to realize this gain does not make the organization a nonprofit. It is merely a for-profit firm that has a loss or is breaking even. Failure does not transform a firm into a charity. Similarly, if the organization was created with a motive of making a profit, its making large charitable contributions does not make it a nonprofit. In this case, it is simply a profit maker with a strong social conscience.

To the for-profit firm, charity may be important, but it is not essential to its existence; the charitable purpose is incidental. Accordingly, many for-profit firms have their own charitable foundations and make sizable charitable gifts to nonprofits. To the nonprofit, charity is the exclusive motive for existing and profits are incidental, although profits are an important means for financing the charitable mission. As seen from these examples, nonprofits may run profitable businesses that may or may not be related to their mission. An example is gaming.

GAMING AND GAMBLING

Many states permit nonprofits to engage in gaming or gambling under regulated conditions. Gambling or gaming are activities in which assets of value such as cash, credit, and checks are placed at risk that is dependent upon chance or lot and may or may not use a gambling device such as a slot machine. These activities may include bingo, bookmaking in sports, card games such as blackjack, keno, dice games such as craps, lottery, raffles, slot machines, festivals, and in some cases door prizes. These regulations may also include certain promotional games—ones in which an individual does not have to pay in order to win—and gift enterprises (one in which a purchase is required). A typical way of regulating these activities is through the requirement that a license be obtained and that the organization file certain reports that are made available to the public.

Even when professional gambling may be outlawed, gambling by nonprofits may be permitted but regulated. Vermont is a case in point. It requires no licenses, but it requires that all funds raised through these activities must be used for the mission of the organization and it allows only 501(c) organizations, civic organizations, schools, fraternal organizations, fire departments, religious organizations, and municipalities to engage in gambling. The dollar amounts in prizes that can be won per game, per day, per month, and per year are limited. The law also limits the number of days per week bingo may be played and casino nights may be held per quarter or per year, and the number of consecutive days that casino nights may be held.

PROFIT-MAKING AS A SOURCE OF REVENUES

What is the legal history upon which the courts and the IRS have held that nonprofits may make a profit? The seminal case is *Trinidad* v. *Sagrada Orden*.[13] The Supreme Court stated that the law

> recognizes that a corporation may be organized and operated exclusively for religious, charitable, scientific or educational purposes, and yet have a net income [profits] . . . it says nothing about the source of the income, but makes the destination the ultimate exemption.

In several cases thereafter, the IRS and the courts have held that organizations dedicated to a charitable, educational, religious, or other tax-exempt purpose could conduct profitable business activities without losing their exempt status and without paying taxes or penalties on these profits. An example is the ruling by the IRS that a tax-exempt museum engaging in the

> sale of greeting cards displaying printed reproductions of art works contributes importantly to the achievement of the museum's exempt educational purposes by stimulating and enhancing public awareness, interest, and appreciation of art. Moreover, a broader segment of the public may be encouraged to visit the museum itself . . . as a result of the cards. The fact that the cards are promoted and sold in a clearly commercial manner at a profit and in competition with commercial greeting card publishers does not alter the fact of the activity's relatedness to the museum exempt purposes.[14]

Accordingly, the IRS concluded that not only should the engagement in these profitable sales by this museum not result in the loss of tax-exempt status, but the profits should not be taxed. The business earnings were related to, but not the motive for, their mission or existence.

Similarly, in *American College of Physicians* v. *U.S.*, the courts held that revenues from advertising in the *Annals of Internal Medicine* were related to its tax-exempt mission. Therefore, the advertising was not cause for the repeal of its tax-exempt status and the profits from the advertising were not taxable. In the words of the court:[15]

> That the primary purpose may have been commercial, however, does not preclude a finding that the activity is substantially related to an exempt function. . . . While the educational function of the advertising may well have been secondary to the purpose of raising revenues, the evidence of record establishes that the advertising in *Annals* fulfilled an important educational function. . . . The evidence of record establishes that the contribution of the advertisements to the exempt purpose is an important one.

The court continued, "We hold that the sales of advertising in *Annals* are substantially related to the exempt purpose of the College to educate internists and, therefore, are not taxable." We shall return to this case. This is not the end of the story.

From these two cases, we see that the two ultimate authorities, the courts and the IRS, both sanction the making of profits by nonprofit organizations. A careful reading of the rulings indicates the separation of two levels of analysis by the courts and by the IRS: (1) Is the tax-exempt mission of the organization threatened or secondary to the for-profit activity? If it is, tax-exempt status is denied or revoked. If it is not, then (2) is the for-profit activity related to the carrying out of the tax-exempt mission? If it is not, the net earnings (profits) from the business are taxed. If it is related, the net earnings are not taxed.

In some cases, both the courts and the IRS rule that the organization may maintain its tax-exempt nonprofit status, but it must pay taxes on the profits. This is so when the business is unrelated to the tax-exempt mission of the organization. Hence, in another case involving a museum, the IRS ruled that an art museum was dealing in an unrelated business when it sold books dealing with science. In the eyes of the IRS, the sale of science books had nothing to do with art. In this case, the museum's tax-exempt status was not threatened, but it had to pay taxes on the profits from the sale of its scientific books but not on the sale of cards promoting art.[16]

To fully appreciate this point, let us go back to the case of the American College of Physicians. Not satisfied with the lower courts, the IRS appealed the case to the Supreme Court. On April 22, 1986, Justice Thurgood Marshall in *United States, Petitioner* v. *American College of Physicians* rendered the unanimous decision of the Court. It held that the advertising in *Annals of Internal Medicine* was unrelated business and that the American College of Physicians must pay taxes on the earnings from such advertising.

The case against the American College of Physicians turned on whether or not the advertising was conducted in a manner that showed that it was not substantially related to the tax-exempt mission of the organization. The Court pointed to an earlier focus of the Claims Court:

> The evidence is clear that plaintiff did not use the advertising to provide its readers a comprehensive or systematic presentation of any aspect of the goods or services publicized. Those companies willing to pay for advertising space got it; others did not. Moreover, some of the advertising was for established drugs or devices and was repeated from one month to another, undermining the suggestion that the advertising was principally designed to alert readers of recent developments [citing, as examples, ads for Valium, Insulin, and Maalox]. Some ads even concerned matters that had no conceivable relationship to the College's tax-exempt purposes. 3 Cl. Ct. at 534 [footnotes omitted]. [*Supreme Court of the United States, United States* v. *American College of Physicians,* No. 84–1737, April 22, 1986, pp. 14–15]

Based on that finding the Supreme Court concluded:

> These facts find adequate support in the record. See, e.g., App. 29a–30a, 59a. Considering them in light of the applicable legal standard, we are bound to conclude that the advertising in *Annals* does not contribute importantly to the journal's educational purposes. This is not to say that the College could not control its publication of advertisements in such a way as to reflect an intention to contribute importantly to its educational functions. By coordinating the content of the advertisements with the editorial content of the issue, or by publishing only advertisements reflecting new developments in the pharmaceutical market, for example, perhaps the College could satisfy the stringent standards erected by Congress and the Treasury. In this case, however, we have concluded that the Court of Appeals erroneously focused exclusively upon the information that is invariably conveyed by commercial advertising, and consequently failed to give effect to the governing statute and regulations. Its judgment, accordingly is *Reversed.* [*Supreme Court of the United States, United States* v. *American College of Physicians,* No. 84–1737, April 22, 1986, p. 15]

Note several points from these quotations. First, the American College of Physicians did not lose its tax-exempt status. Second, it may continue a business of advertising for a profit although it must pay taxes on these profits like any other business. Third, the Court did not ban advertising and did not rule out that this could be a related business of a nonprofit and therefore free of taxes. Fourth, the Court suggested how the American College of Physicians may accomplish this objective. In other words, the specific facts and circumstances surrounding an activity determine whether it is related or unrelated.

It is important to appreciate the purpose of this unrelated business income tax. It is not intended to stop the nonprofit from making a profit. This would be a silly prescription, because it implies (at the extreme) that the nonprofit should aim at making losses or, at the other extreme, commit the organization to breaking even. Planning for such exactitude whereby costs just equal revenues every year is humanly impossible. A nonprofit, to be safe if such a prescription were in place, would create a loss every year. It would then go bankrupt and close, serving no useful purpose.

Rather, it is to avoid unfair competition by making sure that if a nonprofit engages in a business unrelated to the promotion of its mission, the profits on that business are then taxed in the same way as all profit-making firms doing the same kind of business are taxed. A second reason, as we have seen in Chapter Four, is to make sure that if such a business swamps the activities of the nonprofit, it loses its exemption and is classified as a for-profit firm.

This thinking is revealed in the *Congressional Record* on the legislation leading to the unrelated business tax on nonprofits.[17]

> The problem at which the tax on unrelated business income is directed is primarily that of unfair competition. The tax-free status of . . . organizations enables them to use their profits tax-free to expand operations, while their competitors can expand only with the profits remaining after taxes. Also, a number of examples have arisen where these organizations have, in effect, used their tax exemptions to buy an ordinary business. That is, they have acquired the business with little or no investment on their own part and paid for it in installments out of subsequent earnings—a procedure which usually could not be followed if the business were taxable.

And the *Congressional Record* continues,

> In neither . . . bill does this provision deny the exemption where the organizations are carrying on unrelated active business enterprises, nor require that they dispose of such businesses. Both provisions merely impose the same tax on income derived from an unrelated trade or business as is borne by their competitors.

In short, a nonprofit may make profits from engaging in a trade or business that is related to its tax-exempt mission without losing its tax-exempt status and without paying taxes on that profit. It may engage in profit-making businesses unrelated to its tax-exempt mission, but it must pay taxes on the profits earned. Neither of these two situations leads to a loss or denial of tax-exempt status.

The status is lost or denied when it appears to the IRS or the courts that the community or public welfare purpose claimed by the organization is nothing but a ruse for carrying on a commercial activity for profit and that the tax-exempt status is intended by the organization simply as a means to evade taxes or to gain a competitive advantage over for-profit firms. Hence, in *Piety, Inc.* v. *Commissioner,* the court held that an organization that did nothing but run bingo games was not tax exempt even though it fed its profits to a tax-exempt organization.[18]

The tax-exempt status is also denied or revoked if the benefits of the organization or the profits of its business inure to private persons. In *Church of*

Scientology of California v. *Commissioner,* the court thus held that the tax-exempt status was to be revoked because the church was operated for a substantially commercial purpose, and its net earnings privately benefited its founder.[19]

To summarize, this section provides legal evidence that nonprofit organizations are allowed to make a *profit* (and the very word is used in the law). But if a nonprofit is allowed to make a profit, what distinguishes a for-profit firm from a nonprofit? Under what conditions will an organization that deems itself to be a nonprofit be considered just another for-profit firm in the eyes of the law and consequently be denied its tax-exempt status?

The critical factors, as we learn in this book, in avoiding revocation or denial of tax-exempt status are as follows:

1. The organization must clearly and unequivocally be motivated by a community or public welfare purpose defined by the *Internal Revenue Code* as worthy of tax exemption or the welfare of its members in the case of associations.

2. The benefits must not inure to private individuals in the case of any type of nonprofit.

3. Commercial activity must not be its primary purpose and must not diminish or rival the ability of the organization to conduct its tax-exempt mission.

4. The activity could not easily be conducted by a commercial firm for a profit.

Note that the community or public welfare purpose to which the organization is exclusively dedicated must also be one that is both defined by law as tax exempt and contained in the organization's charter as described in Chapter Two. Accordingly, in the example of the second museum, the court held that the sale of scientific books would have been tax exempt to another organization that was scientific in its orientation, but not to an art museum. It is not simply the activity that counts, but the combination of considerations mentioned in the preceding paragraph. Hence, in the case of the American College of Physicians mentioned earlier, the fact that the principal objective of the advertising was to raise money is not separated from whether the purposes served by the advertising are defined as tax exempt. Is it education as defined?

To illustrate further, the community welfare purpose may be stated in the charter of the organization but not be defined as a tax-exempt activity by the law. Thus, in Society of Costa Rica Collectors, both the court and the IRS concluded that tax exemption was not warranted by the philatelic society that primarily engaged in sales that were indistinguishable from commercial sales. Merely the sale of philatelic materials is not by itself defined by law as a tax-exempt purpose.[20] And the training of dogs, as we saw earlier, is not recognized as a community or public welfare purpose (a charity) that is tax exempt.

The Use of the Profits Must Be to Advance Public or Community Welfare and the Mission of the Association

A distinguishing characteristic between a nonprofit and a for-profit firm as an economic institution is that nonprofits may not distribute their assets, profits, or other benefits to individuals as owners. They may not advance private welfare but must only utilize profits to carry on their mission to improve public or community welfare or those of their members. In this sense, there are the following important differences between a for-profit and a nonprofit.

1. The for-profit obtains revenues strictly from sales of assets, goods, and services; from sale of equity or debt; and from investments. The profits may be distributed to individuals because they are the owners of the assets and earnings of the firm. A stock certificate is evidence of ownership, and the payment of dividends to stockholders is a distribution of assets and earnings.

2. In contrast, the nonprofit can obtain revenues from sale of assets, goods, and services; debt and investment; but not equity. There is an alternative source, gifts and contributions. The balance among revenue sources (other than debt) is critical to how a nonprofit is classified and whether it qualifies for tax exemption. Furthermore, the nonprofit may not distribute its assets, income, or earnings to individuals or to any other entity that is not a similar nonprofit except the state or unless the distribution is compensation for goods or services bought.

Costs and Revenue Perspectives of Being an Economic Institution

As an economic institution, nonprofits have expenses as well as revenues. A firm may seek profits simply to increase the rate of return to its investors. A nonprofit seeks profits and other revenues to secure the attainment of a mission, that is, to finance it now and in the future. Hence, current and future costs are compelling stimuli to fund-raising. Major costs are plant, equipment, and labor in the form of salaries and benefits. Salaries in some nonprofit organizations are very high because nonprofits must compete for labor.[21] Rentals may also be high because nonprofits must compete for space. Neither a gift of labor nor space is deductible.

It is sometimes said that the word *voluntary* best distinguishes the nonprofit from the profit sector, but this is not totally accurate. Workers in the nonprofit sector are not all volunteers. Even the most charitable of charities, religious organizations, pay their workers.

The problem with the use of the word *voluntary* is best described by a long-time and well-respected observer of the nonprofit world. Alan Piper, writing for the Foundation Center, asserts:[22]

> The term itself is elusive. Theoretically, it includes not only all kinds of private enterprise, both nonprofit and for-profit, but even the institutions of a democratic form of government as well—in short any activity by private citizens undertaken in concert and on their own volition.

True, membership in nonprofit associations is voluntary, but most nonprofits are not membership organizations. Moreover, membership in many nonprofits, such as labor, professional, and trade associations, are only nominally voluntary because failure to join is to deprive oneself of employment, advancement opportunities, and information. Indeed, some associations have certifying powers, and without being certified a person cannot work in some professional capacities.

And though it is true that some participation in a nonprofit is voluntary, this does not distinguish nonprofits from for-profit organizations or market transactions from transactions in the nonprofit sector. To illustrate, participation in the ownership of corporations is voluntary. All market transactions are voluntary. People are not coerced to buy or sell, as this is illegal. Producers and workers make voluntary decisions about all their activities in a market economy. Indeed, without voluntary initiatives, the market system is an oxymoron. It is precisely the voluntary aspects of the market economy (to be described in Chapter Eighteen) that open opportunities for nonprofits.

From a revenue perspective, all nonprofits may charge a price for the assets or goods or services they sell. The range of prices a nonprofit may charge varies from nothing to the competitive price that is being charged by for-profit firms. What gives nonprofits that are charities and 501(c)(3)s this range is that they have one source of income that for-profit firms do not have—gifts and contributions.[23] For-profits do not have gifts and contributions and must sell at a price that absorbs all costs and makes a profit for the owners. In contrast, nonprofits do not have individuals as owners and may not distribute profits to anyone.

For-profit firms do frequently charge below going market price (discounted sales) and give products and services away (donations). The difference is that the nonprofit can sustain this behavior as modus operandi, and for-profit firms cannot. At some point the operation must turn and sustain a profit even at discounted prices.

COSTS AND OTHER STIMULI
TO GENERATING BUSINESS REVENUES

Again, unlike a firm, a nonprofit does not seek to maximize revenues for rewarding investors. A major stimulus for revenue generation is to obtain revenues to expand the ability to carry out the mission. It is also to meet costs, some of which are fixed and must be paid regardless of the level of activity of the organization. Hence, viewing the nonprofit as an economic institution that has costs and needs revenues to meet them should be an objective of management. Let us enumerate:

1. The concept "ability to carry out its mission" means having the required money. It also means having the essentials to do the job conveniently. A university needs a bookstore. What is a university without a bookstore? But there is no need to run a bookstore as if it were a charity. It can be run profitably. Hence, one of the skills of nonprofit management is to isolate those activities that are essential to the mission of the organization, that enhance the ability of the organization to carry out its mission, but that need not be run at a loss. Run them profitably to generate revenues for the mission.

2. Another type of revenue-generating activity comes from observing that there is unused capacity. This capacity may be idle all of the time or just some of the time, for example, the church hall, the fax machine, the computer, the stadium, the classroom. Note that even though these are not being used they generate costs every single day. Lease them.

3. The value of property rights of all kinds are examples of hidden costs that have revenue-generating potential. Take a look at all those sweaters that carry names of colleges and universities. Suppose the university fails. Would you buy the sweater? The university does not fail because millions of dollars are spent every year for it to carry out its mission successfully and therefore the names on those sweaters have a value. Property rights should be sold or leased. Property rights cover royalties, real estate, art, copyright, trademarks, the name of the organization, mailing lists—all of which can generate income.

4. Joint or common costs is another cost stimulus to revenues. Take a journal or magazine produced by a nonprofit. The journal or magazine deals with the mission of the nonprofit, be it wildlife, religion, health, or what have you. It costs. Selling some of the pages of that magazine to an advertiser provides revenues that can help cover the total cost of the magazine. The printing and distribution costs are joint both to the articles and the advertisement. Hence, they can be shared.

5. Every program has costs. Part of these costs can be met by charging a fee to the extent that such fees do not discourage needy clients and diminish the

mission. Many goods and services are appropriately distributed free, but they can be sponsored by individuals, firms, or foundations.

All five of the above examples demonstrate a cost situation that is converted into a business revenue stream, which may appropriately be, depending on the circumstance, very small. Yet they help to cover costs. The ability to do this is part of managing the mission of the organization when the organization is viewed as an economic institution with a benevolent mission, that is, conscious of costs and revenues.

Some nonprofits' cost advantages are obvious. Postage is lower and so, too, are some labor costs because of volunteers. A skilled worker, such as a lawyer, who may charge hundreds of dollars per hour may, as a matter of professional ethics, work pro bono for a nonprofit. Football players through the National Football League promote contributions to the United Way. Business Volunteers for the Arts is a group of approximately 1,000 bankers, lawyers, accountants, and other business managers who assist over 600 art groups in fifteen cities in marketing, finance, and other management services.

The exploitation of any one or a combination of these cost factors can make the mission more "doable." For example, being able to utilize volunteers to lower costs and exploiting a special relationship with the public, as evidenced by hospitals selling tickets to a golf tournament, can turn a needed profit for both the private sector and nonprofit participants in a joint venture, which carries out the mission of the organization.

There are other examples of exploitation of these factors. Hospitals rent space to physicians, run parking lots and physical fitness centers, give lessons in yoga, run gift shops and refreshment outlets, and charge fees to profit. As many nonprofits have discovered, the quickest way for a nonprofit to run a profitable business is to charge a fee for some of the services it provides. If the fee is based on a percentage markup on its costs, the fee not only covers costs but contributes to the organization's mission.

There are other illustrations. *Audubon,* owned by the National Audubon Society, *National Geographic,* owned by the National Geographic Society, and the *Smithsonian,* owned by the Smithsonian Institute, are magazines that have earned millions of dollars in profits. This is done in part by having a special relationship with the public, including a large membership that purchases the magazines, and through lower postal rates for mailing the magazines. And as in the case of the American College of Physicians, magazines owned by nonprofits are not forbidden from selling advertising space at a profit.

Again, it is not profits for the sake of profits. Some of these activities are an integral part of the mission of the nonprofit, but they need not be run at a loss. We shall discuss more about generating business revenues in the next chapters and distinguish between related and unrelated business income even more than we have done in this chapter. The principal purpose of the preceding discussion is to point out that when a nonprofit is managed as an economic institution, it has a better chance of fulfilling its mission by remaining financially sound. One strategy is to control costs, as we shall see in Chapters Twelve, Thirteen, and Fourteen; another is to convert costs into revenue streams, which has been the topic to this point.

Prepared in a Socratic format, the objective of the following discussion is to come as close as possible to actual questions the management should ask when considering any business income. The questions are followed by answers or the accepted procedures for working out an answer. The questions are as follows:

1. How will the investment affect the tax-exempt status of the organization?
2. How should a business be acquired?
3. Should the business be related or unrelated?
4. Should the business be incorporated as a for-profit corporation?
5. Where does the money come from to acquire the business?
6. Is the business profitable?
7. Is profitability enough?
8. What will the investment cost?
9. Will the expected benefits exceed the costs?
10. Is the investment worth it?
11. When will the organization recapture its investment?
12. What are the risks?
13. What will it take to break even?
14. What can be done with the earnings of the business?
15. How will entry into the business be made?
16. What is the nature of the competition? Is it fair?
17. What do the trustees think of the plan?

HOW WILL THE INVESTMENT AFFECT THE TAX-EXEMPT STATUS IN CANADA AND IN THE UNITED STATES?

If this is not the first question to be asked, it surely is the last. As we shall see in the next chapter, although investment in a business is not barred and is encouraged by the law, income from such investments can seriously affect the tax-exempt status of the nonprofit.

In Canada, charities and public foundations are not allowed to conduct any business unless it is related to their missions. Related businesses include those derived from the direct carrying out of their missions, such as admissions fees or the sale of albums or almanacs. Related businesses also may include income from the rental of their underutilized capacities or equipment as long as this does not impede fulfillment of the organization's mission. Private foundations are not allowed to carry on any business whatsoever. Nonprofits in Canada (like associations in the United States) may have business income.

The circumstances are very different in the United States. Any charitable organization can not only conduct related businesses but also businesses unrelated to their missions. But this must be done in proportion to public support through gifts and contributions, as discussed in Chapters Two through Four. Associations may carry out business activities whether or not they are related to their missions. In the United States, the restraint on business activity is primarily on private foundations. But they, too, may carry on either unrelated or related businesses with a cap on their excess (unrelated) business holdings.

All nonprofits have to consider the relationship of business income to their charters and mission. Here are different required perspectives for United States organizations.

1. If the nonprofit is a private nonoperating foundation, it has to consider the excess business holding rules and plan for an orderly divestiture (Chapter Four).

2. If it is a private operating foundation, not only does it have to consider the more lenient excess business holding rule, but that these rules relate to the extent to which the business is integrated into its mission and can influence the organization's election of what test, in addition to the income test, will justify its tax-exempt status (Chapter Four).

3. For 501(c)(3)s other than private foundations, there is no excess business holding rule. There is, however, the need to balance business income with public support or involvement in the activity of the organization in order to justify tax-exempt status (Chapter Three).

4. In addition, for 501(c)(3) organizations the type of business income affects its classification into 509(a)(1) or (1)(2) (Chapter Three).

5. For all exempt organizations, including associations, the type of business income is important in the determination of the organization's tax liability (Chapter Ten).

6. For associations 501(c)(4)s, (5)s, and (6)s, there is no excess business holding rule. For all of them, however, including 501(c)(3)s and business associations, profit-making cannot be a principal function, since this would be a reason for the denial of tax-exempt status (Chapters Two through Five).

7. The way the business is incorporated into the organizational structure makes a difference. The business may be created as a subsidiary, as a close affiliate, a holding company, and these may be singularly or jointly owned or operated (Chapters Ten and Nineteen).

8. Opportunities for gaining business revenues arise from the exploitation of the mission of the organization and from cost-sharing (Chapter Nineteen).

9. The impact of unrelated business income is taxation on all tax-exempt organizations, whether they be 501(c)(3)s, (4)s, (5)s, or (6)s. Therefore, understanding what constitutes unrelated business income is important to managers of all nonprofits (Chapter Ten).

10. Every nonprofit that has organized and operates business activity will some day face the issue of reorganizing it (Chapter Nineteen).

The impact is not always negative. A private operating foundation can meet the asset test, for example, if at least 65 percent of its assets are stocks of a corporation that it controls (that is, it owns at least 80 percent of the corporation's voting and other stocks) and if at least 85 percent of the assets of that corporation are devoted to the tax-exempt purpose of the private operating foundation or to a related business.

Also, income from businesses is considered to be part of the support justifying classification of a nonprofit as public foundation, for example, under Section 509(a)(1) or (2)(2). In short, the answer to this question depends on the tax-exempt classification of the nonprofit and the balance between business income and other types of support, such as gifts and contributions. But in no case is business or investment income barred, and in no case is there an absolute limit on the number of dollars that can be earned. The limit is relative to (1) the ability of the organization to pass the tests shown in Chapters Two and Three, and (2) its ability to carry out its mission with integrity.

To summarize, aside from the unrelated business income tax, business income affects public organizations via classification as 509(a) or (a)(2); private nonoperating foundations via excess business holdings; private operating foundations via meeting the asset test and excess business holdings; and has no legal limit or classification impact on associations to the extent that it can be defined as membership support. (See Chapter Five.)

HOW TO ACQUIRE A BUSINESS

Ownership or control of a business can be acquired as a gift, by purchase, or by starting it up from scratch. It can also be done by transforming a product or service that is provided free to one that has a price tag. All these involve investment decisions. With a gift, the management has to take into account the tax consequences and costs of operating the business and its development and ultimate disposition. Recall, for example, that a business that is acquired through debt, even if it is a gift, can produce taxable income from activities even though they are closely related to the tax-exempt mission of the nonprofit.

In starting up a business from scratch, the management has to incorporate, register, certify, and obtain licenses where these are required, hire employees, locate and acquire plant or office space, invest in inventory, establish lines of credit, establish relationships with suppliers and distributors, develop a market and a clientele, and work hard to establish credibility and name recognition. These are expensive and time-consuming activities. Each involves a risk and each delays the flow of revenues into the coffers of the nonprofit.

An alternative is to buy an existing business. In that case, the nonprofit purchaser avoids the difficulties and risks of starting from scratch. The seller of the business will include those start-up costs in the selling price as part of what is known as *goodwill.*

If the business is to be bought, the nonprofit may use one of two approaches. It may buy the stocks of the business if it is a corporation, or it may buy the individual assets—plant, equipment, and land. This second approach has the advantage that the purchaser does not have to assume the liabilities of the business that are not related specifically to the assets that it is purchasing. For example, if a nonprofit buys all the machines in a business and all the plants, it has to consider only the liabilities (debt) that relate directly to those assets.

However, this approach to buying a business does have its disadvantages. First, all the assets have to be individually valued, and the seller may be reluctant to finalize the sale if there are assets that the nonprofit does not want to buy. It is easier and often less expensive to sell the entire enterprise. Second, the nonprofit purchaser does not get the benefit of having a fully operating business in place, that is, one with a clientele, a line of suppliers, distributors, creditors, experienced workers, a reputation, and other favorable intangibles known as goodwill.

Hence, the option of purchasing the stocks of the corporation and thereby the entire corporation is often used. Buying the entire corporation, however, means (unless specifically excluded) assuming all its assets and liabilities. The advantage of this approach for a nonprofit is that it gets a running start by acquiring an operating business.

Starting from scratch is best accomplished when the business is related without requiring large investments of capital and when the necessary skills are closely allied to those the nonprofit has or cultivates in satisfying its tax-exempt mission.

SHOULD THE BUSINESS BE RELATED OR UNRELATED?

To begin with, we recognize that this choice is subject to the legal definitions to be discussed in the next chapter. Whether a business is related or not is a legal question based on the facts; when in doubt, a private letter ruling should be obtained. It is also evident that when capacity and capital are scarce there is less risk in conducting a related business. Such a business also provides for tax-exempt income, and this income flows directly from the business into the organization.

An unrelated business can be equally simple given that its key difference from a related business is that it is unrelated to the tax-exempt mission of the nonprofit. "Unrelated" has nothing to do with the capacity, capital, or complexity that characterizes the enterprise. It has to do with regularity and relevance. Does it rival the mission for attention and resources? If it does, think twice and incorporate the business as a separate corporation.

SHOULD THE BUSINESS BE SEPARATELY INCORPORATED?

The income from an unincorporated business flows directly to the nonprofit. When a risky and complex business is being contemplated, however, it might be best to incorporate it so as to separate it from the nonprofit. Such action shields the nonprofit from the liabilities and risks of the business. If the business fails, the nonprofit is not in jeopardy. It is not necessary that the new corporation be a for-profit firm. A nonprofit that qualifies under Section 509(a)(3) as discussed in Chapter Four may conduct a related or unrelated business to benefit its parent nonprofit. It may make a profit, but the profit must be used to support the parent organization and its tax-exempt mission. Unrelated net income (profits) of these corporations is taxable; related income is not.

If a for-profit corporation is acquired, its income is taxable at the level of the for-profit.[24] Dividends to the nonprofits may be received tax free. By creating a separate corporation to do its business rather than doing it itself, the nonprofit interrupts the direct flow of income from the business activity into its coffers. This is because the created corporation must have a board of directors who decide on the dividends the corporation will pay to the nonprofit owner.

The absence of a direct flow is not necessarily a meaningful disadvantage compared to a direct flow of revenues from the business to the nonprofit when the business is unincorporated. First, corporate board members with a sympathetic ear to the nonprofit can be chosen, although their first responsibility is to the for-profit corporation. Second, even if dividends are lower than the revenues in a direct flow, they are likely to be more steady. In a direct flow, the receipts of the nonprofit go up and down, reflecting the net revenues of the business each year. However, dividends can be declared in dollar terms (so many dollars per year) rather than as a proportion of earnings. And dividends can be paid out of past earnings retained by the corporation and even out of new debt. Financial planning is easier when flows are steady and reasonably predictable year to year.

WHERE DOES THE MONEY COME FROM TO ACQUIRE THE BUSINESS?

One deterrent to the purchase of a business is the lack of initial capital. Also, a leverage buy out (borrowing) can be arranged. When this is done, the assets of the business are used to make the sale by securing a loan for the purchase. A second approach is to use an installment sale, which may require little or no down payment. The seller receives an annual payment comprising three parts: (1) a return of the capital invested in the company, (2) capital gains or the amount the business increased in value over the seller's basis (initial investment plus improvements and minus depreciation), and (3) interest on the outstanding portion of the payments. An installment sale is attractive to the seller because it constitutes a regular annual payment; the portion that is a return of the capital is not taxable. The return of the owner's investment is not taxable.

In some cases, a business reorganization plan may be used to acquire the enterprise. In this case, the owners give up their common stocks in the business to the nonprofits for preferred stocks that the nonprofit would create and issue in the business. These latter stocks have preference over common stocks in receiving dividends and in protection if the business goes bankrupt, hence the name preferred stocks. This exchange gives the seller an annual income (the dividends) and gives the buyer (the nonprofit) control. The nonprofit also gets all the capital gains resulting from a future sale of its common stocks. It retains the expertise of the business owner, who will remain interested in the future of the business because the payment of dividends depends on it. Moreover, if the exchange is prepared properly the seller will not have to pay taxes on the gains received in the swap of stocks at the time that the swap is made, but will be taxed at a future time if and when the preferred stocks are sold.

IS THE BUSINESS PROFITABLE?

The answer is in terms of for whom, when, and how much. Imaginative entrepreneurs have been able to turn losing enterprises around, and new businesses often experience losses.

Immediately high levels of profitability might not be a good reason for buying or starting a business. High levels of profitability may be only temporary because they tend to attract other investors. The more investors there are, the lower the amount of profits each receives; the large profit eventually disappears.[25]

Similarly, low levels of profits are not necessarily permanent. Profits can be low because of bad management, high costs, and limited markets, all of which can be reversed. Profits can also be affected by the method used to value inventory. In a period of rising costs, a method that values the inventory of a business at the current market price deflates profits. This is because all goods would appear to cost more than they actually did when the business bought or produced the goods sold. A method that values inventory at the original, lower cost inflates the true levels of profits.

Moreover, the earnings of a corporation may be affected by extraordinary nonrecurrent factors. The sale of a piece of land or a plant may result in an extraordinary loss or gain. Such losses and gains are not derived from the operation of the business and will tell us nothing about whether the business is being operated profitably. Also, we must distinguish between after-tax and before-tax earnings of the business.

To illustrate, the gross profit is the difference between the revenues from sales and the cost of the goods sold. Remember that the cost of goods sold is partly determined by the value of those goods in inventory. This gross profit, however, is not the complete story. When other operating costs such as labor, utilities, and insurance are deducted, income before taxes is derived. If the corporation is running an unrelated business, taxes must be paid. Only after these factors are taken into account do we get after-tax net income from operations.

In certain years, the corporation may have extraordinary gains or losses due to damage, the sale of assets such as plants and equipment, and so on. The gains must be added and the losses must be subtracted from income from operations to calculate the net income of the corporation. Hence, in evaluating the income performance of a corporation, its own or one that it wishes to buy, the management ought to focus on income from operations. What the business will have to offer the nonprofit, barring an extraordinary event, is net income from operations, specifically, income from operations minus expenses (except depreciation) and after taxes. This approximates what is sometimes called *free cash flow*.

IS PROFITABILITY ENOUGH?

Looking at the income from operations (after taxes if the business is unrelated and pays taxes) of the business in only one year will not suffice. Any one year may be an aberration. Moreover, the nonprofit is interested in the flow of income during the years in which it will remain invested in the business. Based on the information in the income statements over several years and an analysis of future operations and markets, let us assume the nonprofit may reasonably expect to receive $100,000 per year for the next ten years. Will it be worth the investment of the nonprofit's money? Remember, the nonprofit is not a gambler, and it handles money in public trust for a public purpose. Although income is necessary, is it worth the investment of public money?

A good manager faced with this question will quickly consider the fact that the same investment could be placed in a U.S. Treasury bond without default risk, but with ultimate safety and a good rate of return. Why put it in a business and take risks? Obviously, this will be done only if the expected rate of return from the business is higher than the Treasury bond and if the rate is also sufficiently high to compensate the nonprofit for the risk it will be taking. The manager will then say that the investment must yield a rate of return that is higher than the opportunity cost (the amount it will give up by not investing in the Treasury bond) plus a premium for the risk. In general, the investment is worth it only if it compensates the nonprofit for the opportunity cost plus any risk premium, and the risks can be satisfactorily minimized. Investment is not a synonym for gambling. If the rate is not sufficiently high, the manager might as well invest in U.S. Treasury securities.

The rate of return in any single year of an investment is calculated by dividing the amount of dividends and appreciation after taxes from that investment by the amount of investment made. Obviously, the significance of this ratio is that it gives a measure of how much each dollar that the nonprofit owner has tied up in the business earns for the organization.

Incidentally, this is one reason that perfectly healthy and profitable businesses are often available for sale. It is not because they are unprofitable, but the rate of return might be too low to justify the investment by a particular investor. Again, an advantage for nonprofits is they do not have to compete for investors' dollars by constantly offering higher rates of return to stockholders, as do firms. They have no individual investors to satisfy. For-profit corporations do, so they often will sell a perfectly profitable subsidiary or operation to seek higher rates of return elsewhere.

WHAT WILL THE INVESTMENT COST?

Sometimes the nonprofit will be a price taker. This means that it faces a price that it must pay because it is not in a position to negotiate or to influence the price in any way. Such is the case when the nonprofit purchases stocks or bonds on the stock market. In other cases, such as real estate, the nonprofit is in a position to negotiate a price and can determine what a reasonable price will be by comparing the market price for similar properties in the surrounding area. In yet other cases, a reasonable price may be ascertained by looking at the performance of the business over the past (usually a minimum of five years).

In still other cases, it is possible to ascertain a reasonable price by looking at the book value of the enterprise. The book value is roughly the owner's equity in the business (the net amount the owner of the business has in it), the assets minus the liabilities. But the asking price by the seller will rarely equal the book value. It would invariably be higher, because the book value does not reflect valuable intangibles such as an existing clientele, lines of credit, or a good name. This additional amount, over and above the book value, is called *goodwill.* The asking price will be the book value plus the goodwill.[26] Whether the seller will get the asking price depends on the ability of the nonprofit to negotiate. This ability is enhanced if the nonprofit has an independent professional appraisal made of the business.

FROM A FINANCIAL PERSPECTIVE, IS THE INVESTMENT WORTH IT?

One of the disciplines learned from the previous chapters is that when a nonprofit enters into an investment or an unrelated business, its main (not necessarily its exclusive) purpose is to earn money. Business is business, and the main benefits are measurable in dollars. If at this point the honor of earning a dollar cannot be accepted by the board of the nonprofit, it should drop the idea of making an investment, for it will fail.

From a strictly financial perspective, both benefits and costs are measurable in terms of dollars. The benefits are the dollars that are expected to flow into the coffers of the nonprofit over the years. The benefits are the net annual revenues equaling sales price minus operating costs and any taxes, including the unrelated business income tax. The annual operating costs are already reflected in the net revenues, so the concern is with the initial or acquisition cost. These costs are the dollars the organization has to lay out today in order to acquire the investment.

Obviously, the nonprofit should not invest in the business if the amount of money it has to lay out initially is higher than the present value of net benefits it expects to receive over the entire life of the business. But note that the initial investment or cost has to be paid today with today's dollars. The benefits will flow over several years, and although a flow into perpetuity may be desired, given inflation, every dollar that is received several years in the future is worth less than the dollar paid today. What is the future flow of benefits worth today? Is it less than, equal to, or greater than the cost that must be met to acquire and operate the business? In the language of business, what is its present value?

To answer this question, we must discount the future flow of benefits by a factor that reflects the rate at which inflation will lower the value of the dollar over time. This discount rate may also reflect the risk and opportunity cost that is involved in the investment; for example, we may take the rate paid on Treasury bonds and add a premium to reflect the risk. In this way we arrive at a discount rate, the rate at which we discount the flow of future earnings from the business to find out what those earnings are worth in today's dollars. This discounted future earnings is called the *present value* of the expected flow of benefits.

Naturally, if the present value of benefits exceeds the costs of the investment or business, then the investment makes economic sense. If it is less than the cost, the investment makes no economic sense. If it is equal to the costs, the investment is marginal, but still worthwhile.

Sometimes the present value of the benefits and the costs are expressed in the benefit-cost ratio. A ratio greater than 1 indicates that the benefits exceed the costs; a ratio of less than 1 implies the reverse; a ratio of 1 indicates that the costs and benefits are equal.

DO THE BENEFITS EXCEED THE COSTS?

Public sector and nonprofits often use the concept of a benefit-cost ratio to evaluate a project. Chapter Seven shows a technique the author has developed for cases in which the calculation cannot be done. Here let us assume that the seller's asking price after negotiation is $700,000, and the independent professional appraiser agrees with this figure. Let us also assume that we may expect $100,000 per year to flow into the coffers of the nonprofit if it should undertake this investment, and that it intends to remain invested in this business for thirty years. Is it worth $100,000 per year for thirty years, given an initial cost of $700,000? The answer depends on the discount rate that reflects how risky the investment is compared to a safe one paying high rates, such as the Treasury bond. It also depends on the expected rate of inflation, which will erode the dollar over time. Suppose we decide that after taking all these factors into account we should discount the future earnings by 15 percent, which is not unusual during periods of high expected inflation. What is the present value of the benefits?[27]

To answer this question, we refer to Table 9.1 and note the number 6.566 in the cell that corresponds to thirty years and 15 percent. If we multiply $100,000 (the annual expected return) by 6.566, we get $656,600, which is the present value of that $100,000 expected over thirty years when discounted at 15 percent. Because this amount of $656,600 is the benefit and the asking price, the cost, is $700,000, the investment is not acceptable to this nonprofit.

Table 9.1. Present Value of an Annuity of $1 a Year.

Years	Interest																	
	1	2	4	6	8	10	12	14	15	16	18	20	22	24	25	26	28	30
1	0.990	0.980	0.962	0.943	0.926	0.909	0.893	0.877	0.870	0.862	0.847	0.833	0.820	0.806	0.800	0.794	0.781	0.769
2	1.970	1.942	1.886	1.833	1.783	1.736	1.690	1.647	1.626	1.605	1.566	1.528	1.492	1.457	1.440	1.424	1.392	1.361
3	2.941	2.884	2.775	2.673	2.577	2.487	2.402	2.322	2.283	2.246	2.174	2.106	2.042	1.981	1.952	1.923	1.868	1.816
4	3.902	3.808	3.630	3.465	3.312	3.170	3.037	2.914	2.855	2.798	2.690	2.589	2.494	2.404	2.362	2.320	2.241	2.166
5	4.853	4.713	4.452	4.212	3.993	3.791	3.605	3.433	3.352	3.274	3.127	2.991	2.864	2.745	2.689	2.635	2.532	2.436
6	5.795	5.601	5.242	4.917	4.623	4.355	4.111	3.889	3.784	3.685	3.498	3.326	3.167	3.020	2.951	2.885	2.759	2.643
7	6.728	6.472	6.002	5.582	5.206	4.868	4.564	4.288	4.160	4.039	3.812	3.605	3.416	3.242	3.161	3.083	2.937	2.802
8	7.652	7.325	6.733	6.210	5.747	5.335	4.968	4.639	4.487	4.344	4.078	3.817	3.619	3.421	3.329	3.241	3.076	2.925
9	8.566	8.162	7.435	6.802	6.247	5.759	5.328	4.946	4.772	4.607	4.303	4.031	3.786	3.566	3.463	3.366	3.184	3.019
10	9.471	8.983	8.111	7.360	6.710	6.145	5.630	5.216	5.019	4.833	4.494	4.192	3.923	3.682	3.571	3.465	3.269	3.092
11	10.368	9.787	8.760	7.887	7.139	6.495	5.937	5.453	5.234	5.029	4.656	4.327	4.035	3.776	3.656	3.544	3.335	3.147
12	11.255	10.575	9.385	8.384	7.536	6.814	6.194	5.660	5.421	5.197	4.793	4.439	4.127	3.851	3.725	3.606	3.387	3.190
13	12.134	11.543	9.986	8.853	7.904	7.103	6.424	5.842	5.583	5.342	4.910	4.533	4.203	3.912	3.780	3.656	3.427	3.223
14	13.004	12.106	10.563	9.295	8.244	7.367	6.628	6.002	5.724	5.468	5.008	4.511	4.265	3.962	3.824	3.695	3.459	3.249
15	13.865	12.849	11.118	9.712	8.559	7.606	6.811	6.142	5.847	5.575	5.092	4.675	4.315	4.001	3.859	3.726	3.483	3.268

16	14.718	13.578	11.652	10.106	8.851	7.824	6.974	6.265	5.954	5.669	5.162	4.730	4.357	4.033	3.887	3.751	3.503	3.283
17	15.562	14.292	12.166	10.477	9.122	8.022	7.120	6.373	6.047	5.749	5.222	4.775	4.391	4.059	3.910	3.771	3.518	3.295
18	16.398	14.992	12.659	10.828	9.372	8.201	7.250	6.467	6.128	5.818	5.273	4.812	4.419	4.080	3.928	3.786	3.529	3.304
19	17.226	15.678	13.134	11.158	9.604	8.365	7.566	6.550	6.198	5.877	5.316	4.844	4.442	4.097	3.942	3.799	3.539	3.331
20	18.046	16.351	13.590	11.470	9.818	8.514	7.469	6.623	6.259	5.929	5.353	4.870	4.460	4.110	3.954	3.808	3.546	3.316
21	18.857	17.011	14.029	11.764	10.017	8.649	7.562	6.687	6.312	5.973	5.384	4.891	4.476	4.121	3.963	3.816	3.551	3.320
22	19.660	17.658	14.451	12.042	10.201	8.772	7.645	6.743	6.359	6.011	5.410	4.909	4.488	4.130	3.970	3.822	3.556	3.323
23	20.456	18.292	14.857	12.303	10.371	8.883	7.718	6.792	6.399	6.044	5.432	4.925	4.499	4.137	3.976	3.827	3.559	3.325
24	21.243	18.914	15.247	12.550	10.529	8.985	7.784	6.835	6.434	6.073	5.451	4.937	4.507	4.143	3.981	3.831	3.562	3.327
25	22.023	19.523	15.622	12.783	10.675	9.077	7.843	6.873	6.464	6.097	5.467	4.948	4.514	4.147	3.985	3.834	3.564	3.329
26	22.795	20.121	15.983	13.003	10.810	9.161	7.896	6.906	6.491	6.118	5.480	4.956	4.520	4.151	3.988	3.837	3.566	3.330
27	23.560	20.707	16.330	13.211	10.935	9.237	7.943	6.935	6.514	6.136	5.492	4.964	4.524	4.154	3.990	3.839	3.567	3.331
28	24.316	21.281	16.663	13.406	11.051	9.307	7.984	6.961	6.534	6.152	5.502	4.970	4.528	4.157	3.992	3.840	3.568	3.331
29	25.066	21.844	16.984	13.591	11.158	9.370	8.022	6.983	6.551	6.166	5.510	4.975	4.531	4.159	3.994	3.841	3.569	3.332
30	25.808	22.396	17.292	13.765	11.258	9.427	8.055	7.003	6.566	6.177	5.517	4.979	4.534	4.160	3.995	3.842	3.569	3.332

Suppose, however, the investment were less risky or that we expected a lower rate of inflation so that our future earnings would not be eroded. In that case, we may use a discount rate of 10 percent, which is not uncommon when inflation is not rampant and investments are not very risky. By referring to Table 9.1, we note that at 10 percent for thirty years the number is 9.427. We multiply $100,000 by 9.427 and get $942,700. In this example, the benefits ($942,700) exceed the costs ($700,000). A good deal!

Try the same example, discounting at 14 percent. Here the present value of the benefits is $700,300 compared to a cost of $700,000. We are at the margin where benefits and costs are about equal and the benefit-cost ratio would be approximately 1. What would you do? It is these marginal cases that are most challenging.

WHEN WILL THE ORGANIZATION RECAPTURE ITS INVESTMENT?

The benefit-cost ratio and methods of discounting future earnings to determine whether the investment is acceptable are based on the assumption that the nonprofit will remain invested for a period of time or for the expected life of the investment. Given the pressures on funds, the need to be prudent, and the need to satisfy a board, the management of the nonprofit may ask another question: How long will it take to get our money out of the investment? Technically, how long is the payback period? For an inexperienced or shy manager or for an organization that takes a conservative approach to investment, it might be ideal to invest only in business projects in which the payback period is short.

It is easy to determine the approximate length of the payback period. Merely divide the investment to be made (the cost or initial outlay) by the amount that can be expected to flow into the coffers of the nonprofit annually. This is the approximate time that it would take to retrieve the investment.

To illustrate, assume a project costing $1,000 as an initial outlay. The net income (revenues minus operating costs) per year is expected to be $500. In two years, the net income will be enough to recover the initial cost. Notice, however, that these are projections. There is no certainty. Notice also that a low payback period implies a high rate of return on the investment, and recall that high rates are associated with risks. They are the rewards for taking high risks in the market economy.

WHAT ARE THE RISKS?

Every investment is subject to risks. One type of risk is that the investment will go sour; another is that the earnings from the investment may be eroded by high rates of inflation; or the investment may be illiquid, meaning that it cannot be converted to dollars easily without a severe penalty; or the investment may not be marketable. Which risk is most important depends on the type of investment. For example, investing in certificates of deposit holds very little risk of total loss of investment compared with investments in hot go-go stocks, as long as the federal guarantee limits are not exceeded. And although stocks are easily marketable, the risk is high because they can fall in price dramatically. Risks have to be compensated for, and the compensation is the rate of return. Would you invest in a high-risk venture if you did not believe that it offered fantastic gains? No, and neither would anybody else. Rational investing is the art involving matching risks and rewards. Would you keep your money in an extremely risky investment for a long time? No, and that is why your organization may want to look at a short payback period when risks are high.

Businesses are concerned with two broad types of risks: (1) financial or money-related risks, and (2) business risks, which are those that are nonfinancial such as shifts in the market for the product or service. A nonprofit must do the same. But the ultimate risk for a nonprofit is that it would lose its tax-exempt status and that management will be held liable as a result. This risk can only be evaluated by understanding the issues in Part One of this book.

Holding idle cash balances is not a way to avoid taking risks. Cash invites theft and mishandling. Uninvested cash erodes in value due to inflation. Holding cash is an opportunity cost, the loss of earnings that the nonprofit organization could use.

WHAT WILL IT TAKE TO BREAK EVEN?

Part of judging the suitability of an investment is knowing what is required to at least break even. It is not enough to know that the recovery period for one's investment may be short or long or that the rate of return might be high enough to compensate for the risk. It might also be important to be able to judge the amount of effort that it might take to at least break even. This means to be able to cover the full cost of operation so that the organization is not dipping into its own pocket or into general support to sustain the business. The business is at least supporting itself.

Recall that the break-even point for a product occurs at the level of sales where the revenues from sales are just enough to cover all costs of producing and selling this product. This is like saying that the difference between the revenues and costs is zero or that total revenues equal total costs.

Total revenues are the quantity sold multiplied by the price at which each unit is sold. Total cost is the number produced times the cost of producing each unit. Once the break-even point is known, it is simple to answer a question that should be significant to every nonprofit owner of a business: How much must be produced to meet a target rate of earnings flowing from the business into the nonprofit? Appendix 9.1 shows how to answer this and related questions.

WHAT CAN BE DONE WITH THE EARNINGS OF THE BUSINESS?

To this point, we have been selfish. We see the after-tax earnings of the business as being the property of the nonprofit owner of the business to carry out its mission. This is technically accurate and should be the primary motive. However, the earnings of a business may be retained in it to make further investments to increase its capacity to finance the nonprofit and its mission. It can also be temporarily invested using cash management tools discussed in Chapters Fifteen and Sixteen.

HOW WILL ENTRY INTO THE BUSINESS BE MADE?

Charles Berry and Edward Roberts developed a typological approach to answering this question.[28] Although their examples pertain to for-profit firms, with some modification they can apply to nonprofits as well. See Figure 9.1. A discussion of a few cells is sufficient for our purposes.

The idea is that when an organization chooses to enter into a new business venture, it should begin with an assessment of its familiarity with the market for the goods and services to be produced by the new venture and with its technical competence to produce the goods or services. When the organization is totally unfamiliar with the technology and the market *(cell C going left to right)*, it would be very risky for the organization to go it alone or even to be a working partner in the business. Wiser strategies would be to invest money in the business (venture capital) or acquire the business but keep its present technical staff to run it (educational acquisition). Cells B and F represent the same type of situation. The organization is unfamiliar with the technology and only slightly understands the market. These cells are risky and depend on the learning curve.

Alternatively, the nonprofit may find itself attracted to a business in which it is already involved in both the market and the technology. It has a base in both *(cell G)*. In that case, it would be sensible for the nonprofit to consider going it alone by building internally or by acquiring additional productive resources, even if this meant purchasing the business of a competitor.

Another possibility is that the nonprofit may have a base either in the market or in the technology, but not both *(cells A and I)*. Joint ventures make sense here. The nonprofit enters into an agreement with another organization that

Market Factors	Base	New Familiar	New Unfamiliar
New Unfamiliar	**A** Joint Ventures	**B** Venture Capital or Venture Nurturing or Educational Acquisitions	**C** Venture Capital or Venture Nurturing or Educational Acquisitions
New Familiar	**D** Internal Market Developments or Acquisitions (or Joint Ventures)	**E** Internal Ventures or Acquisitions or Licensing	**F** Venture Capital or Venture Nurturing or Educational Acquisitions
Base	**G** Internal Base Developments (or Acquisitions)	**H** Internal Product Developments or Acquisitions or Licensing	**I** "New Style" Joint Ventures

Technologies or Services Embodied in the Product

Figure 9.1. Optimum Entry Strategies.

Source: Reprinted from Charles A. Berry and Edward B. Roberts, "Entering New Businesses: Selecting Strategies for Success," *Sloan Management Review,* Vol. 26, No. 3 (Spring 1985), 13, by permission of the publisher. Copyright © 1985 by Sloan Management Review Association. All rights reserved.

takes responsibility for either the technology or market, whichever it does better, and the nonprofit takes responsibility for whichever it does better. Notice that what makes a joint venture practicable is that each party has what the other needs to be successful. A joint venture is frequently attractive in business deals because each party maintains its own corporate identity. They merely choose to work together on a specific project. To protect themselves, they might form a whole new corporation or partnership simply for the purpose of carrying out that one business deal.

The nonprofit may be attracted to a business opportunity in an area in which it has familiarity both about the market and the technology. Although the market and technology are familiar, the business would be risky because the nonprofit has never been actively involved in it *(cell E)*. For protection, the nonprofit may form a separate group or corporation (internal venture) to engage in the business. Or it may acquire an outside firm through purchase that is already in the business. It could also enter the business be acquiring all rights or a license and lease them to a firm that can actually do the production. Marketing can be done through a wider network than the nonprofit has. Owning a copyright, permitting manufacturers to use your logo whether on mugs, pens, or shirts, amounts to pursuing this type of strategy.

The attraction of this strategy is that production and market risks and costs are shifted from the nonprofit to a commercial enterprise. Unfair competition is avoided, and the nonprofit gets a risk-free untaxed flow of income called *royalties.*

In yet another scenario, the nonprofit may have a good sound footing in the technology but has never marketed the product, although it has some familiarity with what the market is like. In this case *(cell D)* the nonprofit may wish to develop an internal marketing department, or it might acquire a firm that specializes in that kind of marketing, or it may establish a joint venture with such a firm to take advantage of its expertise.

In *cell H* the organization is solidly grounded in the market, but the technology is new. Here the possibilities for internal development of the technology may be considered, although this may be expensive and risky. Better alternatives may be to acquire a firm that is already producing the product or control of the license of such a production. A joint venture may also be possible here, with the nonprofit doing the marketing and the for-profit providing the products. This is precisely what happens when books, insurance, travel plans, and the like are offered through associations. They are actually doing the marketing of a product or service produced by a for-profit firm.

WHAT IS THE COMPETITION? IS IT FAIR?

This question comes in three parts: business, legal, and public relations. The business question is strictly, is there a market for this business? Chapters Seventeen and Eighteen on strategic planning shows how to go about answering that question.

The legal question deals with the Sherman and the Clayton antitrust acts. These laws make it illegal for firms to impede competition either by price fixing or restricting the market. Though we are wont to think of these laws as strictly relating to for-profit firms, in recent years we have seen them increasingly applied to nonprofit organizations, including several well-known colleges for fixing tuition by sharing tuition and financial aid information. Such anticompetitive collusion is as illegal for colleges and universities, museums, and hospitals—any organization operating in a competitive environment—as it is for firms such as airlines and automobile companies.

Likewise, setting prices below cost so as to create a restricted, monopolistic market is illegal. Note that it is not just low prices, but prices that are below cost. This is normally not a concern of nonprofits dealing primarily with the poor. It should be to others, since one way to demonstrate public welfare is to set lower than commercial prices. Such low prices may be offset by lower costs. Operating costs of nonprofits may be lower by use of volunteers and less attractive facilities.

The antitrust laws can also be infringed on by market share. Using this theory, the court in *U.S. v. Rockford Memorial Corporation*, 1989, barred the expansion of this nonprofit hospital by arguing that its expansion would result in its having 90 percent of the market, which it could potentially control. Chapter Nineteen delves further into these questions.

Markets can be controlled in other ways. In Virginia, a medical supplier charged a number of nonprofit hospitals with unfair competition. It appears that these hospitals used to refer clients to him. Later, these hospitals concluded that they would set up their own business and service their patients directly.

Can't the hospitals argue that they could better serve their patients in this way? Isn't competition healthy? What was the quality of work being done by the private firm? Is the need for additional revenues by the hospitals so great that they could not have foregone this commercial activity? Was the fray foreseeable?

These questions are not easy and this is why many of these cases end up in court. But they demonstrate why, even for the smallest nonprofit, dealing with the appearance of unfairness is important. Here are 3Ps to guide your decision.

Three Ps for a Decision on a Business Venture

1. *Propriety:* Does it fit the nonprofit's image, its mission, and the law? Is it fair? Does it place the organization and its natural clients at risk?

2. *Profitability:* Does the venture cover all its costs and make a worthwhile monetary and nonmonetary contribution to the nonprofit?

3. *Practicability:* Does it work?

Of the three Ps, violation of propriety is the most dangerous because it can lead to the loss of exemption—even if the other two Ps are met.

WHAT DO THE TRUSTEES THINK OF THE PLAN?

The trustees have the final word. They must make investment decisions usually with a social conscience and often governed by the "prudent man's rule" stating, in effect, that overly risky use of the organization's resources and energies are to be avoided. The ultimate risk is not financial, although it can be considerable, but the loss of tax-exempt status.

Furthermore, the charter and bylaws of the organization may designate what types of investments are permissible. State and local laws may limit the type of investments the nonprofit may make, and there might be restrictions in the agreements under which trusts, endowments, and gifts were made.

Furthermore, no good manager attempts any meaningful investment without consulting a lawyer, an accountant, and the investment or financial committees of the nonprofit. In short, a business plan containing more than projections of costs, revenues, clients, and financing needs is advisable. The plan should also answer the questions in this chapter to the critical approval of trustees guided by informed advisors. Once all this has been done, the decision can be made by the trustees.

ETHICAL DILEMMA OF BUSINESS COMPETITION

Unfair competition has been a charge levied by small businesses against nonprofits ever since New York University law school owned Mueller Macaroni Company, which it eventually sold. Spokespersons for coalitions of small businesses charge that nonprofits are able to use their tax-exempt status to acquire capital and their close relationships with their members to create a "halo" effect and that along with their tax-exempt status and nonprofit mailing privileges, they compete unfairly with firms.

Proposals placed before Congress went to extremes, including barring nonprofits from entering certain businesses and taking away some of their tax-exempt privileges. The small business coalition moved its fight into the state legislatures, and has generally not been successful.[29]

Basic to any action, as the U.S. House Ways and Means committee members have said, is the absence of a clear picture of how extensive this abuse is. The IRS now requires more detailed reporting by nonprofits of their business activities. But there are other serious issues.

Does the enforcement of present law offer a better alternative? Is the issue one of enforcement rather than the need for new legislation? Would the legislative proposals put forth by some severely, and perhaps unconstitutionally, restrict trade? What do we do about small communities in which the nonprofit is really the principal business? Is the secondary income stream to a community from a university's running an unrelated business (such as having a professional team use its athletic facilities) something the community is willing to give up? Who in the community would put up facilities to be used a few weeks in a year? Is it ethical to bar an organization from participating in the fruits of an economy it helps to generate and in which (in the case of research and sports) it is also the primary risk taker and cost absorber? What may be the consequence?

A museum that took its vending outdoors and competed with outside vendors by selling articles that were subjects of the museum was informing people and not involved in unrelated business.[30]

However, is it proper that a nonprofit should be selling insurance, given the millions of insurance agents in the country and the fact that these policies sold by nonprofits are often not superior? The same insurance company that produces the policies sold by a nonprofit organization produces competitive policies that their agents sell in the open market. Who is responsible for the inequality? Who benefits?

This is not atypical. Companies other than insurance companies do the same thing and usually can justify this arrangement on a cost basis, that is, lower costs of marketing through nonprofits. Therefore, they are in conformity with antitrust laws. Who is creating the advantage, the nonprofit or the company that supplies both the nonprofit and the for-profit firms and therefore gains multiple marketing channels?

What do you think?

Remember, first, what may be profitable for a nonprofit, given the factors discussed in this text that can reduce costs and therefore make them profitable, does not necessarily apply to a for-profit firm. Second, many activities in which nonprofits are engaged are not attractive to for-profit firms. Third, the size of the retained earnings is not the point. Organizations must justify excessive accumulations to the IRS, for example, to finance new buildings, purchase equipment, pay staff, and have strong financial profiles to influence creditors and credit agencies.

Whatever your arguments, respect case facts and history.

SUMMARY AND PREVIEW

We should now appreciate that the nonprofit is a corporation with legal limits and powers. Its *raison d'etre* is its mission, which has the force of a social contract.

But the nonprofit has costs and needs revenues. Moreover, by being tax exempt and utilizing society's resources, it must also economize. Hence, it is an economic institution. A major and rapidly growing source of revenues is business income or profits. This chapter deals with the conditions for the pursuit of business income.

We now turn to the important classification of business income into related and unrelated income and the effects of this classification on the nonprofit regardless of whether it is an association or a charity. We turn to the tax consequence of business income.

CHAPTER TEN

Organizational and Tax Consequences of Business Ventures

After reading the previous chapter, there should be no question that the decision to conduct a business activity has legal and tax implications and, further, that the exclusive motivation for launching a business activity should be to help finance the cost of operating or growing the organization in the conduct of its mission. This chapter relates to all U.S. nonprofits (charities as well as associations).

What does this chapter have to say to the manager? All business transactions by a nonprofit entity, be it a charity or an association, must be classified into one of two groups: either related or unrelated. This classification is based on specific definitions used by the IRS and interpreted by the courts when there is a dispute between the IRS and the organization. In addition, certain types of business activities meet the definition of unrelated but are treated as exclusions. Therefore, as you may guess, managers and their tax advisers are constantly trying to have their business income fit either the definition of related or one of the exclusions. This allows them to avoid taxes.

As we saw in Part One, however, for the publicly supported organizations, this definition has another importance. It is used to figure the structure of its revenues and therefore affects its classification. Consequently, the good manager is not only concerned with making or losing money, or paying taxes, but with how the classification of the organization is affected. As we saw in Part

One, an excessive amount of unrelated business income quickly gives the organization the profile of a firm. Why should it be given tax exemption?

The overwhelming emphasis of this chapter is on describing related and unrelated business income—the basic rules and exceptions—and how they are treated for tax purposes. The previous chapter gives several questions an organization needs to raise before embarking on a business activity.

THE IMPORTANCE OF BUSINESS IN THE NONPROFIT CORPORATE STRUCTURE

In accessing a business opportunity, we should keep three critical differences between a charity or an association and a business firm in the forefront of our thinking: (1) The charity or association can tolerate a lower than competitive rate of return, (2) it cannot distribute gains or assets to shareholders, and (3) it may not have a substantial or primary commercial motive. It must use its resources to further public rather than private welfare, as discussed in the previous chapter.

But this does not imply (1) that the nonprofit should not seek a positive rate of return on its activities and investments or that (2) there are no claimants on its assets and earnings. The interests of these claimants are a dominant force. Nonprofits, like firms, must have earnings targets and cost discipline. These are imposed internally by staff and directors and indirectly by external claimants. There are two groups of claimants who place constraints and pressures on the performance of nonprofits. One group of claimants has a legal claim; the other, an ethical or moral expectation.

First, the legal. Any nonprofit that has tried to borrow a significant amount of funds either through the sale of bonds or from a bank will testify to the fact that lenders are no more generous simply because one is a charity. They charge competitive rates and expect to be paid on time. Therefore, any nonprofit that has a significant loan must have some way of financing it, either through gifts and contributions or through earned revenues. In short, although the rate of return (financial performance) does not have to satisfy shareholders, it must be good enough to pay all creditors—landlords and lenders, managers and workers, vendors and fee collectors, all of whom are legal claimants.

Second, the nonprofit by its very existence and previous operations cultivates an expectation and a clientele. This group does not have a legal claim on the assets or financial performance (income) of the organization. They have a moral claim, which might, in the case of the needy, be stronger than the legal claim. In short, as a business, a nonprofit has to see that its income (revenue and support) is sufficient to satisfy creditors and clients as claimants.

A businesslike perspective is even more clearly applicable in nonprofits that are 509(a)(2)s. For, as we saw in Chapter Two, running as a business is what they do. If it were not a contradiction in terms, they could be described as businesses with public welfare missions. What would this mean? It means that they are organizations that have public missions, a substantial part of which can be covered by a price. Therefore, it makes sense to encourage these organizations to finance themselves principally by charging. Museums charge fees; universities, tuition; orchestras, admission.

Admittedly, this argument is less true of 509(a)(1)s, but even among these organizations, there are those better able to support themselves by prices than by gifts and donations. "Better" means that they can depend less, not rely exclusively. Short of running its blood service as a business, the Red Cross would have had to close it down a long time ago. Gifts and donations do not come close to covering costs. Can you imagine how inefficient this service would be if it had to depend on the federal budget and bureaucracy?

Some 90 percent of the total revenues of Consumer Union, publishers of the *Consumer Report,* is business income from sales of that publication. Does this offend you? Now, ask yourself, if Consumer Union were relying on contributions, how free would it be to review, rate, and reject products? With what credibility? Business income has its place. It buys objectivity, continuity, growth, and freedom.

Some 43 percent of the total revenue and support of the Salvation Army is from sales of its publications to its members. Sales of supplies to its members account for 44 percent of the revenues and support of the Girl Scouts, and 41 percent of the revenues and support of Father Flanagan's Boys Home is investment income primarily in its endowment fund.[1]

Suffice it to say that this and the previous chapters are not intended to induce nonprofits to plunge willy-nilly into commercial activities but deal with a reality: Earned income is a necessary ingredient for nonprofits no matter how charitable their missions. Both chapters, consistent with this entire book, are about managing costs and revenues in the context of furthering the mission of nonprofits. We begin our journey by looking at organization, because managing costs and revenues may mean operating certain activities as though they were a separate business. Where do these fit in the nonprofit organization?

DEFINITION OF RELATED AND UNRELATED NONPROFIT BUSINESSES

Does it fit? A related business is one that fits integrally as part of the mission of the organization. That is, the income it generates is directly a result of the organization's conducting its community or public welfare mission. Appropriately, the income from this kind of business is not taxed, and it is also categorized as public support for 509(a)(2) organizations.

An unrelated business is one that is not integrally related to the mission of the organization. Its principal purpose is to generate income. A net income (profits) generated from an unrelated business is taxed. Income from an unrelated business is classified as support in 509(a)(1) organizations.

An unrelated business is a trade or business regularly conducted by a nonprofit for the purpose of making a profit. The unrelated business makes little or no substantive or programmatic contribution to the exempt mission of the organization. Its primary contribution is money. A program-related business, on the other hand, is directly and integrally related to the programmatic and substantive goals of the nonprofit. Hence, program-related business would be carried on even if it were not profitable. An unrelated business is pursued because it is expected to be profitable. Interest earned on loans by a nonprofit that has lending as its mission is related business income. It is related to the mission.

There are three keys to determining whether an activity is an unrelated business. First, it is a trade or a business conducted to generate a profit. There must be a clear profit motive. It is the intent, not the size of the profits, that matters.

Sometimes a nonprofit might find itself trying to convince the IRS that an activity is for profit. This allows the organization to use the losses to offset gains in other unrelated businesses and therefore reduce the taxes due. In accessing whether an activity is for profit, the IRS may resort to a nine-prong test:

1. The manner in which the activity is carried on should be businesslike, with the maintenance of complete records, advertising, setting prices rationally, and so on.

2. There should be some expertise in the enterprise and a knowledge of what makes the enterprise successful.

3. There should be enough time and effort spent to make the activity profitable.

4. There should be some expectation that the assets will increase in value.

5. The prospects of profits are enhanced if the taxpayer had related experience, whether profitable or unprofitable.

6. An abnormal string of early loss for the enterprise may indicate a lack of a profit motive.

7. Whether there are changes in the method of operation to improve profitability.

8. An occasional profit of some significant amount may indicate a profit motive; that is, if it shows a profit in three of the past five years, including the current.

9. If the taxpayer has considerable other income such that this source may be deemed as purely a tax-avoidance activity.

In looking at profitability by individuals or from the perspective of compensation, the IRS may be suspicious if the existence of considerable elements of personal pleasure implies that pleasure is the motive—not profit-making.

Second, an unrelated business is a regular activity, not a one-time or occasional event, where the event normally will occur with greater frequency. It is regular if it is conducted by the nonprofit with the same frequency as would a for-profit firm. A one-time bake sale is not an unrelated business. *Regularity, what does it mean?* An example will help.

Once a year the National Collegiate Athletic Association (NCAA) holds a basketball tournament culminating in the Final Four. It arranges with a for-profit corporation to advertise in its program for the Final Four. This advertisement was ruled an unrelated business even though the Final Four is held but once a year. It is regular, it happens every year. In all sports, a tournament once a year is regular. The World Series and Super Bowl are once a year. Finally, the NCAA regularly has tournaments, one for every sport. The NCAA won its case on appeal. The judge ruled that the "duration" of the advertising was not long enough to constitute regularity and that this practice by the NCAA was not significant enough to constitute unfair competition with publications such as *Sports Illustrated.*[2]

Regularity is measured by the norm for that activity reflecting frequency and duration. Regularity does not mean every day. It means the frequency and duration that is customary among for-profit firms in the same trade or business. Therefore, the IRS has counted the number of real estate sales a university made in twenty-five years to determine whether its real estate sales were regular.[3]

Third, an unrelated business is not substantially related to the tax-exempt mission of the nonprofit. It may raise money but is not programmatically integral or related to the tax-exempt mission. Some examples will help clarify this point.

A halfway house organized to provide room, board, therapy, and counseling for persons discharged from alcoholic treatment centers also operates a furniture shop to provide full-time employment for its residents. The profits are applied to the operating costs of the halfway house. The income from this venture is not unrelated trade or business income.

An exempt organization, organized and operated for the prevention of cruelty to animals, receives income from providing pet boarding and grooming services for the general public. This is an income from an unrelated trade or business. But a prison that imports prisoners from other states is not only a 501(c)(3) because it is substituting for government, but the profits from this activity are related business income.[4]

An exempt organization whose purpose is to provide for the welfare of young people rents rooms primarily to people under age twenty-five. This income is not considered unrelated business income, since the source of the income flow is substantially related to the purpose constituting the basis for the organization's exemption.

A hospital with exempt status operates a gift shop patronized by patients, visitors making purchases for patients, and employees and medical staff. It also operates a parking lot for patients and visitors only. Both of these activities are substantially related to the hospital's exempt purpose and do not constitute unrelated trades or businesses.

These examples offered by the IRS illustrate the differences between a program-related business and an unrelated business. The former is an extension of or part of the tax-exempt function of the organization. The latter is not.

The same activity can be either a related or unrelated business depending on how it is handled. A service run *exclusively* for *members* of an organization or completely provided *voluntarily* by them is a related business. But the same services provided by the same nonprofit for the public or by paid employees could be an unrelated business.

A service such as a laundry or store operated exclusively for the membership of a tax-exempt organization is not an unrelated business. The rental income to a nonprofit created by a local government to provide public facilities, including a police station, is not unrelated business income.[5]

Services only for the *convenience* of members, for example, dorms for students, are related businesses. Services by members or volunteers, the sale of donated property, trade shows that are educational, and the rental or sale of mailing labels to other nonprofits are also related businesses. The rental of a mailing list for commercial purposes has been an unrelated business, but a recent Tax Court decision, *Disabled American* v. *Commissioner,* said, at least in this case, it was to be treated as a royalty, which is not taxed. This was reversed on appeal by the IRS.

EXCESS PROFITS: A DISTINCTION BETWEEN RELATED AND UNRELATED INCOME

An IRS regulation announced in the *Internal Revenue Bulletin* is instructive.[6] The case is that of a large metropolitan hospital that provides services such as data processing, food service, and purchasing services to other hospitals. The IRS rules that the earnings would be related income if all of three conditions hold: (1) the hospitals purchasing the service have a maximum capacity for inpatients of 100 persons; (2) the service, if performed by the recipient hospital, would have been a normal service for it; (3) the fee in excess of actual cost is not more than one and one-half times the average rates of interest on public debt obligations issued by the Federal Hospital Insurance Trust Fund.

If all these conditions do not hold, then the earnings are unrelated business income and taxed. This case not only shows the thin line between related and unrelated business income, but also shows that although an absolute dollar level of profits is not stipulated, any profit above a normal rate of return is likely to be considered unrelated business income. It implies a profit motive.

INTEGRATION OF BUSINESS OPERATIONS INTO A CONGLOMERATE STRUCTURE

Figure 10.1 shows a possible configuration of for-profit unrelated businesses and nonprofit entities in conglomerate structure of a nonprofit corporation under Section 501(c)(3). A nonprofit that is a public charity as defined by

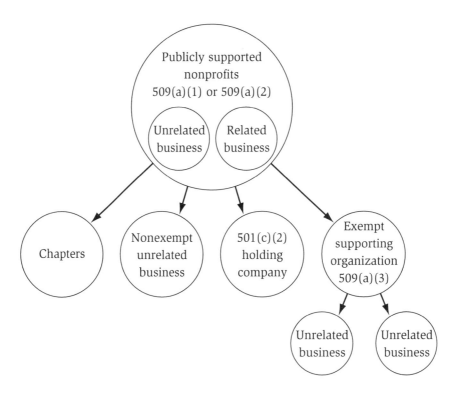

Figure 10.1. Structure of Nonprofit Corporation or Conglomerate.

Section 509(a)(1) or (a)(2) may not only have its internal departments within its corporate corpus but may also house both unrelated and program-related businesses.

In addition, the 509(a)(1) or (a)(2) may have chapters. These are not necessarily separate entities having their own tax-exempt status; rather, they may fall under the umbrella of the parent organization. (See Chapter One.) The 509(a)(3) organizations have subsidiaries or corporations wholly beholden to them. Unlike chapters, these are independently chartered and tax-exempt organizations whose existence relies on their relationship with a publicly supported organization. Furthermore, it is acceptable that these 509(a)(3)s run both program-related and unrelated businesses. Picture it this way. An incorporated chapter could break off or be expelled and run programs on its own behalf. A 509(a)(3) cannot. It is beholden to its parent.

The 509(a)(1) or (2)(2) may also run an unrelated business outside of its immediate corporate corpus. For example, an organization may advertise in its journal. The advertisement could be an unrelated business, but the articles could be related to its educational mission. This is best done within the corporate structure of most nonprofits. The same nonprofit, however, may be part or sole owner of an apartment building or hotel. This is best done outside the immediate corporate structure of the organization.

Note that it does not matter whether the unrelated business is within the corpus of the organization or whether it is a separate corporation owned or controlled by the nonprofit. In either case, it pays taxes. What does matter is that, as independent entities, a corporation outside the structure of the nonprofit shields the latter from liability, provides for separate management and labor contracts, can raise its own capital, shields the nonprofit from unwanted publicity, and provides for the participation of individuals as owners and profit makers.

Figure 10.1 also shows that the 509(a)(1) or (a)(2) may also own a holding company. This company may be exempt or nonexempt. If exempt, it merely serves as a holder of title of property consistent with the tax-exempt function of the parent organization and reports its taxes in combination with the parent. As a nonexempt organization, it may hold title to other properties and report its taxes as a separate corporation. Hence, a nonprofit could have a holding company that is also exempt hold title to all its real estate.

Holding companies are very important to nonprofits, particularly hospitals. Holding companies may be 501(c)(2)s holding real estate. But some holding companies are 509(a)(3)s, which are not holders of real estate but are financial and supporting entities. The likelihood is that the nonprofit hospital in your community is an operating unit of a holding company.

The existence of a holding company is a clue that the nonprofit organization has a far more legally complicated structure than meets the eye.

This structure, as we shall more clearly see when we discuss reorganization, mergers, consolidations, and divestitures in Chapter Nineteen, is intended to accomplish a number of objectives, from efficiency in meeting the mission of the organization to protection of the assets of the organization from lawsuits.

Viewing the complete Figure 10.1 and imagining all of the subordinate circles that could be drawn, it is obvious that an imaginative nonprofit could easily create a conglomerate.

Now that we have juxtaposed a for-profit and a nonprofit, it is worth remembering that a significant difference between the two is that the income and assets of a nonprofit cannot be distributed to individual owners as they can be in the for-profit sector. Accordingly, the nonprofit, being one or the sole owner of the for-profit corporation, gets annual dividends and also capital gains from the appreciation in the value of the stocks. But unlike other stockholders, nonprofits are given better tax treatment. Nonprofits pay no taxes on dividends or capital gains unless they are generated by property subject to debt, as discussed later in this chapter, or unless they are a private foundation paying taxes on investment income. Dividends and capital gains are fully taxable to individual taxpayers. Corporations can only exclude from taxation a portion of dividends they receive from other corporations—and 100 percent of those from wholly owned subsidiaries.

An example is your college bookstore. The National Association of College Bookstores is a tax-exempt organization of over 3500 affiliated stores. It provides educational, research, and trade shows for its members—all within the nonprofit mission and organization. It owns a for-profit subsidiary that purchases computer software, books, and calendars at a substantial discount because of the size of the orders for the member stores. It also has a computerized resume referral service and joint ventures with Publishers' Clearinghouse in the fulfillment of magazine orders. It also sells Value Packs—a collection of coupons from various vendors. What are some of the advantages of this arrangement?

1. Basically commercial and business activities are separated from educational activities, thus allowing managerial focus and making the issue of unrelated business nearly moot. The subsidiary is a business and is taxed accordingly.

2. The subsidiary can share its profits (through dividends) with its parents, which are the college bookstores.

3. The subsidiary can share costs—paying its share of the rent.

4. The liabilities and losses of the subsidiary do not affect the nonprofit parent.

5. The for-profit can raise funds on its own; and the parent organization could even sell interests in the subsidiary or sell it off without affecting its own nonprofit status.

THE ORGANIZATION OF AN UNRELATED BUSINESS

In the for-profit world, businesses are organized as corporations, sole proprietorships, or partnerships. Joint ventures may be undertaken between two or more organizations on a specific project. A trust could also be created to hold and exercise the rights of ownership of those who own a business organization. Except for sole proprietorships, these organizations are adaptable to an unrelated business owned and operated by a nonprofit.

A common way of organizing an unrelated business is as a corporation. A corporation, unlike a partnership or a sole proprietorship, is an independent legal and tax entity. Liabilities for failure and error of the corporation do not extend to its owner, as with partnerships and proprietorships. Corporations have centralized management and do not have to share management decisions with all owners, as with general partnerships. Unlike proprietorships, a corporation can raise capital by issuing and selling shares of stocks in itself. A partnership may do so by selling partnership interests, but such interests rarely have as wide a market as a public corporation's stocks. Unlike a general partnership, a corporation does not have to be dissolved in the case of withdrawal of an owner. It has a perpetual life of its own, and ownership can be easily transferred from one person to another. A corporation is easier and safer than other forms of business organizations. What is most important, even if the nonprofit organized its business as a partnership, it would be taxed as a corporation.

A nonprofit may choose to be a minority, majority, or even sole owner of a for-profit corporation. Its minority ownership may be significantly small or significantly large, but a critical concept of ownership is control. A nonprofit is said to be the controlling owner of a for-profit corporation if it owns at least 50 percent of its voting stocks and 50 percent of all other stocks. How a nonprofit is treated for tax purposes depends not on whether it is a minority or a majority stockholder but on whether it is the controlling organization. In the case of non-stock corporations, which nonprofits are, control means controlling 80 percent or more of the board of directors or trustees.

How the unrelated business is treated depends on the form of business organization. If it is a corporation or partnership, it will face the same tax rate as other corporations. It will also be subject to a minimum tax. In a recent ruling, the IRS required a nonprofit to create a separate for-profit subsidiary or lose its exemption. Accordingly, how the nonprofit is treated may also depend on how the business is organized.

BENEFITS, CONSEQUENCES, AND OPPORTUNITIES OF UNRELATED BUSINESSES

Obviously, the single most important reason for running an unrelated business is because it is profitable and it fits. The income from these enterprises not only finances the activities of the nonprofit but may also satisfy the requirement of demonstrating public support. The reader should recall our earlier discussion in Chapter Two of the role of unrelated business in defining support and determining whether a nonprofit can demonstrate that it is publicly supported.

Yet another perspective is worth noting. Let's go back to the principles in Chapter Two. Nonprofit A, which receives $100,000 in investment income, $40,000 from a community chest, $50,000 from Beverly, $10,000 from Audrey, and $1,000 from Anhela, would fail the one-third support test. Now assume that it had an unrelated business with a net income of $400,000. Now its total support is $601,000. One-third of this is $200,333. Each individual donor's contribution is not valued at more than 2 percent of the total support, or $40,066. This means that instead of being valued at $4,020, Audrey's contribution is now valued at its full $10,000 and Beverly's at $40,060. Now add the contributions of the community chest, $40,000, Beverly at $40,066, Audrey at $10,000, and Clive at $1,000. The sum is $91,000 and the organization fails the one-third test and passes the 10 percent test as before. However, there is a subtle difference. Since each individual's contribution can receive a higher true value closer to the actual contribution made by the donor, the organization may be able to pursue a strategy concentrated more toward larger contributions than it could otherwise have done and still demonstrate public support.

Another benefit of an unrelated business other than support is that it enables the organization to carry out some of its programs by subsidizing them. The advertising in a magazine published by a nonprofit for its members subsidizes the magazine. The advertising may be an unrelated business if it is unrelated to the mission of the organization. A pharmacy catering to the general public but located in a hospital is an unrelated business, although without the pharmacy the hospital could not provide its services as well. Tours unrelated to the tax-exempt mission of the organization that are conducted by a nonprofit for its members and others are unrelated businesses, but they help maintain contact and cohesion and provide a basis for future fund-raising.

An unrelated business can also extend the social involvement of a nonprofit while making a profit. An unrelated business corporation can make tax-deductible charitable contributions to tax-exempt organizations other than its parents. Similar transfers to its parents are not payments for services or goods or return of capital. Therefore, they are not deductible by the corporation and not taxable to the charity.

An unrelated business can also be used to hire disadvantaged workers and receive a tax credit for doing so, thereby reducing the tax liability of the unrelated business. The credit also means that the full wages of the worker are not paid by the business but shared with the federal government. They also qualify for a credit for improving access for disabled persons.

Consequences of Unrelated Businesses

Related business profits are not taxed, but unrelated business profits are. For 509(a)(1) organizations, unrelated businesses are considered to be support, whereas related businesses are not. For 509(a)(2) organizations, unrelated business has a limit to the extent to which it is included in support, whereas a related business income is generally included fully. Unrelated businesses take the nonprofit beyond its tax-exempt purpose; related businesses by definition do not.

A nonprofit may simultaneously run related and unrelated businesses. The accounting must be kept separate and time of employees or use of facilities must be properly allocated if they are shared by both types of businesses. The nonprofit may operate several unrelated businesses. The tax is imposed on the net profit of the combined unrelated business income of the organization. The organization cannot subtract from the net income or profit of an unrelated business those losses it incurred in a business in which there was no intent to make a profit.[7]

Hence, the West Virginia State Medical Association and the North Ridge Country Club were stopped from subtracting losses of one business from that of another.[8] In each case, the court ruled that only one of these businesses was operated with a profit motive. An unrelated business must have a profit motive, be regular, and be substantively unrelated to the mission of the organization. The absence of any one of the three means the business is not unrelated.

Benign Origins of Unrelated Businesses

The entry into unrelated business is rarely a deliberate attempt to compete with for-profit firms. Sometimes it is purely defensive to protect one's space or market; for example, buying the real estate in the neighborhood of one's facilities for future expansion. Sometimes it is to capture some of the financial benefits from one's large and risky investments and to maintain property rights and control; for example, universities' licensing the products of research. It may also be the result of trying to cover large fixed and overhead costs.

The insert that follows shows eighty auxiliary services operated by universities and colleges throughout the country. They are not all carried out by the same university. Many of the seemingly outlandish examples may be related businesses. Some may be an integral part of the curriculum, such as a bowling alley in a physical education curriculum. A bowling alley may be operated for the convenience of students and staff in a community where an alternative is

The Scope of Auxiliary Services

Eighty Operational Categories

1. Food Service, Contracted
2. Food Service, Residence, Self-Op
3. Food Service, Cash, Self-Op
4. Cookie Stand
5. Ice Cream Shop
6. Candy Shop
7. Bakery, Retail Store
8. Bakery, Production
9. Vending, Contracted
10. Vending, Self-Op
11. Amusement Games, Contracted
12. Amusement Games, Self-Op
13. Beer Clubs
14. Night Clubs or Bars (Full Alcohol)
15. Student Unions/Campus Centers
16. Faculty Clubs
17. Faculty Dining
18. Laundry, Contracted
19. Laundry, Self-Op
20. Laundry Machines, Coin-Op
21. Bookstores, Self-Op
22. Bookstores, Contracted
23. News-Stands
24. Press, University/College
25. Print Shops
26. Duplicating Service
27. Word Processing
28. Copy Machines, Coin-Op
29. Typing Service
30. Typewriters, Coin-Op
31. Office Machines Repair Service
32. Housing, Student
33. Housing, Faculty
34. Housing, Married Students
35. Post Office
36. Mailing Service
37. Banks
38. Check Cashing Service
39. Airports
40. Transportation, Air Service
41. Transportation, Ground Service
42. Bus Service
43. Motor Pools
44. Travel Service/Agency
45. Van Rentals
46. Parking Garages, Pay
47. Parking Lots, Pay
48. Recreation, Indoor
49. Recreation, Outdoor
50. Recreation, Camps
51. Bowling
52. Golf Courses
53. Billiards
54. Swim Centers
55. Skating Rinks, Ice
56. Skating Rinks, Roller
57. Arenas
58. Bike Shop, Sales/Rentals
59. Sporting Goods Store
60. Photo Shops
61. Gift Shops

(continued)

62. Concessions, Athletic	71. Microcomputers, Housing
63. Concessions, Other	72. Radio Station
64. Ski Lodge Operation	73. TV Station
65. Telecommunications	74. Furniture Repair Service
66. Computers, Coin-Op	75. Insurance, Student
67. Computers in Dormitories	76. Central Stores
68. Computers, Rentals	77. Day-Care Centers
69. Microcomputers, Food Service	78. Conferences, Summer
	79. Conference Centers
70. Microcomputers, Bookstores	80. Real Estate

Source: *Journal of National Association of College Auxiliary Services,* June 1987, p. 33.
Reprinted by permission of the National Association of College Auxiliary Services.

not readily accessible. It may be open at noncompeting hours of the day. A business run for the convenience of members or part of a curriculum (the mission) is classified as related.

Evidently, (1) there is a thin line between a related and unrelated business, and the difference is not in the name but in the relevance, frequency, and motive, and (2) frequently, unrelated business ventures can arise from an attempt to extend and serve the mission, although the legal or tax judgment is that the relevance is not strong enough to be considered integrally related. Here is an example: the Seventh Day Adventist's Living Faith, Inc. operates a health food business that is consistent with the doctrines of the religion. The Tax Court ruled that this was a commercial activity, that the connection with religion was not strong enough.[9] Consequently, they must pay unrelated business income tax on the profits. Should they stop? Obviously not.

An unrelated business can arise from a tax-exempt organization using its position, process, goodwill, or reputation to make money in a way that is not directly related to its tax-exempt mission. The IRS gives the example of exploiting a mission.

An exempt scientific organization enjoys an excellent reputation in the field of biological research. It exploits this reputation regularly by selling endorsements of various items of laboratory equipment to manufacturers. The endorsement of laboratory equipment does not contribute importantly to the accomplishment of any purpose for which exemption is granted to the organization. Accordingly, the income from the sale of endorsements is gross income from an unrelated business.

An unrelated business can arise from wisely trying to cover costs while carrying out a charitable mission. This is evidenced by the opportunity nonprofits have to make dual use of plant and equipment. The same plant or equipment that it uses for conducting its tax-exempt mission can also be used to produce unrelated business income rather than sit idle, generating costs but no revenues. The university stadium may be used for professional football. When this is done, the nonprofit must separate the two types of income and expenses for reporting purposes. The use of university facilities for professional sports is commonplace. The revenues from these leases help cover fixed costs.

Unrelated Business for Cost-Sharing Purposes

Still another example common to nonprofits is the use of their publications to generate income. This can be done by selling advertising space. The income from the advertising can be unrelated income. But the ads help advertisers speak to an audience. Let's hear the U.S. Supreme Court:

> There is no merit to the Government's argument that Congress and the Treasury intended to establish a blanket rule requiring the taxation of income from all commercial advertising by tax-exempt professional journals without a specific analysis of the circumstances. There is no support for such a rule in the regulations or in the legislative history of the Internal Revenue Code.[10]

Furthermore, the publication's income and costs are divided into portions, so that if the readership portion (its tax-exempt purpose) is operating at a loss, all additional costs above that loss level may be deducted from the advertising portion (its unrelated business) as long as such a deduction does not result in the unrelated business showing a loss for tax purposes. In short, the cost of serving the readership may provide a tax deduction to the unrelated business. We shall take a deeper look at advertising in the next section.

There are several variations to this example. The basic rule is that if an unrelated business exploits the activities of a related business, the losses from the latter may be deducted from the former if such a deduction does not lead the unrelated business to report a loss. In short, the IRS is willing to reduce the taxes of the unrelated business to the extent that such reduction has a legitimate economic basis.

Accordingly, the tax-exempt mission is subsidized by the unrelated business, and the tax liability of the latter is reduced by the losses of the former.

TAX TREATMENT OF DIFFERENT TYPES OF BUSINESS INCOME

In this section we discuss various types of income and arrangements and what exposes them to unrelated business income tax.

Passive Income

Royalties, rents, interests, dividends, and annuities, all passive income, are generally not considered unrelated business incomes and therefore are not taxed as long as the nonprofit maintains a passive role. The promotion of the credit cards carrying its name will convert a royalty (a passive income) into a sale that is taxable. The first caution in avoiding the tax is to avoid an active role.

Dividends are not taxed unless they are received from property subject to debt. This means that a rich source of income for nonprofits is dividends from controlled corporations or profit-making subsidiaries. Certain guidelines may help in setting up these subsidiaries so that the dividends from them will not be taxable to the nonprofit. These guidelines are as follows:

1. Although the parent (nonprofit organization) may appoint the board of the subsidiary for-profit corporation, the majority of the members of the board of directors, the employees, and the officers of the for-profit must not be related to or be agents of the nonprofit organization.

2. The parent organization must not participate in the daily activities of the for-profit firm.

3. Any business transaction between the subsidiary and the parent nonprofit organization must conform to strict business principles similar to those governing two organizations that are independent of each other. Transactions must be at arm's length.

4. The subsidiary must be organized for the purpose of conducting a legitimate business that is truly unrelated to the business of the nonprofit organization. Its purpose must be to make a profit through a trade or business unrelated to the mission of the nonprofit parent.

Under the above conditions, expressed in the General Counsel Memorandum 39326, the dividends received by the nonprofit from its for-profit subsidiary are received tax free. The for-profit subsidiary, however, is subject to all taxes of normal corporations.

Interest earnings, royalties, and rents are taxable to the nonprofit if they are payments from an organization that the nonprofit controls, whether the organization is itself tax exempt or a for-profit firm. These revenues, like dividends, are also taxable if they are derived from a debt-financed property.

Capital gains from selling property are not subject to tax as unrelated business income unless the property was part of an inventory, acquired by debt, or is sold as an ordinary practice in a trade or business. This again puts a nonprofit corporation in a position superior to most owners of property, including stocks.

The use of property that is contiguous to other property owned by a tax-exempt organization even for an unrelated business purpose may escape being treated as unrelated business if there is a clear intent to use that property within the subsequent ten years for a tax-exempt purpose. The IRS must be convinced of this intent every five years. Churches have fifteen years to use the property to generate income without being taxed.

Some types of activities receive favorable treatment. Income from bingo is not taxed if for-profit firms within the local jurisdiction are barred from holding bingo games to make a profit. If they are permitted, then the nonprofit must pay a tax. The idea is to avoid placing the for-profit firm at a disadvantage.

Speaking of bingo, the city of Spokane, Washington taxed a local chapter of the American Red Cross for income derived from bingo, pull-tab, and punch board games. The unrelated business income tax was overruled by the Ninth Circuit Court, arguing that the Red Cross, a congressionally chartered nonprofit, was exempt because it was an instrumentality of the federal government.[11]

Income derived by agricultural groups from growing and selling crops contiguously to a retirement home is specifically excluded as unrelated business income if the income provides less than 75 percent of the cost of running the retirement home. Income earned by religious organizations with a federal license is excluded if that income is used for charitable purposes and the prices charged are neither significantly higher nor lower than commercial prices. Research conducted for the U.S. government, its instrumentalities or agencies, or any other level of domestic government, is not considered an unrelated business. Furthermore, fundamental research is not an unrelated business, and organizations such as hospitals and educational institutions are not subject to unrelated business tax on the income derived from research, whether fundamental or applied.[12]

Tours

The basic tests for determining whether a tour leads to unrelated business income are (1) its time commitment to an educational or religious purpose, (2) the legitimate content of the courses conducted on the tour, (3) the degree to which the tour is unlike commercial packages, and (4) the degree to which the course is connected to and is a clear part of the exempt purpose of the organization.

An organization that conducts travel study tours as its primary activity was granted exemption for carrying on an educational mission. Its courses were taught by certified teachers and were conducted for five to six hours a day, library materials were available, exams were given, and the state board of education allowed credits for the courses taken.

An organization conducting weekend retreats is also given tax exemption for advancing religion. The participants meet on an hourly basis for seminars, lectures, prayer sessions, and mediation. No recreational activities are scheduled but individuals are free to engage in these activities on their own time.

The Cecil Bowman Queler Institute is exempt for the purpose of conducting geographic education. Teachers who are experts on the geographic area being visited conduct the tour. Only those who enroll in the courses can participate in the tour. During the tour, the students devote five or six hours per day to organized study, preparation of reports, lectures, instructions, and recitation. Library and related readings and video materials are available during the tour. Examinations are given and the state board of education awards credits for the course. A hypothetical example such as this, according to the IRS, is not likely to lead to unrelated business income.

Property Subject to Debt

Certain properties owned by a nonprofit may be subject to acquisition indebtedness. All earnings derived from such properties are considered unrelated income and subject to tax. Acquisition debt is any debt incurred (1) to acquire or improve a property, (2) in anticipation of acquisition or improvement, or (3) because of the acquisition or improvement. For example, if a nonprofit incurred a debt to acquire or improve a property, that is an acquisition debt. Or if after acquiring a property that might be free of debt the nonprofit enters into debt directly linked to its decision to purchase the property, that is also acquisition indebtedness. In all these cases, the property is said to be debt financed.

Again, the consequence of acquisition indebtedness is that income derived from the property in interest, rent, royalty, dividends, or capital appreciation is, with some exceptions, unrelated business income and taxed. It does not matter whether the income is recurrent or nonrecurrent. If during the taxable year the property is subject to debt, all income that it yields during that year is unrelated business income.

There are some modifications to this seemingly harsh rule. One very important one is that property obtained upon death (bequest and devise) is not considered subject to debt for ten years after its acquisition if (1) the donor held the property for at least five years, (2) the debt is at least five years old, and (3) the nonprofit did not agree to be responsible for the debt.

Another exception to the general rule of debt-financed property occurs when the entire property (at least 85 percent) is used for a tax-exempt purpose by the organization itself or by an organization that it controls. In addition, there is a ten-year grace period with mortgages unless the nonprofit, having received real estate from a donor, assumes the mortgage payment. If it does, it is taxed under the debt-financed rule.

Finally, rents from personal property, earnings from thrift shops, and property used in research are not considered debt-financed property and, therefore, are not subject to tax as unrelated business income. Concern should center on rents and proceeds from the sale of real estate, income and proceeds from the ownership and sale of securities, and proceeds from the sale of personal property (as opposed to rents from such property).

Rental Income

Income from renting real estate shows how easy it is for a nonprofit to operate an unrelated business even when it does not intend to do so. Seek advice. It should also alert nonprofit managers to the questions that should be raised before accepting real estate as a gift. Here are some complexities. A simplified view is given at the end of the chapter.

What is rent? If a nonprofit owns a parking lot and operates it, this is rent. If it leases it, then the income is not rent from real property.[13] The IRS has to know the facts and circumstances.[14]

As stated earlier, generally income from the rental of real estate is not unrelated income. However, if the rental is from a property subject to acquisition indebtedness, then all rental income derived from the property could be unrelated business income after ten years and immediately if the nonprofit assumes the debt.

If the rental income is from a related organization carrying out its exempt mission, it is not treated as debt financed even if the property is acquired by debt. Yet the income can be taxed if the organization is *controlled* by the nonprofit because, in general, all rents from a *controlled* organization are taxed regardless of whether the organization that pays it is tax exempt or whether it is subject to debt.

Rental from real estate is also subject to unrelated business income tax if the use of the space is coupled with a service, such as room service in a hotel. Furthermore, if the rental income is combined with a rental fee for the use of personal property such as equipment, the entire income would be subject to tax if the personal property (equipment and machinery) part of the rental exceeds 50 percent of the total. If the personal property part is less than 10 percent of the total, the entire rental is exempt. If it is 10 percent, then only this personal property portion is taxed.

If the rental is from an organization that is *controlled* by the nonprofit, the rental income is unrelated business income regardless of whether the organization that pays is a for-profit or a nonprofit.

If the space is used for both tax-exempt and for-profit activities, the amount of the rental must be allocated between the two uses and taxes paid on the part that is for-profit in origin.

If the rentals are from a tax-exempt–related organization and are used for research or for a thrift shop, it is not treated as debt financed and not subject to unrelated business tax under the debt-finance rules. However, it could be considered unrelated business income if the organization paying is controlled by the nonprofit landlord.

If the parent organization uses a debt-financed property (in which case it does not pay rent to itself) exclusively for research or thrift shop, income derived from the use of that property is not necessarily unrelated business income.

If the property was obtained through a bequest or devise and was held by the donor for at least five years, and the debt is at least five years old and the nonprofit does not agree to assume it, then it is not immediately treated as unrelated business income. There is a ten-year grace period.

Rent becomes unrelated business income if it is tied to profits. It can be a fixed percentage of sales or receipts, but not of the profits of the occupant.

There are infinite combinations of these confounding circumstances. Some of the key questions that must be raised are as follows: Is it debt financed? Is it to be leased along with personal property and, if so, what will be the percentage of the total rental that could be deemed to be derived from the real estate portion of the package? Are the tenants controlled by the nonprofit? Is the rent related to the profits of the tenants? For what purpose is the space being used? How much of the total space is being rented? All of these questions have been answered in this chapter.

Gaming

Any nonprofit, including a charity, an association, social club, or a veterans group, that conducts gaming as a primary mission is likely to be deprived exemption and so, too, those that fail to keep proper records. These records should include prize paid, cash receipts, and disbursement journals, accounts payable journals, general ledgers, detailed source documents, and copies of any federal tax returns filed. These records must be kept for at least three years.

How a specific form of gaming is treated for tax purposes depends upon the type of game, whether it is conducted by volunteers, allowed by state law, and treated as an exception. See Table 10.1 for the list of forms that must be filed and Exhibits 10.1, 10.2, and 10.3 for the records that must be kept.

Bingo is exempt if it is allowed by state law and only if nonprofits may conduct gaming in that state. In general, gaming that is conducted purely by volunteers is exempt. However, an "excess" amount of food or beverages may be considered compensation. And tips may be considered compensation. A person receiving any of these compensations is not considered a volunteer, so the volunteer exemption does not apply. No wonder that some gaming sites post signs prohibiting tipping. It also explains why tips are collected in a vessel: because the operator also needs to report the tips an employee gets for his or her income tax purpose. Once tips exceed $20, the person is required to inform the operator.

Qualified public entertainment may also be an exception. Public entertainment refers to fairs and expositions. Here the gaming must be in conjunction with a regional, national, state, or local fair or exposition. It must also be

Table 10.1. Forms That Organizations Conducting Gaming Activities Generally File.

Form 990	Return of Organization Exempt From Income Tax, or
Form 990–EZ	Short Form Return of Organization Exempt From Income Tax
Form 990–T	Exempt Organization Business Income Tax Return
Form W–2G	Certain Gambling Winnings
Form 11–C	Occupational Tax and Registration Return for Wagering
Form 730	Tax on Wagering
Form 940	Employer's Annual Federal Unemployment (FUTA) Tax Return
Form 941	Employer's Quarterly Federal Tax Return
Form 945	Annual Return of Withheld Federal Income Tax
Form 8109	Federal Tax Deposit Coupon
Form 1099–MISC	Miscellaneous Income
Form 1096	Annual Summary and Transmittal of U.S. Informational Returns
Form 5754	Statement by Person(s) Receiving Gambling Winnings. *(Note: This form is not filed with the Service.)*

Note: The use of a promoter or contractor to operate gaming for an exempt organization does not relieve the exempt organization of its responsibility to file the appropriate forms.

Source: Internal Revenue Service Publication 3079, p. 11

conducted according to and by permission of state law allowing only the non-profit to carry on the gaming at that event. The only organizations that qualify are 501(c)(3)s, labor and agricultural associations, and civic leagues and associations (c)(4)s and (5)s, respectively, that conduct agricultural or educational fairs as one of their substantial exempt missions. Under these conditions, parimutuel betting may also escape treatment as unrelated trade or business.

But then there is the North Dakota exception. Only the state of North Dakota qualifies for exemptions of games of chance. Only that state enjoys the exemption from non-bingo gaming.

Besides the paying of taxes (if due) and the filing of forms, the organization assumes certain other responsibilities when it indulges in games. These include paying withholding taxes for winners (whether or not the organization collected it). The organization is also required to make sure that no part of the proceeds is used for personal inurement. The trustees are expressly required to oversee the games as part of their duties.

Two types of taxes can result from wager. The wager tax is an excise tax imposed on the gross amount of the wager received or the total potential. In pull-tabs, for example, it would be applied to the total number of tabs times the dollar value of each.

Exhibit 10.1. Spreadsheet Example: Games Played and Receipts per Game.

If you are reporting games lost or destroyed, skip column D and columns I through O.

Circle Game Played: •Pull-tabs (circled) •Tipboards •Paddlewheels •Other

These games have been: (check only one) •played (circled) •destroyed •lost

Month 10   Year 98   Page _ of _ Pages

A	B	C	D	E	F	G	H	I	J	K	L	O
Mfg. ID	Part Number	Game Serial Number	Date Put in Play	Ideal Gross Receipt	Ideal Prizes	Total Value Unsold Tickets	Gross Receipts (E minus G)	Total Value of Prizes Paid	Net Receipts (H minus I)	Cash in Hand	Cash Over or Short	Date Removed from Play
1 INS Double		030964	100297	1320	924	20	1320	924	396	393	−3	100498
2												
3												
4												
5												
6												
7												
8												
9												
10												
11												
12												
13 Add the amounts in columns J, K, L, M, and N and fill in the total of each column here...............................$								924	396	393	−3	
14 If you are attaching other pages, add together the totals of columns J, K, L, and N to all attached pages and fill in total of each column here ....$												100498

Source: Internal Revenue Service, Publication 3079, p. 28.

Exhibit 10.2. Spreadsheet Example: Report of Games Played, Lost, or Destroyed.

Circle Game Played
(•Pull-tabs) • Tipboards • Paddlewheels • Other

Page _ of _ Pages

	A	B	C	D	E	F	G	H	I	J	K	L	M	N	O
	Name of Game & Form #	Registration Stamp #	Game Serial #	Date Put in Play	Price per Ticket	Number of Tickets	Ideal Gross Receipts	Ideal Prizes	Total Value Unsold Tickets	Gross Receipts (G minus I)	Total Value of Prizes Paid	Net Receipts: (J minus K)	Cash in Hand	Cash Over or Short	Date Removed from Play
1	INS	57216	03096	10/02	1.00	1,320	1,320	924	–	1,320	924	396	396		10/04
2	Hi Lo	57219	02285	10/02	1.00	984	984	739	–	984	739	245	245		10/04
3	Hi Lo	57220	03159	10/03	1.00	984	984	739	–	984	739	245	245		10/05
4															
5															
6															
7															
8															
9															
10															
11															
12															
13	Add the amounts in columns J, K, L, M, and N and fill in the total of each column here..............$									3,288	2,402	886	886		
14	If you are attaching other pages, add together the totals of columns J, K, L, and N to all attached pages and fill in total of each column here ....$														

Month 10   Year 98

Source: Internal Revenue Service, Publication 3079, p. 29.

Exhibit 10.3. Spreadsheet Example: Bingo Inventory and Receipts.

Date of Bingo Session: 10/04/98

	A	B	C	D	E	F	G	H	I
	Name of Game	Mfr. ID	Serial Numbers in Game	Serial Numbers Sold	Cost per Sheet	Number of Sheets Sold	Gross Receipts (E times F)	Prizes Paid	Net Receipts (G Minus H)
1	Postage Stamp	Bingo			.50	300	150	125	25
2	Crazy L	Bingo			1.00	400	400	200	200
3	Small PKg	Bingo			12.00	510	6,120		
4	Large PKg	Bingo			18.00	222	3,996	3,000	7,116
5									
6									
7									
8									
9	Add the amounts in columns G, H, and I and fill in the total of each column here. ....$						✕ 10,666	3,325	7,341
10	If you are attaching other pages, add together the totals of columns G, H, and I and fill in here. ....$						✕		

Source: Internal Revenue Service, Publication 3079, p. 30.

Bingo is exempt from this tax, but lotteries, pull-tabs, and raffles are not. In general, exempt organizations (charities and associations) do not pay this tax on activities not exempt unless there is some personal benefit that inures. This personal inurement does not have to be direct. Hence, if a social club conducts one of these nonexempt activities and places the gains in the general fund, this will be considered personal inurement because so doing would reduce the cost of operating the club and therefore reduce the cost of dues and other assessments to the members. Reasoned from the opposite direction, it would increase the amount of benefits such clubs can offer members with no offsetting increase in cost to each of them.

A second tax is the occupational tax (stamp tax). This tax is applied to each person or entity that receives wagers. This is paid as an annual fee. The tax is applied on an entity or agent of that entity that accepts the wagers. A paid bartender in a social club would be such an agent.

Both of these taxes are significantly increased when the games are not authorized by state law (being run illegally) or operated in a way that is contrary to state law. An example of the latter is using a paid person when the state law requires that only a volunteer or member be used to accept wagers.

One way to construct a gaming activity used by some organizations, is to incorporate a separate taxable corporation. It conducts the games, does the required work, plus pays the taxes. These so-called "feeder organizations" are not exempt. However, the money they pass on to their parents can be received tax free. The caution here is that the parent may nevertheless carry the responsibility to ensure tax and reporting by the feeder. The reader may wish to refer back to the discussion in Chapter Nine on gambling and gaming.

Dues

Any payment that exceeds a certain threshold that is required for an individual or entity to become an associate member of an association, particularly a business or a civic association, will be considered unrelated business income if the principal purpose for forming the associate membership class was to produce income.

The motive for creating the class is deduced from the facts and circumstances, including the minutes of the organization. But central to the determination is whether the creation of the class was motivated to enable the organization to fulfill its mission. Therefore, it is possible that in a profession where there is a recognized ladder of progression, a class of membership could be created if that allows the organization to better fulfill its mission.

Other factors that lead to an interpretation that the membership class is unrelated to the mission are the size of the differential in the fees, kinds of core services, participation in governance, and core organizational offerings between full and associate members. An associate membership that purely gives access, as opposed to benefits and participation in core programs related to the mission of the organization, will quite likely lead to a conclusion that it is unrelated business income and taxable. Such "dues" are nothing more than prices charged to outsiders to gain incidental access to a single or limited services (for example, for admission to showings).

Portfolio and Endowment Income

Certain types of income flow into an endowment or a nonprofit's investment portfolio free of unrelated business income taxes. These are incomes from rent, royalties, annuities, interest, dividends, and capital gains unless these are from controlled groups or from properties acquired by debt, as discussed earlier.

In short, it is possible to run a tax-free endowment. The tainting of any one source of income in such an endowment by its being unrelated business income could subject the entire endowment to unrelated business income tax.

Certain investment-related transactions appear to have elements of unrelated business income but are not treated as such. Income derived from lending a security by the nonprofit to an investor is not treated as unrelated. This includes the interest, fees, and dividends on the security loaned or the earnings on any security the investor may have put up as collateral. Further, the return of these collateral securities by the nonprofit to the investor is not treated as the settlement of a debt in which the security was loaned. Neither is the lapse of an option or the exercise of an option by the nonprofit treated as unrelated.

In these transactions, the nonprofit needs to be careful to have an arm's length arrangement and to avoid dealing with a disqualified person. Moreover, the lending of the security must be subject to a written contract. This contract must include a promise that the security returned to the nonprofit be identical to the one loaned, that risks of loss or gain by the nonprofit are not changed by the loan, that the nonprofit will receive all payments to which it is entitled, that the nonprofit will receive collateral not less in value than the amount loaned, that the value of the collateral be determined daily and adjusted upwards if necessary the following day, and that the nonprofit be able to terminate the loan with five days' notice.

Magazine and Advertising Income

To understand the unrelated business income tax as it relates to magazines and advertising, it is important to see a magazine as composed of three tasks: advertising, articles, and circulation. In the setting up of the magazine there should be a good cost accounting system that recognizes these functions because they affect the potential tax. Each function has costs and revenues. When all three are put together, we have a periodical called a magazine. The periodical's costs and revenues are, obviously, the sum of these parts.

The concept of unrelated business income as it relates to the periodical presumes that the articles are written for the members or the clients of the nonprofit and are therefore related to its mission. Accordingly, it concludes that if there is unrelated business income it is due to the net income from the sales of advertisements or that the subscription price is well in excess of what is needed to support the mission (the articles), or a combination of these.

The unrelated business income of a periodical can be divided into two categories. That related to advertising and that related to the entire periodical largely because the circulation income exceeds the readership costs; that is, the earnings of the periodical are in excess of the amount needed to carry out the organization's mission.

Advertising

1. If the direct advertising costs exceed the gross advertising income, the advertising loss can be used to reduce any other unrelated business income the nonprofit may have.

2. If gross advertising income exceeds direct advertising costs, the balance can be used to cover the costs of readership as long as it does not produce a loss. This is done by deducting the cost of the readership portion of the magazine (articles) from the gross income of advertising.

Entire Periodical

1. If the circulation income (all income other than advertising; that is, income from sale, distribution, and production) is equal to or greater than the readership costs, the unrelated business income is the gross income from advertising minus the direct cost of advertising. Put another way, the advertising income is not necessary to the carrying out of the mission.

2. If readership costs exceed the circulation income, the unrelated business income is the total income of the periodical (advertising plus circulation income) over the total cost of the periodical.

The reader should see that the rules have certain consistency. The second rule under Entire Periodical implies that the advertising income is generating the excess and because total periodical cost is being subtracted and that contains readership costs, advertising income is subsidizing the readership income, just as under the first rule under Advertising.

What is *gross circulation income?* Mainly, it is the price of subscribing to the magazine. For a commercial magazine, this is not a problem. For a nonprofit the subscription price depends, in part, on whether nonmembers pay a higher price for the magazine than do members. If this is the case, and at least

20 percent of the subscribers are nonmembers, the price they pay is considered to be the subscription price. If 20 percent or more members pay a lower membership dues and this is because they do not get the magazine, the difference in dues is considered to be the subscription price. Otherwise, the subscription price is obtained by taking the total membership dues and multiplying that by the cost of the magazine divided by the total cost of conducting the organization's exempt mission (including the magazine). The idea is to get a subscription price that is equivalent to what a magazine sold by a for-profit publisher would charge.

Corporate Advertising or Sponsorship

Acknowledging a corporate sponsor will not be called unrelated business income if there is no language or action to induce the audience to buy the product or service of the sponsor. Inducement can occur by mentioning price or by making qualitative comparisons with other products. An exclusive contract with the corporate sponsor so that no other sponsorship may be included in the event or in the production of a printed matter will cause the transaction to be classified as an unrelated business. Any statement of endorsement will have the same effect. So, too, will pegging the amount the organization is paid to the exposure or potential of it, such as how many people may attend, see, or hear it, will have similar results.

Otherwise, prominently displaying the sponsor's logo or name and describing the sponsor's activity in a noncomparative manner and in a manner not to promote will not be a problem. Neither will giving some special considerations to the sponsor, such as free tickets to the event being sponsored, preferential tickets, or even a thank-you reception. It is within bounds to negotiate where, how, and what language will be used in the acknowledgment. An organization may do well to stick to language such as "supplying this service for so many years" or "supplying an extensive array of such services" or "dedicated to doing their best" as opposed to "being the best."

Mortgages: Income Subject to Debt

It is easier to deal with this topic by raising a set of questions and giving some preferred answers—assuming that the objective is to avoid unrelated business income tax by conforming with existing rules. Because a mortgage (and a lien) are debt instruments, a property acquired through the signing of a mortgage or that has a lien placed on it can yield unrelated business income in its sale or in the income it generates.

1. Is at least 85 percent of the property to be used by the organization for its exempt purpose? Yes.

2. Is at least 85 percent of the property to be used by an organization related to the mortgagee? Yes.

3. Is the mortgaged property one obtained by bequest and did the donor have the property and the mortgage for five years or more before dying? Yes.

4. Is the property adjoining to or the next closest possible parcel to the one occupied by the organization for its exempt use and is the property to be converted to exempt use in ten years (or, if a church, fifteen years without regards to the contiguity of the property)? Yes.

5. Is the property to be used as medical clinic? Yes.

6. Is the property to be leased to a disqualified person or the person who sold the property? No.

7. Is the mortgage gotten from a disqualified person? No.

8. Is the organization one that has gotten a specific authorization or qualification to purchase, restore, or repair homes without being subject to mortgage-related tax? Yes.

9. Is the income or sale of the property being taxed as unrelated for some other reason than the existence of a mortgage and therefore will not be taxed again? Yes.

10. Is the use to which the property acquired by debt one that is exempt? Yes.

A related organization, for the purposes of debt acquisition, has a definition that is different from those we referred to in Part One of this book. Two organizations are related for mortgage purposes if 50 percent of the members in one are also members of the other. This is analogous to the so-called brother-sister relationship among firms. In addition, organizations are related if they are associated with a common state, federal, or international organization, or if one controls the other, or one organization is a holding company and the other is part of that system.

It is not necessary to assume a mortgage to have it cause unrelated business income. All that is necessary is that property has a mortgage—no matter who holds the mortgage and whether it is converted, changed, or refinanced. It is the existence of the mortgage that matters. Further, a property that is exempt because it is used for an exempt purpose becomes taxable once its use is changed. It is the use, not the property itself, that matters. Therefore, question 10 above is key.

Income from Mailing Lists, Logos, and Affinity Cards

Usually there is no problem if the organization leases its mailing list or the use of its name or logos only to exempt organizations, or if it leases to a commercial enterprise at a fixed and fair market fee without getting involved beyond that point. A problem arises when there is any attempt to control the use of the mailing list or logo (for any reason whatsoever) or when there is a participation in the profits (that is, percentage of profits paid to the nonprofit), or when the nonprofit becomes involved in promoting the use of the product or service (for example, credit card) for which the for-profit corporation leased the list, logo, or name. A problem can arise even if the nonprofit works through its own subsidiary. (See the following section.)

Active Participation and Agency Income

Active participation in a transaction unrelated to the mission of the organization will probably trigger the unrelated business income no matter how subtle the activity. But will this tax be triggered if some other entity, even a for-profit contractor, is used as an intermediary or representative of the nonprofit? Here the question rests on whether the intermediary, a subsidiary or an independent contractor, is serving as an agent for the nonprofit.

The facts of each case as viewed by the IRS and the courts are determinative. In Mississippi State University Alumni, Inc., Technical Memo 1997–397, the IRS argued unsuccessfully that putting applications on a table and the carrying of a newspaper article about a credit card using the university's logo were services to the issuer. It argued that allowing the bank issuer to use the mailing list of the university along with the logo on the credit card amounted to a service. It even argued that a service was provided by the university when one of its employees reviewed the endorsement letters prepared and distributed by the bank. Disagreeing with the IRS, the court argued that these were too insignificant to convert a royalty to taxable income.

One of the most arduously fought cases is *Sierra Club, Inc.* v. *Commissioner.* The club, a 501(c)(6), owns a mailing list that it sells to one of its subsidiaries at a fixed and fair market rate. The subsidiary markets the list to firms as it sees fit. The club exercises control over the dates and contents of the message for which the list is to be used. One use of the list was by a bank issuing credit cards. The club was paid a fixed percentage of the total amount charged on the card. The IRS argued that these payments to the club were not royalties exempt from tax because the club merely used the subsidiary as an agent.

But the club argued that they were merely exercising quality control and that it was a "passive" participant. They were not doing the marketing or renting and did not exercise managerial control over the vendors. The courts agreed.

In *State Police Association of Massachusetts* v. *Commissioner* we see the opposite results. The association contracted with an outside vendor to solicit advertising for its journal that was distributed free by the association at its annual event. Advertising fees were paid directly to the association and it paid the vendors a fixed percentage. The president of the association wrote letters to potential advertisers encouraging them to buy spots in the journal. Both the IRS and the courts concluded that the income was taxable because the outside vendor was just an agent of the association.

In *American Academy of Family Physicians* v. *United States,* the academy sold its mailing list to a for-profit subsidiary at a fair market price. This subsidiary marketed an insurance program. The insurance premiums were paid directly to the insurance company (not the subsidiary or the academy). The insurance company paid the academy a fixed percentage of the insurance reserve. The court concluded that this fixed payment was not unrelated business income. The academy's participation in the program was not a trade or business and their payments were not for services rendered.

The IRS will challenge an arrangement in which the nonprofit attempts to be "passive" by using an intermediary if that intermediary can be considered an agent or under the control of the nonprofit. A for-profit subsidiary is considered to be under the control of a nonprofit when the nonprofit holds at least 50 percent of the voting shares of the for-profit company. With the 1997 law, this ownership is attributed to any subsidiary owned by the subsidiary that the nonprofit owns. Control is also implied when the suggestions discussed under the dividend portion of Passive Income, a section earlier in this chapter, are not observed.

That the courts or the IRS may conclude that a transaction is not unrelated business income merely means that the nonprofit does not pay an income tax on the transaction. It does not exempt the subsidiary (whether nonprofit or for-profit) or independent vendor. Consequently, many transactions of this type are set up so that the payment from an independent vendor to the nonprofit is in the form of royalties or interest rather than in the form of dividends. Dividends cannot be deducted by the for-profit, but interest and royalties can. And interest and royalties are also received tax free by the nonprofit in a clean transaction in which they are passive. Consequently, the parent avoids taxes and the subsidiary reduces its taxes by paying royalties and interest rather than dividends. See our discussion below for more on for-profit subsidiaries.

Income from For-Profit Subsidiaries

In Chapter Three we discussed 509(a)(3)s as nonprofit subsidiaries. If they earn unrelated business income they are taxed. What if the subsidiary is a for-profit corporation? How is this setup treated?

Figure 10.2 shows what could have happened under past laws. A nonprofit could form a for-profit subsidiary and own 79 percent of its voting stocks,

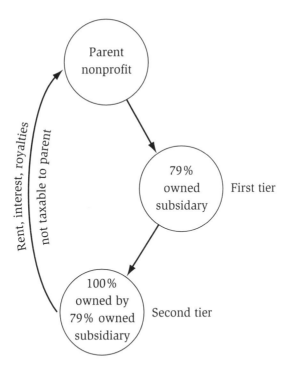

Figure 10.2. Old Law of Subsidiary and Income Flow.

the remainder of the voting stocks being owned by some friendly party or parties. The subsidiary could then own 100 percent of a for-profit firm that would pay interest, royalties, and rents to the nonprofit organization. These income flows would be received tax-free because the nonprofit owned less than 80 percent of the first-tier subsidiary (so by law it was not considered to be in control of that subsidiary). Because none of the latter's ownership of the second-tier subsidiary was attributed to the parent, the parent was not considered to be in control of this second-tier subsidiary either.

Under current law this is no longer possible. The nonprofit is considered to be in control of the first-tier subsidiary once it owns 50 percent of the voting stocks of the first-tier subsidiary. Furthermore, a part of the stocks of the second-tier subsidiary owned by the first is attributed to the nonprofit. This means if the first-tier completely controls the second-tier subsidiary, the nonprofit is considered to be in control of both once it controls 50 percent or more of the voting stocks of the first tier.

Note that this rule omits reference to dividends. Dividends from a for-profit corporation to its parent and only stockholder are not taxable regardless of whether the parent is a for-profit or nonprofit corporation. Furthermore, dividends are not deductible by the paying corporation. But interest, royalties, and rents are deductible by the paying corporation. Therefore, the incentive of the nonprofit was to win both ways: to have its subsidiary pay interest, royalties, and rents to it, which the subsidiary would then deduct from its income tax. These payments would then be received by the parent nonprofit tax free under the unrelated business income tax rule.

The new law still allows the payments of royalties, interest, and rents to be deducted by the for-profit subsidiary, but these are now taxable to the nonprofit, since they control the subsidiary. Note when control is absent, these flows would remain tax free unless made taxable under some other condition, such as being debt acquired.

Income from Holding Companies of Multiple Parents

Title holding companies, as described in Part One, are tax exempt as long as they stick to their mission—acquiring and holding title to real estate, collecting income and passing it on to the parents. If a 501(c)(25) should vary from this, it loses its exemption. Technically, therefore, there is no unrelated business income arising from activities unrelated to their mission. Since the 501(c)(25)s are expected to be active and are controlled by their parents, these activities would hardly give rise to unrelated business income.

But what about property acquired by borrowing? The rules allow that these properties would not yield unrelated business income for certain types of nonprofits—particularly educational institutions. For all other institutions, their liability for this type of unrelated business income will relate to their pro rata share of ownership of the holding company.

SOURCES OF UNRELATED BUSINESS INCOME: A SIMPLIFIED VIEW

There are three main sources of unrelated business income: (1) unrelated business activities, (2) debt-acquired property, and (3) controlled organizations. Some general rules follow.

1. All profits from unrelated business activities are taxable to the nonprofit unless they are passive income such as rents, dividends, interest, royalties, and annuities. Profits from unrelated sales, for example, are taxed.

2. Profits from debt-financed properties are usually taxed as unrelated business income unless they are already being taxed under source 1

or 2 or arise from a tax-exempt mission or fall into an exception. (See Appendix 10.1.)

3. All rents, interests, royalties, annuities, and other payments (excluding dividends) to the controlling organization from its subordinates are taxed regardless of whether the subordinate is tax exempt.

TEN QUESTIONS TO JUDGE WHETHER BUSINESS WILL BE UNRELATED

Based upon the preceding discussion, the following ten questions should be asked to gain an inkling of whether an activity is at risk of being declared unrelated business. If the answer is other than the preferred, as indicated next to each question, reread this chapter to see whether you are an exception and check it out with a competent attorney and accountant. The final judgment is based upon the facts and circumstances in each case. Hence, the individual exceptions in the long list shown the appendix to this chapter get their meaning from how the activity is actually conducted and by the specific mission of the organization in question. After all, *unrelated* means unconnected to the carrying out of the organization's mission.

1. If this project had *no* profit expectations or possibilities, would you have undertaken it purely and legitimately as a part of your mission? Preferred answer, yes.

2. Do you know of any examples of an organization similar to yours in mission that is conducting that activity as part of its mission? Preferred answer, yes—especially if the organization has defended the activity on the basis of a Revenue Ruling from the IRS.

3. Can a reasonable person without stretching his or her imagination see the connection between the activity and your mission? Preferred answer, yes.

4. If this activity is being conducted by a local commercial firm or could easily be conducted profitably by one, does yours differ in size, scope, frequency, market, clients, price, advertising, payment of workers, profit margin, and character? Preferred answer, yes.

5. Does the activity involve expending or using the organization's assets, name, goodwill, employees, or space to help a for-profit firm make a profit even if the activity serves your organization? Preferred answer, no.

6. Do you promote or *share* in the profits of a for-profit venture as opposed to recovering costs and charging a flat fee? Preferred answer, no.

7. Is the activity carried on by paid employees? Preferred answer, no.

8. Is the activity one in which persons *other* than those vital to your mission—that is, employees, volunteers, students, patients, the needy—are beneficiaries? Preferred answer, no.

9. Does the income (other than dividends) flow from a controlled group as defined? Preferred answer, no.

10. Does the income flow from an activity or property subject to debt? Preferred answer, no.

THE FEDERAL TAX

Whenever an exempt nonprofit has *gross* unrelated business income of $1,000 or more, it must file an income tax form. Although net income or profits determine the tax liability, gross income determines whether or not filing is mandated. Failure to file, file on time, or file quarterly estimated income tax may draw penalties and interest charges unless the failure was due to reasonable causes. The tax form (Form 990–T) must be signed by hand by the president, trustee, treasurer, vice-president, or some other officer designated by the organization.

If it has more than one unrelated business, even if they are separate for-profit corporations, it may consolidate all into one. This permits the organization to reduce the taxable income of one business by the losses from the others. For-profit corporations can also do this.

If the organization is a corporation, it is taxed at the corporate rates; if a trust, it is taxed at the rates for trusts.

Calculating Unrelated Business Income

Taxable net income from the sale of services or products is calculated, as per for-profit corporations.

Gross Sales

   Minus discounts and returns

   Minus cost of goods sold

   Minus general and administrative expenses

   Minus operating expenses

   Plus net income from investments

   Plus net income from other sources; that is, capital gains

Total Net Income (taxable income)

   Multiplied by tax rate (stepwise as shown in tax table)

Tax Liability Before Credits

   Minus credits (those available to all corporations in a similar line of business)

Unrelated Business Income Tax to Be Paid by Nonprofit

Taxable Income

A nonprofit is taxed for unrelated business income just as though it were a firm. From gross sales, discounts and returns are subtracted and then allowable expenses are deducted. But a nonprofit gets a $1,000 deduction called a *specific deduction*. But only one specific deduction can be taken, no matter how many unrelated businesses the organization runs. However, a religious association—for example, a diocese, synod, district, and the like—can take one $1,000 specific deduction for each of its churches that is not separately incorporated. The churches that are separately incorporated must file their own tax form and take their own specific deduction.

For all officers and trustees who are paid by the nonprofit and also work for the unrelated business, their names, the amount of time spent on the unrelated business, and their compensation must be reported to justify their deduction as part of the business expense of the unrelated business. Otherwise, the business could end up subsidizing the nonprofit and also taking a deduction for an expense it did not legally incur.

Now, what is taxable? Unlike a for-profit corporation, a nonprofit, other than a private foundation, does not pay taxes on its investment income. However, there are some important exceptions. Such gains are taxable when they are debt-financed. Hence, capital gains resulting from the sale of a debt-financed stock are taxable if the debt was outstanding during the twelve months prior to the sale. Gains from debt-financed properties, in general, are taxable.

If an organization has more than one periodical, it may report on a consolidated basis, thereby offsetting the gains of one with losses from the others. This offset is only permitted if all of the periodicals to be consolidated are published with the purpose of making a profit. This is deemed to be the case when gross advertising income is at least 25 percent of the readership costs. If the organization elects to consolidate these profit-oriented periodicals, it must include all such profit-oriented periodicals it runs.

Surtax

Nonprofits with unrelated income tax liability of at least $100,000 must pay an additional 5 percent surtax.

Sharing the Taxes

A nonprofit that operates several for-profit corporations may allot the total tax bill, including the surtax, from its consolidated tax calculations to the various members of the controlled group. To understand this, go back to the tax rates. Notice that they are in brackets. Naturally, it is better to be in the 15 percent bracket. Hence, the regulations limit the group to one $25,000 and one $50,000 bracket use. Assume, for example, that there are two corporations in the controlled group. It could be decided that they would apportion equally. Each would thus have their first $12,500 (half of $25,000) taxed in the $25,000 bracket and each would have $25,000 (one half of $50,000) taxed in the $50,000 bracket.

The controlled group can divide this up by prior signed arrangement among the members. The group could thus reduce its taxes by having the one with the largest taxable income taking the entire bracket; that is, using up the privilege of the group to have its first $50,000 taxed at 15 percent.

OTHER COSTS OF UNRELATED BUSINESS INCOME

Before closing this chapter it is worth noting that the federal income tax and even the state income tax may not be the only consideration of this kind that must be taken into account when an activity yields unrelated business income. That activity may also not be exempt from property or sales taxes on the state and local levels. In addition, the activity may be subject to higher postal rate. This can also be true if the mail advertises a commercial partner. Furthermore, the activity may be subject to state and local fees. This does not imply that unrelated business income is unworthy of the organization. In a Virginia case, the judge held that gross income could not be treated as charitable income if any portion of it was used to pay the expenses of a commercial vendor because such a payment was not a charitable use of these funds.

SUMMARY AND PREVIEW

Business operation is important to many nonprofits, even as they carry on their missions. This chapter, of concern to all nonprofits, focuses on unrelated businesses. It discusses their definition, how various types of transactions are treated, the tax implications, and the implications of these on the tax-exempt status. But unrelated business income is not the only concern of management. Is business income worth pursuing? What should be the consideration?

CHAPTER ELEVEN

Pitfalls in Marketing, Lobbying, and Solicitation

This chapter addresses the pitfalls of which management has to beware in marketing the organization, its mission, or its products or services in soliciting charitable contributions, political and membership contributions, or dues and in lobbying. It discusses designing policies to protect the organization and what I referred to in the second edition as the 5Ms of marketing a nonprofit—whether charity or association. The chapter also gives tips on using a commercial fund-raiser to solicit on behalf of the organization.

Some years ago, the National Easter Seal Society sued the American Lung Association for using a seal in its fund-raising. It claimed that a seal was its trademark and therefore its use by the American Lung Association represented a trademark infringement that would cause confusion and a diversion of donations. Marketing decisions have organization-wide implications. All of the activities described in this chapter have legal implications. What are the rules?

Aside from these civil issues, there are federal and state laws concerning what may be and what must be said in certain types of solicitations and how these must be presented if the organization is an association or a political action committee (PAC). In addition, states and the federal government have certain tight rules concerning charitable marketing (in which a product or service is being sold) and in charitable solicitations in which donations are requested. These rules and the consequences of disobeying them are the concerns of this chapter. Indeed, the rules of exchange between a marketing transaction and a charitable contribution are distinctly different.

THE EXCHANGE

It is fashionable to view marketing as an exchange of values. Such a concept applies very well to a business and to those activities in a nonprofit organization that are businesses. It does not apply equally well when what is being marketed is an opportunity to give, that is, to make a tax-deductible donation. For this reason, the concept of an exchange needs to be understood by managers of nonprofits and applied differently when the marketing applies to a gift and when it applies to a sale or an exchange of equivalent value. The consequences of error are not trivial.

Neither in the United States nor in Canada can a tax-deductible gift or donation involve an equivalent exchange of values, whether tangible or intangible. Put otherwise, a pure gift is a transfer of property from a donor to a donee with no expectations or actual receipt of benefits by the donor from the donee for that transfer.

The Sadie Wattley Malcom family makes a gift to St. Gibson's parish for masses said for her and other deceased members of the parish. The IRS ruled that such a gift is tax deductible, since the church established that it did not sell or charge for masses and because the donation could be used at the discretion of the parish for its other charitable activities. The donation was not tied to the intangible benefit of a mass.

An exchange is different. It involves a transfer of a property from one person to another with the expectation of something of equivalent value in return from the recipient. When the property expected to be received is cash or something of equivalent or superior value, what we have is a sale. Sales are not gifts. They are not tax deductible. Indeed, the gains on a sale may be taxable by federal, state, and local governments.

Sales are subject to consumer protection laws such as the ones described in the sidebar from the State of Idaho Statutes.

Some exchanges are for properties of like kind and of equivalent values, for example, a rental property for a rental property with the same market value. Such exchanges are also not deductible. They are not taxable because there was no gain and not deductible because there was no measurable economic sacrifice. Each person received an equivalent (no more and no less) of what he or she gave the other. These exchanges are not tax deductible.[1] There is no gift in this transaction.

Some transfers of property are so complex that they involve a sale, an exchange of equivalent value, and also a gift. Such complex transfers are dissected into parts for purposes of identifying each portion, placing a value on it, and determining whether it generates a tax, a deduction, or neither. We saw such strategies (bargain sales) in Chapter Seven. For purposes of marketing, it is

---

Title 48: Monopolies and Trade Practices

Chapter 6: Consumer Protection Act

48–603A. Unfair Solicitation Practices. (1) It is unlawful for any person to solicit a sale or order for sale of goods or services at other than appropriate trade premises, in person or by means of telephone, without clearly, affirmatively, and expressly revealing at the time the person initially contacts the prospective buyer, and before making any other statement, except a greeting, or asking the prospective buyer any other questions, that the purpose of the contact is to effect a sale, by doing all of the following:

(a) Stating the identity of the person making the solicitation;

(b) Stating the trade-name [trade name] of the person represented by the person making the solicitation;

(c) Stating the kind of goods or services being offered for sale;

(d) And, in the case of an "in person" contact, the person making the solicitation shall, in addition to meeting the requirements of paragraphs (a), (b), and (c) of this section, show or display identification which states the information required by paragraphs (a) and (b) of this section as well as the address of the place of business of one (1) of such persons so identified.

(2) It is unlawful for any person, in soliciting a sale or order for the sale of goods or services at other than his appropriate trade premises, in person or by telephone, to use any plan, scheme, or ruse which misrepresents his true status or mission for the purpose of making such sale or order for the sale of goods or services.

(3) It is unlawful in the sale or offering for sale of goods or services for any person conducting a mail order or catalog business in this state and utilizing a post office box address to fail to disclose the legal name under which business is done and the complete street address from which business is actually conducted in all advertising and promotional materials, including order blanks and forms.

Source: State of Idaho Statutes.

---

important to be mindful that there is a distinction with serious consequences both for the organization and the donor.

An error can (1) deprive the "donor" of a deduction or cause the donor to misrepresent facts when filing income tax, (2) cause taxation if the donor received a gain, and (3) cause the nonprofit to be liable for sales and income taxes if in fact it made a sale that is outside its line of work[2] and a violation of law if it fails to make the proper disclosure, to which we now turn.

Exchange of Values and the Law

The distinction between an exchange (a sale) and a gift is not petty theory. Accordingly, once the IRS sent 400,000 nonprofits its Publication 1391 informing them that a gift and an exchange are two different things. In a gift, there is no quid pro quo to the donor, but in an exchange one thing is given up for another. In a charitable gift, the donor gives something of value to a nonprofit without the expectation or receipt of anything of value in return.

The publication points out that each nonprofit must determine the fair market value of any property it gives to a donor in connection with his or her gift. The donor must be told by the nonprofit that only the amount of the donation that exceeds the fair market value of such property is a tax-deductible donation because this portion is a gift. The remainder is an exchange of equivalent value or a sale.

A simple example: In a fund-raising dinner, the meal and entertainment are benefits or values received by the attendees. The per-person cost of both the food and the entertainment can be ascertained. Only the amount paid by the attendees that exceeds this cost is a tax-deductible gift. The amount that is equal to the per-person cost of the food and entertainment represents an exchange of values—dollars for food and fun—and is not deductible. Your nonprofit hospital makes no pretense that its charges to you are anything other than a payment for medical services, a benefit received, and not a gift.

Some exchanges are so insubstantial that they can be ignored.[3] But what is insubstantial is defined by the IRS. For example, Dillan gives as part of a campaign and receives a benefit from the nonprofit. The benefit is valued at less than 2 percent of the total amount she gave that nonprofit. Because (1) it was a gift in a campaign and (2) her benefits were 2 percent or less, the entire amount she gave that nonprofit is tax deductible as long as this benefit does not exceed $50.

The exchange is also insubstantial when the benefits are token items such as mugs, chains, pens, posters, and T-shirts. A nonprofit can thus avoid problems for its donors and at the same time do relatively less expensive marketing by offering inexpensive objects of gratitude. Observe this strategy as used by your public radio station.

Newsletters are special. The nonprofit does not have to give the fair market value and the donor does not lose the deduction if the newsletter that is given is unavailable commercially on newsstands or to nonmembers of the organization through subscription, and if the purpose of the newsletter is to inform about the organization. Examples are the books and other literature television ministers send in return for cash contributions. Listen carefully.

Exchange of Values, Accounting, and Ethics

Not only the IRS is concerned about exchanges and the need to disclose what values are being exchanged. The standards of ethics of the watchdog agencies do as well. Furthermore, accounting principles call for distinguishing and accounting for gifts differently from exchanges.

Exchange of Values: Churches as Examples

Two religious cases illustrate the legal pitfalls. The first case is about a church that offers full-tuition scholarships to children of its members. It also asks these parents to increase their donations to the church by at least the amount they would have to pay in tuition. The court held that the donations were not tax deductible because they were made in anticipation of a benefit—education and zero tuition.[4]

The second case is about the Church of Scientology. The church offers its members classes designed to increase their spiritual awareness by teaching them church doctrine. As a result of this training, attendees may qualify to teach. The mother church sets fixed tuitions, which vary with the length and sophistication of training. In *Robert L. Hernandez* v. *Commissioner* and *Katherine Jean Graham et al.* v. *Commissioner,* the U.S. Supreme Court denied any deduction for these payments. It argued that the transactions presumed a quid pro quo (exchange of values) and therefore are not deductible, even though what was being exchanged was religious.

Exchange of Values: Limitation to Marketing Strategy

The examples given should be sufficient to illustrate a legal pitfall in approaching charitable donations as though they were exchanges of values. There is another problem. Most nonprofits have nothing to exchange with those whose dollars they most need. Therefore, for them, a marketing campaign based on the concept of exchange will fail.

To illustrate, Bill Cosby gives $20 million to Spellman College. True, his daughter attended that college. But paying tuition (an exchange of values—dollars for education) is cheaper than giving $20 million. Certainly, it cannot be suggested that he personally wanted something from the college that was worth $20 million. The same is true of former owner of *T.V. Guide* Walter Annenberg's gift of $50 million to the United Negro College Fund. What could he have been exchanging? It is obvious that if either of these approaches were dependent on an exchange, the gift would never have been made. Neither man needed an exchange—not even recognition. Television provided enough for both men.

A symphony orchestra exchanges music for dollars. It therefore sells tickets and admits only those who have tickets and only to the section of the auditorium where the quality of the enjoyment matches the dollars paid. Values are thereby exchanged. But the purchase of a ticket does not provide the purchaser with a deduction. It is a sale because values (dollars for musical entertainment) are exchanged. But gifts to the symphony are philanthropy, not exchanges.

Exchange of Values Applied

We have seen that approaching nonprofit marketing as an exchange of values can be seriously flawed when used outside those activities that are businesslike. We have seen that the consequences could include (1) loss of a tax deduction for the would-be contributor, (2) a possible sales and income tax on the donor if there is a gain and on the nonprofit if it gained in an unrelated business, and (3) frustration when the nonprofit has basically little or nothing to exchange with major donors.

However, some nonprofits can use this approach successfully. These are nonprofits that charge fees in the form of tuition, entrance fees, or prices. They are clear exchanges. It is also applicable when organization offer meaningful prizes—cars, trips, houses.

One final word. Do not confuse a recognition with an exchange of values. The naming of a building at a university or college, a room in a hospital, or a scholarship for a major donor is not an exchange. It is a recognition. If it were an exchange, the person would end up owning the building, room, or scholarship. Recognition is an effective inducement. Few would choose to have that marred by public knowledge that they "sold out."

Similarly, do not confuse opportunity with exchange. Often, especially at the end of the year when preparing for taxes or after some emotional event such as death or joyful event such as winning the lottery, people seek opportunities to give. They are less likely to be interested in what the organization offers them than what it represents and its ability to accommodate their gift. For these people, the last thing in the world they are seeking is an exchange because this would merely complicate their dilemma.

CHOOSING AN OBJECT OF MARKETING

It is the responsibility of the nonprofit management to make the final decision on what is marketed and how tastefully and accurately. It must choose from a menu of choices offered by the staff persons and their consultants. It must also sign the contracts.

A nonprofit has a choice of marketing its name, its mission, its product or service, or a combination of all of these. "Harvard" is a name that has recognition and therefore value. It can be marketed. The American Red Cross, the American

Cancer Society, and the American Heart Association are all marketable names. What's in a name? Money. This is reflected in the large markup on sweatshirts when they carry the name of a school—any school.

Alternatively, a nonprofit may choose to market what it does. "A Mind Is a Terrible Thing to Waste" is a message marketing the educational services of historical black colleges and universities. It is a powerful message, reportedly the most sought-after public service ad of the Advertising Council.[5]

As a group, these black colleges market their mission through a conduit, the United Negro College Fund (now called the College Fund), which collects and disburses the gifts and donations induced by the message. It is easier for the general public to recognize a single name and mission—if both are attractive.

A nonprofit may also choose to market an individual product or service. Hospitals do this when they send mailings about specific services. Universities do this when they advertise summer and special programs or curricula. Museums do this when they advertise specific exhibits. Many nonprofits have a problem that is analogous to multiproduct firms. They must choose which product or combination of products to push. This decision is based on a number of considerations, but central to any list should be (1) how well they produce the product or service and (2) how satisfied they are in being identified with the product or service being promoted.

The decision to market a specific product or service carries the pitfall of misrepresentation of the quality or characteristics of these products and services. The decision to market the name of the organization places the image of the organization in jeopardy and should never be done without board approval. The decision to market a mission identifying the organization as capable of carrying out the mission is most desirable for the majority of nonprofits because it carries the least risk and gives the organization the best opportunity of receiving secondary benefits from events. An organization that is solidly identified with disasters is remembered when there is a disaster.

A Girl Scouts of the U.S.A. ad reflects a combination of these objects of marketing even in its simplicity and brevity. "Girl Scouts . . . As Great as You Want to Make It" capitalizes on the well-known name, mission, and service.

CHOOSING A TARGET

All marketing efforts should be targeted. Private foundations, corporate donors, and individuals have preferences, and each varies in its willingness and ability to respond positively to any fund-raising campaign. Some, by virtue of their charter or goals, give only to local nonprofits, to the arts, or to certain ethnic, national, or religious causes.

Targeting increases the efficiency and effectiveness of marketing. Obviously, one question managers should raise is, To whom is the message being sent? Is the target group large enough and significant enough to the mission of the organization to warrant the effort?

Targeting of the organization's clientele is also implied in the mission of many nonprofits. This is sometimes referred to as *market segmentation*—isolating a special portion of the overall market for attention. Nonprofits that serve the needy have, by definition, a defined client group. Those founded to serve the homeless, say in Cleveland or Los Angeles, have an even more specifically defined target clientele. Hence, an essential difference between targeting in a for-profit and in a nonprofit corporation is that the latter often has no choice. It is its mission. Consequently, for each nonprofit, targeting should have at least three of the following four facets: (1) targeting donors for fund-raising purposes, (2) targeting volunteers for their assistance, (3) targeting clients for programs, and (4) targeting potential members. Each may demand a different marketing strategy.

It should be obvious that targeting is more endemic to nonprofit organizations than to firms. A hardware store or barbershop is not required to specify its target group in its charter or annual report. Most nonprofits are required to state the persons or locality they exist to serve. Not focusing on their target client group can be construed as a violation of their charter and a misuse of their assets.

Targeting avoids conflict. In many communities nonprofits are accused by small businesses of infringing on their markets. A good deal of public goodwill can be achieved and also taxation of revenues avoided by proper targeting. Therefore, a college does not advertise the availability of its dormitories to the general public as a less expensive substitute for local hotels. To do so would not only be bad public relations but would lead to taxation of the income derived from such advertised activities, and they would probably be attacked as unfairly competing.

An organization can target based on a number of dimensions simultaneously. We have already mentioned mission and geography. Two other dimensions are crucial to most nonprofits. These are income and price, to which we now turn.

Targeting by Income Levels

Appeals also vary according to income. Rich folks give to art more than poor folks do. One study has even shown that there is a sharp distinction between the giving patterns of blacks and whites, the kinds of appeals that are effective with them, and the causes to which they give.[6] Another has examined the giving patterns of physicians by specialty, age, sex, and religious orientation.[7] Biennial surveys by the Independent Sector show the age and ethnic characteristics of donors and volunteers.

In determining a marketing strategy, the organization should bear in mind that some goods, services, and purposes vary in intensity of need and according to income. Income affects the life cycle of a product. The need for most goods changes as income changes. During recessions and when a community is depressed, its needs are more basic and simple. Many inner-city churches in Detroit and other cities experienced a sharp change in their fiscal ability as well as their functions as those communities became poorer. The reverse is also true. Hence, targeting, based on strategic planning as described in Chapter Seven, helps the organization meet changing community needs and, consequently, its mission.

A nonprofit does not necessarily risk its tax-exempt status by serving the rich, because, as stated in Chapters Two through Four, not all nonprofits are charities. In fact, many nonprofits, including religious congregations, do target rich populations as their principal clientele. A nonprofit places its status in danger, however, if it was created to serve the needy and fails to do so by shifting resources to attract and serve the rich. Some organizations cast a wide net to obtain a diversity, others to obtain scale. Megachurches might be examples.[8]

Targeting by Price Levels

With for-profit firms a price is not only a way to recover cost plus make additional gains, but it works to exclude or deny anyone who cannot pay. You cannot get into the movie theater unless you pay. Indeed, one reason for firms charging high prices is to exclude certain people. Restaurants and apartment buildings that cater to higher-income people do exactly this.

For many nonprofits, the very idea of charging a price that works to exclude is an anathema. This is true of those nonprofits that serve the needy; for surely if the price is set so low that the very poor can afford it, then certainly everyone else can. Hence, although a price can be used deliberately to exclude with for-profit firms, it cannot be similarly used by all nonprofits.

Even among those nonprofits that use exclusionary prices, there is a tendency not to do so completely. Universities, hospitals, museums, and even civic centers find ways to give access to some needy persons. The failure to do so, especially with hospitals, health care centers, and universities, is to risk loss of their nonprofit status and access to government payments. Observe that not all exhibits at a museum require an entrance fee. The Metropolitan Museum of Art in New York City uses a suggested donation that varies by age. This is artful pricing.

The upshot is that price plays a role in the marketing strategies of nonprofits different from that of for-profit firms. Therefore, nonprofits that rely on the exclusionary aspect of pricing risk the loss of their tax-exempt status as their pricing strategies make the discharge of their mission impossible. Hence, the management of all nonprofits must assess their marketing strategies to see whether they are appropriately targeted.

It should be obvious from what has been said that the management of a non-profit needs to target both its clientele and its sources of funding. Failure to do the former may violate its mission. Failure to do the latter is wasteful.

UNLAWFUL MARKETING AND SOLICITATION
AND THE FIRST AMENDMENT

Giving and receiving are subject to federal and state laws. Recall that the primary purpose for permitting tax exemption to nonprofits is to encourage their work and to encourage citizens to give to them. The purpose of the laws that limit giving and receiving is to defend against the abuse of this exemption. The laws that limit giving generally limit the percentage of income an individual or corporation may give in any one year. These are federal laws. The laws that limit receiving and generally limit fund-raising behavior are state laws. It is not uncommon that a nonprofit would obtain 20 percent of the proceeds from a fund-raising activity. Detractors of this type of law argue that this ratio is not unreasonable because of the cost of some fund-raisers, because what constitutes "cost" is often arbitrarily determined, and because it limits freedom of expression; that is, it rules out those fund-raising events that are very expensive or that are being conducted not for immediate revenues, but for public relations purposes.

The State of Maryland enacted such a law in 1976 after a religious group was convicted of misuse of funds. The law limited administrative expenses for fund-raising to 25 percent. The law provided that the secretary of the State of Maryland could waiver the 25 percent at his or her discretion. It also provided that certain expenses such as feasibility studies, planning, and counseling for fund raising would be excluded in calculating the 25 percent limit.

On June 26, 1984, in *Secretary of State of Maryland* v. *Joseph H. Munson Co., Inc.,* the Supreme Court of the United States in a five to four decision held that the law is unconstitutional on its face. In the majority's view, the Maryland law could not distinguish between organizations that had legitimately high administrative costs in pursuit of their First Amendment rights and those that did not. The lack of precision of the Maryland law, according to the majority of the Court, meant that its application always risked the suppression of constitutional rights. Whether other state laws placing limitations on fund-raising are consequently unconstitutional will depend on the individual state law. In *Riley* v. *National Foundation of the Blind of North Carolina,* 1988, the U.S. Supreme Court concluded that a requirement that nonprofits disclose the percentage of fund-raising receipt they will receive is a violation of the First Amendment.

Solicitation practices have come under more and more scrutiny by the federal, state, and watchdog agencies. The IRS has put nonprofits on notice that it will strengthen its compliance investigations. It expects answers to about 100 questions. These are consolidated in the sidebar. But the laws also require 501(c)(4)s, (c)(5)s, and (c)(6)s to make clear that contributions to them are not deductible as charitable contributions.

Most states require nonprofits that solicit contributions to register and annually disclose their solicitation and operational activities. They may require licensing or registration of fund-raisers and counsels. Some nonprofits, specifically hospitals, are exempted from these requirements. Table 11.1 (on pages 360–362) has been prepared to alert the manager to where there may be a specific state provision that ought to be carefully checked before launching a solicitation campaign. A telephone number is also supplied. The table is based on a more complete body of information supplied by the American Association of Fund-Raising Counsel.

Nonprofits are not legally or morally immune from prosecution for violations of laws concerning advertising. They should not misrepresent the facts or give assurances they cannot keep. Such interstate misrepresentation would contravene Federal Trade Commission (FTC) rules on advertising, in addition to being unethical and perhaps ultimately counterproductive. The FTC rules apply to sales, not contributions.

Neither should they engage in collusion to set market prices and market conditions—hence the U.S. Justice Department's investigation of colleges and universities for possible violation of the Clayton and the Sherman antitrust acts. They prohibit collusion in setting prices (in this case, tuition and scholarships). They also prohibit the corollary, which is to control market share (in this case, enrollment levels). In the same vein, the Federal Trade Commission unleashed an antitrust action against the College Football Association and Capital Cities/ABC for illegally restraining competition by their exclusive broadcast agreement. In 1984, the Supreme Court put an end to the National Collegiate Athletic Association's monopoly over broadcasting of games of college teams.

Other possible violations can arise from marketing techniques that violate Federal Communication Commission rules as far as broadcasting is concerned, and the failure of educational institutions to advertise that they are not discriminating. Statements of nondiscrimination are required of these institutions.

The U.S. Post Office in some regions tightened their enforcement of postal rates in cases of nonprofits that do joint marketing with for-profit firms. Many of these nonprofits are being charged regular commercial rates on these joint mailings, rather than the lower nonprofits rates. One culprit appears to be envelopes displaying the name of the for-profit firm. This is seen as advertising.

The Omnibus Budget Reconciliation Act (OBRA) of 1987 introduces two new laws concerning advertising by nonprofits. It says that nonprofits to which

Consolidated Checklist of Compliance with IRS Solicitation Rules

1. List the fund-raising activities of the organization.

2. Does it maintain records of (a) names and addresses of donors, (b) solicitation materials, tickets, and receipts used in fund-raising, (c) did it state that membership dues are deductible, and (d) what are the benefits of membership received by donors?

3. Did it conduct any fund-raising activities that were part gifts or payments such as for admissions or merchandise? What did it say?

4. When donors received benefits for their donations, (a) what was the nature of the benefit including things such as free tickets, subscriptions, and discounts, (b) did the charity refer to the deductibility of amounts in its solicitations or thank-you communication?

5. Did the charity receive noncash contributions with a fair market value greater than $500?

6. Did the organization sell, exchange, or dispose of any noncash contributions within two years of receipt of the noncash property?

7. Does the charity acknowledge receipt of cash and noncash donations in writing?

8. If the charity accepts noncash donations, (a) does it keep a list of the names and addresses of the donors and fair market value of the gifts when the fair market value exceeds $500, (b) who determines the fair market value, (c) can the organization provide the same information for the noncash gifts exceeding $500, and in addition was there any agreement between donor and donee about the disposition of these latter goods, and (d) did the organization file Form 8283 and give Form 8282 to donors of these latter goods?

9. Was a professional fund-raiser hired? If, yes, (a) the name and address, (b) the nature of the contract, including the amount and basis for computing compensation, and (c) if a mailing list was used, its size, cost of mailings, number of donor responses, and the total dollar amount generated by the mailing.

10. If a professional fund-raiser was used, was there (a) any business or family relationship between any officer or employee of the fund-raiser and the nonprofit, and (b) was the fund-raiser the creator of the nonprofit?

11. Did the professional fund-raiser have check writing or cashing authority?

12. Did the charity conduct bingo and other games and (a) were these subject to unrelated business income tax, and (b) were the required income tax forms filed?

13. If the charity conducted one or more travel tours, (a) did it do so with a for-profit travel agency, with which it or its officers had a connection,

(continued)

such as sharing the same address or building, personnel, space, officers or other personnel, (b) was there a contract, and (c) did the written promotional material indicate that there were educational, social, or recreational aspects of the tour?

14. If the charity ran a thrift or gift shop, (a) did the charity solicit used clothing or other property from donors for resale by a for-profit firm, (b) did the firm pay the charity and what were the terms of compensation, (c) what is the relationship between the thrift shop and the charity and any for-profit firm, and (d) if the charity received surplus or nonsalable goods from a for-profit firm, what was the fair market value and how were the goods used by the nonprofit?

Source: Prepared by author from Form 9215 (1–90) from the Department of the Treasury–Internal Revenue Service.

contributions are not tax deductible (those described in Chapter Five) must state that fact clearly in all advertising. They should not, for example, leave any doubt that the attendance at a dinner, the purchase of an item, and even a contribution would lead to a tax deduction when it would not.

The act also requires that if the tax-exempt nonprofit markets a service or product that is readily obtainable from the federal government to an individual about himself or herself (such as a Social Security number or other personal record) the advertising must contain "an express statement in a conspicuous and recognizable format" that the same product or service can be obtained from the federal government. This rule applies only to a service or product relative to the individual client and only when it can be supplied by the federal government for $2.50, including postage and handling costs. This $2.50 limit will be adjusted upward for inflation.

MARKETING AND LIABILITY

With regard to liability, a group of doctors called Doctors Ought to Care sold T-shirts making fun of Miller Lite and its marketing campaign. The T-shirt said, "We're grabbing a potty" and showed a man vomiting in a potty. The doctors argued that beer was detrimental to health and therefore physicians ought to care about reducing or moderating its consumption. They were sued by the beer producer who charged slander, damage to the company's goodwill, and the illegal use of the company's trademark, Miller Lite.[9] Although the case was settled, it does show the need to scrutinize marketing campaigns, especially for those nonprofits that are advocacy groups. All nonprofits need the same vigilance over their marketing.

Table 11.1. State Laws Regulating Charitable Solicitations.

State/Regulatory Agency	Charitable Organizations				Paid Solicitors	Fund-Raising Counsel
	Registration or Licensing Requirements	Reporting Dates and Requirements	Exemptions	Solicitation Disclosure Requirements	Registration/ Licensing and Bonding Requirements	Registration/ Licensing and Bonding Requirements
Alabama	X	X		X		
Alaska						
Arizona						
Arkansas	X	X	X	X	X	X
California	X	X	X	X	X	
Colorado	X					
Connecticut	X	X	X	X	X	X
Delaware						
District of Columbia	X	X	X	X		
Florida				X		
Georgia	X	X	X	X	X	X
Hawaii	X	X	X	X	X	X
Idaho						
Illinois	X	X	X		X	X
Indiana	X			X	X	X
Iowa	X					
Kansas	X	X	X	X	X	X

State					
Kentucky	X		X	X	X
Louisiana	X			X	X
Maine	X	X	X	X	X
Maryland	X	X	X	X	X
Massachusetts	X	X	X	X	X
Michigan	X	X		X	X
Minnesota	X	X	X	X	X
Mississippi					
Missouri	X	X	X	X	
Montana					
Nebraska	X		X		
Nevada	X				
New Hampshire	X		X	X	X
New Jersey	X	X	X	X	X
New Mexico	X	X	X	X	X
New York	X	X	X	X	X
North Carolina	X	X	X	X	
North Dakota	X			X	X
Ohio	X	X		X	X
Oklahoma	X	X	X	X	
Oregon	X	X	X	X	
Pennsylvania	X	X	X	X	X
Rhode Island	X	X	X	X	X
South Carolina	X	X		X	X
South Dakota					
Tennessee	X	X	X	X	X

(continued)

Table 11.1. (*continued*).

State/Regulatory Agency	Charitable Organizations				Paid Solicitors	Fund-Raising Counsel
	Registration or Licensing Requirements	Reporting Dates and Requirements	Exemptions	Solicitation Disclosure Requirements	Registration/ Licensing and Bonding Requirements	Registration/ Licensing and Bonding Requirements
Texas	X			X	X	
Utah	X		X	X	X	
Vermont						
Virginia	X	X	X	X	X	X
Washington	X	X	X	X	X	X
West Virginia	X	X	X	X	X	X
Wisconsin	X	X	X	X	X	X
Wyoming						

x indicates a regulation exists.

Sources: Adapted with permission by author from complete data published by American Association of Fund-Raising Counsel, Inc. (AAFRC), 25 West 43 Street, New York, NY. AAFRC updates and provides details of these regulations.

UNRELATED BUSINESS INCOME TAX: ADVERTISING

Keeping the warnings in Chapters Nine and Ten, it is probably true that for most incidental carrying of advertisements there would be no threat of a taxation. Let us review three cases. In the first case, Richardson William Charity enters into an agreement with Benjamin's Publishers. The publisher solicits ads, collects fees, and gives the organization a percentage and free copies, since these appear in the organization's annual program. The publisher has sole control over ads but makes them conform to the culture of Richardson William's Charity, which gets free copies and a cut in the advertising fees charged by the publisher. The IRS ruled that there were so many ads on a page that not one constituted a significant revenue generator. The amounts were too small to be of any commercial significance.[10]

In the second case, the Byrnes Parchment Walters Artists, a nonprofit, enters into a contract with a firm, the Carlogh Corporation. The firm does very much the same thing as described above. The nonprofit does not pay overhead, production, or distribution costs, but gets free copies and a share of the total net revenue, including subscriptions, from the publication—not just a share of the advertising income. Here, again, the IRS ruled that this was not unrelated business income.[11]

In a third case, the results were different. An organization leases its mailing list to an insurance company. The company uses the list to actively solicit life insurance among the members of the organization. The organization not only endorsed the company and permitted it to use its logo, it also promoted the sale of the policies. The IRS ruled that two aspects of this transaction created unrelated business income—the mailing list rental for commercial purposes and the active promotion of the insurance sales.[12]

All three of the above cases point to one fact: Before undertaking significant advertising and marketing, consider the tax implication. Again, taxation, by itself, should not defeat a good idea. Pay it.

THE IMPORTANCE OF TRUSTEE POLICY

So much of marketing is based on timing and opportunity that it is judicious for a board of trustees to lay broad policy guidelines. Two events, occurring almost simultaneously in the middle of 1990, are instructive. At the very same time that Volvo was withdrawing a commercial because it falsely "demonstrated" that its car could withstand being driven over by a substantially heavier vehicle, a nonprofit was being sued because an ad in its magazine was allegedly responsible for a boy being shot to death. We need not judge either of these cases here. The message is very similar: Marketing is not risk-free. Couple this fact with the enforcement of rules governing solicitation and "exchanges," we see the need for trustees to lay down broad guidelines. The reasons are clear. An ad carried by a magazine or publication owned by a nonprofit can (1) mar its reputation, (2) expose it to unrelated business income tax as discussed in Chapter Twelve, (3) expose it to legal action, (4) expose its donors to taxation when an exchange is implied, and (5) probably eventually cause the revocation of its tax-exempt status. The trustees cannot shield themselves from these consequences.

Policy Guidelines for Advertising and Marketing

To assist trustees, here are five topics on marketing and solicitation for which they may someday have to develop a policy:

1. The use of the organization's name, logo, and resources, and the control of prohibited expenditures, particularly on politics and lobbying

2. The meeting of legal requirements on disclosures to donors

3. The filing prior to soliciting and the reporting to the governmental authorities as required

4. The avoiding of transactions not at arm's length, and without regard to an ethical and moral code

5. The image the organization wishes to project to whom, and with what purpose

EVALUATION

Every marketing program should be evaluated by management. The evaluation should consider costs, results, and public acceptability. I refer the reader to various marketing texts that discuss the technicalities of evaluating marketing depending on what is being marketed and the strategy employed. Evaluation methodologies are readily available to any nonprofit. How much was raised? How much was raised relative to the cost of raising it; that is, what was the *fund-raising yield?* How many people respond by requesting more information? What response do we get from a focus group of persons who represent the population to which we are targeting our message? Management needs evaluation of marketing because marketing uses the organization's resources and goodwill.

FIVE Ms FOR SUCCESSFUL NONPROFIT MARKETING

In the marketing of an organization, begin with the mission. People give to causes in which they believe. Foundations, whether corporate or private, focus on certain missions. One study found that 86 percent of its respondents rated the mission and the programs that support the mission to be extremely important in influencing their decision to give.

Public perception of the management is important. When the public loses confidence in the management, it reduces its gifts. Foundations and corporations do not give to those in whom they have little confidence. Gifts to the United Way, a very worthy cause, dropped precipitously once negative news about the management hit the streets. Confidence in the ethics as well as the competence of the management is essential.

Another key factor is the fiscal integrity of the organization. David Rockefeller in his founding address to the Business Committee for the Arts, Inc., 1966, was on target when he said, "Even the most public-spirited corporation has, I think, a right to expect the organization seeking its help to prove that it has competent management, a realistic budget, and workable plans to attain immediate objectives as well as long-range goals." The hardest organizations to market are those that have long-lasting deficits. Potential donors view their gifts as going down a drain rather than propelling new initiatives.

A good plan stating the mission of the organization, what and how it intends to do something about it, a competent and trustworthy management, a budget that shows that the mission is fiscally possible, and financial statements that show the organization is fiscally sound are the sine qua non of marketing a nonprofit. Fancy brochures sometimes draw attention, but they may backfire. They do not hide faults and do not communicate need. Let the organization speak for itself.

Finally, it is important to remember that the essential difference between marketing for a for-profit firm and marketing for a nonprofit is that in the former, an individual expects to and does have a right to some property or service equal to the value of the money he or she paid. The exchange is based on an assumption of quid pro quo. In nonprofit marketing, the challenge is to have someone give up cash and receive absolutely nothing or something that is noticeably worth less in return. Quid pro quo is not the motivation.

I recommend that successful marketing for a nonprofit organization be based on 5Ms:

1. *Mission:* The purpose to which people are called should appeal to a meaningful segment of people.

2. *Management:* The ethics and the skills of those who manage the organization and its resources are important assets in marketing.

3. *Money:* Organizations that are broke have a hard time raising money. Money attracts money.

4. *Message:* The message should communicate a name, mission, product, or service, or a combination of these.

5. *Method:* The way the message is communicated should be cost effective and in keeping with legal and ethical standards and yet make it convenient for the audience to respond.

These 5Ms do not describe marketing techniques, which are best discussed in a separate text. These are the principal policy concerns for any nonprofit contemplating a marketing campaign. Bear in mind that a marketing campaign can be ineffective if it does not include opportunities for the target group to respond, and if the resources derived from the response, either through sales or donations, are mismanaged due to unsound management principles or ethical standards.

AN ETHICAL DILEMMA IN MARKETING

Many difficult ethical issues can arise in any marketing activity, from the sale of mailing lists of members, subscribers, and donors and the associated personal information that these lists may contain, to ethical issues that hit at the heart of the organization's mission. Let us take the following cases.

Do Not Eat Your Heart Out

Today we see seals of approval by nonprofit organizations on all kinds of products. This practice has not been without controversy. Some years ago, the American Heart Association (AHA) announced that it would endorse specific products by brand name based on how healthy these products were. Immediately, the organization was denounced by companies that were to be excluded and questions were raised by the Federal Food and Drug Administration and some state attorneys general about the propriety of this decision. Some of these complaints had to do with the possibility that the AHA's message would lead people to believe that just because some food was not listed it was not as healthy.

Ethical questions were raised about whether this was an appropriate role for a nonprofit to play and whether this would compromise the organization. Companies that were excluded from the approved list complained: Was AHA selling out? Was this ethical? Was this product endorsement? Was this another scheme to raise money, requiring companies to pay AHA for their seal of approval? Or was the identification of healthy products just useful information for the public to have?

Before you agree with the complainers, consider that the highly regarded and reputable *Consumer Reports* is published by a 501(c)(3) nonprofit, the Consumer Union. What may be the salient differences if any? So-called "seal of approval" labeling is also being considered by other groups.

Do Not Sell Your Soul

The Sunbeam Corporation sued the American Medical Association, which withdrew from an advertising endorsement of its products. The withdrawal occurred subsequent to disapproval of the arrangement by members of the AMA.

Florida and eleven states shared $1.9 million paid by SmithKline Beecham for falsely characterizing its relationship with the American Cancer Society in the promotion of its antismoking products. The charges of misrepresentation against the company were as follows:

1. The use of the American Cancer Society logo and the phrase "Partners in Helping You Quit" to suggest that the nonprofit organization had endorsed the products when it had merely allowed SmithKline Beecham to display its name and logo in exchange for a fee.

2. Claims by SmithKline Beecham that its smoking cessation products were more effective than those of another manufacturer's when the company could not scientifically demonstrate such superiority.

3. Claims that consumers would be able to quit smoking permanently by using two of its products when in fact the majority of consumers who initially quit smoking after using these products resumed smoking within one year.

The American Cancer Society was praised by the Attorney General of Florida for cooperating with it in the suit against SmithKline Beecham.

STATE CHARITABLE SOLICITATION REQUIREMENTS

Why do managers of nonprofits need an appreciation of solicitation laws? Because most states have charitable solicitation laws that oversee solicitation for contributions as well as sales. If the organization is an association, it is also subject to solicitation laws with respect to membership and sales. If the organization is an association, with a foundation, and it also is involved in interstate sales, it is also involved in rules on interstate commerce in addition to all other solicitation rules in each and every state. We focus here on charitable solicitation.

What is solicitation? Massachusetts law, Chapter 68: Section 2, which I shall describe below, defines solicitation to include:

1. Any oral request that is made in person, by telephone, radio, or television or other advertising or communications media

2. Any written or otherwise recorded or published request that is mailed, sent, delivered, circulated, distributed, posted in a public place, or advertised or communicated by press, telegraph, television, or other media

3. Any sale of, offer, or attempt to sell, any advertisement, advertising space, sponsorship, book, card, chance, coupon, device, food, magazine, merchandise, newspaper, subscription, ticket or other service or tangible good, thing, or item of value, or

4. Any announcement requesting the public to attend an appeal, assemblage, athletic, or competitive event, carnival, circus, concert, contest, dance, entertainment, exhibition, exposition, game, lecture, meal, party, show, social gathering or other performance or event of any kind

When is registration required and what is the registration process? Oregon requires that all nonprofits, for-profits, and mutual benefit organizations and individuals who solicit funds for nonprofit organizations in that state be registered to do so in that state and pay a fee. It exempts volunteers and paid employees of the organizations from registering.

All registrants must submit a notice before starting the fund-raising campaign. It must include

1. The contract with the nonprofit and what name will be used in the solicitation

2. A good-faith projection of campaign revenues and expenses

3. Telephone scripts

4. Written materials to be used with required disclosures

If the fund-raiser rather than the nonprofit handles the proceeds of the campaign, it must submit shortly after the campaign ends the following:

1. Amount paid to the nonprofit for which the campaign was held

2. Total cost of the goods and services sold

3. Total direct costs of solicitation

4. Amount retained by fundraising firm as profit

5. Gross revenues from the campaigns

The above revenue-expense data are common requirements among several states. The attorneys general of these states annually summarize these data. Using this resource, a nonprofit can compare the performance of fund-raisers along various dimensions such as what is their typical percentage take, how much they have raised in other states for other, similar-type organizations, and the total dollar volume of donations they raised across states in a given year.

A common soliciting requirement is public disclosure. In Ohio, prior to making any solicitation verbal or written the solicitor must disclose (1) his or her name, (2) a statement that the solicitation is being conducted by the person as a professional solicitor, (3) the name and address of each charity on behalf of which any portion of the solicitation is being made, (4) whether these organizations are not 501(c)(3)s and therefore the charitable tax deduction will not be available, and (5) the percentage of the gross revenues that the charity will get if the person being solicited wants to know. Ohio, like Pennsylvania and other states, also requires that the fund-raising firm carry a surety bond to insure its performance.

In Massachusetts, any person, organization, or association, foreign or domestic, that solicits for itself, or has another solicit or collect for it in any public space, must keep a record of the name and addresses of these solicitors-collectors and the amounts they collected. It must also keep a record of how these funds are used and who were the recipients of them. This record should be available to the Attorney General at all times.

Massachusetts requires that all charitable organizations doing public solicitations register annually. An organization is exempt if it is a religious corporation, a trust, a foundation, an association or organization organized for religious purposes or to support organizations with religious purposes. Organizations that do not raise more than $5,000 per calendar year or receive contributions from more than ten persons, and that do solicitations by use of unpaid persons are also exempt. All other charitable organizations must register annually by giving the following information:

1. The name of the organization and the purpose for which it was organized

2. The Massachusetts address of the organization or the person having custody of its financial records

3. The place and date that organization was legally organized and the category of its exemption

4. The name and address of the principal officers and trustees and their compensations

5. A copy of its financial report for the immediately past year

6. Whether the organization intends to solicit from the public

7. Whether the organization has the permission or authority of any agency other than the Attorney General to solicit and whether the courts have enjoined the organization from soliciting

8. The charitable purposes for which the solicitation is being made

9. The name or names under which the solicitations will be made

10. The names of the officers of the organization that will have final custody of the funds collected

11. The names of the officers of the organization that will have final decision-making powers about how the funds will be disbursed

Registration must be done under oath by two officers of the organization and in the Commonwealth of Massachusetts and a fee is required. The organization can file on behalf of itself and its affiliates, chapters, or branches in the state. Registration may be revoked if the registrants fail to comply with the law or indulge in deceptive practices, false pretenses, misrepresentation, or misleading presentation.

All contracts between the organization and the commercial fund-raiser has to be in writing, signed by two officers of the nonprofit corporation, and filed with the Attorney General before starting the solicitation. The contract should contain a description of the charitable purpose for which the proceeds will be used and the fixed percentage guaranteed-minimum of the total collection that will be given to the organization. The total compensation to the solicitor, its employees, or agents cannot exceed 2 percent of the total pledges and contributions they collected minus all (noncompensation costs) of the solicitation.

Each commercial fund-raiser must file annually with the attorney general, pay a fee, and have a surety bond. In addition, the fund-raiser must file a financial report showing the amount raised, expenses, and the amount awarded to the organization for charitable purposes. The report must be cosigned by the fund-raiser and the representative of the organization.

Any person who is compensated to solicit door-to-door contributions for any charitable civic or political organization must reveal that fact. The person might choose to wear a badge that says "Paid Solicitor." The person need not do this if all he or she receives is paid expenses or if the person is an officer of the organization or a member of the clergy collecting for his or her religious organization.

States vary in the penalties they impose. The attorney general of Pennsylvania announced that it had imposed a $60,000 fine on a telemarketer and the firefighter group on whose behalf it raised funds. They were accused of failing to conspicuously disclose to consumers that the caller was a paid professional solicitor and not a firefighter affiliated with a local fire department. They were also accused of misleading potential donors by stating that a solicitation would benefit a local fire group when it did not, and stating that the firefighters would receive a higher percentage than they did. It is apparent that this was a collusive effort to mislead. Such suits concerning policy and firefighter organizations have taken place in other states. The fact that such an important public service group would be targeted is attestation of the importance of the issue.

Format of Disclosure for Donative Solicitations

The Omnibus Budget Reconciliation Act of 1987, as amended, requires that any organization with gross annual receipts of at least $100,000, a donation to which does not qualify for a charitable contribution, to disclose that fact in any solicitation as described above. The format of the disclosure depends upon the medium used in the solicitation.

If the medium is print, then the disclosure must

1. Say, "Contributions or gifts to (name of organization) are not deductible as charitable contributions for federal income tax purposes," or "Contributions or gifts to (name of organization) are not tax deductible," or "Contributions or gifts to (name of organization) are not tax deductible as charitable contributions."

2. The above statement must be in at least the same size print as the remainder of the message.

3. The statement must be on the message side of any printed material the donor is to return with the contribution.

4. The sentence must either be the first in a paragraph or be a paragraph.

If the medium is the telephone, the disclosure must

1. Say "Contributions or gifts to (name of organization) are not deductible as charitable contributions for federal income tax purposes," "Contributions or gifts to (name of organization) are not tax deductible," or "Contributions or gifts to (name of organization) are not deductible as charitable contributions."

2. The statement must be made in the same telephone conversation by the same solicitor near to the statement of request.

3. Any written bill or follow-up must conform to the requirements pertaining to print.

If the solicitation is by television, the disclosure must

1. Say, "Contributions or gifts to (name of organization) are not deductible as charitable contributions of federal income tax purposes," or "Contributions or gifts to (name of organization) are not tax deductible," or "Contributions or gifts to (name of organization) are not tax deductible as charitable contributions."

2. If any of the statement appears on the television screen, it must be there for at least five seconds and in easily readable type. If it is spoken, then it should be said close to the request for donation.

If the solicitation is by radio the disclosure must

1. Say, "Contributions or gifts to (name of organization) are not deductible as charitable contributions for federal income tax purposes," "Contributions or gifts to (name of organization) are not

tax deductible," or "Contributions or gifts to (name of organization) are not tax deductible as charitable contributions."

2. The statement is made close to the solicitation in the same radio program.

Format of Disclosure for Membership Solicitations for Associations

Associations, specifically, labor, agricultural, and business associations, must conform to certain disclosure rules with respect to membership solicitation. Some membership fees, though not deductible as charitable contributions, may be deductible as a business expense and may not be deductible even at that to the extent that it is used to defray lobbying expenses. The format for this type of disclosure is

1. "Contributions or gifts to (name of the organization) are not deductible as charitable contributions. However, they may be tax deductible as ordinary and necessary business expenses."

2. "Contributions or gifts to (name of organization) are not tax deductible as charitable contributions for federal income tax purposes. However, they may be tax deductible under other provisions of the *Internal Revenue Code*."

3. "While contributions or gifts to (name of organization) are not tax deductible as charitable contributions for federal income tax purposes, they may be tax deductible under other provisions of the *Internal Revenue Code*."

The Internal Revenue Service promises that the use of the specific language described above under the conditions to which they appertain would not evoke a penalty for violation of the OBRA. Alternative language may be used but depending upon all of the facts and circumstances may or may not evoke a charge from the IRS. Of course, no disclosure of this type is required on a solicitation that is a bill for a payment arising from a commercial transaction.

DISCLOSURE OF LOBBYING

Both state and federal laws require nonprofits that lobby to disclose and register that activity. Clearly, state laws vary. One example is given below. The disclosure and registration are in addition to the entries on the 990 forms, in addition to the 1120 Forms alluded to in Chapter Two, and are not dependent upon the formula or word "substantial" discussed in that chapter.

Rhode Island 22–10–3 requires all persons, organizations, and associations that lobby to register. Individuals whose sole lobbying activity is testifying in a public hearing of a legislative committee or commission on behalf of a nonprofit and who receive no compensation from that organization and for whom that organization expends no money related to the appearance are exempt.

For obvious reasons, lobbying at the state and local levels is not defined as it is on the federal level. Rhode Island 22–10–2 defines lobbying as "acting directly or soliciting others to act for the purpose of promoting, opposing, amending, or influencing in any manner the passage by the general assembly of any legislation or the action on that legislation by the governor."

FEDERAL RULES ON SOLICITATION BY ASSOCIATIONS AND PACS

We shall discuss federal and state laws having to do with charitable solicitation. These laws apply also to organizations that are not qualified to receive tax-deductible contributions. Note words such as "all solicitations" and some specific reference to associations as covered by such laws. The federal government, however, as a result of the Omnibus Budget Reconciliation Act of 1987, required all organizations that do not qualify for tax-deductible contributions to disclose that fact prominently in all solicitations. It suggested how this should be done to ward off the possibility of federal action. These so-called "safe-harbor" (meaning that the government won't fuss if you follow) rules are as follows:

• The Lobbying Disclosure Act of 1995, as amended in 1998, requires certain organizations to semiannually register with the Secretary of the Senate and the Clerk of the U.S. House of Representatives as lobbyists. Any organization with lobbying expenditures at the federal level of $20,500 or more semiannually that makes contacts to influence high executive-branch employees or Congress may be required to register. The key areas covered by this registration are the subject matters of the lobbying activities, the expenses, the persons lobbied, and the role of foreign entities.

• In calculating lobbying expenditures, an organization has to include the amount it expends on hiring an outside lobbyist. In the case of churches and church affiliates that are normally not required to register, their outside lobbyists may have to include them among its reported clients. Whether an outside lobbyist includes an organization as its client depends upon two facts—it receives at least $5,000 semiannually from the organization, and its lobbying effort is at least 20 percent of the effort it expends for the organization.

- To calculate its own lobbying expenses, the organization must include that which it expends on outside lobbyists. To calculate its internal lobbying expenses, it may take the percentage of time spent by each worker involved in lobbying and multiply that by the average salary to get the worker costs. But supplies, communications, support staff, and overhead should also be added. Alternatively, if the organization has an office that has lobbying as its principal function, it might use the entire cost of that operation. Further, if there is a central organization that controls the lobbying of a number of its units, it can file a consolidated report. Finally, if a 501(c)(3) has to report lobbying expenses to the IRS it may use that amount in reporting its disclosure.

- Often organizations form coalitions for lobbying purposes. The coalition must report any organization that donated $10,000 or more to its efforts. It must also report any foreign participant and its contribution.

- All new lobbying arrangements must be reported after the first contact is made or the lobbyist is employed or retained. If an organization hires an outside firm and pays that firm at least $5,000 semiannually and at least 20 percent of the work it does for that organization is lobbying, it must file a report indicating that that organization is its client. Hence, using an outside firm may not obviate the need to register.

- Section 18 of the Lobbying Disclosure Act makes 501(c)(4) organizations that lobby ineligible for federal grants, awards, or contracts. The False Statement Accountability Act of 1996 makes it unlawful for any person or organization to knowingly file false statements. Failure to comply with the Lobbying Disclosure Act is subject to civil action and a fine of no more than $50,000.

SOLICITING THROUGH A FUND-RAISER

Managers and trustees of nonprofit organizations need to be aware that hiring a fund-raiser exposes the organization to certain serious risks. Virtually every state holds the nonprofit responsible for some part of the transaction between hiring the fund-raiser and receiving and expending the funds with appropriate accountability to the state. Therefore, hiring a fund-raising firm should be done with complete awareness of risks and a design to manage these risks.

The hiring of a fund-raiser is governed by the solicitation laws of the state. Pennsylvania's solicitation laws are rather extensive and contain many of the items we shall discuss below. A few need to be stated here. First, the law makes it unlawful for a Pennsylvania organization to contract with a non-registered fund raiser. Second, it makes it a requirement that the nonprofit organization report any relationships between the organization or its officers and trustees and the fund-raiser. Third, it requires the organization and the fund-raising firm to report if any legal actions have been taken against them or their officers in respect to fund-raising practices. Fourth, it requires that the organization maintain control of the funds. Fifth, it gives the attorney general wide powers, including that of appointing a receiver, sequestering the funds, reimbursing the persons who gave, and assigning penalties.

Many attorneys general of states offer brochures on tips in hiring a fund-raiser in conjunction with the state law. The following list is taken from the tips offered by the attorney general of the State of Michigan offers the following tips to nonprofits seeking to hire a fund-raising firm:

1. Comparison shop

2. Insist on a written contract

3. Do not relinquish control to a professional fund-raiser

4. Contact the office of your state attorney general to get a list of fund-raisers licensed to do business in your state.

Regarding the contract:

1. Identify parties by correct, complete, and legal names and addresses

2. Clearly describe the duties and responsibilities of both parties

3. Identify the compensation to be paid—a flat fee and/or percentage

4. Describe the flow and control of money

5. Specify the split of funds—how much the organization will get

6. Clearly identify who will pay expenses—set limits if possible

7. Clearly specify the contract period, including settlement dates

8. Specifically authorize or prohibit subcontractors

Regarding questions to ask:

1. Will the solicitation be done by mail, telephone, personal contact, or another method?

2. Who will develop the script, invoices, and brochures?

3. Will your organization have the opportunity to approve all materials?

4. Is there a standard contract that you can preview?

5. Who will handle the money?

Among the advice given by the attorney general is that the organization should have the checks sent to a mailbox that it controls—but most important, that the officers of the organization remember that it and they are ultimately responsible for what is said and done in the organization's name.

For this reason, I believe that a nonprofit should also consider including in the contract certain warrants (promises) and representations (assurances). I have developed the following:

1. That the fund-raiser warrants that it will comply with all state and local laws in each state and jurisdiction in which it raises funds for the organization.

2. That the fund-raiser will conform to a code of ethical practices acceptable to the organization.

3. That the fund-raiser will not co-mingle the activities of the organization with that of another without express prior approval.

4. That the fund-raiser is in good standing with the states and federal authorities that oversee its activities. (Good standing implies more than registration; it also implies that they are current in taxes.) The fund-raiser ought to be able to produce a certificate of good standing issued by the state of its incorporation. (See 8 below.)

5. That the fund-raiser's financial statement for itself is reliable.

6. That the fund-raiser carries appropriate insurance to cover its performance and its employees.

7. That the fund-raiser will hold the organization harmless for its negligence or wrong doing.

8. That the fund-raiser is up to date in the payment of its taxes, fees, and other legal obligations and that funds raised for the organization will not be pledged in support of these.

9. That the fund-raiser will provide reports on a timely basis and in a form that enables the organization to comply with its legal reporting requirements and bylaws.

10. That the fund-raiser will clearly identify and describe and make known to the organization any restrictions a donor places on funds.

11. That the fund-raiser is an independent contractor and not an employee of the organization.

12. That the fund-raiser will refrain from the use of certain language, the conduct of certain behavior, the use of certain materials, the solicitation of certain types of gifts, and similar restrictions that do not meet the approval of the organization, its trustees, membership, or the law.

13. The fund-raiser covenants not to use the space owned, leased, or occupied by the organization to carry on its campaign without expressed written permission and limitations on liability.

14. The fund-raiser promises not to use the name of the organization in its own advertising without permission.

15. The fund-raiser promises to meet all public disclosure requirements by state.

16. That the membership list is the property of the organization and may not be used for other purposes than those agreed to in the contract.

17. That there are no outstanding court actions against the fund-raiser that impinge on its ability to fulfill its contract.

18. That the contract can be terminated by the organization for good cause and a specific compensation may well be charged to the fund-raiser if it is in violation of the contract and caused economic harm to the organization.

19. That there will be no business relationship between the nonprofit board, officers, and trustees and any party of the fund-raising firm that would lead to self-dealing or the suspicion of it.

20. That all current relationships relative to 19 have been revealed and found to be fair and appropriate given the self-dealing rules of the states involved and the federal government.

These warrants and representations are intended to protect the organization against that which it cannot see, scrutinize, substantiate, supervise, stop, or substitute once the campaign has started but must rely upon the skill, goodwill, and honesty of the fund-raiser and yet remain subject to legal and public sanction.

ETHICS AND THE DONOR'S RIGHT

A group of organizations, including the American Association of Fund Raising Counsel, the Association for Healthcare Philanthropy, the Council for Advancement and Support of Education, and the National Society of Fund Raising Executives, developed "A Donor Bill of Rights." The Bill was endorsed by the Independent Sector, the National Catholic Development Conference, the National Committee on Planned Giving, the National Council for Resource Development, and the United Way of America. They agree that donors have the following rights:

1. To be informed of the organization's mission, of the way the organization intends to use donated resources, and of its capacity to use donations effectively for their intended purposes.

2. To be informed of the identity of those serving on the organization's governing board, and to expect the board to exercise prudent judgment in its stewardship responsibilities.

3. To have access to the organization's most recent financial statements.

4. To be assured their gifts will be used for the purposes for which they were given.

5. To receive appropriate acknowledgment and recognition.

6. To be assured that information about their donations is handled with respect and with confidentiality to the extent provided by law.

7. To expect that all relationships with individuals representing organizations of interest to the donor will be professional in nature.

8. To be informed whether those seeking donations are volunteers, employees of the organization, or hired solicitors.

9. To have the opportunity for their names to be deleted from mailing lists that an organization may intend to share.

10. To feel free to ask questions when making a donation and to receive prompt, truthful, and forthright answers.

SUMMARY AND PREVIEW

In Chapter Seven we saw that the strategic planning process is employable in determining general management strategies, as well as some specific tasks such as marketing. This chapter focused on caveats that the management of the nonprofit should allow to influence their marketing strategies, warned of the dangers of the concept of exchange of values, elaborated on the role of targeting and the need for management to decide what is to be marketed and to whom, and reminded the reader of laws that affect the marketing activities of nonprofits. Keep the mission preeminent. To grow an organization and conduct its mission, money is a must. Its use also must be controlled. Controlling costs and revenue allocation within and outside the confines of a contract is our next topic.

PART THREE

CONTROLLING ORGANIZATIONAL COSTS AND RISKS

The power of the budget is not that it allows managers to control programs or people, but costs and perspectives. A manager who has no appreciation of the hidden concepts behind the numbers can neither control present nor prospective costs and places the financial well-being of the organziation at considerable risk.

CHAPTER TWELVE

The Budget as a Tool
of Control and Contracting

A budget is probably the single most important tool a manager has for shaping the direction of the nonprofit. The budget is a financial plan for the organization. Constructed properly, it is the organization's business plan. It is a tool of control. A budget tells a lot about an organization's ambition. It can also be fiction.

This chapter goes beyond counting beans and putting them into categories. The fundamental question it addresses is, How can a budget serve the purposes of management? It begins by showing the various purposes a budget can serve, from being a historical device to a tool of communication and control. But it also deals with certain technical subjects such as budgeting for different types of costs and the rules for cost allocations—even if the organization is an indirect recipient of federal monies. Appendixes 12.1 and 12.2 are about treatment of costs and revenues under the realm of federal contracting rules.

THE BUDGET AS A MANAGEMENT TOOL

A budget is a projection of costs and revenues approved by the board of trustees. It is the financial game plan for carrying out the mission of the organization. At the end of the year, the financial statements tell how well the organization did in meeting its targets.

A budget is the basis on which actual performance is periodically measured against projected performance. The budget is a tool of continuous management control. Variances between actual and planned expenditures or receipts indicate the organization is off course and should sound an alarm for the attention of management.

For management, the process of budget formulation is part of the planning process. The budget is the monetary translation of the strategic plan described in Chapter Seventeen. Accordingly, a preliminary budget for each program the organization is considering during the strategic planning process is necessary so that the organization may compare expected benefits and costs before choosing among programs.

Before the chosen programs can be implemented, a final budget must be adopted so that the managers may know the amount of resources planned for their programs, the sources of those dollars (from grants, fees, and so on), how those dollars are expected to be allocated among competing uses within each program, and a schedule of expenditures and receipts over the life of the program. As a planning document, a budget has no legal force.

As a management tool, the budget is a political document. It expresses a policy decision about the priority of some programs over others, and it increases the power of some managers over others. Programs can be dropped or added, weakened or strengthened by using the budget as the rationale, for example, "It is not in the budget."

As an instrument for managerial control, actual spending and receipts can be tracked against planned targets. Variances between actual and budgeted performance signal the need to slow spending or increase receipts, or to shift resources from one category to another, or the need to raise more funds.

Variance from budgeted amounts should be of concern to management, even though the variance may be positive. Actual spending that is lower than planned amounts could be the result of laggard performance in program implementation. But it could also indicate greater than expected cost savings in program implementation. In short, all variances in spending or revenues that are more than incidental departures from the planned amounts demand management's attention. Variances are often an early warning that something could or has gone wrong. They can alert managers to the possibilities of cost overruns for which the organization may not be reimbursed. These overruns can create serious financial problems. Much of the deficit that nonprofits experience may well represent sloppy financial and operating management rather than benevolent overspending.

Although it is not audited, the budget as an instrument of control may be used by auditors to judge the extent to which the organization exercises forethought and control over its spending and revenues. Does the organization display reasonable management that plans and sets targets? Does it keep regular and systematic track of its financial performance?

THE BUDGET AS A SUM OF PARTS

For those nonprofits that operate several different programs, endowments, or businesses, the organization's final budget may be a composite of several sub-budgets: (1) one for each activity within each program or functional area, (2) one for each program or functional area, and (3) one for the organization as a whole, which is a composite of all functional or program areas plus general administration. A functional or program budget merely refers to one that is set up according to programs or activities, rather than according to objects such as paper, pencil, books, and other items. Each function will have its own detailed budget, and the organization's budget will be a composite of these individual, functional budgets.

The nonprofit budget is the sum of restricted and unrestricted amounts. Budgets in nonprofits should distinguish between restricted and unrestricted sources and uses of funds and show any anticipated transfer from one to the other. This is important because the management of the nonprofit has no discretionary use over the restricted funds. These funds must be used for the purposes for which they were received. To use them otherwise is to violate the contract under which the funds were obtained. Therefore, when the amounts of restricted funds are shown as receipts in the budget it is imperative that they are shown to be restricted; that is, their planned use is predetermined. I shall say more about restricted funds in Chapter Fifteen.

Restricted funds do not always come from outside the organization. Sometimes the board of directors may choose to set aside a certain portion of the annual revenues of the organization for some special purpose and restrict the management from using it for any other purpose. Here, again, it makes no sense to include such funds as revenues without indicating that their use is restricted. Nonprofits without an independent flow of funds from investments, unrelated or related businesses, or institutional gifts frequently find themselves with relatively little discretionary budgetary power. They function, but with little budgetary discretion.

THE BUDGET AS CONTEMPORARY HISTORY

It is frequently helpful to put the current year's budget into historical perspective. This can be done by showing the budget for the previous five or ten years. By so doing, the board of the organization can get a picture of where the organization has been, how it is growing or declining, and how resources have shifted from one functional use to another. Is the organization changing emphasis or direction? Have some programs been sufficiently funded and emphasized such that now they should be less dependent on the organization's general funds?

This historical perspective can also provide a basis for forecasting and projecting financial changes in the organization. By comparing how far off last year's planned amounts were from actual, senior management can obtain a picture of how realistic their and their subordinate managers' projections are. Are they consistently overoptimistic or overly cautious? By how much?

To facilitate comparisons over time, budget figures should be shown in current and constant dollars. Constant dollars are current dollars adjusted for inflation. The fact that current budget is 20 percent higher than last year's would not mean that the organization is expanding in real terms if the inflation rate is 20 percent. The organization is standing still. One way to assess this is to show both the dollar and the physical amounts. Accordingly, rent may be shown as $2,500 per month and the number of square feet as 1,200. Every year, show both the square feet or full-time equivalent for employees and the dollar amounts.

CAPITAL AND OPERATING BUDGETS

Another useful comparison in some nonprofits is between capital and operating budgets. Capital budgets, to be discussed later in this chapter, relate only to the acquisition or disposition of assets that have a useful life of more than one year. Planned acquisition or disposition of cars, buildings, furniture, and computers will be included in the capital budget. Operating budgets, the subject of this chapter, are prepared annually for showing expected revenues, support, and expenses for the current year. Nonprofits that are on a cash basis with very small planned capital expenditures may not need to separate capital from operating budget, but nonprofits with large capital programs must separate these two. Failure to do so would distort the annual operating budget. For example, a building purchased for $1 million is paid for over several years. In an operating budget, this transaction would be shown as a planned expenditure of $1 million in the current year, which is incorrect information.

Now we see a significant difference. To *capitalize* a cost implies paying for it over several years. To *expense* it is to pay for it in a year. The budgetary implications, you can now see, are very dissimilar.

BUDGETS AS BASELINE

A budget can commence from the bottom up. Each center gives estimates, which are then aggregated at the top. They may also flow from the top down. The management gives scenarios that reflect a broader reality of the environment and the responsibilities of the mission of the organization, the constraints and pressures upon it, and the marching orders of the trustees. It is conciliatory within the limits set by the trustees. Managers of centers with specific responsibility (called "responsibility centers") tell how they plan to enforce trustee guidelines by how they compose their center's budgets. They are responsible for micromanagement of the budget for their units, given the aggregate limits and policies set by the board. But the board and top management always reserve the right to review and authorize the budget of each center. A good budget will be the product of both flows. It reconciles differences.

BUDGETS AS FICTION

Budgets may reflect the aim of program managers to occasionally set low expectations so as to avoid the appearance of failure. They also set targets to attract more resources. Budgets are also fictitious in their appearance of accuracy, yet budgets are imperative to rational management.

PRINCIPLES UNDERLYING BUDGETS

Budgets of nonprofits should be formed according to two distinct principles: policy and efficiency. On the policy level, the trustees should be concerned with what programs will be undertaken in keeping with the organization's mission, how much of the organization's resources will be allocated to each program, and what will be the sources of funds for financing each program. As we saw in Chapter Four, the sources of support and the nature of the programs have implication beyond the budget. They affect the tax-exempt status of the organization and are therefore policy questions.

On the level of efficiency, questions to ask are the following: How much will it cost? How much money must be raised? What will be the schedule of disbursements and expenditures over the life of the program? These questions are not resolvable by policy debates without specific technical estimates.

These two principles, policy and efficiency, undergird all budget formulation processes and techniques.

ZERO-BASED BUDGETING AND PPBS

One budgeting technique is zero-based budgeting (ZBB). This technique requires the organization to pretend that it is starting from scratch. In every budget formulating period, each activity must be ranked in terms of its expected contribution to the organization's mission. Programs that cannot be justified or are of low priority are dropped or their resources are decreased. This ingredient should be present in every budgeting session, whether zero-based or not.

Another technique is program budgeting (planning, programming, and budgeting systems, or PPBS). PPBS rests heavily on measures of costs and benefits. One of its main contributions is that it integrates planning, programming, and budgeting. It forces us to see these as related rather than disjointed processes. In PPBS, programs are ranked, and those with the highest ratio of benefits to costs are assumed to be superior.

Regardless of the approach, however, the ultimate programming and financing decisions are based on policy and efficiency considerations, as described in the preceding paragraphs and in Chapter Seventeen. Accordingly, it is conceivable that the program with the highest benefit-cost ratio may be rejected because it does not fall within the policy range preferred by the organization. Similarly, the most justified program in a zero-based planning exercise may not be one that the organization can implement with the level of investment or efficiency required.[1]

Furthermore, the essence of both approaches should be present in every decision-making exercise. Programs must be justified and given priority ratings. They should be well integrated and planned for, and efficiently run. Both approaches are especially useful in long-range planning and in periodical program review.

EFFICIENCY: COSTS AND SUPPORT

In earlier chapters we dealt with policy questions. What should the organization's mission be? How should it be funded? What type of tax-exempt status is most appropriate? Let us focus for a moment on the efficiency aspect of the budget. Efficiency may be technological or economic. Technological efficiency refers to the use of the most advanced and appropriate techniques, machines, and tools for getting a job done.

The other type of efficiency, economic efficiency, is concerned not merely with dollar costs, but with an additional question: How many dollars must the organization raise today or on a periodic basis if it is to meet a certain target funding level by some specific date in the future?

Other types of capital budgeting questions are the following: How much can a nonprofit extract annually from an endowment that is earning interest at a specific rate before the endowment runs out? How should the capital budget be funded? Should the organization borrow? If so, by note or bond, and of what maturity? Would revenue bonds be wise? How will the loan be amortized? What percentage of the project should be paying for itself? How should the nonprofit invest the funds for the capital project while waiting to start the project?

These are examples of tough questions that pertain to capital planning. They are efficiency-related and technical in nature and should be resolved first in a technical manner. I shall show how in Chapter Sixteen where I discuss setting capital budgeting targets. Some questions require a clear understanding of discounting, present value, and annuity techniques. Without an understanding of these, no sensible policy decision can be made; the objective will not be met and the endowment will be wiped out. Indeed, if the organization is a private foundation, it could be liable for taxes on benefits. Economic efficiency means lowering costs and increasing benefits. Technological efficiency, as opposed to economic efficiency, is concerned only with lowering costs. When constructing its budget, a nonprofit must be concerned with economic efficiency; that is, it wants to provide the greatest amount of help (benefits) at the least cost.

THE IMPORTANCE OF DISTINGUISHING BETWEEN CASH (EXPENDITURES) AND COSTS IN BUDGETING

In January 2000, Pringle Theater contracts for 900 hours of work by actors in a production of *Gone With the Wind,* which is to take place in November 2000. In January, Pringle had to come up with the reservation price (down payment). The production takes place in November as planned and Pringle receives a bill at the end of December payable by January 30, 2001. On January 19, 2001 Pringle makes payment in full.

There is nothing unusual about the structure of this transaction. From a budgeting and management perspective, however, it is significant that the cost occurred in 2000—that is when the production took place. The commitment also took place in 2000. But the bulk of the cash expenditure took place in 2001.

This very common example illustrates (1) there is a difference between costs and cash expenditures; (2) that the budget of year 2001, when the money had to be expended, was actually determined by actions taken in the past, 2000, when the commitment was made; (3) to control costs is different from controlling expenditures, for the former could only have been controlled during or prior to the year the production was actually taking place; (3) at the point of actual cash expenditure, January 19, 2001, the organization was constrained—not to controlling costs—but to controlling the allocation of revenues among various expenditure categories that year, given that it had to pay the actors and continue its regular operation.

Lesson: Today's cash expenditures and operating budget are substantially a reflection of yesterday's decision about which costs would be incurred and how they would be controlled or minimized. For this reason we shall begin this discussion with a heavy emphasis on understanding costs. This observation is less true, of course, among nonprofits operating completely on a strict cash basis—committing and spending in the same narrow period and only to the extent that actual cash (not credit) is in hand. There aren't many of these.

CLASSIFICATION AND TREATMENT OF COSTS IN BUDGETING

Let us look at the cost aspect of efficiency. What are the important concepts from the point of view of practical budget-making?

Fixed, Variable, and Semivariable Costs

One way to view cost is as either variable or fixed. A *fixed cost* is one that does not vary with the number or amount of production or services produced. If the concert is to be held in Chanel Hall, the cost of Chanel Hall is fixed. If Chanel Hall has a capacity of 590 people, the rental for the hall is the same whether 590, 400, or zero persons attend the concert. The rental does not vary by the number of attendees. It is also a direct cost to the concert, for without the concert there would be no need to rent the hall. This says that in budgeting, a program should be fully charged for its direct cost, part of which could be fixed.

In contrast to fixed costs, *variable costs* vary with the amount that is produced or service rendered. A true variable cost will change for every single unit change in the output. Hence, the cost of stage lighting will vary depending upon the number of times a play is performed because each time it is performed we need stage lighting.

In between these two extremes are *semivariable costs,* such as the tickets. For any given production, we estimate the number of tickets needed. The printing cost of tickets does not vary with each ticket but does vary for bulk quantities; that is, the cost is so much for the first 500 and so much for the next 500. Given a choice, we would, for simplicity's sake, think of semivariable costs as variable because, unlike fixed costs, they have an important element of variability; that is, we can vary the cost of tickets by printing only 500.

What does this discussion have to do with budgeting and planning? It reminds us that we do not have the same discretion over all costs once a program gets started; therefore, we ought to take planning seriously. We have one good shot: At the outset all costs are variable because we can decide how much to do and at what scale. (We can even decide what theater capacity we need and which theater or auditorium we need.) Once that commitment is made, costs are fixed for some time. Our only other option for cutting costs are the semivariable and variable. But the semivariable requires us to have a minimum (500 tickets) or to buy in additional bulks. There is limited variability. The theater has true variability in the stage lighting.

Notice that *stage lighting,* not *electricity,* is the cost used. Electricity is also semivariable. Can you tell why? Does the electric bill for the theater have a fixed component? Does it have a component that is unrelated to the specific production being performed? While we are at it, is the payment to the actors group totally variable? Do actors require a minimum just to show up so that if the production is canceled they will have to be paid a minimum? Why do they do this? Because in accepting your offer to play in your community, they had to reserve that time and therefore had to forego something else. This allows us to sneak in a new concept, a *reservation cost or price.* Reservation costs are examples of fixed costs. Airlines use it, too, when they refuse to refund your ticket. You made a reservation.

Direct and Indirect Costs

Direct costs are those that relate to a specific project or activity. A nonprofit may, for example, hold a concert. The payment to the musicians to perform in that specific concert, aside from all other performances, is a direct cost of that activity. (For more on definitions, see Appendix 12.1.)

Indirect costs are costs that do not relate to the specific activity but to the administration and management of the organization or to the group of activities—not just one. These costs, usually called *overhead costs,* cut across all activities and would exist even if one or the other activity is discontinued. For example, even without a concert the nonprofit would have to pay salaries and benefits to a core staff (the management of the nonprofit), pay rent, and buy supplies and equipment for the general operation of the organization. Lavalas Caron's salary as music director would have to be paid, but his payment as a musician in a specific concert is due solely to that concert. Hence, part of Lavalas's work is a direct cost of a specific concert in which he performs and part is indirect—that portion as a music director that includes but goes well beyond the specific concert.

Common and Joint Costs

Two types of indirect costs are *common* and *joint.* Here is the idea: Basically, by the time we do *A* we have incurred a substantial part of the cost of producing *B.* Why not do *B* and add to our output, especially if the additional cost for completing *B* (its marginal cost) is small and can generate additional revenues (marginal revenue) equal to or greater than the additional cost? Doing two is slightly more costly than doing one. As a matter of fact, the revenues from *B* might cover its additional cost plus the common costs it shares with *A.*

Hence, two products or programs are said to have a *common cost* when they share an identical cost factor so that the production of one of the programs means incurring part if not most of the costs of producing the other. The same thing is true with joint costs. However, with joint costs, unlike common costs, the ratio of the output of the two products remains the same. To illustrate, the production of beef and hide are *joint costs* because they have the same cost factors (the production of cattle) and they occur roughly in the same ratio: so many pounds of beef and so much hide in an animal.

The important aspect shared by common and joint costs is that they provide ways of fulfilling and financing the charitable mission of the nonprofit and cost sharing of projects. The selling of advertising space in the nonprofit's publication is an example. The advertising (business) and the articles (nonbusiness) activities share common costs: printing, editorial, circulation, material, and space costs.

These costs are important in accounting and in budgeting. We must determine what portion of the common costs is to be allocated among the activities before we can calculate the total cost for each. Obviously, if *A* and *B* share a common cost, we need to decide how much of that cost is to be covered by *A* and how much by *B*. The more of the common cost we allocate to *A*, the more costly we make it. We may choose to allocate most of the common costs to *A* if *A* can be sold and generate revenues to help pay for *B*.

Here is an example. Reach for your local newspaper. Notice that it has a section that contains only classified ads. Physically separate the ad from the news section. What you have are two products, news and ads. These products are produced by two units (called responsibility centers) in the newspaper offices, the news and the classified. Each product therefore has direct costs of its own: staff time, the additional paper, since news and classified ads are printed on separate pages, and telephone costs traceable directly to ads or to news.

The two products, ads and news, also have certain common or shared costs, most notably distribution; the paper was sent to you in one piece and as a package—not two pieces, ads and news. The common cost is shared, and accountants must use some formula to allocate this joint cost between the news readers and advertisers. In addition to these common and direct costs, the newspaper has indirect costs. These include the personnel department, the publisher, the legal department, and others who would be there if only the ads or the news were published. They serve all products and services of the newspaper—the ads, news, distribution, and so on. These costs also have to be allocated or attributed. The full cost of ads and readership news is then determinable for budgeting, for accounting, and in determining unrelated business income. (See Chapter Eleven.)

Rationale for Allocation of Indirect Costs

But who pays for the indirect cost? Who pays the overhead? Someone has to pay the salaries of the nonprofit management and for the office space in which the nonprofit works. Indirect costs are those that exist even in the absence of the particular activity. These costs are not the result of the specific concert. But the concert is being conducted by the nonprofit and the latter needed a staff and offices to function, not only for the concert but also for the general mission of the organization. Therefore, the indirect costs are allocated (when possible) among all projects of the nonprofit. All projects benefit from the existence, operation, and management of the nonprofit. The concert is charged its share of indirect cost, its full share of direct fixed costs, and its full share of direct variable costs.

Calculating and Reporting Indirect Costs: What Managers Should Know

Allocating indirect and common or joint costs is basically an accountant's job. It must conform to contractual definitions, accounting rules and to IRS rules in the case of a cost relationship between unrelated and related businesses.

Within these rules, managers have discretion and should know that depending on how overhead and shared costs are computed and allocated, some programs can be subsidized by others. This occurs because the method chosen determines how these costs are divided up among programs—evenly or very unevenly among them. Which program should bear the burden, and how much? This is a managerial decision, not the accountant's, whose job it is to find the acceptable allocation procedure to fulfill the manager's aim.

Since overhead cost is included in determining the overall cost of a project, it can also determine how successful a nonprofit is when bidding. Therefore, managers need to know the following methods for allocating overhead costs.

One method of allocating indirect cost is the *simplified method*. It is applicable when every responsibility center or program contributes roughly the same to the overhead costs or according to one simple index. The overhead or indirect cost is divided up either evenly or according to the index.

For accounting and contracting purposes, overhead or indirect costs are usually stated as a percentage of direct labor costs or a percentage of total direct cost (labor, materials, and other costs directly and exclusively caused by an activity). These simple indexes are referred to as *overhead rates*. For example, based on the previous year's experience, the organization may find that its indirect cost was $200,000 and its direct labor cost was $100,000. Its overhead rate (sometimes called a burden rate) would be 200 percent of its direct labor costs. If total indirect costs (labor and materials) were used as the base and we presume that it amounted to $150,000, the overhead rate would be 133 percent. This total direct cost would then be used for all projects, even though they use different amounts of materials and labor. In both cases, the heavy user carries the greater burden.

A second method, known as the *multiple allocation method* or *Activity Based Costing (ABC) method,* is applicable when there are different pools of indirect costs (depreciation, personnel and administration, utility) and the responsibility centers are unequal in their contribution to each cost pool. Therefore, the allocation of overhead should be based on some basis that reflects accurately the different contributions to each pool. Under this method, the organization could allocate one set of indirect costs based on direct labor, another set based on direct materials, and still a third or more sets based on other indexes (for example, duration of use in the case of a computer). This simply says that the pool should be allocated to the center and according to the factor (labor, material, time) that causes the cost to rise. These are called *cost drivers.*

A third type, known as *direct allocation,* is applicable when the nonprofit divides up its activities into major responsibility centers, such as fund-raising and general administration, and requires each to consider its contribution to overhead as part of its own direct cost.[2] This method transforms an indirect to a direct cost by concentrating the activity into an identifiable, manageable, and controllable responsibility center. This is analogous to setting up a fund-raising center to handle all fund-raising. All fund-raising costs will now become direct costs of the center, hence one consequence of reorganization is to shift costs between direct and indirect.

The nonprofit must choose among these and frequently can do so with the aid of an accountant and the association to which it belongs. Sometimes the task is made easy because it is possible to attribute overhead costs to an activity because there is a clear and reasonably unequivocal cause-and-effect line between the activity and the indirect cost. Often this facile solution does not present itself, and some arithmetic method of allocation such as those we have discussed is used.

The major conceptual task in calculating the overhead rate is the proper classification of costs between direct and indirect. For this reason an independent judgment, perhaps through an audit, of how the organization classifies costs is necessary before an overhead rate is established. In federal government contracting, an agency may accept an overhead rate at the inception of a contract. It may change it if an audit of the organization's books by the agency shows that the classification of direct and indirect costs or the amounts assigned to each were incorrect or inconsistent with the actual cost experience of the organization. Unlike the government, many foundations do not pay overhead when financing specific programs. These programs are financed by restricted funds, and overhead must be covered by unrestricted funds (sometimes called general funds) from other sources.

UNALLOWABLE INDIRECT COSTS

Foundations frequently refuse to finance indirect costs. The government allows nonprofits to charge indirect costs to the extent that these indirect costs are generated by programs financed by the government. Certain costs may not be acceptable to the government. These costs are given in OMB Circular A–122. They may include the following:

1. Advertising and public relations costs including those to promote the organization

2. Alcoholic beverages

3. Automobiles furnished by the organization for personal use

4. Defense and prosecution of criminal and civil proceedings, claims, appeals, and patent infringements

5. Goods and services for personal uses

6. Housing and living expenses of an organization's officers

7. Insurance against defects

8. Memberships in any civic, community, or social organization, dining or country club

9. Selling or marketing of goods or services

10. Trustees' travel

11. Payments of fines and penalties resulting from violations of, or failure to comply with, foreign laws and regulations

12. Costs of some severance packages

13. Costs of commercial insurance that protects against the costs for correction of defects in materials or workmanship

More is said about cost definitions and denials in the next chapter and in Appendixes 12.1 and 12.2.

MANAGERIAL USE OF ACTUAL INDIRECT COST ALLOCATION

In planning, the managers may decide on how they would like indirect costs to be allocated, although the actual allocation must conform to accounting convention described in this book and contractual allowances. The way indirect costs actually occurred across programs can be used by management to control these costs in the future.

Controlling costs is facilitated by a grid such as in Table 12.1. It takes numbers for each type of indirect cost (telephone, janitorial services, electricity, ordering, or whatever the indirect cost is) and shows how those costs were distributed over each major responsibility center of the organization and within each center by the different types of programs. Some programs may be low-overhead programs across the board. Others may be low overhead only in reference to a specific type of cost. Some costs may be more heavily the result of a specific program—not just the center.

Table 12.1. Distribution of Actual Indirect Costs.

Centers of Responsibility	Indirect Costs (Percentage Distribution of Each Type of Indirect Costs)				
	A	B	C	D	E
Center 1	50	20	30	70	10
Program 1	25	09	01	30	04
Program 2	10	10	23	05	05
Program 3	15	01	06	35	01
Center 2	20	30	30	10	40
Program 4	04	09	11	01	01
Program 5	04	04	08	04	03
Program 6	06	09	10	01	35
Program 7	06	08	01	04	01
Center 3	15	25	20	10	50
Program 8	08	13	08	03	06
Program 9	05	11	03	05	01
Program 10	02	01	09	02	43
Total	100	100	100	100	100

ALLOCATING JOINT COSTS WHEN FUND-RAISING IS AN ACTIVITY

The American Institute of Certified Public Accountants (AICPA) has issued guidelines to accountants about how joint costs are to be allocated whenever fund-raising is done jointly with any other activity; for example, marketing.[3] The next few paragraphs are directed at the question of how these rules will affect the modus operandi of the organization. Accounting rules have impacts for management aside from where to put numbers.

By allocating part of its fund-raising costs to programs and management, the organization can charge external sources for at least part of its fund-raising expenses. By putting a fund-raising message in an educational brochure, an educational or a program being run by the organization could be charged part of the postage, printing, and composition costs of the fund-raising activity. This has the effect of subsidizing fund-raising. This lower cost gives the organization a more favorable profile in the eyes of potential donors and watchdog agencies.

Because of the new rules, the packaging of fund-raising campaigns will now have to be done with more concern for the content, purpose, audience, and medium of whatever other activity is jointly done with fund-raising.

For example, a solicitation in which the nonprofit includes a brochure that merely educates the reader about a problem will no longer be able to be charged to a program or management account. For example, a nonprofit treating drug abusers will not be able to charge any account other than that of fund-raising if it includes with the solicitation a brochure simply describing the evils of heroin.

Such a brochure may effectively educate people about the problem and get them to contribute financially to the organization, and that may well be its intentions. For this very reason it would be considered fully chargeable to fund-raising. The bottom-line of the new rules is that any joint activity, the principal purpose of which is to promote fund-raising, is fully charged to fund-raising. The rules presume that general public information accompanying a fund-raising activity promotes fund-raising.

For an activity to be allocated part of the joint cost when fund-raising is involved, the activity must be used by the audience or recipient, must cause the recipient to provide more than financial assistance to the organization in the conduct of its mission, or cause the audience to direct this information to others who would either use or direct others to use the program or help the organization carry out its mission other than by just sending it money.

Under the new guides the nonprofit may be better off including a brochure recruiting clients or volunteers than merely telling a horror story. The litmus test for allowing cost sharing is that the recipient must act in a meaningful way to participate in, assist, or direct others to do either in a substantial mission of the organization.

The new guidelines will also affect compensation contracts. If the joint activity compensates those who are involved in it on the basis of fund-raising proceeds, then the activity is fully charged to fund-raising. This alone is sufficient to require that no part of the charge be allocated to any other activity but fund-raising. Therefore, now the compensation clause of independent contractors doing the activity attached to the fund-raising must not calibrate their fees to the amount raised in the fund-raising portion of the joint activity or else the entire activity will be charged to fund-raising.

Indeed, to charge another activity, the independent contractor would have to be a specialist in the other activity, devote his or her effort exclusively to that activity in this joint effort, and be paid on a basis other than fund-raising.

The new guidelines do not require measurement. But they do state that one of the factors that would justify allocation is that the portion, say of a program, that accompanies the fund-raising activity has performance measures associated with a substantial program the organization conducts. In general, the portion accompanying the fund-raising must be a part of a bigger program or management activity inherent to the mission of the organization.

In addition to the content and purpose issues, the organization must also take care in the choice of audiences. An educational message sent primarily to past donors could be considered solicitation and would be fully charged to fund-raising. The audience must be made up of people able to assist management in a nonfinancial way, or use the program, or direct those who would do either for the cost to be shared.

Finally, the rules require good record keeping. This is so because an auditor may resort to minutes of meetings and internal memos and other organizational records to determine the motive behind the joint activity.

Allocation of Common or Joint Costs

A simple way to allocate common costs is as a corresponding percentage to some measurable unit. If the common cost is, for example, that both programs share a room, the rental is divided up according to the amount of space in the room used or the length of time the room is used, and cost is allocated according to these percentages: 90 percent of the space, 90 percent of the cost, and so on. The allocation of common costs causes the same concerns about one activity subsidizing another as we learned in the discussion of indirect cost allocation.

Marginal or Incremental Costs

Related to variable costs are marginal or incremental costs. This is the increment in cost due to the production of an additional unit of good or service. By how much does variable cost increase if one more unit of the good is produced? This is marginal or incremental cost. When marginal cost is increasing rapidly, variable cost and total costs are increasing rapidly. In the example of Chanel Hall, the manager knows that once the decision to use Chanel Hall is made, costs can only be lessened by reducing variable costs. But how much can he save by having one less show? This is the marginal cost of an additional show. In other words, by knowing marginal cost the manager will know how much can be saved by reducing the variable costs (the tickets) one by one and, conversely, how much costs will increase should he increase the number of shows even slightly.

Marginal cost is important for another reason. It tells the manager how much additional support may be needed as the output of goods or services increases. If a nonprofit produces housing units and the marginal cost of a unit is known to be $4,000 (that is, the next unit will add $4,000 to total costs), then the minimum amount of support that the nonprofit must raise to fully cover the cost of that additional unit is $4,000. By knowing how much variable costs increase as output increases (marginal cost), the manager can tell how much must be raised to cover that additional cost. Any additional amount above the marginal cost contributes to the reduction of overhead or fixed costs.

Average Cost

Marginal costs show only the variation in variable costs as the number of goods and services produced varies. Another concept of costs is average cost. This tells the unit cost of each output. Average cost is the sum of variable and fixed costs or the sum of direct and indirect costs divided by the number of units. For most planning purposes, a nonprofit manager may find it easier to calculate average costs rather than marginal costs. Furthermore, for many reporting purposes, average costs are requested. Often, marginal and average costs are about equal so that one is a good approximation of the other. The astute manager should realize, however, that there is a difference between the two concepts, and a familiarity with both will improve decisions.

Total Costs

The total cost of goods or services produced is the sum of variable and fixed costs, just as the total cost from an earlier perspective is the sum of direct and indirect costs. One perspective shows how cost varies as output varies. The other distinguishes between costs directly and exclusively due to a specific project and therefore a direct cost of that project, and those due to the existence and operation of the organization. Both perspectives give important information to the manager.

Opportunity Costs

Another concept of cost is opportunity cost. This is the true economic cost of a project. Because every organization has a limited amount of resources, any decision to undertake one project means that another project has to be reduced or totally sacrificed. Opportunity cost tells the management in monetary or programmatic terms the consequence of its decisions on the ability of the nonprofit to meet all facets of its mission.

In a similar manner, when measurement permits, opportunity cost can be measured in terms of the net present value of benefits foregone by choosing one program over another. Even when measurement is not fully possible, the concept of opportunity cost is important in reminding decision makers that the choice of one program over another is not costless. This question should be an explicit part of the decision. What are we giving up to pursue this course of action? The answer is the opportunity cost.

Opportunity cost is applicable every time the management thinks, "We could have done X if we didn't have to do Y," or, "In order to do X we cannot do Y." Opportunity cost forces management to see the consequence of its decisions on the ability of the organization to fully meet its mission or the targets decided on in the strategic planning process, as seen in Chapter Seventeen.

Capital, Operating, and Replacement Costs and Expenses

Costs are not always instantaneous. Some costs flow over several years. This is not simply because the cost is associated with a capital item, the payments of which extend over years, but because once a project has been launched it sets into place a stream of costs from which the organization may not be able to extricate itself. Once a building has been bought, the mortgage must be paid regardless of whether the building is used. This is related to an initial capital expenditure, which also sets off the need for various types of operating expenses—insurance, janitorial, utility, security. Similarly, once a journal or newsletter has been launched, the organization must be prepared to carry it through for some time or lose face (a small price to pay compared to bankruptcy).

In planning, programming, and budgeting, it is important to take into account the operating as well as capital expenditures that flow over time. Often these costs increase rather than decrease as time passes. Inflation and deterioration requiring maintenance are two reasons these costs increase.

This brings us to another element of costs, *replacement* costs. It is important for the reader to appreciate that the term *cost* could refer to the original cost of the item or the replacement cost at a given period in time. The replacement cost of a machine today would be the price one has to pay to replace it today with at least a comparable machine. The replacement cost tomorrow may be higher. The original historical cost (what one paid for it in the past) is lower. In capital (*not* operating as in the discussion here) budgeting, replacement cost is sometimes better to consider than original cost because the organization is looking into the future. In accounting, original cost is used because the organization is depreciating or recovering its expenditure on a capital item for which it has already paid. This means that the cost in the balance sheet of an organization may be quite different from the cost in its capital budget for a similarly named asset.

Sunk Costs, Reservation Price, and Risks

Another concept is sunk cost. Once an expenditure is made it represents a sunk cost if it cannot be retrieved. It should therefore have no further impact on future choices. It is done. This is another way of saying that today's choices should not be burdened by yesterday's decisions. More precisely, it means that we should evaluate today's options on their own merits and not based on the quality of decisions we made in the past.

The concept of a sunk cost reminds us that we frequently have to forego an option into which we have sunk money and organizational energy. Sometimes we do this because the initial decision was bad. We do not pursue a bad decision just because we have put money into it. Sometimes a sunk cost arises because a superior option is now available. The concept of sunk cost is important in budgeting because it relieves us of the errors of the past when planning the future.

But a sunk cost remains an obligation when financed by debt that is still outstanding. The cost may be sunk for the organization, but not for the creditor who must still be paid. A cost may thus be sunk in terms of its impact on planning but not in its impact on budgeting. Sunk costs financed by debt constrain today's budgetary decisions to the extent that the budget must reflect the legal obligation to pay that debt.

Sunk costs also become a problem when they contain restrictions or constraints that prohibit the organization from taking action. For example, when undertaking large or cooperative projects, the organization may have signed a contract that prohibits it from undertaking a similar competitive project. This is not unusual when a project is financed by debt or through a joint arrangement. It is a way in which partners and financing sources protect themselves. The project may be sunk, but the restrictions under which it was undertaken may be very much alive. The restrictions cannot be ignored in planning because they may prohibit certain actions, require others, and allow others only after permission is obtained.

Some sunk costs have to do with a reservation price paid to insure an outcome. Assume that Clive III makes an application to six colleges. His top five choices place him on their waiting lists. So he sends the deposit that his fifth choice requires as a reservation price—a premium to insure against the risk that he will not attend college at all this year. A month after, his very top choice sends him a registered letter certifying that he has now been granted admission and requires him to send in his deposit. Would Clive be wise in responding that he is no longer interested because he has already made a deposit to his fifth choice? No, he would consider that a sunk cost and move on. Every reservation price (the cost of making every reservation) is a potential sunk cost to the extent that it is not reimbursed. In that sense, it is an insurance premium.

Illustration of Costs: Program Termination

As will be elaborated on in Chapter Seventeen, knowing something about the life cycle of a program alerts management to make required adjustments, which may be to amend, abolish, or add to the program. Adjustments may be in the form of *incremental* or *total change.* If the decision is to terminate a program, incrementalism implies phasing it out, thus prolonging both fixed and variable costs.

In either an incremental or total approach, we must know fixed costs; that is, a contract must be honored whether we phase out gradually or end abruptly. Hence, in terminating programs, isolate the fixed costs. They are sunk. They must be paid regardless of the approach taken. Focus on direct and variable costs. They can be stopped abruptly or gradually.

All the concepts described are helpful, at least conceptually, even if they cannot be precisely measured and even if in some organizations the activity and budgetary levels are so small and simple that they do not justify expensive calculations.

Costs and Responsibility Centers

There is yet another way in which costs are reported for purposes of control and accountability. Many organizations find it wise to set mission or responsibility centers. Accordingly, instead of showing costs simply by function or object, costs are shown by centers of program activity. The center of activity might be a department or a unit that conducts more than one program or project. By doing this, the senior management can hold subordinate managers responsible for cost variations. In very large and complex organizations, this decentralization into centers is often preferred, since the central management cannot keep track of all the details of a program or unit. Within each unit, however, there might be a functional and an object budget so that the manager of that unit can keep track of financial and operating details.

The more an organization is divided up into centers and the more transactions among these centers, the more the need for transfer prices. To illustrate, assume that the organization has a reproduction center. Other units in the organization use this center. The reproduction center can recover its costs by charging these other units. These are called *transfer prices*. One effect of transfer prices is that they turn indirect costs into direct costs. Billing calls to specific phones is an example. They also control use; that is, you can't deny having used the item unless you cheat.

Sometimes a center is assumed to have no control over its costs or revenues. Control is a matter of discretion, hence these are called *discretionary cost centers.* This method should be used only when everything else fails, because it invites arbitrary decisions and unaccountability. Decisions are ruled by negotiation.

In developing transfer price, the price that one department in the organization charges another, think of these 5Cs:

1. *Costs:* What does it cost to produce the service?
2. *Competition:* Is it cheaper to use an outside provider?
3. *Conservation:* Having to pay may reduce wasteful use.
4. *Congruence:* A transfer price should not hinder organizational cohesion and attainment of goals.
5. *Capital:* Transfer prices should be high enough to allow the cost center to buy new equipment if necessary.

TEN STEPS TO COST BUDGETING

In what follows, we apply the preceding cost concepts to a real situation. Let us assume that our association got direction from its board of trustees to create a new function called membership services. We have done all the preliminary work and now we are prepared to put pencil to paper.

1. Federal government rules for dealing with costs tell us that functions such as membership services are part of the association's mission and must be

considered a *direct* cost. But membership services is a constellation of functions—holding conferences, sending out publications, answering letters, and the like. The way we treat a direct cost that is a constellation of functions is to create a *cost* or *responsibility center.* For budgeting purposes membership service is a cost or responsibility center, and those costs exclusively arising from its operations are its direct cost.[4]

2. We must *identify* all the *inputs* necessary to carry out the responsibilities of the membership center. These inputs have a relationship among themselves. Some are complementary, others are substitutes, and still others may be independent. An employee who has a desk must also have a chair. The chair and the desk are *complementary.* The simple example is magnified: a school that decides on a chemistry program must also provide the complements of a laboratory and equipment; a museum that decides on certain precious art pieces must also have specific rooms and temperature control; a school that decides on a driver training program must also decide on cars, specialized teachers, and a lane. The failure to detect complementary inputs is a prescription to disaster; dollars can be spent on a project that cannot operate because all the *necessary* inputs are not in place.

Special stationery for the director of membership services may be a *substitute* for regular organizational stationery; one type of desk for another. When we identify substitutes, we identify ways of saving money. Other types of inputs are independent of any other. A training text or desk reference for nonprofit management is *independent* of any other expense. It is also not necessary, although it may be helpful.

3. Once we have identified the *necessary* inputs, we need to *classify* them. The best way to do this is to begin by distinguishing those that are *direct* and those that are *indirect* costs. Recall from our discussion that direct costs relate only to the responsibility (*cost objective*) being carried out. Put another way, if a responsibility center does not have the objective or membership service, then certain costs necessary to carry out a membership service objective would not exist. These costs are therefore directly related to the membership objective (cost objective) and are therefore direct costs to that center. All other costs are indirect.

From a *control* perspective, identifying the direct cost of membership services tells management what costs can be brought down to zero by not having such a service. Since such a service also has indirect costs, not having the service will reduce the indirect cost of the *entire* organization, but only by the amount *traceable* to the membership service. The sum of the increase in cost of the organization (direct and indirect) is the *marginal* cost of having the membership service. Put another way, we can only reduce the total cost of the organization by this *marginal* amount by not having a membership service center.

4. Now, step back. The sum of direct and indirect costs is the *total* cost of running the responsibility center called membership service. Management's job

at this stage is to assess the *opportunity cost.* Do we have better use for that money? What are we giving up by allocating resources to this membership service objective? Is it still worth it?

5. Let's say that the answer is to go forward in establishing the membership service center either because there is no choice or because the opportunity cost is acceptable. The center is both *feasible* and *desirable* (per Chapter Seventeen).

6. We continue our classification. We need to distinguish between *fixed* and *variable* costs. The best way to do this is to go into the category of costs called direct and separate the fixed from the variable costs and then do the very same thing for the indirect-cost category.

How we do this will depend on management's policy, cost-accounting convention, and government regulations. But the manager has tremendous latitude. Here is another point where the smart manager exercises control over a budget and builds in defenses. This is done by recognizing that at the outset all costs are variable, and that it is within the manager's *discretion* to determine which will be fixed. That discretion has to be exercised before commitments are made. An often unrecognized consequence of every commitment is to automatically put a cost factor into either the fixed or variable, direct or indirect cost category.

Let me give you an example and show its implication. The membership service director needs a computer. If the computer is to be bought in the future, it is listed in the *capital budget.* If it is to be paid for in one payment, which is possible with most PCs, it becomes a *capital cost* and it is also a *fixed* cost. If the computer is leased and the lease is year to year and paid in that way, it creates an *operating expense,* which is also *fixed.* This is true even though the computer is a capital item. It is the commitment, not the size or the flow, that makes a cost fixed. The implications here are significant. Being fixed by commitment, the cost must be met no matter how much the membership director uses the computer, and there is virtually no chance for quick cost cutting.

If it is leased, this fixed cost is part of the monthly *cash out flow.* A monthly payment must be planned for in every year's *operating budget.* Failure to make payments can lead to loss of the computer, a bad credit record, and attorney's fees. But paying for it in a lump sum involves an opportunity cost, roughly the difference between the month's lease payment and the lump sum paid that month. We could have invested that difference. Hence, every purchase needs to be weighed against a lease alternative.

Furthermore, once it has been acquired the computer is a *sunk* cost. It is a done deal. But we cannot allow ourselves not to think of better ways of doing things just because we bought a computer. If it turns out to be too expensive to run our own computer, the fact that we own one should not stop us from contracting for computer services if that proves to be superior. In other words, we cannot be trapped by a sunk cost. The concept of a *sunk* cost is best used to avoid being trapped by the past. It does not rectify a bad decision—it mentally frees us from it, even though we cannot escape paying for it.

Alternatively, the use of a computer could be made a *variable* cost by contracting to pay on a per use basis rather than purchasing the machine. Which is the better treatment? It depends on the organization and the specific situation. The only point being made is that management has *discretion* over whether a cost is fixed or variable, and how that discretion is exercised has significant financial implications for the organization.

7. Once all costs are identified and classified, we need to *measure* them, to put a dollar value on each. We do this by calculating *standard* costs. The standard labor cost for doing a job is the amount of time that job usually takes multiplied by the hourly wages of the type of personnel needed to do the job. We can do the same for materials costs and computer costs, and so on, in calculating their standard cost. Adding all these, we get an estimate of total direct cost. No magic.

8. Now we have identified, classified, and measured all direct cost. We are not through. Remember membership service? It doesn't exist by itself. It is part of an organization, the nonprofit, which probably has other responsibility centers such as research, publicity, and fund-raising. All these responsibility centers are served by the organization and coordinated by the central administration. It also has costs. If these costs are not covered, the whole organization collapses.

The central administration's costs are made up of trustee costs for overseeing the mission, legal fees and payroll services to each of its responsibility centers, supplies and equipment costs, space costs, employee welfare and benefits, and so on. In short, the central administration is an accumulation of the *indirect* costs of all the responsibility centers plus its own *direct* and *indirect* costs.

This combined cost of the central administration (both its direct and indirect) and the indirect costs of each of its responsibility centers, including the membership service, are *pooled* into one or more gigantic *indirect cost pools* and divided among the various responsibility centers; each is *assigned* or *allocated* some percentage of this big indirect cost pool according to one of the three methods discussed earlier. Hence, the final budgeted cost for the membership service center will be its own *direct* and *indirect* costs *plus* its share of the cost for the *total indirect cost pool* of the organization.

Again, various methods are used for allocating or assigning these costs to the individual responsibility centers. From the perspective of management, the method chosen is very important. It provides a means through which some weak but necessary responsibility centers can be supported by others. Let us use the simplified method we introduced earlier in the next step.

9. Calculate an *overhead rate* as a percentage of *direct cost*. A simple way to do this for illustrative purposes is to remember that total cost is equal to direct plus indirect cost. So if we subtracted direct from total cost we should get indirect cost. We can thus divide indirect by direct costs and get the overhead rate to be used in subsequent periods to multiply direct cost to get indirect cost. This

is a simplified illustration. Recall that in an actual situation direct and indirect costs are first determined by classification and then by division. First classify costs between direct and indirect. Next select a ratio that reflects reality and is consistent with the policy aims of the organization.

10. Periodically, this process, particularly the method of allocating *indirect costs (overhead)*, should be reviewed with a good accountant to see whether your overhead rate is working to cover full cost. The federal government will accept a provisional rate while the organization determines a more permanent one.

Rates may have to change as the organization grows or changes in complexity. Failure to calculate good rates can mean (1) the organization fails to cover full costs on projects and fails to subsidize some projects while indirectly subsidizing others; (2) the organization overestimates the cost of every project if the rate is too high, and therefore the organization fails to win programs, or the cost is underestimated, and each time the organization wins a program it loses money; (3) the organization has to reimburse the federal government for mischarges. Usually, this occurs because the indirect costs are inappropriate or misclassified. (See Appendix 12.2.)

HOW TO ESTIMATE COSTS

The cost concepts give us a rational basis for estimating the expenditures to be put in the annual budget:

Step 1. Begin with fixed cost. The best approximation of this is all the costs we incurred last year that we cannot escape this year. Do this for each item in the budget.

Step 2. For variable costs, determine a standard quantity that will be used and multiply it by a standard cost. For example, determine how many hours of computer time you will need and multiply it by the cost per unit of time. Do this for each item.

Step 3. Add steps 1 and 2. This is the total cost.

Step 4. Separate out the indirect (overhead) from the direct costs for the organization as a whole and allocate them to each program. Ignore the programs that have an uncertain probability of being funded, because if they fail to be funded you will have underallocated your indirect costs and therefore will not recover the whole amount.

Step 5. Attribute the remaining direct cost to its program of origin.

Step 6. Verify that the sum of your direct and indirect costs are equal to the sum of your fixed and variable costs.

KEY TO CONTROLLING COSTS

From the above we should easily discern that to control cost we must first be able to identify and classify it. It is easier to control costs when they are variable than when they are fixed. It is easier to control direct costs since their source is more identifiable. It is easier to control costs when we have a base to estimate what it should be and therefore can compare actual performance against expectations, a topic discussed later in this chapter under the heading Variance.

Table 12.2 shows direct costs divided up into fixed and variable portions and the same for indirect costs. It also shows that the easiest costs to control are direct variable costs because you know exactly what program or service is responsible for it and you can increase or decrease it.

The most difficult costs to control are those that are indirect and fixed. These costs appear some distance from individual programs. They are often administrative. Even though programs are partly responsible, the precise amount each program contributes to the indirect cost may be indeterminable. How much of the cost of the personnel department is attributable to the chemistry department? Because they are fixed, there is nothing you can do about getting rid of them during the relevant period. They are hard both to allocate and to cancel.

LEASING AS A FIXED-COST STRATEGY

Organizations should not presume that purchasing an asset is necessarily better than leasing or vice versa. There are two types of leases—a capital lease and an operating lease. A capital lease is nothing more than an installment or conditional sale. Actually, you bought the asset but are paying for it on an installment basis and will not get full ownership of it until sometime specified in the future. With an operating lease, you never get ownership. The lease may be terminated at an agreeable juncture. It modifies the time over which a cost

Table 12.2. Total Cost Ranked by Ease of Control.

		Total Cost	
		Variable	Fixed
Total Cost	Direct	1	3
	Indirect	2	4

Note: 1 is easiest; 4 hardest.

is fixed. What should management consider in choosing between leasing and purchasing?

1. Does the life of the asset exceed our needs for it? If it does, then a lease is indicated unless the asset appreciates in price and would make a good investment.

2. Does the asset depreciate and how rapidly? A for-profit firm can use depreciation to reduce taxes. A nonprofit, unless it is operating an unrelated business, cannot. Actual depreciation, such as an automobile, results in lower resale price of the asset.

3. Is the asset subject to rapid obsolescence and therefore cannot be sold at a good price? Worse still, is it incapable of meeting the needs of the organization?

4. Is there a high maintenance cost and possibilities of breakdowns? Assets leased from a reputable dealer can often get repaired and replaced.

5. Is there risk in the design of the asset? Leasing might allow risk-sharing. Who carries the title?

6. Is there a significant cost difference? Bear in mind that the only costs that count are those which are different under one option as compared to the others; for example, the space needed for the equipment may be the same no matter how it was acquired.

7. How is the asset going to be used? Can you justify cost?

8. What are the cash-flow requirements? Operating leases may not include any interest cost, which is a significant cost if the property is bought on an installment basis.

9. What is the interest cost? For a firm, this cost is deductible. It is not for the nonprofit except against unrelated business income.

10. Is there reason to use a master lease? Master leases are an umbrella lease contract—a line of credit that covers all properties the organization leases. These may have very stringent terms, such as a minimum commitment.

A very special type of leasing arrangement is called tax-exempt leasing. A supplier would lease more favorably to a nonprofit than to a for-profit firm because the interest earned on the note signed by the nonprofit is not taxable if certain conditions are met. One of these conditions prohibits the supplier from reclaiming the property just because, in the case of government-supported organizations, the legislature did not provide funds to make the monthly payments. These leases, called tax-exempt leases, do permit the nonprofit to eventually own the equipment. These leases are conditional sales.

OUTSOURCING AS A COST STRATEGY

There are certain economies to be gained from outsourcing—having certain functions be performed by external business providers. These economies are derived from lowered need to invest in space, personnel, liability insurance, workmen's compensation, utility costs, automobile insurance, personnel benefits, and the demands on internal management.

The core idea of outsourcing is that being highly specialized and often with better trained workers, more sophisticated equipment, and access to better and lower priced materials because of volume of orders, external sources can often provide better quality, just-in-time performance.

Some nonprofits have turned to outside providers for printing, order fulfillment, legal and accounting assistance, and even for the entire management of the nonprofit organization. Many associations contract with an association management corporation to do all their administrative work.

Outsourcing should be done within the confines of a carefully written contract that specifies measures of performance and time of evaluation, opportunities for inspection and grace period for correction, specific period of commencement of the contract and of its termination, protection of property and intellectual rights, material to be returned, timing and method of compensation, clear identification as an independent contractor, types of liabilities, and insurance that might be necessary.

Nonprofit organizations using outside for-profit providers must determine whether the outside contractor is disqualified because it is owned or materially controlled by an "insider" in the nonprofit. This insider may be a board member, a manager, a relative of one of these, or even the outside source itself if it is a substantial contributor. This could give rise to self-dealing.

SUPPORT AND REVENUES

The word *support* is used intentionally. For nonprofits, the critical revenue data for the organization are sources of support. In Chapters Three and Five, we described what is included in support for different types of tax-exempt qualifications. We now take a budgetary perspective on the same concepts.

In the for-profit sector, firms have only one principal source of revenues and that is from sales. In the public sector, the principal source of revenues is from taxation. In the nonprofit sector, revenues may come from a variety of sources. What is critical is the balance. Good budgeting for a nonprofit means more than showing numbers; it means being alert to the balance required to maintain the nonprofit's classification.

For the management of the nonprofit, this balance has an important effect not intended by the law. The law intended this balance to assure that the nonprofit was not a sham for a profit or private money-making activity designed to avoid taxes. It turns out that this balance also means that support can be diversified. The more diversified support is, the better, because the nonprofit is not overly exposed to the influence of one supporter and to the risk that it would collapse if that supporter declines.

Support falls into several categories. The first category is the *fees* from or assessments of the membership. These can be a steady base of support and can be seen as an offset to fixed costs. Fees do not ordinarily go up or down depending on the amount of output of the organization. Obviously, fees relate to the kinds of service the membership gets, but small variations in that quantity do not appreciably affect the number of members. Disputes over particular services do affect membership, and recession does cause a drop in membership as members or the agencies or corporations that pay their membership dues fall on hard times. During deep recessions, association membership may decline, as it did from 1981 to 1982. Not all nonprofits have membership and therefore not all get membership fees.

A second category is *gifts* and *contributions.* In writing a budget, estimates from past experience should be made concerning amounts of gifts and contributions and their sources. As stated earlier, in dealing with gifts and contributions, it is important to distinguish between those gifts that are made to the general fund of the organization and are unrestricted and those made with restrictions about the uses to which they may be put.

A third source of support is *revenues* from related and unrelated businesses. One advantage of revenues from these sources is that their use is totally at the discretion of the board of trustees of the organization. They are also reasonably predictable in the same sense (and using the same techniques) that for-profit businesses project their earnings. The simplest way for a nonprofit to make these projections is by evaluating past trends and asking whether there are any reasons to believe that there would be significant variations from past trends. If there are not, the trend line would be adequate. If variations are expected, then a judgment can be made to adjust the trend line. This is a judgment call. When the issue is more complex than this, it is up to the management of the business to supply its nonprofit owners with better information. As a matter of fact, this information should always be demanded from the business manager.

A fourth category is *contracts* and *grants.* These may be from the federal, state, or local governments or from a for-profit firm or another organization. Some grants are unrestricted and are given to enable an organization to get off the ground by having resources that the management needs to build and support the organization. Other grants and all contracts are awards for performing a specific task. The task may be broadly defined, but the money cannot be shifted from that intended by the contract or grant. Even these elements of revenues have a degree of predictability, because many are multiyear grants or contracts.

Investments in securities and *royalties* are a fifth source of revenue. Many securities have fixed terms and set rates of interest or dividends to be paid over a specified period. Some organizations (such as those in research) get royalties, which are also predictable. The royalties that may be less predictable are production royalties that come from oil, gas, and other materials. Gains and losses in the sale or purchase of securities are unpredictable.

ALLOCATING DOLLARS ACROSS PROGRAMS

Within any department of the nonprofit, the problem of choosing options sometimes can be reduced to a simple form. Sometimes the problem is nothing more than how to spend the last dollar on programs to which the organization is already committed by virtue of its mission or the demands of its membership. This is very common in associations because the mission of an association often involves an explicit or implied commitment to certain groups of activities, for example, education, lobbying, and so on. In short, the organization is committed to offering a combination of activities, not just one. How does one choose among the activities in this committed combination when the sole issue is the relative costs of these activities?

This problem is different from the long-run or strategic problem described in Chapter Seventeen. There, the organization is considering weighing activities not only in terms of their costs and benefits, but also in terms of desirability and feasibility. Once programs are chosen and assigned to the departments, however, it is the responsibility of the department to allocate the budget assigned to it so as to get the best results, given that it is committed to this combination. A membership department is committed to produce a variety of membership services. But how should it allocate its funds among these services?

Let us take any two programs: A and B. The department can spend all of its dollars in one or the other or it can allocate its budget between the two. How it allocates its dollars between the two is partly a function of the cost of one relative to the other—how much A must give up or sacrifice in order to get more B and vice versa. How much it must give up of one in terms of the other is clearly the cost of one in terms of the other. If a dollar on A can purchase 5 As and a dollar on B can purchase 6 Bs, then every other dollar spent on A means sacrificing 6 Bs in order to get 5 As and vice versa.

A smart manager would recognize that the department could produce various combinations of As and Bs given any budget. All it does is shift dollars from one program to another. Shifting dollars from A to B means producing more B and less A. The question is what should be the combination chosen by the manager?

Let us see. If the manager could get more benefits from spending one more dollar on A than on B, the manager would wisely choose to spend that dollar on A and would continue to do so as long as this is true. If the manager could get more benefits by choosing B over A, the manager would wisely continue in choosing B if this is true. When the point is reached that the last dollar would buy exactly the same additional benefit in either program, the manager has allocated the last dollar in a way that maximizes the department's benefits from the dollars allocated to it.

Why? At this point, the manager can get the very same additional benefits from choosing either program. There is no further additional benefit to be gotten from one over the other. Consequently, the manager has maximized the benefits from the budget that was assigned to him or her because no reallocation of dollars from A to B or from B to A will give any higher results than what he or she has already attained. Few managers ever reach this complete state of accomplishment. But that is not the point. The point is that as long as the manager follows this line of thinking, he or she is thinking in a way that moves the department toward doing the most with the dollars it has.

In flexible budgeting the manager would think: Let me do this for every possible level of budget that may be assigned to me. So for every possible budget amount, the manager would have planned to allocate that budget level so that no reallocation of A to B or B to A at that level would yield greater result at that budget level.

Accordingly, Table 12.3 shows that once the most efficient allocation (the one in which no additional greater benefits can be gotten by reallocating dollars between A to B) is attained, by simply forming the ratio of A to B or B to A one can determine how a fixed number of dollars assigned to the department as its budget can be allocated between the two. This can be done by finding the ratio of A to B at the point where reallocation, as described, is attained and then allocating the total budget accordingly.

Table 12.3. Results of Efficient Budget Allocation Among Programs.

	Program A	Program B
Budget Levels		
100,000	20,000	80,000
200,000	40,000	160,000
300,000	120,000	180,000

Assuming ratios of 1A to 5B (1 to 5, or 20 percent to 80 percent) is found to be the most efficient allocation of dollars between programs A and B.

It is too easily and erroneously claimed that the preceding discussion is mechanistic and does not take into account aspects of the problem that are not measurable. A ratio does not necessarily require that everything be measured. Indeed, often a good manager bases a calculation on a best-educated hunch. So knowing A is probably valued at five times B is sufficient basis for saying that the ratio is one to five. We make these types of decisions every day.

PERMANENT REVENUES AND FIXED COSTS

An implication of the above discussion is that some revenues are more permanent and predictable than others. Previously, we saw that some costs are more fixed than others. Please turn now to Table 12.4, which combines costs and types of revenues.

Good budgeting and financial planning would argue against financing fixed costs by reliance on transitory or unpredictable revenues (−), but would support pegging it to a predictable or permanent base (+). And when the income is transitory, costs are best treated so that they are variable rather than fixed. This strategy gives flexibility. The organization may be in a better position to reduce cost in response to a decline in income. Naturally, in the best of all worlds, one would always prefer an abundance of permanent, predictable income. But that is never the reality.

FORECASTING

Implicit in much of the previous discussion is the question of how we know what future revenues and expenditures will be. Answers to this type of question require forecasting or projecting.

The science of revenue and expenditure forecasting can be very complex or very simple. For most nonprofit organizations, simple methods are applicable. One method is to assume that last year's accomplishment will be the same or increase or decrease by a certain percentage. This percentage can be based on

Table 12.4. Matching Costs on Revenues.

Total Costs	Type of Income	
	Permanent	Temporary
Fixed	+	−
Variable	−	+

+ is preferred; − is unpreferred.

the previous year's performance adjusted by expectations of some unusual event. For example, just by taking a look at how the receipts have grown per year over the past five years is an indication. The simple average of that amount could be used.

Going up the ladder of sophistication one step, the management could look at the weighted average of the past five years. For example, the management may say that we are less likely to perform as we did in the first year, and more likely to perform as we did in the most recent ones. Therefore, we may give more credence and weight to the latter than to the former years.

Another step up the ladder of sophistication may involve some form of an equation. The simplest form is a linear regression model, but we will not discuss that here. However, imagine that the organization has ten years of experience. It may plot its performance each year, as in Figure 12.1. Then it may run or calculate a straight line through these points. The slope of this line is the average rate that the performance may be expected to change over time. This slope can then be used to project the future. Simply move up along the line.

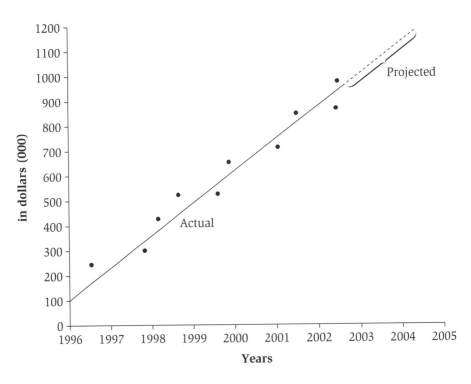

Figure 12.1. Scatter Diagram of Annual Receipts of Expenditures and Projections into Future.

However this is done, forecasting is judgmental. A new organization may simply make a modest guess year after year, and this experience over the years becomes the basis for its projections. Projections should never yield to mathematics even though the latter is important in avoiding wild guesses. Comparing the actual with the projected, we get a variance that tells us how good our forecasting is. But the past is not necessarily prologue.

For most organizations there is an element of stability. From past experience with commitment, a bottom level of revenues to be received is known. Several grants are multiyear. Some costs are so critical to the organizations that they will never run to zero. If it cannot afford office space, it cannot function. Hence, it is impossible to approach forecasting with the notion "We have no idea." Management may not know it all, but they most surely know the minimum performance in revenues beyond which the organization must close down and the minimum performance in expenditures below which it is a useless organization and should close down anyway.

ILLUSTRATION: COSTS AND REVENUES AND THEIR RELATIONSHIP TO THE BUDGET

The final budget disguises the concepts of costs and revenues that we have just discussed. Let us see the relationship.

Budget

The Budget We See		The Hidden Concepts	
Items		Fixed Costs	Variable Costs
Rental	$45,000	$38,000	$7,000
Telephone	10,000	3,000	7,000
Supplies	3,000	2,700	300
Travel	4,000	0	4,000

What we generally see in a budget can be broken down into two portions: the fixed and the variable. The fixed portion is the result of past commitments. It is the starting point for today's budget. It has to be met. Most annual budgets are really arguments over the *variable* portion. Start each year's budget by accounting for the fixed portion. The clearer this distinction is made, the more the focus can be on manageable costs and the more unlikely underbudgeting (which is inherently fatal because the fixed cost was ignored) becomes.

The importance of this can best be seen with rental income. Many organizations have long-term or capital leases of space. This means that they have to project their rental fees over the terms of the lease and account for that schedule and its current portion not only in their budgets but in their financial statements. It is recorded as a liability or a debt in the financial statement. It is a legal obligation, and therefore it must be met.

Similarly, a part of the telephone service is fixed. The telephone company charges a fixed fee no matter how many calls you make. Hence, annual budgeting first involves establishing the fixed cost coverage and then debating about the variable. Many of the supplies budgeted in an annual budget can also be split, because part of the cost is nothing more than accounting for supplies already on the shelf. Only a small amount may, under ordinary circumstances, be variable. Budgeting sunk costs, especially when they are already paid for, is a common although often undetected and unintended way of padding a budget. Travel is almost all variable.

In the same way that costs can be broken down usefully for budgeting, so can revenues.

Budget

The Budget We See		The Hidden Concepts	
Item		Permanent	Transitory
Gifts	$10,000	5,000	5,000
Contracts	45,000	35,000	10,000
Membership fees	7,000	6,000	1,000

Note here that *permanent* means that there is a firm commitment that extends well beyond the current year. The income is reliable. Endowments provide permanent income of gifts. An organization must always take into consideration that some part of their gifts budget is soft money that could disappear through a recession, a change in interest, or the intensity of fund-raising. Contracts may be multiyear and therefore permanent (even though the risk of revocability should be taken into consideration). Some contracts are transitory in that they are for a few days, months, or even revocable upon notice.

Organizations have a membership base that provides a relatively stable income, but this, too, may have a soft portion. Good budgeting must take these factors into account. It is risky budgeting to finance permanent projects with transitory income, or to fix costs at levels beyond which the income stream is unreliable. This is a sure invitation to bankruptcy.

Take a look at Figure 12.2. This concept is so important it deserves a name. Let us call it Simon's Dilemma: As we get a higher and higher ratio of fixed to *total* costs, we move closer to zero discretionary budgeting and zero organizational initiative at the same time that we increase the intensity of fund-raising, particularly for permanent funds to bail us out. However, few foundations, corporations, or individuals will knowingly make such gifts because the organization is inherently risky. Furthermore, large gifts are usually not unrestricted; therefore, they only add to the pressure because they are fixed commitments.

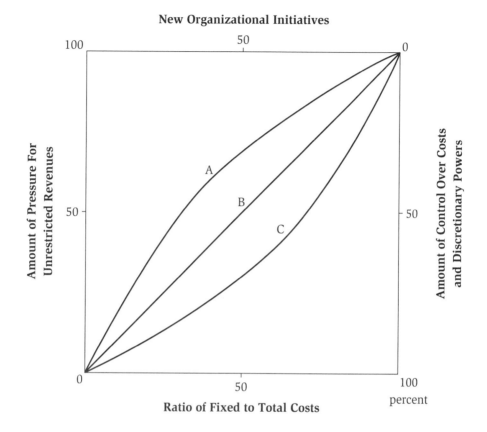

Figure 12.2. Simon's Dilemma.

Note: A, B, C show that organizations may move through dilemma at different rates. The effect is the same.

Let's look behind the numbers from the perspective of direct and indirect costs:

Budget

		The Hidden Concepts			
The Budget We See		Program 1		Program ... *n*	
Items		Direct	Indirect	Direct	Indirect
Rental	$45,000	$1000	500	We can break down	
Telephone	10,000	2000	300	the total to the left	
Supplies	3,000	800	200	even further.	
Travel	4,000	90	500		

The direct cost for Program 1 occurs, for example, if this program requires something special, such as a special security that is unrelated to other programs, and its indirect cost of $500 is allocated or attributed to it as part of the entire rental bill of the organization. Supplies and other items can also be broken down. The $800 may be special paper needed by the unit—say, photographic—while its allocated share of the total stationery and other general supplies used by it and the rest of the organization is $500. From this we see that individual programs have cost consequences for the entire organization.

Budgeting must recognize this fact lest the consequence of every program is to add to an ever increasing hidden cost burden and eventually to the collapse of the organization. In sum, behind the simple numbers in a budget are important cost consequences.

BUDGETING BY SCENARIO

An alternative to forecasting as we described it is budgeting through alternative scenarios. We can assume three or four different scenarios. In one the total resources that would be available to each responsibility center would (1) decline by some percentage, say 10 percent, (2) remain the same, or (3) rise by, say, 5 percent.

Let us assume that last year the organization hit its target so that there is no variance of actual from expected or planned expenditures. It spent exactly the amounts that it projected in every line. (This is an unnecessary assumption; we do it only to avoid having to produce another table of the actual amounts.)

Now let us calculate percentages by row and by column. These are shown in Table 12.5. From these we know the composition of costs in each activity area and the distribution of costs across activity areas. We can now take a total sum, say $5 million, and see how a budget of that size would be allocated under different scenarios.

Armed with these percentages, it is easy to use a spreadsheet and calculate what any change in any of the components would do to the budget. We can answer any of these questions: (1) What would be the effect of a change in the size of the overall budget? (2) What would be the effect of a change in any component of the budget (program or any of the items such as salaries, postal rates, and so on)? By having these percentages, we can postulate various changes or scenarios and see their impact on expenses. Accordingly, not only do we have a baseline for next year's budget, but we also have a *living budget* because we can make adjustments throughout the year. Budgeting becomes *flexible.*

You have noticed that this procedure does not give details such as how much should go to each program. At some point, budgets must deal with magnitudes or aggregates before and after details. This is what allocation is all about.

Table 12.5. Percentage Distribution and Composition of a Hypothetical Operating Budget by Function.

	Program	Manage-ment	Fund-Raising	Total	Program	Manage-ment	Fund-Raising	Total
Salaries	53.18	29.53	36.82	46.45	77.00	12.00	11.00	100.00
Payroll taxes and benefits	12.40	11.04	8.35	11.58	72.00	18.00	10.00	100.00
Consultant fees	1.94	6.90	2.56	2.96	44.00	44.00	12.00	100.00
Professional fees	0.00	20.56	0.00	3.88	0.00	100.00	0.00	100.00
Supplies	1.15	1.19	1.80	1.25	62.00	18.00	20.00	100.00
Telephone	1.46	1.51	2.28	1.58	62.00	18.00	20.00	100.00
Postage	1.52	1.57	2.37	1.64	62.00	18.00	20.00	100.00
Occupancy	12.49	12.92	19.54	13.55	62.00	18.00	20.00	100.00
Equipment rental	1.27	1.32	1.99	1.38	62.00	18.00	20.00	100.00
Printing	8.92	3.35	9.10	7.89	76.00	8.00	16.00	100.00
Travel	0.00	1.74	7.11	1.32	0.00	25.00	75.00	100.00
Conferences, meetings	0.00	1.59	0.68	0.39	0.00	76.00	24.00	100.00
Mail	4.58	0.42	5.69	3.95	78.00	2.00	20.00	100.00
Insurance	0.00	5.23	0.00	0.99	0.00	100.00	0.00	100.00
Interest	0.00	0.00	0.00	0.00				
Miscellaneous	1.09	1.13	1.71	1.18				
Total expenses	100.00	100.00	100.00	100.00				

Discretionary Forecasting and Budgeting

When forecasting and budgeting by scenarios, computer technology cannot supplant common sense or strategic thinking and decision making. Return to Table 12.5. Some entries have zeros. Take *interest expense*. A strategic decision to borrow would change that zero to some positive number. Not only will that change the distribution and composition of costs, even if only slightly, but such a number is reasonably fixed or known. Therefore, for every period a reasonably certain number can be inserted. It is independent of the mechanistic forecast. It is known.

Budgeting and forecasting are discretionary in yet another way. Management has discretionary flexibility over how much of any cost falls into any program, service, or responsibility center. This can be done in basically two ways: (1) reclassifying or relocating a person or activity from one center to another—not just calling it something else; (2) allocating costs when billings are not exact. For example, how much of a long-distance call was really fund-raising as opposed to service? At the next budgeting session of your organization, watch how many times and how passionately program managers raise the question: Why should this be charged to my budget?

BUDGET FORMATS: FORM FOLLOWS FUNCTION

No one budget format fits all functions. The purpose of this section is to discuss formats that can be used to set up and analyze budgets for presentation to the trustees. This is not a difficult task once the basic aim, as discussed earlier, is understood.

Combinations of Program and Item Budgets

Table 12.6 shows a functional or program budget combined with an object or item budget. Such a display gives management a view of how much of the organization's dollars are being spent on each program and their distribution among various items. It enables management to get to the nitty-gritty of each program cost, particularly direct costs.

In accounting, each program is referred to as a cost objective. It is the set of actions that generates costs. Each unit that generates these costs or runs a program is called a *cost center*. We can see that through a form such as Table 12.6 it is possible to pinpoint which cost center (staff units) is mostly responsible for each type of expenditure.

Each program may have more than one objective. For example, we show that program C has three objectives. Suppose that program C is for operating a new site for a nonprofit organization that runs a chain of day-care centers. Each objective under program C may be a site. Note that other programs are given

Table 12.6. Example of Program or Functional Budget and Object or Item Budget Combined.

Object or Item Budget

Classification of Program	Salaries and Benefits	Rent and Utility	Supplies and Materials	Travel	Equipment	Totals
Program A						
Program B						
Program C Objective 1 Objective 2 Objective 3						
Program D						
Program E						
Totals						

one objective. Whether each should be broken down into objectives is a matter of judgment. In general, a program should not be broken down into multiple objectives if each cannot be clearly defined and clearly and separately evaluated.

Many programs in nonprofit organizations are classical cost centers because they generate no revenues. For such centers a budget format such as the one shown above suffices. Other programs, indeed the organization itself, must consider both costs and revenues. Yet some centers such as fund-raising are mostly revenue centers; their aim is to generate revenues. In short, it is useful to look at costs separately and to do the same for revenues before combining the two.

Table 12.7 is an example of a form that may be used to analyze the inflow of expected or budgeted money into the organization. This inflow may be divided between restricted funds such as gifts, contracts, and endowments, over which the nonprofit has no discretionary control, and unrestricted funds. The latter are inflows from fees, business income, investments, gifts, and contributions that have not been designated exclusively for some specified purpose. The ratio of the two gives an indication of the amount of discretionary authority the management has over its budget. It is possible to have a wealthy nonprofit with minimal discretionary authority if most of its funds are restricted by donors or terms of contracts.

The first two columns give a historical backdrop for the budgeted amount in the third column. By doing this, management has some basis for judging the

Table 12.7. Example of Horizontal and Vertical Presentations of Actual and Budgeted Receipts.

Classification of Support	Actual Receipts		Budgeted Receipts 2002	Change in Receipts		Distribution of Dollars by Sources (in percent)	
	2000	2001		2000–2001	2001–2002	2001	2002
Restricted							
Total restricted							
Unrestricted							
Total unrestricted							
Total						100.0	100.0

reasonableness of the budgeted amount. Why should we expect this amount of money from gifts and contributions when we have not had anything close to it in the past? Is the staff serious, or do they have something planned? What is it? Is it feasible? Will it generate that much revenue? Is it consistent with the mission of the organization? Will it infringe on the organization's tax-exempt status? Is it desirable?

The next two columns give the rate of growth in past years, as well as the budgeted rate of growth. Rates of growth (occurring across columns) are examples of what accountants refer to as *horizontal analysis;* that is, one column is divided by another. Again, by setting up the budgeted rate of growth next to the past rate of growth, it is possible to judge the reasonableness of the expectation. By looking down the rows, it is possible to ascertain which sources of support are expected to grow fastest.

The last two columns show the percentage that each source will contribute to the overall expected revenues of the organization during the year for which the budget is made. This is called a *vertical analysis* because it shows how much each row contributes to the total. Each of these columns will add up to approximately 100 percent. Again, reasonableness can be disclosed by comparing the budgeted amount with the past year's performance. It is important to indicate that once these figures are accepted by the board they become targets. Accordingly, in the next budget cycle, appropriate questions would be, Why did we not attain our financial objectives? If we outdid our expectations, can we do it again?

A similar type of analysis can be done in Table 12.8 for expenditures. Note that in both the cases of expenditures and revenues we are concerned with the rates and distribution of growth or decline. Variances, discussed next, are concerned with actual performance.

Variances

Variance analysis can be viewed as a form of record-keeping for the purpose of setting off alarms when the organization's performance is off course. The reader

Table 12.8. Example of Horizontal and Vertical Presentation of Actual and Budgeted Expenditures.

Classification Programs	Actual Expenditures		Budgeted Expenditures 2002	Change		Distribution of Dollars by Programs (percent)	
	2000	2001		2000–2001	2001–2002	2001	2002
Program A							
Program B							
Program C							
Program D							
Program E							
Totals						100.0	100.0

may wish to preview the section on monitoring in Chapter Seventeen. Now for a simple, useful method of flagging performance deviation through the budget and financial statement. Earlier we discussed variances. In this section, we discuss some forms that may be used. From a policy perspective, management should be concerned with at least three types of variances: variances in overall program expenditures from the budgeted amount, variances in receipt from the expected amount, and variances from alternatives, especially those that would have been acceptable if the expected expenditures were lower. Operationally, managers may also be interested in variances in actual costs from standard costs, where standard costs may be the list price of an item or the usual and reasonable current cost multiplied by the number of the item used.

Table 12.9 shows a format that may be used to look at variances in expenditures. Note that the advantage of putting all this information on one sheet is that it is easily compared. Each program being implemented (A to E) is assessed at least every six months by comparing the budgeted amount with the actual expenditure. The difference is the variance, which should be shown both in dollars and in percentages. At the end of each year, this is also done so that an annual summary is available.

There is no hard and fast rule saying this analysis must be done every six months. In some cases, it might be wise to do it quarterly or even monthly. The critical factor is that it is done with sufficient frequency that the information needed to generate corrective action is available in time for action to be taken. There is little value in knowing that a program is off target when the program is already ended. The tradeoff is interruption in the flow of work and the resistance of many managers to report data accurately and frequently.

At the bottom of the form is room for explanation. This may be insufficient room. Both positive and negative variances (undershooting or overshooting targets) need to be explained. As stated earlier, spending less than budgeted may be a sign that the program has been delayed and will not meet its deadline. Overshooting may mean that the program was badly designed and needs revamping and will lead to a deficit. To appreciate this latter point, recall that contracts are often negotiated at a fixed price. This means that if the organization overshoots and ends up in a deficit there is no way to recover the money from the donor or the contracting agency.

A similar type of form can be used for analyzing variances of expected from actual receipts (Table 12.10). In this case, the receipts should be divided into the two basic groups of unrestricted and restricted funds. Restricted funds are from endowments, gifts, or decisions of the board to set aside funds to be used only for specific, designated purposes. Unrestricted funds are those that go into the general account of the organization and can be used in the way management chooses. These are discretionary funds. Here, too, the arguments of the previous paragraphs, including the frequency of collecting and reporting these

Table 12.9. Example of Variance Between Budgeted (Expected) and Actual Expenditures.

Classification of Programs	First Six Months			Second Six Months			Cumulative Year End		
	Budgeted	Actual	Variance	Budgeted	Actual	Variance	Budgeted	Actual	Variance
Program A									
Program B									
Program C									
Program D									
Program E									
Comments: Explanation:									

Table 12.10. Example of Variance Between Budgeted (Expected) and Actual Receipts.

Classification of Support	First Six Months			Second Six Months			Cumulative		
	Budgeted	Actual	Variance	Budgeted	Actual	Variance	Budgeted	Actual	Variance
Restricted									
Total restricted									
Unrestricted									
Total unrestricted									
Total									
Explanation:									

data, pertain. It is obvious that if receipts are lagging behind expenditures the organization is heading for trouble. The purpose of these forms is to give an early warning of what is ahead.

For this reason, a separate summary sheet is necessary for the end of every period to show what the projected deficit or surplus is likely to be based on that period's and the past period's performance. An example is Table 12.11. The unrestricted account shows the individual program period and a cumulative deficit or surplus, since all funds in that account may be used for any general purpose. Not so with the restricted account; therefore, each has its own expected deficit or surplus.

A RECOMMENDED FORMAT FOR USING THE BUDGET AS A CONTROL TOOL

Let us consider the difficulty placed on an executive whose organization conducts many programs. Each responsibility center or mission center in the organization may oversee several cost objectives or programs. If the manager oversees ten mission centers and each has ten programs, such a manager would

Table 12.11. Example of Summary Showing Deficit or Surplus by Program.

Classification of Programs	Summary First Six Months		Summary Second Six Months		Summary Cumulative	
	Deficit	Surpluses	Deficit	Surpluses	Deficit	Surpluses
Unrestricted						
Program A						
Program B						
Program C						
Total unrestricted						
Restricted						
Program D						
Program E						
Explanation:						

either have to look at one hundred different budgets or ten summary budgets, one for each responsibility center summarizing all the activities in that center. One hundred budgets are too many to consider in detail, and ten summary budgets are, by definition, too broad to grasp the essential details.

From a control point of view, the financial manager needs to identify quickly and flag those programs that are in jeopardy of overspending and those that are moving so laggardly that they are not likely to spend the money committed to them in the time period allotted and may therefore need an extension to keep from loosing their allocation.

Let me recommend a way for you to do this for each program. It was introduced in the first edition of this book. Refer to Table 12.12. It shows a list of over 100 programs according to the responsibility centers under which they fall. Each program has a control number to identify it. The first two digits identify the responsibility center and the other digits identify the specific program within the center; hence 0110 is a program in the responsibility center designated 01. The number 10 identifies the program. In this display we show each responsibility center as having twenty-seven programs. It is not necessary for purposes of financial flagging to deal with specific program names.

The program code is followed by a code such as 2/4/80/70. The first number represents the current year of the program; 2 would mean that the program is in its second year, the year for which the present budget is being submitted. The second number indicates the expected life of the program; 4 means that the program is planned for four years. The third number is the percentage of the total allocation that will be consumed by the end of the year for which the budget is being submitted; 80 means that by the end of this year 80 percent of the budget allotment would have been used up. The fourth number indicates the program manager's assessment of the amount of work that will have been done by the end of the budget year; 70 percent means that by the end of this present budget year only 30 percent of the promised activities will be left to be done.

This technique provides several advantages. First, the financial manager can focus on the possibilities of cost overruns on each program within the organization because the pertinent information is given in simple form. Second, it gives the individual program manager, the manager of the responsibility center in which the program falls, and management of the organization an early warning of trouble. Third, it forces the program manager to assess how much has been accomplished and how much is still left to be done and, consequently, to be accountable as to how the remaining task will get done.

Now, it is not unusual to find program managers who would try to escape this responsibility by saying that "it is hard to measure how much is left to be done." Such a plea of impotence is often no more than a sign of incompetence. The fact is that you cannot manage a multiyear program under a budget

Table 12.12. Format for Flagging Potential Budgetary Problems.

Program Code	Responsibility Center-01 Status	Flag	Program Code	Responsibility Center-02 Status	Flag	Program Code	Responsibility Center-03 Status	Flag	Program Code	Responsibility Center-04 Status	Flag
0100			0200			0300			0400		
0101			0201			0301			0401		
0102			0202			0302			0402		
0103			0203			0303	2/4/80/70		0403		
0104			0204			0304			0404		
0105			0205			0305			0405		
0106			0206	3/4/99/50		0306			0406		
0107			0207			0307			0407		
0108			0208			0308	1/2/110/60		0408	3/5/80/60	
0109			0209			0309			0409		
0110	3/4/10/90		0210			0310			0410		
0111			0211			0311			0411		
0112			0212			0312			0412		

constraint if you cannot see the end of the project and cannot ascertain where you are, where you are going, and roughly what it will take to get there. The judgment does not have to be 100 percent accurate. It has to be reasonable. The users of such information should keep in mind that an objective of all control systems is to be able to flag and avoid potential problems. Control systems do not give answers as much as they flag situations where managerial attention ought to be focused and questions raised.

In addition to reducing the probability of cost overruns, this system also alerts managers to projects that are lagging behind the funding schedule. Some contracts are written such that they terminate at a specific period and must be renegotiated at the risk that they will not be extended. Unspent funds may be lost. So a program that shows 3/4/10/90 is as much a potential problem as one that shows 3/4/99/50. The first has to find a way to justifiably use 90 percent of the funding in one year when only 10 percent of the job is left to be done. This is not a problem only if the last 10 percent can justifiably use the remaining funds. The latter has to do 50 percent of the work with 1 percent of the funds.

A display such as 1/2/110/60 would raise serious questions about cutting losses. This is a two-year program that at the end of its first year would have overspent its budget by 10 percent and still have 40 percent of the expected work to be completed. A program of 3/5/80/60 is a five-year program that already in its third year shows a sign of a potential need for more funding. This process of seeking additional funding can be started well before the project enters into serious cost overruns.

A BUDGET FORMAT FOR THE BOARD

The formats we have discussed are well suited for daily management. The board of directors needs less detailed information and can request it if it does. The board needs to evaluate the overall direction of the organization.

One format for presenting a budget to trustees is to show simultaneously the revenue, support, and expense expectations and how they are distributed by program and support categories. This is shown in Table 12.13.

This format shows the organization's revenues and support by source and how they are distributed across programs and support activities; at the same time it shows how the organization plans to allocate its dollars, not only by expense category but also by program or support category. This budget format may omit considerations of the different objectives of each program. The objectives can be given as part of the supporting document accompanying the budget.

Table 12.13. A Budget Format for the Board of Trustees.

	Program Services					Supporting Services			Total Expenses	
	Program 1	Program 2	Program 3	Program 4	Total	Fund-Raising	Management and General	Total	2000	2001
Support and revenue:										
Support-contributions and grants and contracts										
Revenue-fees and investment income										
Total support and revenue										
Expenses:										
Salaries										
Employee benefits and payroll taxes										
Fees to consultants and contracted services, including expenses										
Fees to authors and speakers, including expenses										

(Continued)

Table 12.13. *(continued)*.

| | Program Services | | | | | Supporting Services | | | Total Expenses | |
	Program 1	Program 2	Program 3	Program 4	Total	Fund-Raising	Management and General	Total	2000	2001
Rent										
Printing and production										
Postage and mailings										
Office supplies and expenses										
Telephone										
Conference on-site expenses										
Committee meetings										
Travel and other meetings										
Books and periodicals										
Advertising and promotion										
Depreciation										
Other										
Total expenses										

The advantage of this format is that it provides the key information needed by top-level decision makers at a glance:

1. It shows the total revenues that are expected during the year, how much will be distributed to each of the various programs or responsibility centers, how much will be allocated to support activities, and the composition of revenues by type. For example, it shows how much the organization expects to receive from contributions. Is this reasonable? Does this help the organization maintain its public support requirements? How will these revenues be distributed across programs? Is this consistent with the mission of the organization and the directive of the board? Should some programs be more self-supporting?

2. It shows the major expense categories of the organization and how much the organization plans to allocate to each category by program.

3. It shows annual changes in allocated amounts by type of expense.

One principal advantage of such a format is that it comes close to the statement of revenues, support, and expenses that records the actual dollars that were received and spent by the organization during the year. Hence, it would be easy to compare actual with planned performance. In Chapter Fifteen we shall look at statements of revenues and expenses and come back to this discussion.

SUMMARY AND PREVIEW

Our discussion of costs, support, and budgets will be integrated into our discussion of strategic planning in Chapter Seventeen. Strategic planning is a process through which programs are selected and designed to execute the strategies to meet objectives, consistent with the mission for which the organization was created.

Any rational choice of programs should be based partly on economic factors. Which program has the greater benefit-cost ratio? Can the organization raise the money to meet the cost? Can it afford the program? Answers to these questions can only be obtained through developing and comparing a standard budget for each alternative. Budgeting and programming are linked, and in the ideal case, when the choice of a program is made, so too is its preliminary budget.

Although it is not necessary to go over the entire strategic planning exercise every year, it is necessary to do a budget every year. In those years when a new strategic plan is not developed and the existing plan remains operative, the budgeting exercise implies the continuation of the organization's strategies and objectives.

Any number of factors make annual budgeting imperative. Changes in the prices of labor, materials, and equipment, increases or decreases in revenues, changes in the size and scope of the activity, errors in the previous budget, the requirements of most major sponsors for annual budgets, and the bylaws of the organization are some of the most important forces that make an annual operating budget an imperative. This does not imply that multiyear budgeting is incorrect. A two-year or biannual budget is a composite of figures for each of two separate years.

The concepts learned earlier in this chapter also apply to planning, programming, and budgeting systems (PPBS). We begin by noting that at the point of choosing among programs we also compare their expected costs and revenues. This is what is referred to as a *differential analysis*. We are comparing the difference between one set of costs and revenues against others.

In determining overhead, what is included is as important as finding out who will pay for it. All charges are not appropriate. Furthermore, overhead must be allocated between the exempt and nonexempt (including unrelated business) activities of the organization. Hence, for example, a university operating a fieldhouse that is used both for exempt and for unrelated business is permitted to allocate the overhead between the two.[5] The effect of this is to reduce the amount of taxes the university pays on unrelated business income because overhead expenses are deducted.[6]

CHAPTER THIRTEEN

Compensation and Employee Benefits

The financial success of an organization depends on its ability to contain costs, the major and most rapidly growing portion of which are employee salaries and benefits and, most controversial, executive compensation. This chapter describes in detail the types of optional benefits available to attract and retain competent employees in nonprofit organizations. Properly structured, the costs of these optional benefits can be contained and tax advantages can be enjoyed by the employees. But the chapter begins with executive compensation and a discussion of what constitutes reasonable pay.

Among the specific questions this chapter addresses are

Why should every nonprofit provide certain benefits?

What are the options and considerations in designing a benefits package?

How does the organization determine executive pay?

It also discussses benefits including life, disability, medical and hospitalization insurance, retirement and pension plans, and other fringe benefits. It shows how some of these can be integrated with Social Security to reduce costs.

EXCESS EXECUTIVE COMPENSATION

Trustees are responsible for negotiating and agreeing to executive compensation contracts. The federal law, informally known as the intermediate sanction rule or "Taxpayer Bill of Rights 2," makes trustees disqualified persons. For purposes of compensation, a disqualified person is any trustee, manager, donor, entity (and in the case of hospitals, physicians) who has substantial influence over the organization in the five years preceding the date of the "excess transaction." The law also states that any corporation in which a disqualified person owns or controls 35 percent or more of the stocks is also disqualified. The law specifically refers to 501(c)(3) and (3)(4) organizations.

The law states that any such disqualified person who obtains excess benefits can be subject to an excise tax of 25 percent of such an excess, and any disqualified person who knowingly participated in this agreement would also be subject to an excise tax of 10 percent of the excess up to $10,000. The focus of this law is on executive compensation but it applies to all kinds of transactions, including the payment of trustees or any other disqualified person as defined above or the payment in a sale of a product or service rendered by them. The law considers excessive compensation to any disqualified person to be self-dealing; for example, using the assets of the organization for personal benefits.

The law defines participation in self-dealing as willful if the disqualified person engaged in the act voluntarily, intentionally, and consciously. But liability also arises from silence and the lack of action to stop or to record objection to an excess benefits transaction unless there is reasonable cause to believe that the trustee or other disqualified persons did not know of the transaction, and did not know that the transaction would be deemed self-dealing. Failure to have inquired about whether the transaction was an act of self-dealing, where this inquiry is clearly indicated, does constitute an act of negligence and could likewise result in being penalized by the imposition of the excise tax.

But when is compensation excessive? When the compensation exceeds the economic value of the benefit the organization got in return, or when the compensation is calibrated to the organization's revenues or reflects personal inurement. In the first, the amount that exceeds the fair market value of the benefits received is the excess. A job that is worth $140,000 but $200,000 is paid to a disqualified person yields an excess of $60,000, which is taxed. In the second case, the total of any payment calibrated to the revenues of the organization (such as a percentage of profits) is, by definition, likely to be considered excess.

The law does provide for the organization to indemnify or insure the disqualified person against the cost of any penalty or taxes due to an "excess transaction." It does, however, also require that this insurance or indemnification be included in the compensation. Hence, the more the organization covers for the disqualified person, the greater the tax or penalty on all disqualified persons found to have knowingly participated in the transaction.

Because executive compensation is so costly, the concept so elastic, and because such compensation must be reported annually on Form 990 to the federal government, this book proposes that the following steps be taken at a minimum by trustees in determining executive compensation and compensation to disqualified persons. A reasoned legal opinion of the deal is a sine qua non for all such transactions, and a private letter ruling from the IRS when such transactions are at the borderline is advisable.

In any event, the trustee should

1. Create a compensation committee that is not composed of individuals who are disqualified persons as described above. This committee would oversee the compensation package for the top 5 percent of the employees and all major independent contractors.

2. Ensure that the entire executive compensation package, including compensation to disqualified persons, is consistent with the bylaws of the organization and is part of a resolution. Further, the bylaws should state a definite procedure for voting on such a package, and it should reflect the prohibitions of state and federal laws on economic benefits such as loans, leases, expenses, insurance, pension, and pay.

3. Instruct the committee to gather information about comparable positions in organizations of comparable asset size, mission, qualifications, geographic location, and duties for each person being considered plus the competitive environment.

4. Make sure that the committee considers the qualifications needed independently of specific candidates.

5. Require the entire board, excluding those who are disqualified persons, to vote on points 1 through 4 above and pass a resolution. All changes in the package from this point on should require a vote by the board at large or an executive committee of the board as provided by the bylaws.

6. Require that any executive search be conducted only within the framework of the resolution and its amendments.

7. Make amendments to the resolution to attract or retain a person already connected with the organization judiciously, even if that person is not already a disqualified person. Such amendments should be clearly justified in terms of the broader needs of the organization.

8. Adopt all perks by resolution and recorded in the books prior to the beginning of the fiscal year, subject to some measurable performance indicator. Otherwise, the perk may appear as personal inurement,

excess compensation, or an attempt to distribute the largess as if it were a special dividend in a firm.

9. Keep records. An auditor ought to be able to ask for a written document that explains the organization's compensation policy. As a matter of fact, so should the IRS, the U.S. Labor Department, a potential major donor, and members of the organization.

10. Meet the reporting requirements. Form 990 does require the organization to report on the amounts paid the highest 5 percent of employees and independent contractors. A badly written compensation policy can convert an independent contractor to an employee for whom the organization owes Social Security taxes.

REASONABLE COMPENSATION

The beginning point of any compensation package is reasonableness. For each employee, particularly executives, the entire package taken as a whole should be reasonable. By this is meant that it should be based on considerations of education, duties, experience, and comparability with the earnings of persons similarly situated in the region. For executives, a departure from this norm can lead to penalties for self-dealing. The IRS in its letter 9008001 issued March 5, 1990 ruled that a nonprofit that argued that its unusually high compensations to its trustees hinged on the fact they were doing a lot of staff work, including reviewing of proposals, was really self-dealing in excessive compensation. The IRS could find no similar setup in the area in which the nonprofit operated.

SOCIAL SECURITY

Nonprofits must make contributions for employees earning $100 or more in a year. Because of the compulsory participation in Social Security, the wise manager of a nonprofit should know how such participation may be integrated into a benefit package to keep costs down and benefits at a desirable level. This is important because benefits are the most rapidly rising costs and are therefore a key to understanding the management and financing of nonprofits.

DISABILITY INCOME INSURANCE

We must distinguish between disability income insurance and worker's compensation. The latter is required by law and covers employees for injury sustained on the job regardless of who is at fault. The premiums are paid exclusively by the employer and are based on the type of work done, the occupational composition of the work force, and the past history with respect to the number and seriousness of past claims.

Disability income insurance (sometimes called income continuation plan) is not compulsory. It covers disability whether or not it resulted from work-related activities. One of its purposes is to protect the nonprofit against the cost of paying both the salaries of an incapacitated worker and a replacement. It also assures the worker of continued income during periods of incapacitation.

Because disability income insurance is not compulsory, the nonprofit may elect self-insurance by having a written contractual agreement with its employees to continue the payment of salary to a worker when incapacitated. Unless this is a written plan, all payments received by the worker during periods of incapacity may be fully taxable.[1]

An alternative to self-insurance is for the organization to purchase a disability insurance policy, particularly for its key employees. An insurance policy may be for long- or short-term disability. A short-term disability policy will cover the worker for approximately five months if the worker is unable to conduct normal functions. A long-term policy may cover the worker usually up to age sixty-five, the expected time of retirement.

Cost Control of Disability Coverage

Cost can be controlled by distinguishing and choosing between long and short coverage and the integration of Social Security. A critical difference between long- and short-term policies is in the definition of disability. Commonly, the short-term definition of disability is the incapacity of the worker to perform normal occupational functions. The long-term definition is most often the incapacity of the worker to perform any occupational function whatsoever, given his or her age, work, and educational experiences. Since these are often subjectively interpreted, a long-term claim could be denied on the grounds that the person can do some type of remunerative work.

In structuring a disability income plan, the nonprofit management may begin by considering the option of not providing it for any employee or only providing for its key or executive employees. The cost savings would enable the organization to hire people it might otherwise be unable to afford. Second, the nonprofit may consider the option of self-insurance, which may be less expensive, depending on the number of employees who have claims and the length of time for which each incident is covered. Self-insurance should only be undertaken if a detailed plan can be written defining disability, what constitutes a new or continued claim, how many claims each employee may make in a period, what constitutes a benefit period, and so on.

Another option is to provide only a short-run or only a long-run policy. Providing only a long-run policy means that the employee would normally have to wait five months before receiving a check from the insurance company, but during this time the nonprofit may continue full or partial salary payments to the employee.

Social Security Integration of Disability Coverage

An alternative is to purchase a short-run policy that has a waiting period. This is a period that the employee must wait before receiving the first check. The policy would most likely cover the employee for five months after the waiting period. At the end of this period, Social Security begins payment if the employee is eligible. Social Security disability income payments are long term (up to age sixty-five). Yet another alternative is to provide no short-term coverage and wait until Social Security payments begin in the sixth month of disability.

It is necessary to understand the rules of Social Security disability if it is to be integrated into the benefits package of a nonprofit. Eligibility depends on the age of the worker when the disability occurred and the number of quarters of credits earned prior to the disability.[2]

The disability must have lasted or be expected to last at least twelve months, be permanent, or result in death. In addition, the worker must be unable to work at any job regardless of age, work experience, and education. Fitness to work is determined by a state agency physician, not by the private physician of the employee. Moreover, the employee must enroll in a state vocational rehabilitation program.

Regardless of which option the nonprofit chooses, it should be aware that other segments of the benefit package may have a disability component. Pension plans and life insurance policies usually provide some disability protection. However, it might not be enough to rely on this simply because it is usually incidental. For example, the most common disability provision in a life insurance policy merely pays the premium on the policy so that it does not lapse. And the most common disability provision in a pension plan is to permit early withdrawals without penalty either by the government or by the company issuing the disability contract.

Disability premiums, as those for workmen's compensation, vary by age of workers, types of occupations, and the location by zip code, reflecting environmental risks. A nonprofit that covers several geographic locations could be faced with a different rate for each, or an average based on all locations, or a rate based on the location where most of its employees are located.

One final word. If an executive wishes a disability contract, it is sometimes wiser first to buy an individual one for him and her alone before creating and enrolling that person in a group policy. The reason for this strategy is that the ceiling (percentage of earnings to be replaced by the disability contract) can be exceeded. If the executive meets the ceiling through a group contract, an insurance company will not sell him or her additional disability. But it would ignore the ceiling reached in the individual contract if he or she subsequently becomes part of a group.

LIFE INSURANCE

Death benefit payments are not compulsory. A nonprofit may or may not choose to make a token gift to the family of a deceased worker.[3] A nonprofit that chooses to be competitive for good workers would also choose the more common alternative, which is to purchase life insurance policies on its workers.

A life insurance policy may be purchased by the nonprofit to protect itself. When a key employee dies, there is work interruption and the need to have an audit and to recruit and train a replacement. A policy bought and owned by the nonprofit on the life of its key employees or on the position held by such a person would, upon the death of the incumbent, provide proceeds that can be used to defray these expenses.

In addition, life insurance may be bought to protect the dependents of the deceased employee against the total loss of income. The life insurance contract may be of two broad types: (1) permanent insurance, or (2) term insurance. There may also be an individual or group policy.

Permanent versus Term

A permanent insurance policy is one that does not have to be renewed or converted. It lasts as long as the premiums are paid, and the premiums are usually the same year after year. These policies are inexpensive. However, a term policy lasts only for a specifically predesignated term—one, five, ten, or fifteen years—and after the predesignated term the policy must be renewed for another term, usually at a higher premium. By agreement with the insurance company, it is possible to convert a term policy to a permanent one.

A disadvantage to the worker of a permanent policy is that the part of the premium that is in excess of what the premium would have been on a term policy is taxable to the worker as income. Therefore, the permanent policy tends to be more expensive to the organization and leads to taxable income on the part of the employee. Yet many employees may prefer a permanent policy because, even with the tax, it is less expensive for the worker to have the organization buy the policy than for the worker to do so. In some instances, a permanent policy for key employees may be an incentive to attract such persons to the organization.

Because of its simplicity and lower costs, the group term policy is best suited for the work force of the nonprofit. The term of the insurance is usually one year. This makes sense because people enter and leave the employ of the organization every year. It is renewed every year, at a higher rate, that the employee remains.

Group versus Individual

The nonprofit may also elect group or individual policies. Group policies are less expensive and often superior in their coverage. They are less expensive because certain administrative costs decline on the average as the group gets larger. Most important, group policies protect the insurance company against adverse selection. This refers to the inclination of individuals who are most adversely exposed to the possibilities of death to be the most eager to select life insurance coverage. If only such persons were covered, the insurance company could find itself continuously paying claims. But the larger the group is the more high-risk workers would be balanced by low-risk workers, and therefore the lower the premium the company will charge because the number of claims will be relatively lower.

For important legal purposes, a "large" group is one with ten or more members. For groups of that size, the nonprofit management may exclude certain classes of workers from coverage. A class may be excluded if it is based on broad definitions such as occupational classification, salary, full-time or part-time employment, or union status. The class must be defined to avoid individual selection and exclusion. Individuals may be selected or excluded because of their membership in a class within the larger workforce of the nonprofit, not because of individual characteristics.

There are important flexibilities with group policies. Upon retirement or separation, the policies may be converted to an individual policy. This conversion is normally possible regardless of the reason for separation, including the demise of the organization.[4] Group policies may have a waiver of premium rider, which waives premiums if the worker becomes permanently disabled so that disability would not cause the policy to lapse.

Cost Control

There may be a probationary period before an employee is covered for life insurance, and employees may also be required to contribute to the premiums. A probationary period often makes sense since it would give benefits to an employee who had made at least a minimal commitment to the organization, even though it could be a hindrance to recruiting workers. Employee contributions are particularly useful if the employee wishes to have the policy cover the life of a dependent or spouse. However, requiring a contribution on the part of the employee to cover his or her own life is a disincentive.[5] Group term is cheaper than permanent.

Death Benefits

The nonprofit is free to choose a policy that would give death benefits that exceed $50,000. For tax purposes, the maximum benefit is $50,000. Any policy that offers a benefit in excess of this amount would create taxable income to the employee. The tax will be levied on the premium paid for the amount in excess of $50,000. Here, again, some executives will gladly pay that tax, since any comparable policy bought on the open market is likely to be more expensive even after considering the tax. Of course, the tax can be avoided altogether. If the policy on the life of the employee has a death benefit that exceeds $50,000 and the policy is donated and owned by a nonprofit as a charitable gift, then the excess premiums are not taxable.

Even though it is a group policy, it is owned by the employee. The employee is thus free to name beneficiaries, change them, or even use the policy as collateral for a loan. If the policy is a permanent policy, not only could it be used as collateral for a loan, but it would also have a loan value, that is, a periodic accumulation (called the *cash* or *surrender value*) that could be borrowed. Term policies (unless of fifteen years or more) have no such value and therefore can at best be used only as security, roughly as credit insurance.

Upon the death of the employee, the beneficiaries may choose one of several settlement options. They may choose to receive the benefits in a lump sum, or over a specific number of payments, or a specific amount per payment; they may guarantee a minimum number or amount of payments; they may take interest, leaving only the principal to another beneficiary; or they may receive payments for the life of the beneficiary, which terminate upon that beneficiary's death.

Each of these has important tax and financial implications. For example, a lump sum leads to no income taxes to the beneficiary, although it could lead to an estate tax unless the individual gave 100 percent to a spouse or a charity. An interest only leads to a $1,000 annual deduction if the beneficiary is a spouse but a tax on everything above the $1,000. Periodic payments are partially taxed. Now that organizations increasingly offer financial advice as one of their benefits, there is an awareness of the income, gift, and estate taxes associated with various death benefit options. For example, the simple act of naming of a clearly identified beneficiary, by full name, birth date, relationship, and social security number would facilitate settlement of death claims.

Social Security Integration of Life Insurance

With compulsory participation in Social Security, a nonprofit manager may find it wise to consider survivorship benefits in determining the percentage of the employee's income that the nonprofit would wish to replace through its own insurance. Here again it is important to consider the Social Security eligibility criteria.[6] A worker might be eligible in one of two ways. To be currently insured, the worker needs to have earned six quarters of coverage during the thirteen calendar quarters ending with the quarter in which death occurred. To be fully insured, the worker must have quarters of coverage that correspond to his or her age. One who is fifty-four must have thirty-two quarters; one who is fifty, twenty-eight quarters, and so on.

A spouse of at least nine months and the parent of a dependent child, whether natural or adopted, are eligible for survivor's benefits. But there can be no duplication for the same person; a person cannot get payments as a retiree and also as a survivor. One check for the higher of the two benefits is received.

Split-Dollar Policies

An organization may wish to recruit or retain a key person through an investment known as split-dollar insurance. In its simplest form, the organization takes out a permanent policy on the life of its executive and pays all or part of the premiums. Upon the death of the executive, his or her beneficiaries receive the death benefit, and the organization is repaid the amount it invested in the premiums. This amount is drawn from the savings portion of the policy. This strategy allows the executive to obtain insurance at a very low price, even after paying taxes for the premiums paid by the nonprofit. This is so because the tax is substantially lower than the premium. Another alternative of a split-dollar policy provides for the executive, upon leaving, to take the policy and repay the nonprofit for its contributions by paying it the cash value of the policy. Yet another alternative, called a reverse split-dollar, makes the charity the beneficiary of the death proceeds and the state (or some other designee) the beneficiary of the cash value upon the death of the executive.

ACCIDENTAL DEATH AND DISMEMBERMENT

A nonprofit may wish to protect its employees who travel or are exposed to risk of injury and death due to accidental causes. Insurance can be bought to protect against losses due to accidental death and dismemberment. This coverage may be bought separately and very inexpensively or as part of the life or health insurance policies.

To some extent, accidental death represents a duplication of coverage. Dismemberment is a real fear in some occupations but not in others; moreover, the disability coverage may well offer sufficient compensation. The full death benefit may be covered on the life insurance policy. If it is not, perhaps it should be. Is it any more expensive to die from an accident than to die from natural causes? Why seek a higher or independent coverage for accidents? One reason for the inexpensiveness of this type of policy is that the probability of collecting is very low.

The conditions under which the beneficiaries or insured may collect under accidental death policies are strict. Death must usually occur within a specific period, perhaps ninety days after the accident. Moreover, death must be due exclusively to the accident and not attributed to or the result of another cause.[7] Also, death resulting from certain types of accidents may be excluded from coverage.

If death or dismemberment owing to travel is the risk of concern, consideration should be given to using a credit card to pay for travel. Many cards include this type of protection.

MEDICAL AND HOSPITALIZATION INSURANCE

Of all elements in the usual benefit package, this is probably the most confusing and difficult because (1) the risk is so high that everybody needs this type of protection, (2) the cost is so high that every employer needs to control it, and (3) every policy is different, with a wide range for comparing seemingly incomparable benefits or costs. Nonprofits that require overseas travel by their employees have the additional problem of being sure that they are covered by an insurer that provides for payment for services rendered abroad, including air evacuation.

Medical and hospitalization costs have been rising dramatically—faster than the rate of inflation. Health and medical benefits are intended to protect the employee against these costs. This protection may be provided through regular commercial or association insurance, Blue Cross/Blue Shield, medical accounts, or through a health maintenance organization (HMO).

Basic versus Major or Comprehensive

Medical and hospitalization insurance policies differ by company, and there may be several different alternative policies from which the nonprofit organization may choose. The simplest and perhaps least expensive insurance plan is the basic plan, sometimes called the indemnification plan. The principal characteristic of basic plans is that they emphasize hospital-related benefits. Such plans cover hospital services, some emergency costs, and basic surgical fees. Basic plans may differ from company to company, and one company may have more than one alternative.

Under the basic plan, hospital room and board are covered. The payments may be for a specified amount per day up to some maximum dollar amount or number of days. Other hospital charges such as medicine, drugs, and x-rays are usually paid as a percentage of the benefits being paid for the room and board. Surgical fees may be paid according to a schedule or according to what is usual, customary, and reasonable for similar surgical services in the geographic area.

Major medical insurance policies cover a larger number of medical events, pay a higher maximum, and are more expensive than basic plans. Major medical protects against catastrophic illnesses. A major plan may be a supplement to a basic plan so that it covers illnesses excluded by the basic plan or picks up payments when the basic plan reaches its limits. In the latter case, there may be a deductible before the major plan kicks in. Alternatively, the major plan may be independent of the basic plan or may incorporate it into a comprehensive plan. Again, there are major differences among major plans.

Tax-Favored Medical Reimbursement Plans

Medical reimbursement plans are an alternative way of financing health care. These plans allow workers to put dollars into an account for paying medical bills. These dollars escape taxation as part of the salary of the employee. The plans work well when the worker has a good estimate of what the annual health bill for the family will be because the amount not used at the end of the year is lost (that is, "use it or lose it"). The amount placed in these plans also counts to reduce the maximum amount the employee can place in a tax-sheltered annuity (discussed in this chapter).

Medical reimbursement accounts are of two types. One is to pay expected dental, vision, and medical expenses that are not covered by a regular insurance plan, and the other is to pay for dependent care including day-care expenses for a child and expenses for an invalid spouse, parent, or child. These are called *reimbursement accounts* because they work as follows. The monthly payment is deducted from the employee's check up to the limit allowed by law. The employee pays no income tax on this amount. Hence, it is said that the payments are pretax payments—reducing the amount of the employee's income subject to withholdings of federal and state income taxes.

When the employee incurs a bill for any of the qualified purposes that would include the deductible or co-payment amounts on his or her regular insurance policy or for any of the dependent needs stated above, the employer would reimburse the employee by debiting the appropriate account. The two accounts are separate and must be billed separately. They cannot be used interchangeably even if one is exhausted and the other is untouched.

The principal advantages of these accounts are that they allow the employee to set aside money for known and predictable expenses in an orderly fashion, and the employee can reduce his or her taxes because this amount is not subject to tax. In this respect, it lowers the cost of meeting predictable medical and dental expenses.

The principal risk for the employee is that any amount not used during the course of a year is lost. It cannot be carried forward to a future year. Each year the employee must re-enroll. During the enrollment period and after the occurrence of certain events—such as death of the employee or that person's covered spouse or dependent, marriage, divorce, birth, and loss of job—the employee has the right to change his or her enrollment.

In deciding on whether to enroll in such a plan, the employee must first itemize known expenses and create a medical reimbursement account to cover them. The tax advantage will have more value to those who do not qualify for itemizing their medical expenses on their income taxes or to those who may have to borrow, for example, use a high-interest credit card, because the interest on these loans may not be deductible.

Since these reimbursement plans may be used alone or in combination with a regular insurance program, giving the employee a choice is worth being considered by the nonprofit organization.

Medical Savings Account

The medical savings account (MSA) is a variation on the theme of the medical reimbursement account. The MSA provides a side account to a medical insurance policy. This side account earns interest tax-free and the employee does not lose the balance if it is not totally spent. The account can be used to pay deductibles or portions of medical costs not covered by the insurance policy.

Cost-Cutting Strategies

Because of the breadth of coverage of major plans, the insurance companies impose cost-sharing devices. The nonprofit may choose how much it wishes to participate in each of these, the net effect of which is to shift costs to the employee. One such device is the deductible and another is co-insurance. A deductible requires the employee to pay the first dollars on a claim, often the first $50 or $100. When the claim exceeds the deductible, the company may share the cost further by paying only a specified percentage of the amount in excess of the deductible, usually 80 percent of that amount. The remaining 20 percent of the claim is paid by the employee. Above the level of co-insurance, the company may pay 100 percent of the claim up to some maximum. The greater the deductible and the co-insurance, the lower the cost to the nonprofit because the lower the exposure of the insurance company.

The insurance company may limit its exposure even further. It may limit the amount it would pay to an employee or a family either per calendar year or per policy year, per medical event, or for all events combined. Similarly, deductibles may be per person, per family, per policy period, and so on. All this is in addition to an overall maximum limit over the life of the employee. Hence, a policy could read that it is limited to $100,000 per calendar year per employee and $400,000 over the life of that person. At this limit the company reserves the right to terminate the policy.

In the same way that the insurance company may wish to limit its exposure, so too should the worker. Therefore, it is wise to seek out a policy that has a stop-loss feature. This means that beyond a certain cost the insurance company takes over 100 percent of payments up to its maximum limit.

In considering medical insurance, the choice is between a basic or a major plan or a combination of the two, either with the major supplementing the basic (which means that the first dollars of payment come from the basic) or a comprehensive plan that contains both the features of a basic and a major plan.

Comprehensive and major plans are expensive. The cost can be lowered if the nonprofit accepts a higher level of co-insurance and deductible and by making the plan contributory (meaning that the employees pay part of the premium, if only for their dependents). Other cost-saving devices include the nonprofit recommending to employees the use of hospitals and physicians who are competent but lower priced and by excluding some routine visits from coverage. The trade-off with cost-saving devices might be the postponement of preventive care.

Partly because of the growth of two-worker families, there is the increased likelihood that each spouse would have independent coverage under the same or different employer plans. This duplication of coverage is costly and wasteful. The rules and practices of health insurance companies require that benefits be coordinated. This means that workers or their dependents can collect from only one policy at a time. A dependent child must first collect from the father's policy; a child of divorced parents may also have to collect first from the father's policy. The rules of coordination of benefits include considerations of divorce, separation, length of coverage, sex of spouse, and so on. In a nutshell, the rules simply remove the possibility of collecting from more than one company at the same time and for the same cause.

A closely related principle is the indemnity principle. This says that the insured cannot collect more than the cost of the health and medical service. When this principle is considered with the principle of coordination of benefits, it becomes clear that there is no way to recover from being overinsured as far as medical and health insurance are concerned. Only one company will pay unless the contract says otherwise. The extra premium is wasted.

Outside the insurance itself, many nonprofits, particularly the larger ones, may benefit from using techniques such as providing workers with a list of preferred medical practitioners and encouraging healthy behavior on the part of their employees and families.

Health Maintenance Organizations

Unlike insurance companies, health maintenance organizations (HMOs) are direct providers of health and medical services. The employee gets a wide range of services, such as hospital care, outpatient x-ray and laboratory services, physical examinations, eye examinations, routine gynecological examinations, and maternity care, all at no extra cost other than the initial fee called the *capitation fee*. Many HMOs are also nonprofit.

Often there is no deductible and no co-insurance, although there may be a copayment for prescription drugs. Unlike in the past, HMOs often offer twenty-four-hour service, even if the person is away from the service district of the HMO in which membership is held. HMOs may require that the enrollee pick up some costs. HMOs may also exclude coverage of things such as cosmetic surgery, some organ transplants, dental care, and custodial services.

Because most of the services are provided without extra charge, HMOs are said to be less inclined to prescribe unnecessary treatment and hospitalization. They must absorb all costs, but in doing so they may limit some services or treatment. However, because the enrollees have prepaid for all services, they may be less reluctant to use HMOs and therefore seek treatment for potential problems early, when treatment is likely to be more successful and less expensive.

When a nonprofit employer is considering a health and medical benefit package, it may be required by law to offer its employees the opportunity to select a federally qualified HMO. This is so (1) when the nonprofit employer has and contributes to a health and medical benefit plan for its employees, (2) if the employer has twenty-five or more employees, (3) if it pays at least the minimum wage, and (4) if a federally qualified HMO in the area where the nonprofit has twenty-five or more employees submits a written request to be considered and if those employees are not presently served by an HMO.[8]

Preferred Providers

This option involves a list of physicians who have agreed to provide services at an agreed upon rate schedule. The enrollee in these plans agrees to see the physicians or dentists on the list first. The employee may be referred to another physician by those on the list. Unlike the traditional HMOs, the employee chooses (but from the names on the list), and the physician or dentist treats without the treatment constraints of the HMO. Point-of-service arrangements allow the employee to go outside the strict HMO service provider but at an additional cost to the employee.

Considerations in Choosing

Recognizing that there is a threshold at which an HMO option must be offered, a nonprofit employer may choose among HMO, preferred provider, or point of service, some combination, an insurance company, or an association of nonprofits that form an insurance pool or multiemployer plan. The choice ought to be made based on the cost to the employer and employee, the package of benefits, the competence of the selling agent, and the experience of others with the equivalent quality of service. Although it is possible for the nonprofit employer to create its own health and medical benefit package or self-insure, this is not recommended. The antidiscrimination laws that are intended to protect lower-earning workers from being excluded and to prevent management from reaping the major benefits are complicated and stiff and apply to self-insured, not to plans with licensed insurance companies. The law presumes that these antidiscrimination restrictions are satisfied if the insuring responsibility falls on a third party (such as the insurance company) rather than on the employer. Moreover, the organization could experience considerable drain on its resources as employees become ill.

In comparing HMOs with other medical and health providers, a criticism that is often heard is that the employee does not have a choice of physicians. This is not altogether true. Physicians may form an HMO among themselves as independent providers. The individual may choose among these physicians and still obtain the benefits of an HMO. Such a group of physicians is referred to as an independent practice association (IPA). Various HMOs may also offer out-of-network service.

COBRA

The Consolidated Omnibus Budget Reconciliation Act of 1985 (COBRA) requires all employers except governments and churches to give employees an extension on health coverage at the point of termination of their employment for any reason, voluntary or involuntary, unless for reasons of gross misconduct. Part or all of the cost of this extension can be shifted to the terminated employee. The ex-employee may be charged a slightly higher premium.

The employer is considered to have a health plan if the employer contributes to premium payments, if the plan is maintained for employees, and if the employee's premium is lower than it would have been on the market. The extension must be for eighteen months. It is for thirty-six months for spouses and dependents due to divorce, death, and legal separation; it may also be for thirty-six months for dependents of the worker who loses dependency status because of turning twenty-five.

Social Security Integration of Medical Plans

The two points of integration of Social Security is with disability, which we have discussed, and with Medicare. We skip discussion of the details of the latter, but point out that it applies only to workers sixty-five years of age or older who have been receiving disability or have kidney defects. Medicare should be considered in the determination of whether the organization wishes to offer postretirement health benefits beyond those required by COBRA.

PENSIONS

The major objective of a pension plan is to provide support for the employee during retirement years. A properly designed pension plan can provide a number of additional benefits, including the deferring of income taxes and the ability to withdraw cash to meet emergencies.

It is possible for a nonprofit to institute a pension plan that would cost it virtually nothing and still benefit employees. Section 403(b), sometimes called TSA for tax-sheltered annuity, was passed by Congress to give nonprofits a special vehicle. Before discussing Section 403(b) in particular, there are some basic principles about pensions that the nonprofit manager ought to know.

Defined Benefits versus Defined Contribution

Pensions are of basically two types: defined benefits and defined contribution. The defined benefit plans stipulate the amount of benefits an employee will receive upon retirement. This may be a flat number of dollars, a percentage of salary earned over the years the employee worked with the nonprofit, a percentage of the employee's final pay, or an amount adjusted for the number of years of service.[9] What is being defined is the benefit to be received several years from now when the employee retires.

Because the benefits to be received upon retirement are stipulated in a defined benefit plan, the nonprofit must resolve an actuarial problem. It must determine how much it has to deposit in each of the remaining working years of the employee so that the promised amount will be available on the date the employee retires.[10] Furthermore, to ensure that the promise will be kept, the nonprofit may have to comply with several regulations, including the need to put up each year sufficient dollars so that future pension obligations can be met. This is called funding future pension obligations. The amount will vary according to the number, age, and life expectancies of workers covered (including those already retired), the amount the pension plan has and is expected to earn, and the amount that is promised to workers at the time of their retirement.

The defined contribution plan differs from the defined benefit plan because it stipulates the amount of contributions that will be made, rather than the amount of benefits to be paid. It is easier to set up and administer and requires less reporting. The only promise that the nonprofit makes is that it will contribute a specified percentage of the employee's salary or a fixed amount of that salary to his or her retirement account each year. The employee chooses how these contributions are to be invested. And each employee has a separate account, rather than being part of a large pool, such as in the defined benefit plan. The Section 403(b) plan, to be discussed later, is a defined contribution plan.

Defined contribution plans are of two types. Money purchase plans make a contribution that is fixed in the sense that it does not depend on the performance of the employee or the organization. The organization may agree to contribute 7 percent or $200 of an employee's salary each month. Alternatively, in profit-sharing or incentive plans, the contribution is based on the fiscal performance of the organization or employees. In addition, the employer may vary the amount contributed each year.

Defined contribution plans that are money purchase plans are usually simpler to administer and therefore are more popular. They are not as regulated by the government as are defined benefit plans and do not require annual estimates about how much the organization must contribute in order to meet its pension promises in the distant future. The only promise is to make an annual contribution of a specific percentage of the worker's base pay.

Another approach is called a target plan. This stands between a defined benefit and a defined contribution plan. In this approach the organization sets a target benefit it would like to meet upon the retirement of the worker and defines its contributions in terms of that target. Unlike the defined benefit plan, however, the organization has no legal obligation to achieve the target.

Contributory versus Noncontributory and Fixed versus Variable

Whether a plan is defined contribution, target, or defined benefit, it may be contributory or noncontributory. A contributory plan provides for the employee to make either voluntary (elective) or mandatory contributions. The latter, which must be set at a low enough level so that all employees may meet it without undue hardship, is simply an amount the employee is required to contribute annually in order to remain in the plan. The voluntary amount is the amount employees may, on their own volition, contribute to build up their accounts.

In a contributory plan, the organization may also make a contribution but in a noncontributory plan, only the organization makes a contribution. The employees make none. This latter approach is often seen as simpler to administer. The contributory plan, however, may have an advantage in that it could be designed to accommodate the employee's savings and individual retirement account (IRA).[11]

The contributions made to the retirement plan may be deposited into a variable or a fixed account as elected by the employee. Deposits into a variable account are used to purchase common stocks, so the rate at which the contributions grow is determined by the growth in value of the stocks.

Contributions made to the fixed account are invested in securities such as bonds and money market funds where there can be some reasonable assurance of earning no less than some specific rate. Insurance companies are willing to guarantee a rate of return for a specified period, and so too are banks on certificates of deposit.

Settlement Options

The employee can maintain a similar distinction between variable and fixed account earnings upon retirement. The first means that each check will reflect the earnings in the stock market; that is, some checks will be higher than others. The fixed amount means that every check will be the same.

The employees may also choose the manner in which they would like to receive payments upon retiring. The entire retirement benefit can be taken in a lump sum, in periodic payments guaranteed either in terms of the number or amount per payment, or in periodic payments that terminate upon the death of the employee or continue after death to a designated survivor. All plans are required to give married employees the option of payments that continue to the surviving spouse upon the death of the retiree. The employee is not required to accept the option, but if the option is rejected, the employee must supply evidence that the spouse accepts this rejection. The aim is to secure a flow of income to a surviving spouse. One reason why the option may be rejected is that the periodic payments are lower than those the worker would obtain under the life option that terminates payments upon the worker's death.

Each option has income-tax and estate-tax implications on which the employee should seek advice.

Rules for Retirement Plan

So far we have discussed the general features of pension plans, but there are also specific rules that must be followed. One set of rules requires annual reporting to the employees on the developments and earnings in the plan during the year, including any pertinent changes. A second set of rules determines whether the plan will be qualified for tax advantages. These rules should be appreciated by managers of nonprofits.

To review the tax benefits, if the plan qualifies, contributions to the retirement plan and earnings of the plan are not taxed to the employee. Taxes are postponed until retirement years, when the worker is supposedly in a lower income bracket. For a young worker twenty-one years of age, taxes could be deferred some forty years until retirement. To be qualified for this tax benefit, the plan must conform to certain rules.

The basic rule is that the plan must not exist only for the benefit of high-salaried workers, directors, managers, trustees, and key supporters (such as disqualified persons discussed earlier). How, then, is eligibility determined?

Aliens, part-time workers, workers who come under a union agreement providing for some other source of coverage, and workers under twenty-one years of age can be excluded automatically from eligibility without fear of violating the rules against discrimination. The effect of this is to reduce the number of persons the organization has to cover and therefore its cost.[12]

Eligibility might be immediate or after one year of service (defined as 1,000 hours of paid employment in a twelve-month period). No more than two years may elapse before the worker becomes eligible. If a two-year waiting period is used, all contributions are 100 percent vested when participation starts, according to the 1986 law. In cases where a defined benefit plan is utilized, the employer is not required to make an employee eligible if that employee is within less than five years of the normal retirement age, which is usually sixty-five.

The reason for putting an upper limit on the defined benefit plan is to avoid placing a financial burden on organizations. For example, if a new worker has only a short time to work before retiring, an organization would have only a short time in which to accumulate the retirement benefits to which it has obligated itself in a defined manner. The amount required, to begin paying a worker

30 percent of his or her final pay for a lifetime only after two years of service, might be very large. This problem does not exist with a defined contribution plan, and such plans do not carry an upper age limit for participation.

The plan must have a vesting schedule. This schedule gives the rate at which the employees acquire ownership over the employer's contributions to their retirement accounts. Note that the vesting schedule refers only to the employer's contributions. All the employees' contributions are 100 percent vested when made. The employees cannot forfeit their contributions.

The 1986 tax law simplified vesting schedules. One provides for 100 percent vesting of all the employer's contributions to the employee's retirement account after five years of service. The other requires vesting of 20 percent after three years, 40 percent at the end of four, 60 percent at the end of five, 80 percent at the end of six, and 100 percent at the end of seven years.[13] This is called the *seven-year minimum vesting schedule.*

An employee can lose vesting credits or eligibility if there is a break in service, that is, if the employee fails to do paid work for the organization for at least 501 hours in a twelve-month period for reasons other than military and jury duty, pregnancy, vacation time, or layoffs. Federal law now requires that people be given a grace period of five years before all previous credits toward vesting or eligibility is lost because of a break in service. Within the five-year period, the employee ought to be able to buy back into the system, picking up all previously earned credits and all credits that may have been accumulated during the break in service.[14]

A pension plan must be permanent unless termination is the result of economic difficulties. Termination of a plan by the employer leads to 100 percent vesting of all accumulated amounts in the employees.

A Funding Agency

A decision has to be made about the funding agency. For most nonprofits, this is done simultaneously with the plan, since they merely accept a prototype plan offered by the company that will manage the funds. These prototype plans permit the organization to fill in certain blanks about eligibility, vesting, and amount of contributions and how the fund is to be invested. In completing these forms, all the above discussions apply. With a defined benefit plan, all the money is placed in one pool and administered by one agency. In a defined contribution plan, each employee has a separate account in his or her name and chooses how that account is managed by the agency. With a 403(b), each employee can choose a different agency (company) to which to have the contributions sent.

There are several alternatives. Banks, mutual funds, and insurance companies are common funding agencies of regular pension plans. With the 403(b), however, banks (unless they sell annuities or mutual funds) are not qualified agents. Insurance companies may offer the widest variations of alternative funding. The best advice to give a manager in selecting among these is to know the services each provides. An insurance company, for example, may have a family of mutual funds and also have a variety of annuities. Nonprofits may also wish to consult association plans.

Social Security Integration of Retirement Plans

Now that nonprofits must participate in the Social Security system, it is wise to integrate the pension plan of the organization with that of the system. Integration of pension plans lowers the organization's costs of providing pension benefits. Basically, what one does in integrating pension systems is to use the Social Security system as a floor. The private plan of the organization provides benefits above that floor. The actual mechanics of accomplishing this depends on whether the plan is a defined benefit or a defined contribution plan. For each, integration is different, but the results are basically the same—using the private system to go beyond the threshold set and paid for by Social Security.

Because participation in the Social Security system was only recently required of nonprofits, workers for these organizations who are fifty-five years of age on January 1, 1984 or older are allowed to retire with full Social Security benefits with fewer years of credit than other workers of the same age who are covered outside the nonprofit sector.

Section 403(b)

Section 403(b) is a special retirement plan for 501(c)(3) organizations available through mutual funds, insurance contracts, and some retirement plans for churches. Only 501(c)(3)s, including public schools, may use this defined contribution plan. Section 403(b) permits nonprofit employers to contribute to a pension contract for their full-time or part-time employees.

Section 403(b) plans have several advantages. The yearly amount contributed by the employer of employee earnings is not taxed until funds are withdrawn. Employees of nonprofits thus get to defer some of their income from present taxes. All employees, regardless of part-time or full-time employment and regardless of age, can be eligible.

Section 403(b) allows withdrawals prior to age fifty-nine and a half without penalty because of death of the worker, disability, early retirement, or medical expenses that are deductible. All other early withdrawals are subject to income tax and a 10 percent penalty.

One disadvantage of the 403(b) is that if on retiring the worker takes all his or her money in one lump sum, he or she is taxed on the entire amount unless it is rolled over into an IRA. But even with an IRA, there is no way to average the income over ten or five years to lower taxes on the lump-sum. To avoid this problem, the worker may wish to take the funds in periodic annual payments, in which case part of the payments will be received free of taxes.

The nonprofit can make a 403(b) plan available to its employees at no cost to the institution, and the organization need not contribute any funds of its own. The contributions can be made through salary reductions, where employees agree to reduce their salaries by a specific amount to be used by the employer to make the contributions.[15] The employee's income for tax purposes is lowered by the amount of the contribution, meaning that this amount is not presently subject to tax—except that it is not excluded in the computation of the Social Security tax. The employee can continue to make contributions while employed, all the while sheltering income and the earnings on the accumulated accounts for taxes. Furthermore, all contributions by the employee and all the interest earned on these amounts are immediately vested at 100 percent. It cannot be forfeited. The employee owns it.

Unlike other retirement plans, the amount that can be contributed through a 403(b) depends on the number of years the employee has worked for the nonprofit in question, length being advantageous because contributions can be made even to reflect back years before the plan went into effect. This is called the *catch-up* feature. Obviously, the greater the number of years, the greater the amount that can be contributed. Annually, a new statutory limit is set on the amount that the employee can contribute. This amount is subject to revision by Congress in order to adjust for inflation.[16]

A worker who wishes to use the 403(b) plan needs to calculate precisely how much he or she can exclude. The annual statutory limit, which is popularly quoted, is the total for all voluntary or elective contributions that the employee makes to all pension plans run by the organization. The fact that this is the statutory elective limit does not mean that any employee may contribute up to that much. For each employee, a specific calculation has to be made. The maximum contribution increases the longer the service and decreases the greater the amount of tax-preferred benefits the employee is already receiving. Publication 571 of the IRS shows how the calculations should be done.

Excess contributions that are not removed before April 15 of the tax year can cause a 15 percent penalty. Church workers have special rules that are especially attractive. For example, even though they may have worked for several churches, they may treat them as one employer, which has the effect of boosting the amount excludable from taxation.

Rabbi Trust

The name derives from the fact that this technique was developed for a rabbi. It is a particular type of retirement plan that is now used widely in corporations (especially where the executives fear an unfriendly takeover), even though it had its legal genesis with a rabbi and his synagogue. Here is how it works. A nonprofit wishes to set up a retirement plan for an executive. If it gives him access to the contributions, he is immediately taxed. If, however, the executive only gets a promise from the nonprofit, then it can be broken, or when he is ready to retire he may discover there are no assets. To protect against this, he has the organization make its contributions to a trust that neither he nor the organization controls. This works for tax purposes, however, as long as the creditors of the organization can have access to the funds should the organization go bankrupt. The objective is to protect the executive against changes in the leadership of the organization and at the same time avoid current taxes to him or her. The law, however, requires protection for the creditors to be superior to that of the organization or the employee.

SIMPLE IRA or 401(k)

Nonprofits are eligible to use the SIMPLE IRA retirement plan—provided that they do not have another deferred compensation plan running at the same time. This plan is particularly suited for the small nonprofit with 100 or fewer employees.

SIMPLE should be considered because it is simple. It involves relatively little paper work, gives both the employer and the employee considerable flexibility, and places the employee in control of all investment decisions. It is particularly useful for small nonprofits or individual independent affiliates of a larger nonprofit. The ERISA nondiscriminatory requirements are not applicable, so the number and rank of employees enrolled is not a consideration. Neither is the vesting nor the extensive disclosure rules of ERISA applicable.

A SIMPLE plan allows an employee of a tax-exempt organization to enter into a written agreement to have his or her compensation reduced each pay period by a specific amount, which is invested in an IRA chosen by the employee and which is in the employee's name. This IRA must be designated by the custodian or trustee as a SIMPLE IRA.

In addition to these elective contributions or salary reduction contributions, an employer must also make a nonelective or a matching contribution to the employee's IRA.

During the sixty days before the beginning of any year, or sixty days before the midyear if the program is to begin at midyear, the employee can choose to request that either a specific dollar amount or percentage of his or her compensation be contributed by the employer to the SIMPLE IRA. Employers do not have to offer the option of a specific dollar amount and they cannot put a lower or upper limit on the percentage contributions except as provided by law. For their part, employees can cancel the request any time during the year.

Assuming that the employer chooses to make a matching rather than a nonelective contribution, the matching contribution must equal the amount chosen as the elective contribution by the employee. All employees choosing an elective contribution must be treated the same. But in no case can the matching contribution exceed 3 percent of the employee's compensation that year. But the matching requirement could fall as low as 1 percent, although this cannot be done for more than two out of five years.

If, however, the employer chooses a nonelective contribution option, the employer must make a contribution to all eligible employees who have at least $5,000 in earnings even if the employees have not chosen a salary reduction option. This distinction is important. A nonelective contribution option requires the employer to make a contribution to all eligible employees without regard to their having to make any contribution themselves. A matching option allows the employer to make contributions only to those who are making contributions on their own behalf.

The amount that can be contributed via the nonelective route is 2 percent of the employee's contribution during the entire year. Any amount exceeding $160,000 of an employee's salary cannot be included in this 2 percent calculation.

Through the use of the matching option, under the current law about the maximum an employee could have contributed is $12,000. This is $6,000 that is the statutory limit on elective contributions plus another $6,000 on a dollar-for-dollar match.

Who are the eligible employees? Employees are eligible if they received $5,000 in compensation from the employer in any two prior years and if they are also expected to receive at least $5,000 in the current year. Those employees covered by a collective bargaining contract or foreign workers who received no income in the United States are excludable by the choice of the employer.

What is important, compensation for the purposes of the SIMPLE include all wages and pay from the employer that are subject to income tax withholding and even amounts that are deferred under plans such as the 401(k), 403(b), or Section 457(b). However, the amount being deferred under these plans must be reduced by the amount being contributed under the salary reduction through the SIMPLE. It is the employee's, not the employer's, responsibility to make sure that these limits are followed.

For tax purposes, distribution to the employee from a SIMPLE is treated just as if it were from a regular IRA. Rollovers from trustee-to-trustee or from custodian-to-custodian are not taxable. But an employee must wait two years after the employer has made its first contribution before rolling over into an ordinary IRA. During this two-year period, however, the employee may rollover from one SIMPLE to another.

When the employee (or his or her estate) takes a distribution from the SIMPLE IRA, all of it is taxed as ordinary income. As in the case of other qualified plans, the employee must begin distributions by April 1 one year after the employee reached age seventy and a half and cannot begin taking distributions before fifty-nine and a half without penalty.

Premature distributions or early withdrawals can be costly if they occur during the two-year period after the employer's first contribution. During this period, the penalty is 25 percent rather than 10. For this purpose, an early withdrawal can occur if a rollover during the two years after the commencement of contributions occurs from a SIMPLE to any other IRA rather than a SIMPLE IRA.

SIMPLE plans are available through mutual funds making available a variety of investment choices, and through insurance companies selling fixed-rate or variable annuities. These products can be obtained from a broker, a bank, or an insurance agent.

The prototype plan that can be used depends upon whether the employer will allow each participant to choose his or her own financial institution for investment or whether the employer will choose one financial institution for all employees. In the first situation, Form 5304–SIMPLE is used and in the second Form 5305. The employer's responsibility is to give sixty days notice before changes in plan and to inform all works about their options and the plan content.

The elective contributions of the employee must be sent to the financial institution within thirty days after the period for which earnings were deferred. The employer's contribution, whether matching or nonelective, must be remitted by the time its taxes are due, including extensions.

The SIMPLE can also be available in the form of a 401(k) rather than in the form of an IRA. It is even possible to convert an existing 401(k) into a SIMPLE 401(k). Such plans must conform to the contribution requirements of the SIMPLE IRA if they are to avoid being top-heavy. A principal advantage of the 401(k) version of the plan is that it does allow for loans.

A "short-term loan" can be gotten with the SIMPLE IRA because the owner is free to take distributions at any time. A distribution that is repaid within sixty days is not taxed. The custodian or trustee, however, may have a penalty for early withdrawal if the IRA is funded through an annuity.

The SIMPLE IRA or 401(k) Compared with Others

The SIMPLE's great advantage is simplicity and, consequently, its lower cost and risks of noncompliance. Here are its specs:

1. It does not require annual reporting to the IRS, only to the employees.

2. It can be operated at zero administrative costs compared with the third-party administrator cost where a 401(k) type program or a 403(b) is used.

3. It does not require any testing for discrimination.

4. It does not require any service hours to be calculated and has no age limit for eligibility. Any person working the previous two years with a

minimum earnings of $5,000 and who is currently expected to receive at least $5,000 in pay is eligible. The employer is free to use a more lenient eligibility rule.

5. Vesting is 100 percent and immediate. There are no schedules to determine how much of the employer's contribution the employees own. It is 100 percent from the day it is made.

6. Integration with Social Security is prohibited, thus making employees better off.

7. The employer has no fiduciary responsibility because the assets are owned by the employee, who makes all investment decisions and who gets an annual or quarterly report from the insurance company or mutual fund in which the assets are invested by his or her choice.

8. Complicated transactions such as loans and the purchase of insurance are disallowed.

9. Currently, the employee can defer up to $6,000. Deferral is not based on a complicated formula.

10. The employer can (a) match up to 100 percent of the amount contributed by the employee but no more than 3 percent of the employee's compensation, (b) contribute up to 2 percent of each eligible employee's compensation when the employee contributes nothing, or (c) instead of 3 percent in (a) the employer matches no less than 1 percent but for no more than two out of five years. The employer must do one of the above.

CAFETERIA PLANS

Cafeteria or flexible plans may be considered by nonprofits as a way of packaging benefits. Cafeteria plans are based on the premise that no two employees may need exactly the same amount of each type of benefit: One employee would prefer more life insurance and less health and hospitalization. Under a cafeteria plan, each employee can tailor his or her own mix among the benefits included in the plan. Each employee creates his or her own package.

With a cafeteria plan, the employer places all nontaxable benefits, including health and life insurance, retirement plans, cash, disability or others, before the employee. Excluded by law are scholarships and taxable fringe benefits discussed later in this chapter. The employee may choose between cash and nontaxable benefits.[17] As in a cafeteria, the employee is given a meal ticket and chooses from a variety of offerings as much as is wanted (within permissible limits).

PROFIT-SHARING PLAN

In more than one ruling, the IRS has stated that a nonprofit may have a profit-sharing plan.[18] These plans are of two major types: bonus or incentive plans, or savings and retirement plans. Basically, the bonus or incentive plans are those that compensate employees on a percentage basis, that is, a percentage of the revenues or cost savings to the organization.

The term *profit sharing* does not mean that it comes from a profit, although prior to the 1986 changes that was basically true. It means that the employer can have annual discretion about how much to contribute and this may vary from zero to some percentage. It also means that the contribution is based on the performance of the organization, unlike money purchase plans, in which the amount is fixed and must be contributed without regard to the performance of the organization. Profit-sharing plans are thus ideal for incentive programs.

A study of one plan approved by the IRS suggests that the plan should have the following properties:[19]

1. The bonus should not make the total compensation of the employee (regular salary and benefits combined) unreasonable compared with another person with similar education and experience in a similar position in a comparable nonprofit in the same geographic area.

2. The organization should not deviate from its tax-exempt mission, and benefits should not inure to private persons. Hence, an unreasonable compensation or one that is solely for the benefit of certain managers unrelated to their performance may be construed as a plan to promote their private welfare at the expense of the mission.

3. The mission should be based on some indicator that proffers benefits to others, such as a bonus plan based on cost savings to patients or clients so that they, too, are beneficiaries.

4. The plan should be so calibrated that if the performance is not achieved, the incentive or bonus payments will not be made.[20]

Two experts caution that the plan should also have the following properties:[21]

1. The organization's management should be omitted from the plan so as to remove suspicion that the plan is to serve them.

2. The plan should be established as a result of an arm's length negotiation between the management and workers of the organization.

3. The plan should contain a statement of how it will help the organization advance its tax-exempt status.

4. There should be a limitation on how much each person can receive in a period so that no one will be unreasonably compensated.

5. There should be a formula for calculating the benefits so they do not result in increasing prices and charges to the public.

6. There should be a system of annually comparing the compensation with those in other organizations to maintain reasonableness in compensation and in the quality and quantity of services being provided.

FRINGE BENEFITS

There are a number of other benefits that a nonprofit employer might offer. These include loans, to the extent that they are permitted by state law and the bylaws. These loans should require repayment, not be habitual to the same persons, charge an interest rate comparable to the rate being paid by the federal government for loans of similar term (which would still be better than what the borrower would have to pay commercially), be reported, require repayment in full by some specific but reasonable date, and be reasonably small, perhaps less than $10,000. Such loans need to be made on a business-like basis. Again, beware of self-dealing and prohibited acts as discussed in Chapter Four. Recall that in Chapter Six we noted that personal loans to trustees are prohibited in many states.

Other benefits include discounts such as tuition, child care, and legal assistance. The objective should be to provide these without causing a tax liability for the employee. How can that be done? By falling into one or more of the following general categories:

1. Employers, the nonprofits, can give services and products to employees, dependents, and retirees without causing them to be taxed as long as there is no additional cost to the nonprofit for doing so and as long as they are made available to all employees on equal basis. The service or product must be in the line in which the employee works. In a nonprofit school, for example, all children and spouses of professors (active and retired) could be given free education without causing that part of the tuition that does not exceed $5,000 to be included in the incomes of these professors. This rule does not require that the gift be exercised at the school offering the fringe benefit.

2. The nonprofit can give equal discounts to all present and retired employees, their dependents, and spouses as long as the discount does not exceed 20 percent of the selling price to customers and does not exceed the amount by which it had marked up the goods in order to have a profit. Theoretically, then, a university could give every one of these persons a discount that conform with these rules without anyone having to report this as income.

3. The nonprofit can offer what is known as *working condition fringes,* benefits of things that would otherwise be deductible, such as uniforms, had the employee purchased it himself or herself. Again, all employees must be treated alike if any is to avoid being taxed.

4. *De minimis:* Some things are so small that nobody fusses. Try to avoid getting above $25.00.

Two types of assistance are worthy of special mention. Educational assistance that falls into any category mentioned above cannot be for graduate school or for dependent children under twenty-five. Generally, preferential treatment of the cost of dependent (child) care is not available to a one-earner family unless the nondependent employee who is the one-earner is disabled or a student.

Adoption Assistance Programs

Adoption assistance programs are not included in the employee's wages, but social security and Medicare taxes must be paid on the value of the assistance given to the employee. The program must have a plan statement that is available to all employees except those excluded by collective agreement contracts. The program must not favor highly compensated employees. These are the top 5 percent employees and persons making over a specified amount set by the IRS periodically. The employees must provide evidence of adoption-related payments.

The Treatment of Thirteen Other Specific Benefits

A fringe benefit is a form of pay made to an individual because of some service performed. The recipient of the fringe benefit may be the person performing the service or a relative of the person. Generally, fringe benefits must be included in an employee's pay and subject to income and employment taxes on the employee. But the following fringe benefits may be excluded from the employee's pay.

1. The use of a car.

2. Airplane flights.

3. Discounts on property or services.

4. Memberships in country and social clubs.

5. Tickets to entertainment or sporting events.

6. Meals furnished to employees because it is convenient for the organization to do so; that is, to keep the employee at his or her task during lunch, late evenings, on weekends.

7. A no-additional-cost service or one that is provided the employee at no cost greater than providing that service to customers. This category of

services usually is the result of sharing unused capacity with the employees; for example, a hospital allowing its employees services of an unused bed at a zero or discounted rate. Employers may have written contracts among themselves to offer these services to the employees of each other. But the service must be the same type provided customers in the organization in which the employee works and the one that is providing the no-additional-cost service. No-additional-cost benefits may be available to the employee, a retired or disabled employee, a dependent child (under twenty-five years of age) or a surviving spouse who died while employed by the organization or who stopped working because of a job-related disability.

8. A qualified employee discount on services or property offered customers during the ordinary course of business of the organization. Property held for investment does not qualify. In general, the discount on a service should not exceed 20 percent of the amount customers pay. For property, the discount cannot exceed the price you charge customers minus the amount of your profit included in that price.

9. As stated earlier, working condition fringes are those that an employee (or independent contractor) or a trustee would deduct if it had been included in their pay. What are specific examples? An organization that pays a stipend to advisory board members would not include parking expenses paid as part of the stipend paid because this amount would be deductible by the advisory board member as an expense associated with deriving that stipend. Among the types of benefits that can fall under this category of working condition fringes are educational assistance, outplacement services (if this benefits the organization by avoiding a wrongful termination suit, or by increasing the employee morale or organization's image), and the personal use of a vehicle by the employee if the vehicle is clearly marked with the organization's name.

10. As earlier stated, *de minimis* fringe benefits are also not included in the employee's taxable wage because they are so insignificantly small. What are specific examples? These include coffee and doughnuts, occasional tickets to entertainment events, occasional parties or meals, or transportation fare or gifts that are not expensive. Also included are picnics or even a group term life insurance policy on the employee or his or her spouse so long as it is not for more than $2,000. Cash is never a *de minimis* gift unless it is paid for purposes such as transportation or meal expenses.

11. Commuter transit pass, parking expenses, rides on commuter highway vehicles of any type that seats six or more persons. These can be

excluded even though they are being provided in place of paying the employee an equivalent amount. These payments cannot be provided to independent contractors and the maximum amount that can be excluded from the employee's pay is set periodically by law.

12. Qualified moving expenses covering the transportation of household goods and personal effects and the travel expenses associated with moving.

13. The use of on-premises athletic facilities made available only to employees and their families, not to the general public or through the sale of membership, are also excluded.

Creating the Fringe Benefits Package

In making the preceding fringes available, there are some general rules that should be followed. These include making them subject to a written plan. Make the plan available to all full-time employees. Leased employees (those hired to replace a full-time employee for a period of twelve months or more) are also eligible. Therefore, for each benefit, determine how the word "employee" is defined in law relating to that specific benefit. If the organization has a profit-making subsidiary or significant unrelated business income, the expenses associated with the benefits may be deductible as business expenses by the subsidiary or against the unrelated business income to the extent that they cover employees engaged in these activities. Finally, the fact that the benefit is not included in the employee income and therefore is free of income tax does not mean that the employee may not have to pay social security and Medicare tax on them.

Fringe benefits are a way of increasing employee morale and retention. They are ways of providing benefits at lower cost than the employee could have gotten them. The savings come from a combination of convenience, discounts, lower taxes. These expenses to the organization can be covered as part of overhead or indirect costs and are therefore chargeable to contracts.

Finally, there is no general rule that precludes the number of fringe benefits that may be offered employees. These important principles should be taken into account. First, fringe benefits are not cost-free to the organization. The package must be priced. But most contracts with governments would cover their portion of these costs. (See Chapter Fourteen.) Second, a fringe benefit should be installed or maintained only to the extent that there is a clear indication that it is not for self-dealing or discriminatory in favor of certain employees. If it is, the fringe should be included in their taxable earnings. Third, the fringe benefit package must be included in the calculation of reasonable earnings. To the extent that this amount is exceeded, self-dealing and excess compensation penalties, as discussed earlier in this chapter, apply.

ERISA AND IRS RULES

Any employee welfare or pension plan that is operated by an employer, whether in the for-profit or nonprofit sector, is subject to the rules of the Employee Retirement and Income Security Act of 1974 (ERISA) unless the program is for an employer with less than 100 employees or, if 100 or larger, the program is for a select group of executives or the program is financed through a licensed insurance company; or is based purely on unenforceable promises and not on actual contributions of cash or property; or the employer simply pays the employee directly out of the assets of the organization.

This means that many employee benefit or pension plans run by nonprofits are subject to ERISA rules on disclosure, requiring that specific information be shared with the employees about how the plan operates. ERISA also will subject the organization to annual reporting to the Secretary of Labor (the Form 5500 for pensions) and also hold the organization, its trustees, and all others involved in administering the plan to fiduciary rules very much as we discussed in Chapters Four and Five. These later rules also contain prohibited transactions very much as in those chapters.

In addition to its zero cost to employer, 403(b) plans can fall outside of ERISA (which we shall discuss later) requirements for disclosure, reporting, and fiduciary because they need not technically be operated by the nonprofit. By this is meant the following:

1. Participation is voluntary.
2. The employee or his or her designee are the only ones who can control the accounts, since each person has a separate account of his or her choosing.
3. The nonprofit is not paid and receives no benefits from having the plan.
4. The employer does not limit which mutual fund or insurance contract an employee may use except for purely administrative reasons.
5. The employer's sole role is to deduct the contributions and transmit the funds to the company chosen by the employee.

Pension and employee welfare plans are tax-exempt organizations operating under private foundation rules. Hence, before undertaking any major employee benefit program, inquire whether ERISA applies. SIMPLE plans are exempt from ERISA by law. The Department of Labor has prepared a list of exceptions to ERISA.

The second set of rules comes from the IRS. Failure to meet them means that the recipients of these benefits are taxed, not the organization, which is not generally taxed anyway. With retirement and pension plans, discrimination (when the plan is top-heavy with highly paid employees and underrepresented by non-highly paid employees) also means that the vesting schedule must provide for 100 percent vesting at the end of three years. This represents a potential cost to the organization, which is the amount that it would have retrieved into the plan for those employees who would normally have left at the end of three years.

An important IRS rule has to do with discrimination. This has nothing to do necessarily with race, gender, sexual preference, or religion, although these types of discrimination are illegal for pension-planning purposes. It has to do with whether highly paid persons are preferred in (1) eligibility, (2) contributions, or (3) benefits—any or all three of these. Are lower-paid workers being discriminated against? This is defined differently for each type of benefit. Let us take two of the three most common.

Discrimination in Medical Benefits

Currently, a health insurance program that is through a licensed insurance company is exempt and does not have to meet a discrimination test. A self-insured organization must. Since few nonprofits would be self-insured for medical benefits, let's go to pension plans.

Discrimination in Pension Plans

The general rule for pension plans is that 70 percent of the nonhighly compensated employees must be covered and 70 percent of all those who are covered by the plan must be nonhighly compensated employees. Hence, both the recruiting and enrollment pool must have participation by nonhighly compensated employees.

On the 403(b), the rules are very simple if the contributions are based purely on an agreement to reduce the employee's income. Then the rules say that all employees must be afforded the same opportunity, and all should be able to reduce this contribution by $200 per year. These are easy to meet by having the board pass a resolution instituting the plan and informing all employees by newsletter or employee handbook of their rights to participate and not setting any organizational limits on contributions, except to advise on IRS limits. It can be even easier. The organization honors the request of the employee to reduce his or her salary and sends it to the mutual fund or insurance agency.

For 403(b) plans that permit other contributions, the rules are more difficult. Other contributions (called *nonelective contributions*) such as matching contributions by the employer or additional contributions (other than income reduction) by the employees are of concern. For example, because the 403(b) is such a good tax-saving device, an employee may wish to periodically add more money to it, that is, after-tax savings, but higher-paid persons are in a better position to do so. Moreover, if matching is permitted, then executives can set higher matches for themselves, and because they can afford to reduce their income more easily than lower-income employees can, they could reap greater benefit. For these reasons, the discrimination rules when these types of non-elective contributions are permitted in the 403(b) plan are tighter. They are described in IRS Notice 89–23 of February 7, 1989.

Discrimination in Group Term Life

The group term plan is discriminatory unless 70 percent of all employees benefit, 85 percent of all employees participating are not upper paid, the plan satisfies the rule for a cafeteria plan, and the IRS approves the classification of employees.

To Discriminate or Not

In deciding on eligibility, contribution, and benefit, the nonprofit must make the decision based on several factors, including cost, purpose, employee morale, ethics. In most instances, a nondiscrimination policy would be preferred by all employees. Yet the overall compensation of key executives should exceed those of other persons. Some benefits such as permanent insurance, split-dollar insurance, rabbi trusts, and disability are justifiably used for meeting this objective of higher pay for greater responsibility. When they are so used, the tax consequence falls on the executive. Yet having that benefit at a very low cost makes the tax worth it. Some plans allow pension preferences by age or by class of employees.

Avoiding Discrimination

Should the decision be to avoid discrimination, there are certain broad beginning points. Require everyone to participate once the minimum legal eligibility requirements are met. Make the cost to the employee for his or her coverage zero; that is, make the plan noncontributory, making the employee's ability to pay irrelevant and therefore not a barrier to participation. The organization pays all.

Use the same contract for all employees. Have contributions based on a similar percentage of compensation up to legal limits. Accordingly, the Boys and Girls Clubs of America "has a noncontributory defined contribution pension plan, called a money purchase plan, covering all eligible employees. Each employee receives the pension purchasable by funds accumulated from annual contributions based on a percentage of compensation."[22]

TEN STEPS TO SETTING UP THE BENEFIT PACKAGE

1. Create a list of compulsory benefits (workmen's compensation and Social Security) and their costs.
2. Prepare a similar list of optional benefits, discussed in this chapter.

3. Commit the organization to the compulsory benefits.

4. Put priority on a health package and apply the cost control measures discussed.

5. Consider group term life insurance rather than permanent, except as an executive perk.

6. If resources do not permit a contribution by the nonprofit to a pension plan, do a 403(b) based only on salary reduction or try a SIMPLE.

7. Minimize exposure to discrimination (if benefit is not an executive perk or too costly) by making participation compulsory once the legally required age and service requirements are met, by using the same contract for managers and low-paid persons, and also by making it noncontributory so that affordability is not an impediment.

8. Give employees choices.

9. Seek outside advice and benefit from the experiences of other organizations. Make the entire package reasonable.

10. Get the vote of the trustees and make their resolution to establish the benefit part of the organization's permanent minutes.

INDEPENDENT CONTRACTORS AND SOCIAL SECURITY

The preceding section was about employees. Employment taxes such as Social Security and unemployment, the cost of some liability insurance, and benefits, including worker's compensation, can be avoided by contracting for services in lieu of hiring employees. Note, however, that the organization must file as part of its annual 990 Form a report on the five highest-paid independent contractors who, individually, receive $30,000 or more from the organization and at tax time it must file a Form 1099 with the IRS and the employee. A 1099, unlike its employee equivalent, a W2, shows only payments to the contractor—not deductions for benefits, Social Security, and state, local, and federal income taxes. For a contractor, the organization pays none of these.

Whether a person is an independent contractor or an employee depends on the facts and circumstances of the specific case. The IRS, through Revised Ruling 87–41, gives the following guidelines to help in the determination. A person may be presumed to be an employee if the organization:

1. Specifies the time, place, method, and person who is to do the job

2. Trains the person to do the job

3. Requires the person to do the job himself or herself

4. Hires others to assist the person who is doing the job

5. Integrates a person into its staff

6. Has a long-standing work relationship with that person even though it may be irregular

7. Sets the hours of work of the person

8. Requires the person to work full time

9. Requires or permits the person to work on its premises

10. Determines the sequence of work the person does

11. Requires oral or written reports from the person

12. Pays the person on a regular and periodic basis, for example, weekly

13. Pays the person's business or travel expenses

14. Furnishes the person tools, equipment, or materials

15. Maintains the right to fire, assign, or discharge the person

16. Has the right to terminate the contract without liability for breach and if the person

17. Has no other customers

18. Makes no attempt to get other customers

19. Makes no profit or losses

20. Has no investment in himself or herself as a business

These latter conditions (17–20) help make sense of the sixteen points that preceded them. To illustrate, take the surgeon. He or she may be an independent contractor even though the hospital provides the beds of the patients, the operating room, and equipment and schedules when the operation may take place. Moreover, the hospital may write and enforce operating rules governing which procedures he or she may conduct within its facilities and it may terminate its affiliation with the surgeon. In short, with the surgeon, most of the fifteen rules would be violated just because of how hospitals and surgeons conventionally operate.

In spite of all this, the surgeon could be, as probably most are, an independent contractor because the four conditions become operative. A surgeon who is an independent contractor works in more than one hospital, reports profits or losses either through his or her closely held professional corporation, or is allocated his or her share of profits or losses by a partnership, or is paid directly as a sole proprietor. The office employees of the independent contractor surgeon are paid by his or her business—not as employees of the hospital.

Now, in all of these cases, common sense must prevail and the facts and circumstances must override motivation. A person may prefer to be treated as a contractor rather than an employee because that allows the deduction of travel and other related expenses. In addition, if, as is sadly true of so many not-for-profits, the organization provides no retirement or medical benefits, the individual may be better off being a contractor, since a tax-advantaged retirement and medical account could be set up by him or her.

Obviously, organizations may prefer a contractor's status in order to lower employee costs if it does provide these benefits. But these motivations are irrelevant to the facts and circumstances of judging if the person is a contractor from the point of view of Social Security. It should be emphasized that it is thoroughly possible for a person to be an independent contractor for the purposes of liability and yet be an employee for Social Security reasons.

Remember, unlike other retirement plans, a nonprofit cannot elect not to participate in Social Security. Unlike other retirement plans, it cannot declare a part-time or unionized or nonresident alien employee ineligible. Unless the organization is exempt (usually for specific religious reasons) it pays Social Security for every employee it paid $100 or more. The only operative question is who is an employee? When in doubt, begin with the above self-administered test.

Ironically, many organizations that may claim that their relationship with a person is one of an independent contractor will discover, at the time of judgment, that they probably made the most fundamental mistake—forgetting to have written a contract that unequivocally proves independent contractor status. Or they may have a perfectly sound contract written by a competent attorney but which the organization contradicts in its actions.

SUMMARY AND PREVIEW

Nonprofits must compete for competent workers. To do this they must devise benefit packages enabling them to attract and retain such workers while controlling costs. This chapter describes various elements of a benefit package. The options are so wide open that there is little reason for a nonprofit not to provide most of these benefits to their employees. Benefits are a form of insurance for the employees as well as the organization. But the organization is exposed to other risks, many caused by errant management. These are the subject of the next chapter.

CHAPTER FOURTEEN

Managing Against Claims
of Negligence and Harassment

A risk is the probability that an event will occur and will result in losses. In the case of negligence and harassment, subjects of this chapter, the relevant loss is personal injury. Nonprofit organizations are exposed to many types of risks that lead to personal injury. Some risks relate to actions or inactions of the organization's agents or representatives. These include workers, volunteers, trustees, and officers. Another set of risks of personal injury arises from the organization's owning or leasing property, including furniture, swimming pools, and buildings. Nonprofits that produce a product are subject to liability from personal injuries that the product may cause. Furthermore, managers expose the organization by the way they treat employees, volunteers, and clients. They also expose the organization to economic losses by mismanaging contracts where the risks of doing so are highly foreseeable by a well-informed manager.

What are the legal risks the organization faces?

How can management lower these risks?

What are the legal shields that protect the organization?

Risk management has become a very important topic among nonprofit managers because many have been sued, because of the cost of insurance, and because without a risk management policy trustees and volunteers are harder to get and some of their facilities are better off closed.

THE BASICS OF RISK MANAGEMENT

Risk management encompasses the following steps:

1. *Identification:* Identify the organizational factors and events that can cause personal injury. In a day-care operation, there are risks of injury to children resulting from lack of supervision, from molestation, or through defects in facilities. In a building there may be fire, lead paint, and asbestos.

2. *Risk evaluation:* How likely is it to occur and what will it cost the organization if it does?

3. *Decision:* Decide on a policy for dealing with each risk.

4. *Implementation:* Once the policy for dealing with each risk is decided on, implement the policy.

5. *Evaluation:* Finally, periodically evaluate and adjust policy to fit experience and expectations of the future. Experience may teach that the risk is either greater or less than thought, that the policy for dealing with it is inadequate or improperly implemented, or that there are new risks not anticipated.

Now, let's go back to item 3. What are our policy options? The options for dealing with a risk are the following:

1. *Ignore it.* This is a perfectly rational policy if the risk is very unlikely to occur or if the cost would be manageable. To ignore a risk is to assume a risk because every event has the potential of being worse than anticipated and of inviting a suit, even though trivial. To ignore a risk without evaluating it in light of its serious consequences is, however, stupid, even though it is impossible to defend against all conceivable events.

2. *Reduce it.* This policy is always wise. Use of protective garments and doing background checks of school staff and armed guards in a museum are ways of reducing risks.

3. *Transfer it.* The risk may be transferred in toto or shared. Obtaining an insurance policy causes the risk to be shared with an insurance company's other policy holders. A school or day-care center that requires parents to provide transportation for their children to and from the school transfers risks associated with busing to the parents. Another way to transfer risk is to form a separate corporation to conduct the activity that is deemed risky (see Chapters Thirteen and Nineteen).

4. *Retain it.* Agree to be totally responsible. To ignore a risk is equivalent to retaining it. But many risks are purposefully retained as a matter of policy. Sick leave pay is an example of a risk that the nonprofit consciously retains.

5. *Avoid it.* It is impossible to run an organization and avoid all risks. Some risks, such as the example of the parents bringing and taking the children from school, are ways of avoiding a specific risk. All risks cannot be avoided. Risks are a part of life.

A Simplified Approach to Risk Identification and Intervention

Refer to Figure 14.1. We can divide the performance of an organization into three sets of intervention points. The first point is at the intake of clients, personnel, supplies, materials (equipment), and visitors. We could view this initial point as an intake valve. Before turning it on, set quality and flow conditions: accept only supplies, equipment, and clients that minimize risks, and set up rules so that high-risk individuals who are accepted are well and properly served but do not exacerbate the risks to themselves or to others.

For many nonprofits, risk taking at the intake point is endemic to the mission. This is obviously true of those that deal with the infirm, the elderly, and with children. Certain risks are commonly associated with these groups, and other risks with other groups. To have a mission attending the infirm means exposure to certain foreseeable risks. The handicapped can fall, the ill die, and so on. The theory of *adverse selection* says that people at risk will, disproportionately to others, seek inclusion where that risk gets attention. Accordingly, a nonprofit

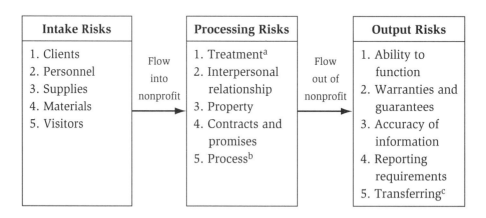

Figure 14.1. Path of Risk Taking.

[a] Treatment includes training or anything done to the input.

[b] Process means the method of treatment; the treatment may be proper but the process is not, or vice versa. The excision of a malignant tumor may be indicated, but the procedure used is riskier than others.

[c] An example is transporting a child from school to home.

that has a mission of caring for a specific risk will attract a disproportionate number of people with that risk. Clearly, risk avoidance is nearly inconsistent with mission compliance. Under these circumstances, minimization of negligent or careless occurrences is doubly important. It is an obligation of the organization to itself as well as to its clients.

Adverse selection makes insurance expensive for many nonprofits. As a rule, their missions are inherently risky. This is so even in a seemingly benign mission such as economic development. Homes can be destroyed by fire. Stores can be robbed. A pedestrian can fall into a pothole.

A second intervention point in the path of risk taking is the processing point. Here the organization is doing its thing. Before starting, set conditions and rules that reduce the probability that the processing will be injurious. Adjust conditions so that the child or senior citizen will not fall from a badly kept platform or so the nurse will be less prone to administer a fatal dose unintentionally.

The third intervention point is the output. Supposedly, the organization has completed its work or the person is no longer under its aegis. But this stage does not free the organization from risk; for example, a child may contract hepatitis in school and discover it at home. As we shall see, it is not necessarily where the event is discovered that matters but that there is a cause-and-effect connection between an event and an injury, making the event what lawyers call a *proximate cause*. Hospitals protect themselves against one type of this risk by using a wheelchair for patients being released, even though they can walk. They escort them to a car—off the premises.

TYPES OF RISKS

Another approach to managing risks is to look at the types as opposed to the specific risks associated with each and every activity. In the following pages we discuss three types of risks of personal injury that are common to nonprofits. These include risks associated with persons who are agents or representatives of the organization, that is, officers, employees, volunteers, and trustees. We shall also discuss risks associated with property and products.

RISKS ASSOCIATED WITH AGENTS AND REPRESENTATIVES

To understand risks associated with agents or representatives—be they volunteers, officers, employees, or trustees—it is necessary to appreciate some rules concerning the concept of agent. An *agent* is someone who is empowered to act on behalf of another, called the *principal*. That empowerment may emanate from an apparent, an actual, or an implied authority conferred by the organization (the principal) to the agent.

The words apparent and implied are not synonyms. A hospital that permits an orderly to dress and act like a physician or a nurse takes the risk of a presumption by a patient that the orderly is a nurse or a physician and therefore may act as one. A hospital that hires a physician or nurse implies that he or she is trained to perform certain technical functions.

A hospital in Alabama hired a practical nurse and assigned her the duties of a circulating nurse, which by common hospital practice must be a registered (RN) rather than a licensed practical nurse (LPN). A surgeon gave her (the LPN) duties common to a circulating nurse for a particular patient. The patient died. The hospital was found negligent but the surgeon was not. The court ruled that surgeons do not normally check the credentials of nurses who circulate. Both the surgeon and the patient had the right to assume that the hospital did, for it was its duty to do so.[1]

Agents have actual, apparent, and implied powers to act on behalf of principals, that is, an employee on behalf of the organization. Hence, in identifying risks, the organization (the principal) must look at the apparent, implied, and actual powers it gives all its agents to act on its behalf. The organization would be barred (estopped) from denying that its agents have these powers if it has permitted them to act as though such powers were conferred. In short, the hospital cannot have orderlies act as though they were physicians or nurses and then, when something goes wrong, tell patients that they had no right to presume that these persons had such power or authority.

Risks Associated with Employees as Agents

There are specific risks to which employees expose a nonprofit. An employee is defined as someone who is under the control and direction of an employer and who works to further the employer's business purpose. Once courts were reluctant to hold nonprofits liable for their employees or volunteers, arguing that neither worked to serve the business purpose of the nonprofit and also because of the fear that damages would destroy nonprofits and discourage volunteerism or employees. We shall discuss federal immunity of volunteers later. States commonly do not limit liability where the act of the volunteer is willful or intentional.

What kinds of risks do employees create? Employees create a potential liability for a nonprofit because the nonprofit hires, pays, directs, and supervises them. Therefore, it is responsible for their actions when these employees are performing job-related duties and when in the performance of these duties they cause personal injury to others. The most common form of liability for its employees, therefore, is called *respondeat superior,* which means that the employee has a servant-master relationship with the employer.

To be liable under *respondeat superior,* the employer-employee relationship must exist, the employee must cause the injury while performing the duties required by the employer, and the negligence (action or inaction) of the employee must be the connecting cause, called the *proximate cause,* of the personal injury.

The above examples show that nonprofits have at least one way of minimizing this risk growing out of *respondeat superior* and that is to contract out activities where the probability of personal injury to anyone is high. Other measures are to make sure that employees are properly trained, procedures are properly developed and carried out, and all employees are competently supervised.

Having an independent contractor does not mean that the nonprofit escapes all liability; it may escape it under the theory of *respondeat superior* and still be liable. A drug dealer was given staff privileges as a physician in a Florida hospital. The "physician" was not an employee but an independent contractor, as are many physicians, who have privileges to hospitalize and treat their patients. A patient under this man's care died. His estate sued and won. The court held that the hospital had a duty to select and retain competent physicians.[2]

Negligent hiring is another risk a nonprofit faces from having employees. Here the risk derives from the hiring practice. The nonprofit employer may not be negligently at fault for what the employee did, but for having hired that person to carry out the function. Clearly, the best way to protect against this charge is to hire competent people whose relevant backgrounds are checked. Day-care centers face this risk if they hire someone who turns out to be a child molester. In avoiding liability for negligent hiring, it is not necessary, for example, to do a complete check, but it is important that checks that would unveil facts relevant to foreseeable dangers be done.

Keeping an employee in a position after the lack of qualification is uncovered exposes the nonprofit employer to *negligent retention.* Here the risk derives from the failure to dismiss that person or stop that person from discharging certain functions on behalf of the nonprofit. This risk is easily avoided. Fire the person or stop him from doing the task for which he is a misfit. Of course, the employee could then sue for discrimination, improper discharge, defamation, and so forth. Risk management is often the substitution of one risk for another.

Finally, nonprofits as employers are exposed to a risk called *negligent entrustment.* This risk does not require that the person be an employee. It has to do with permitting someone to use equipment or a tool for which that person has no skill or competence. Letting a person (stranger or employee) drive a car or use an x-ray machine are possible examples.

In all these types of risks, the evidence must demonstrate a proximate cause. That is, there must be a clear connection between the negligence and the injury. A common defense, therefore, against claims of negligence is to suggest that something else caused the injury. When evidence is not clear, however, the nonprofit could be found liable under the principle known as *res ipsa loquitor.* This is Latin for "it could only have happened by negligence."

To illustrate, a patient went to a New York hospital to have foot surgery. The patient entered the hospital with all her natural teeth. She came out of surgery with them missing. I swear this is true. The court ruled negligence under *res ipsa loquitor.* It concluded that it is not normal for a patient to lose all her natural teeth when having foot surgery, so negligence must have occurred in that operating room.[3] That makes sense to me.

PROTECTING AGAINST LIABILITY OF INDEPENDENT CONTRACTORS

Because nonprofits do so much outsourcing and because the previous paragraphs do connote that an independent contractor could expose the organization to less risk than an employee, we need to elaborate. An employee is an agent. What is an agent? An *agent* is someone who has the authority (a) to act on behalf of, (b) who is controlled by, and (c) who acts with the mutual consent of the *principal*—the organization or person on whose behalf the agent acts. When these conditions hold, whether expressly or implied by the nature of the relationship, your contractor is really your agent and therefore you are directly liable when that person is acting on your behalf. Not only can you be sued by a third party to whom this person does damage, but you cannot in turn sue the agent to recover your losses.

Furthermore, in some cases you can be held *vicariously* liable for the actions of an independent contractor. For example, if the work to be done by the contractor is particularly hazardous to others, you must exercise due diligence in selecting that contractor. We saw that rule applied in one of the cases above. You may also be vicariously liable if, given the hazards of the work to be done, you failed to take due precaution to protect others. And there is what the lawyers refer to as *nondelegable duty,* which means that the facts show that the danger is endemic in your activity and the resulting damage might have occurred whether it was this contractor or any other competent person doing the work. The responsibility is yours. All said, a contract with an independent contractor should include certain items to protect against exposure to liability associated with independent contractors:

1. A limitation on any authority, implied or expressed, beyond that needed to do the job.

2. A limitation on the amount of control the organization exercises over the independent contractor.

3. A careful definition of the job to be done, when and where, and the responsibility of the independent contractor to choose and compensate the workers.

4. A statement of compensation for the job.

5. A declaration of your right to be held harmless (not responsible) for certain events and to be indemnified (paid) if the contractor does certain harm.

6. A declaration that the contractor is responsible for paying all taxes and insurance.

7. A declaration that the person who signs the contract is acting as a dutifully empowered agent of himself or herself, or the company, to do the job.

8. An affidavit or proof that the independent contractor has the required licenses, permits, and insurance.

Risks Associated with Property

Owners or occupiers of property face certain risks. Nonprofits own buildings and run swimming pools, playgrounds, stadiums, dormitories, and so on. What are their risks? Clearly, they take risks of damage and destruction to the building as well as misuse. But they also have certain duties to those who use that property. Hence, a major source of risk is that they would negligently fail to comply with those duties.

Who are the users of property and what duty does the nonprofit have to them? One user is a *trespasser.* Even though this person is an uninvited guest and comes on the property without permission and for his or her own purpose, the nonprofit still has a duty not to injure that person. The nonprofit does not have a duty to keep the place safe for the use of a trespasser. But it cannot injure or create opportunities for that person to injure himself or herself, that is, as a penalty for trespassing.

The situation is very different with other users. A *licensee* is someone who comes on the property with the expressed or implied consent of the owner but for his or her own purposes. This category of user includes sales people and social guests, such as off-campus students coming to a fraternity party.

The duty of the nonprofit to *licensees* is to warn them of hidden but foreseeable dangers. Three words are important in the preceding sentence: *warn, hidden,* and *foreseeable.* The nonprofit has to warn of (not necessarily correct) the danger; the licensee takes his or her own risk with visible dangers; but the nonprofit must warn of those dangers that are not visible but that are foreseeable—can be reasonably expected by it.

Most persons who come on to a property, however, do so because they are invited as clients, members, or students, or to provide security and repairs, or to attend lectures or an exhibition, and so on. The nonprofit occupier has its strongest duty to these *invitees.* Basically, invitees have a right to assume that the organization would not invite them to a place that was dangerous without forewarning them. They also have a right to assume that the organization would take all prudent and reasonable steps to remove or correct all dangers.

There are special relationships, each implying a duty of the nonprofit to the invitee. Hence, before the courts decided that students were grown-ups who came to colleges and universities for education rather than in search of parental care, these institutions were said to have had a special relationship known as *loco parentis*. In essence, the college took the place of the parents and had a duty to act as if it were the parent.

Both students and colleges are glad that this duty has all but disappeared. Nevertheless, the college may have a special relationship to students and others even though they cannot invoke *loco parentis*.[4] Hence, a court found Montana State University liable because a minor in a teenage program got drunk and died in an accident. The court held that the university should have supervised these students because they were minors.[5] In another case of a "special relationship," a court held the University of Kansas liable because a person fell and got injured while visiting a student. The court held that the university had a duty to keep the hallway safe.[6] It had a special duty to the students and their guests.

Nonprofits that have tenants have a duty to them because of the relationship of landlord to tenant. The landlord does not have a duty to the tenant beyond turning the property over and calling the tenant's attention to any latent or hidden but foreseeable danger. Again, *foreseeable* implies that there are reasons to expect a perilous event or situation. Therefore, the State University of New York at Stony Brook was found liable for the repeated rape of a student. The court held that it had a duty to warn students because, in this case, the peril was foreseeable. There had been several complaints about strangers roaming through the dormitory prior to the rape.[7]

The occupier of the property also has a duty to children who may be attracted to the property. This is called the *attractive nuisance* doctrine. Basically, this requires that a child be attracted to a danger on a property where the conditions leading to an injury are not purely based on nature and where the occupier, but not the child, could foresee the possibility of injury. This is why people put fences around swimming pools. Note that this special duty to children is not restricted to schools.

Risks Associated with Products

Product liability is important to nonprofits because some are manufacturers, distributors, or sellers of products. One does not have to be the producer of a product to be liable for injury caused by its use. Sellers are also liable. Furthermore, liability extends beyond the sale contract. This means that a third party, not necessarily the original purchaser, can sue for personal injury caused by the product. Hence, a worker can sue both his or her employee as well as the manufacturer of a machine that did the employee bodily injury.

What are the different sources of product liability? Product liability may arise out of

1. Negligence—the failure to exercise proper care in the manufacture or design of a product, that is, recklessness.

2. Failure to live up to a warranty—an assurance that a claim made about the product is true—whether that assurance is expressed or implied. A warranty is said to be expressed if it is an affirmation, part of the description, or part of the sample or model used in the sale or bargain. It is implied when the buyer is depending on the seller's knowledge or because the good can be assumed to have certain safe or usable qualities when sold for a specific use unless these qualities are specifically denied. A dealer's sale of a car has an implied warranty that the brakes will work. Cars are not ordinarily sold without working brakes.

3. Misrepresentation, whether such misrepresentation be purposeful, innocent, or negligent—lies upon which people base judgments are gross misrepresentations.

4. Application of *strict liability* theory—the so-called "no fault" liability in which the injured person need not establish fault. The manufacturer is liable because it is in the best position to exercise care or to foot the bill.

Nonprofits may face product liability as defendants or as plaintiffs. The American Red Cross and other nonprofits in the blood business faced a serious potential liability question from contaminated blood (hepatitis and AIDS). They were sued, but legal interpretation came to the rescue. The generally acceptable legal solutions today are "blood shield laws," which hold that these organizations do not produce blood and therefore they do not create a product subject to product liability. Furthermore, blood transfusions are services, not sales. Therefore, two criteria—a sale and a product—needed to form the basis of product liability suits were removed by definition, as long as proper and up-to-date procedures are used.[8]

LEGAL SHIELDS

The case of blood just cited reminds us that nonprofits do enjoy some shield from legal action. But this is a dangerous basis on which to set policy, because shields may be punctured. For example, the blood shield law does not protect against willful misconduct, only against unintentional negligence.

Immunity

States that offer partial immunity often do so with some conditions. They may require a risk management plan; they may offer immunity to nonprofits only if similar immunity is offered a for-profit employer; they may offer immunity to the extent of insurance coverage. They may offer immunity to a volunteer but not to an employee or officer under the same conditions. They may give immunity to a person but not to the organization. They may specifically protect only certain types of organizations and not others.

Under the federal Volunteer Protection Act of 1997, volunteers (persons earning less than $500 per year or who get paid only expenses) are immune from economic and punitive action by an injured party resulting from the inflicting of harm or acts of omission as long as such an act occurred while the volunteer was carrying out a duty for which he or she was approved and certified, and as long as the action was in connection with his or her duty as part of the mission of the organization.

Volunteers are not immune under this law when acting under the influence of alcohol or other drugs, or when the person lacks the proper licenses, or carries out a willful act or one that was hateful or violated the civil rights of another, or if the act involved a sexual offense or was a crime of violence or terrorism, and if the act represented a flagrant disregard for the safety of the injured, recklessness, or gross negligence.

This federal law leaves open the possibility that the organization (as opposed to the injured party) may sue the volunteer and may itself be sued by the state or local government in a civil action. It also leaves open the possibility that the injured may sue for noneconomic damages such as mental anguish, loss of enjoyment and of consortium, physical damage, and the like. For these, the volunteer is liable proportionately to his or her contribution to the resulting damage. Therefore, insurance protection may still be needed.

The Volunteer Protection Act covers all nonprofits, including associations. It covers volunteers, not employees or the organization. In most states, the organization and its employees remain fully liable.

Under state law a nonprofit organization is not liable for its volunteers if under a similar situation a business is not liable for its employees. It is not liable if it had no reasonable expectations of the unfitness of the volunteer and did not use the volunteer in a manner for which the volunteer is unfit.

The volunteer may not be liable under federal law as explained, or under state law. Utah 78–19–2 is an example. It gives volunteers immunity for acts of omission while rendering services for the nonprofit, and shields volunteers from personal financial liability for any claims of negligence or other action seeking damage for any injury arising for any act or omission while the volunteer was in the service of the nonprofit organization. But the following conditions must prevail:

1. The volunteer was acting in good faith and must have reasonably believed that he or she was acting within the scope of his or her official functions in the organization.

2. The damage or injury was not caused by an intentional or knowing act by the volunteer that was illegal, willful, or wanton.

The protection is not applicable if

1. The injury resulted from a volunteer's operating a mode of transportation without a license.

2. The suit is brought by state or local government to enforce a federal law.

3. The organization fails to provide a reasonable recovery to the individual suffering the loss due to the action of the volunteer.

Standing

In addition to partial and absolute immunity, nonprofits are protected by what is called *standing*. This is just a legal term to say that the courts do not view the individual who is bringing the suit as being among the injured. Hence, when a pro-choice group brought suit against the Catholic Church, alleging that it had violated the lobbying rules for nonprofits as described earlier, the courts held that the pro-choice group had no standing. It was not injured and it was not prevented from doing the same as the Church did. When their lawyers argued that they were taxpayers and therefore had a right to bring the suit, the court maintained they had no standing here either, because they could not (as individuals apart from the Congress) tell the U.S. government how to spend tax money.

First Amendment

Another way in which nonprofits are shielded from suits is the First Amendment to the U.S. Constitution, which guarantees freedom of speech, association, and religion. As noted in preceding and following chapters in this book, state challenges to fund-raising are frequently defeated on the basis of the First Amendment freedoms.

Courts are usually reluctant to judge religious principles or doctrines in civil matters, so they are reluctant to decide whether an individual who is a voluntary member of a church has been wronged by virtue of its doctrine. They are reluctant to go inside the doctrine. Yet there have been several cases brought against Christian Scientists for failure to seek medical assistance for children. The Amish have been sued for their position on education.

Limited Recovery

Nonprofits are also protected by limitation on damages. States in recent years have placed limitations on the amount that can be recovered in a successful negligence case against a nonprofit. In the state of Massachusetts, for example, a limit on nonprofit hospitals for malpractice is $20,000. In Virginia, settlement of a case in which a hospital gave parents the wrong babies was stymied by the legal limits that can be received from a nonprofit hospital.

Waiver

Another way nonprofits may be shielded from damages is through a waiver, basically a declarative warning that it will not be responsible and that the person acts at his or her own risk. How good waivers are depends on state law. In New York, for example, waivers (sometimes called *releases* or *hold harmless clauses*) are unenforceable as to the use of swimming pools, gyms, and places of recreation. Yet in a California case, a waiver signed as a condition for using the pool at a YMCA was upheld.

A ruling in New York state is instructive. Arthur Ashe (not the late tennis player) went to a clinic that charges poor people half price as long as they sign a waiver. When the dentist and his dental students got through, Mr. Ashe's two gold crowns ended up in his lungs. The Appellate Court concluded that to honor the waiver would be to deprive the poor of a protection accorded the rich.[9] How good are waivers? It depends on the state and the circumstances.

Indemnification

Finally, there are specific indemnifications. Take the Arts and Artifacts Indemnity Act of 1975. Through this act, a museum can obtain a certificate that causes the Federal Council of the Arts and Humanities to pledge the full faith and credit of the United States to indemnify lenders for losses of items of educational, cultural, historical, or scientific value. Such indemnification covers international lending. But some states, Florida, Iowa, and Texas, provide coverage for some noninternational lending.[10]

COVERAGE: SHIELDS CAN BE PENETRATED

Wise trustees will not blindly depend on shields, even those state protective laws discussed in Chapter Six that shield trustees and volunteers from negligence. A case in point: A volunteer for a nonprofit and a boy in his charge had a fatal accident. After considering all the evidence, the estate of the volunteer was assessed by the U.S. Circuit Court in Chicago. Fortunately, the nonprofit had insurance to cover the bill. Little wonder that virtually every major nonprofit's annual report contains language such as "Litigation: . . . is a defendant in a lawsuit. The amount of possible liability has yet to be determined. However, in the opinion of management, there appears to be adequate insurance to cover any eventual judgment."

Therefore, seek shelter, not a shield, and be guided by the adage that an ounce of caution is better than a pound of cure.

The Right of the Volunteer to Sue the Organization

A volunteer may sue an organization for a variety of reasons, including sexual harassment and discrimination. A volunteer can also sue the organization if it misrepresents the facts that a financially secure source of recovery for injury to the volunteer or to a third party by the volunteer does not exist when such was promised as Utah 78–19–2 illustrates.

Put another way, a nonprofit does not have to have insurance to protect a volunteer, but it should. If, however, it indicated that it does, the volunteer accepts to do service, something happens, and there is no insurance, then a suit is possible. Being a volunteer does not necessarily imply that the organization does not have to provide certain protection to make the property and environment safe.

In some cases, the nonprofit may have partial immunity. Hence, some states (Illinois, for example), though not making a hospital totally immune to suit, would protect the hospital against a physician who sues because of being dismissed or sues the hospital or a peer review board. The latter is generally immune form such suits, and the former need only demonstrate that it has followed the procedures laid down in its bylaws.

In Pennsylvania, Section 7107 of the code holds that canon law applicable to a corporation that is a religious organization will hold if such law is in conflict with specific state laws on nonprofits, as long as the law is not inconsistent with the state constitution and the Constitution of the United States of America. Hence, in Pennsylvania a local law is subordinate to a canon law on religious matters if the latter does not violate either the state or national constitutions.

Years ago, nonprofits did not have to worry about suits because most states held them absolutely immune to suits. This is no longer the case in most states. Yet even when absolute immunity from suit is available by state law, risk management is necessary because of the economic costs; that is, the nonprofit may still have a moral obligation to pay for its damages to others, and to avoid injury to them.

RISKS OF SEXUAL HARASSMENT

By their duties, managers expose the organization to several risks. These include (1) discrimination by sex, race, creed, or origin and sexual preference or harassment, (2) libel, slander, and flawed dismissal recommendations, (3) failure to report, (4) failure to exercise supervisory care, and (5) failure to conform with laws protecting the disabled. A detailed discussion of these should be part of management training.

RISKS OF HARASSMENT

Every employer is exposed to the risk of being sued because of sexual harassment. The Equal Employment Opportunities Commission (EEOC) has issued new guidelines on how the employer may protect itself against liability for harassment by the supervisors it hires and who work with its authority and on its behalf. These guidelines are relevant whether the harassment is sexual or racial. The guidelines assert that an employer is liable if an employee brings about a successful case against a supervisor and if the action of the supervisor directly or indirectly leads to some significant and tangible change in the employee's current or future employment situation. It is irrelevant whether the employee suffers a salary loss or gain. Under these conditions, the employer has no defense and is liable.

If, however, there is no significant change in the employee's job situation, the employer may (even after a successful charge has been made against the supervisor) defend itself by arguing that (a) it had taken substantial steps to prevent or to mitigate such harassment and (b) the employee unreasonably failed to avail him- or herself of these measures. This two-prong defense is called an *affirmative defense.*

These rules are so important that I have replicated the guidelines here (with substantial abbreviation). Take note of who is considered a supervisor, what types of claims are actionable, what types of policies are recognized as preventative, what types of remedies are deemed adequate, what types of investigations must be made, and how to judge the credibility of those involved even as witnesses. The following is verbatim, but abbreviated.

ENFORCEMENT GUIDANCE ON VICARIOUS EMPLOYER LIABILITY FOR UNLAWFUL HARASSMENT BY SUPERVISORS

I. Introduction

In *Burlington Industries, Inc. v. Ellerth,* 118 S. Ct. 2257 (1998), and *Faragher v. City of Boca Raton,* 118 S. Ct. 2275 (1998), the Supreme Court made clear that employers are subject to vicarious liability for unlawful harassment by supervisors. The standard of liability set forth in these decisions is premised on two principles: (1) an employer is responsible for the acts of its supervisors, and (2) employers should be encouraged to prevent harassment and employees should be encouraged to avoid or limit the harm from harassment.

The question of liability arises only after there is a determination that unlawful harassment occurred. Harassment does not violate federal law unless it involves discriminatory treatment on the basis of race, color, sex, religion, national origin, age of 40 or older, disability, or protected activity under the anti-discrimination statutes. Furthermore, the anti-discrimination statues are not a "general civility code." Thus federal law does not prohibit simple teasing, off-hand comments, or isolated incidents that are not "extremely serious." Rather, the conduct must be "so objectively offensive as to alter the 'conditions' of the victim's employment." The conditions of employment are altered only if the harassment culminates in a tangible employment action or is sufficiently severe or pervasive to create a hostile work environment.

II. Who Qualifies as a Supervisor?

A. Harasser in Supervisory Chain of Command. An employer is subject to vicarious liability for unlawful harassment if the harassment is committed by "a supervisor with immediate (or successively higher) authority over the employee." An individual qualifies as an employee's "supervisor" if:

a. The individual has authority to undertake or recommend tangible employment decisions affecting the employee; or

b. The individual has authority to direct the employee's daily work activities.

If the harasser has no actual supervisory power over the employee, and the employee does not reasonably believe that the harasser has such authority, then the standard of liability for co-worker harassment applies.

III. Harassment by Supervisor That Results in a Tangible Employment Action

A. Standard of Liability. An employer is always liable for harassment by a supervisor on a prohibited basis that culminates in a tangible employment action. The Supreme Court recognized that this result is appropriate because an employer acts through its supervisors, and a supervisor's undertaking of a tangible employment action constitutes an act of the employer.

B. Definition of "Tangible Employment Action". A tangible employment action is "a significant change in employment status." Unfulfilled threats are insufficient. Characteristics of a tangible employment action are:

1. A tangible employment action is the means by which the supervisor brings the official power of the enterprise to bear on subordinates.

2. A tangible employment action usually inflicts direct economic harm.

3. A tangible employment action, in most instances, can only be caused by a supervisor or other person with the authority of the company.

Examples of tangible employment actions include:

- Hiring and firing
- Promotion and failure to promote
- Demotion
- Undesirable reassignment
- A decision causing a significant change in benefits
- Compensation decisions
- Work assignment

Any employment action qualifies as "tangible" if it results in a significant change in employment status. Similarly, altering an individual's duties in a way that blocks his or her opportunity for promotion or salary increases also constitutes a tangible employment action.

On the other hand, an employment action does not reach the threshold of "tangible" if it results in only an insignificant change in the complainant's employment status. The Supreme Court stated that there must be a significant *change* in employment status; it did not to require that the change be adverse in order to qualify as tangible.

C. Link Between Harassment and Tangible Employment Action. When harassment culminates in a tangible employment action, the employer cannot raise the affirmative defense. This sort of claim is analyzed like any other case in which a challenged employment action is alleged to be discriminatory.

A strong inference of discrimination will arise whenever a harassing supervisor undertakes or has significant input into a tangible employment action affecting the victim. However, if the employer produces evidence of a nondiscriminatory reason for the action, the employee will have to prove that the asserted reason was a pretext designed to hide the true discriminatory motive.

IV. Harassment by Supervisor That Does Not Result in a Tangible Employment Action

A. Standard of Liability. When harassment by a supervisor creates an unlawful hostile environment but does not result in a tangible employment action, the employer can raise an affirmative defense to liability or damages, which it must prove by a preponderance of the evidence. The defense consists of two necessary elements:

a. The employer exercised reasonable care to prevent and correct promptly any harassment, and

b. The employee unreasonably failed to take advantage of any preventive or corrective opportunities provided by the employer or to avoid harm otherwise.

B. Effect of Standard. If an employer cannot prove that it discharged its duty of reasonable care *and* that the employee unreasonably failed to avoid the harm, the employer will be liable. In some circumstances, however, unlawful harassment will occur and harm will result despite the exercise of requisite legal care by the employer and employee. For example, if an employee's supervisor directed frequent, egregious racial epithets at him that caused emotional harm virtually from the outset, and the employee promptly complained, corrective action by the employer could prevent further harm but might not correct the actionable harm that the employee already had suffered. Alternatively, if an employee complained about harassment before it became severe or pervasive, remedial measures undertaken by the employer might fail to stop the harassment before it reached an actionable level, even if those measures are reasonably calculated to halt it. In these circumstances, the employer will be liable because the defense requires proof that it exercised reasonable legal care *and* that the employee unreasonably failed to avoid the harm.

C. First Prong of Affirmative Defense: Employer's Duty to Exercise Reasonable Care. The first prong of the affirmative defense requires a showing by the employer that it undertook reasonable care to prevent and promptly correct harassment. Such reasonable care generally requires an employer to establish, disseminate, and enforce an anti-harassment policy and complaint procedure and to take other reasonable steps to prevent and correct harassment. The steps described below are not mandatory requirements—whether or not an employer can prove that it exercised reasonable care depends on the particular factual circumstances and, in some cases, the nature of the employer's workforce.

Alternatively, lack of a formal policy and complaint procedure will not defeat the defense if the employer exercised sufficient care through other means.

1. Policy and Complaint Procedure
Generally it is necessary for employers to establish, publicize, and enforce anti-harassment policies and complaint procedures. An anti-harassment policy and complaint procedure should contain, at a minimum, the following elements:

- A clear explanation of prohibited conduct.

- Assurance that employees who make complaints of harassment or provide information related to such complaints will be protected against retaliation.

- A clearly described complaint process that provides accessible avenues of complaint.

- Assurance that the employer will protect the confidentiality of harassment complaints to the extent possible.

- A complaint process that provides a prompt, thorough, and impartial investigation.

- Assurance that the employer will take immediate and appropriate corrective action when it determines that harassment has occurred.

2. Questions to Ask Parties and Witnesses

When detailed fact-finding is necessary, the investigator should interview the complainant, the alleged harasser, and third parties that could reasonably be expected to have relevant information. Information relating to the personal lives of the parties outside the workplace would be relevant only in unusual circumstances.

The following are examples of questions that may be appropriate to ask the parties and potential witnesses. Any actual investigation must be tailored to the particular facts.

3. Questions to Ask the Complainant

- Who, what, when, where, and how: *Who* committed the alleged harassment? *What* exactly occurred or was said? *When* did it occur and is it still ongoing? *Where* did it occur? *How often* did it occur? *How* did it affect you?

- How did you react? What response did you make when the incident(s) occurred or afterwards?

- How did the harassment affect you? Has your job been affected in any way?

- Are there any persons who have relevant information? Was anyone present when the alleged harassment occurred? Did you tell anyone about it? Did anyone see you immediately after episodes of alleged harassment?

- Did the person who harassed you harass anyone else? Do you know whether anyone complained about harassment by that person?

- Are there any notes, physical evidence, or other documentation regarding the incident(s)?

- How would you like to see the situation resolved?

- Do you know of any other relevant information?

4. Questions to Ask the Alleged Harasser

- What is your response to the allegations?

- If the harasser claims that the allegations are false, ask why the complainant might lie.

- Are there any persons who have relevant information?
- Are there any notes, physical evidence, or other documentation regarding the incident(s)?
- Do you know of any other relevant information?

5. *Questions to Ask Third Parties*
   - What did you see or hear? When did this occur? Describe the alleged harasser's behavior toward the complainant and toward others in the workplace.
   - What did the complainant tell you? When did she or he tell you this?
   - Do you know of any other relevant information?
   - Are there other persons who have relevant information?

6. *Credibility Determinations*

If there are conflicting versions of relevant events, the employer will have to weigh each party's credibility. Factors to consider include:

- *Inherent plausibility:* Is the testimony believable: Does it make sense?
- *Demeanor:* Did the person seem to be lying?
- *Motive to falsify:* Did the person have a reason to lie?
- *Corroboration:* Is there *witness testimony* or *physical* evidence that corroborates the party's testimony?
- *Past record:* Did the alleged harasser have a history of similar behavior?

The fact that there are no eyewitnesses to the alleged harassment by no means necessarily defeats the complainant's credibility, since harassment often occurs behind closed doors. Furthermore, the fact that the alleged harasser engaged in similar behavior in the past does not necessarily mean that he or she did so again.

7. *Reaching a Determination*

Once all of the evidence is in, interviews are finalized, and credibility issues are resolved, management should make a determination as to whether harassment occurred. The parties should be informed of the determination.

Assurance of Immediate and Appropriate Corrective Action

An employer should make clear that it will undertake immediate and appropriate corrective action, including discipline, whenever it determines that harassment has occurred. Management should inform both parties about these measures.

Remedial measures should be designed to stop the harassment, correct its effects on the employee, and ensure that the harassment does not recur. In determining disciplinary measures, management should keep in mind that the employer could be found liable if the harassment does not stop. At the same time, management may have concerns that overly punitive measures may subject the employer to claims such as wrongful discharge.

To balance the competing concerns, disciplinary measures should be proportional to the seriousness of the offense. Remedial measures should not adversely affect the complainant. Remedial measures also should correct the effects of the harassment. Such measures should be designed to put the employee in the position she or he would have been in had the misconduct not occurred.

Examples of Measures to Stop the Harassment and Ensure That It Does Not Recur

- Oral or written warning or reprimand
- Transfer or reassignment
- Demotion
- Reduction of wages
- Suspension
- Discharge
- Training or counseling of harasser to ensure that she or he understands why her or his conduct violated the employer's anti-harassment policy
- Monitoring of harasser to ensure that harassment stops

Examples of Measures to Correct the Effects of the Harassment

- Restoration of leave taken because of the harassment
- Expungement of negative evaluation(s) in employee's personnel file that arose from the harassment
- Reinstatement
- Apology by the harasser
- Monitoring treatment of employee to ensure that she or he is not subjected to retaliation by the harasser or others in the work place because of the complaint
- Correction of any other harm caused by the harassment (e.g., compensation for losses.)

Other Preventive and Corrective Measures

An employer's duty to exercise due care includes instructing all of its supervisors and managers to address or report to appropriate officials complaints of harassment. Furthermore, due care requires management to correct harassment regardless of whether an employee files an internal complaint, if the conduct is clearly unwelcome. Reasonable preventive measures include screening applicants for supervisory jobs to see if any have a record of engaging in harassment. Finally, it is advisable for an employer to keep records of all complaints of harassment.

D. Second Prong of Affirmative Defense: Employee's Duty to Exercise Reasonable Care

The second prong of the affirmative defense requires a showing by the employer that the aggrieved employee "unreasonably failed to take advantage of any preventive or corrective opportunities provided by the employer or to avoid harm otherwise." *Faragher,* 118 S. Ct. at 2293; *Ellerth,* 118 S. Ct. at 2270.

Proof that the employee unreasonably failed to use any complaint procedure provided by the employer will normally satisfy the employer's burden. However, it is important to emphasize that an employee who failed to complain does not carry a burden of proving the reasonableness of that decision. Rather, the burden lies with the employer to prove that the employee's failure to complain was unreasonable.

1. Failure to Complain. A determination as to whether an employee unreasonably failed to complain or otherwise avoid harm depends on the particular circumstances and information available to the employee *at that time.* An employee should not necessarily be expected to complain to management immediately after the first or second incident of relatively minor harassment. Workplaces need not become battlegrounds where every minor, unwelcome remark based on race, sex, or another protected category triggers a complaint and investigation.

There might be other reasonable explanations for an employee's delay in complaining or entire failure to utilize the employer's complaint process. For example:

- Using the complaint mechanism entailed a risk of retaliation.
- There were obstacles to complaints.
- The complaint mechanism was not effective.

To establish the second prong of the affirmative defense, the employer must prove that the belief or perception underlying the employee's failure to complain was unreasonable.

SUMMARY AND PREVIEW

This chapter has introduced the reader to the basic concepts in risk management. Although our examples are drawn principally from mental health, hospitals, higher education, and day care, they apply to all types of nonprofit organizations. The key point to remember is that no nonprofit can carry out its mission and avoid all risks. Some risks are inherent in the mission, and others are created by management. In both cases, the organization must identify at least the most serious of these risks and design policies to deal with them. This is what the present chapter has been about. In the next chapter, we are concerned with the risk of financial ruination.

PART FOUR

MANAGING THE ORGANIZATION'S FINANCES

*Those who manage or oversee the management of a nonprofit
have an inescapable legal duty to its financial integrity.
The successful discharge of this duty depends upon
the devotion to clearly defined details.*

CHAPTER FIFTEEN

Financial Statements as Tools of Conversation and Control

The manager who does not know accounting need not be afraid of this chapter. It focuses on the managerial use of financial statements rather than on teaching accounting rules and procedures. The first part of the chapter discusses the basic statements and how they are used. This is followed by mock dialogues (a board meeting) illustrating how these concepts can be used by the manager not only in assessing his or her organization, but in defending its asset management, debt management, and revenue performance. This discussion is basic to all types of nonprofits—charities and associations alike.

The second part of the chapter focuses on special problems in the accounting and use of financial statements when donors place restrictions on how contributions can be used. This discussion is particularly applicable to organizations for which contributions are tax deductible—501(c)(3) organizations.

The discussion in the third part of this chapter is applicable to all organizations. It has to do with audits and the managerial responsibility attendant to anticipating, preparing, conducting, and responding to an audit, especially when federal funds are directly or indirectly involved.

Appendix 15.1 is a summary of the accounting rules for the treatment of gifts and contributions.

FINANCIAL STATEMENTS AS AN AID TO MANAGEMENT

The budget of the organization is a financial plan. It is analogous to the business plan of a firm. It contains estimates of the organization's best guess of the future.

What do financial statements tell us about the nonprofit organization?

How can they guide decisions and make them better?

How do we use them to alert us of impending financial disasters?

Budgets are financial plans indicating the level at which the nonprofit plans to operate, how its resources will be allocated among various programs within its mission, and from where those dollar resources are expected to come. Budgets have no legal force in nonprofit organizations and they are usually never audited.

This is not so with the other financial documents that will be studied in this chapter. These documents are audited, they have some legal force, and unlike the budget they are made up of actual numbers rather than projections or estimates. These documents have legal force in the sense that to propagate them knowing that the numbers are wrong is an act of misrepresentation with serious legal consequences, for example, if those figures are used to support financial transactions. It is these financial statements, not the budget, that creditors and donors to the organization often require. They are also often required by sponsors of programs. While sponsors may ask for a budget of the program they expect to support, they usually also ask for a picture of the overall financial condition of the organization to be sure that they are not pouring their dollars into a sinking ship. These documents also give management an early warning of impending financial disaster and signal the possibilities of financial opportunities. Finally, they are the bases for annual financial reporting to governments and for evaluation by watchdog agencies. We begin with the balance sheet.

THE BALANCE SHEET OR STATEMENT OF FINANCIAL POSITION

The balance sheet (Table 15.1) is a statement of the financial position of the nonprofit on a given date, in this case, December 31, 2000. This balance sheet as presented assumes that the nonprofit sells a product in a related business. It also assumes that there are no donor restrictions on its use of funds. Many associations and 501(c)(3) organizations fall into this category. We shall deal with donor restrictions later.

There are alternative ways to present a balance sheet.[1] All highlight certain points. As a basic rule, the information in the balance sheet is divided into three major categories: assets, liabilities, and fund balances. The amount of funds the use of which was restricted by donors must be shown. The amount that is tem-

Table 15.1. Example of a Balance Sheet of a Nonprofit Corporation, December 31, 2000, or Statement of Financial Position.*

Current Assets		Current Liabilities	
Cash	$ 1,000	Current notes payable	$ 8,000
Membership	50,000	Accounts payable	600
(minus allowance for	(5,000)	Wages and salaries	55,500
uncollectibles)		Deferred revenues	700
Marketable securities	5,000	Total current liabilities	64,800
Receivables	400		
(less uncollectibles)	(40)		
Inventory	900		
Supplies	500		
Prepaid items	1,000		
Total current assets	53,760		
Long-lived assets			
Long-term investments	3,000	Long-term debt	1,000
Property and equipment	8,000	Total liabilities	65,800
(less accumulated	(800)		
depreciation)			
Leasehold improvements	3,000	Funds balance; excess	5,260
Deferred charges	1,500	(deficit) of assets over	
Other long-term assets	2,600	liabilities	
Total long-term assets	$17,300	Total liabilities and fund	$71,060
		balance	

* Assuming zero restrictions of any kind.

porarily restricted must be separated from the amount that is permanently restricted. Thus the balance sheet also tells the manager how much discretion he or she has over the assets of the organization and how much, if any, is restricted temporarily or permanently by donors.

Current assets include

1. Cash and accounts on which checks may be drawn

2. Marketable securities (treasury bills, certificates of deposit, repurchase agreements or any security with a fixed date, usually no more than a year for its redemption)

3. Membership fees showing the amount that may not be received as members fail to pay

4. Prepaid items such as insurance when payments are made in advance, usually to cover the current year's costs

5. Supplies: paper, pencils, pens, whatever is consumable in the work process

6. Accounts receivable: payments expected from others for goods or services rendered minus the uncollectibles

7. Inventory: the stock of goods and services the organization has to sell

Since all claims are not collectible because some clients do not pay, the accounts receivable should be adjusted to reflect the uncollectibles. The same is true for pledges. All other assets are listed at fair market value except that marketable securities (stocks and bonds) are either listed at fair market value or cost, whichever is lower.[2] Inventory may be listed according to the latest or earliest price of the item making up the inventory.[3]

Fixed or long-term assets include items such as

1. Building and equipment—these items are listed at cost and the depreciation on them is shown in an accumulation account just below their entry on the balance sheet. The cost (the amount paid for it by the organization) minus the depreciation is known as the *book value* of the asset.

2. Deferred charges—advance payments by the organization for goods and services that will not be delivered to it during the year.

3. Copyrights and leasehold improvements—long-term leases on real property whereby the nonprofit maintains the property and remodels it as if it were the owner.

The total assets owned by the organization are the sum of the current and long-lived or fixed assets. In the balance sheet shown in Table 15.1 this amounts to $71,060. Some balance sheets will separately show *intangible* assets, such as copyrights and trademarks, to be differentiated from physical assets such as land and buildings.

Other major areas of information in a balance sheet are liabilities of the nonprofit and funds balance. *Liabilities* are claims against the nonprofit and may be divided into current and long-term claims. Current liabilities include

1. Current notes payable—payments to be made this year. These might be short-term notes or the current portions of long-term debt that are payable in the current year, such as mortgage payments to be made this year.

2. Accounts payable—payments due creditors who have extended goods and services to the organization.

3. Wages and *salaries*—payments to the employees for services rendered and accrued vacation time.

4. Deferred revenues—amounts received but not yet earned by the nonprofit. The nonprofit may receive subscription dollars for a publication not yet produced and distributed. Such revenues are said to be deferred and create a liability or claim of the subscribers against the organization until such time that the goods or services are produced and delivered.

Long-term liabilities include debt and other obligations such as long-term leases that must be paid to others in future years. (Note that the current years amortization of debt is listed as current liability.) Total liabilities are the sum of long-term and current claims. For this organization on December 31, 2000, they are $65,800.

The difference between total liabilities (current and long term) and total assets (current and fixed) is the *fund balance,* which may be an excess or a deficit. This nonprofit has an excess of $5,260. Its liabilities are less than its assets. A deficit is easy to spot, since it is usually placed within parentheses ($5,260).

Managerial Use of the Balance Sheet

The balance sheet tells how financially sound the organization is on a specific date. We know from Table 15.1 that as of December 31, 2000, the assets of this organization exceed its liabilities. For most uninformed observers, this nonprofit is economically sound. If it had to close down tomorrow it could meet all of its liabilities and still have $5,260 left over. But there is more to the story.

Liquidity and Cash Management

A balance sheet can give other critical information about a nonprofit. It tells how liquid or solvent the organization is on the date the balance sheet was prepared. Can the organization pay its current bills? Does it have sufficient cash or liquid assets that it can sell easily in order to raise enough cash to pay its current liabilities? In short, is the organization solvent? This organization is not.

There are several ways to use the information in the balance sheet to determine how liquid or solvent the organization is. One test is the size of the *net working capital.* This is the difference between current assets and current liabilities. The larger the net working capital, the greater the liquidity. The net working capital for this organization is a negative of $11,040. This is the amount by which its current liabilities exceed its current assets. It cannot pay its bills this year. It must borrow, sell assets, raise more funds, or use a combination of these. An existing line of credit can back up low working capital.

Another way of expressing the same dilemma in which this organization finds itself is to calculate the current or the working capital ratio. This is the current assets divided by the current liabilities for each year in question. Ratios are better than absolute numbers for making comparisons. The ratio for 2000 was 0.286, meaning that the assets were about 83 percent of the liabilities. The organization was 17 percent short of just covering its debts, including paying its employees.

Liquidity is also measured through what is called a *quick ratio* or *acid test.* Instead of using all current assets, as is done in calculating working capital, only cash and assets that are easily converted to money (those that have a fixed redemption date, preferably in the current year) are used. In the balance sheet of Table 15.1, this would include cash, marketable securities, pledges (minus the expected uncollectibles), and accounts receivable (minus the uncollectibles). The amount, $51,360 in this example, is divided by the current liabilities ($64,800). The ratio is 0.792. It is worse than the working capital ratio. The amount of money or near money the organization has is $51,360, but it is 20 percent short of what it needs to pay its current debt. The amount of cash or near cash the organization has must be viewed in terms of the current claims against it. Can it pay the monthly bills?

Note that we speak of monetary assets—cash and assets easily converted into money—and not just cash. As we have discussed under Liquidity and Cash Management, a large amount of cash on hand is not necessarily good. The excess cash could be invested in marketable securities, thus earning interest for the organization. However, a shortage of cash portends a serious solvency problem if the organization does not have marketable securities that it could readily sell to raise the needed cash. Like the working capital, the quick ratio is a warning signal. There is no magical level that is good or bad. Obviously, however, the lower the cash or working capital relative to the current liabilities, the greater the risk of insolvency.

Here are some illustrations of the use of working capital or quick ratios. Suppose the organization has a current ratio of 2:1 and the assets that yield this ratio are principally receivables, only half of which are collectible. How liquid is this nonprofit? Not very. The true ratio, given the uncollectible receivables, would be closer to 1:1. The lesson: No ratio, no matter how high, is better than the quality of the assets behind it.

Would you be willing to lend a nonprofit money if its quick ratio is less than 1 or its working capital is negative? You probably would not without substantial collateral, because a negative working capital figure or a quick ratio that is less than 1 is a sign of probable insolvency because current liabilities exceed current assets.

As a matter of fact, short-term borrowing would not help because it increases current liabilities by the amount of the debt and interest, thus increasing the demand for cash. But long-term borrowing may be helpful. It increases long-term rather than current liabilities and provides cash that increases current assets. The debt ratio of this organization (long-term debt divided by total assets) is .014. Not bad. Over the long run the organization is not overleveraged in excess debt relative to its assets. But still, would you want to make the loan? How will the organization pay the interest and the principal? One possibility would be to use the long-term loan to meet its current obligations and begin to restructure its balance sheet so that it will avoid the same dilemma in the future.

One way of restructuring the organization is to increase revenues from its business. Another way is to sell some of its assets; still another is to increase gifts and contributions. In all cases, the objective of the organization should be to increase its cash or near-cash items. To illustrate, a gift in the form of a building would not help. It increases fixed assets rather than current assets. Furthermore, if a debt is assumed or if there are current operating costs exceeding current revenues from the building (a negative cash flow), the situation is worsened.

Similarly, a gift that is restricted may not help. To illustrate, suppose that the organization has a cash shortfall. It gets a gift of $1,000,000 from Cita Mathew Landers, but this gift is restricted to the building fund. These dollars, whether received in cash or deferred, cannot be used to meet current expenses unless the restriction can be legally broken.

Equity and Debt Management

The balance sheet also tells us something about the claims others have against the organization. Liabilities are claims against the organization. The total liabilities, $65,800, is roughly 60 percent of the total assets, $71,060. This debt ratio may be too high for a nonprofit.

Let us explain. Large nonprofits such as hospitals, universities, and housing that raise money in the bond market, as for-profit firms do, receive credit ratings, and so what is a good debt ratio depends on the rating systems view. Therefore, there is a market discipline to the debt ratios of these nonprofits.

With other nonprofits, such wide market discipline does not exist, so it is more imperative that market discipline be internally imposed. The amount of debt that can be carried, whether by a household, firm, or nonprofit, depends on several factors: the cost, the use, and, what is most critical, the level and steadiness of earnings. Debt, short or long, must be paid according to schedule.

Debt that generates income is superior to debt that does not; that is, debt for an investment is better than debt for a consumer good. The organization that has a high steady monthly income, after all operating expenses are accounted for, is in a better position to carry debt than one that has an erratic or low net revenue flow. It is precisely these latter organizations that tend to suffer short-term cash flow problems that generate more debt, because their current assets fall below their current liabilities. The need for controlling debt becomes imperative. This should begin by monitoring the debt-to-equity ratio and keeping it low (below 30 percent). It should also be done by monitoring the revenue, support, and expense statement (which we shall be discussing) to be sure that the debt, whatever its size, can very easily be covered because of a large and dependable net cash flow. We refer you to the discussion in Chapter Twelve about matching fixed costs with permanent income.

Comparative Balance Sheets

The critical differences between the balance sheets of a for-profit and a nonprofit corporation are in the line items referring to gifts and contributions and in the balancing entry. For-profits do not attract gifts and contributions even when they are insolvent. Nonprofits do not have stockholders and therefore there is no stockholders' or owners' equity (net worth) shown on their balance sheets. This is central to the definition of a nonprofit: Its income and assets may not be distributed to individuals. Any excess of assets over liabilities is reflected in fund balances to be used to further the mission, not to increase stockholders wealth.

However, even this is a matter of degree. Some nonprofits have members who are not owners in the sense of for-profit stockholders. Yet the organization (an association) may be thought of as having earnings that are at the disposal of the membership as a group. Hence, the excess shown in the balance sheet may be labeled "funds balance and membership equity."

STATEMENT OF SUPPORT, REVENUES, AND EXPENSES OR STATEMENT OF ACTIVITIES

Another important financial statement for nonprofits is the statement of activity or statement of expense, revenues, and support, as shown in Table 15.2. This is an annual statement produced by the nonprofit and is analogous to the income statement of a for-profit firm. The statement is a year-end depiction of the financial operation of the organization during a year. Again, we assume that this organization has no donor-imposed restrictions on its funds.

The support and revenues of the organization may include

1. Fees from admissions to events
2. Government contracts, state, local, or federal
3. Gifts and grants from institutions and from individuals
4. Membership fees (if applicable)
5. Investment income (dividends and interest) on marketable and long-term securities
6. Net realized investment gains or losses from the sale of the securities
7. Royalties; that is, income from permitting others to use logos, trademarks, and other copyrighted materials
8. Revenues from sales of publications and the like

Table 15.2. Statement of Support, Revenues, and Expenses of a Nonprofit Corporation, January 1, 2000, to December 31, 2000.*

Support and Revenue**		
Admissions	$ 2,235	
Government contracts	20,000	
Gifts and grants	230,000	
Membership	38,000	
Investment income	10,000	
Net realized investment gains (losses)	4,000	
Royalties	1,000	
Revenue from sales	5,000	
Total		$310,235
Expenses		
Programs	290,000	
Supporting services	48,000	
Cost of sales	1,000	
Total		339,000
Fund balance at beginning of period		(30,000)
Fund balance at end of period		$279,235

* Assuming no restrictions on the use of funds.

** If this were a 501(c)(3), the entry would show public support, with a subset of contributions.

The statement does not show that these revenues and support (except the government contract) are restricted to a specific fund or use, which I shall say more about later. Generally, these revenues and support are available for use by the organization as it sees fit in the conduct of its mission. This nonprofit had unrestricted support and revenues during the year January 1, 2000, to December 31, 2000, of $310,235, minus the $20,000 for government contracts. Contracts are restricted to the performance of a specific task.

There are also expenses. For nonprofit organizations, expenses are generally classified by function or program, general administration or supporting services, and the cost of sales (items sold in a business). This organization had a total operating expense of $339,000. Its operating expenses exceeded its revenues and support by $28,765. It operated in the red.

This operating deficit had nothing to do with the related business that yielded sales of $5,000, for the cost of such sales was $1,000, giving a gross profit (defined as the difference between the two) of $4,000. As these businesses become larger, it will be important for the organization actually to itemize costs such as insurance, wages, rents, and interests that are specifically attributed to the business as for-profits do. A more accurate measure of the profitability of the business can then be obtained.[4]

This organization has two strategies available to it. It can seek to bring its expenses into line or increase its revenues and support. This latter approach would work only if the organization increases its unrestricted funds. Funds restricted by donors for other purposes cannot be applied to general operations.

An organization can sustain a deficit and still survive. The question is, How long?

A special class of revenues and support is called *capital additions.* These are receipts, usually in the form of endowments, the use of which are restricted by the donor. The restrictions are expressed in the agreement that leads to the gift, bequest, or contribution. The use of the funds may be restricted in several ways. The restriction may apply to specific purposes, such as the construction of a building. The restriction may require the passage of time or the occurrence of an event before the restriction is lifted. The restriction also may be permanent— a stipulation that the funds (and earnings they're from) can be used only as specified.

The capital additions include

1. Restricted gifts received during the year

2. Net investment income earned on these gifts and similar ones received earlier

3. Gains or losses realized from the sale of assets related to these restricted gifts

Managerial Use of the Statement of Support, Revenues, and Expenses

The most basic use of this statement is to determine whether the organization operated efficiently during the year. To do this, we must distinguish between operating and capital performance. Each has its bottom line.

This organization operated at a deficit ($28,765). It spent more than it took in for current program and support activities. The interpretation of deficits and surpluses depends on the facts and circumstances. Every organization can expect a deficit to occur now and again over its lifetime. The objective should be to have surpluses in both the operating and capital accounts every year, as long as the organization is carrying out its mission satisfactorily. Surpluses provide savings for financing the future and are an indication of the ability to pay off debt.

A nonprofit that conducts many programs may strategically plan for surpluses in one or more of them as a way of financing or subsidizing other programs. A full-blown revenue statement would enable management to distinguish between these two.

It is important to recognize that the statement of activity gives hard facts predicated on reasonable accounting practices, not estimates as in the budget.

The data on the statement of activity can therefore be used to compare the actual with the projected figures shown in the budget. The statement of activity thus tells whether the organization operated efficiently, met its budgetary targets and limits—and how. Moreover, as we can see here, the statement of actual activity, if used properly, would also form the basis for budgetary targets. This organization needs to review its revenue and expense performance and set new, achievable budgetary targets on each if it is to escape the fate now facing it. This organization would benefit from considering Chapters Twelve and Sixteen.

The statement of activities, when compared over several years, gives a picture of the trend toward the diversification of income and support. Is the organization becoming more or less dependent on admissions or fees? Is this a good trend? Is it sustainable? Which expenses are rising faster, which programs? Why? Is this what we want?

Comparative Statement of Activities

There are differences between the income statement of a for-profit firm and the statement of activity of the nonprofit. The revenues of a firm are earned from the sale of goods or services (called *revenues from operation)* or from the earnings on investment or the sale of assets (called *other* or *extraordinary or nonrecurring revenues*). For-profit firms do not get support from deductible gifts and contributions.[5]

In many nonprofits, this support is the only meaningful form of income. In others, there are both contributions and earned revenues. It is the ability to rely on contributions that permits the nonprofit to operate and sell its goods and services below market price. The price might even be zero, indicating that the nonprofit does not charge at all. It can do this because of its reliance on gifts and other contributions. A for-profit cannot do the same. It must operate at or above market price because it must bear all costs and provide a fair rate of return to its investors.

At the risk of being repetitious, another difference between for-profit and nonprofits is in the bottom line. The income statements of for-profits normally end with an entry that is called net income. This is the bottom line because it shows whether the organization operated at a loss or a gain during the course of the year. If there is a gain, that amount can be retained by the firm, distributed to the shareholders in the form of dividends, used to purchase other assets, and used to pay off debt at the discretion of the board of trustees.

A nonprofit has as its bottom line "funds deficit or excess," or a similar phrase. Note that for both a for-profit and nonprofit, the possibility of having a positive or negative bottom line exists. Either may have a surplus (called a *profit* in a for-profit firm) or a deficit (called a *loss* in a for-profit firm). The major difference is in the use of the surplus or profit. Of all the possible uses, one does not pertain to nonprofits: Nonprofits may not distribute their surplus to individuals or use it other than to foster their mission. Of all the possible ways of dealing with a deficit, the one that cannot be used by nonprofits is that they cannot issue shares of stocks but they may rely on gifts. Just the reverse is true of a for-profit firm: They may raise additional funds by selling stocks but cannot rely on gifts.

A final difference between the for-profit and nonprofit statement of activity is that the former will have an allowance for taxes whereas the latter, unless a private foundation or the operator of an unrelated business, would not normally have such a line item.

STATEMENT OF CHANGES IN FINANCIAL POSITION

The principal purpose of the statement of changes in the financial position of the organization is to show how resources were acquired and how they were used during the year and, consequently, why the organization finds itself in either a favorable or unfavorable financial position at the end of the year. Unlike a budget, it is not a projection of the sources and uses of resources. It is an actual accounting of major resource uses and acquisition during the fiscal year of the organization. And, unlike a budget, this statement is subject to audit.

The statement of changes in the financial position of the organization also differs from the balance sheet. The latter describes the financial status of the organization at a point in time. The former shows the flows that contributed to the attainment of that financial status. In short, what are the major financial flows that resulted in the picture portrayed in the balance sheet? Both statements are subject to audit.

The statement of changes in the financial position of the organization differs from the statement of activities just analyzed. The latter shows the dollar expenditures of each set of activities by type of expenditure (salaries, rent, supplies, and so on) and the sources of revenues by type. The latter focuses on broader categories of resource flows.

Sometimes the statement of changes in financial position may be combined with the statement of activities. Instead of a statement of changes in financial position, an organization may report a statement of changes in working capital. This latter statement merely shows the changes in current assets and liabilities that the organization experienced during the year. A statement of changes in financial position is broader than a statement of changes in working capital because it includes all major resource flows, not just those in current assets and liabilities.

Managerial Use of Changes in Financial Position

Like all financial statements, the statement of changes in the financial position of the organization contains information in the form of numbers, and the interpretation of these numbers is the responsibility of management. Instead of looking at an example of a statement of changes in financial position, let us focus on some of the major resource flows that may appear in the statement. What are some of the major uses and sources of financial resources for the nonprofit organization during the course of its fiscal year? What resource flows may bring about a change in its financial position?

Note the use of the word *resources*. It is intended to imply more than the word *cash*. Changes in resources may or may not be reflected in the change in cash. This is illustrated below.

Sources of Resources

Here are eight sources of resources for the organization:

1. The operating excesses from the organization's performance during the year arise because the organization's revenues and support from operations exceeded its expenditures. These revenues and support may include sales and contributions that are unrestricted; that is, available to be used for the general operation of the organization. An excess implies that the organization did not spend more than it brought in during the year, so the excess can be used to strengthen its financial position. If the organization operated at a deficit, this too would represent a change in financial position, thus implying, at least in the short term, a weakening of the financial position of the organization.

2. Decrease in inventories (when the organization runs a related business) implies that sales are made. Therefore, a reduction in inventories implies positive change in the financial position of the organization. An increase in inventories, particularly if such increases were unintended and merely represent the inability to make planned sales, implies a weakening of the financial position of the organization. The organization is less liquid and had to use its resources to build up unintended inventories, which it has been unable to sell.

3. Increases in deferred amounts (such as unfilled orders for the organizations publications) represent changes in the financial position of the organization. By deferring payments or the fulfillment of orders, the organization has more financial resources available to it now. A decrease in these amounts, however, implies that payments were made and, therefore, the organization has less resources available to it.

4. Returns on the organization's investments may be from the sales of investments, interest earned, and dividends received from corporations in which it owns stocks. Returns on investments represent a positive increase in the financial position of the organization and an improvement in its ability to advance

its mission. However, losses represent a deterioration of the financial position of the organization.

5. Increases in contributions and bequests that are restricted to specific purposes, such as a building fund or a scholarship fund, represent improvements in the financial position of the organization. These are known as *capital additions*. One aspect of capital additions is that the funds may not be used for operating purposes at the time they are given, and their uses are restricted to those stipulated by the donor. Hence, although capital additions improve the long-term financial position of the organization, they may do little to improve its liquidity unless the terms of the gift provide for the transfer of these funds and earnings from them for operating purposes.

6. Sales of the long-term assets of the organization also bring about a change in the financial position of the organization. Such sales bring in cash. This is not to imply that selling the assets of the organization is necessarily good. In some cases it might be a strategy forced by the need to raise cash. But in others, selling long-term assets might reflect a decision that they are no longer needed or they may be divestitures required by law, such as the excess business holding law of private foundations discussed earlier in this book.

7. The organization deducts depreciation every year in determining whether it operated at a deficit or a surplus. But unlike other expenses, the organization does not pay out any money to anyone when it incurs a depreciation expense. Technically, it withholds the amount depreciated to be used to finance the replacement of the equipment or property depreciated. The depreciation is thus a "source" of resources.

Recall that when the organization records a depreciation expense, it does not make a payment to anyone such as it does when it incurs a salary or benefit expense. In these latter cases, payments are made. Because no payments are made in depreciation, even though it is deducted as an expense, this deduction represents a source of resources.

8. By acquiring debt (borrowing), the organization increases the amount of resources available to it in the short run. At the same time, it increases the claims of others over the future resources of the organization. Debt may be necessary because the organization does not have needed resources. But long-lived assets also are better financed—not by current income but by income the assets generate over their lifetime. If debt is incurred to purchase an asset that appreciates, the effect is to increase the total financial resources of the organization by more than the debt.

Uses of Resources

What are some major uses of resources of the organization that result in a change in its financial position? Such uses include the following:

1. Resources may be used to purchase new assets such as buildings and equipment. To say that such a transaction represents a change in the financial position of the organization is not to imply that the organization is worse off. The organization is merely less liquid, having used its cash to purchase long-term assets. The transaction may have limited effect on the organization's immediate liquidity position if the purchase is financed totally by long-term debt such as a mortgage. Future liquidity will be affected because the interest and principal on the notes will have to be paid. Whatever method is used to finance the purchase, a change in the financial position occurs.

2. Reductions in short- and long-term debt represent a change in the financial position of the organization because a reduction in debt implies a payment, that is, a use of the organization's resources.

3. The purchase of investments such as bonds and certificates of deposit represents the use of cash for the acquisition of an income-producing asset, thus changing the financial position of the organization. This act does not drastically change the organization's liquidity if the investment is short-term and very marketable.

4. The resources of the organization are also used to the extent of increasing receivables, including pledges of contributions not received. To understand this, consider that a receivable, whether it is called *accounts receivable* or *pledges due,* is really a payment due to the organization. Technically, that payment is due because the organization expended resources either to create and sell a product or service or to create a situation to which a donor wishes to give. The act of creating the product, the service, or the purpose to which the donor wishes to give could only occur by the use of the organization's resources. Put another way, the organization's resources may be used to create a product or service or to create a purpose for giving. If an immediate sale were made or if the donation had been received, this would have represented an increase (a source) of resources. Since no money is received by the organization, technically all the organization has done is expended its resources in expectation of receiving money. It has incurred costs. These expectations are receivables. Where there is a sale, collection is legally enforceable; a promise of a gift may not be.

5. The transfer of funds from restricted accounts to the unrestricted operating account (a source of resources), or vice versa (a use or application of resources), is a flow of resources that is unlike the others because it does not represent bringing in additional resources to the organization or transferring the organization's resources to an outsider. It is a flow of funds between one set of accounts of the organization and another. The organization thus changes its financial position without necessarily adding or subtracting from the total amount of resources it commands. These interfund transfers are governed not only by accounting principles but by the legal agreements that set up the funds.

For example, the organization may transfer funds from an endowment to the operating fund either because the terms of the endowment provide for such an amount to be transferred at that time or because the organization is borrowing the funds for operating purposes—as long as the terms of the agreement that set up the endowment permit such loans.

Resource Use and Opportunity Costs

Changes in uses of resources are not cost free. To demonstrate, based on the above discussion, we know that building up inventory is a use of funds; therefore, it has a cost. One cost is an opportunity cost because resources could be used for something else. Inventory has other costs, which we shall discuss later. Building up accounts receivable (while there are claims against others) also has a cost. Take the organization that charges for its newsletters. It can build up readership by building receivables—extending credit by making it easier for people to pay. In the meantime, the organization has to pay its bills and foregoes earnings on the interest it could have received had the payments been received and banked.

Rises in inventories and receivable must therefore be monitored. A rise in receivables, for example, could occur because the organization has a bad collection policy. Bills go out late, there is no follow-up, or the organization extends credit to the wrong people. Such lax management of credit consumes resources. The statement of changes in financial position gives us a clue.

Comparative Statements of Changes in Financial Position

A principal difference between the for-profit firms statement of changes in financial position and that of a nonprofit is that the former can increase resources by issuing stocks, thus producing cash. It can also use resources to pay dividends, which induces some people to purchase and hold the stocks. Neither of these entries will appear on the books of a nonprofit. The nonprofit may not issue stocks to increase its cash and may not pay dividends. It has no individual owners.

GENERAL ASPECTS OF INTERPRETATION

In using financial statements, the management must know whether the accounting is on a cash or an accrual basis. If it is on a cash basis, all accounting entries represent actual cash receipts or outlays. If the organization is on an accrual basis, there is a definite commitment to pay or to receive payment. The transaction may be completed but no cash has been transferred. In this case, the amounts shown as accounting entries represent commitments rather than cash. Small nonprofits tend to operate on a cash basis, whereas the larger, more complex ones operate, like for-profit firms, on an accrual basis.

When using financial statements, managers should also be aware that as in budgets, vertical and horizontal analyses can be helpful. This is especially true if the data are presented for more than one year. For example, in the support, revenue, and expense statement, a horizontal analysis for more than one year could reveal whether the proportion that each line item contributes to expense or revenues has changed. Similarly, a vertical analysis of the same factors over the same number of years could reveal which line items are growing fastest and which are declining. The question for management is, Why? Is this in the best interest of the organization? Is this what we planned in our strategic planning process? Do we need to change our plans?

Using financial statements may also involve comparisons with other organizations. This is not necessary but it is often advisable. In so doing the underlying differences in the organizations ought to be kept in mind. Moreover, when possible, ratios rather than absolute numbers ought to be used to reflect the differences in sizes of the organizations. Because nonprofits tend to be so different from each other and data and accounting procedures are less standardized, comparisons among organizations ought to be done with utmost care.

On the point of standardization of accounting procedures, I reiterate that the examples given in this chapter are intended to highlight concepts. All nonprofits do not use exactly the same accounting procedures or reporting format. The mastery of the information as presented in this chapter, however, should be a firm basis for dealing with individual organizations.

FUNDS: A MANAGERIAL ACCOUNTING PERSPECTIVE

Fund accounting refers to a system of financial record keeping and reporting that is common among nonprofit organizations. The basic characteristics of fund accounting is that certain accounts must be kept separate, funds cannot be commingled except in an approved investment pool or through authorized and documented transfer of funds from one account to another, and the financial activity in each separate fund is subject to independent accounting. Interfund transfers, the movement of money from one fund to another, must be authorized by the board of trustees. Accounting principles require nonprofits to classify all of their funds into one of three categories: (1) permanently restricted, (2) temporarily restricted, and (3) unrestricted. For internal managerial purposes, other types of fund classifications may be used. We begin with the managerial perspective.

Managerial Types of Funds

For managerial purposes, funds may be classified as expendable or nonexpendable. *Expendable funds* are those that may be totally spent. *Unexpendable funds* are those of which typically only the income to the fund may be spent, but the principal and sometimes the gains from sales of the assets of the funds must be spent so that the fund may have a perpetual life. True endowments are examples of nonexpendable funds.

Endowments, as we discussed earlier in Chapter Eight, are of several types. A university may have an endowment fund for scholarships, land acquisition and building construction, athletic purposes and facilities, lectureships, and for professorships. Although we may speak of the endowments of Harvard or Columbia universities to be a certain dollar amount, we are actually speaking of the composite of several separate endowments.

Within any category of endowments are numerous separate accounts. For example, a modest endowment of $100 million may have thousands of separate restricted accounts. Some are restricted for scholarships, some for academic prizes, and some for financing academic events. Each account represents a specific donor or cause for which a specific endowment has been established, not just a gift but an endowment, that is, a gift that is expected to have a lengthy life whose principal would not generally be spent, but the income of which will be used to support a specific cause specified by the donor or donors.

Each of these separate accounts technically has a balance sheet, an income statement, a financial report, and perhaps a statement of changes in financial position. Each must be kept separate and generally bears the name of the donor. The Simon and Myra Bryce chair, the Carlos Gill chair, the Orvin and Sylvia Gaustad chair, and the Mabel and Mary Laporte chairs may be in the same university, but each is a separate endowment subject to separate accounting. Each is also subject to a separate agreement between the donor and the donee. It is this separate, written legal document that determines how a fund may be used.

Managers may use another important classification of funds. Funds may be restricted or unrestricted. Restricted funds are those that can be used only for purposes that are specified in the agreement at the time the gift was made or the contract was signed. A grant or payment to a nonprofit to provide research on the topic of AIDS uses its restricted funds. An unrestricted fund is one that can be used to finance activities at the discretion of the board of trustees of the organization. These unrestricted funds can be used to pay salaries, provide scholarships, make investments, take advantage of unanticipated opportunities, meet emergencies, fund scholarships, begin new programs, and finance general activities.

Sometimes the term *general funds* is used to denote unrestricted funds used for general operations. The term *operating funds* may include general funds and restricted funds used in current operations but for the specifically restricted purpose for which they are given. Hence, in a current year, a university operates using restricted funds to finance scholarships and lectures and also uses unrestricted funds for these and other purposes, including salaries and maintenance.

It should be kept in mind that the terms *restricted* and *unrestricted* are not synonymous with *budgeted*. An organization may budget $1 million for salaries and benefits. What makes the amount restricted is a legal force. A restricted amount cannot be used for any other purpose than those for which it was given. Variations from this intended purpose legally occur only by an act of the board of trustees when it imposes the restriction, the court, and the donor, directly or through a representative. Again, a budgeted amount is a planned or anticipated amount. It is not a legal restriction. There are no legal contracts or consequences from their variations. The misuse of a restricted fund is a violation of a contract and can be subject to both civil and criminal penalties.

The fact that the funds are unrestricted does not mean that discretion is absolute. These funds cannot be used for purposes that contravene the mission of the organization or violate the terms discussed in Part One of this book. *Unrestricted* merely means that the management may use its discretion about how the funds can be used as long as the use is consistent with the mission of the organization and the terms under which it was given legal and tax-exempt status.

Unrestricted funds come from gifts and contributions of donors and the earnings of the nonprofit. Many nonprofits conduct special campaigns to increase the size of their unrestricted funds. Others obtain unrestricted funds almost exclusively through fees and sales.

In addition to giving the organization fiscal discretionary powers, unrestricted funds also have the advantage that there is no legal ratio of unrestricted to restricted funds that it must maintain. Hence, financially skillful nonprofit management can maintain the support ratios discussed in Chapter Four and still maintain discretion. For example, it is possible to meet the one-third public support test and still have a large percentage, even 100 percent, of the assets of the organization as discretionary. It is possible and customary, for example, to emphasize unrestricted gifts in any contribution campaign the organization conducts.

Many nonprofits do run campaigns for unrestricted gifts at the same time that they seek out funds for restricted purposes. They are two different tracks upon which chapters on giving and on soliciting in this book are based.

The previous discussion on fund restrictions, emphasizing managerial use, is summarized in Table 15.3. The accounting requirements will soon follow.

Interfund Transfers by Managers

The transfer of money or assets from one fund to another is a formal financial transaction with at least three requirements: (1) a vote or standing permission from the board to allow such a transaction, (2) permission from the donors or broad language in the terms of the gift to allow such transactions or an act by the court or state, and (3) a clear and specific accounting of such transactions in the year-end financial statement.

Table 15.3. Summary of Managerial Approach to Funds Restriction and Use.

Type of Fund	Use of Funds
Unrestricted	Determined by management via budget
Board restricted	Determined by trustees
Expendable	Both principal and income spendable
Unexpendable	Only part of income spendable
Donor preference	Moral obligation to follow preference
Donor restricted	Determined by legal contract
Expendable	Both principal and income spendable
Unexpendable	Only part of income spendable
Contract and grant	Determined by terms of acceptance

Note: Unexpendable or inexhaustible funds may, by provision of the contract, permit occasional spending of principal. The aim is to avoid this since perpetuity of the fund is the objective.

Interfund transfers occur for several reasons. An expense may be paid from general funds and then recouped from the specific fund to which it belongs. This avoids having to sell securities to make immediate payments. It also allows parking funds in short-term interest-earning accounts. Sometimes the maintenance of a separate fund is no longer economical, legally or managerially necessary; that is, the objective is satisfied or obsolete. Transfers are frequently made into the current accounts to provide cash to carry on current operations consistent with the terms of restriction. There are also interfund loans to cover cash shortfalls.

Funds as an Accounting Concept: The Meaning and Treatment of Restrictions

For internal purposes, organizations may defer in how they account for and treat funds as a managerial method of classifying resources. Accounting principles, however, require a specific treatment of funds for public reporting purposes. Funds must be classified in financial statements as unrestricted, restricted, or temporarily restricted. Here the concept of a restriction refers solely to the restriction imposed by the donor, not the board or the organization.

A donor may make a restriction based on the lapsed or passage of time. For example, the donor may say that the gift cannot be transferred to the control of the organization for ten years, or twenty years, or some other period. Alternatively, the donor may say that the gift cannot be transferred until the occurrence of some event. An event may be the death of a person, the completion of a building, or the start of constructing a building.

A restriction may be permanent or it may be temporary. A restriction that is based on not expending any of the funds until a building has already been constructed is a temporary restriction—assuming that there are firm commitments. A restriction that funds may never be used but in a specific fashion—scholarships for senior tennis female students—is a permanent restriction. If there are neither temporary nor permanent restrictions placed by the donor or if these restrictions are already met, the accounting must show the funds as unrestricted.

The accounting segregation of restricted funds must appear in the financial statements of the organization. The accounting statements, such as the statement of activities and the statement of financial position, show the amount of permanently restricted, temporarily restricted, and unrestricted funds. The notes to these financial statements will detail the nature of these restrictions. Again, and by definition, if assets or revenues are not restricted temporarily or permanently by the donor (not the trustees), they are by definition unrestricted.

There are six points to bear in mind about the accounting concept *restricted:*

1. Accounting restrictions occur within the scope of contractual law. The restriction occurs because the donor (not the trustees) imposed it and the gift was accepted with the promise that the restriction will be obeyed by the management and enforced by the trustees.

2. When in doubt, the organization has to consider the probable intent of the donor in deciding the character of the restriction.

3. This way of segregating funds does not deny the organization the chance to use other methods of classification, such as those described earlier, as long as it is understood that they are for managerial purposes and cannot replace the restrictions required by accounting conventions.

4. Because the restrictions are contractual, they can only be changed by the donor (or permission given by the donor in the contract transferring the gift) or by the court. When the court relaxes or nullifies these restrictions it does so through a *cy pres* decision. Such a decision is granted, not for the convenience of the organization or to relieve it of the burden of conforming, but because the restriction is contrary to public policy or economically detrimental to the organization.

5. As restrictions are satisfied, funds may move from one restricted category to another and finally into unrestricted. These interfund transfers are formal accounting procedures that must be documented in specific ways. See the earlier discussion on Interfund Transfers by Managers.

6. Management has full discretion only in the use of unrestricted funds. But these funds may be subject to managerial restrictions by the trustees even though they appear as unrestricted in the accounting statements. Managerial restrictions are thus of two types—those imposed by the donors, and those imposed by the trustees—even though only the first appears in the accounting statements.

Managerial and Solicitation Implications of Restrictions

Some years ago, I sat on a board that was the official issuer of billions of dollars in tax-exempt bonds. The bond consul prepared a draft of the prospectus to describe the bond. It said that all of the income and assets of the organization for which the bond was being issued was pledged to support the bond. I objected. Why? Because assets acquired with other restrictions cannot be used to support a bond unless the contract accompanying the gift permitted such use.

The prospectus had to be amended to show that the use of certain assets was restricted and technically could not be pledged in the support of the bond, yet the assets could be reported as part of the overall assets of the organization. Today this problem is lessened by the requirement that the restricted asset totals must be identified in the financial statements.

The list below shows some examples of different types of permanent restrictions.

Illustration of Permanent Restrictions

Scholarship	To support the athletic program
Permanent gift to purchase roses	To buy flowers
Gift for purchasing windows	For maintenance of building
Purchase science books	To purchase books for the library

It should be clear that the accounting rules are more than a technical issue for the manager. Compare all of the above with an outright gift to the same school. Then compare each of the permanent restrictions in the first column with the change in discretion that is attained by a slight change in language in the second column. Yet in both cases the restrictions are permanent.

Consider also what a big difference would have occurred if the language of the gift said that the restriction would be temporary and then the residue would be used by the management to support the organization. The lesson: The amount of discretion, even though stipulated by the donor, is often the consequence of how the idea was presented and eventually worded. The consequence of all this falls on the managers and restricts the ability of the organization to create its own initiatives without seeking specific funding for each and every purpose. See Simon's Dilemma (Figure 12.2).

AUDIT

The various sectors in the nonprofit world apply different accounting standards. One standard is "Audits of Voluntary Health and Welfare Organizations" of the American Institute of Certified Public Accountants; another is *Accounting Principles and Reporting Practices for Churches and Church Related Organizations* by the Catholic bishops.

General Characteristics of Audits

Audits are done to determine whether the accounting procedures used by the organization conform with the generally acceptable accounting principles (GAAP). The aim of these principles is to be sure that the accounting of the organization is objective, fair, complete, and accurate. These are the four criteria used to judge the accounting practices of the organization.

In assessing the organization's conformity with these four standards, the auditors look at expenses and revenues of the organization. In investigating the expenses, the auditors seek clear evidence that the expenses were authorized and approved by a responsible person of the management team, are correctly classified by function (program) or object, are recognized in the correct accounting period, and are justified or supported by documents such as invoices. Auditors are instructed to pay particular attention to the existence of controls over expenditures. These controls include the existence of an organizational chart and a clear line of responsibility for decision making, recording, and monitoring expenses. The auditor may also compare the extent to which actual expenditures deviate from planned or budgeted expenditures. The auditors may also be expected to see whether the factors that are included in the overhead of the organization are properly classified as such or whether they should be classified as part of the direct cost of a specific project. Conversely, they will check to see that items treated as direct costs are properly classified and charged to the correct project. The auditors can be expected to look at operating expenses to be sure that they are properly classified as unrelated or related and that there is compliance with the payment of taxes.

On the revenue side, the auditors will be concerned with the accurate recording of the amounts of revenues, in the proper time period and in the proper classification by type such as fees, gifts, and contributions, income from investments, sales, and so on. The auditors will also check to be sure that there are proper controls set over the receiving of revenues, including the persons who are so authorized, and that there is a chain of command within the organization to control the receiving, recording, and accountability for such revenues. Where applicable, as in the case of endowments, the auditors will assure that accounts are segregated and independently recorded.

Where cash is involved, the auditors may want to be sure that there are physical safeguards for keeping cash and procedures that control and limit petty cash to a reasonable amount. Where securities are concerned, the auditor will verify the type and the reasonableness of their reported cost and return.

In carrying out their function, the auditors focus on financial statements, such as the balance sheet, that tell them about the treatment of the assets and liabilities of the organization. They focus on the revenue and expense statements, which tell them about the flow of revenues from various sources and the expenditures of the organization for various purposes. They examine those and other statements that explain how the financial position of the organization has changed over a period that is usually one year. Their only use of the budget is as a standard through which they may judge departures from the organization's commitments, what the organization thought was reasonable, and as evidence that there is some credible attempt to control both the revenues and expenses of the organization.

At the end of the audit, the auditors may render an opinion in writing to the organization. The opinion is divided into a section that describes the scope of the audit, a disclaimer, an explanatory paragraph, and an opinion. The scope tells what financial statements were audited and for what period; the disclaimer tells what was omitted from the audit and why; the explanatory statement explains departures or peculiar aspects of accounting by the nonprofit and why they may be justified; and the opinion is the judgment of the auditors as to the conformity of the organization with generally acceptable accounting practices. An opinion may be "clean," meaning that the organization conforms with the GAAP, or it may be "qualified," meaning that it expresses concern about the practices of the organization.[6]

The Scope

The scope statement gives the period and the specific fund being audited, as well as the basis for the audit. Note that the scope is limited to a certain period, but it may also be limited to a particular fund and be conducted for a specific purpose.

The Explanation

The explanatory paragraph further defines the scope of the audit. In some cases, it emphasizes that the audit is not of the entire organization, which is not unusual. As we recall, endowments are accounted for separately, and often periodic auditing may be called for in the contract. Alternatively, the audit could have been for the organization in general rather than for a specific endowment alone.

The Opinion

In a clean opinion, there are no qualifying statements. The auditors may state: "In our opinion, the financial statements referred to above fairly present. . . ." Take note that the opinion does not use words that imply that the financial status of the organization is strong or weak or precarious. An audit does not make judgments about the financial strength of the organization. Only those who interpret financial statements make such judgments. Note also that the audit does not say that the numbers used by the accountant or bookkeepers for the nonprofit are right or wrong. Even a clean audit does not verify that the numbers are right. An audit gives an opinion about the soundness and merits of the procedures and practices used.

Audit Trail

In assessing the practices used, the auditors attempt to establish what is known as an audit trail. That is, they try to trace each revenue item and each expense item from its inception. In an audit trail, auditors may discover sloppiness and embezzlement as the perpetrator fails to provide acceptable evidence of the justification, authorization, and disposition of the nonprofit's money.

PREPARING FOR AN AUDIT

What is management's responsibility in preparing for an audit? It varies depending upon the scope of the audit. One of the broadest audits is that done of nonprofit recipients of federal assistance.

Circular A–133 of the federal Office of Management and Budgets describes the auditing of programs that are financed by the federal government. It offers a useful protocol for all organizations and managers whether or not they receive such funds. The financing by the federal government may be through cash payments, loans or loan guarantees, cost-reimbursement, the transfer of property or other types of noncash assistance, or the use of these assets directly by the organization or by its subcontractors.

The circular sets certain requirements with which the management of the organization to be audited must comply. Management must prepare and give the auditor a schedule of expenditures of federal awards it has received during the period to be audited. Management is expected to disclose to the auditor the terms of the contracts and to demonstrate compliance with these terms. Management is also expected to provide effective internal control over the federal assets, to be able to demonstrate this control, and to provide the auditors with copies of correspondence that are material to the management of the contract.

In addition, management must also provide all financial documentation including reports, claims, books, and other records that provide the basis for the financial statements. If there is a pass-through, records pertaining to transfers from and to the nonprofit must be surrendered even if these transfers or communications occurred electronically. If the subcontractor's auditors have findings, the nonprofit being audited must demonstrate that it acted expeditiously upon these findings. It must also reveal all contracts with the subcontractor.

If there were previous audit findings about the organization, these must be surrendered to the auditor with a description of any ameliorative actions taken. Changes in internal control that could materially affect the federally assisted program must also be given to the auditor. Of course, the management must always warrant to the truth and accuracy of all these statements and documents it gives the auditor. Failure to comply or to cooperate is sufficient reason for a qualified opinion or a disclaimer and a reason for pursuing the audit. The Circular A–133 audit is not only about accounting procedures, it is also about contract compliance and internal control.

ILLUSTRATION OF MANAGERIAL USE OF FINANCIAL STATEMENTS

Let us role play. Let us pretend that the board of directors of a nonprofit organization is meeting. We have just entered the room when the board is about to listen to an extensive report by the CEO about the state of the organization at the end of the year 2004. Notice how the concepts discussed in the past chapters of this book are put into play in a conversation between a smart manager and a board that is doing its duties at a board meeting. There is full participation—across the board. Members try to explore the meaning and implications of what they are viewing for the welfare of the organization. The financial statements are not divorced from planning or from the current or future budgets.

A secure CEO would rarely enter such a meeting without his or her executive staff and would expect them to be able to explain technical matters. In such a meeting, each financial statement has a specific story line. The balance sheet tells about the status of the organization, the income statement about the operations of the organization, and the changes in financial situation about how or through what major transactions these changes in the financial status were brought about. In a well-balanced board, a conversation can be conducted without talking in technical tongues. The formality of the conversation enhances its seriousness.

> CHAIRMAN EUGENIA NORMAN-RUBY: Let us come to order. I would like to ask Victor Alexis, our new CEO and president, to give us a complete rundown on the financial state of our organization. As a board, we are concerned because of the increasing demand on our resources, and we brought Mr. Alexis because of his confidence that he could reverse our past few years of deficits. We were all very conscious of the fact that years of deficits would eventually destroy this organization and its ability to carry on its important mission. Furthermore, I remind each and every one of you that part of the duties of a trustee is the duty of care. This implies our unequivocal involvement in the financial health of the organization.

> BOARD MEMBER DELFINA ATHERTON: Does this mean that we can't snooze through this boring stuff?

CHAIRMAN RUBY: Ms. Atherton, I promise you that it will not be boring. It is a legal and inescapable part of our duty as trustees. Mrs. Norma Reginald-Sadie who is chair of our finance committee, Mr. Millett Clifford, chairman of our audit committee, and I, as chairman, have gone over these financial reports that were audited by Ezra, Ford and Chambers a reputable CPA firm with a specialty in our line of work. Ms. Olivia Fibuiel-Innis who was in charge of the audit for the firm is here with us today and so, too, is Mr. Thomas Beckels who is one of our two attorneys.

Discussion of the Balance Sheet

MR. ALEXIS: Thank you, Mr. Chairman. I would like to ask you to turn to the balance sheet or statement of financial position that we sent each of you in advance of this meeting. We are conscious of the fact that we have a responsibility to inform you, and that is the only way you can exercise your duties properly.

This statement summarizes our financial health as of the end of the past year. It tells us that our assets exceeded our total liabilities—we owned more than we owed. This difference means that we achieved a positive fund balance at the end of the past year. Our unaudited report for the past six months suggests that this positive fund balance is growing.

Before we go further into detail, let me call your attention to the bottom lines in the balance sheet. They show that a majority of the assets that we have are unrestricted funds, followed by those that are temporarily restricted, a substantial portion of which would be released from the donor-imposed restrictions during the year. The remainder are restricted.

BOARD MEMBER DOROTHY JOHNSON-BOSTIC: I interrupt to remind the board that the restrictions we imposed last year on the $4 million check that we got from Clark Smythe is reported as unrestricted. He graciously gave the money without restricting how it is to be used. We imposed the restriction. Therefore, while for our managerial purposes we treat it as a restricted amount, for accounting purposes it is unrestricted. Our financial statements report donor restrictions because of the legality of such restrictions. As a board, we can remove our own restrictions, but we can't remove a restriction or disobey a restriction that a donor sets.

VICE CHAIR OF THE BOARD FRANCIS COX-DYLAN: That's an important reminder. I saw some of you look with wonderment at those figures. It is one of those peculiarities of 501(c)(3)s and other organizations that receive tax-deductible gifts. Please be assured that the decision that we made last year about the $4 million is being honored. We have supplied a separate report showing these managerial restrictions and the variances between our actual and budgeted expenditures for the year. We'll get a chance to question the President about these variances later.

Balance Sheet: Asset Management

PRESIDENT ALEXIS: Let us turn our attention to how we are managing the assets of this organization. How are these broken down? Basically, our assets, as are those of other organizations and associations, are broken down into two large classes—those which we call current because they are readily accessible and those that are fixed or long-lived.

We closed the year with current assets equaling more than $10 million. This number, as all other numbers, should not be held as implying either that that was the average amount we held during the year or that that amount was constant. It changed from time to time, but that is the amount we ended the year with, and it is considerably greater than what we had last year.

BOARD MEMBER ALBERT VAN HORN: Does this mean that you may very well have operated with substantially less during the year but closed the year up with $10 million?

CHAIRMAN RUBY: That is correct, and the reverse is also true.

PRESIDENT ALEXIS: Thanks. As I was saying, our current assets are broken down into the usual categories: cash, marketable securities, receivables from sales, contributions and pledges, dues, and inventory. Please note that we have decreased the amount we hold in cash. With the market being as good as it is, we have tried to follow Mr. Kenneth Sandiford's recommendation to hold more marketable securities, and that strategy explains the figure—not only do we own more but what we own has appreciated considerably. We account for our holdings at their market price at the close of the year. We did well.

BOARD MEMBER HECTOR HOGAN: I wish to remind the board that the policy to invest more was not the only thing we voted upon. We voted upon setting up a guideline for allocation of our investments among certificate of deposits, stocks, bonds, and treasury notes. This diversification will help us to meet our obligations if the market turns down. It is wasteful to carry so much cash as we did. The earnings from these investments will enable us to do our work in the future. Also, because we did not borrow to make these investments, all of the earnings from them—interest, dividends, capital gains, and even the rentals from lending of our securities—are tax-free. They are not subject to the unrelated-business income tax.

If we were a political action committee, however, we would have had to pay income taxes on this amount. Furthermore, if we were a 509(a)(2) organization, there would have been a limit to the amount of these earnings we could use to demonstrate that we are publicly supported, and if we were a private foundation, it would affect the amount that we have to distribute annually.

BOARD MEMBER WINSTON OAKLEY: And it would also have increased our need to get in more dues or gifts and contributions so that we can meet our public-support test.

BOARD MEMBER THELMA DACOSTA: By the way, does my association have this problem? I am also on its board.

BOARD MEMBER SONIA LESLIE-FERNANDEZ: Associations also have to worry about setting and following investment policies, unrelated business income, and demonstrating that their membership financial support is a considerable part of their total income. But let us not jump the gun. The fact that these appear in our balance sheet does not imply that we would make these gains when we actually sell. Today's balance sheet shows the investments that could lead to gains or losses in our income and expense statements next year.

BOARD MEMBER JOSEPH MORRELL: What is this about inventory?

PRESIDENT ALEXIS: As you know, we carry large inventories of a variety of properties from personal properties such as uniforms to books that we sell. Since we run a cafeteria, we also carry inventories of food. Clearly, we cannot count each item and value each item everyday because we purchase them at different days and some of our inventories perish, some we must sell at a discount after a period of time, some we must dump, and some increase in value. We try to get a value of our inventory taking these factors into account, for example, discounting some for loss of value and using a technique to assume that the value of the last unit of an item purchased is the value of all similar items in our inventory. We could, of course, have used an equally acceptable technique of valuing all similar items by the price we paid for the first of such items. Is this what you are referring to, sir?

BOARD MEMBER MORRELL: Not exactly. What concerns me is the tremendous growth in inventory. As you know, such a growth is not cost free. There is the ordering or purchasing cost of the items. There is the holding cost, including storage and insurance. And there is the risk that the inventory would become damaged or even obsolete. There is also the question as to whether the inventory increase resulted from our inability to move it, our producing and acquiring the inventory in anticipation of sales this year. You see, an increased inventory is not by itself a sign of progress.

VICE PRESIDENT OF OPERATIONS CYNTHIA EDGEHILL: Your point is well taken, sir. We sought to significantly increase a large part of our inventory in November because we got a good discount and we believed that we can exhaust it in the first quarter of the year with little additional holding cost. Frankly, by the middle of the quarter, most of that inventory should be sold and you would see a reduction in inventory and an increase in cash or accounts receivables to the extent that we extend credit that we need to do. Unfortunately, as you are well aware, we did not receive payment for 100 percent of the credit that we extended. Thus, our receivables (as incidentally our pledges) must always be discounted for amounts we will not collect.

CHAIRMAN RUBY: Please summarize quickly your comments on fixed assets, which is the other category of assets you mentioned, and move along to the liability side.

PRESIDENT ALEXIS: I shall be happy to do so. We made no major changes in our fixed assets last year. We acquired and disposed of no buildings or equipment, which are the major components to our fixed assets. We do want the members to appreciate, however, that we use the original cost of these assets in our accounting and decrease them by the amount of their depreciation. Of course, we depreciate a building, but not land. Therefore, the accounting data sort of understates the real value of our properties. These, because of a very strong real estate market, are actually higher than shown. We do not know exactly what the values are.

BOARD MEMBER VIOLET GUSTAVE RUDOLPH: I guess we don't get tax appraisals from the local government, because we are exempt from property taxes because all we use all our properties for is to carry out our mission.

BOARD MEMBER ROSA BROWN: And we don't pay unrelated-business income taxes either for the very small portion that we rent out to Jocelyn, Sinclair and Scantlebury even though they are a very profitable for-profit firm.

BOARD MEMBER DOROTEA MEDFORD GIBBS: Please remember that the balance sheet simply tells us what we owe and own. These questions about the character of actual earnings, while important and accurate, will have more to do with the income statement. In that statement we will learn how much we actually earned and what the character of these earnings are for tax purposes.

I would like to have the President tell us more about the liabilities. What are the claims against these assets on the right-hand side?

Balance Sheet: Debt Management

PRESIDENT ALEXIS: Like the asset side, the balance sheet shows liabilities as either long-term or current. As you all know focusing on the liabilities side tells us about our debt and the claims of others against us.

The current liabilities are mostly made up of accounts payable. These are the amounts we owe people who sell us things such as goods and services. Incidentally, it includes our compensation. It also includes our interest payments during the period. This is both our interest payment to the bank for the line of credit that we took out and the payments to our bondholders—those holding our revenue bonds.

MEMBER BETTINA JONES-MAYNARD: I don't recall. Didn't we have to use our accounts receivables and out inventory as collateral for that bank loan?

CHAIRMAN RUBY: Yes, we did. They used 80 percent of the value of both on the date that the loan was closed for collateral purposes. Of course, that does not infringe on our use of these in the ordinary course of operation. We still want to move this inventory, get the cash even from those who purchased on credit, and pay the bank.

BOARD MEMBER LAURA LAYNE-CAMPBELL: If my arithmetic is correct, our current assets were five times as large as our current liabilities. If I remember my accounting, this is good because it tells me something about our ability to pay our current debt. That is, for every one dollar in debt at the close of last year we had five dollars worth of readily available assets to make such payments had we chosen to do so. Is that correct?

PRESIDENT ALEXIS: Yes. The arithmetic difference between those two numbers is called the net working capital and the ratio of current assets to current liabilities is called the liquidity ratio. But what impresses me more is the fact that we had sufficient cash on hand to meet those liabilities. We wouldn't have had to sell our securities, depend on a fast sale of our inventories, or hound our customers and members to pay up in order to meet those debts. In short, we managed both our short-term or current debt and our current assets wisely, and we were shrewd enough to get a line of credit to back up our cash position.

BOARD MEMBER LORD TOMLINSON ROMERO: Let me congratulate the managers on keeping us liquid and afloat. But I am reminded that this is a year-end report. Were we that liquid throughout the year?

PRESIDENT ALEXIS: Frankly, we almost had a shortfall and were able to get a government advanced payment. We also had to draw on our line of credit. It is our insurance and our first line of defense so that we do not have to touch our investments or endowment.

BOARD MEMBER ANITA THEOPHOLOUS: I seem to remember that Mr. Teddy Gillette, our Treasurer, was adamant about our performing in a way that would keep up our credit rating. Have we done so?

PRESIDENT ALEXIS: Yes. As you know, the purpose of our issuing those bonds was to develop a massive community for the elderly. I have asked our accountants to prepare a separate set of financial statements of that project. The balance sheet for that project shows that our total debt outstanding is $12 million. That is in the lower left. If you go up to the upper left, it would show that our payment of interests during that period was $157 thousand. Our payment of principal was $100 thousand. These were all current liabilities—claims that our borrowers had against the project over the past year.

Please turn to the upper left of the balance sheet, and it shows the total cash and marketable securities and outstanding rents due as receivables associated with that project alone. That amounted to $800 thousand. Thus, our current assets for that project were more than three times what we owed our bondholders and more than two times what we owe all of our creditors combined—including the maintenance service. If we look at the income statement, our rents were more that nine times the interest we owed. This index, sometimes called times interest earned, is very favorable.

But that is not all. Our credit rating also depends upon the quality of income. By that I mean its steadiness and dependability. Our account receivable is very low because our renters pay their rents. Moreover, their rents are partly guaranteed by the government. They are steady. Let me add that if you go back to the balance sheet of this project you would discover that the ratio of debt to total assets is less than two percent. The project owns substantially more than it owes.

BOARD MEMBER DOLORES DUDLEY TROTMAN: Let me interject to say that the fact that the organization's overall financial statements are strong also helps. These things tend to impact each other in the minds of the bondholders. Moreover, that such a large part of our income, as we shall soon see, is unrestricted means to the bondholder that the parent is not only financially strong but has discretion to use those funds to ensure paying off the debt. I am feeling more secure about our debt management.

Discussion of the Income and Expense Statement

CHAIRMAN RUBY: In the interest of time, let us turn to the income statement.

PRESIDENT ALEXIS: The income statement tells the source of all of our revenues during the last period. This includes revenues from our net sales (sales minus discounts and returns), gifts and contributions, contract income, investment income, and income from the sale of our fixed assets—if any. There was no sale of the assets. Therefore, there is no income from such sales we have to report on our income statement and no decline from such sales on our balance sheet.

Again, I call your attention to the bottom lines. We operated efficiently. Our revenues from operation exceeded all our expenses by four to one. As you are aware, one of your responsibilities would be to decide how that excess is to be used. We shall visit that issue when you set broad guidelines for our next budget or amend this current budget later in the year.

It is important that you note that the majority of funds that came into the organization from donors was unrestricted. Again, accounting rules require our income statement to separate funds that donors restrict the use of permanently from those that are restricted by the donors temporarily or that have no donor restrictions at all. The lack of restriction allows us to exercise discretion and avoid the Simon's Dilemma as described by Professor Bryce in *Financial and Strategic Management for Nonprofit Organizations.*

Fortunately, the format we use for reporting income and expenses segregates those revenues that are considered public support from others. As you may recall, we need to pass a test showing public support and we need to try to achieve that every year.

Also, I do wish you to note that the $5 million promise that has been pledged to us by Sybil of Jamaica, Ltd., is reflected as a receivable. We have not received it, but there are no contingencies or reasons to doubt its receipt. As you know, a promise to give can only be recorded as such if there are no conditions that would reasonably place its receipt in doubt.

BOARD MEMBER JAMES SMITH: Sir, I find it helpful that your statement allows us to look at certain types of expenditures across major categories. We can look at salaries across fund-raising, management, and programs, for example, and we can total up the expenditures on each of these categories. Are there any general rules on the distribution among or between categories that we should be following?

BOARD MEMBER ENID JONES DEBRATHWAITE: No, there aren't. I jump to answer the question because we had a strong debate in another organization and came to learn from Attorney Janet Stewart-Williams that even the Supreme Court and the IRS realize that organizations can be so different that to come up with one ratio is unwise. Expense ratios should reflect the operating realities of each activity. Some activities are more labor intensive and involve more skilled personnel than others. We trust that our accounting staff is allocating costs correctly.

BOARD MEMBER SYLVESTER PRINCE: Our job is to use these numbers in the income statement to ask the following questions: (a) Are we producing a surplus for the organization at the same time that we consciously carry out our mission? (b) Is some of the income taxable and are we paying the unrelated-business income tax? (c) Can we control these expenses better? (d) Does the composition of our income stream allow us to pass the support test? (e) Are we allocating costs properly? On this last point, it seems to me that what we have are actual expenditures (not true costs) and that we do not know enough about how indirect costs are allocated across these various groups.

PRESIDENT ALEXIS: Your points are on target. As you know, indirect cost allocation is important for our survival, our ability to recover the full costs of our activities from those with whom we have contracts, and that the failure to recover these costs will eventually create financial problems. The notes to our financial statement describe the method of indirect cost allocation that we use.

As to the other points you have made, you are correct that the financial results have far-reaching consequences. We must report these in our 990 forms, which are made public and which are the bases of IRS decisions about our classification. Part of our financial planning must be to ensure that we meet these tests. I am fully aware that the details of doing so are part of our responsibility as management, and we appreciate that the board does not micro-manage these details.

While we report financial results to you today, we calculate these figures throughout the year and use them to develop variances from the budgetary targets that the board sets. Let me emphasize that your question as to whether these operational results actually meet our targets is very much germane and so, too, are your questions about whether they meet our requirements to keep our tax-exempt status or bonding rate or covenants surrounding the outstanding loans. They do. Thanks for your appreciation of the fact that the glow of a financial performance is not all there is to what we are about. These financial statements and budgets are instruments for keeping control and guiding the organization. As management, we are constantly comparing them and are accountable to you.

BOARD MEMBER ROY WOOD: Am I correct in concluding that at some point we, as trustees, must look at these results again from what the Form 990 and budgets say?

CHAIRMAN RUBY: Your question applies to all financial statements, and we have one more to look at. But I wish to respond affirmatively to your question at this point because the income and expense statement is actually the fulcrum of all financial statements, and it is so easy during the discussion of this statement to become either saddened or overjoyed with the bottom line.

As a matter of fact, I have requested that we obtain a full financial statement for our stores so that we can look at those in detail. We may want to consider subcontracting the operations of these stores. I got to this idea from looking at the data for its expenditures and revenues along with the other "program" in this financial statement and notice that it is not as financially prosperous for us. Okay, I don't need to be reminded that we don't have a profit motive. But neither do we have a pledge to be losing money. A properly constructed subsidiary or contractual relationship would not necessarily change our tax-exempt status or the taxability of the earnings we obtain from this enterprise.

BOARD MEMBER HARRY TAIT: Some of our new members may be wondering, as I did when I first got on the board, why the income statement can show such an apparent imbalance between our earnings and our taxes. Perhaps we ought to be reminded, Mr. Chairman, that as a tax-exempt organization we do pay taxes on earnings unrelated to our income. Furthermore, but for the grace of good management, we could have ended up paying taxes on interest, dividends, capital gains, royalties, and rental income if the management were not careful not to violate the rules that make those specific classes of income exempt.

VICE PRESIDENT FOR FINANCE AND PLANNING GOODEN WALTERS: We make those considerations part of our overall planning. We always have to consider how what we do impacts our financial position but also our tax-exempt status. That is why we retained the tax-law consultants Charlotte, Melvina and Kelly.

Discussion of Changes in Financial Position

PRESIDENT ALEXIS: Before proceeding to look at the statement of changes in financial position or cash-flow statement, let me expand on the idea of the income and expense statement as the fulcrum—a word used by the chairman. The balance sheet tells us about the status of the organization at the end of an operating period. The income and expense statement tells us about how we operated to achieve that status. These other statements tell us which resources were used during this operation and where they came from.

I may live to regret saying this, but often a board becomes so enamored with the positive surplus that was achieved without ever asking how it was gotten. Such a surplus could be gotten, for example, by selling more bonds because this brings in a heavy cash flow at the time of sale. It could have been gotten by our selling some property, or it could have been gotten because we carried out our mission efficiently. The next statement we are about to discuss, changes in financial position, helps us to understand the sources and uses of resources during the period and to uncover where they came from.

I want to call your attention to the fact that, as in the previous two statements, we report permanent, temporary, and the absence of donor restrictions.

BOARD MEMBER HARRIS SOLEY: I thought that depreciation was an expense. That is what it shows in the income and expense statement. Why are we adding it back in to determine the source of our resources?

BOARD MEMBER MITCHELL SCOTT: As an accountant, I can tell you that this is common and reasonable. Depreciation is not a cash expense. It is merely a bookkeeping or paper expense. No money is ever used up in paying someone for depreciation, therefore, none of the organization's cash is used. If we didn't add it back in, we would have implied that the cash left the organization. It didn't.

This does not mean that depreciation has diminished actual operational importance. We actually used up the physical capacity of our equipment—we just didn't pay out cash in doing so. Because this equipment and building would some day have to be replaced, the board passed a resolution that a "capital replacement fund" be set up and that that be funded partly by a fraction of this depreciation. Again, however, this does not imply that the funds leave the organization. There is just an inter-fund transfer, so to speak. The organization has lost no cash, it merely placed part of it in a different pocket for a rainy day.

PRESIDENT ALEXIS: This has been an open, not an executive, meeting, and our visitors must leave shortly. Let me quickly summarize the sources and uses of our resources during the past year. I call your attention at this point to the fact that all our resource uses were consistent with our mission. There were no dividends because that would have been personal inurement and illegal. Further, note that our main resource was internal—from our own operations. I call attention to inventory because a question was raised earlier about the size of our inventory. Do note that the turnover or sale of our inventory was a major source of funds for us, and so was the collection of receivables associated with those sales.

BOARD MEMBER POLLY VERONICA WELCH: You say that these were major sources. I notice that all sources show decline over the past year and all uses show rises—at least for the assets, and the reverse is true for liabilities. Please explain.

BOARD MEMBER GASKIN DIAZ-LOWE: Let me explain. For assets that decline, say for inventory or receivables, are sources because we sold the inventory we had and got cash or gave credit. Then we collected the credit and we got cash. Similarly, when we sell some of the stocks or bonds we own, we will reduce our holding of these and report that we got cash for them. I hope that this would be more than we paid and we would get a substantial realized gain. As it stands in the balance sheet at this point, the gains are unrealized as we still own the securities. In the case of liabilities, notice just the opposite is true. Notice that our payables went down sharply and that was possible only because the staff used cash to pay off our debt to others. When we purchase goods or services on credit we are temporarily using other people's cash to finance our organization.

CHAIRMAN RUBY: Thanks for this discussion. Please remember that we will have to revisit some of these findings when we submit our Form 990, our taxes, and when we prepare our budget. Our budget should reflect the reality of our recent experience.

Discussion of Audit and Impact of Financial Statements

BOARD MEMBER RICHARD GOODING: Mr. Chairman, just before we bring this discussion to an end, I would like to applaud the staff for an excellent job. I note that the financial recording and reporting they have done meet the generally acceptable principles in accounting, and we have gotten a clean audit. I hope that when we audit our endowment and when the federal government audits our accounting for their programs that we shall have the same results. I am mindful that these are independent and separate audits. But we need to applaud not only the general management that provides us with outstanding operating performances, but with the management of our finances, and the financial recording and reporting systems. At least we did not get an opinion that our accounts could not be audited because there was no way of tracing expenditures or receipts.

CHAIRMAN RUBY: I totally agree with you. We often forget that our financial statements are public through the Internet and may be used by watchdog agencies and both state and federal governments. The contents of these statements give confidence not only to knowledgeable donors and, therefore, increase our fund-raising yield, but they are also important to foundations and to those with whom we contract. Again, thanks.

PRESIDENT ALEXIS: Thanks for the fine compliments. But the staff needs to express its own thanks. One of the reasons why our unrestricted funds have grown so much as a percentage of the total is because of our concerted efforts to solicit such contributions. It was just two years ago that this board directed us to focus our soliciting campaign on unrestricted gifts. What happened in the past is that our funds were generally restricted by donors to our most popular and, perhaps, our single best program. But a dynamic organization that is full of imagination does need unrestricted funds, and we have been successful in using the two best sources for us—our revenues generated from our own fees and sales and our campaign that encourages unrestricted gifts without detracting from the eminence of our main and best known programs.

The Impact of Transactions

BOARD MEMBER SANDRA CUMMINGS: Mr. Chairman, we are grateful for the large gifts that have made our financial statements so much more attractive and for the work the staff has done in increasing the financial efficiency of the organization in general. Because he recognized that large gifts such as the ones we have reported could have significant impact on the organization, Mr. Frederico Larson urged this board to create a subcommittee to look at the possible impact of these gifts on the organization.

As a result, a subcommittee was formed with Mr. Evans Coloute, Ms. Lynnette Benjamin, and me to look at ways to integrate these gifts. Our subcommittee report is not yet due. However, I would like to alert the board to routes of investigation we are now pursuing and to accept any recommendations. First, we are aware that such large gifts, if not balanced by others, could impact our ability to pass the public-support test. Second, we have to avoid being categorized as a private foundation and the donors as disqualified persons. Third, should these or similar gifts not materialize, just as they boosted our financial statements this year, we would have to discount them in the future causing a negative picture of our statements. These are just three of the directions, esoteric as they might be, that we are following.

BOARD MEMBER JOHN CUMMERBACH: I hope that you would also look at our ability to meet the terms of the gifts—if any. Even though these funds are unrestricted, donors can be angered when their gifts are used in certain ways. Unrestricted does not mean disinterested. Furthermore, gifts of the size that we are reporting tend to impact the program direction of the organization even though we would remain within the broad terms of our mission.

BOARD MEMBER WAITE CARR: I hope the ad hoc committee formed to shepherd in the gifts and to consider their integration will soon meet with Mr. Lloyd Sobers's and Mr. Cedric Ferraro's committees on strategic planning and budgeting with the aim of asking not only whether these gifts are consistent with our long-range plan, but how we may modify these plans given the new opportunities that arise with these gifts.

CHAIRMAN RUBY: I trust that Mr. Sidney Henry has gotten this discussion properly recorded in our minutes.

HOW MUCH DO FINANCIAL STATEMENTS TELL?

Financial statements show the organization's status at the start and end of a period. They say little about the interim. Financial statements sometimes exclude facts, show them in favorable light, or are dressed to present the best picture of the organization. Sometimes they legitimately give incomplete information. For example, it is not customary for museums to report the value of their collections. Therefore, a museum's balance sheet will frequently underestimate its assets.

Depreciation is now expected of all long-lived assets except rare pieces of art and historical assets. But how a nonprofit chooses to depreciate, whether it considers the asset depreciable, is a matter of discretion. Land may be depreciated if its quality is used up, as in farming. But for a building site, its quality remains reasonably constant once construction is completed. Therefore, there may be no depreciation charges shown in the balance sheet.

Similarly, accounts receivables and pledges are not all collectible; how much to report as such and how much to report as uncollectible are matters of judgment based on the history of the organization. Financial statements might be the next best thing to truth. What protects the user and justifies the patience in analyzing them as we have done is not only that they are the best information available. The misrepresentation of the facts in these accounts is illegal. The threat of the law constrains falsehood. The threat of an unfavorable audit constrains material incompleteness.

To gain greater uniformity and greater reliability in the interpretation of financial statements of nonprofits, the Financial Accounting Standards Board (FASB) has promulgated some changes. These include requiring most nonprofits to report (1) depreciation, (2) gifts when they are deemed to be actually received and free of conditions, and (3) the value of volunteer services when these services can be priced, such as fees for attorneys because even though these services are not deductible, pricing and including them give a truer picture of the cost of running the organization.

Take a simple case. Frances Williams makes a gift to Gertrude and Louisa School for the Handicapped in the form of a pledge of a $1 million to be provided through the proceeds of a sale of Francess mansion. Should the school report this $1 million in its current balance sheet? Should it report it in the year the sale actually takes place? Should it report it in the year the hard cash is received? Each of these projects a different financial picture of the organization.

THE NOTES

The notes to financial statements can provide insight into the meaning of these statements. They give explanations, expand on some accounting procedures and content matters, give definitions, and explain procedures commitment. Did you ever want to know whether an organization is a 501(c)(3), (4), (5), or (6) and what type of 501(c)(3), as discussed in Part One? Check the note.

SUMMARY AND PREVIEW

The budget (as discussed in Chapter Twelve) and the financial statements are similar in the sense that both are expressed in dollars and cents. The budget, however, is a financial plan and it may or may not be realized. If there are variances from the plan, the manager will wisely ask why. The financial statements discussed in this chapter, however, are factual representations of what occurred financially in the organization during a given time. The budget charts the course, and the financial statements reveal whether the course was actually maintained.

Unlike the budget, the financial statements must conform to generally acceptable accounting principles. These principles are intended to ensure consistency, objectivity, fairness, and completeness in the reporting of financial data. The purpose of an audit is to ascertain whether the practices of the organization conform to good practices. In conducting an audit, auditors seek evidence to confirm that accounting entries are supported by the facts and by authoritative decision making on the part of responsible managers. We have also seen how these statements can be used to assist in the debt and asset management of the organization. We shall turn next to the use of financial statements and budgets in setting operating targets.

CHAPTER SIXTEEN

Evaluating, Setting, and Implementing Financial Goals

After the financial statements have been interpreted, decisions have to be made about how the organization will proceed. Should new financial objectives be set? What should be the new targets? With a good system of reporting information, the board of directors and managers of the nonprofit should have financial statements at least every six months. On the basis of the information in these statements, financial goals and targets can be modified. These modifications feed right back into the system and, in this sense, financial management is a loop.

Periodic evaluations during the fiscal year lead to the setting of new targets or the affirmation of old ones, which themselves will later be reaffirmed or modified. This chapter is about evaluating old targets and setting new ones and the menu of short-term investment strategies that is available in this process. It is also about capital budgeting and endowment planning, both of which involve setting long-range targets and strategies.

Targets may be set for investment, disbursement, and fund-raising objectives, the subjects of this chapter. Setting targets begins by assessing the status of the organization.

QUESTIONS FOR EVALUATING OLD TARGETS

The end of every fiscal period marks the commencement of a new one. A new fiscal year begins at the very moment that the old one ends, thus giving an uninterrupted continuity to the financial function. Having the financial data from the closing period means that the managers of the nonprofit organization are now armed with real data that indicate the actual financial performance of the organization. Management can also assess actual accomplishments. The balance sheet will tell the present situation of the organization: What does it have with which to launch the new year? One way to use these data is to amend or reaffirm old targets. These will be reflected in the new capital and operating budgets. The first step, however, is asking the right questions.

The following are examples of the questions that must be answered in evaluating financial targets:

1. Was the revenue target in the budget met? If not, by how much was it missed and what was the reason? Does it make sense, in light of recent experience, to continue believing that such a target is reasonable? Should it be increased or decreased, or should it remain the same? Why? Are we on course?

2. What form and sources of giving showed the greatest increase? Is this a promising new area of emphasis? Is this where the organization has its best shot? In what form of giving did the organization underachieve? What can be done to get greater support from this form of giving or from this sector? What new strategies shall we try?

3. What is the distribution of support by source? Is there too much dependence on one source or form of giving? Should the organization diversify its base of support? Does the mix of support leave the organization in jeopardy of its tax-exempt status?

4. What are the major cost factors in operating the organization? Can anything be done to contain costs without reducing the productivity and commitment of the organization to its mission?

5. What cost factors are rising and at what rate? Why? Is there a less expensive substitute?

6. What cost centers are exceeding their budgets? Why? Was the budget allocation unreasonable? Should these allocations be realigned? Do some centers need less while others need more? What programs should be dropped?

7. Is it time to put some functions on a self-financing basis? Could they survive? Could they provide revenues for the organization?

8. If there is a deficit, how will it be financed? How long can it be sustained before destroying the organization?

9. Is it time to change investment advisors? Is it time to change banks, insurance companies, or the financial committee of the organization?

10. Is there a cash surplus? How can it be used to the best interest of the organization?

These questions feed back into the strategic planning process from the interpretation of the hard facts in the financial statements. Once decisions are made about targets for the new year, renewed efforts must be made to raise money and contain costs, gather financial data and interpret them, and then begin the cycle all over again setting new targets. The process continues as long as the organization lasts.

CONSIDERATIONS IN SETTING NEW TARGETS

Based on the answers to the preceding questions, the management may set new targets and restrictions.

First, there are policy considerations based on the mission and philosophy of the organization. For example, this organization will not invest in overly risky investments, certain corporations, or countries.

Second, there are legal considerations. New targets should not jeopardize the tax-exempt status of the organization or its charter or place it unwittingly at odds with ethical standards.

A third type of consideration is contractual. Do these targets commit the organization unwisely? Do they threaten existing commitments?

A fourth consideration is the capacity or knowledge of the organization. I hope that this book has broadened the horizon of management. Yet some may not have learned, others will fear, and yet others will reject. The point as noted in the strategic planning chapter is that an organization is constrained not only by what occurs externally but by its own internal capacity, imagination, and initiative.

A fifth and realistic type of concern is that the organization may simply not have the financial resources to be flexible. It is common for an organization to receive a high percentage of its support in the form of restrictive gifts, grants, or contracts. Hence, the room for discretionary decision making is limited. Ironically, however, it is these very organizations that need to push toward the development of unrestricted money to be used for the general support and development of the organization in the conduct of its growing mission. Recall Simon's Dilemma (Figure 12.2; also discussed in Chapter Fifteen).

Within this broad set of constraints, decisions have to be made and targets set. This chapter gives examples of six common types of financial target-setting problems in nonprofits and shows how they can be resolved.

To set financial targets, the organization has to have a firm vision of what it is and what it can do (Part One), because this vision must fit within these legal boundaries that shape the range of strategies at its disposal. The management will want to consider these options systematically (Chapters Seventeen and Eighteen), decide what investments to make (Chapter Sixteen), or how to strengthen their fund-raising activities (Chapters Seven through Ten). Management must also know how to control costs and attract good personnel (Chapter Thirteen). After these managers have had a chance to implement the programs, they must evaluate the fiscal performance of the organization (Chapters Fifteen, Seventeen, and Eighteen) and then reassess targets, set new ones, and make new investment decisions to help meet the targets. The process is continuous and circular and answerable to the trustees (Chapter Six).

THE TREASURER'S REPORT

The treasurer's report highlights the financial experience and status of the organization over a specified period. It is given legitimacy by the signature of the treasurer of the organization and (if used externally) may require the signature of each board member and the CEO of the organization. The report may contain the following:

1. A highlight of significant changes in assets—specifically those that are material to some policy declaration previously made by the board, some change in direction that was taken or that the management deems desirable, or in such assets that are critical to the financial and operating health of the organization.

2. A similar highlight of liabilities—including contingent liabilities (such as lawsuits and outstanding pension obligations) that are critical to the organization. This may include the rate of disposing of liabilities or drawing down on the assets created by and to pay off such liabilities.

3. Changes in restrictions or the impact of restrictions on the organization.

4. The investment experience of each portfolio and of the endowment.

5. The liquidity of the organization and its ability to meet upcoming obligations.

6. The meeting of capital campaigns or fund-raising targets and the need to accelerate such activities if desirable.

7. Extraordinary claims or receipts of the organization.

8. The results of implementing and monitoring past policy initiatives of the board so that they may evaluate their decisions.

9. The results of the disposition of certain assets of the organization.

10. Major acquisitions—financial and otherwise—and their impact on the organization.

11. New financial risks, credit ratings, and collateral requirements.

12. Board contributions to the organization.

13. Reports of consultants, lawyers, and auditors as they pertain to the financial performance of the organization and status of filings the organization must make requiring the signature of the board or for which it is liable.

14. Changes in bank and other depository relationships.

15. Report on or request for new financial authorizations—who may sign, limits on amounts, methods to improve cash management, investment policies, and changes in auditors, investment, or financial advisors.

16. The financial outlook of the organization, including opportunities, threats, needs, and targets.

17. Changes in revenue sources, including subscriptions, membership fees, and assessments.

A thorough treasurer's report should increase the trustee's ability to comply with the duty of care. It should also prepare the trustees by laying the foundation for financial recommendations to be made by the investment advisor, auditor, and CEO. Unlike the mere presentation of financial statements or the mere analysis of such statements, the treasurer's report tells a story that goes beyond the numbers.

ASSESSMENT OF REVENUE ALTERNATIVES

In setting new targets, it is important to reassess the revenue structure of the organization. I recommend the following questions:

1. Is the overall revenue stream sufficiently diversified to meet the tax-exempt requirements if the organization is a 501(c)(3)?

2. Is the overall revenue stream sufficiently diversified to reduce a financial risk?

3. Is the overall revenue stream sufficiently coordinated with cost expectations?

4. Is the revenue stream sufficiently coordinated to meet covenants and other agreements of the contract? Does it impede other contractual agreements?

5. Is the organization exploring all of its most potentially fruitful sources?

6. For each potential source, what is the answer to each of the following:

What is the normal range of its giving or support for the activities in which the nonprofit is eligible?

What would it cost the organization in money and other resources, including time to apply?

Are the funds discretionary? If not, what are the constraints? Can the organization comply? At what costs?

How long will the funds last? Is the organization penalized for achieving savings if it spends less?

When will cash begin flowing? Will costs be incurred before cash is received? If so, how will cash need be covered?

Can the funds be leveraged?

Will the amount received be sufficient to cover indirect and direct costs?

What are the risks that promised funds will be recorded but not received?

This last question is important because a sizable promise that has been recorded in the books but not kept has the potential effect of causing the organization to show a decline in assets. Such an unkept promise also has the effect of reducing the ability of the organization to make commitments planned on the strength of that promise and could, if large and significant enough, affect the debt rating of the organization. If it is a matched gift, it has the potential effect of having the organization renegotiate a restriction on the match or even losing the match.

CASH MANAGEMENT AND INVESTMENT STRATEGIES: INCREASING CASH

Having set revenue targets, the next question is, What do we do with the cash? One set of strategies that must be continuously assessed is what to do with the organization's money (cash management) so that it might multiply until it is used to meet the organization's targets. To appreciate the challenges of cash management, it is necessary to revisit the sources and uses of cash. Aside from donations and business income or membership fees, how does the organization get more cash?

Sources of Cash

In Chapter Fifteen we looked at sources and uses of cash for detecting the changes in the financial condition of the organization. Now we shift from analyzing past actions to the planning of present and future ones.

A source of cash is the operation of the organization. The organization may operate at a deficit or surplus. To this deficit or surplus we add depreciation, since it was an expense charged but no cash was actually spent. Hence, two sources of cash are the surplus (the total revenues and support that exceed expenses) and the depreciation.

A third source of cash is the net decrease in all current noncash assets. A decrease in inventory implies that the organization had sales that yielded cash; a decrease in marketable securities implies they were sold for cash. A decrease in accounts receivable means that cash was received. A decrease in prepaid items and supplies is a source of cash savings and therefore a source of cash. If the organization had increased these current assets instead of decreased them, this would cause a decrease in its cash position. It can only buy more marketable securities or prepay items by spending cash.

A fourth source of cash is the increase in current liabilities. An increase in notes payable implies a loan of cash that would otherwise have been used to pay a bill. An increase in accounts payable means that the organization has increased its cash position by not paying for its purchases. Similarly, an increase in salaries and wages owed implies that the organization has kept cash by postponing the payment of these expenses. If it had paid any of these expenses, its cash position would have decreased. Expenses can only be paid with cash.

A fifth source of cash is the sale of fixed or long-term assets. The sale of the organization's furniture, automobile, and building will all lead to an increase in the organization's cash.

A sixth way to increase cash is to enter into long-term loans. These loans may even be from insurance policies given to the organization or they may be from a lending institution such as a bank. Let us take a deeper look at loans.

Preparing to Borrow

Organizations should prepare for borrowing by taking certain steps. An organization should

1. Obtain a resolution by the board authorizing it to borrow.
2. Have its financial statements, tax statements, and filings in order.

3. Obtain, if necessary, a letter of good standing from the state of incorporation. This is a certificate from the state indicating that it has filed annual reports and taxes as required.

4. Determine whether there are outstanding encumbrances to its going into debt. An outstanding debt may prohibit further bother without the authorization of the creditor.

5. Ascertain whether it will have the cash flow to make debt payments.

6. Determine the length of time for which it needs the loan and match it with its ability to pay.

7. Decide whether it has collateral for the loan and the extent to which it may wish to encumber that collateral. Collateral may be accounts receivables, future grants or contract revenues already committed, or contributions.

8. Determine whether the loan would lead to opportunities for self-dealing and devise a preventative strategy.

9. Understand, before closing the loan, the conditions under which the loan is being made. These conditions may state what the organization must do to get the money, what it must continue to do while the loan is enforced. This may involve holding cash in the bank, it may require the board making annual restrictions on specific monies, it may even prohibit the organization from making significant increases in salaries. Please note that the breaking of a condition in the contract amounts to defaulting on the loan.

10. Learn what the penalties are.

11. Be prepared to do the annual reporting that may be required.

12. Consider getting a financial advisor, if the loan requires the issuing of a bond or is sizable.

13. Be prepared to be truthful with the lenders and in applications. Lenders will require the management of the organization to make certain warranties and representations. It is a crime to misrepresent the facts and this may be punishable both by jail time and penalties.

BORROWING AS A SOURCE OF CASH

It is normal for nonprofit organizations, as well as firms, to run into cash flow problems and have to borrow. They also borrow to meet capital projects, such as purchasing a building or equipment or making leasehold improvements (improvement in office rental space when the lease runs several years). Loans may be for a short or long term. What are the mechanics and strategies?

Short-Term Borrowing

Short-term borrowing refers to loans that are for approximately one year or less. The need for these loans may be indicated when the organization cannot meet current payments, such as for supplies, a month's rent, payroll—basically payments that are periodic and current. These loans are sometimes called *working capital loans* and arise most commonly from cash flow or liquidity problems. That is, the organization is not necessarily broke; it simply is not receiving cash at the same time that it has to pay it out, or wisely chooses not to liquidate assets.

Calculation of Interest

When negotiating a loan, it is important to determine how the interest rate is calculated. One way is to calculate the interest in dollars based on a nominal (stated) rate and then add it on to the amount of the loan. The amount "borrowed" is thus the amount asked for plus the interest on it. In short, the amount actually borrowed will exceed the amount you wanted.

This is a common way of determining interest on installment loans. When this is done, the annual percentage rate (APR) is the important number to know. It may be higher than the annual interest rate quoted and is required by law to be given.

Sometimes the interest is simple. That is, it is calculated and paid at the end of the term of the loan. Another form of calculation, called *discounting,* is to determine the interest and subtract it from the loan; therefore, the borrower gets less than requested. Simple interest is the least expensive, but it is not always available.

Which balance is used also makes a difference. Does the interest apply to the balance at the beginning or end, or is it an average of the daily balance during a period? Which will work better for your organization depends on the pattern of borrowing and repayment during the course of the month. See the upcoming discussion on average daily balance in the following section, Lines of Credit.

Sometimes, even though these are unsecured loans (meaning that no collateral is required), the bank may require a compensating balance. This means that the bank requires the organization to keep some total in its checking account at all times, for which it receives no or a lower interest than is being charged for the loan.

Lines of Credit

The following insert of a line of credit reflects many useful concepts; for example, compensating balances, prime rate plus, and encumbering certain assets as collateral. A loan contract is often referred to as an *indenture* and the conditions under which the loan is made are called *covenants.*

> ### Line of Credit
> A working capital line of credit is maintained with Bowman, our primary banking relationship that allows for borrowing up to $1,250,000 at the prime rate plus 4.5 percent. In connection with this agreement, the Hilton Cherie Organization has agreed not to encumber certain real estate without approval of the bank. In addition, the Organization is to maintain at least $250,000 in net-free demand deposits as a compensating balance. This agreement expires January 1, 2009, and is expected to be renewed. No debt was outstanding on this line of credit as of January 1, 2004.

Again, establishing a line of credit when the organization is in the strongest financial position is a good strategy. Managing so that the debt does not overwhelm the organization is a necessary strategy.

One way to obtain a short-term loan is to request one, called a *negotiated term loan,* when it is needed. One problem with this is that the organization most needs a loan when it is also least attractive to a lender and the loan is thus seen as very risky. Second, the term of the loan may be very unfavorable at that time. Third, the situation may be urgent (for example, to meet a payroll) and there just isn't time. For these reasons, organizations should establish lines of credit when their financial statements and outlook are most favorable.

Because cash flow problems are so common, every organization should consider a line of credit for short-term borrowing. Credit cards are a form of such credit, but these generally have such low limits that they cannot be used for major organizational purposes such as payroll. It is therefore good for the organization to negotiate a larger credit line. The question is whether the temptation to use it willy-nilly can be contained. To protect against this, lines of credit should probably require the signatures of two authorized persons, just as checks should, when the amount being drawn exceeds, say, $1,000.

The bank is a common source of short-term loans whether they are in the form of a credit card or a line of credit. Basically, the bank approves the nonprofit to draw a check on the bank without having to negotiate a loan each time. Lines of credit are good to have as long as they are not abused. Such loans are negotiated well in advance and are formalized by an agreement that is a promissory note. This note lays down the conditions under which the line is established, how the interest and finance charge will be determined, and the rights of both the borrower and the lender:

> This is an agreement between Dylan Bank (the Lender) and Carla Carter Charity, as Borrower, for the establishment and use of a line of credit. This agreement constitutes a promissory note executed under seal, and we may enforce it to the full extent allowed by law for the enforcement of promissory notes. The credit

line that the lender makes available to you permits you to borrow on a revolving basis up to the maximum indicated in this agreement. The credit line is secured by . . . .

Many types of assets may be used to secure a line, for example, inventory, the income from a contract or a grant already awarded the organization, real estate, or equipment. When an asset is used as security, the lender gets the right to inspect it and to require you to insure and to maintain it so that its value does not fall. The lender also reserves the right to foreclose and to demand that the property be sold when it appears that the loan is not likely to be paid. Under these circumstances, it can also call the loan, demanding full payment. It will demand to receive information if the property is to be sold by you and may prohibit its use as security for other loans without prior approval. Permission may also be required to move or modify the property.

When the organization's property is used to secure a loan, be sure that all legal steps are taken to record and free it once the loan has been repaid. In some cases, for example, on real estate in the District of Columbia, papers releasing the property must be filed. Because of the encumbrance, called a *lien,* placed on the organization's property or future income, loans must be approved by the trustees.

The lender may also retain the right to assign or sell your promissory note. The sale of your note, normally not a problem, may occur without your knowing it because the terms of the loan will not change and because the lender may continue to service the loan, meaning that you will continue to pay the original lender and receive bills from it. The original lender then passes your payments to the institution to which it sold your loan. This is a common and usually harmless procedure.

The interest rate on lines of credit will normally vary according to some index. One commonly used index, the T-bill rate, is the rate that the federal government is paying to borrow money on a three- or six-month basis. Another index is the prime rate of some major bank, the rate that the major bank is charging its best customers. Usually, a credit line will charge a rate at least one and one-half percentage points higher, that is, the prime plus one and one-half.

Because rates may rise while a loan is outstanding, it is smart to choose a credit line that has a maximum by which it can increase per year and a ceiling. Hence, the contract may say that the rate is one and one-half percentage points above prime but will not rise more than 2 percent per year and will never exceed 21 percent.

But two other concepts are important, partly because they affect your finance charge but also because they are useful information to have in controlling and managing your short-term finances. One of these concepts is the *average daily balance.* Every day the institution calculates the balance in your line of credit by adding what you borrowed that day to the outstanding balance at the beginning of that day and subtracting the amount it received from you as payment. It does this every day for the billing period—the period that the bill covers. Let us say that the billing period is thirty days. Then it sums up each day's balance over the thirty-day period. Since the billing period is thirty days, it divides the total by thirty and that gives the average daily balance. It tells the nonprofit what its outstanding debt was per day on average during the period.

The finance charge for the period is obtained by dividing the annual percentage rate by the number of days in a year, 365 or 366. If the interest rate is 10 percent, dividing by 365 gives a daily rate of .027. This is the amount of *interest* your organization paid every day on its outstanding balance for that day during the billing period. By adding up all these charges for the thirty-day period, the total finance charge for the period is obtained. In short, you can reduce the cost of the loan to your organization by paying early in the billing period. This would reduce the amount outstanding, assuming no further borrowing.

Trade Credit

Another form of short-term loan is trade credit. This occurs, for example, when the organization purchases supplies and has thirty days to pay. If it pays within those thirty days, it pays no finance charge. This is free trade credit.

A variant of this involves discounts, say of 2 percent, if the organization pays in ten days or else it has to pay the full amount due in, say, thirty days. The discount lost by not paying within the ten days is actually an interest charge for a loan for twenty days (the 30 minus the 10). So delaying beyond the discount period implies paying a finance fee.

Every organization should take advantage of discounts to the extent that by so doing a serious cash flow problem is not created. These discounts may also not be worth it if the organization has to liquidate accounts or assets that are earning higher rates than the organization is being charged by the vendor, or if it has to borrow from the bank at an unfavorable rate. In these cases, it is better to wait thirty days. The cost of a bounced check is usually higher than the implicit cost of foregoing the discount.

Advances

One of the least cumbersome ways of getting a short-term loan is through an advanced payment on a contract or grant. Sometimes it is possible to arrange these before the contract or program period. Other times it is done when money is needed. This is not cumbersome, except one should be aware that when money is advanced, interest can be charged and specific performance may be required. That is, repaying the advance may not free the organization from performance should it decide it does not want to go through with the contract. Consider an advance as a retainer. It is also a debt.

The IRS, Trustees, and Officers Not Lenders

An illegal form of short-term loan is borrowing from the IRS. This occurs when payroll taxes are not paid even though collected by the organization. The penalties on the organization, its management, and trustees can be severe. They are all liable. Do not use payroll and other taxes to meet short-term obligations. See our discussion in Chapter Six.

Borrowing from trustees or officers of an organization may be convenient but not always wise. It encourages a merging of identities between persons and the organization they manage. Moreover, when loans are paid back they may give the appearance of self-dealing. Such loans, if they occur, should be documented and should not encumber the organization with any promises or obligations beyond repaying the loan; interest should be at or below market rate, should be authorized by the board, and should not violate state law, which may not permit them. Borrowing from trustees or officers should be a very last resort.

Cash Value Insurance

A source of short-term (or long-term) capital can be the cash value of insurance policies donated to the organization. As stated in Chapter Eight, these cash values can be borrowed. All that is required is a written request to the insurance company. No collateral is necessary because the security the insurance company has is the insurance contract itself. The rates are usually below the commercial rates, and such loans do not have to be repaid. At the time of death, the total amount owed, including accumulated interest, is deducted from the face value of the insurance before the proceeds are paid to the organization. Policies more than seven years old are generally best for these purposes if a tax on such loans is to be avoided.

Foundations, Government, and Nonprofit Loan Funds

Occasionally, foundations will provide short-term loans to nonprofit organizations. In Minnesota and some other states, nonprofits have another option. The Minnesota Nonprofit Assistance Fund provides loans with terms ranging from thirty days to five years and for amounts ranging from a couple hundred dollars to hundreds of thousands of dollars. The intent is to provide financial stability to nonprofits, particularly 501(c)(3)s in Minnesota. As is similar in some foundation cases, loan recipients can also receive technical assistance.[1]

Long-Term Loans (Revenue Bonds)

Long-term borrowing occurs principally for long-term reasons, such as the purchase of a building. These are usually secured loans. A common way of securing these loans is by pledging the property owned by the nonprofit, including land, equipment, and building. These can be sold to pay off the creditors or can be assigned to the creditors if the organization is unable to pay off the loan or meet scheduled interest payments.

Long-term borrowing is also secured by the income stream of the project, rather than the project or property itself. Dormitories, hospital buildings, and low-income housing are good examples of uses of long-term borrowing secured by the income stream of the project. These are called *revenue bonds*. The loans are made because the lenders believe that the income stream (revenues) from these projects will be high enough to pay the interest and the principal on a timely basis. Income from the project is the only collateral. These bonds are attractive to buyers because they do not have to pay income tax on the interest they earn. Accordingly, the cost of borrowing is lower. These bonds are sold on the capital markets just as every corporate board is. See our discussion in Chapter Five.

Any organization that contemplates this type of borrowing will soon learn how important it is to put together a good financial structure for the organization and a good reporting system. These nonprofits must compete with government agencies and corporations in the capital markets and therefore must be able to demonstrate financial stability. People buy these bonds not because of the mission of the organization but because they expect a competitive rate of return after accounting for the tax-free rates.

Leasing is an alternative to long-term borrowing. Basically, the nonprofit needs to compare the cost and advantages of leasing with the costs and advantages of purchasing. This type of financing is not for small nonprofits, but is of increasing use by housing authorities, hospitals, universities, and other large nonprofits.[2]

Borrowing and all the other approaches lead to an increase in the cash position of the organization. Note that the receipt of gifts and contributions is not ignored. As stated under Sources of Cash, an excess from operations is a source of cash. This excess is defined as the amount of all revenues and support (including gifts and contributions) minus all expenses. So the organization does increase its cash by increasing its receipt of gifts and contributions and other forms of support, including business income. But the actual amount of cash available at the end of any fiscal year depends on the timing of disbursements and receipts and their volumes. I'll say more about this later. But first, what are the competing uses of cash?

USES OF CASH

Here are some of the ways the organization may opt to use its cash, whether it is gained from operations or a loan.

It can increase its fixed assets by buying more or better types of plants, equipment, or buildings.

It can increase its current assets by buying more marketable securities, making more prepayments, increasing inventory, buying more supplies, and financing more accounts receivables.

It can decrease its current liabilities by paying off notes, accounts payable, salaries, and wages, and decrease its deferred revenues by spending what it takes to produce and deliver those items for which it has been paid but has not delivered.

It can pay its long-term debt.

The organization can also use cash to finance the operating deficit. The fact that an organization has a deficit does not mean that it does not have to pay bills. The deficit may be financed by using previous years' cash accumulations or what would have been this year's cash accumulation.

Alternatively, if there is a surplus, cash could be saved. As we discussed previously under Cash Management and Investment Strategies, holding excess idle cash is usually unwise. But using excess cash to begin a program for which future support has not yet been identified or secured may be equally unwise.

Cash management is a skill. It involves increasing the total volume (sources) and the rate (acceleration) at which cash flows into the organization. At the same time the volume (uses) and the rate (deceleration) at which cash flows out must be prudently tempered to meet the obligations and mission of the organization. Unlike government agencies, nonprofits are not "required" to disburse or obligate their funds at the end of the fiscal period. This is even illegal in federal agencies. Some surplus shown in the financial statements of nonprofits results form expenditures lagging behind receipts. This is good management and it provides cash for short-term investment opportunities. The lag might be due to time needed to build the organization's capacity to carry out a program successfully. The gain might be nothing more than interest arbitrage (the interest earned is higher than that due to the delay in paying a bill). Let us look at alternatives for investing excess cash.

LIQUIDITY VERSUS INVESTMENT AND RISK VERSUS SAFETY

The following steps may be taken once cash is available: First, the board of trustees of the organization may elect to have a part of the cash placed in a restricted fund. This fund may be restricted so that withdrawals can occur only at the discretion of the board or to finance some specific activity in the future. Accumulation of this type is generally no problem for public charities, except it could affect their meeting watchdog standards. For private foundations, as explained in Chapter Four, any attempt to set aside large amounts of cash should be done only after getting specific authorization from the IRS. Obviously, if accumulation is the choice, holding cash and currency makes no sense. The money ought to be invested.

Second, an amount of cash of approximately six months of the organization's cash need should be kept in a highly liquid asset that earns interest with a very low risk of loss. Negotiable order of withdrawals (NOW) and money market accounts available at banks and through mutual funds are examples.

Third, beyond this amount, cash should be invested so as to stagger maturity dates. That is, some cash should be placed into instruments that have a thirty-, sixty-, ninety-, and 360-day maturity. Repurchase agreements (as will be explained), certificates of deposit, Treasury bills, and commercial paper (short-term loans to corporations) are examples. These instruments pay higher rates of interest than NOW and money market accounts but are less liquid.

TEN CONSIDERATIONS IN SELECTING AND MAINTAINING A BANK ACCOUNT

The most direct way of dealing with cash is to put it into the bank. The bank debacles of the 1990s are reminders that banks are not risk-free. Here are ten rules that should be helpful:

1. Be sure the bank is insured, preferably by the federal government.

2. Determine dollar limits of the insurance and whether the limit is per depositor, per bank, or per account.

3. Because of items 1 and 2, try to maintain no more than the limit in any one bank—diversify. If more than this amount must be kept, try to have separate accounts and indicate that each account is being held in your capacity as a fiduciary; it is thus being held for another entity. Using different branches may not help unless they are separately chartered; for example, in different states.

4. Balance checks monthly and check each entry.

5. Compare fees, free checking, and interest payments. They differ among banks.

6. Be sure that your bank will be willing to make a short-term loan, or at least provide a line of credit. You may need it.

7. Hold money for investment and retirement in a bank different from that holding money for check-writing needs. This relates to items 1 and 2, but it is also important because the same bank may not be equally good at both.

8. Check the investments of the bank. Some banks are risky. Banks are rated according to performance and risk exposure.

9. Check the investment and performance of the parent if the bank is a part of a holding company, that is, part of a larger bank family. Children can inherit the problems of their parents.

10. Check to determine whether the bank has a social investment policy compatible with your interests. How much does it invest in the local community? Does it cater to nonprofits?

Near-Cash Investments

One possible use of cash is to hold it to meet the known cash needs of the organization and to meet emergencies. There is no magic to determine what this amount should be. This depends on the experience of the organization. Aside from putting money in the bank, the organization could buy securities. Bank accounts rise because of the interest earned. A security may earn interest or dividends and rises if buyers bid up their prices and falls if any of these is reversed.

Treasury bills are the lowest-risk securities. They are issued by the U.S. Treasury weekly and carry a three-, six-, or twelve-month maturity. They are sold in $5,000 multiples with a $10,000 minimum required. Repurchase agreements have short (overnight) maturity. A borrower gives security to the nonprofit. When the loan is repaid the nonprofit returns the security. The risk of loss of any portion of the investment in commercial paper (a short-term loan to a corporation) can be reduced by buying only the shortest-term papers of the strongest companies. The risk of loss from buying certificates of deposit can be reduced by buying them from institutions covered by federal insurance.

Bonds

U.S. Treasury notes mature in two to five years and are sold in minimums of $1,000 to $5,000. Bonds may be bought from the Treasury, a government agency, state and local governments, or a corporation. Newly issued bonds mature in twenty to thirty years. This is a long time to commit the organization's money, and although we would like to think of bonds as having little risk, this is not the case. There are risks of default, and there is a risk of inflation, with not only a decline in the real value of the interest earned, but a fall in the bond prices as investors seek to make up for the low interest by lowering the price they will pay for it. Why pay $1,000 for a bond that offers 7 percent, when you can get 10 percent on another bond? Hence, if the organization needs to sell before maturity, it will have to take a loss unless interest rates have declined, in which case it might make a gain as the price of the bond rises to reflect the fact that this bond earns more interest than ones issued at a lower coupon (interest) rate.

Low-grade corporate bonds (rated B or under) pay attractive rates but are highly risky not only of default, but also of loss of principal if the corporation collapses. These are junk bonds. True, bondholders have a claim on the assets of the corporation, but this claim may be long in exercising and may be worthless.

The riskiest of the corporate bonds are subordinated debentures that have a below A rating. *Subordinated* or *junior* means that claims, in the event of bankruptcy, will be among the last honored. A debenture means that the bond has no collateral behind it. Below A means the firm is not among the financially strongest. These bonds pay high interest rates because of their high risk. They, too, are junk. Nonprofits interested in these bonds would do well to purchase them through a mutual fund, thereby reducing bond-specific risks.

Another risk that bondholders face is that the bond may be called by the issuers. Bonds are called when the issuer sees that it can issue a new bond at a lower rate of interest. Consequently, a bondholder who is getting abnormally high rates of interest may not have that bond for very long, as it may be called by the issuer. Unfortunately, it is usually impossible to reinvest the proceeds at similarly high rates and low risks because calls occur when interest rates have fallen. The inability to reinvest at a comparable rate and risk is called *reinvestment risk.*

Even state and local government bonds have risks. Not all are backed by the full faith and credit of the issuing government. That is, not all are backed by the full taxing powers of the jurisdiction. Those that are reduce the risk of loss of principal investment or interest because the issuing jurisdiction is required by law to fully utilize its taxing powers to pay bondholders. But the fastest growing type of jurisdictional bonds have no such backing. These are called *revenue bonds* because they are backed only by the revenues from the project (housing, dormitories, hospitals) they finance. To reduce the exposure to risk, the managers of the nonprofit may obtain information on how the bonds are rated, keep to AAA or AA or A ratings, and take an additional precaution by being sure that the bond is part of an insured fund.

Stocks

Listed stocks are easily marketable because they can be bought and sold every working day unless some special event causes their trading to be suspended. Stocks are highly volatile. Preferred stocks (stocks that are given preference in the receiving of dividends and in the settlement of claims should the business collapse) are less risky than common stocks. The latter has lowest priority in exercising claims if the firm folds and no preference in the payment of dividends. Usually, the dividends paid are low and may be changed at any time by the board of directors of the corporation. Both types of stocks, but especially the common, offer the possibility of appreciation in their prices as the company's expected earnings are favorably valued by investors. They also have the possibility of decline as they become less favored, and common stocks are more volatile than preferred because, even in a decline, the investor can expect higher dividends from the preferred.

Stocks are dubious investments for some nonprofits because of their long-term perspective, volatility, and the capital needed to diversify among many companies so as to reduce the risk associated with any one (called *nonsystematic, idiosyncratic,* or *diversifiable risks*). Moreover, a number of nonprofits and foundations have sizable ownerships of businesses and indeed were originally founded by gifts of stocks in these businesses. Playing the stock market, however, requires a lot more expertise and involvement than some nonprofits have. For many, their involvement should not go further than accepting gifts of stocks and investing in mutual funds.

Mutual Funds

Mutual funds, other than money market funds, are of all types. There are corporate bond funds, municipal bond funds, energy funds, gold funds, and aggressive common stock funds, bond funds, and emerging markets income funds, to name a few. There is virtually a mutual fund for every investment taste. Mutual funds are marketable in that they can be bought and sold with relative ease. They avoid the need for investment expertise on the part of the organization because they are managed by professional investment advisors.

Mutual funds reduce the risks of losses associated with individual common stocks because they are very large and highly diversified. Even a mutual fund that specializes only in gold will carry the stocks of several firms involved in gold. Mutual funds do not generally invest more than 10 percent of their portfolio in any one company so the individual investor in one of these funds is not overexposed to the risks of collapse by any one company. Mutual funds move faster, slower, or are indexed to move in speed and direction of the general or some specific market. There is a fund for every investment taste.

Partnerships

Investing in tax-sheltered partnerships is another option, but this serves no useful purpose to most nonprofits except pension funds. These partnership interests cannot be redeemed without considerable penalty and only in the amounts and at the times stated in the contract. Moreover, the need of nonprofits for a shelter is less than it is for tax-paying entities, and the use of such shelters may be challenged by the IRS.

The preceding paragraph refers to partnerships for tax purposes. These are very different from the types of partnerships discussed in Chapters Nine and Fourteen, where the partnership is for a productive purpose or for producing rental income, as discussed in Chapters Eleven and Eighteen. Several nonprofits engage in the latter types of partnerships. They are common in the nonprofit housing and health sectors.

Buying Guide

Ratings can be used as a guide to determine the investment quality of bonds, commercial paper, municipal notes, and stocks. These ratings are not recommendations and they are not forecasts of how well the security will perform in the future. They are evaluations of the financial integrity of the issuer and the issue. In the following, we summarize certain ratings, beginning with the Moody's rating of corporate bonds.

Aaa: These bonds are judged to be of the highest quality. The interests are believed to be protected by exceptionally stable profit margins and the principal is deemed to be secure. The chances that the fundamental financial qualities of the issuer will deteriorate are deemed unlikely.

Aa: These bonds, like Aaa bonds, are considered high-grade bonds. They are not graded Aaa because their underlying financial position is subject to wider changes than the Aaa bonds, but they are of high quality.

A: These bonds are backed by the sound financial situation of the issuer, but some of these conditions may be subject to change in the future. These bonds are said to be of medium grade.

Baa: These are also medium-grade bonds but they are more speculative, since it is believed that some of the underlying factors that protect principal and interest could deteriorate in the foreseeable future.

Ba: These bonds are characterized as uncertain. They are speculative, with very modest protection of principal and interest.

B: These bonds are speculative and there is limited assurance that the principal or interest will be forthcoming in the future or that even the terms of the contract under which the bonds were purchased can be met.

Caa: These bonds may either be in default (interest has not been paid) or there are visible dangers that a default or the inability to pay principal may be imminent.

Ca: These are very speculative. They are either in default or seriously flawed.

C: These bonds have little likelihood of ever being upgraded to investment standing. They are the most speculative.

Sometimes Moody's will show the letter grades and a numerical grade. An Aaa 1 rating means that the security is in the top of the Aaa ratings and a C3 means that it is the lowest of the C-rated bonds.

Standard and Poor's has a similar rating system except that it uses pluses and minuses instead of a numerical grade to indicate the standing of each security within its generic class, and the letter grades are somewhat different. For instance, instead of Aaa, it uses AAA, and instead of Ba, it uses BBB. Ratings of securities do change. Fitch is also a well-respected rating agency.

Again, the major purpose of these rating systems as far as the financial manager is concerned is an indication of the investment worthiness of securities. It is often unnecessary, unwise, and sometimes illegal to invest the dollars of a nonprofit organization in a highly risky (below A) security. Another way to reduce risk is to purchase securities that are insured. Even municipal bonds may be insured so that the purchaser's risk is reduced. A good investment strategy is an excellent source of unrestricted income for running an organization. The earnings can generally be used at the discretion of the management to carry out the mission. Table 16.1 displays some typical investments and their risks.

Volatility of Security

The organization should also be concerned with the degree of volatility or systematic risks; that is, changes in the value of a security as the overall market changes. This feature of a stock or mutual fund can be ascertained by checking out its beta coefficient. The more the beta exceeds one, the more the stock moves (up and down) relative to the market. A negative beta means the stock or fund moves in the opposite direction to the market. With bonds, the duration is the index of volatility. Hence, the more the duration is above one, the more a change in the interest rate would affect the price of that bond. When a small increase in the market interest rate causes a large fall in the price of an existing bond so as to compensate new buyers of these bonds for the lower rate the bond carries on its coupons, the bond is said to have a long duration. These indices, durations and betas, are easily obtained and a diversified portfolio will have a combination of them. In the final analysis, the structure of a portfolio is dependent upon its intended use and the purpose for which it was constructed. These indices help to coordinate use with market risk. The risk of being invested in a single company or industry can be reduced by diversifying the investment portfolio. The latter should reflect investment objectives and risk tolerance.

SETTING UP A PORTFOLIO: FIRST STEPS

Creating a portfolio involves the following steps. First, the organization needs to have an estimate of the total funds available to it for investment. Then it has to divide this sum up into portions that are for the current year, some intermediate periods, and for the distant future. The division into these periods will vary depending upon the budgeting and program responsibilities of the organization. Some private foundations budget over a two-year period and they must take into account the legal requirement that they distribute the higher of 5 percent of their net investment income or adjustable gross income. See Chapter Four.

Table 16.1. Securities: Their Typical Minimum Maturities and Risks.

Securities	Typical Minimum Maturity Period	Comments
Negotiable order of withdrawal*	Immediate	Low risk, especially if institution is federally insured
Money market mutual fund	Immediate	Low risk, especially if portfolio is weighted toward U.S. Treasury paper
Repurchase agreements	1–90 days	Risk depends on security backing agreement
Commercial paper	20 days or more	Risk depends on issuing corporation
Certificate of deposit	90 days	Low risk, especially if institution is federally insured
U.S. Treasury bills	90 days	Low risk
Negotiable certificates of deposit	90 days	Low risk, but requires large initial amount of $100,000
U.S. Treasury notes	3 years	Low risk, but long holding period
U.S. Treasury bonds	30 years	Low risk, but long holding period
State and local government bonds	30 years	Varying risk depending on issuer; long waiting period
Mutual funds (other than money market)	Immediate	Risk depends on investment philosophy of fund
Corporate bonds	20 years	Risk depends on issue
Common stocks	Immediate	Wide fluctuations
Preferred stocks	Immediate	Fluctuate like bonds; risk of dividend default
Tax-sheltering partnerships	Indefinite	Risky and redemption depends on terms set in contract; early redemption will lead to losses
Guaranteed investment contracts	3–5 years	Fixed interest; should be considered long term

*By law, available only to individuals and nonprofits.

Some organizations have very strong current needs, but have an endowment that allows them to invest over the long haul. Some organizations have program needs that are neatly divided into the short-run, intermediate run, and long run. Hence, the meaning of a period in terms of years depends upon the underlying facts about how the organization operates.

Once this breakdown into periods is determined, a second step will be to decide how to allocate the funds set aside for each period among various types of assets appropriate for that period. The most important principle here is that the funds are available when needed and that they are generating income for the organization while being held.

Given this orientation, we can think of the following periods and allocation of funds at the beginning of each period. Allocations will vary upon the risk tolerance of the organization, the rate of return that can be gotten, and the schedule at which the accounts will be drawn down to pay bills. But the availability of a line of credit to the organization to make up for its inability to cash in the assets without loss at the time the money is needed can serve as a good hedge.

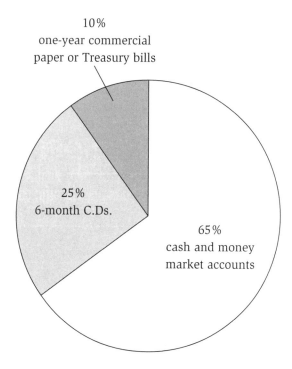

Figure 16.1. Funds Needed Within One Year.

Legend: Spending begins with the cash and then the money market, and by the time these amounts are exhausted, the CDs should mature and be ready to enter the spending stream. By the time that amount is exhausted, the commercial paper and Treasury bills should be ready.

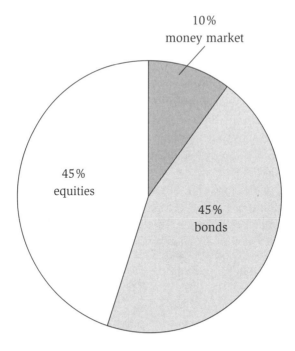

Figure 16.2. Funds Needed in Ten or More Years.

Legend: Money market accumulates dividends, interest, and capital gains to finance new investments.

The short-term portfolio is also dependent upon the cash management arrangements the organization can make—and its ability to postpone payments without penalty or at a cost is less than the cost of delaying payments.

In Figure 16.2 most of the portfolio can be put in longer-term assets that are likely to have greater rates of return and more risk. The organization can wait out turns in the market. This kind of allocation is appropriate for a nonexhaustible endowment—one that does not require complete draw-down of the amounts in the funds described in this chapter. This is so not only because of the long holding period it allows, but also because the trustees can set draw-down rates to match the earnings of the portfolio. Hence, in a bad year, the amount that will be drawn will be lower than in a good year.

Once these major broad asset allocations are made, the real technical skill is in determining the choices within each asset class. Which bonds and which stocks? Here are some simple rules that would help the manager:

1. Get a good investment advisor (or preferably separate portions of the account among several of them).

2. Get a board that is diligent and prudent.

3. Recognize that investment decisions are ultimately that of the board.

4. In general, oppose giving unconstrained rights to investment managers or advisors to make decisions about the portfolio. If an unconstrained approach is desirable, think of a mutual fund.

5. Place limits on the amount of the portfolio that can be invested in any one company and sector. Check state law on this. This book discusses these laws in various places, including in this chapter and in the chapter on trusts (Chapter Eight). Most times, a manager would rely on an investment advisor in or outside the organization. The manager must be approved by the board and must report to it.

6. Require the investment manager to give presentations that are understandable. Most investment options that are too technical or too difficult to understand are too risky for those who are being asked to undertake them and who are bound by oaths of prudence and care.

7. Although investment advisors are required to disclose any relationship they or their firm may have with a security or its issuer, it is wise to include that disclosure requirement in any contract. Beware of self-dealing when such a relationship exists.

8. Do not let a commission come between you and a good deal. In my view, as one who has marketed, served as a trustee for issuers, and also has bought securities, the concern about commission is often misplaced. The investor should ask these questions: Is this deal for me? Does it make me significantly better off even after the commission is paid? Is this a relationship that can serve my information needs beyond this trade? Is there a possibility of a charge of self-dealing by management or the trustees?

9. Every decision should be prefaced by education and no decision can be so urgent that it cannot wait. The market creates opportunities every day.

10. Make sure that the investment advisor is acquainted with state and federal laws related to the investment of institutional funds.

If the money will not be needed for some time in the future, most of it can be invested in assets that have maturities of one year or more. As one invests in these longer term fixed assets, the risk is that the interest rate will rise above that which the organization is getting. But because the portfolio is rolling, some of this loss will be reduced as the organization places money at these higher rates.

The opposite risk, discussed earlier, is the *reinvestment risk*. This refers to the occasion that the nonprofit is getting a higher rate than the market is

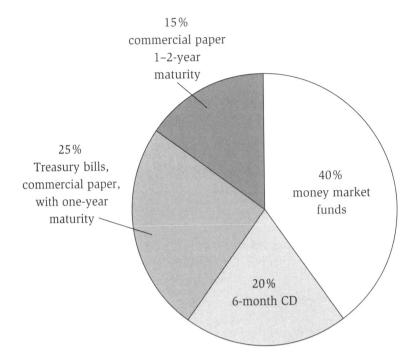

Figure 16.3. Funds Needed in Two to Three Years.

Legend: Because cash is not needed for a year to date, the 40 percent can be placed in money market accounts. The CDs will be ready at least six months before the year begins and can join the money market pool. This would provide a strong cash buffer for supporting the longer-term investments.

currently paying. Therefore, the funds that mature can be reinvested only at lower rates. Spreading the portfolio over different maturity periods dampens these types of risk. Figures 16.3 and 16.4 show intermediate portfolios.

SELECTING SECURITIES AND REBALANCING PORTFOLIOS

In several places in this chapter we describe concepts that would help the manager in selecting securities. The principal rule to follow is that this is not the manager's job. A smart manager would exercise his or her duty of care that compels an understanding of what is going on. He or she will also rest on the law's protection if the manager relies on the recommendations of a carefully chosen advisor. The trick is to set hurdles and prohibitions. A very simple one is to insist that the primary purpose of the entire portfolio strategy is *capital preservation*. This is a message understood to mean moderate risk.

The descriptions used in this text in the discussions of volatility of security, buying guides, ranking of securities, and especially in the rebalancing of

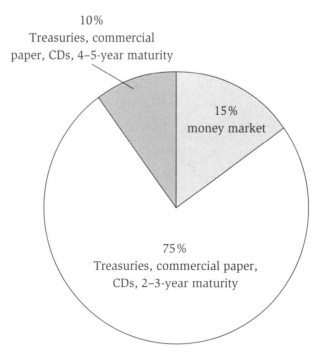

Figure 16.4. Funds Needed in Four to Five Years.

portfolios (see the next sidebar on pages 562–563) would help the manager understand and participate in the decisions about the securities that will populate the portfolio. There is no advantage to trying to be your own investment advisor, but there is total disadvantage in not understanding.

INVESTMENT POOLS

Managers of small organizations may wonder whether investment strategies such as those used by larger organizations may be available to them. The answer is yes, through an investment pool. Such pools provide for several organizations to invest as a group. By doing this, they share risks and are able to diversify among several investments, hire an investment advisor, and trade at a lower commission rate.

The National Conference of Catholic Bishops, the United States Catholic Conference, the American Board of Catholic Missions, the Campaign for Human Development, the Committee for the Church in Latin America, and the Catholic Communication Campaign, for example, have a short-term

Rebalancing Portfolios

Rebalancing of portfolios is a way of managing risks. It is also a strategy for preserving past gains and minimizing future losses. Rebalancing involves not only giving a new structure to a portfolio and a new risk profile, it also involves the timing of these changes.

Here are some thoughts that a board of trustees of a nonprofit organization ought to consider in thinking about rebalancing the organization's portfolios—a process that should be ongoing regardless of what the market does.

1. Setting portfolio ranges is the duty of trustees. Every organization needs an investment policy. It should be passed by a resolution of the majority of the board of trustees. A vote of the board is also required for resetting the parameters in that policy. A good policy provides ranges that are broad enough to be useful and narrow enough to be confining. Hence, a policy may say 30 to 50 percent in stocks rather than 30 percent or 30 to 35 percent.

2. A guiding principle of all investment policies and of all rebalancing is prudence and preservation of the assets of the organization. This is the duty of care.

3. The overall policy should reflect diversification across types of assets—such as common stocks, bonds, and money market assets such as treasury notes, short-term certificates of deposits, and checking accounts. Diversification should take into account that within each class of security further diversification is prudent. For example, bonds of different investment grades such as AAA, AA, and A and of different issuers, maturities, and durations (a measure of how volatile the price of the bond is with respect to small changes in the interest rate) are bases upon which bond diversification can be accomplished.

4. Similarly, stocks can be differentiated by industry, the dollar size capitalization of the firms such as small, mid-cap, and large cap or blue chip. An important diversification can be between preferred and common stocks. The former is usually bought because it provides a more stable dividend.

5. The overall policy should reflect diversification across geographic lines and may well include some global investments. It may also be consistent with the social policy of the organization.

6. The overall policy should reflect the financial needs and capabilities of the organization and the particular purpose of each program. Some activities of an organization might be heavy cash users on a monthly basis; their portfolio needs would require a considerable amount of

liquidity. Long-term investments should be considered only after the organization's liquidity needs are fully satisfied.

7. The trustees must decide how much rebalancing can be done automatically; that is, how much discretion they wish to retain for themselves, and how much they wish to give to their investment manager. In each case, the composition of the portfolio is adjusted as changes occur either through relative growth or decline in one part of the portfolio relative to others. Rebalancing can also occur by changing the formula for distributing new contributions to the overall portfolio.

8. The past is no predictor of the future. An investment mix that worked well in the past may not work well in the future. During periods of great uncertainty, the holding of larger cash or money market assets to preserve past gains, invest as market opportunities arise, and assure liquidity for future needs is not necessarily imprudent.

9. The excess holding of cash may create an opportunity cost or loss— the possibility that cash may be held for too long and in too large an amount.

10. Since index funds (those that are set up to have the same composition of some broader index such as the Russell 5000, S&P 500, or the Dow Jones) sometimes do better than managed funds (those that have portfolios that change at the discretion of managers), the need for continuous rebalancing might be reduced when investments are made according to these indices. This does not eliminate the need to consider rebalancing. But it reduces the range of discretion, since the aim is to mimic the index.

11. Rebalancing is not cost-free even though there may be no charge. Investment managers earn fees when funds are turned over. This should not stop management from exercising the prudence of rebalancing but it should be considered in assessing the motive or advice to rebalance and the returns from rebalancing.

12. Beware of being a victim of fast-talking investment advisors, fads, and the lure of high returns. At the same time, beware of paying a premium for rights never used. The right to withdraw or to have access is worth as much as the probability that such a right will be exercised. However, a good reason for rebalancing a portfolio is to have access to meet a known future expenditure.

13. There is no substitute for beginning with a thoughtful policy, having patients, and yet recognizing the need to change when that need is clear. For trustees of nonprofits, this is part of the duty of care.

and long-term investment pool for themselves. This assists them in conducting a wide range of charitable missions here and abroad, including financial support of other charities. Section 501(d) organizations (see Chapter Two) are specifically organized to permit religious organizations to have a common treasury and carry out investments.[3]

CAPITAL PLANNING

To top management, capital planning must precede capital budgeting. It should contain at least the following considerations:

1. Determine that there is a need that is likely to endure for some time. By definition, capital projects are long-lived and therefore so should the intensity and quantity of the need.

2. Determine the desirability of the project. Does the need comport with the mission, culture, and philosophy of the organization under current conditions and in the foreseeable future?

3. Determine the feasibility of the project. Can the project, conceived in a manner that is acceptable, be done?

4. Determine alternative cost scenarios within the range of feasibility and desirability.

5. Determine operating and maintenance costs and inputs.

6. Determine requirements and their costs. For example, a construction project may pass all of the above tests and the capital budgeting hurdle but be completely handicapped by the inability to get a license or a permit to operate as quickly as desired.

As a reminder of point 6, note that most building-related expenditures are subject to zoning laws. This kind of violation occurs much too often and represents bad capital planning. So even though the budgeting may have appeared to have been perfect, if point 6 occurs and endures, the cash inflow projection upon which the capital budget was done would be wrong. The organization will face a financing problem it did not plan to entertain.

CAPITAL BUDGETING AND ENDOWMENT PLANNING: SETTING TARGETS AND IDENTIFYING SOURCES OF CAPITAL

The operating budget that we described in Chapter Twelve is concerned with the annual operation of the organization. It shows planned inflow and outflow of the organization's resources during the course of the coming year. Some organizations, but not many, have a multiyear operating budget. These budgets show the plan for annual operation of the organization for each of the next five years.

A capital budget shows the planned acquisition, disposition, or reconstruction of capital items. A capital item is one that has a useful life of more than one year. Furniture, equipment, buildings, automobiles, and computers are examples of capital items. The launching (not operation) of large, flagship, or sustaining programs that are at the core of the mission of the organization should also be considered a capital expense, especially if such programs are associated with endowments or capital expenditures such as the acquisition of new buildings or equipment.

Expenditures on capital items are called *investments* or *capital expenditures.* These are different from expenditures planned in the operating budget, which are *operating expenses*. An investment is an expenditure on an item that may change in value over time and that is not all consumed or used up in one year. A building is not used up in one year. It has a useful life of decades. But each year, a portion of the building, the computer, or the automobile is used up; that is, there is wear and tear. The dollar approximation of this wear and tear is called *depreciation*. Because depreciation arises as a result of annual operation, depreciation is shown as an annual expense in the operating budget and financial statements of the organization.

Furthermore, once the capital item is placed in service, it requires maintenance, and the principal and interest on the loan used to purchase the asset (mortgage in the case of a building and car loan in the case of an automobile) must be paid annually. These become annual operating expenses.

Capital planning and budgeting require analyses not only of when and how the capital asset will be obtained, but how it will affect the annual operating budget. Two routes through which this impact occurs are by way of maintenance and amortization costs (payment of principal and interest). Another source is through insurance premiums. Credit and liability insurance premiums must be paid annually; they may increase as capital expenditures increase. An additional building means greater exposures to liability and credit risk.

From a financial point of view, several questions arise in capital budgeting. Let us put ourselves in the position of the board of directors of a nonprofit organization considering the acquisition of a building. What are some of the questions that may arise?

One question is the source of the required funds. One potential source is through gifts and contributions of money, including a large gift obtained in trust or by running a special gift campaign, that is, a capital campaign.

A second potential source is through the accumulation and setting aside of part of the annual earnings of the organization. Recall that with private foundations, such accumulations must be authorized by the IRS.

A third source of capital acquisition may be the physical gift of a building, which may be used, sold, or leased by the organization. Be reminded, however, that if the building is obtained through a gift and has a mortgage on it, the income from the rental could be subject to an unrelated business income tax and this annual tax payment would affect the organization's operating budget.

A fourth source that provides the basis for systematic accumulation is depreciation. By depreciating existing assets, an expense is written off current operations. But depreciation does not represent the kind of expense that requires the organization to draw a check. It is a paper expense. Therefore, one way to finance new acquisitions is to accumulate these paper expenses—actually setting aside each year the amount of depreciation so that these amounts may be used to purchase new assets.

A fifth source is debt: Borrow the money. This source would also have an impact on the organization's operating budget since the principal and interest on the debt must be paid annually.

A sixth source is a leasehold arrangement. This is a cross between a lease (a long-term liability) and ownership. Basically, the owner of the property makes physical changes in the building to suit the specific needs of the nonprofit with the commitment from the nonprofit that it would stay for a specific number of years, pay rent according to a specific schedule, and leave a security deposit. In this case, the source of cash for rental payments is a capital fund or the operating revenues of the organization.

As stated earlier in this book, nonprofits may not sell stocks in themselves. Therefore, this source of financing capital projects is not available to them as it is to for-profit corporations. As Chapter Eleven describes, a company that they control can issue stocks, or they can sell partnership interests in a project such as the housing case discussed under "Coexistence of Charity and Capitalism" in the next chapter.

ACCUMULATION AND DISBURSEMENT STRATEGIES

A related set of questions has to do with the schedule of accumulating the funds needed to acquire the building. For example, the organization could collect all the money it needs in one year or it could collect it over a number of years. How much does it need to collect in each year if it chooses the latter course? How much does it need to collect by the end of the first year if it chooses to collect all the money at the end of that year?

Both answers depend on the rate of interest, for the smart financial manager would invest the collected sum in a safe investment paying a relatively predictable fixed rate. By doing this, the amount that has to be collected, borrowed, or taken from the organization's savings or shifted from the monies available for the daily operation of the organization would be lessened.

Let us assume that the rate of interest is 10 percent, the planning horizon (the time over which to accumulate the money) is four years, and the amount needed to acquire the building is $5 million. What are some of the alternative targets for accumulating the funds?

Present Value of Single Sum

One option is to have a fund-raising drive that ends at the end of the first year and to put that money into the bank so that, at 10 percent, it will accumulate the money needed to acquire the building over a four-year period. If the organization can be successful in doing this, it will be able to avoid debt, shift its fund-raising efforts to another program, and avoid using any of its operating income or savings from operations to buy the building. How much must it raise in the first and only year of its fund-raising effort for this strategy may be successful? What is its target amount?

A strategy such as this obviously depends on the amount of money that must be collected in the first year so that when it is invested at 10 percent over a four-year period it will equal $5 million. This is called the *present value of a single sum*. It is the dollar value of a single amount of money that, if invested, would yield the targeted amount at the end of some specified period (in this case four years) when the rate of interest per year is some specific amount (in this case 10 percent).

This problem can be solved by going to a table such as Table 16.2, which can be found in interest rate books. We look under the column called *single payment present worth* and the row that applies to four years, and we find a factor .6830. We multiply $5 million by this factor and get $3,415,000. This is the amount that must be raised and invested in the beginning of the first year at 10 percent annual rate of return each year if the $5 million target is to be met by the end of the fourth year. Of course, the board could significantly reduce this amount and still not take the greater risk of looking for a higher rate of return if it stretches out the time it has to accumulate the funds. If they chose to wait eight rather than four years, their fund-raising target would be (.4665 × $5,000,000) or $2,332,500.

Future Value of a Single Sum

Alternatively, the organization may already have a large gift that it can invest in the first year. The question that the board of trustees is faced with is, Will this be sufficient when invested at 10 percent over the four-year period to meet our target? Would we have to raise more money? How much more? This type of problem is called *finding the future value of a single sum*. That is, how much is a single sum invested today at, say 10 percent, worth in the future, say four years? Once we have found the answer to this, we can subtract this amount from our required amount and determine whether we are going to meet, exceed, or fall short of the target.

Table 16.2. Time Value of Money Assuming 10 Percent Interest Factor.

n Years	Single Payment Compound Amount Future Value of $1	Single Payment Present Worth Present Value of $1	Uniform Series Compound Amount Future Value of Uniform Series of $1	Sinking-Fund Payment Uniform Series Whose Future Value Is $1	Capital Recovery Installment to Amortize $1	Uniform Series Present Worth Present Value of Uniform Series of $1
1	1.100	0.9091	1.000	1.00000	1.10000	0.909
2	1.210	0.8264	2.100	0.47619	0.57619	1.736
3	1.331	0.7513	3.310	0.30211	0.40211	2.487
4	1.464	0.6830	4.641	0.21547	0.31547	3.170
5	1.611	0.6209	6.105	0.16380	0.26380	3.791
6	1.772	0.5645	7.716	0.12961	0.22961	4.355
7	1.949	0.5132	9.487	0.10541	0.20541	4.868
8	2.144	0.4665	11.436	0.08744	0.18744	5.335
9	2.358	0.4241	13.579	0.07364	0.17364	5.759
10	2.594	0.3855	15.937	0.06275	0.16275	6.144
11	2.853	0.3505	18.531	0.05396	0.15396	6.495
12	3.138	0.3186	21.384	0.04676	0.14676	6.814
13	3.452	0.2897	24.523	0.04078	0.14078	7.103
14	3.797	0.2633	27.975	0.03575	0.13575	7.367
15	4.177	0.2394	31.772	0.03147	0.13147	7.606
16	4.595	0.2176	35.950	0.02782	0.12782	7.824
17	5.054	0.1978	40.545	0.02466	0.12466	8.022
18	5.560	0.1799	45.599	0.02193	0.12193	8.201

19	6.116	0.1635	51.159	0.01955	0.11955	8.365
20	6.727	0.1486	57.275	0.01746	0.11746	8.514
21	7.400	0.1351	64.002	0.01562	0.11562	8.649
22	8.140	0.1228	71.403	0.01401	0.11401	8.772
23	8.954	0.1117	79.543	0.01257	0.11257	8.883
24	9.850	0.1015	88.497	0.01130	0.11130	8.985
25	10.835	0.0923	98.347	0.01017	0.11017	9.077
26	11.918	0.0839	109.182	0.00916	0.10916	9.161
27	13.110	0.0763	121.100	0.00826	0.10826	9.237
28	14.421	0.0693	134.210	0.00745	0.10745	9.307
29	15.863	0.0630	148.631	0.00673	0.10673	9.370
30	17.449	0.0573	164.494	0.00608	0.10608	9.427
35	28.102	0.0356	271.024	0.00369	0.10369	9.644
40	45.259	0.0221	442.593	0.00226	0.10226	9.779
45	72.890	0.0137	718.905	0.00139	0.10139	9.863
50	117.391	0.0085	1,163.909	0.00086	0.10086	9.915
55	189.059	0.0053	1,880.591	0.00053	0.10053	9.947
60	304.482	0.0033	3,034.816	0.00033	0.10033	9.967
65	490.371	0.0020	4,893.707	0.00020	0.10020	9.980
70	789.747	0.0013	7,887.470	0.00013	0.10013	9.987
75	1271.895	0.0008	12,708.954	0.00008	0.10008	9.992
80	2048.400	0.0005	20,474.002	0.00005	0.10005	9.995
85	3298.969	0.0003	32,979.690	0.00003	0.10003	9.997
90	5313.023	0.0002	53,120.226	0.00002	0.10002	9.998
95	8556.676	0.0001	85,556.760	0.00001	0.10001	9.999

To answer this question, turn to Table 16.2 and look under the *single payment compound amount*. Assume that the amount the board of directors has on hand is $2 million. What would this amount be worth in four years invested in a manner that yields 10 percent per year? The factor is 1.464. Multiply $2 million by this factor and get $2,928,000. Since $5 million is needed, the board knows that it cannot rely merely on its initial investment. It must raise more money to meet its target.

Future Value of a Uniform Series of Payments

The board of directors may conclude that they prefer not to deal with a single sum. Rather, they would prefer to have a fund-raising campaign that is annual and stretches over a four-year period. This has the advantage of being less pressing on them and the staff. They can assume, based on past experience and on their contacts, that they could raise a specific amount of money every year, say $800,000 per year. Would they meet their target if they collected that amount every year and put it into an investment paying 10 percent per year? Would they overshoot their target, fall short of it, or just meet it?

This type of problem requires finding the dollar value that a series of uniform payments made at the beginning of every year for a specified number of years would be worth on a specific future date. To solve this we go to Table 16.2 and the column that shows a *uniform series compound amount*. We see the factor 4.641. Multiply this by $800,000 and get $3,712,800, which is how much $800,000 raised and invested each of four years will be worth at the end of the fourth year. The board will fail to meet its $5 million target unless it raises more money or stretches out the period of raising and investing funds.

Sinking Fund

The reciprocal of the same uniform series of payments problem stated above is a *sinking-fund problem*. In this case, the trustees are less interested in whether they will exceed, fall short, or miss their target. They wish to give a clear and specific annual target to the fund-raising manager. "We have a target of $5 million that we must have in four years. We know that the safest rate of return we can get on our money is 10 percent. To accomplish this, we give you a directive to set a fund-raising target of X number of dollars per year." The director of fund-raising retorts, "I shall be happy to follow your orders if you could specify how much must be raised each year under the conditions you have set."

The answer can be found by resorting to Table 16.2. The column entitled *sinking-fund payment* tells how much money must be sunk into a fund each year if a specific target is to be met over a specific number of years and when the rate is 10 percent. Multiply the factor shown for four years, .21547, by $5 million. The fund-raising team must come up with $1,007,350 per year. Notice that this is substantially lower than the fund-raising target when the money is expected to be raised only in one year (the example given earlier), but to accomplish the objective, the fund-raising campaign must last at the same intensity for four years.

Capital Recovery

The board of directors may follow another option. They may decide that they would rather go out and borrow the money to acquire the building. They know that if they do this they will have to pay principal and interest on the loan each year until the loan is paid off. This is called *amortization,* the paying off of a debt. They will borrow the entire $5 million. How much will be their annual payment in principal and interest? In other words, how much will the lender charge per year so as to recover the full amount loaned plus the interest charged? This is called a *capital recovery problem.*

To solve this problem, go to Table 16.2 and locate the column showing *capital recovery.* The factor is .31547, which when multiplied by $5 million gives $1,577,350. This is how much the organization would have to come up with each year if it borrows the funds at 10 percent and pays off the mortgage in four years. More realistically, it may choose a thirty-year mortgage. The factor there is .10608. Multiply it by $5 million and get $530,400, the amount it must come up with each year (its target) to pay off its principal and interest.

Present Value of a Uniform Series

The reciprocal of the capital recovery problem involves finding out how much money the organization could borrow given its capacity to pay a total sum of money each year. Would the amount of money we can afford to pay each year for the next specific number of years be sufficient to pay both principal and interest on our loan so that at the end of that period our loan would be paid off?

In this case, the trustees are willing to commit to a specific annual payment, but only if it would be enough to pay off the principal and interest on the debt. To answer the question, turn to Table 16.2 and the column showing *uniform series present worth.* Assuming that the organization is willing to come up with $200,000 per year for the next ten years, what size mortgage could it afford assuming a mortgage rate of 10 percent? The factor is 6.144, which when multiplied by $200,000 gives $1,118,800, the maximum mortgage it can afford.

Perpetual Endowment

Once a building is built it has to be maintained for the remainder of its life. It has to be painted, remodeled, refitted with heating and air conditioning systems, and so on. Good planning will involve a strategy not only to raise the funds to construct a building but also to do the maintenance for the life of the building. Once the building is in service, the trustees won't have to search for funds to keep it maintained. It is a farsighted and wise strategy. Hence, a good building program may have both an exhaustible (construction) as well as an inexhaustible (maintenance) endowment invested and managed differently for their different purposes.

Since a building could conceivably last forever, the board may well ask, assuming that we have a fund of $4 million that we intend to last forever, how much would we have per year to take care of maintenance and repairs if we use just the earnings of the fund for repairs? By using only the earnings, the principal amount we invested in the fund would last forever. It will always be there earning money to pay for the maintenance and repairs. This is called the *perpetual endowment* problem. Funding scholarships and professorships are of this type.

The answer to this problem is not found in Table 16.2. It is simple. Multiply the principal amount by the rate of interest expected per year and we get the target. If the rate of return on the invested $4 million is 10 percent, $400,000 would be available each year to maintain and operate the building.

Capitalization

Capitalization is the opposite of a perpetual endowment. In capitalization, the board of trustees is asking, How much must we put up in an endowment if we know that the annual cost of repairs and maintenance or of scholarship awards is $200,000 per year? In other words, how much capital must we put in an endowment if we intend to use only the earnings of the endowment so that the principal will last forever, earning the required amount of money we need to do maintenance and repairs or to award scholarships so that we might never have to undertake (unless in an unusual circumstance) to borrow, use operating funds, or have another fund raiser for this specific purpose?

To answer this question, let us assume that the expected rate of return on the investment is 10 percent. Divide this required amount of $200,000 by 10 percent and get $2 million. This is the target amount by which an endowment would have to be capitalized if it is to yield sufficient money annually to pay for the repairs and maintenance of the building.

Disbursement in Practice: Simple Rules and Practices

In practice, trustees are responsible for setting disbursement schedules and procedures for capital and endowment funds. Beginning with the foregoing exercise, they set simple rules. Note one thing about all these rules: They aim to have the endowment last forever. They also assume that a 10 percent rate of interest is available every year and inflation does not erode the value of the earnings by causing the cost of the repairs, scholarships, or other reasons for withdrawal to escalate. In actuality, these do happen, and so trustees monitor annual performance and requirements particularly over withdrawals, which, unlike earnings, they control. How do they do it?

The American Red Cross uses what is known as the total return method for withdrawing and disbursing funds from its endowment. At the beginning of each year, the trustees set a spending or withdrawal rate, called a *target withdrawal rate,* which is a percentage of the market value of the portfolio at the beginning of each year.[4] Under this method, disbursements to meet this target are made first from net investment earnings of that year. If this is insufficient to meet the target, the rest is taken from cumulative realized gains (the amounts accumulated from the past sale of assets and securities). This preserves the original principal, which grows whenever current investment income equals or exceeds withdrawal needs.

A variation of this approach using moving averages is used by many colleges. It works this way. A policy setting a fixed percentage of 5 percent of the earnings of the past five years is the withdrawal target. This means that in 2000 the withdrawal was based on 1994–1999 earnings, in 2001 on 1995–2000, and in 2002 on 1996–2001. This dampens the impact of erratic earnings—when they are in a valley or peak—on how many dollars can be disbursed.

Disbursements conform to contingencies set up by the board or by the grantor of the endowment. To illustrate, the endowment set up by the National Urban League based on a grant from the Ford Foundation, under terms of the grant, prohibited disbursement from the principal for five years. Such terms are based on the calculations that we discussed earlier and are intended to give the endowment an opportunity to grow and to last into perpetuity. The League is permitted to expend, for operational purposes, any net realized gains. The basis for calculating this gain is the dollar value of the endowment when it was started. But it is also required to plow into the endowment over a five-year period cash and securities matching the $4.5 million of the original gift.[5]

Finally, when starting a new endowment, postponing all disbursements may be a good strategy. Accordingly, the board of trustees of Camp Fire Boys and Girls prohibited any disbursements from its endowment until it reached $750,000.[6]

PRESERVATION OF THE TERMS OF ENDOWMENT

The law requires that endowments be prudently administered to preserve the intent of the donor and that the trustees act with loyalty toward the public purpose of the endowment. The list of actions given in Chapter Six that could be cause for suit applies to endowments.

When we say that endowments must be administered by the terms of the contracts that create them, we are making reference to law. The borrowing of money that is in an endowment, shifting it to some other use, and closing an endowment are all legally prohibited transactions unless allowed in the endowment contract. Otherwise, the management, trustees, or board can be sued by the donors or their public beneficiaries. To make such unspecified transactions legal, the trustees or board may have to get permission from a court. Such permission is usually granted if a financial crisis that cannot be satisfied in some other manner can be demonstrated; if the purpose of the endowment no longer exists or is impracticable, contrary to public policy, or financially infeasible; and when actions required by the endowment would lead to its destruction. Under what the lawyer's call a *cy pres* ruling, the court may give authority for the funds to be used in some manner other than that stipulated in the contract but consistent with the mission of the organization.

To illustrate the need for abiding with public policy, in one case the IRS concluded that a charitable trust, though established and functioning for decades, was no longer qualified for tax exemption and its donors no longer qualified for tax deductions because the fund's mission was to aid "worthy white people."[7]

To avoid these types of problems, attorneys try to eliminate this type of language, which was perfectly acceptable at the time that the trust was set up. Of course, the problem can be reduced when the fund is created by the board of trustees of the organization by transferring operating surpluses into a restricted fund. Yet it is not uncommon that universities and other nonprofits run into serious problems with their own restrictions. Times change.

Some endowments are set up under terms that stipulate that they will not commence making awards or cash payments until the passage of some time. This gives the fund an opportunity to grow, establish some critical level based on a calculation of the future value of a single payment, and then make perpetual awards based on the amount that is needed to sustain a perpetual payment of some specific amount.

The terms under which an endowment is established will include accumulation, investment, and disbursement policies. Some of these may have the force of contractual law.

Members, officers, a single trustee or a group of trustees, an individual with reversionary rights, and the attorney general may sue an organization, its officers, and trustees if restrictions are broken without the authority of the donor or the authority of the court; except trustees of religious organizations in California can in good faith find that the restriction is contrary to public policy and, after making a written explanation and decision, remove the restriction.

TIME AND RISKS IN ENDOWMENT PLANNING

It should be obvious from what has been said in this section that capital planning and endowment management are related to sustaining the growth and performance of the organization over several years. It has not only to do with buying buildings, equipment, and machines but with creating funds that can finance the mission of the organization well into the future.

In all capital planning problems, as we saw above, the pressures on the fund-raising campaign can be reduced by stretching out the time required to accumulate a targeted amount of money or by investing the money in assets that pay a higher rate of return. But a higher rate of return always implies a greater risk. When an investment is risky it must pay high rates so as to attract money. Because securities of the federal Treasury are generally considered to be the lowest risk, a rate approximating their prevailing rate is what should be used as a basis for judging the relationship between risk and return.

Moreover, because the rate has to be presumed to prevail for the length of the planning horizon, the investment that should be made is one that is likely to keep a relatively fixed rate for that period. The accumulated funds should be invested in reasonably safe fixed-rate assets that mature at about the time the money is needed. Notes, bonds, U.S. Treasury securities, securities of government agencies, certificates of deposits, even high-grade zero-coupon bonds and municipal bonds are examples.

Stretching out the time reduces the pressures on the fund-raising efforts and may perhaps make the project more realistic. This has to be weighed against other factors. Stretching out the time increases risk: inflation would cause the cost of the project to rise. If the assets held are fixed rate, then their value will decline or probably will not keep pace with the rise in inflation. Hence, the earnings to finance the project will not keep pace with its rising costs and more, not less, fund-raising will be necessary, and common stocks may be a superior alternative to bonds. If bonds are used in volatile markets it is important to know their duration—a measure of how much the bond price changes as a result of changes in the interest rate.

Stretching out time also risks loss of interest on the part of donors and, in the case of buildings, changes in zoning or building codes that could increase costs. However, stretching out time does have an advantage—feasibility; but as argued earlier, stretching out time is not riskless.

SETTING TARGET PRICES, FEES, AND DUES

For a nonprofit organization to do well selling its goods and services requires a rational approach to the setting of prices and fees. In this section, I describe some approaches.

Prices and Fees

It is essential to note that all prices are eventually determined by the market, some prices more so than others. In a very competitive market, the price or fee that a nonprofit will be able to charge will depend on the prices or fees being charged by its competitors. Even in a monopoly situation where the nonprofit sets a price and does not have to worry about competition, market forces will determine how much of that good or service will be sold. If there is no demand for the product, it will not sell. If the demand is limited by a very high price, only a few will be purchased. If the price is low enough and consumers are very sensitive to prices, more will be sold. This is the basic law of supply and demand.

Not only does the market set limits on prices, but so too do the laws and regulations from federal, state, or local authorities. For example, where there is rent control, nonprofits may not exceed it unless by special exemption.

In short, whatever the price or fee level set by the nonprofit and whichever of the methods it uses to determine those prices or fees, they must eventually be adjusted to the realities of the market and the law. Therefore, the methods to be discussed may best be viewed as rational ways to determine target prices or fees.

The rational setting of prices and fees means that they should have some relationship to costs. To simplify matters, let us describe the full costs of producing a good or service as composed of (1) direct costs resulting solely from the production of the good or service, and (2) indirect costs only partly related to the production of the good and service. Put another way, direct costs exist only because the good or service is being produced. Indirect costs would exist whether or not a specific good is being produced because the organization has to incur costs to exist and to carry on its nonprofit mission. See Chapter Twelve.

Various price or fee targets can be set depending on the amount of the direct and indirect costs the organization wishes to recover. On one level, the nonprofit may set a fee or price that does not meet even its direct costs. It can do this only to the extent that gifts and contributions or some other source of income—for example, membership fees, endowment income, business income, or government grants—make up the difference. This is in fact what many nonprofits do. When they set the price of their goods or service at zero (or no charge), they are totally dependent on other sources to pay for the cost of the service they provide.

On a second level, the nonprofit may set a price or fee that only recovers its direct costs. When this is done, less pressure is placed on other sources of income to support that particular activity. These sources would be needed only to cover the indirect costs, a portion of which would exist even if the good or service were not being produced.

On a third level, the price or fee could be set so that the full costs, both direct and indirect, are being covered by the price. In this case, the activity is self-supporting. The other sources of income can be used to advance other missions of the organization.

On yet another level, the price or fee may be set so that the organization not only recovers its full costs (direct and indirect) but more. It can do this by adding a percentage to its full costs. In the for-profit world, this percentage reflects a gross profit margin. This margin is also permitted to nonprofits. In the

General Council Memorandum 39346, dated March 15, 1985, the IRS concluded that the provision of veterinary service for a fee of cost plus a percentage was not in violation of the tax-exempt status of 501(c)(3) organizations formed to provide veterinary services. Moreover, the IRS concluded that given the facts and circumstances of that organization, the markup did not constitute an unrelated business and therefore it was not taxable.

The significance of this last level of setting a target price or fee is that this extra percentage can be (and virtually must be if it is not to be taxed as an unrelated business) used to support the advancement of the mission of the organization. Hence, the pricing levels described progress from losses that impose a burden on the organization to one that provides a legal surplus helping to support the organization in its mission.

Setting of prices or fees does not necessarily subvert or destroy the charitable character of a 501(c)(3) organization or its mission. The fees or prices may be set according to some means test. Clients are charged according to their ability to pay. Those who cannot pay are served without charge, and the charge rises as the ability to pay increases. In setting rental levels in homes for the elderly, the nonprofit must set the prices so that they fall within the financial reach of a significant proportion of the elderly population in the community. Should a resident not be able to pay, the organization should be prepared to make necessary arrangements to continue to provide housing even in a housing project operated by another organization. The organization should also operate at the lowest feasible cost. This does not mean that it does not provide amenities, but that the cost of these plus other necessary costs should not become so high that the subsequent price is out of reach of a large segment of the elderly population.

Prices can be set in a deliberate attempt of the organization to meet its mission and to demonstrate public support. The John F. Kennedy Center for the Performing Arts sells tickets at half price to seniors, low-income groups, students, military, and handicapped persons. The cost of doing this is considered by the Center as part of its educational and public service mission. The Metropolitan Museum of Art in New York "suggests" an entrance fee to its visitors on a sliding scale—lower rates for senior citizens and zero for children.

Dues

Membership dues are prices—the cost to an individual or entity to be a member. For nonprofits, setting these dues should balance the ability to pay with the benefits received. Partly because of the support rules described in Chapters Three and Four and the rules on deductions, as well as for marketing purposes, it helps to separate these two considerations.

Accordingly, part of the dues should be based on the average (per person) total cost of running the organization and providing benefits from which people cannot be excluded. This part of the dues should be based on a sliding scale according to the ability to pay. This portion could very well have a value of zero for the least able to pay.

The second component of the dues may reflect benefits received. Hence, we may tilt higher dues to those who receive the greater benefit. For most organizations, this runs counter to the ability to pay and, unlike a firm, a nonprofit should place more weight on the ability to pay.

One way to reconcile this difference is to structure the dues based on the ability to pay. Then take all those benefits that can be priced and make them available to the membership at a price. Hence, there is an annual dues according to a sliding scale; but if one wishes to attend a conference or receive a publication, a price is charged. The target dues, like the target price, are subject to market considerations. It will be lowered if people do not value the organization's services as highly as it does or cannot pay, in which case the organization will have to return to the point from which we began this book: Whose welfare is it advancing?

Dues, Donations, and Taxation

Ruling 407–95–03 of New Mexico makes an unusual but interesting point about the definition of dues and includes a reminder of the importance of state laws. It reads, "Exempted from the gross receipts tax are the receipts from dues and registration fees of nonprofit social, fraternal, political, trade, land or professional organizations and business leagues. . . . [D]ues means amounts that a member of an organization pays at recurring intervals to retain membership in an organization where such amounts are used for the general maintenance and upkeep. . . . Under the Internal Revenue Code a 501(c)(4) is a civic league or organization. . . . X is not a nonprofit social, fraternal, political, trade, labor or professional organization, nor a business league. . . . The voluntary payment made by the community members do not fall with the definition of 'dues'. . . . Therefore X's receipts are subject to the gross receipt tax."

The IRS is also concerned not only about differences in dues—arguing that charging associated members a different dues amount could be unrelated business income (Chapter Ten)—but that discounted prices and fees could also be a problem. Therefore, when using a discount for members, be sure that it is reasonable and that the event is financed primarily by the members. If this is not done, the higher rate charged to nonmembers will be construed as personal inurement; that is, the higher rate of nonmembers was a benefit in the form of a lower rate passed on to the members. Also be sure that if differential dues are used, these are not subject to the same argument and are not seen simply as a way of increasing revenues. If this turns out to be the interpretation, Revenue Procedure 95–21 calls for the reporting of an unrelated business income and a tax on that income. Further, if nonmember fees and charges become a principal source of gross revenues of associations, the exemption can be lost.

SUMMARY AND PREVIEW

This chapter has shown how the financial function of the nonprofit organization is continuous and feeds back into the planning of the future of the organization and the continuous search for new opportunities.

The successful search rests on the ability of management to expand its view of what the organization can and cannot do legally and the identification of appropriate niches within and outside the boundaries of the marketplace. However, merely identifying these potential niches is not enough. The organization needs to have a well thought out set of financial strategies and targets that is consistent with its mission and capabilities and objectives. This chapter focused on setting financial targets and the management of cash to meet these financial targets. Now we turn to nonfinancial targets.

PART FIVE

STRATEGIC PLANNING FOR GROWTH AND SURVIVAL

The law requires every organization to have a written plan
for disposing of its assets when it is dissolved.
The demise of an organization may occur prematurely
by management's failure to plan for organizational
growth, transformation, and reinvigoration.
The options are no secret.

CHAPTER SEVENTEEN

Strategic Planning as a
Management Tool
for Growth and Survival

In Part One we saw how the nonprofit is formed, discussed certain basic legal operating rules, and finalized the discussion with overseeing this elaborate or (in some cases) embryonic organization. We now turn to growing the organization. Our interest begins with strategic planning. We are less concerned with the mechanics of this method than we are in its usefulness to the manager in growing the organization, or at least in giving it a fighting chance to survive.

To the manager, the beginning question should be, How can the organization get the most out of its mission? Other questions follow: What are the options and how does one make choices among these options that are desirable, effective, feasible, and consistent with the mission of the organization? How does one follow up to monitor, evaluate, and report these outcomes in a way that is advantageous to the pursuit of the mission?

THE IMPORTANCE OF STRATEGIC PLANNING: GROWING
THE ORGANIZATION COHESIVELY

The principal purpose of strategic planning is to help the organization systematically arrive at important decisions while involving as many as possible in the deliberations. The following from the National League for

Nursing is apropos because it revolves around concepts included in this book: markets, information, feedback, bylaws, trustees, and holding company structure. Notice the dynamics of growth: "flexibility in reaching new and different markets."

> The Long Range Planning Committee presented a proposal for a new structure for the League. At that time, information was provided and feedback was sought. In the intervening years, the committee worked diligently at refining the proposal and at educating our members. This year the proposal and the new by-laws were passed. One of the goals of the new structure includes greater flexibility in reaching new and different markets. Another goal was to streamline the board to a workable and cost effective size. Another goal was to take advantage of the benefits incurred by having a holding company structure. [*Nursing Health Care,* Vol. 10, No. 7, September 1989, p. 380]

THE IMPORTANCE OF STRATEGIC PLANNING TO ASSOCIATIONS

Winnowing down choices (and choosing options) are also very important to associations—and in many respects more difficult for them. Associations tend also to have very broadly defined missions to represent and to serve a constituency that may be very broad, even though bound by a common interest. Take, for example, a trade group that has a common interest the improvement of U.S. foreign trade. Such a group may contain bankers, steel manufacturers, users of steel, users of substitutes for steel, other manufacturers that export to a steel-producing country but who are willing to sacrifice the exportation of steel in order to favor their own interests in the steel-producing country, and so on. The point is that below the common interest may be very strong, conflicting, idiosyncratic interests. Sometimes these problems can be resolved by creating caucuses or single-interest groups or by broad resolutions of commitment. Not infrequently, these underlying conflicts give rise to the formation of a more narrowly defined or competing association.

Associations are continuously faced with the need to make choices where the competing demands are strong and consequential to the group or to subparts of its membership. Hence, after lobbying and successfully having the U.S. Congress pass a strong health care law for the elderly, an association for retired persons was faced with asking Congress to repeal that law because its members rejected it. No association, even religious organizations bound by a common belief and a hierarchial structure of decision making, is immune to this problem. Strategic planning in associations is often as important in coordinating, congealing, and consolidating the organization as it is in finding new directions and finding ways to deal with common threats to the membership.

STRATEGIC PLANNING AS A WINNOWING TOOL

Let us take a mission of a 501(c)(3) organization:

The *mission* of the Myra Simon Institute for Children, Inc., is to advance the development, horizon, and accomplishments of disadvantaged boys and girls. They do this by developing, conducting, disseminating, evaluating, discharging, recognizing and publicizing programs, community or corporate projects and individual actions that are consistent with the advancement of disadvantaged youth and the section 501(c)(3) of the Internal Revenue Code, or the corresponding section of any future federal tax code.

How many ways can the mission be satisfied by the Myra Simon Institute for Children? When resources are scarce the organization has to make choices. It might focus on disadvantaged children in a specific state, county, or urban or rural area. It may focus on children within a specific age bracket. Further, it may choose between developing or conducting or disseminating or evaluating or discharging or recognizing or any combinations of these.

But a good mission statement is broad but consistent with the criteria of a mission statement discussed in Chapter Two. To allow growth and change, it must admit to an infinite number of possibilities. But the mission must be met in a noncommercial manner. This does not mean that a price cannot be charged, but that profits cannot be the motive and competition with market-oriented firms should be minimized. Therefore, part of the strategic decision is whether to charge a price and if so how much. Accordingly, choosing programs that are (1) consistent with the mission of the organization, (2) noncommercial, (3) feasible, (4) desirable, and (5) designed to meet the competitive threats of the nonprofit's market is one use of strategic planning. It is a deductive process through which the organization moves from an infinite number of strategic options to a finite number with the best chances for success.

If this were a membership organization, the choice among these various options would also reflect the diverse and often conflicting interests of its members. Thus, strategic planning for this organization would encourage participation, help make rational choices among competing groups and ideas, and stimulate a consensus is not merely a way of stimulating consensus. When the community participates in the process, strategic planning also becomes a way of demonstrating public support needed by 501(c)(3) organizations and cohesiveness needed by associations.

For another view of how strategic planning can be helpful in winnowing down options, take a look at Table 2.2, which lists the variety of activities that can be conducted under the 501(c)(3) label. Imagine that there are an infinite number of ways of doing each. How many ways can a synagogue or church serve its congregation and its community? Let us recommend a minimum condition for choosing rationally. Obviously, if strategic planning is a tool for making choices in a rational and participatory manner, there must be some rules. What conditions should the choices satisfy? In this and earlier editions of this book, we advocate that the choice must be simultaneously desirable, feasible, effective, and consistent with the mission, and we develop a technique for meeting these criteria simultaneously.

STRATEGIC PLANNING: PURPOSES AND APPROACHES

Strategic planning is a process through which a nonprofit organization may do any of the following:

1. Identify needs
2. Define its mission
3. Evaluate its capabilities
4. Assess its external environment
5. Set objectives
6. Select strategies
7. Design programs
8. Determine a budget
9. Evaluate performance

In the strategic planning process, it is possible to use the most sophisticated techniques in research, group dynamics, logic, argumentation, program planning, and evaluation. These techniques are discussed in standard texts. But the purpose of this chapter is to develop and illustrate a step-by-step strategic planning process that may be applicable to the successful management of nonprofits. The litmus test of any strategic planning process is whether it flows logically toward a participatory decision that makes sense and is applicable to the organization. Below I recommend a process and explain why it may be best for many nonprofits. The chapter highlights certain concepts upon which nonprofit managers should focus (see Figure 17.1).

The reader will observe that the strategic planning process that is recommended begins with an identification of a need consistent with the mission of the nonprofit. This is significant. A for-profit firm is not bound by a mission statement. A nonprofit is. Recall from earlier chapters that for a nonprofit, a mission is tantamount to a social contract. It should therefore begin every planning process respecting this constraint. From a marketing as well as from a production perspective, this initial step is equivalent to asking what we should consider

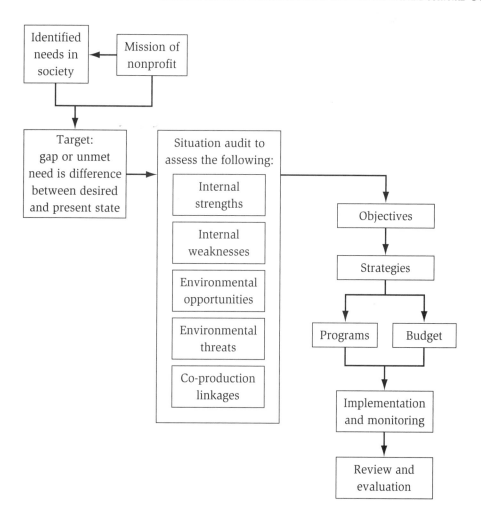

Figure 17.1. Strategic Planning Process.

producing that is permissible (consistent with our mission). We can make a list of possibilities. Our next step will be to narrow the list.

Logically, the strategic planning process then proceeds to reduce the need to a manageable form for the nonprofit. Only then can realistic programs be designed. This is equivalent to saying that the mission statement, as indicated in Chapter Two, is broad and permits the organization to attack a need from various perspectives. But the organization only has limited resources. Therefore, which aspect of the need shall it be? At this stage, it is sufficient to narrow the list to include only those needs that are most consistent with the mission and represent a real need in severity or quantity worthy of the organization's attention.

Put another way, because most social needs are complex and stretch well beyond the resources of any one organization, it is important for each nonprofit to identify a specific gap that it may be able to fill. This gap becomes the focus of the planning process. It is the organization's target, for it is the difference between what is being done to meet the need and what is necessary to fully diminish it. The gap is a measure of an unmet need.

Having identified a gap and an unmet need consistent with its mission, the nonprofit must now assess its ability to successfully fill a portion of that gap. This leads to an assessment of the internal weaknesses and strengths of the organization. Does it have the necessary management experience or capacity to fill all or a portion of the gap? What aspect of the gap, from the perspective of its mission and capacity, is it best suited to fill?

The management may decide that the current capacity of the organization is nadequate to meet the task. Therefore, it is necessary to identify what is required in addition to existing capacity and how it will be acquired. Is the acquisition of the necessary capacity within the reach of the organization? If not, is there another way? We shall see a strategy of cooperation or joint ventures that permits organizations to go beyond their own capacity to do good.

Similarly, it is necessary to assess the external environment. What opportunities exist in the world at large that are available to the organization so that it may successfully fill the gap it has identified and targeted? What are the external obstacles or threats the organization will face once it has attempted to fill the gap? Are other organizations operating in the same area of unmet need and specifically in the gap targeted by the nonprofit? Is there room for one more nonprofit? Are there licensing laws or political and locational factors that would impede the nonprofit's attempt to fill the gap?

Sometimes these threats and obstacles come in the most oblique and disguised way. Take the case of *Christian Gospel Church Inc. v. City and County of San Francisco.*[1] This case is not about religion or meeting a religious need. It is about an environmental obstacle, something external to the church. The court supported local officials, indicating the church had to move from its present location because it created traffic and was noisy and parking was inadequate. These are discoverable in planning. The problems are all external to the organization and led to a costly court case.

Next, the organization must take into account the interaction between itself and a number of external forces. This is particularly important in nonprofit organizations because many of their activities depend upon coproduction. *Coproduction,* to be discussed later in this chapter, means that the organization's success or failure in supplying a good or service depends on the participation of others, including the clients, in the production process. Therefore, the nonprofit must be certain about its coproducers as well as the linkage or interaction that brings all factors together to make the production process successful.

An example of this is education. For a school to rank high in the educational performance of its students depends on the quality of the faculty, the facilities, parental support, and the quality and dedication of the students. The students are more than passive clients. They are critical to the production of high scores, for if all the other factors were present and the students were of low intellectual capability or uninspired, high scores would be impossible.

Another example is the resolution of crime. Students of police performance have discovered that the ability of the police to respond quickly and solve crimes depends heavily on the nature and speed of response and cooperation of the victims. The victims, by virtue of their cooperation with the police, are coproducers of police performance.

This concept of linkage is so important. Beaufort Longest, in his article "Interorganizational Linkages in the Health Sector," identifies twenty-seven linkages involved in the operation of a hospital.[2] These linkages include insurance companies, governments, employee unions, joint venture partners, suppliers, accrediting agencies, affiliates, and consumers and their representative organizations. Each has its time to be most important in a decision the hospital makes. Each has its opportunity to determine the success or failure of the hospital. Like the hospital, nonprofits should identify their linkages and co-producers and articulate a policy for dealing with each.

The organization is now prepared to state its objectives. Notice how late in the recommended process this comes. Objectives are statements of intent to meet specified unmet needs or to fill specified gaps. Objectives are meaningful if they reflect the internal and external constraints (opportunities, weaknesses, and threats) to the organization. This is why it is best to state objectives only after the gap is clearly analyzed and identified and after a complete assessment of the organization's capacity and environment, including the strength of linkages among coproducers, has been made. To do otherwise is to waste time debating meaningless if not impossible options.

Once the objectives have been specified, the strategic planning process may proceed to develop strategies. Strategies are statements of how the objectives will be accomplished. They are statements of mode or direction. How will the unmet needs be met? Strategies should be broadly stated to provide room for imagination, flexibility, and realism in the design of programs.

Programs activate strategies. Programs are clusters of action that, when implemented in the mode or direction specified by the strategy, enable the organization to meet its objectives.

Programs are of two types. Action programs are clusters of interrelated activities as described. Financial programs are budgets. They tell how much will be needed for what purposes, when and where the money will come from, and in what form. Assuming that the staff of the nonprofit has designed a set of action programs, the next step is to identify the benefits to be derived from each and the feasibility and desirability of each. The challenge for the nonprofit is to select the best program. We show later in the chapter a simple technique for making this choice (see Chapter Twelve for discussion of formulating budgets).

Once the preferred programs are chosen, strategic planning moves toward implementation. The length of the implementation process depends on the type of program, but it also depends on decisions concerning the availability of resources, the duration of unmet needs as targeted by the nonprofit, and the effectiveness of the programs. Accordingly, implementation should be accompanied by continuous monitoring and periodic reviews and evaluation. Through this process, the need for adjustments can be detected and the adjustments can be made before resources are wasted. I shall provide helpful steps later in this chapter; for now, let's proceed with the process.

With the information provided, any manager ought to be able to employ a strategic planning process that is beneficial. More sophisticated processes do require technical assistance and more research on needs assessment, program planning and evaluation, and the subject matter (the gap or unmet need) of the planning process.

Regardless of whether the processes are sophisticated or not, some basic concepts deserve further elaboration for the nonprofit manager. One is the selection of strategic options because this is what decision making is all about. A second essential concept is coproduction because this is central to the operation of most nonprofits. A third basic concept is the life cycle of needs because their fulfillment is the ultimate mission of nonprofits. We shall discuss each in turn.

MISSION, ETHICAL CODES, AND STRATEGIC OPTIONS

Strategic planning decisions should be consistent with the ethical codes of the organization. It is also possible to use strategic planning to develop such a code. The code of ethics adopted in April 1991 by the American Association of Community and Junior Colleges (AACJC) is noteworthy because it manages to be brief, all-encompassing, very clear, and yet it recognizes an important fact: An organization's ethical code must be based on shared values. Hence, it begins with the following shared values: trust and respect, honesty, fairness, integrity and reliability, commitment (to community, self, college, intellectual and moral development), openness, and diversity.

On these values are founded certain responsibilities to trustees, administrators, staff, faculty, students, other educational institutions, the community at large, and the chief executive officer of the college. The code says all of this in two easily read pages. How can an organization develop its own ethical code consistent with its mission and unique character?

Step 1. State the mission

Step 2. Identify the shared values on which commitment to the mission rests

Step 3. Identify the principal classes of people and entities (including animals and the environment where these are principals) involved and the principal communities affected

Step 4. Identify the interaction—that is, duties and responsibilities—each to itself and to each other

Step 5. Stipulate the ethical norms that should govern these duties and responsibilities

Step 6. Obtain consensus and commitment

Step 7. Assign enforcement and overseeing responsibility to a respected authority (even the board of trustees) within the organization

Step 8. Review and update periodically

The organization's ethical code should guide its strategic options.

STRATEGIC OPTIONS: PROFITS VERSUS MISSION

Before an option is selected, it must be compared with other options along a number of dimensions simultaneously. One dimension is nonmonetary: Is the option feasible, desirable, ethical, and consistent with the mission of the organization? As we saw earlier, veering from its mission can have dire legal and tax consequences for a nonprofit.

Another dimension along which options should be compared is monetary: Do the monetary benefits exceed the monetary costs and, if so, by how much? This does not mean that the managers always have precise measurements of the benefits, costs, feasibility, or other criteria. It means only that they are able to make some reasonable judgment, such as, "We believe that the benefits are five times the costs."

But the fact that the benefits may exceed costs is not enough information to make most decisions. Often monetary considerations conflict with the mission and the manageability or feasibility of an option. To appreciate this, let us consider a case in which a nonprofit has six options for tending to an unmet need.

Assume that the six, A through F, have the following benefit-to-cost ratios: A = 5, B = 4, C = 3, D = 2, E = 1, and F = 0.1, meaning, for example, that in A the benefits are five times the costs and in D the benefits are only twice the costs. Is A to be chosen over D? To answer this, see Figure 17.2, which shows these options as they fall on a graph that simultaneously considers the feasibility and desirability of the options.

Option A has the highest benefit-cost ratio and, according to Figure 17.2, is very feasible but not desirable. Many options are economically sound but do not comport with the organization's image or value system; moreover, some options not only lead to tax consequences for nonprofits but may even cost them their tax-exempt status. The viability or acceptability of options change from time to time.

At the other extreme, although D has the third lowest benefit-cost ratio, it is more desirable and feasible than A. D is superior to A. Although C's benefit-cost ratio is only average, it is more desirable than A. C ranks second to D.

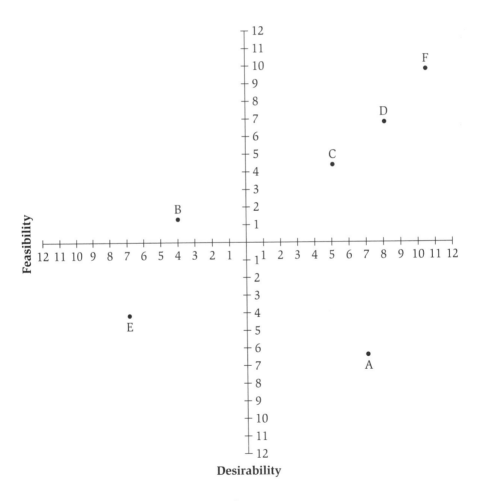

Figure 17.2. Desirability-Feasibility Coordinates.

F is both the most feasible and desirable option. However, F has a benefit-cost ratio of less than 1. Its costs exceed its benefits.

Option B is desirable and has the second highest benefit-cost ratio, but the organization is incapable of implementing it. E is infeasible and undesirable; its benefits equal costs, thus leaving C and D. Both may be chosen because they may be complementary; pursuing one enhances the success of the other. A secondary school could use a primary feeder school.

Both C and D may be chosen if they are independent of each other because this reduces the risk of failure. This is a diversification of options. Or both may be chosen because together they will share costs. Finally, both may be chosen even if they are contradictory, because the selection of options is often based on political considerations; that is, pacifying the opposition, or compromising between opposing but legitimate viewpoints.

The lesson for this exercise is that the choice of options is rarely based on the simple calculations of costs and benefits; sometimes the attractiveness of choices may be influenced by other considerations. This does not mean, as is usually implied, that nonprofits should not be motivated in their decisions by dollar costs and benefits and should not try to maximize the difference between the two so that dollar benefits far outweigh costs. It merely means that often such programs are not within the realm of feasibility or desirability of the organization from the point of view of its mission. We discuss strategies to deal with necessary infeasibilities (joint ventures) or undesirabilities (separate corporations) in Chapters Eighteen and Nineteen.

STRATEGIC OPTIONS: COMPETITORS AND COOPERATORS

One important factor in the selection of options is the role of other organizations. The choice of options is influenced by other organizations, whether they are competitors or allies of the nonprofit. How do other organizations influence the choice of options?

Zero-Sum Games Among Competitors

Although nonprofit managers may at times be oblivious to it, they are often more exposed to competitors than for-profit firms. The capital requirements, technology, licensing, and regulations that affect the rate of entry of new firms in the for-profit market do not exist to the same extent in the nonprofit sector.[3] To see this, list the number of organizations that cater to your different attributes, such as age, sex, income, religion, political identification, job, residence, ad infinitum. In many ways, entry of new competitors into the nonprofit market is relatively easy. Nonprofits cannot stop the entry of new competitors, and the laws are often not so stringent as to be prohibitive to new organizations.

Aside from the rate of entry of new organizations (both private and non-profit) over which a nonprofit may have no legal control, there is the task of how to compete with an actual or potential competitor once entry has occurred. The basic question is what the reaction of a competitor will be if the nonprofit should pursue a particular strategy. Suppose, for example, nonprofit A decides to target a specific income group to give drug counseling. Will nonprofit B, in order to justify its funding, intensify its efforts to give drug counseling to the same group? Will it choose a narrower group, such as teenagers? Will it focus on specific neighborhoods, or drugs, or sex?

Notice that each of these counterstrategies of B chips away at the overall clientele of nonprofit A. If the size of the drug population in the community is relatively fixed, say 1,000 people, A can only increase its clients of drug abusers by reducing the number available to B, and vice versa; if A chooses a strategy, any counterstrategy of B that is successful will reduce the extent to which A will increase its clientele.

This is known as a zero-sum game because the overall size of the market is fixed, so one group can only grow at the expense of the other. This is captured in Figure 17.3, which is called a payoff matrix. The rows show the strategies, 1 through 6, that A may choose. The columns show the strategies available to B. The number in each cell is the percentage of the market that A will gain when it chooses a specific strategy that is countered by B's choice of one of its six strategies.

Strategies of Nonprofit B

	1	2	3	4	5	6
1	5	90	48	39	19	27
2	7	38	75	1	33	79
3	94	4	88	19	42	39
4	67	85	22	50	80	0
5	57	8	37	40	0	10
6	53	0	69	29	50	40

(Rows labeled 1–6 under "Strategies of Nonprofit A")

Figure 17.3. Payoff Matrix of Nonprofits in Highly Competitive Zero-Sum Market.

The number of cells depends on the number of strategies available. Obviously, the greater the number of strategies under consideration, the greater the number of cells. For this example we assume that each nonprofit has six options. One option may be to do nothing. Options may be active, passive, defensive, or aggressive.

Accordingly, if A chooses strategy 1, it will gain 90 percent of the market only if B chooses strategy 2, but only 5 percent if B also chooses strategy 1. If A chooses strategy 3 and B chooses 1, A gets 94 percent of the market; but if B counters with 2, A only gains 5 percent. Likewise, if A chooses 6 and B counters with 2, A gains nothing; but if B chooses 3, A gets 69 percent. The three cells with zeros indicate that it is important to identify and avoid strategies that can do you no good.

The central utility of payoff matrices is that they discipline strategy choices so that managers take into account the consequences of counterstrategies by competitors. Hence, the choice of policies 1 through 6 by A will partly depend on what strategy it expects B to most likely pursue either in response to its own pressures or because of the threat posed by A. Hence, A will not choose 5 if it believes that B will also undertake 5. In the drug example, A will not focus on teenagers if B has a competitive advantage working with teenagers (strategy 5). If, however, A feels that B will counter with 4, A may still pursue 5 and split the market somewhat evenly. A may choose to deal with teenagers if it believes that B will shift its focus to adult alcoholism.

An Example of Competitive Strategy in a Zero-Sum Situation

An educational academy in my home town is proof that theory meets reality even in a religious context. The academy was a very good Catholic girls' school in the Washington, D.C., metropolitan area. But Catholic schools in the area were experiencing declining enrollment, which threatened their existence. Within a few miles was a Catholic school for boys that was beginning to feel the same decline. The priests made the first move. They went co-ed. The prestidious girls' academy is now pleasant history.

Nonzero-Sum Games Among Cooperators

Nonprofits may have a cooperative relationship so that if A and B undertake supporting strategies they could expand the market for both of them. Suppose that A and B are nonprofits with a mission to eradicate smoking. Suppose that the total number of smokers is 50,000, but A only reaches 5,000 and B only 10,000. There are 35,000 more persons to be reached. A and B may decide to cooperate in advertising, in seminars, or by each specializing in a particular subgroup of the 35,000. The situation is depicted in Figure 17.4.

We see that if A chooses strategy 7 and B chooses strategy 3 they are relegated to the small inner circle; that is, the market share of both is small. But if

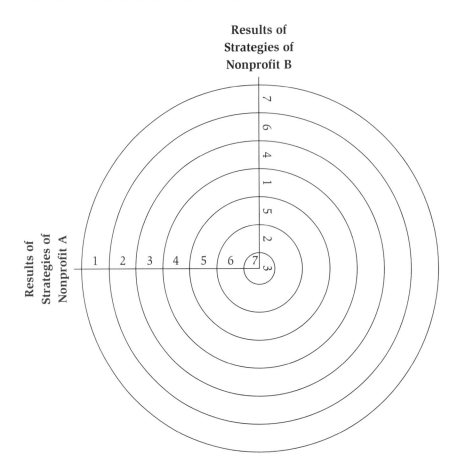

Figure 17.4. Schematic of Nonzero-Sum Game Among Cooperative Nonprofits.

A chooses 4 and B chooses 1, the frontier is expanded and both organizations increase their range. They can reach the entire market if A chooses 1 and B chooses 7. If in a moment of noncooperation A should choose 7 and B chooses 1, both are hurt relative to where they were when A had chosen 1 and B took 7.

Fortunately for nonprofits, until recently they were not constrained as for-profits firms are through rigid application of laws prohibiting collusion in cooperating to expand markets. The law seems increasingly less lenient. Yet cooperation is still possible as long as it does not unfairly defeat competition. The object of the cooperation cannot be to defeat competitors, to restrict the market, or to set prices.[4] By cooperating, organizations can reach the outer boundaries of their market. Hence, nonprofit A may decide to focus on teenage smokers if doing so has a particular advantage in working with youth, and B may focus on adults if this is its comparative advantage.

An Example of Cooperative Strategy

Again, theory meets reality. Data collected by the Council for Aid to Education show two trends. Public schools are getting a larger and larger share of corporate donations. In the mid-1950s, public four-year institutions received about 14 percent of total corporate contributions. By 1988, their share was slightly over 50 percent. But during the same period, the total pot available to all institutions more than doubled, from $76 million to over $1.5 billion. Even though the share of the private institutions fell from 86 percent to about 50 percent, their dollars received rose more than ten times to be divided by the same number of schools as in the 1950s. By increasing the size of the pot, everybody was made better off. What accomplishes this? Campaigns that promote "college education" as a worthy cause, not competitive campaigns—public versus private.

Cooperative Strategies When There Is Mistrust

Under certain conditions, the nonprofits may face a "prisoner's dilemma." Suppose nonprofits A and B could benefit by doing nothing once A is at 1 and B is at 7 because they have expanded their market to its maximum. It could occur, as it often does, that both A and B become suspicious of each other so that A believes that B will change its strategy. B may rationally choose to do so because it believes it can exist without A or can outdo A, or because there are pressures for it to shift course. B may harbor the same suspicions about A. Being suspicious, they both act. The consequence of this is that they are both worse off.[5] Any combination of policies other than A taking 1 and B taking 7 is inferior.

The prisoner's dilemma does not have to be so extreme. It is also possible for events to occur in this sequence: A chooses 2 and B chooses 6. Suspicion and discontent arise between the two. A decides to move to 1. What is the probability that B, without knowing that A was going to move to 1, would counter by moving to 7? The probability is small. The chances are that B's countermove would be something other than 7 (if all choices are randomly chosen). The consequence is that both would be worse off.

Strategies for Competitors and Cooperators

In Chapter Eighteen we see more formal cooperative strategies such as joint ventures and partnerships. Another formal alternative is forming a new corporation. For example, 501(e)s are nonprofit corporations created by hospitals for the purpose of carrying out activities such as record keeping, purchasing, data processing, warehouse, billing, training, printing, and laboratory work for the hospitals that own the corporation. Cooperative efforts by these hospitals help reduce total cost because volume reduces the cost to each hospital. It also allows the sharing and development of specialization and efficiency. Yet these hospitals are competitors for clients and medical professionals.

Coproduction: Working with Clients and Community

Strategic planning is of particular applicability to nonprofit organizations because it is a method that promotes participation and focuses on a mission.[6] As we saw throughout Part One of this book, a nonprofit, unlike a for-profit, must justify its existence and tax-exempt status by demonstrating public support and participation and by adhering closely to its mission. One form of public support, under the 10 percent test described in Chapter Three, is public participation.

Throughout the strategic planning process, a wide level of participation by the public as well as the leadership and staff of the nonprofit is to be encouraged and is easily accommodated by making them part of the strategic planning group. I say more about this later in this chapter in the discussion of needs assessment.

One aspect of participation common to many nonprofits is coproduction. Figure 17.5 shows interaction when coproduction is absent. A private or public foundation, for example, may provide funding for a nonprofit to produce a newsletter, poetry, a play, a painting—products that the nonprofit can produce without direct involvement of clients in the creative process. A newsletter can be produced without its readers writing, printing, or distributing the articles.

Illustration of Coproduction

Contrast this simple process with Figure 17.6, which is a depiction of an actual coproduction process involving a nonprofit. It is a description of the National Urban Policy Roundtable funded by the Charles F. Kettering Foundation and coordinated by the Academy for Contemporary Problems (ACP), now called the Academy for State and Local Governments.[7] The mission of the Roundtable was to produce policy analyses and recommendations for federal, state, local, and private leaders in a steering committee and in a roundtable. Working papers were prepared, published, and disseminated. Many of the products of the Roundtable were utilized in the annual report of the president of the United

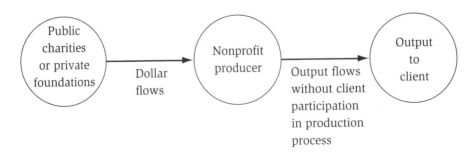

Figure 17.5. Schematic of a Simple Production Relationship in the Nonprofit Sector.

States to the U.S. Congress and by the associations of state and local governments that were represented on the governing board of the Academy and the
steering committee of the Roundtable, whose members were frequently a target group of clients. Figure 17.6 traces the complex coproduction relationship:

1. The Charles F. Kettering Foundation, a private operating foundation,
finances a project. But as we saw in Chapter Four, the law requires that such
foundations directly participate in many of their projects. It is insufficient to
send a check; it is necessary that their assets and staff be directly involved. The
consequence of this is intersection A, which shows both the private operating
foundation and the nonprofit (ACP) as coproducers.

2. To ensure the policy relevance of the project as well as public participation, both the nonprofit and the private operating foundation encouraged the
participation of the clients, which in this case were the public, publicly elected
and appointed officials, and private sector leaders. In the parlance of strategic

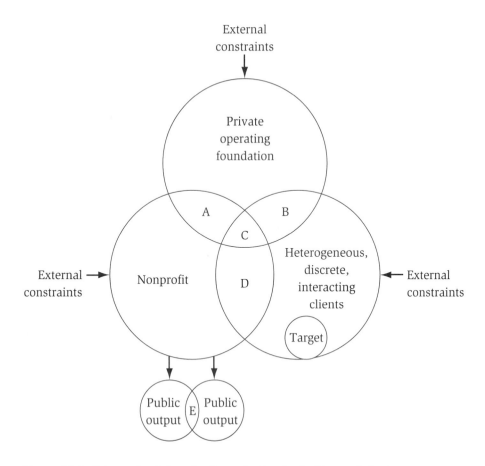

Figure 17.6. Schematic of Complex Coproduction in the Nonprofit Sector.

planning, these are called *stakeholders* because they have a stake in the outcome of the process.

Because the clients were persons from different sectors (public, private, and community) and different groups within each sector (bankers, builders, governors, state legislators, mayors, citizens), these groups are referred to as *heterogeneous, discrete,* and *interacting.* Indeed, these groups could also be described as *atomistic* because they were independent of each other. They sometimes cooperated, but at times had radically divergent and antagonistic positions on the same issues. No issue was equally relevant to all groups. Consequently, for each issue a prime target group was identified.

3. The coproduction process also involves direct relationships that the client group may have with the private foundation, either as a group or as individual constituencies within the group. This is represented by intersection B. Though not directly involving the ACP, the nonprofit, the influences of such relationships were always indirectly felt. For instance, the coproduction activity had to be defined so that it did not infringe on other relationships between the private operating foundation and the clients. In effect, this partly defined the boundaries of the ACP and circumscribed the scope of activity of the Roundtable.

4. Similarly, the clients may have direct relationships with the nonprofit outside the direct coproduction relationship. This is represented by intersection D. In the case of the Roundtable, many members of the client group were also members of the board of directors of the ACP and were conducting other joint programs among themselves and with the ACP.

5. Intersection C is the core of the coproduction activity. It is the interaction among the client, the private operating foundation, and the nonprofit. In the case of the Roundtable, the ACP (the nonprofit) is the principal producer; the private foundation is both the funding source and a coproducer, and the clients are both consumers and coproducers.

6. As a result of this interaction, a final product E is obtained. The final product—the production and dissemination of the policy documents—is not unrelated to other products being produced by the ACP. This is often the case, since one activity of an organization draws on and contributes to other activities of the organization. Note that by the very nature of nonprofits, the products, even though targeted to a specific population, may have positive external effects.

A factor that makes coproduction difficult is that the actual interaction among all parties, C, may represent a small part of the activities of any one of the organizations. Yet it brings the central producer, the nonprofit, under the influence not only of its external constraints, but also of all coproducers. One example is worth noting. The Roundtable produced a study listing the cities with greatest potential for fiscal default. One of the cities was vitally related to the client group and the private operating foundation. The morning the study was released, the city announced its intentions to offer a new issue of municipal bonds. Although not required to rescind its results, the nonprofit ACP, as coordinator, not just the Roundtable, expended a significant amount of energy explaining its results and the timing of its release. The actions of the Roundtable, though honoring its own constraints for objectivity, affected the external constraints of a key member of its client group to raise badly needed capital at favorable lending rates and involved the entire corporate body of the ACP, of which the Roundtable was only a part.

LIFE CYCLE OF NEEDS: TIME TO CHANGE

The level of need (the gap) that a nonprofit addresses can be expected to change over time. It may increase or decrease at a rapid, slow, or constant rate. Some needs may remain constant for a long time, whereas others may be fleeting. It is important that strategic planning for the nonprofit reflect how the needs it plans to address will change over time. The ability to answer these questions, even in general terms, helps the organization avert disaster. Imagine investing in meeting an "unmet need" when the need has already been fulfilled or failing to prepare properly for a need that is rapidly escalating. Indeed, the plight of many nonprofits stems from their inability or unwillingness to track the decline in public ranking of the need to which the organization was dedicated or a change in the true level or intensity of the need.

Consequently, it is useful to know the approximate life cycle of the need being addressed by the nonprofit. This involves two questions: How long will the need last? How will it change over time? Figure 17.7 shows some possibilities. It is possible that once the program is launched the need for it declines uninterruptedly. The pattern of decline may be as in line *a* in the first panel or like lines *b* or *c*. The decline in line *a* begins rapidly and then flattens out so that a very low level of need is maintained until the end of the planning period, which, in this example, is the twelfth year of the program.

Alternatively, the decline could be steady but rapid as in line *b* or steady but slower as in line *c*. These are not simply geometric expressions. The point is that how rapidly a need disappears has an important bearing on how the organization should plan for it. A nonprofit should not go into debt or assume an obligation for more than five years if the need is likely to have a life cycle such as that depicted in line *b*. Its commitment would outlive the problem. However, if the life cycle is like line *a*, a long-term commitment of up to ten years can be made, and the organization can gradually extricate itself year by year from such commitments.

Alternatively, the need could increase over time. Here, too, the life-cycle pattern is significant. The increase could be at an increasing rate such as line *d*, a constant rate such as line *e*, or a decreasing rate such as line *f*. If line *d* is

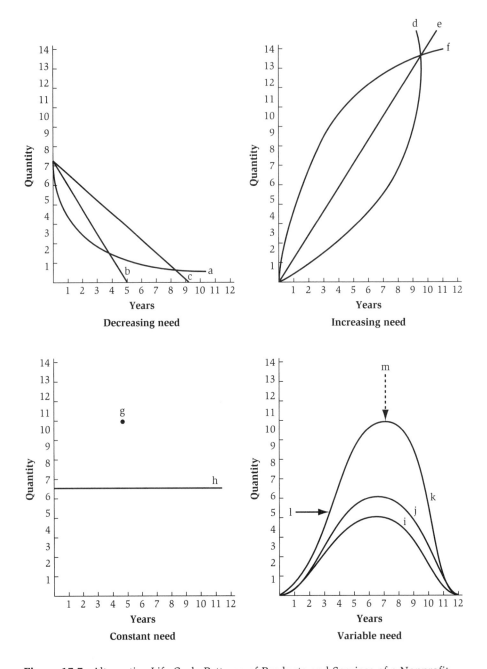

Figure 17.7. Alternative Life-Cycle Patterns of Products and Services of a Nonprofit.

applicable, the organization must plan to increase its capacity rapidly over time. This can place great strain on the internal factors, which may now become the major constraints. If, however, the life cycle is as depicted in line *f* or *e*, the strain would be less.

Another possibility is that the life cycle is as shown in the third panel, indicating that it remains constant for the planning period. The dot *g* indicates that the life of the need expires at the end of one year, whichever year the need arises. In this case, the need is anticipated to occur in (not over) five years and will expire in that year. The dot indicates that during the year it may be at only one level. Is this unlikely? Many of the local activities for the Olympics are precisely of this nature. Activities celebrating the bicentennial of the birth of the United States of America were also of this type. They started and ended. They had a known and predictable short life. A profit was made partly because management knew the life cycle of events. Special fund-raising events are often dots!

A constant pattern is represented also in line *h*. In this case, the need remains fairly constant over the planning period. Planning for schools in a community that is relatively stable is an example. The need for additional facilities may remain stable for a long time until it is affected by dramatic population changes.

The need may be one that varies over time. This is reflected in the patterns shown in the fourth panel. The need may rise rapidly at first up to point *l* and then increase at a slower rate, eventually reaching a peak *m* and thereafter declining. The need may reach its peak very rapidly as in line *k* or less rapidly as in line *I* or *j* and be more prolonged as in the case of line *I*, which gives the lowest peak but the most sustained one, lasting roughly two years as opposed to one year in line *k*. The organization would then have to plan its capacity so that it would meet the rapid and short peak as in line *k* or the slow rise but prolonged peak such as in line *I*. Can you give examples? Natural disasters?

Being able to spot the turning points such as at *l* and *m* is important in the ability of the organization to adjust quickly and efficiently to changing needs. It is possible, for example, that once the peak has been reached, the nonprofit would begin planning to shift its resources toward meeting new and emerging needs, perhaps even in the same general field. A drug-abuse center could begin shifting its attention from LSD to PCP, from marijuana to crack.

It is not likely that any nonprofit or for-profit firm will know the exact rate at which the need for its services or products changes. But as economists who estimate demand over time know, it is infinitely better to make plans based on rational expectations of how needs will change over time than to have such changes occur unexpectedly. If the change is a rapid rise in need, the nonprofit will be unable to meet the escalation, which opens the door for dissatisfaction and the entry of new competitors that will quickly displace the existing nonprofit. If the change is a rapid decline, the nonprofit will find itself having invested scarce resources to meet a need that no longer exists at the levels it once did.

ILLUSTRATION: LIFE CYCLE AND DISASTERS

Go back to the graphical display of life cycles. It would be tempting to conclude that an event of such short duration that it can be represented by a dot does not lend itself to strategic planning. Nonetheless, planning is justified whenever an event has a probability of occurring, and if it occurs, the cost is significant to the person or entity that bears it. The issue is not if planning should be done, but how.

The Olympics is a short-lived event. But planning is continuous because the event is reasonably certain to occur and the stakes are high. An earthquake, eruption of a volcano, storm, flood, or airplane crash—each can occur and each extracts a high toll. The probability of each is small. We therefore do not plan continuously and do not plan for each separately, but we do plan for their common requirements that are generally applicable to any one of these emergencies—evacuation and medical assistance; that is, we plan more frequently for disasters as a whole, not specifically for an earthquake.

We can also budget for these short-lived events. The American Red Cross has a special fund, earmarked exclusively to be used in "disasters." Funds in this account can be used for several types of disasters.

In conclusion, life cycles determine how we plan, the duration of the plan, its contents, and how we budget for it. They do not determine whether we should plan. Planning is a form of risk management.

PLANNING PERIOD

This brings us to a more formal treatment of the concept of *planning period.* Every strategic plan should have a predetermined life cycle. Each program in the plan should have its own planning period, which may be coterminous with the program life. But for the organization as whole the planning period should be independent of the life of any one program.

The planning period is the time over which a plan is expected to last before it must be formally reviewed and revised. A strategic plan may be a five-, ten-, or fifteen-year plan. It gives the long-range view. The longer the range, however, the more important that it be divided up into short-range perspectives. Below we shall discuss milestones related to this concept. The point is that a set of targets should be established for each year in a fifteen-year plan. At the end of each year, actual performance should be measured against these targets and revisions should be made. Each major planning period should involve an assessment of needs consistent with the mission of the organization.

CONDUCTING NEEDS ANALYSIS

To make needs analysis useful, the nonprofit should do a lot of up-front work. Perhaps the following paragraphs will help. Begin with a clear picture of what the mission of the organization is. It makes no sense to discover needs that are outside your mission. You cannot address them unless the mission is changed or the organization is willing to risk losing its exemption.

Select a group of stakeholders. These are people who can be affected by the organization positively or negatively. They include community people, staff, trustees, and members. Brainstorm in a disciplined manner so that the conversation does not flip-flop or touch every irrelevant issue. Listen particularly to the members and the community. In the final analysis the organization exists to serve them. Phrase the question that stakeholders should address. For example: "This organization, the Paula-Lugades-Lewis Art Center, exists to advance awareness and appreciation of the arts in the southern states. Can you tell us some specific ways in which we might do precisely that?"

Notice that the question is constrained, yet it gives people an opportunity to think and to recommend—but within the framework of the mission of the organization. Think of this question for a moment. There are an infinite number of recommendations possible. "Southern" covers a number of states. One state or a combination might be the new market—perhaps just the largest cities or small towns. "Arts" covers a number of fields—modern, dance, music, Byzantine, vocal, instrumental (and there are numerous types of instruments). Moreover, the target population can be the elderly, the Indians (and there are many tribes), minorities (of any or a combination of descriptions), children (preschool, elementary, high school), or the mentally or physically impaired.

From these "needs," create a list. The list ought to be unpurged. Have this same group and some additional persons representing the same stockholders rank the recommendations after first trying to combine them. Listen to the arguments and record them. Prepare a listing by rank with some of the reasoning under each rank. Get this same group or some other to review and ratify what you have done.

Now have your staff review it. Warning: Staff should not be assumed to be objective or the most informed. To assume this is simply to defeat the purpose of having others who have a stake express their points of view. Many of these persons are daily witnesses to the problems and have frontline information. The most precious input of staff is that it can assess what it would take to accomplish any of the needs—objectives gleaned from the steps mentioned previously—and highlight the possible impact on the organization of each item on the menu of needs, at least from the operational perspective. This is precious. It is a way of assessing internal capabilities and organizational risks.

With this information, have an executive-level meeting in which all these bits of information are narrowed and made comprehensible for policy-level decision by a board of trustees that cannot possibly handle all the details. This means that the executives must be willing to express their choices—at least to make recommendations or helpful comments, even subjective ones.

The role of the CEO is not to ignore subjective information but to put it into perspective. Why? Because failure to do so is to put inaccurate, incomplete, and sometimes misleading information before a board of trustees so that planning is incomplete.

This topic is worth a short deviation. Suppose an operational manager opposes a new program. Suppose that the reason she does so is because she knows that the consequence of its adoption would be that resources would be shifted from her program. This view may be disguised in her comments. But can it be ignored just because it is self-serving? No. The point of fact is that part of the judgment that the organization has to make is the opportunity cost. Is it worth shifting those resources in terms of the activities that will be given up by her group? Moreover, is the gap that will remain worth filling? Does it negatively affect other parts of the organization in terms of their ability to perform?

Finally, the material should be put before the board of trustees. They should vote on the needs that the nonprofit will address as part of its mission.

What is accomplished through this process? The organization reduces the risk of straying from its mission, and it involves the community and membership that it exists to serve. Surely, this has political and public relations value, but the bigger value is that the organization becomes more relevant and gains wider internal and external support. The staff had an opportunity to assess its capabilities and to express its views. The trustees have met their responsibility, and the organization has met its responsibility to the trustees. Insight is gained.

Now, armed with this information, the organization can do a structured survey if thought necessary. It can focus on asking respondents about the needs that the organization is willing and able to meet. Such a survey, if conducted, should permit the respondents to express orders of preference or strength of needs. For example, which of these do you least (or most) need? Which of these needs are currently being adequately met?

SETTING PRIORITIES: AN ILLUSTRATION

Setting priorities is difficult when there is no framework. Let me share an experience. Many years ago, I was assigned to developing priorities for the educational system of a developing country. A thorough study had been done of the system and a list of over thirty recommendations was made. The Ministry of Education had indicated that it could not respond to all the recommendations because resources were limited. To which should it give priority?

To answer this question, we formed a team of four officials from the Ministry who knew the system and understood how it functioned and knew the priorities of the government and the political realities. We proceeded as follows:

1. We spent the first few days discussing how the system works. This provided a common reference for our thinking.

2. We concluded that a working hypothesis was that the overall priority of the educational system was to improve the quality of people and their productivity in the work force—economic development.

3. We designed a simple flow chart of how the system in step 1 works to accomplish the objective in step 2. This is represented in Figure 17.8. Being simple, the flow chart was workable and did not become an issue in itself; rather, it

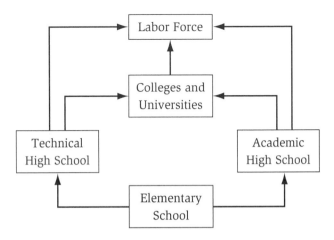

Figure 17.8. Flow Chart for Priority Setting.

became a tool. A hammer is a simple tool that does marvelous work. The chart shows both the linear and collateral relationships of how a student flows through the system into the workforce. We thus identified impact points.

4. We placed each of the thirty recommendations in the box representing the impact point in which it was most appropriate. Some recommendations belonged in more than one box.

5. We set the order that the recommendations within each box must take for the box to fulfill its mission: What is the order necessary for technical schools to produce a better student?

6. Based on step 6, we had the priority for each box. Based on the flow chart, we had the priority for the system. We had solved both simultaneously. Because the people who did it were the officials responsible for implementation, we had agreement that respects reality. Hence, the final step.

7. Is the result practicable? Is it acceptable? After making any adjustments for the answers to these questions, we wrote our final report. It was the product of a consultant facilitating the decisions of people responsible for turning a plan into priorities, policy, and ultimately practice.

MONITORING FOR PERFORMANCE

We monitor the flow of relevant information in a timely fashion to enable decision making and to provide information that must be incorporated in reports, whether to the trustees, funding agency, or the government or regulatory body, such as the annual report alluded to in Chapter Two. Through adequate monitoring, the organization can determine when to shift course, intensify, or keep going as is. (See the life-cycle discussion in this chapter.) It can also take corrective action. Monitoring should be done in the most efficacious way possible, for collecting and processing information is costly.

To appreciate what is involved in monitoring, let us presume an organization such as that shown in Figure 17.9. Every method of monitoring depends on the

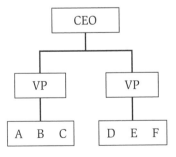

Figure 17.9. Organizational Chart.

size and complexity of the organizational structure, the volume and scope of the activities it conducts, the frequency with which it conducts each, the extent to which the information is required for managerial as well as public reporting purposes, and so on. Therefore, there is no one best way. Figure 17.9 helps us focus on this situation.

A, B, C and D, E, F are on the operating level. Their managers are equivalent, but they supervise distinctly different, but related activities. A, B, C are more like each other than like D, E, F and therefore they are grouped accordingly and report to a different vice-president. The fact that A, B, C are alike does not mean that they do the same thing, have the same external reporting requirements, or are funded in exactly the same way. A, B, C may, for example, be three separate wards in a children's hospital.

The data needed on this operational level are basically information that permits each operation (or each program) to be carried out efficiently. How often these data must be collected and in what form depends partly on the nature of the activity. In a hospital ward, the head nurse needs to take inventory of the medicines, the operating level of each piece of equipment, bed vacancies, turnover of patients, and so on. Furthermore, this level of monitoring occurs at least three times a day, upon the change of each shift. Although many of these data may be quantitative, some are also qualitative, such as reporting the status of patients and noteworthy changes in their condition. Basically, the data are operational rather than financial. Each of the three wards (A, B, C) dealing with orthopedic services will report similar types of data, while each of the three wards dealing with cardiac services (D, E, F) will do roughly the same—but they will differ to the extent that each is specialized.

But the flow is not one way. Just as each feeds its information up to its supervisor, the vice-president, information must be fed backward. The backward flow should give each manager a trend, an average, and a per unit cost. This information does not have to be daily or even weekly. Monthly may be sufficient. These figures are intended to give the operational manager some picture of performance over time. Is it on par, deteriorating, or improving? The figures are also intended to give these managers some insight as to the cost of their operation. To the extent that there is the possibility of discretion, the manager can contemplate alternatives for reducing the cost of his or her operation.

On the level of the vice-presidents, a different type of information is needed to monitor the activities being overseen. Not only are the numbers generated by the lower levels important, but also they must be compared if possible. The manager must also obtain data to monitor the markets for what is being offered by his or her units, how well these units are integrated, whether one has excess capacity and the other is idle, which needs additional persons or machines. In short, the level and kind of information needed tends to be almost equally weighted between physical numbers and dollars. The objective is not simply to determine levels of activities, but to choose among reporting operations, difficult as this might be.

In doing their job, the vice-presidents also need information flowing back from the top. This information should emphasize at least three things: (1) changing legal, marketing, and financial realities of the organization as a whole and their implications for each vice-president's operations; (2) the financial, public relations, and marketing impact on the organization of those activities for which each vice-president is responsible (that is, how they generate overhead cost); and (3) the need to meet the mission of the organization.

The top officer of the organization has the responsibility for keeping the organization relevant. Perhaps the low intake rate for the cardiac service has to do with competition or the narrowness of the service area of the hospital. What changes are appropriate? If the service area is too narrow, is it cost effective to have three or zero wards? Is it cost effective to have to have certain types of specialized but low-volume cardiac services? What is the cost to the overall organization—not just in dollars, but in opportunities lost or, as described in Chapter Fifteen, opportunity cost? Is the organization properly financed so that there are sufficient funds for the operational level staff to do their job? And, an often overlooked factor among nonprofit managers, to what risks (including the possible loss of exemption) are the operational, supervisory, and top-level persons exposing the organization?

The central objective of the monitoring by the top-level persons is to keep the organization alive and well, both financially and legally. It is also to keep it relevant. This completes the flow upward and downward, because the basic source of all such information is the operational level persons—the nurses, social workers, classroom teachers, and counselors. It is their reports as conformed to organization purpose by the vice-presidents that tell what and how much the organization is doing, how successfully, and the market reaction. They provide frontline intelligence.

The vice-presidents add to this by translating some information to dollars, showing trends within the organization and comparable organizations, and recommending through qualitative judgments courses of action or causes for concern.

When a nonprofit fails on the operational level, it is useless, because the basic purpose of a nonprofit, unlike a firm, is not to advance individuals as proprietors or to accumulate wealth through investments, but to advance public welfare. To be useful, it must serve a meaningful public purpose; it must do something of public value. The reader may wish to turn to the discussion of variance analysis in Chapter Twelve. It is a form of keeping tally and setting off alarms when performance is being monitored.

Monitoring for Planning

Monitoring the activities of A, B, C and E, D, F has planning purposes, some of which were mentioned; for example, the life cycle of activities and the shifting of resources among operational units. But monitoring has other planning dimensions. Imagine, for example, that the organization has a meeting or convention facility. Monitoring helps to determine peak and low levels of use. Therefore, the allocation of personnel, vacation time, special marketing efforts are all more intelligently planned for if data are available that reveal trends and patterns. Monitoring provides data for short-term and long-term planning. Monitoring for planning is sometimes equivalent to finding the life cycle of a product or service. The cable and transportation engineers near your intersection or traffic light are monitoring to plan traffic patterns and the signal cycle. By sitting there all day, they can plot traffic size by time of day; that is, the shape of the life-cycle curves discussed earlier.

MONITORING FOR RISKS AND CONTROL

A program should be monitored to ascertain whether proper controls are being applied, whether there is conformity with established rules and regulations, and whether new ones are needed. Monitoring for risk management helps uncover potential problems and develop policies for dealing with them.

When we start a recreational program, build a swimming pool, start a new treatment, have a new exhibit, remove a gate—all of these create and change our risk exposure. Moreover, our risks change as we and others learn more about what we are doing. If we keep records in a hospital, there is a risk to confidentiality just as there is in a school and in the military. Are our procedures adequate? If we are running a museum, is the security sufficient? A building inspector, whether for asbestos, fire hazard, or building code violations, is implementing a risk management policy in no less a critical way than a nurse who monitors the progress of a patient to stabilize his or her condition, or the food inspector who is concerned with the quality of the food we eat. The answers sought through risk management and monitoring are variations on the same theme: What shall we do to avoid a problem? What are new developments in the administration of the organization or program that affect our risk exposure? What shall we do?

Monitoring and Marketing

Monitoring also helps in marketing. Who uses the service of the nonprofit and therefore to whom must it reach out? What time is the service used and by whom and for what purpose? Are users satisfied? Are there improvements to be made? Therefore, what service shall the organization offer to whom? What is its best message in a marketing campaign? I shall say more about marketing in the next two chapters. Let us close this discussion of monitoring by saying that it should be more than collecting data for data's sake.

EVALUATING, BENCHMARKING, AND REPORTING

Much of evaluation is measuring actual performance against expectations. But what determines the level of expectations? *Benchmarking* is using the performance of an external peer to set these levels of expectations. Benchmarking requires the selection of a comparable peer (or target). The choice of these is always imperfect, but the process of choosing can uncover processes that are worth copying even when the comparison is imperfect.

Evaluation is important, and we have discussed cost-benefit analysis in this chapter and have touched on other techniques in the discussion of budgeting in Chapter Twelve. What we view evaluation from the perspective of the chief executive officer of most nonprofits. Rarely, and for some, never, do they have the time or resources to conduct comprehensive textbook evaluations. What then to do?

The simplest way to conduct an evaluation is to set milestones in physical and dollar units and also in terms of customer satisfaction at the very outset of the program. For example, if enrollment declines in a day-care center with no evidence that the population of eligible children has declined, and there is no physical obstacle to the children's getting to the center, this is indeed an inkling of disapproval by somebody and certainly of a probable problem. The failure of a play to attract an audience or woo the critics is also a measure of dissatisfaction, no matter how misguided.

At the end (and intermittently as a monitoring objective), compare what actually happened with what was planned. This device may seem too simple to suit some analysts; but the fact is that when CEOs are called forth to justify their programs before their trustees, the public, or their funding agencies, there is no time to do complex analyses. The question is simple: What did you do with the money? The answer cannot be: Wait, let me do a cost-benefit analysis.

Try this technique. At the outset, list a set of benefits or outcomes that are reasonably attainable. These should be separated into direct and indirect. The number of welfare mothers attending a class is a direct outcome of a program aimed at training mothers on welfare. That so many got jobs may be an indirect effect if the program was only to train, not also to place. In setting targets, put the emphasis on the direct benefits because these are the ones the organization can control and for which it is ultimately accountable. Try to report direct and indirect benefits in numbers, not narratives.

Place targets on the costs of running the program and also on required revenues. This should be relatively easy because no funding agency will give you money unless this is forthcoming. These costs should also be classified as direct or indirect. (See Chapter Twelve.) At this point, let it suffice to think of direct costs as those that the organization would not have had if your program were not adopted. And let us call indirect costs *overhead*. In short, at the outset you must determine how much the program will cost. At the end of the program, compare these costs, and do so intermittently for monitoring purposes. If the two are way off, you should be concerned.

Finally, prepare a narrative. This is the opportunity to tell your story in words that should not all be apologetic. Part of the narrative is to help the reader and planners for the next round of planning to understand what is behind the numbers. For example, cost might have risen. It may be that to enroll one welfare mother is to also incur costs of transportation, baby sitting, and so on that might have been unplanned for but later authorized with no supplemental budgeting. It may be that because of funding delays the program got off to a slow start. Do not fail to evaluate and report surprises. They form the basis of new programs, directions, and strategies to avoid risk.

Why do we suggest trying to report numbers? Compare the effects of alternative reporting of exactly the same event, which is that 100 families were served three meals a day from January 1 to December 31:

1. We fed 100 families during the year.
2. We served an average of 9,000 meals per month.
3. We served 108,000 meals.
4. We served 324,000 meals.
5. We prepare and serve hot meals to needy families.

Alternative 1 is not only the least impressive, but it is the most subject to error. How large is each family? Is it the same family that gets the meal day after day? Are there different families? How about single persons? Alternative 5 has a lot of emotion, but it does not communicate that the organization is doing very much. Alternative 4 may seem large but it is the most informative, impressive, and accurate. Try multiplying 100×3 meals a day $\times 30$ average number of days per month $\times 12$ months in a year $\times 3$, the average size of a family. Poor families tend to be larger than the 3 in the formula, but this is offset by single, elderly persons. So 3 is not bad. Put yourself in the position of the funding agency. Having this number affords easy calculation. Let us put a figure of $3 per meal. Now, we have the minimum basis of a grant, $972,000.

Guidelines for Evaluating a Program

Every program should be evaluated over the course of its life. Some evaluations are very extensive and may involve years of study, the collection of extensive amount of data, the following of numerous subjects, the participation of a diverse number of stakeholders whose interest in the program are often conflicting. The results of the study may be for improvement of the program or for the satisfaction of the funding source. No matter the reason, an evaluation ought to conform to rules of logic, relevance, and appropriateness.

The U.S. Department of Health and Human Services is well experienced in funding evaluations of its programs and in assessing these evaluations. Here are some of its guidelines paraphrased. These guidelines should help every not-for-profit organization. Obviously, not every word stated below may be applicable to your organization; for example, your organization may not be one doing the kinds of service that requires large-scale data collection and sophisticated scientific analyses.

Nevertheless, you will find the guidelines below, which paraphrase the original, helpful in thinking about your programs and how they might be evaluated if they are funded by a large funding agency. They may also help you write better proposals and program reports.

Because a study is composed of several parts, such as the literature, data collection design, analysis, findings, recommendations, and so on, some of these guidelines may seem repetitive and easily collapsed into a few. This is not the case when an evaluation is being done. Each part has to be treated eparately and then the interconnections have also to be assessed.

The Significance of the Evaluation

1. The evaluation should be of a significant public policy issue.
2. The findings of the evaluation ought to be potentially useful.

Conceptual Criteria

1. The evaluation should contain a review of the relevant literature.
2. The evaluation ought to be drawn on previous findings and it ought to be based on a theory or a model or both, thus providing a logically consistent foundation for the study.
3. The assumptions upon which the program is based should be stated.
4. The evaluation should draw from previous evaluations, if any, or from similar ones.
5. The evaluation ought to be linked closely to the program described.
6. The evaluation ought to present several perspectives.

7. The various stakeholders should be consulted in the preparation of the evaluation.

8. The program being evaluated should be mature enough to be evaluated.

Questions the Evaluation Raises

1. The aims of the evaluation should be clear and testable.

2. The questions raised by the evaluation should be significant and linked to the program and the conceptual or theoretical basis of the evaluation.

3. The questions should be creative.

Findings and Interpretation

1. The conclusions should be justified by the analysis.

2. The summary should not go beyond the findings of the evaluation.

3. When qualifiers are appropriate, they should be used.

4. The conclusions should follow from the analysis.

5. Findings that are doubtful should be expressed as such.

6. The findings should answer the questions that launched the evaluation in the first place.

7. The interpretation of the findings should tie in with the conceptual foundation of the evaluation.

8. Whether the findings deviate from the literature or support the literature should be stated.

9. The presentation should be understandable.

10. The results should have practical significance.

11. The implications of the program should be assessed.

Recommendations

1. The recommendations derived from the study should be deserving of being carried out, affordable, timely, feasible, useful, and appropriate.

2. The recommendations should be relevant to the questions of the evaluation.

3. The recommendations ought to be clear and specific.

4. The recommendations for future evaluations or improvements in the program or both should be stated.

Methods

1. The evaluation design should be appropriate, sound, feasible, timely, applicable for cultural diversity, valid, feasible for data collection, and reliable for measurements, and the sample should be appropriate for the study.

(continued)

2. The variables should be clearly specified and fit the design and questions of the evaluation.

3. The design should fit the program and its implementation and the questions of the evaluation.

Data Collection

1. The data collection should be from the units being measured, there should be controls for participant selection and bias, and allowance should be made for the proper handling of missing data or, in the case of longitudinal studies, attrition of subjects.

2. An appropriate sample size should be used with a proper response rate, and information about the sample should be part of the evaluation.

3. Data collection should be faithful to the research design but it should also be consistent and maintain proper confidentiality and be collected with the cooperation of the relevant community.

4. The quality of the data must be addressed in the evaluation report.

5. The method of data collection should be appropriate to the evaluation being done.

Data Analysis

1. The data analysis should take into account the effect of the size of the sample, the limitations of the study design, and the statistical methodology used, and should match the study design.

2. The analysis should show sensitivity to various cultural groups.

3. The study should not go beyond warranted generalizations and inferences.

4. The analysis should be simple and efficient.

At every stage of the study certain factors ought to be guiding. These include clarity, logic, the use of state-of-the-art techniques, innovation, notation of deficiencies in the study and its approach, and the notation and adherence of cultural and ethical correctness.

Source: This is adapted from "Appendix C: Evaluation Review Panel's Criteria for Assessing Program Evaluations," in *Performance Improvement 1998*, U.S. Department of Health and Human Services, 1998, a report to the U.S. Congress. NFS.

SUMMARY AND PREVIEW

This chapter has examined strategic planning as a process that can be used by managers of nonprofit organizations to identify unmet needs and so grow the organization, assess the ability of their organizations to meet those needs (given both internal and external constraints), develop strategies and programs, and make necessary evaluations and adjustments. The next chapter takes us from process to content. How does the organization identify growth opportunities? Where are they found? These are the concerns of the next chapter.

CHAPTER EIGHTEEN

Searching for Strategic Opportunities and Alliances

The manager who masters strategic planning is still stuck if he or she does not know how to apply it in search of opportunities to grow the organization. Many nonprofits do not appreciate the need to constantly search their environments for new opportunities consistent with their missions. This search is needed for purposes of growth as well as survival in a world where programs can quickly become dated and irrelevant. This is why, as discussed in the previous chapter, learning something about the life cycle of programs is so important.

In this chapter we turn to an analysis of the environment—the search for a niche. To a nonprofit, the discovery of a niche is the discovery of relevance. To be relevant, a nonprofit needs to be useful to society, although the societal benefits it confers need not be immediate. Therefore, to be operating within its niche, the nonprofit must simultaneously (1) have a relevant mission, and (2) run programs that are feasible, desirable, and consistent with that mission. We discussed methods for doing this in the previous chapter. Furthermore, the discovery and exploration of our niche open possibilities for productive partnerships that are within the tight perimeters of law.

How do we go about finding our niche? The organization has to be able to comb the environment for those tasks that are meaningful to society that consistent with its mission, feasible, and desirable for it to undertake. The previous chapter taught how to select options. But what are the real options in the real world? How can strategic alliances, particularly with for-profit firms, enable a nonprofit to do its job better? When, specifically, do such alliances threaten an organization's exempt status? What are the rules?

THE IMPORTANCE OF IDENTIFYING
NEW NICHES IN OLD MISSIONS

To understand what this chapter is all about, first recall our discussion in the last chapter on life cycles of programs. Then read the following:

> Goodwill's strength lies in its ability to train people to meet *real, identified* labor needs in the community. . . . Goodwill's service programs have changed with the changing times, and will continue to do so.
>
> While Goodwill's traditional "client" population has been people with physical, mental, or emotional disabilities, the people Goodwill serves today increasingly include those who face other disadvantaging conditions—illiteracy, a history of substance abuse, advanced age, or a history of welfare dependency and an accompanying lack of work experience. As labor needs change and as the United States continues to face a critical labor shortage, Goodwill will be there to provide training and to help match the work to the job.[1]

Or consider a shorter version of a publication that laid out the public policy agenda of the YWCA at the turn of the decade, the section titled "Optimum Functioning of the Economy":

> The interdependent functioning of the economy affects women as workers, consumers, and mothers . . . . We therefore support . . . adequate guidance and counseling services, training, and retraining opportunities at every level for women and girls confronted with new demands and new opportunities in the work world.[2]

The preceding statements reveal (1) a concern for change and a strategy for adjustment to it by the organization, (2) a relevance of the organization to the larger world of which it is a part, (3) programs that are marketable because they are relevant to a larger, changing world, and (4) programs that are consistent with the mission of the organizations. Dynamic organizations adjust to changing environments.

We will not undertake an analysis of culture, politics, or international relations here, but will focus on the economy because it is so central to the environment in which nonprofits throughout the world, even in emerging markets, function. We shall systematically dissect the economy with the purpose of asking what relevance each part has for our own nonprofit organization. This is what environmental scanning is all about. Please go back to Table 2.2. Note the number of specific purposes that relate to the economy. How does your organization fit? Why is it relevant?

ECONOMIC PURPOSE OF NONPROFITS

Attempting to find a theoretical foundation for the laws on nonprofits, legal scholars have turned to economics.[3] One argument is that nonprofits exist because of "contract failures."[4] This means that there are a number of situations in which the purchaser is uncertain of the quality of product or service that a for-profit producer would provide. The producer is seen to be motivated by profits and not necessarily by what is in the best interest of the public. Under these conditions, some contracts with a for-profit firm would fail. In these cases, a nonprofit is said to be superior to a for-profit producer because it has no profit motive, just the single mission or purpose of improving the welfare of the public.

This view is sometimes seen as too narrow. Another legal scholar takes the view that the economic role of a nonprofit is that sometimes it is in the best interest of the customers to own the producers.[5] This view rests on the idea that customers often find among themselves a mutual or common interest that cannot be appropriately satisfied by the market. In such a case, through a nonprofit mode they can join together to produce the product or service themselves. For instance, in the case of a day-care center, a group of working mothers may join together to create a cooperative center responding to their specific needs and desires for the kinds of services they wish for their children. In the normal operation of the market, they cannot control the production process; they can only choose among alternative offerings, none of which may be satisfactory.

Even the view of nonprofits as collectives or voluntary associations to exercise individual beliefs or expressions (the First Amendment) is consistent with economic theory.[6] The economic theory of collectivity argues that people come together in groups or collectives because of interdependencies, or what is known as *externalities* and *economies of scale*. An externality in economics means that the action of one person affects another person. For example, a thousand persons of the same religious belief may not only find greater religious satisfaction by worshiping together, but they would find it cheaper to build a house of worship in which they all worship together rather than for each person to build an individual house of worship.

Nonprofits do play a central role in the market economy. Even in the market economy's symbolic core, the stock market, nonprofits are major holders of stocks and debt. They were also major sources of funds in leverage buyouts as well as major beneficiaries as the value of endowment portfolios appreciated as raiders bidded for stocks they held. Furthermore, the National Association of Security Dealers (NASD) regulates security dealers and brokers and carries the most up-to-date and complete price quotations on the over-the-counter stock exchange. NASD has been a nonprofit association.

SYMBIOTIC RELATIONSHIP

A good starting point of any environmental scanning exercise focusing on the economy is to acknowledge that the economy is mixed. The public sector relies on the private sector. It is the latter that produces the goods and services, creates income, and makes the profits that are taxed as corporate and personal income, the two major sources of revenues of the public sector. One way in which the public sector uses its revenues from taxation is to support nonprofits through contracts and grants.

The support that nonprofits get from nongovernmental sources comes form individuals and firms. Individuals can make gifts and contributions because they earn an income from the for-profit sector that pays its own workers and supplies the revenues that government uses to pay its workers. These workers, in both the public and private sectors, make contributions and gifts to the nonprofit sector.

The gifts and contributions made by firms to nonprofits come from their income or profits. Hence, whether the support comes from the public sector or individuals or directly from profit makers, the ultimate source is exactly the same: the for-profit firm.

The reliance on the for-profit sector goes beyond support. It extends to opportunities created by the way for-profit firms operate. Opportunities are also created by the limited effectiveness of government action. To detect the new opportunities for nonprofits requires the ability to appreciate two trends: (1) the dynamics of for-profit firms, that is, of the market economy, and (2) the limited effectiveness of government action. To do this requires dissecting the economy and finding niches and linkages. There is a future for those who can visualize cooperative connections earlier than others.

NONPROFIT OPPORTUNITIES GENERATED BY THE MARKET ECONOMY

The market system internally generates and satisfies many needs. Often, however, capacity and efficiency considerations mean that for-profit firms cannot fully satisfy all market needs, even though there is no lack of ability to pay on the part of those whose needs must be satisfied. Economic growth creates a demand for sudden increases in capacity, information, and other resources often existing in the nonprofit sector. To appreciate this fully, let us look at the economic behavior of each of the major actors in the market economy. We begin each section with specific real-world examples; then we present the basic theory and show how other opportunities may be generated to the discerning and dynamic management of nonprofits. What is our niche?

Consumers

What can the consumer-oriented nonprofit do for the consumer? Try Codes 530 and 402 of Table 2.2 or 905 and 906. Do you see others?

There are several real-world examples of nonprofits intervening in the market process to assist consumers. A nonprofit group was given tax exemption as a charity because it gave education on personal financial management to low-income households.[7] Another nonprofit was similarly classified because it provided guidance and information to low-income households on building their own home.[8] These are examples of nonprofits, to benefit the community, providing information and education of the dangers of certain foods, behaviors, and environments that put people at risk. A good example is *Consumer Reports,* published by the Consumer Union, a nonprofit.

How does the economy operate to provide these types of opportunities for nonprofits to assist consumers? What are the points of opportunity for a nonprofit? To spot these, we must know how consumers behave and how the private market responds or affects that behavior. From this general framework, each organization can identify and develop its own point of entry. To make this easier, key words in the description below are in italics. Think of the number of permutations and combinations in which these words can form a mission statement! Can you make a purpose in Table 2.2 qualify? This is what creative nonprofit management must do to remain relevant. It must pinpoint a niche.

A consumer can *buy* a good only if he or she has an *income.* The goodwill is bought only if its *price* does not exceed the dollar value the consumer places on it—that is, its *utility* to the consumer. The money used to make *purchases* is from the earnings of the consumer as a worker.

Consumers are *free* to choose how to spend the income they earn as workers. *Low-income consumers* buy fewer *luxuries* and more *low-priced* or inferior goods but spend just about the same proportion of their income as higher income persons do on *necessities,* such as food, soap, and shelter.

As do other commodities, soap comes in numerous sizes, shapes, brand names, scents, and chemical compositions. Each of these *characteristics* is represented in the price. Similarly, cars come under different *brand* names with different characteristics, which are reflected in differences in price. Yet one can be *substituted* for another. They all provide the same utility or *use,* transportation, but some more comfortably than others. The same thing holds for soap. All can be used for cleaning, but one gives a more favorable scent than the other.

Hence, if the price of one brand of car or soap *rises,* consumers who want basic *transportation* or cleanliness would buy more of the less expensive brand if it has maintained comparable *quality.* They will behave in this way as long as they are *aware* or have *information* on the prices and the brands they want are *available*. In short, consumer *choice* depends on information as well as income, prices, and the availability of substitutes and complements.

Hence, as the for-profit sector grows, producing goods that are *substitutes* for each other or *complements* to each other, some of which are unrelated to each other, the opportunities for nonprofits are also increased. The home computer industry is an example. As for-profit firms produce more models that are really varying degrees of substitutes, there is also a rise in the demand for complements (software), which are also varying degrees of substitutes for each other. This has spawned countless opportunities for nonprofits to provide the computer-related complements of information and education. Carnegie-Mellon, for example, owns a subsidiary that develops and licenses the use of its software to for-profit firms.

Education and training even for a fee (as many educational institutions charge) are acceptable functions of nonprofits. Education is defined, for tax-exempt purposes, as instruction, information, and training that benefits an individual and the community.[9] It should be evident from the framework just described that the economy generates an endless number of these opportunities. Hence, the basic question for a nonprofit is, Which of these varying degrees of consumer needs best meet our mission? How will these needs change?

Producers

Codes 180, 200, and 207 in Table 2.2 are real-world examples of nonprofits assisting producers. One type of nonprofit, called an *incubator,* is credited with spawning nineteen new corporations, creating over 1,800 jobs and $80 million income for a depressed Kentucky community.[10] Incubators are nonprofit organizations that finance, assist, and rent space to a cluster of growing firms so that they can interact and nurture each other.

One of the best examples of a cooperative relationship is between McDonald's and the Environmental Defense Fund (EDF), who formed a team to study ways to reduce trash. After two years of study, the McDonald's reduced its volume of packing by 80 percent by using new wraps, more recycled paper products, and recycled tires for nonskid surfaces for playgrounds at the more than 1,700 McDonald's restaurants. McDonald's, in its 1990 Annual Report, notes that it does not own or purchase cattle that has been grown on rainforest land—only on corn and grass (alfalfa). What are the gains for McDonald's? Lower costs, higher profits, greater market share—all while advancing public welfare.

On a smaller scale is an organization that was awarded tax exemption for marketing cooking and sewing done by low-income women. On a larger scale is the organization that does research on color science and technology[11] or the society that was formed to do scientific research on air conditioning and ventilating.[12] On even a larger scale are the universities that conduct research that benefits producers. The most rapidly growing and controversial aspects of this relationship are in pharmaceuticals and biogenetics, where the ethical issues have been, to some, bothersome.

What is the basis of missions that aid producers? How about 230 through 249 in Table 2.2? To maximize their *profits, producers* create the mix of goods consumers want at the lowest *cost* possible by using the best *technology* and *workers available* and by *selling* the goods at the highest price consumers will pay in a very competitive world market. Nonprofits have contributed in every phase, including product development in agriculture.

Research to develop technology (*R&D*) requires *specialized skills.* Research and development are acceptable functions of nonprofits as long as the results are made public, that is, *disseminated.* A very high percentage of the research and development that eventually leads to commercial *applications* is done at universities and other nonprofit laboratories. This is in fields including engineering, crop development and land conservation, medicine and medical procedures, and science in general. A laboratory can be used for teaching and for product development and testing.

Workers

An organization that provided a registry of available nurses was given tax exemption because the registry was seen as assisting the community to find nurses, rather than assisting the nurses to find jobs.[13] The registry was not viewed as self-promotion of the nurses, in which case it would not have been exempt, but as information to the public. An organization formed to transport low-income workers to jobs because of inadequate transportation was also granted exemption.[14] An organization formed to give career counseling and distribute educational publications was also granted exemption, even though it charged a fee.[15] Day-care centers are granted exemptions if nearly all the child-care service is provided to enable parents to work and if the service is available to the general public.

What are the factors that give rise to opportunities to assist workers? An *individual* in the market economy acting *freely* and *knowledgably* would *choose* the occupation for which he or she is best suited because this would improve the chances of maximizing the *benefits,* including *income,* and minimizing the *unpleasantness* of work. Once in that *occupation* or *job,* the person would seek to work for the highest-paying producer. And naturally, the higher the pay, the greater the willingness to work.

This economic behavior of workers depends on a number of factors: having adequate *information* about occupations and employment, having *access* to *training* and to jobs, being *compensated* according to *productivity,* having information and access to *leisure,* and being able to make a rational judgment between leisure and *work.* Meeting these training, informational, *search,* and employment needs is an acceptable function of nonprofits. Codes 566, 126, 159, 568, and 031 in Table 2.2 are examples.

This is precisely what job training schools do. They train and help in job search. Some nonprofits aid older workers, the disabled, veterans, women, and the disadvantaged in career development and in finding jobs. In this regard, they work to help expand the for-profit sector and to improve its efficiency by training and placing workers. Not only do nonprofits train the input necessary for growth, but they can also assist in matching input availability (supply) with demand.

Investors

Economic growth cannot occur without new *net investment* in *plant* and *equipment*. As economic growth occurs, it stimulates more investment as investors begin to expect acceptable *rates* of *return* on their investments. Producers must borrow to invest because the initial cost of most projects is large. They will *borrow* only if the expected rate of return on their investments equals or exceeds the rate of interest they have to *pay* for borrowed funds. It makes no sense, for example, to borrow at 15 percent and get only a 5 percent return on the investments made.

Nonprofits do have a growing opportunity to affect investment decisions. Economic development corporations and community development corporations are nonprofits that can make investments that are beneficial to the community but that for-profit firms will not make because the project is too risky or the rate of return too low. See 400–429 in Table 2.2 and 533 for examples.

In addition, these nonprofit corporations can lower the cost to the for-profit firm by putting up seed money, making loans at below-market rates, packaging and preparing land, and giving *technical* assistance. By lowering costs, these actions increase the profitability of the project and make it more attractive to private investors. A real case will be presented at the end of this chapter.

Savers

Investment dollars come from the savings of workers. To get more savings for investment, consumers must be encouraged to save by having safe vehicles for saving and earning high rates of interest. Encouraging effective saving strategies through education is an acceptable function of nonprofits. Hence, the organization that assisted low-income households to improve their *money management* was granted tax exemption.[16]

By referring again to Table 2.2, we see that there are types of savings-related institutions, Codes 921, 251, and 565, that are nonprofits. Pension trusts, Code 268, have billions of dollars in assets and are nonprofit organizations.

Deposits to these trusts and pension funds are regular, predictable, and dependable. Withdrawals from these trusts are orderly and extend over many years. Therefore, pension trusts are a primary source of dollars for long-term investment. Mutual insurance companies and credit unions are also examples of nonprofit associations operating to stimulate saving and provide loans.

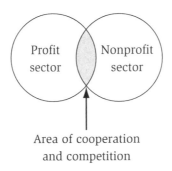

Area of cooperation
and competition

Figure 18.1. Interaction of Profit and Nonprofit Sectors.

These discussions indicate that within the market structure itself are potential opportunities for nonprofits to assist (1) consumers, (2) workers, (3) producers, (4) investors, and (5) savers. In a growing economy, these opportunities increase, not decrease. Many of these opportunities exist in the shaded area in Figure 18.1. In this area, nonprofits and for-profit firms may be competitors or collaborators, such as joint partners in research, information dissemination, and community development.

The competition even within the shaded area is limited. It often means that the for-profit and nonprofit corporations divide a market for the same product or service. Constrained by their need to make a profit, the for-profit firms would almost automatically focus on the more profitable segment of the market, whereas the nonprofit, able to rely on gifts and contributions as supplementary support and being constrained by IRS rules to demonstrate that they are not just another commercial firm but are catering to a clientele that such firms do not reach, will focus on the less profitable segment. Witness the difference between privately owned (for-profit) hospitals and many, admittedly not all, community or nonprofit hospitals. Notice also that this does not necessarily mean economic disaster for the nonprofit.

Before proceeding to the next section, the reader may wish to revisit the section on internationalization in the Preface of this book. Nonprofits are fantastic buffers when the market fails. They are also fantastic boosters of dynamic change.

NONPROFIT OPPORTUNITIES GENERATED BY MARKET FAILURES

Economists use the term *externalities* to denote the effect that one entity's or person's market behavior has on others.[17] In a market economy, each person or entity acts in a manner to meet his or her economic objectives with only limited regard for its effects on others; that is, the market fails to control the impact that individuals or firms have on society. The existence of these externalities creates a need for nonprofits. They imply that given its profit-motive, firms may supply too much or too little of a product, for example, tobacco, or that consumers would use too little or not enough of a product.

Negative Effects of Consumption

The use of automobiles (emitting carbon dioxide, making noise, requiring the conversion of open space to roads and highways), airplanes (noise and air pollution), and tobacco and the abuse of alcohol and other drugs are said to result in *external diseconomies of consumption* because they have *harmful* or *deleterious* effects on persons other than the user. When external diseconomies of consumption exist, the obvious reaction is to *curtail* consumption and the negative effects of it. Look at Codes 536 (intoxication), 537 (drugs), 538 (tobacco), 539 (erotica) in Table 2.2.

Governments can impose laws and regulations and may even tax the purchase of the commodity with the hope that the higher price will discourage consumption—that is, sin taxes. Under certain conditions, such as designating no-smoking areas in public places and in airplanes, the intervention by the public sector may only be partly effective. Experience has shown that public sector actions insufficient and often ineffectual. Producers and consumers of products that have strong external diseconomies are usually successful in resisting any truly impeding law or tax, not only by virtue of their political power, but by calling on the constitutional protection of their rights.

Because there are usually *no profits* to be made in restricting consumption resulting in external diseconomies, for-profit firms are usually not attracted to such activities. On the contrary, there are often more profits to be made in the production and sale of commodities and services such as cigarettes, alcohol, and drugs than in curtailing their use. Mothers Against Drunk Driving (MADD) and Alcoholics Anonymous are examples of nonprofits working to solve problems of diseconomies of consumption.

Again, the agreement between the Environmental Defense Fund and McDonald's Corporation alluded to earlier is proof that nonprofits and for-profits can work together in this area, as well as others. Noting the waste produced by the over 1,000 stores, the two agreed to cooperate in formulating conservation strategies. The creation of *waste* (a problem for others) by customers at these and similar stores is a form of external diseconomy of consumption.

If the government taxing and rule-making powers have limited effect, and if the profits to be made in curtailing consumption are also limited, even though curtailing consumption is socially desirable, a natural opportunity then arises for nonprofit organizations. Examples of these are nonprofits using their education and training authority to educate people about the dangers of smoking and drugs, and the organization that received tax-exempt status because it provided funds to owners of cats who could not afford the cost of having the pets spayed or neutered.[18]

The tasks before the management of the nonprofit when external diseconomies exist are (1) to identify the aspect of the external diseconomy that the organization can address, (2) arrive at an appropriate strategy for dealing with it, and (3) use the social merit argument as well as the merits of the organization to justify cooperation and support, as the Environmental Defense Fund did.[19]

Positive Effects of Consumption

External economies exist when the consumption by any one person of a good or service has a *positive* effect on others. Your use of a deodorant or fragrance is appreciated by others. Vaccinations against communicable diseases benefit both the client and others with whom he or she may come in contact. Many health and educational programs fall into this category; for example, an organization formed to give counseling in employment, citizenship, language, medical information, and housing to immigrants is of this type. The more the immigrants partake of these offerings, the easier their adjustment and the lower the need for social assistance and the possibilities of infractions against the law. Consequently, the entire community is better off.[20] The objective is, therefore, to *increase* such behavior. But who will do it? Perhaps, a nonprofit.

Returning to the case of inoculations, *profits* may be made by inoculating individuals who are *limited* by their ability to pay, have an awareness of danger, and have a willingness or ability to make themselves available for shots. Because it is to the advantage of society to have as many persons as possible inoculated, and because for-profit firms are limited by their need to earn a profit, some needs will remain unmet. One possibility is for the public sector to answer these unmet needs directly. Another is for the public sector to subsidize both for-profit firms and nonprofits so that the unmet needs will be addressed. A third possibility is for the nonprofit to meet these needs by relying on below-market rate fees, using gifts and contributions to make up the difference. Through its normal operation, the economy generates or leaves unanswered a number of consumption externalities or *spillovers,* as they are sometimes called, for which fees can be charged by a nonprofit provider.

Negative Effects of Production

External diseconomies occur when the production process results in *negative* effects on others. Smoke emission from a plant and chemical and industrial wastes dumped in waterways are examples. Economic growth, if only by increasing the rate at which facilities are used, generates diseconomies of production. See Code 351 in Table 2.2, combating air pollution.

One reason external diseconomies of production such as air and water pollution persist is that they bring down the cost of production to the producer. It is cheaper to dump wastes in rivers than to dispose of them properly. In short, producers have limited incentive to *curtail* external diseconomies of production. When such incentive exists, it often is brought about by external forces.

One external force is the government. It can impose fines, taxes, and jail sentences. Another source is for-profit firms that produce substitutes or use substitute methods of production—disposable diapers, biodegradable soap, no-lead paint. The production of substitutes is not enough, as can be seen in the different grades of gasoline. Moreover, the initial force for bringing about change is often a nonprofit movement, as in the fields of environment and energy.

Often there are no profits to be made by discovering these diseconomies, monitoring and reporting them, or even creating solutions to them. Hence, an organization that is *not* constrained by *profit* considerations must often come to the fore. The environmental movement, from monitoring to the development of alternative energy sources, in large measure represents reactions to external diseconomies of production. Hence, when external diseconomies of production exist, a need for nonprofit organizations to reduce them arises, perhaps under Codes 350 through 379 or even 203 of Table 2.2. The nonprofit does not have to be in a confrontational position. There are many industry-supported nonprofits that regulate their members. The challenge before the nonprofit management is, again, to answer the three-part question: (1) what is the specific feature of the diseconomy that the nonprofit is capable of addressing, (2) what is the best strategy, and (3) what are the merits upon which funds can be obtained? A specific example of a nonprofit organization that has received tax exemption to meet this challenge is one that was formed to inform the public about the destruction of the environment from solid-waste disposal and that obtained revenues by collecting and selling solid waste for recycling.[21]

External Economies of Production

External economies arise when the production process of one firm creates *benefits* to other firms. There are benefits that the firm is *incapable of* harnessing and *selling*. Hence, it has very little incentive to produce them at any level greater than what is incidental to its normal production, even though society may benefit from more. As in the case of the consumer, the government could try subsidizing the firm to induce it to do more, but this is expensive. A less expensive way is often to increase the intervention of a nonprofit organization.

As an example, grocery stores always experience spoilage or the need to reduce the price of inventory such as baked goods after they have been on the shelf for some time. A nonprofit, viewing this as an opportunity, entered into an agreement whereby these day-old or damaged foods are distributed by the nonprofit to the poor. Here, what would ordinarily have been a loss is converted to an external economy of production and a social gain. The management of this nonprofit knew (1) where an external economy of production existed or could be created from a potential loss, (2) how the nonprofit and its clients could benefit from it, and (3) how it could raise the very modest support needed. The goods were obtained free and volunteers were used to collect and distribute them. This activity attracted clients to the organization, many of whom purchased commodities received as gifts and sold them at bargain prices in its thrift shop, thereby generating revenues.

PURE PUBLIC GOODS AND NONPROFITS

Even though they might be of *inestimable value,* pure public goods are not produced by for-profit firms because the principal characteristic of a pure public good is that once it is provided, no one can be *excluded* from its enjoyment. Clean air is an example. Once the air is clean, anyone who lives in or visits the vicinity can enjoy it. Because there is no way to exclude anyone, everyone will enjoy it regardless of whether he or she is charged or pays a price. Who will voluntarily pay a price for something that can be had without paying? Public goods are sometimes seen as *free* goods to the consumer, even though they are *expensive* to provide.

A corollary characteristic of pure public goods is that they are usually *indivisible.* It is not possible to split them up into units that can be distributed one to an individual. Who will pay for a commodity that cannot be *owned?*

Another corollary of a pure public good is that the consumption by any one individual of that good *does not diminish* the consumption by any other person. When one person breathes fresh air, that does not diminish the amount available to any other person. As a result, there is no bidding because the good does not run out.

These features mean that *pricing* of public goods by a for-profit firm *is impossible.* How can a profit be made on a good that no one is willing to pay a price for? How can a profit be made on a good if ownership cannot be sold? Who will buy it? How can a profit be made if no buyers will bid? Since the pure public good cannot be sold, a profit cannot be made and for-profit firms will not produce it.

Yet there is a cost to producing pure public goods. Clean air is maintained at a cost. Who pays? Generally, the government pays through imposing compulsory taxes and by contracting with or subsidizing for-profit or nonprofit organizations to do the work. Public goods such as clean air are appropriate functions of nonprofits and so, too, are neighborhood development programs (Codes 400, 401, and 402) and public radio and television (Code 121).

Associations are one type of nonprofit that produce pure public goods on a smaller scale. Associations of employees, employers, counties, and cities are all examples of nonprofits providing public goods. They are listed in Table 2.2. To understand a public good, we only have to see that, once a union wins benefits for workers, those benefits can be enjoyed by workers in the trade or industry regardless of whether or not they are members of the union. This technique is used in automobile and airline negotiations. Unions pick one company to set a pattern. When the American Medical Association fights for and wins a legislative position favorable to doctors, all doctors potentially benefit whether or not they are members of the association.

Associations also provide some private goods. They can charge a fee for the association's magazine because the magazine is not a public good. As is increasingly the case, members who do not pay a special fee for the magazine will not get it. The magazine is divisible so that many subscribers may be served, each with an individual copy. Members who do not pay conference charges cannot attend; that is, they can be excluded.

However, the representative effort of the association is a pure public good. No actual or eligible member of the association can be excluded from the representative benefits. Accordingly, associations commonly place a price on some of their activities such as seminars and journals, which are private goods, but not on their representative efforts, which are public goods. These are covered by membership fees.

Another example of a nonprofit providing public goods is an organization of physicians that oversees the quality of health care in a particular community.[22] The same is true of an organization created to do improvements on municipally owned property.[23] An organization created to preserve lakes for public recreation is also an example.[24]

In general, public goods offer opportunities for nonprofits because for-profit firms have no price incentive to produce such goods. A price cannot be charged. In this sphere, nonprofits have an advantage because they can charge a general membership fee and also seek additional support in the form of gifts and contributions and special assessments as ways of paying for the public good.

NONPROFIT FINANCING OF PUBLIC GOODS AND RESPONSES TO EXTERNALITIES

Why, it may be asked, would nonprofits be able to find profitable opportunities in externalities and public goods when for-profit firms cannot? The answer is that nonprofits can rely on combined support from individuals, firms, and government and a below-market price to cover costs and produce a surplus. Private firms must rely only on market price.

Does it make sense to speak of reliance on support when such support, at least from the government, is becoming less reliable? This means that nonprofits must increase their persuasion and diversify their revenue base, a major concern of this book.

Why would an individual give to a nonprofit that produces a public good or responds to an externality when neither may be particularly profitable? The answer is that "giving" is only related to economic considerations in a limited way. Moreover, an activity might have too low a return to attract a particular investor. Yet that investor could reap significantly high tax savings and public goodwill by making a contribution to a nonprofit that would make the investment. Indeed, the individual may be a beneficiary of the mission of the nonprofit.

NONPROFITS AND MARKET MONOPOLY

The best way to visualize this subject is to think of medicine, and one of the best examples is AIDS. A company has exclusive rights to produce and market a medical device or cure. It has monopoly power. It can therefore set prices as high as it wishes. The result is that only a few persons have availability to the product or cure, and many of these have it for only a short period because their resources will soon be totally depleted. This situation would be described by economists as one in which social benefits exceed the amount that can be satisfied at high monopoly prices.

The government can break up the monopoly. But this is hard to do, expensive, and time-consuming in litigation. It can encourage nonprofits to enter the market either by producing a competitive "generic" product or cure or by taking over one of the logistical functions, such as distribution, which would lower cost. Either way, the role of the nonprofit is to produce social benefits by being an alternative to the monopoly. Many life-saving products will be financed on the strength of this reasoning. The nonprofit is used to reduce monopoly power.

NONECONOMIC CONSEQUENCES OF MARKET BEHAVIOR AND OPPORTUNITIES FOR NONPROFITS

As the market system functions, it produces a number of noneconomic consequences. One is inequity. The market system pays people only if they work. Pay is determined by the value of the contribution of the worker to the value of the final product. Some individuals are unable to work for reasons of disability or age. In a strict market economy, only those who work are able to consume because only they will have income with which to make purchases. Moreover, in a strict market economy, people who are less productive than others would not only be paid less than others but may very well be paid below the amount necessary to afford a socially accepted minimum standard of living. Poverty is thus consistent with a market economy. There are both working and nonworking poor.

The consequence of this is that many persons are unable to afford even basic necessities. The most efficient market economy distributes income according to productivity, not according to need. A producer cannot pay purely by need. A producer can pay according to the value of the product the worker produces, since this is the main source of revenues for the producer. For-profit firms do not get gifts and contributions.

But equity and the needs of individuals cannot be ignored in any humane society. Consequently, there are organizations such as the Samaritan Ministry of Greater Washington, a partnership of thirty-one Episcopal churches with the goal "to provide services to persons in need which enable self-sufficiency, independence, and dignity." A mission such as this is clearly noncommercial.

Because revenues place a limit on what firms can pay, a need arises for an entity that is not limited by its earnings. Nonprofits are not so limited. They have other sources of support—gifts and contributions. Therefore, nonprofits are very suited for dealing with issues of equity.

Admittedly, the dimension of the equity problem may be too large for the nonprofit sector alone or for any one specialty within the nonprofit sector. Note the number of codes in Table 2.2 that are reserved for making life fair. This is why understanding these complex problems is important.

SOCIALLY COMPLEX PROBLEMS AND THE NEED FOR NONPROFITS

Whether opportunities appear within or outside the perimeters of the market system, they are likely to present themselves as complex problems. In the view of Horst Rittle, *complex* does not mean *difficult*. A complex problem is one that is (1) subject to many definitions, (2) with each definition requiring a unique set of solutions, (3) with each solution creating its own set of side problems, and (4) with each of these side problems (like the original problem) subject to many definitions and solutions, and so on in a circular fashion.[25]

Rittle describes these problems in terms of energy and the urban environment. Using a similar approach, we can see that poverty is a complex problem. It has many facets, including health, education, nutrition, employment, law, and culture. Each aspect presents a set of specialized challenges; that is, the legal questions are different from the medical and nutritional factors. Each set of specialized solutions represents a role for a special type of nonprofit. Having undertaken the challenges of one solution, a new set of problems arises. For example, setting up a health clinic does not solve the problem of getting people to attend, but it does create the need for a link between their social and health needs.[26]

Moreover, the very definition of poverty is temporal and spatial; that is, the poverty level for an urban family of four is different from that of a similar family in a rural area. The poverty threshold changes every year, and the cash definition of poverty is different from the cash-plus-assistance-received definition.

The point is that a truly complex problem creates a wide range of interrelated needs—each set of needs requiring a different specialty and each specialty requiring an organization with a specialized mission. All complex problems are not purely charitable, but even noncharitable complex problems create the need for nonprofits.

The production and use of automobiles, nuclear plants, and a residential development are truly complex problems and create a need for nonprofits, partly because of the externalities as we discussed them and partly because of the creation of pure public goods. An automobile is a private good that creates external diseconomies of consumption through gas emission and reckless driving. It also gives rise to public goods, such as the creation of antidrunk-driving nonprofits. Complex problems, obviously, are also related to the operation and growth of the economy.

Imaginative management of nonprofits requires the ability to detect the existence of a complex problem, systematically dissect it, and identify the aspects of the complex problem that the organization can adequately address within its mission and resource capabilities.

OPPORTUNITIES FOR PROFITABLE COOPERATION BETWEEN NONPROFIT AND FOR-PROFIT CORPORATIONS

In the previous section, we showed how nonprofits may intervene in the market process to carry out their charitable missions while at the same time earning revenues and public support because they are relevant. To do this, it is unnecessary and often inadvisable for the nonprofit to go it alone or try to compete with for-profit firms. This section demonstrates several levels of cooperation that can benefit both the for-profit firms and the nonprofits. But why would these for-profit firms and nonprofits have any incentive to cooperate with each other?

Every successful partnership requires the intermeshing of interests among the parties involved. Chapters throughout this book make it clear that a nonprofit may make a profit, but the profit must be used to carry out the tax-exempt mission of the organization. The dominant motive is public welfare, not private profits. However, for-profit firms are driven by the profit motive, not public welfare. A profit is a possible shared interest even though its use, once obtained, may vary.

The successful partnership combines the interests of the nonprofit as an economic institution that needs revenues to conduct its mission with that of for-profit firms that need markets from which to derive a profit. The market is composed of the clients and potential clients of the nonprofits. By serving the clients or mission of the nonprofit, revenues are generated for both the for-profit and nonprofit partners.

What makes these arrangements possible is that neither the for-profit nor nonprofit organization disagrees about the need for revenues. Both are interested in containing costs and in a good public image, and both are economic institutions, but neither maximizes profits.[27] Herbert Simon, a Nobel prize winner, noted that firms engage in "satisficing" rather than in maximizing profits. By this he means that for-profit managers try to accommodate a number of competing constituencies both within and outside the firm, and that this attempt to satisfy rarely leads to maximum performance.

For any partnership to succeed, all parties must contribute something. What the nonprofits contribute is their advantage in meeting certain needs that the regular commercial market cannot profitably satisfy. This advantage derives basically from the following:

1. Nonprofits can sell a product or service at a lower price than for-profit firms can because nonprofits can subsidize their lower price by gifts and contributions.

2. Nonprofits often have a built-in clientele, not only from their membership but from the fact that the relationship that people develop with these organizations is rarely based solely on the quality of product or services they produce or the price at which they sell them.

3. Nonprofits are in a better position to lower costs of production by using volunteers, obtaining plant and equipment as gifts, being eligible for lower postage rates (often challenged by postal authorities), and by not having to pay taxes under certain very circumscribed conditions, even when they run a business for profit.

4. Nonprofits such as research organizations often hold licenses or patents that can be used by for-profit firms to produce a product or service while providing the nonprofits with revenues in the form of nontaxable royalties. (See Chapter Ten.) A relevant example here is the licensing of use of software by for-profit firms by nonprofits such as universities.

For-profit firms have no such advantages, but they can deduct interest and other operating expenses from their taxes, subtract depreciation in calculating their taxes, and, prior to the 1986 tax reform, take an investment tax credit on the equipment they bought. The investment tax credit varied from 6 to 10 percent of the purchase of old or new equipment, which could be deducted from their tax bills. Nonprofits could not use these tax credits unless they ran a for-profit business that paid taxes. The net effect of tax breaks such as interest, depreciation, and investment tax credit (when it was legal) is to reduce costs and increase the after-tax rate of return on investments. In addition, for-profit firms can contribute expertise and capital.

For-profit firms can contribute marketing skills, logistical and transportation capacity to move a product or service across the globe, technological and production capacity, expertise, and capital. By exploiting the main differences between these two sectors, there are endless opportunities for cooperation, sometimes called *strategic alliances,* between for-profit firms and nonprofits. Let us take a look at three levels of cooperative efforts. Chapter Nine discusses a matrix that helps managers decide when cooperation is advisable.

Transactions

On the transactional level, a for-profit and nonprofit merely engage in a transaction that is mutually beneficial. A nonprofit may use its fund-raising advantage to construct a building. It can then sell that building to a for-profit firm and rent space within the same building. The deal involves the nonprofit getting a low rent and getting back the capital it invested in the building and an additional amount of money representing a gain from the sale. The for-profit buyer gets rental income from the building from the nonprofit and other tenants. The taxes on the rental income are reduced by the deduction for interest, depreciation, and investment tax credit, when it applies.[28] If the depreciation is sufficiently high to represent a paper loss for tax purposes, the for-profit investor is also able to shelter income from other sources from taxes. Both parties gain by utilizing their comparative advantages. These sale-leaseback arrangements are profitable for both parties when appropriately structured.

Joint Ventures

On this level, the for-profit and nonprofit organizations work cooperatively toward a common goal. They share authority, risks, costs, and benefits. They do not, however, form a separate legal organization. They merely work together. One study identifies five types of joint ventures between universities and corporations:

1. Research done at universities but sponsored by corporations

2. Corporate use of licenses and patents owned by universities to produce goods for commercial sales and for which the universities get royalty payments

3. Consulting agreements between the corporation and the university faculties for which the university charges a fee

4. Sharing of laboratory space and facilities between the university and corporation

5. Ownership by universities of either the majority or minority share of a for-profit corporation[29]

ILLUSTRATIONS: COEXISTENCE OF CHARITY AND CAPITALISM

A nonprofit ballet company has a contract with a for-profit firm. The nonprofit is a major customer but is having financial problems. The firm does not want to lose a client. So it undertakes to share part of its profits with the nonprofit and induce others to contribute. The firm was allowed to deduct this as a business expense, not as a charitable donation, and the nonprofit got help.[30] We shall describe this pioneering case later in this section. The firm's charitable and commercial motives merged. Let's turn to an example in housing.

Joint ventures are also possible among nonprofits. 509(a)(3)s are vehicles for joint ventures for 501(c)(3)s and for certain associations. Hospitals are increasingly entering into joint ventures with nonprofit (or for-profit) corporations owned by physicians. Joint ventures and partnerships, to be discussed next, are motivated by (1) a desire to share costs and risks, (2) the sharing of assets, technology, and management that one party has and the other finds too costly to develop, (3) confidence in each other, and (4) a market for the finished product or service.

Partnerships

One form of working jointly is through a partnership arrangement. In such an arrangement, the nonprofit enters into an agreement with one or more nonprofit partners to create a separate legal organization to carry out a trade or business. The partnership is not, however, simply an agreement to work together, such as a joint venture. It is a legal organization with its own identity and staff.

The partnership has one or more general partners. These are organizations or persons who are fully liable for the losses of the business and who manage it cooperatively. General partners also decide how to distribute the earnings and tax benefits among themselves and how to share the responsibility for coming up with the capital required to get the business going. Unlike a general partnership, in a limited partnership the partners cannot participate in the management and are not liable for any losses beyond the amount of money each has invested. If the limited partner invests $1 million, it cannot be held liable for any amounts over $1 million. In contrast, the general partner's liability may go beyond the investment. For example, a general partner who puts up $1 million

Joint Ventures for Affordable Housing: Solving a Major Problem

Many cities—large and small—have substantial stocks of abandoned homes which impair the attraction of the city, its communities, and neighborhoods, cost millions of dollars to protect and millions more in lost revenues since these abandoned units produce no tax dollars.

Rehabilitation of these housing stocks has been one major approach to bringing these unused houses back on the tax rolls and to answering the quest for affordable housing. Rehabilitation is not as expensive as new housing starts, and rehabilitation that includes the public and nonprofit sectors usually assures that some of the units will be made available to the needy, elderly, and the young. Rehabilitation also tends to retain the character of a neighborhood— often an important consideration.

One approach is an agreement that involves the City of New York, the State of New York, Enterprise Foundation (a nonprofit), its subsidiary Social Investment Corporation (a for-profit), the Federal National Mortgage Association (a for-profit) and eligible community development corporations (nonprofits) and their for-profit subsidiaries.

The City of New York has agreed to provide 1,000 rental units which it has in its possession because their owners have failed to pay taxes and which are presently unfit for rental. As is, the city not only loses because these properties are not on the tax roll, but the abandoned properties are havens for crime and fire and are a blight on the city.

The recycling process will begin with a community development organization CDC submitting a proposal to the city and state to get the units rehabilitated, occupied, and managed.

The city and the state will make a loan at 1 percent for the initial investment in the rehabilitation project. Because the loans provide that regular payments of the principal do not have to be made, future rent charges can be held comparatively low and yet some cash flow may be provided.

The CDC then submits its proposal to Enterprise Foundation, a nonprofit, for evaluation. Should Enterprise conclude that this project can attract private investor interests, it passes it on to Social Investment Corporation (a for-profit subsidiary of Enterprise) to raise the funds to do the rehabilitation.

The remainder of the costs of rehabilitation (usually a minimum of 25 percent) is obtained from private sources. The Social Investment Corporation will syndicate interests to for-profit corporations. Thus, the Federal National Mortgage Corporation (Fannie Mae) has agreed to invest up to $28,000,000 through the purchase of ownership interests in these properties. The proceeds from the sale of these interests to Fannie Mae by Social Investment Corporation will provide the additional funds needed for rehabilitating these and future units.

There is no gift. Fannie Mae becomes a limited partner. The CDC forms a for-profit subsidiary to be the general partner.

By not making itself a nonprofit, the general partner, the CDC, avoids liability should the project fail. It also avoids mixing the daily tasks of running a nonprofit with those of running a business.

What are the incentives for each of these partners? Yes, the city gets taxes and so does the state. The neighborhoods and people get better housing. The private developers get jobs and profits. Enterprise Foundation gets to fulfill its mission and may obtain dividends from Social Investment Corporation. The latter gets a fee for syndicating the interests and for putting together the deal. The CDC does not rely on gifts, and it meets its mission.

What does the private investor such as Fannie Mae get? It gets tax credits. It may reduce its total tax liability to the federal government for each of the next nine years by 9 percent of the qualified rehabilitation costs. Almost all of the tax credits generated by the project will go to the private investors.

Let us take another look at this financing structure. It is particularly attractive to corporations or individuals seeking tax credits. The typical private real estate investment offers possibilities of returns through cash flow (monthly net income through rents that exceed operating costs), capital appreciation (or capital gains when the property is sold for a price higher than acquisition and rehabilitation costs), and tax benefits (principally through depreciation and tax credits). Traditionally, low-income property offers limited opportunities for cash flow because rents are low relative to expenses and appreciation is limited or nonexistent. These New York properties are no exceptions.

But tax credits are important considerations because they do not rely on charging high rents to low-income persons in order for the private investor to get an attractive return. Investors not heavily dependent upon immediate cash flow can obtain an acceptable return by using the tax credits to increase their income retention after taxes.

Note: I am grateful to Heidi Most of Enterprise for her cooperation.—HJB

Source: Herrington J. Bryce, Bureau of Business Research, School of Business Administration, College of William and Mary, Williamsburg, Virginia, October 1987.

---

is liable for more than that amount if the business is sued or if creditors demand to be paid. One way to protect against this limitless liability is for the general partner to be insured or to be a corporation that has limited liability in the sense that creditors cannot reach the assets of the owners of the corporation. Under ordinary circumstances, the assets of the corporation must do.

This description of a partnership arrangement reveals some of the concerns that the IRS and the courts have about partnership involvements by nonprofits with for-profit firms. The nonprofit's strongest position is in being general partners because they can influence the management. But a general partnership also exposes the nonprofit to limitless losses. Moreover, the motive of the for-profit partner is distinctly different and sometimes in conflict with the assumed motive of the nonprofit. The former seeks profits for private individuals as its primary purpose for engaging in the partnership, while the latter seeks profits as a mean of financing a tax-exempt mission. In the latter case, the profits are only incidental to the mission. There is thus an inherent conflict between the two goals. Accordingly, when the facts and circumstances of the partnership arrangement are such that they jeopardize the requirements of a nonprofit organization, the IRS will deny or revoke the tax-exempt status of the organization.

Let us proceed to look at some accepted partnership arrangements in housing and neighborhood development. In one case, a nonprofit and a for-profit firm entered into a partnership to construct and operate a housing project exclusively for the handicapped and the elderly. The nonprofit is responsible for marketing and renting units, enforcing leases, supervising repairs and maintenance, and conducting social programs for the tenants. In ruling favorably on this arrangement, the IRS noted that providing housing for the handicapped and the elderly is a defined charitable goal and is consistent with the charitable purpose of the nonprofit in question. See Codes 380 through 390 in Table 2.2. It also noted that there were sufficient safeguards to protect the nonprofit, because one for-profit general partner had pledged to cover all operating deficits for a specific period. The risk of unlimited liability was reduced by the existence of other for-profit general partners who had agreed to share it, and the mortgages were insured by the federal government in case of default by the project.[31]

Partnerships have also been used in the arts. In *Plumstead Theatre Society* v. *Commissioner,* the court ruled in favor of a partnership between a theater that clearly operated as a nonprofit and private individual investors who put up $100,000 in return for a sizable percentage of the profits the theater was expected to make.[32] The court ruled that the theater was not controlled by the private investors, was not required to pay them for losses, and did not depart from its tax-exempt purpose of promoting new and experimental productions and its involvement in the community.

Similarly, the court has ruled in favor of joint ventures in the field of medicine. It ruled that a nonprofit hospital that entered into a joint venture to construct and manage rental office space to its affiliated physicians had not violated its tax-exempt status. The hospital was paid a management fee and its proportionate share of the profits, was protected against losses, and could provide better service to patients by having the doctors around.[33]

It is not simply the activity that counts. The courts and the IRS have also not denied or revoked the tax-exempt status of nonprofits entering into joint ventures in housing, the arts, medicine, and so on. The following factors matter:

1. The organization must not depart from its tax-exempt purpose or subvert it to the profit motive of the for-profit partner.

2. The organization must remain free from the control of the for-profit partners and be able to withdraw from the group.

3. The assets of the organization must not be exposed to cover the liabilities of the venture and its private partners.

4. A significant portion of the activity must be dedicated to the charitable purpose of the organization.

5. There must be a demonstrable advantage to the nonprofit in having a for-profit partner.

Internal Revenue Ruling

With 95–15, the violation of condition 1 is sufficient to doom the partnership's tax-exempt status. This ruling is discussed later in this chapter.

Basically, the IRS uses a two-part test to determine the acceptability of an investment partnership to qualify under Section 501(c)(3). First, it must be demonstrated that the organization is legitimately serving a charitable purpose. The housing need of the elderly, for example, is a charitable purpose. But if a housing partnership provides only a token proportion of its housing units to the elderly, this would not qualify.

Second, while recognizing that in a partnership the nonprofit will have some legitimate economic and fiduciary relationship to its partners whose motives are strictly profits, the partnership agreement should insulate the organization from obligations that serve to increase the profits of its for-profit partners or that cause the organization to veer from its mission. Hence, an arrangement whereby the nonprofit is placed at risk of guaranteeing profits or covering the losses of the for-profit partners is not acceptable. Neither is it acceptable that the for-profit partners receive a disproportionate share of the profits or losses, that the nonprofit will sell assets such as land and equipment or rent space or make loans to the partnership at below-market rates, or that the profits to either the nonprofit or for-profit partners are excessive. The IRS looks skeptically on partnerships between the founders and managers of a nonprofit and the nonprofit organization they are supposed to be managing.[34] Remember self-dealing?

DESIGNING A PARTNERSHIP: ILLUSTRATIONS

In July 1999, the United States Tax Court rendered a decision in Redlands Surgical Services, *Petitioner* v. *Commissioner of Internal Revenue Service,* Respondent, Docket No. 11–25–97X, Filed July 19, 1999. I have distilled five points that this well-argued, lengthy document makes that should discipline every attempt of a nonprofit to enter into a joint partnership with a for-profit firm. The organization in this case is a 501(c)(3), and therefore the reference to *charitable* in what follows:

1. An organization would fail to qualify for tax-exempt status if it has a substantial or exclusive purpose of participating in a for-profit activity. This is so

even if the organization is a silent partner and even if all of the income the organization receives is used for an exempt or charitable purpose.

2. Such an organization is neither likely to pass the organizational test nor the prohibition against personal inurement (see Chapter Three). It is likely to fail if a principal purpose of the partnership is a nonexempt activity or performed with a profit motive. It is also likely to fail because the sharing of the income generated by that activity with a for-profit partner means that the gains would inure to the benefit of that partner. Therefore, it follows that a principal purpose of the activity would be personal gains. Such gains are completely contrary to the charitable purpose for which exemption is given and of the organizational test that requires that the exclusive purpose of the organization be charitable.

3. If the nonprofit partner is incapable of unilaterally shifting the focus or of modifying the operation of the partnership toward a community benefit (the rationale for tax exemption), then, any assets that the nonprofit partner has contributed to the partnership are placed under the control of the for-profit partner. Since the motive of a for-profit partner is profits, not charity, the assets would have to be construed to be used principally for a for-profit, not a charitable, purpose.

4. The fact that an operating agreement may be negotiated at arms-length between the for-profit and nonprofit partners cannot be used to supplant the realities of the agreement that creates the partnership. If the nonprofit lacks control in the partnership agreement, it may be presumed to lack control in all other subsidiary or collateral agreements. How the partnership is initially put together is key.

5. The partnership agreement cannot restrict the nonprofit from carrying out its mission. For example, it is not uncommon for a partnership agreement to restrict the partners from carrying out activities that are competitive. The question is, does such an agreement restrict the reaching out of the nonprofit through the conduct of similar but potentially competing activities? It should not.

With this court decision in mind, let us now turn to examples (with names changed) that the IRS offers as guidance in the formation of partnerships between nonprofits and for-profit entities. Two cases, based on the facts in Revenue Ruling 95–15, illustrate partnership arrangements. Notice how carefully the nonprofit remains loyal to its mission even when its assets are managed by a corporation with a profit-making motive. Notice that the mission is better served by the formation of the partnership and that the nonprofit does not subvert itself or its assets to the role of the for-profit. The first deal survives scrutiny because the for-profit (for a fee) is actually helping the nonprofit meet its mission better than it could have done by itself and the deal is arranged in such a way that the nonprofit is unequivocal in its commitment solely to its mission.

Observe that this commitment is more than words. It is built into the operational arrangement of the partnership.

A nonprofit corporation, exempt under 501(c)(3), owns and operates an acute care hospital described in Section 170(b)(1)(A)(iii). A firm, let us call it Gisselle–Canales de Marquis, Inc. (GCI), is a for-profit corporation that owns and operates a number of for-profit corporations. The nonprofit believes that it can better serve its community if it could attain additional funding. GCI is willing to provide the additional funding provided that it earns a reasonable profit.

GCI and the nonprofit form a limited liability company. The nonprofit contributes all of its operating assets, including its hospital, to the partnership and GCI also contributes assets. Accordingly, they share ownership of the new entity, called Cecil-Cockburn Health Care (CHC) proportionately to their contribution of assets to its formation. Further, the distribution of capital and earnings must also be proportionate to their ownership of CHC.

According to its governing agreement, CHC will have a governing board consisting of three individuals chosen by the nonprofit and two chosen by the for-profit, GCI. The nonprofit promises that its three designees to the board will be community leaders with experience in hospital operation but with whom it has no business connection. The agreement also requires that any amendment to key parts of the governing document will require a majority vote. These key elements include

1. The annual capital and operating budget of CHC

2. Distributions of CHC's earnings

3. Selection of key executives

4. Acquisition or disposition of health care facilities

5. Contracts in excess of some specified amount

6. Changes in the types of services offered by the hospital

7. Renewal or termination of management agreements

The governing document also requires CHC to commit themselves to operating to further community welfare and to do this even if it means sacrificing profits. In the case of a conflict between community welfare and profits, the latter must yield to the former.

CHC enters into a management agreement with a for-profit company, Enrique Hospital Management (EHM), which is unrelated to any of the other companies or to the nonprofit. EHM will provide daily management. The contract is for five years and EHM will be paid a fee based upon the gross revenues of CHC. The terms are reasonable and usual within the industry and the agreement may be terminated by CHC for cause.

None of the officers, directors, or key employees of the nonprofit who were involved in making the decision to form CHC was promised employment or any other inducement to approve the contract. None of the directors of the nonprofit has any interest, even by attribution, to any of the other entities.

The nonprofit intends to use all of its distributions from the venture to support activities that promote the health of its community and to help the indigent obtain health care. Substantially all of the nonprofit's grant making will be funded by distributions from CHC. Making these charitable grants will be the only activity of the nonprofit.

The second example of partnership arrangements is tricky. It looks almost like a carbon copy of the first. But something is wrong. Can you spot it?

Lucrecia Marva of Marian (LMM) is a nonprofit corporation that owns and operates an acute care hospital. It decides that it could better serve its community by additional funding, which will be provided by Ada, Aldrich & Adele (AAA), a for-profit hospital corporation that owns and operates a number of hospitals and also provides hospital management services to hospitals it does not own.

AAA requires a reasonable rate of return. Consequently, a limited liability company was formed. Let's call it STMA. LMM contributes all of its operating assets, including its hospital, to STMA. AAA contributes other assets that are needed. In return, they both share ownership interests proportional and equal in value to their individual contributions.

The governing documents of STMA state that it will be managed by a governing board that is made up of three individuals chosen by the owners, LMM and AAA. LMM will appoint community leaders who have experience with hospital management but are not engaged with or have business dealings with the hospital.

The governing document also specifies that the majority of the board must agree on decisions relating to

1. STMA's annual capital and operating budgets
2. The distribution of STMA's earnings over the minimum required in the document
3. Unusually large contracts
4. The selection of key employees

The owners of AAA, the for-profit partner, share the returns of capital and other distributions of earnings (dividends) proportionately to their ownership of AAA. AAA enters into a five-year renewable contract with one of its wholly owned subsidiaries for the subsidiary to provide day-to-day management services to AAA. The contract can be broken by AAA for cause. The subsidiary is paid a reasonable fee based on the going rate for such services. The fee is based on the gross revenues of the hospital it manages.

Lucrecia Marva of Marian approves the appointment of executives who worked for the subsidiary and who would oversee the day-to-day management of the hospitals. These executives will be paid the going rate for such persons in similarly situated hospitals.

LMM will use all of its earnings from the partnership to support its grant-making to health-related charitable programs in its community. Grant-making will be the only activity it will engage in as part of the partnership.

LMM will be sharing control of STMA with AAA in addition to making grants. But the organizing document does not commit STMA to a charitable purpose. Even though LMM has that purpose, it cannot enforce it on the STMA because it does not have a majority of the board. To get a majority on a vote it would need at least one vote from a member of the board appointed by AAA. Since the subsidiary that manages day-to-day operation is a for-profit owned by AAA, the information that LMM will be using to make judgments can be information tainted by a profit motive, not a charitable one. Therefore, it was concluded that STMA was not organized exclusively for a charitable mission and exemption was denied it.

STRATEGIC ALLIANCES, CONTROL, AND OTHER CONCERNS

Nonprofits engaging in strategic alliances with for-profit partners must be careful that they do not surrender control directly or indirectly over the assets of the organization. If control is surrendered, the consequence is loss of tax exemption. Accordingly, joint ventures, including those that bring the facilities of the nonprofit under the management of a firm, can cause a loss of exemption. Partnerships are not only of concern to the IRS, but also of state governments, and they are within the scope of interest of the Federal Trade Commission and the Justice Department as part of their antitrust responsibilities. Does the partnership violate antitrust laws? Does it impede competition? Is it so large and powerful to affect prices and choices?

In South Carolina, for example, the attorney general ruled that the leasing of a hospital property to a for-profit management firm led to a loss of the tax-exempt status of the hospital because, as the attorney general argued, the law reads that such exemptions are available to a hospital "owned and operated" by a nonprofit group. The attorney general in Michigan had brought a similar suit (described in Chapter Nineteen) because a nonprofit hospital had contracted with a for-profit firm, giving the latter management control over the nonprofit hospital. Who controls the assets is the key. The consequence can include loss of exemption and a fine on the trustees and officers for shifting control of the assets of the organization without prior consent of the state attorney general. The motive behind most state laws is not to stop strategic alliances but to avoid shifts in mission and the subverting of the assets of the organization to profit-makers and self-dealing by trustees and officers. The kinds of transaction that bring concern are those that involve all or substantially all of the assets of the organization such as placing a hospital under contract to be managed by a for-profit firm. This type of an arrangement must be done very carefully and will be further discussed in Chapter Nineteen.

MARKET ACTIVITIES AND THE THREAT TO NONPROFIT STATUS

In this book we give examples of nonprofits operating within the market economy and making a legal profit. To keep things in perspective, it would be wise to remember that the nonprofit exists to carry out a welfare or social mission and the profits are incidental to the discharging of that mission. In *Copyright Clearance Center* v. *Commissioner,* the court said:[35]

> Although an organization might be engaged in a single activity, such activity may be directed toward multiple purposes, both exempt and nonexempt. But in the case of multiple purposes, it must be kept in mind that qualification for exemption depends upon whether the entity in question is organized and oper-ated "exclusively" for one or more of the exempt purposes in the statute.

The court went on to state that there is no stringent definition of the word "exclusive" and that it may also be interpreted as meaning "primary." Whichever word is used, the legal interpretation is equivalent to substantial. The nonprofit may be said to exist exclusively for a tax-exempt purpose if it has no substantial activity that is nonexempt; that is, the commercial activities that are undertaken cannot be a substantial part of the activities of the nonprofit.

ESSENTIALS OF A PARTNERSHIP AGREEMENT

The Uniform Partnership Act of 1976 and its subsequent amendments descri-bes the contents of a partnership agreement. This section is concerned with some essentials of such an agreement from the perspective of a nonprofit manager:

1. A partnership agreement spells out the purpose of the partnership, for example, what operations it is formed to carry out. This relates to the mission of the organization.

2. A partnership agreement describes the specific assets that each partner is to contribute to the partnership and the value of such assets. It stipulates if these assets are loaned or contributed to partnership.

3. A partnership agreement describes types of partners and assigns respon-sibilities, rights, and liabilities of each type. Essentially there are two types of partners: (1) a general partner, who is responsible for the management of the business and whose contribution to the partnership may include its

management expertise, and (2) a limited partner, who is not involved in the management of the partnership and whose contribution is almost exclusively an asset other than management.

4. A partnership agreement describes the voting powers. It is not true, as is commonly stated, that limited partners have no voting power. They may vote particularly with respect to the naming and discharging of the managers and in the determination of management fees, and they may have certain limited powers over specific assets or changes in the scope or mission of the partnership and also in the final distribution of assets. They simply do not become involved in the everyday management operating decisions.

5. A partnership agreement describes how the assets of the partnership is to be distributed. With respect to the operation of the partnership, the agreement may distribute profits or gross revenues. The distribution of profits implies that the recipient is a partner, whereas the receipt of gross revenues does not necessarily lead to such an implication. Where distributions are based on profits, it is presumed that the distributee—whether a for-profit or nonprofit organization—has a profit motive and, logically, seeks to maximize it.

6. A partnership agreement describes how losses and expenses are to be distributed. It is not unusual in a partnership that binds a for-profit and a nonprofit that the former contributes real assets that are depreciable because such a partner can get 100 percent of the distribution of depreciation expenses. A for-profit organization can use such expenses to reduce taxes, a nonprofit organization, unless operating an unrelated business at least one of which is the partnership, cannot ordinarily use these expenses, because its income is tax-exempt.

7. A partnership agreement describes the sharing of risks and assessments when something goes wrong. This includes the issue of who is liable and the extent of such liability.

8. A partnership agreement describes the kinds of information to which each partner is entitled.

9. A partnership agreement describes the terms for disposing of partnership interests. The terms may include the actual price or formula for calculating the price and who may acquire the interests. A partner is often required to sell its interests only to the partnership.

10. A partnership agreement describes the conditions for withdrawing or being forced to surrender a partner's interests and for closing down.

SEVEN KEY QUESTIONS ABOUT PARTNERSHIPS

There are at least seven questions that should be raised before a nonprofit enters into a partnership—including a management agreement—with a for-profit corporation. A "no" answer to any of these questions is likely to threaten the tax-exempt status of the partnership. If the partnership is the principal purpose of the nonprofit organization, then the tax-exempt status of the nonprofit will be threatened. The seven questions are:

1. Is the exclusive purpose of the partnership identical to the principal mission of the organization?
2. Does the nonprofit control the use of its assets?
3. Is the nonprofit unconstrained by the terms of the agreement in advancing its mission?
4. Is the agreement in writing and was it negotiated at arms-length?
5. Is the nonprofit able to withdraw from the contract?
6. Is the nonprofit able to out vote the for-profit when it comes to what the partnership does and whom it serves?
7. Is the compensation of the partners unrelated to the size of the profits such that the implicit motive is not to maximize profits?

The answers to these questions are to be attained from the facts and circumstances of the agreement. There is a subtle implication: to assure its maintenance of control, the nonprofit may have to consider being a general partner or having the agreement so well drawn that, while it does not have management control, it has the unequivocal power and obligation to automatically end the partnership. Being the general partner possesses its own problems, as discussed earlier in this chapter.

LIMITED PARTNERSHIPS FOR THE PURPOSE OF GIVING AND POLITICKING

Partnerships may be challenged on the basis that they involve activities such as politicking, which are in violation of the tax-exempt rules. Thus in a lengthy *Washington Post* editorial, I wrote that one of the problems Speaker Gingrich faced is not that he used a nonprofit shell, but that the purpose of that nonprofit was to help inner-city children read—which is unrelated to teaching adults a political philosophy.

Partnerships have also been used for the purpose of making gifts. A business owner, having formed a partnership of his or her business, donates a limited partnership interest to a nonprofit, and the donor gets a charitable deduction. Being a limited partner, the nonprofit does not participate in the management of the business, because the power of managing is exclusively held by the general partner. Hence the donor, having retained the general partnership, continues to run the business and receives not only fees for doing so but may participate in the gains. Indeed, the nonprofit may not be the only limited partner. These partnerships, which possess their own problems, are different from the type of operating partnership that has occupied our attention in this chapter.

SUMMARY AND PREVIEW

In most societies, the economy is a dominant sector. By understanding how it operates, nonprofit managers are able to detect new opportunities. These opportunities derive partly from the imperfections of the market—the inability of the economy to fully satisfy important needs of the public or community.

One set of opportunities exists within the market structure itself. These relate to the needs of consumers, producers, investors, workers, and savers. Another set of needs relates to effects that are nonmarket related. Being able to identify specific opportunities within these environments means that the nonprofit can benefit from the dynamic growth of the economy by being relevant and by being an attractive ally. After all fails, the organization may decide that the best solution is to reorganize—the subject of the next chapter.

Reorganization: Mergers, Divestitures, Sale of Assets, Acquisitions, Conversions

This chapter is about reorganization and the restructuring of the organization. It is about the legal requirements on managers and trustees when such actions are undertaken. These concern antitrust law, violation of the fiduciary responsibilities of the managers and the trustees, self-dealing, and improperly dissolving of a nonprofit organization and conversion of public assets to private use.

A principal motive of carrying out a reorganization of the nonprofit organization is to gain economic efficiency through a new structure. Why is structure so important? What specifically does it yield?

THE IMPORTANCE OF STRUCTURE

We have met the concept of corporate organization in Chapter Five, where we talked about affiliates and chapters. There, the bonding was a common mission. As a consequence, a number of good things, including local responsiveness, occurred. In Chapter Four we talked about corporate organization in which the purpose was primarily to separate political, lobbying, and advocacy functions from fund-raising and tax-exempt purposes. In Chapters Nine and Ten we looked at organization as a means of accommodating business. Now we shall examine corporate organization from the perspective of economics and markets.

In the following two sections, I describe hospital systems. These are not static. They change. Changes are brought about partly for the reasons and by the processes described in this chapter.

Illustration: Riverside Health System

The Riverside Health System is a holding company offering a wide range of health care including acute, long-term, mental health, ambulatory, preventive, education, home care, and rehabilitative services. In addition to owning and managing its hospitals and health care centers, Riverside also manages a city-owned hospital. It manages the latter through a wholly owned corporation, Riverside Health Care Services. In addition, it manages a joint venture providing laundry, printing, and microfilming services for a group of hospitals. This eliminates the need for each to do its own, with resulting unused capacity and high fixed costs, which would eventually have been reflected in higher prices to patients.

By having several dozen units, the system can cover a large geographic area—market. But these units are in turn grouped under specialties. There are geographically dispersed convalescent centers that form one or more corporations. The board of directors to which this group responds is different from the board of each of the independent hospitals, each a corporation with its own board. This structure permits separate units to spread across several markets or service areas. But the units are grouped according to specialty, thereby gaining both diversity in service and markets as well as managerial efficiency.

One of the ways in which costs are further reduced is through the Riverside Food Production Services, a separate corporation. This is a centralized food production service for the various units. The capital costs of food storage and preparation in each unit are thus eliminated. Further, economies are achieved through large procurements and centralized billing.

Illustration: Carilion Health System

Let us look at another example. In Figure 19.1 the separate tax-exempt hospitals, each a corporation, are under the Carilion Health System, which is a holding company. The Carilion Health System, the holding company, is the sole member of the individual corporations under it. In for-profit terms, the holding company is the sole owner or stockholder of the individual corporations that make of the system. The individual corporations do not necessarily own any portion of each other. As the sole member, the holding company has the powers to appoint and remove board members of any of these corporate subsidiaries and to approve changes in their articles of incorporation. We have already seen that different hospitals may serve different areas and specialties. Giles Memorial in Figure 19.1 is an acute care facility; Gill is an eye, ear, nose, and throat facility; Burrell provides long-term care for the elderly.

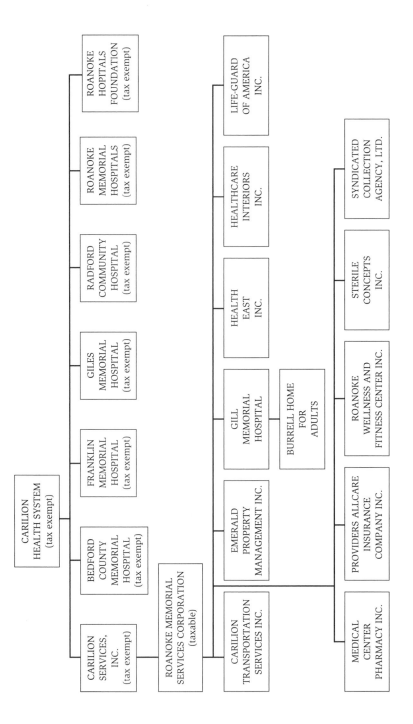

Figure 19.1. Carilion Health System Corporate Structure.

Source: From the *Carilion Health System 1988 Annual Report*, Roanoke, VA. Reprinted with permission.

Note: This structure may undergo change as time passes. Hospital systems are dynamic. See Figure 19.2.

Please turn your attention to the three last lines in the chart. Notice that these individual corporations, though specialized, fit into the overall role of running a hospital service. Carilion Transportation Services, Inc. provides non-emergency ambulance service to hospitals, which do not have to be part of the Carilion system. Emerald Property Management, Inc. holds title to property, such as apartments, where medical residents and students live. Health East, Inc. provides management consulting services and mobile imaging services such as x-rays and scanners to smaller hospitals that cannot afford the equipment. Health Care Interiors Inc., provides specialized interior decorating for hospitals and medical facilities. Medical Center Pharmacy, Inc. sells durable medical equipment such as wheelchairs and beds. Providers Allcare Insurance Company, Inc. manages claims of companies that are self-insured. Sterile Concepts, Inc. sets up specialized and custom-made surgical trays for hospitals throughout the country. Trays are prepared according to the individual needs of a surgeon, thus reducing the time required for a nurse to put a tray together and cutting down on waste of sterilized materials. Syndicated Collection Agency, Inc. is a collection agency that removes the chore and onus of forcing payment from the hospital.

Now, turn your attention to another specialized corporation, the Roanoke Hospital Foundation, which is a supporting organization under 509(a)(3). It, too, has a separate board that determines how the funds will be used. Again systems are not static. As these two systems did, they all undergo changes.

Hospital systems are not static. We have just described the Carilion Health System as it was ten years ago. Now, please turn to Figure 19.2. It reflects some of the significant changes that occur in large nonprofit organizations and in hospital systems in particular. Many of these changes occurred through the processes and for reasons to be described in this chapter. But the reader may want to refer back to the discussion of holding companies in Chapter Five or to the consolidation of Alabama hospitals also described in the chapter and to the complex structure of organizations described and demonstrated in Chapters Nine and Ten.

Figure 19.2 shows that CHS has three new corporations—two of which are nonprofit hospitals. In one of these, Wythe County Community Hospital, CHS has a minority interest. In the other, Smyth County Community Hospital, it has a 50 percent interest. This last arrangement was motivated by the fact that the local community and the board of directors of Smyth was not willing to relinquish full ownership or control because of fear of unwillingness to risk the cessation or modification of hospital services to the community. We shall see later in this chapter that this type of concern is part of the fiduciary responsibilities that some states impose on hospital boards. The third corporation, Carilion Health Plans, Inc., is 63 percent owned by the system. This is a for-profit corporation. It deals with the contracting between physicians and insurance companies.

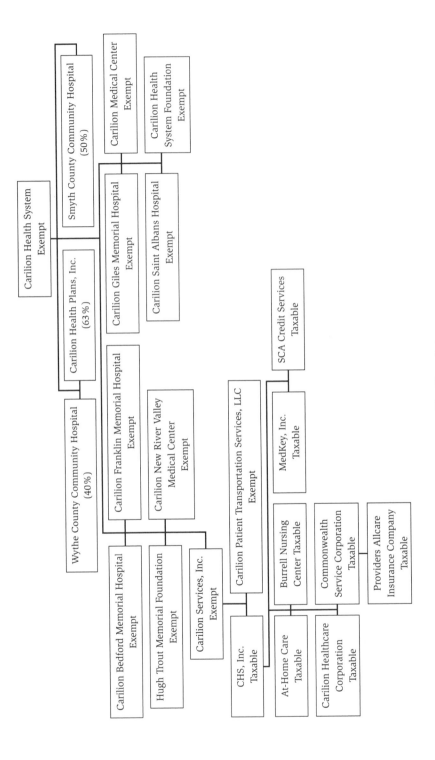

Figure 19.2. Carilion Health System Corporate Structure—Ten Years Later.

Source: Carilion Health Systems. Reprinted with permission.

The reader would observe that the holding company, CHS, has a subsidiary, Carilion Services, Inc., that itself owns several wholly owned subsidiaries, most of which are for-profit. These provide a range of services on a competitive basis and pay taxes. At-Home Care provides medical equipment. Burrell Nursing Center is a long-term nursing care facility. MedKey, Inc., is a credit card corporation that extends credit to patients unable to pay bills and who have no or insufficient medical insurance. SCA Credit Services is a credit collection service to physicians and to others. It also issues credit cards. Carilion Healthcare Corporation owns and operates private physician practices. Commonwealth Service Corporation serves businesses that are self-insured. Commonly, such businesses would contract with a hospital that either debts a pool of funds created by such businesses to pay for their employees and/or through a type of preferred contract receives billing for services to their employees. Providers Allcare Insurance Company is a company that issues and markets health insurance policies.

Principles Behind Corporate Organizations

By now you may be asking: When does creating these complex structures make sense?

1. When it is important to separate out liabilities so that the liability of one function does not spill over and ruin other essential parts of the mission; for example, flying helicopters expose the organizations to special risks and high operating costs.

2. When specialized management and staff are required and may have to be treated under separate labor-management agreements.

3. When it is necessary or possible for the unit to develop its own financing and have access to capital that the other units may not have; for example, foundations can get grants and donations whereas hospitals can charge fees and sell bonds.

4. When the relative size of the organization is too dominant and could change the central core of operation and therefore threaten the carrying out of the principal charitable mission.

5. When there are costs and tax implications; for example, by filing a consolidated statement, the loss in one corporation can be covered by the gains in another. It is thus possible to carry out an essential service even at a loss as long as it can be partly subsidized by another subsidiary without destroying the profitable one by having it conduct activities that are losers.

6. When there is a fit, but not a direct one; for example, insurance is a way to secure payments of patients and to self-insure, but it does not heal illnesses.

7. When there is a perfect fit, but some consideration such as 1 above or 8 below dominates.

8. When the markets are identifiably separate in location, specialty, or clients.

9. When it is anticipated that the service may have to be sold; it is sometimes easier to dislodge a corporate unit from the rest than it is to dislodge unorganized pieces of a corporation. In the for-profit world, a firm takes a service that it wishes to dislodge, turns it into a separate corporation, and sells the corporation. These are called spin-offs.

10. When there is corporate dissonance or an image problem for the parent corporation, isolation of the infant institution is invariably indicated as the treatment of choice; for example, a collection agency.

Sometimes nonprofit corporations must reorganize. Let us turn to the subject of corporate reorganization in the nonprofit world.

THE IMPORTANCE OF REORGANIZATION

Reorganization has been important not only for hospitals and other nonprofit health providers. In the case of Salem University in West Virginia, reorganization took place to avoid a disaster. The university merged with Teyiko University of Japan. As a result, faculty salaries went up over 25 percent. Some $400,000 was added to student scholarships; the university, which was deep in debt, had all its debt paid off. New programs were added. A small West Virginia community was faced with a brighter economic future. The principal purpose of mergers, acquisitions, and corporate reorganization in the nonprofit world is the same as in the for-profit world: economic. Among the reasons for corporate reorganizations are (1) to increase revenues, (2) to reduce costs, (3) to bring about better performance through consolidation of activities, (4) to separate and isolate liabilities and different types of risks, (5) to create different management structures, and (6) to deal with ethical and public relations problems. I will illustrate many of these points through real cases of corporate reorganization of nonprofits.

There are five dangers in corporate reorganization. The first is that the nonprofit institution may lose its tax-exempt status either entirely or it will be shifted from one category to another; for example, from a public to a private foundation or from a 509(a)(1) to a private foundation or something of the kind. Second, there may be unrelated business income created because of the gains resulting from the shift in assets from one corporation to the other or because of payments from one to the other. Third, self-dealing may occur due partly to interlocking directorates. Fourth, the organization may end up violating the

Sherman Antitrust and the Clayton Antitrust acts prohibiting the restriction of competition. Fifth, the legality of the reorganization may be successfully challenged by the state. These last two dangers are fundamental. If either challenge is successful, the deal as proposed is dead. Hence, these last two dangers deserve special attention. A common reason for state challenges are that control over the organization's assets have fallen into the hands of private interests in violation of all I stated in Part One of this book.

ANTITRUST

Antitrust cases are resolved around the issue of whether a proposed combination would be able to determine prices of specified products or services in a specified market because consumers cannot substitute other products or services or because new firms cannot easily enter the market to compete. Let us see how this is applied to nonprofits.

In one case, the Federal Trade Commission (FTC) sought to prevent the merger of two nonprofit hospitals in Michigan, Butterworth Health Corporation and Blodgett Memorial Medical Center. The FTC argued that the merger would result in a concentration of extraordinary market power in the new combination, that the consumers would not have alternative outlets or treatments even in the form of outpatient care, prices could rise as they usually do in such dominated markets, and that new hospitals could not be expected to enter the market given the capital requirements and the size of the market.

The judge relied on the fundamental differences between for-profit and nonprofit corporations in his decision. The presiding judge, the Honorable David W. McKeague, concurred with the FTC's basic argument. But he reasoned that although data for for-profit firms show that prices often rise subsequent to increase market power, there is no comparably strong incentive for nonprofits to do the same because they are motivated by community and charitable purposes rather than profits as explained throughout Part One of this book.

Further, he argued that if the merger would lead to higher prices that consumers cannot escape because there is no other provider, the results may not be necessarily bad even if these higher prices led to higher profits. This is so, he argued, because the nonprofit, unlike the for-profit firm, cannot distribute these profits to investors. They must be used to advance the mission. Therefore, the higher profits would lead to better care for the community.

Furthermore, he argued, as the FTC claimed, the higher prices would fall on third parties such as governments and insurance companies, thus implying that there would be a transfer of wealth from the rich to the poor. Isn't this charity?

In addition, he argued that unlike the board of a for-profit hospital, the board of a nonprofit hospital, in particular these two, is made up of prominent community people. Their fiduciary interest is not personal profits but community betterment. Therefore, a pledge by them to use the increased market share to help the community, rather than reward investors, is especially meaningful when they also pledge to make this a legally binding commitment.

Finally, the court argued that there are clear economies to be gained from the proposed merger. The savings would come from the fact that absent the merger, the two hospitals would revert to competing with each other by building more and more expensive facilities, which each had already planned.

Let us not read into this judgment some new standard of judging antitrust cases involving nonprofits. What is important is the demonstration that the concepts in this book are applicable. So, too, are the specific facts and circumstances to be interpreted. Accordingly, in another case in Rockford, Illinois, the courts banned the expansion of Rockford Memorial Hospital because through its acquisition it would have dominated 90 percent of the market share.[1] A similar case, *United States of America* v. *Carilion Health System and Community Hospital of Roanoke Valley*, shows that the definition of the "market" is critical: "When the various hospitals in the market area surrounding Roanoke are included, however, defendants' market share, even adjusted for the six other hospitals in the market that are owned or managed by Carilion, cannot be expected to approach the estimates advanced by the government."[2]

HOSPITAL MERGERS THE FTC WILL NOT CHALLENGE

Because of the spate of joint ventures, acquisitions, and mergers of hospitals—including nonprofit hospitals—the Federal Trade Commission issued a statement about the types of hospital mergers it will not challenge for possible violation of federal antitrust laws. According to that statement, hospitals that have fewer than 100 licensed beds and a daily census of 40 or less patients are not likely to be investigated. Hospital mergers can bring lower costs to consumers, may save a hospital that may otherwise not have survived, and may not have any anticompetitive effects if there are strong competitors or if the two hospitals are sufficiently different in their services. The FTC asserts that it is likely to use the following rules in analyzing a joint venture or merger of hospitals:

1. It will seek to define a relevant product and geographic market.

2. It will then determine the anticompetitive effects of the merger or joint venture on that market.

3. It will investigate the procompetitive effects of the proposed transaction.

4. It will determine whether any agreement that is part of the deal will have an anticompetitive effect.

These rules form a good foundation for all nonprofit mergers of meaningful size.

CENTRAL ROLE OF STATES IN REORGANIZATIONS

Just as a successful antitrust suit can terminate a proposed reorganization, so too can the state's refusal to approve the proposal for any number of reasons. The type of reorganization that may be subject to such approval and the nature of such approval vary from state to state.

The transactions that call forth the attention of the law and the need for approval in Georgia include the sale or lease of assets of a hospital owned or operated by a hospital authority to an individual, business corporation, general partnership, limited partnership, limited liability company, limited liability partnership, joint venture, nonprofit corporation, hospital authority, or any other for profit or not for profit entity.

Any of the previously described transactions requires a public hearing in Georgia. The purpose of the public hearing is to ensure that the public's interest is protected when the assets of a nonprofit hospital are acquired by an entity by requiring full disclosure of the purpose and terms of the transaction and providing an opportunity for local public input.

Below I present four examples of state laws dealing with hospitals: Connecticut, Ohio, Washington, and New York. Notice the concerns for control over the assets of the nonprofit, the various forms through which control can be shifted, the value of the assets, the role and duty of the trustees, and the stipulation of permanence in the mission to which the assets were dedicated (all discussed in Part One of this book).

Connecticut

A nonprofit hospital is not permitted to enter into an agreement to transfer a material or substantial amount of its assets or operations or submit such assets to the control of a for-profit entity without first getting the written permission of the commissioner of health care access and the attorney general.

The latter has the power to amend or disapprove the transaction if it is determined that it does not conform with the promotion of the public interest in any of the following ways:

1. The transaction is prohibited by Connecticut's common or statutory law governing nonprofit corporations, trusts, or charities.

2. The nonprofit hospital governing body failed to exercise due diligence in making the decision to transfer the assets, in selecting the purchaser, in obtaining a fair evaluation from an independent expert, or in determining the terms and condition of the transfer.

3. The nonprofit did not disclose any conflict of interest, including those related to board members, officers, key employees, experts of the hospital, the purchaser, or any other person.

4. The nonprofit hospital will not receive fair market value for its assets; that is, the value that it would have received in an open competitive bid given the same facts and circumstances.

5. The price has been manipulated to cause it to be less than it would otherwise have been.

6. The form of financing the sale would place the nonprofit hospital at unreasonable risk.

7. Any management contract associated with the sale is for unreasonable compensation and arrangements.

8. A sum equivalent to the sale price is not being transferred to an entity or entities not associated with the corporate structure, governance body, or membership of the for-profit purchaser or the nonprofit.

9. The above sum is not being used for charitable health care consistent with the nonprofit hospital or nonprofit health care center's original purpose, or for the support and promotion of health care generally in the affected community, nor does it abide with any prior asset-use restriction intended by the donor.

10. The hospital or the purchaser fails to provide the attorney general with the data needed to make the above assessment.

Finally, prior to approving or disapproving the transactions according to the above criteria, the attorney general must have at least one public hearing.

Ohio

The Ohio law refers not only to transfer of assets to a for-profit but also to certain combinations of nonprofit hospitals. Further, in Ohio any transfer of ownership or of control of assets of a nonprofit health care entity—whether by purchase, merger consolidation, lease, gift, joint venture, or other transfer, including any binding obligation in furtherance of future transactions that involve at least 20 percent of the assets of the entity—will trigger the need for the approval of the attorney general.

In addition, the nonprofit must submit

1. Names of all parties to the transaction, including the boards of directors and officers of all parties in the proposed transaction

2. The terms of the transaction and the amount that is to be paid in the form of compensation to all parties, including the boards, officers, other entity and experts involved

3. A statement acknowledging the power of the attorney general to approve, disapprove, or amend the transaction and to require more information from the parties

4. Audited financial statements for the three past fiscal years

5. A valuation statement prepared by an independent qualified expert

6. Copies of all contracts and agreements between the entities and persons such as officers and directors

Within seven days after filing the required documents with the attorney general, the nonprofit must publish a description of the proposed transaction in a newspaper of general circulation within its primary place of business.

These are the factors that the attorney general will consider in coming to a decision:

1. Whether the transaction would result in a breach of the fiduciary duties, including self-dealing, by the individuals involved, including officers, directors, and experts

2. Whether the nonprofit hospital will receive full and fair market value for its charitable or social welfare assets

3. Whether the proceeds of the transaction will be used in a manner consistent with the original charitable purpose of the nonprofit entity

4. Any other criteria the attorney general may reasonably choose to be sure that points 1 through 3 are respected

With respect to point 3, the Ohio law states that the proceeds of the transaction may be dedicated and transferred to one or more existing or new charitable organizations exempt under 501(c)(3) of the U.S. *Internal Revenue Code.* This is the charitable section of the code under which most nonprofit hospitals are exempted.

But the attorney general may authorize a transfer of all or part of the proceeds to a 501(c)(4), which are civic and welfare membership associations including some HMOs and health associations not open to the general public. He or she may do the latter only for the amounts necessary for efficient management and "monetization of the equity ownership, if any, in the nonprofit health care entity." To explain, a civic association can form a charitable hospital—a 501(c)(3). It can, for example, at a later date sell that hospital. The proceeds from the sale can be directed to the civic association, a 501(c)(4), assuming that it is no more than is enough to compensate that association for its assets in the hospital.

In addition, this amount must only be equal to that which is necessary to fund that association's activity under its tax-exempt status. Presumably, this cannot be used to create or purchase a for-profit corporation. Further, the receiving 501(c)(4) must pledge not to use any portion of this amount in lobbying, politicking, or any other political activity, and agrees to abide by the requirements imposed on 501(c)(3) organizations. This has the effect of relegating the use of the proceeds only to charitable purposes.

Finally, no officer, director, or person with fiduciary duties with respect to the organization may receive anything of substantial value or that is of such a character that it could influence them in carrying out their fiduciary responsibilities.

In doing this analysis, the attorney general may engage any expert, at the expense of the nonprofit parties. Within forty-five days after receiving notice of the approval by the attorney general, the nonprofit must hold a public hearing within the county of its principal operation. In some states, for example, Oregon, this public hearing is required before approval can be gotten.

The State of Washington

In this state, approval is needed by the acquiring party if it is not a nonprofit corporation having a charitable health care purpose substantially similar to the hospital being acquired, is government owned, is tax-exempt as a 501(c)(3), and will maintain representation from the affected community on the local board of the hospital.

An acquisition includes a purchase, merger, lease, gift, joint venture, or otherwise if it results in a change of ownership or the transfer of control or ownership to the acquiring party of 20 percent or more of the assets of the hospital, or results in the acquirer controlling 50 percent or more of the assets of the hospital.

The acquirer must submit the acquisition agreement, an analysis of the financial and economic impact of the proposed acquisition, and the acquisition price. The evaluation and analyses must be prepared by an independent expert or consultant.

Within five working days of receiving a completed application, the state department of health must make a public announcement in the localities where the hospital does business. This announcement must describe the proposed acquisition and seek public comments within a specified time frame. The department must hold hearings within forty-five days of receiving a completed application. The department has the power to subpoena witnesses, take depositions, and take statements under oath. The department also has the power to use consultants and experts at the expense of the acquirer.

The health department will transmit all these data along with its own assessment to the attorney general for review. Within forty-five days the attorney general must make a recommendation to the department of health, which makes a decision to approve the proposed acquisition with or without modification or to disapprove it.

The department of health (not the attorney general's office) makes the decision. To approve, the department must, "at a minimum," show:

1. The acquisition is consistent with the state's nonprofit corporation laws and those state laws concerning trusts, estates, or charities.

2. The nonprofit owner of the hospital to be acquired has exercised due diligence in authorizing the acquisition, selecting the acquiring person, and negotiating the terms and conditions of the acquisition.

3. The nonprofit board of trustees and its officers have fulfilled their fiduciary duties, were sufficiently informed about the proposed acquisition and alternatives to it, and utilized appropriate experts.

4. No conflict of interest exists on the part of any party, officers, directors, experts, involved in the transaction.

5. The nonprofit will receive fair compensation.

6. Charitable funds will not be placed at unreasonable risk, if the acquisition is financed in part by the nonprofit corporation.

7. Management contracts will be at market rate.

8. The proceeds of the acquisition will not be controlled by any of the parties involved and will be used for charitable health purposes consistent with the nonprofit's original purpose, including health care to the disadvantaged, the uninsured, and the underinsured, and providing benefits to improving health in the affected community.

9. The charitable entity established to receive the proceeds of the acquisition must be broadly representative of the community.

10. A successor nonprofit hospital or foundation has the first right of refusal to repurchase the assets if they are subsequently sold to, acquired by, or merged with another entity.

Further, for the department of health to approve an application the acquisition cannot be detrimental to the community. At minimum, the department must have included in the application

1. Sufficient safeguards to assure the affected community continued access to affordable care and availability of alternative sources of care.

2. The acquisition will not result in the revocation of hospital privileges.

3. Sufficient safeguards are included to maintain appropriate capacity for health science research and health care provider education.

4. The acquirer is committed to providing health care to the disadvantaged, the uninsured, the underinsured and to improving health in the affected community.

5. There are sufficient safeguards to avoiding conflict of interest in patient referral.

The Washington law also provides for follow-up after the acquisition. The department of health must require periodic reports from the nonprofit or its successor corporation or foundation and from the acquirer to ensure compliance with commitments made in the approval process. If there is a failure of compliance, the department can hold hearings. Then, if the acquirer continues out of compliance, its hospital license may be revoked by the department and further action to insist on compliance may be taken by the attorney general.

New York State

In 1956 New York State passed Section 2801 of the Public Health Law barring partnerships that are not of natural persons and corporations owned by other corporations from establishing hospitals in the state and running them for profit. Only natural persons (physicians) or a partnership (of physicians) may establish and run a hospital in the state for profit. A business corporation may, however, operate (as opposed to establish) a hospital for profit. The exceptions are those hospitals established prior to 1956; but the law requires that any contemplated transfer of 10 percent or more of the ownership, voting powers, or interest in a partnership or corporation running a hospital or residential center must get the approval of the public health council.

This set of restrictions effectively limits the transfer of nonprofit hospitals to the for-profits. For example, in *McNelly* v. *De Sapio*, 1958, the courts, relying on the 1956 law, held that even though an individual physician may own a hospital, that physician cannot transfer the stocks to a stock corporation so that it, in effect, becomes the owner-operator. The effect of the law, therefore, is to restrict business corporations from owning hospitals in New York either by the transfer of assets to them or by their establishing a hospital.

At the same time, the state encourages strategic alliances, including mergers, acquisitions, consolidations, and cooperative arrangements among two or more nonprofit hospitals or other health-related agencies. It does this under the New York Prospective Hospital Reimbursement Methodology by offering financial assistance out of a statewide pool to hospitals undertaking these alliances as strategies to cut administrative, management, and operational costs and improve the quality of patient services.

TYPES OF REORGANIZATION

The reader of the following cases should keep three things in mind. First, the complexity and interconnections of organizations are often the result of growth and change in environments rather than trickery. This is one reason why strategic planning, as discussed in Chapter Seventeen, is important. It helps organizations restructure themselves as a consequence of their own internal changes and the changes in their environment.

Second, as we implied above, corporate reorganization is a legal matter requiring changes in the charter of incorporation and bylaws of the organizations involved, even if one organization is under the control of the other. This is not like changing around departments or branches.

Third, the reader should be aware that the cases are based on examples in the IRS files where names are generally not used. All the organizations are described in the original by statements such as "M is an organization exempt under section 501(c)(3) of the *Internal Revenue Code,* and described as not being a private foundation under Sections 509(a)(1) and 170(b)(1)(A)(iii)," or "C is . . . . under Section 509(a)(3)." Do you recall what these numbers mean?

Hint: Do not read the following to memorize the details of what was done to what organization. Read (1) to get a sense of the complexity of structures and (2) to learn what each type of reorganization can accomplish for you.

Case 1: Affiliation

Observe that the organizations keep their independence but gain economies and enter into a formal legal arrangement. This is perhaps the most simple form of restructuring.

The World Wildlife Fund entered into an affiliation agreement with the Conservation Foundation, a nonprofit 501(c)(3) organization. The objective of the affiliation is to provide the ability of doing joint biological and social science activities on key conservation issues and to take advantage of economies resulting from shared management, development, and communication expenses. The two share the same board of directors but remain separate legal corporations.[3]

A second example is the agreement between the Kennedy Center and the National Symphony Orchestra Association of Washington, D.C. The purpose, among others, was to reduce operating costs, increase fund-raising or development capabilities, and "to add to the artistic luster and potential of each organization and, thus, improve the Center's and the Association's long-term prospects." Both organizations maintain their separate corporate structure and identity.[4]

Case 2: Restructuring[5]

Observe the repositioning of organizations.

LaPorte Samaritan Hospital has three nonprofit corporations under it. One of these nonprofit corporations, Jason Foundation, controls a for-profit corporation, which is a holding company. This for-profit corporation, called Nia Enterprise, has nine for-profit corporations under it. It owns 100 percent of their stocks, so it is the sole owner of each of the following:

1. A same-day surgery center

2. A collection agency that collects from patients of physicians at LaPorte Samaritan and other for-profit affiliates of LaPorte

3. A clinical laboratory that performs tests for LaPorte and others

4. A firm that manages industrial medicine for a group of physicians

5. Four corporations that are inactive

In addition to Jason Foundation, the other nonprofit controlled by LaPorte is Dylan Educational Center, which provides health-care education. The third nonprofit it controls is Carla Charity, which is a fund-raiser and manager of investments for LaPorte Samaritan and Jason Foundation.

As a result of the reorganization, Jason will become the parent corporation and LaPorte will be under it and so will the Carla Charity and the Dylan Educational Center, and it will continue to hold all the stocks of the for-profit corporations. The organizations will continue to have interlocking directors.

The reorganization calls for Jason to carry out certain functions that LaPorte, a hospital, could not do as well. These include strategic planning and financing for the entire group and representing the groups before industry, government, and citizens; and it will act as an intermediary between LaPorte and the for-profits within the system to make sure that LaPorte gets a fair deal.

There will be several commercial transactions between members of the system, such as renting space. Nia Enterprise, which is a for-profit holding company of the nine corporations, will rent space from LaPorte. This, however, needs to be done in an arms-length transaction, and Jason is responsible for seeing to that. LaPorte's loan to Nia Enterprise must also receive a fair rate of interest and so, too, must be the charge of the collection agency to LaPorte and its physicians. These were the arguments placed forth for the restructuring:

1. It assured LaPorte's commitment and leadership to its health-care mission.

2. It facilitated compliance with government reporting.

3. It segregated hospital assets from nonhospital assets to limit liability.

4. It segregated regulated from nonregulated activities.

5. It increased investment opportunities.

6. It facilitated long-range planning.

7. It improved recruiting.

8. It increased flexibility in capital expenditure projects.

9. It isolated unrelated from related businesses.

10. It removed the management of nonhospital activities and assets from LaPorte.

Case 3: Mergers

The simple schematics of mergers are as follows. Nonprofit *A* acquires others but does not merge with them. It keeps them as separate corporations and may elect to report a consolidated 990 tax form, and others may be part of group for exemption purposes.

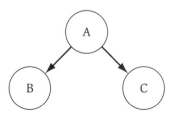

Nonprofit *A* acquires another and they consolidate through a merger. In this case, one or the other nonprofit disappears into the other. A new corporation is formed made up of the two. Which will be the surviving corporation is decided by the parties to the transaction by comparing a number of factors, including the name, asset size, and reputation.

Nonprofit *W*, which is a subsidiary of nonprofit *A*, acquires nonprofit *P* and merges with it. These types of mergers involving subsidiaries are called triangular mergers. The surviving corporation may either be *W* or *P*.

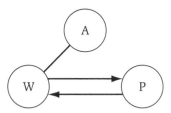

Nonprofit *W*, a subsidiary of *A*, acquires *R* and the latter merges into *A*.

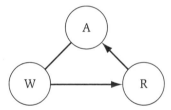

MERGER OF FOR-PROFIT WITH NONPROFIT

When a for-profit corporation, Lucrecia & Giselle, acquires a nonprofit corporation, it pays for those assets to a nonprofit with a similar mission (including a foundation created for receiving the payments). It then converts the latter to a for-profit corporation, and then it may merge it or leave B as a subsidiary of A. A merger of a for-profit and a nonprofit is illegal. The process takes at least three distinct legal steps.

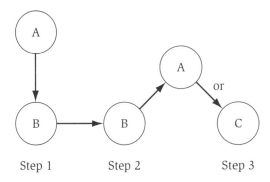

Now let's look at a more complex but real case.[6]

Observe the disappearance of an organization and the creation of one that is composed of two or more preexisting legal organizations.

n is a nonprofit organization. It is the parent holding company of a health-care system that controls acute care hospitals and other health service organizations. It provides overall management to and direction for the system and conducts certain community health programs. *n* had another nonprofit *p*, which was a regional holding company for acute care hospitals and other health service corporations that were a portion of *n*. Under *p* was a nonprofit *m* that operated an acute care hospital.

The nonprofit *n* had another affiliate *t* that was formed under the group 501(c)(3) authorization of the U.S. Catholic Conference. Its sole purpose was to be a charitable trust operating solely for the benefit of and in connection with *s*, which is a nonprofit operating an acute care hospital serving certain areas served by *m*. When *t* became affiliated with *m*, another nonprofit *q* was made inactive. This nonprofit *q* had a nonprofit under it called *r*, which operated an acute-care hospital serving the same areas as *m* and *s*.

s gets its support services from *u*, which is another nonprofit organization formed under the umbrella of the U.S. Catholic Conference. This nonprofit *u* owns the real estate around *s* and a medical clinic *e*, which is also a nonprofit organization. But *s* is a nonprofit under *p*.

Are we clear? Now, the merger.

Three of the nonprofits, *p, q,* and *s,* are merged into *m.* As a result of the merger, all the assets, liabilities, operations, and employees of *p, q,* and *s* are transferred to *m,* and the new entity now takes on the name of *p.* In addition, *r* and *q* will amend their charter to show that they are now under *p,* and *t* will amend its charter to show that it is a supporting organization for *p,* which will remain under the nonprofit *n.*

The merger was undertaken for the following reasons:

1. To simplify operations
2. To share employees, facilities, and services
3. To facilitate certain Medicare savings
4. To improve the availability, efficiency, economy, and effectiveness of delivery of health services in the community previously served by duplicate organizations under the same nonprofit umbrella

Case 4: Divestiture and Sale of Assets

A divestiture refers to the sale of an operating business unit. In popular parlance, it is a "spin-off" of that unit from its parent. Thus, a university—after establishing its hospital as an identifiable legal and separable business unit—can spin it off in a sale to a third party. When a nonprofit or a firm is planning to spin-off a unit, it prepares for the separation by making the unit attractive to potential buyers and takes steps to bring about a legal separation. A firm may require a vote by its board and its shareholders. A nonprofit would require a vote by its board and members. Some members, as some shareholders, may have a greater voting power (called preferred rights) than others, and the same is true for shareholders of a for-profit corporation.

The sale of an asset is different. In a sense, every spin-off is a sale of an asset, but every sale of an asset is not a spin-off. The university could sell its stadium, a building donated to it, a dormitory, and even the hospital as a building. As a matter of fact, it could chose to follow the sale by renting that building from the buyer and continue to operate the hospital as a business unit. Why is all this important? Because a nonprofit, unlike a firm, has community and donor accountability to satisfy. The sale may also be opposed by members, the community, or the state on one or all of the following common grounds: (1) the sale of the asset or the divestiture hinders the ability of the nonprofit to carry out its mission and commitment, (2) the asset is undervalued, and (3) the sale violates donor restriction on the use or disposition of the asset.

The trustees of the Poynter Institute for Media Studies, a journalism school in St. Petersburg, Florida, wrestled with whether the sale of the *St. Petersburg Times* in response to a very attractive offer would hinder the school's ability to teach journalism. The sale was never consummated.

The Barnes Foundation had to wrestle with whether the lending of certain pieces of art reduced its capacity to conduct art education and whether the removal of the art from the building was consistent with donor restrictions.

In neither of these two cases was the amount of money the deal-breaker. For a nonprofit, a divestiture or sale of a key asset goes to the heart of its mission and to donor restrictions. Furthermore, there may be standards that must steer these sales. Museums generally would not sell a piece of art unless the proceeds are intended to purchase another piece or art. With this understanding we proceed to look at divestitures.

Observe that an organization, assets, or business is sold or transferred to someone else.[7] It is no longer the property of its previous owner. Divestiture is exemplified by the sale of excess holdings as described in Chapter Four; it is sometimes required by law. Divestitures can also occur because a nonprofit system or holding company decides to sell one of its members to another nonprofit.

The Simon Foundation is a nonprofit educational foundation that runs not only educational functions, but also a separate nonprofit hospital called the Exalter Memorial. The Simon Foundation proposes to sell its hospital assets (Exalter) to a separate corporate nonprofit entity known as Baxter, which was created by the trustees of the Simon Foundation. Baxter and Simon will be separate entities with distinct boards with no overlaps. The board of Simon does not have the power to appoint or remove a member of the board of Baxter, and no board member of Simon works for or acts as an agent of Baxter. (Do you see the avoidance of self-dealing?)

The Simon Foundation will sell (divest itself of, a divestiture) of the following assets to Baxter: an annex, a professional building, a parking garage, radiation therapy buildings, and all associated hospital equipment. The sale will be made at a fair market value. The sale will be made partly by Baxter's signing a note (a loan) for the real estate and equipment. These notes will bear interest at 6 percent per annum, which is payable monthly. The note payments will be for interest only for three to five years. (Do you see the continued avoidance of self-dealing?)

At the end of this divestiture, Baxter Memorial will be the nonprofit hospital in existence, Exalter Memorial's assets will have been sold to Baxter, and Exalter will be a defunct corporation without assets. Simon Foundation will continue to exist, but only as an educational entity.

The divestiture accomplishes the following:

1. Simon can focus on its educational mission without the complexity of running a hospital.

2. Since Baxter will be separate, its medical staff will now be granted a greater voice, and even serve on its board of trustees.

3. The management of Baxter will be able to focus on carrying out its medical mission without being burdened with considerations of the educational mission of Simon.

4. Simon Foundation can consider requests for assistance to Baxter in the very same way and under the very same rules it considers such requests from other qualified nonprofits.

When divestiture occurs by the sale of the nonprofit member to a for-profit concern, a very common transaction, the concerns under the Ohio, Connecticut, and Georgia laws discussed earlier in this chapter are operative. The proceeds of this divestiture may be paid to the holding company, the other members of the system, or by the creation of a private foundation.

Case 5: Acquisition

Observe that an organization, assets, or business is acquired.[8]

The Lorina Conservation Institute promotes interest in and knowledge of a historical community originally established as a social experiment. In carrying out its mission, Lorina operates a building and the grounds around it, all of which are part of the exhibit, lectures, tours, and other activities integral to Lorina's mission.

Jeremiah's enterprise is a for-profit corporation. Lorina proposes to purchase all the stocks of Jeremiah's (which means that Lorina, a nonprofit, will now become the sole owner through acquisition of a for-profit corporation). When the acquisition is completed, Jeremiah will operate only unrelated businesses. The purchase is paid for by Lorina through the transfer of a portion of the building referred to above to Jeremiah, which will turn it into a multiunit condominium. The other portion of the building will be kept by Lorina and used for its mission.

The majority of the directors of Jeremiah's will not serve on the board of Lorina. The latter's board will control the day-to-day activities of Jeremiah's independently of any relationship with Lorina. All business activities will be conducted on an arm's-length basis and based on fair market values. These business activities include maintaining guest and boarding rooms and meal service.

A board of managers for the condominium units will be created with responsibility for maintenance, insurance, and the management of common elements, but it will not be subjected to day-to-day control by Lorina. Expenses will be allocated among the units on an arm's-length basis.

The acquisition permitted the following:

1. Lorina will be in a better position to carry out its mission and more efficiently. (It does not have to provide guest room services.)

2. There will be separation of the assets and liabilities.

Case 6: Partnerships and Joint Ventures

See Chapter Eighteen for cases and discussions in addition to the state laws in this chapter.

Case 7: Conversion

Observe the change in character of the organization from tax exempt to profitable, or reverse.[9]

In November 2001, the Tybalt Corporation changed its articles of incorporation to indicate that it was from henceforth a nonprofit. Prior to this it was a for-profit corporation.

To implement this change, Tybalt changed the nature of its stock from transferable, proprietary business corporation stock entitling the holder to dividends and a share of the assets upon dissolution to restricted, nontransferable stock that does not entitle the holder to either dividends or a share of the assets upon dissolution. None of the assets of the Tybalt Corporation was distributed to the shareholders because of or in conjunction with the conversion.

At issue was whether the collection of accounts receivables (outstanding amounts owed by customers of what was previously a for-profit firm) constituted unrelated business income. The ruling was that the collection by an exempt organization of its accounts receivable is a necessary day-to-day administrative function and not an unrelated business.

This case involves the conversion of a for-profit into a nonprofit. Admittedly this is less common than the previous cases. But it is described here to reinforce our understanding of the importance of the ownership of assets in nonprofits. The conversion resulted in the organization getting tax-exempt status.

Conversion also occurs when a nonprofit organization changes from one form of a nonprofit to another. This is exemplified by the private foundation that wanted to go public. It was required to demonstrate public support, as discussed in Chapter Three, and file a new application.[10]

A principal reason for converting a nonprofit organization into a for-profit firm is to gain access to capital. Recall that a nonprofit cannot sell capital stocks; therefore, its sources of capital are earnings on its investments, its membership fees, debt, business income, and contributions if the organization is a 501(c)(3). Nonprofits such as Blue Cross–Blue Shield, which are 501(c)(6)s, cannot receive tax-deductible contributions. This is also true of nonprofit mutual insurance companies. Hence, in recent years, with the high values that initial public offerings of stocks have fetched, many nonprofits have consummated conversions. Conversions have given these used-to-be nonprofits greater access to the capital market. They can now issue stocks in addition to bonds, and they can still charge fees and even higher premiums.

Other effects of conversions are that they allow directors and officers to be paid more. As managers of firms, not only are their salaries likely to be higher, but they can also be compensated in stock options and given other compensation rights associated with the appreciation of their newly formed company's stock. Such stock appreciation rights are impossible in nonprofit corporations.

How does the conversion of associations work? Associations and mutuals convert from nonprofit to for-profit status through a process known as *demutualization*. (Charities often convert to for-profit status for the same reasons as these other nonprofits.) In demutualization, capital stocks are exchanged for membership shares. All assets owned by the nonprofit are the properties of the community—not of private individuals. Therefore, the new private owners must pay a fair market price for it. These assets include real estate, equipment, furniture, mailing and client lists, and all of the intangible assets the organization acquired. These have to be valued and a price set for them.

But to whom is the price to be paid? It is possible, as in the case of Blue Cross–Blue Shield of Virginia, to turn over the sum to the state and ask it to distribute it to the worthy nonprofits. More often, the converting organization and the state will come to an agreement about a foundation that will receive the fair price of the assets being bought from the nonprofit by this new firm, that is, the one being converted from a nonprofit.

States follow the norm, based on the IRS tax code, that the funds must be used to continue the mission of the nonprofit—at least in its broad general form, such as for "the promotion of public health." Therefore, the proceeds from the conversion of an insurance company can be placed in a health-related private foundation and do not necessarily have to be placed in an insurance company.

The central problems that arise in these conversions are

1. Is the property being transferred fairly valued?
2. Is there self-dealing on the part of the management?
3. What should be the mission of the foundation (or organization) into which the assets will be transferred and who should be on its governing board?
4. In what form will payment be made and on what schedule?

The currency of payment may be in cash or stocks or a combination of the two. When cash is used it may be borrowed or it may be the result of either an initial issue of the stocks of the new company or, as in the case of Blue Cross–Blue Shield of Missouri and California, the result of spinning off a for-profit subsidiary and using both the cash and stocks of that subsidiary to fund the private foundation.

When stocks are used, there have to be at least three considerations. First, there can possibly be a taxable event if at the initial moment of the spin-off 80 percent of the subsidiary's stock is not retained by the nonprofit before it converts. Second, if the stocks either of the subsidiary or the newly created firm received by the foundation amount to more than 20 percent of the voting stocks of the newly formed firm, the foundation will eventually have to divest itself of some of these stocks so as to avoid the excess business holding rule unless it is an operating foundation (Chapter Four).

The selling of some of these stocks to meet the excess business holding requirement can be negotiated with the state and the IRS to avoid major capital losses upon their sale or avoid major taxable events. Furthermore, the eventual selling of these stocks may be an act of prudence to achieve greater portfolio diversity and larger cash to carry out the private foundation's mission of financing charitable organizations.

Case 8: Dissolution

When a dissolution occurs, the entire asset of the organization is involved. The dissolution plan has primacy as long as it remains consistent with state law. (See Chapters Two and Three.) A dissolution means that the organization, as this book, has come to an end.

ISSUES FOR THE TRUSTEES IN ALL DISPOSITIONS

Charges brought by the Attorney General of Michigan against a proposed joint agreement of Columbia/HCA and Michigan Affiliated Healthcare System, Inc. along with the earlier discussions of the rules in Connecticut and Ohio provide a good catalogue of what should concern trustees. The reader can refer back to Connecticut and Ohio laws in this chapter. Here is a paraphrasing of the issues in Michigan.

1. Failure to represent state laws on charitable organizations and trusts
2. Abusing, exceeding, or ignoring the charter of the organization
3. *De facto* dissolution of the organization
4. Failure to seek a private ruling from the Internal Revenue Service
5. Illegal transfer of assets received as gifts
6. Failure to secure a *cy pres* as explained in Chapter Seven
7. Failure to get judicial release of restricted funds
8. Violation of contractual agreements consistent with the mission of the hospital

9. Failure to hold a public forum

10. Failure to protect charitable assets

Again, every case is driven by its own details but the basic principles apply.

FORMAL PLANS FOR REORGANIZATION

Divestitures, mergers, conversions, whole partnerships or management contracts over the entire nonprofit organization, particularly if it is a 501(c)(3), represent a change in control over "public" assets. These changes are particularly worrisome when the control is acquired by a for-profit entity. When the assets became public, the attorney general of the state, as the legal representative of the public, became a party to any transaction that would lead to a change in control. Changes of this nature involve at least two written plans.

First is the plan of dissolution referred to in Part One. We have reproduced a dissolution plan. Note, as described in Chapter Two, that the first few lines cover the total transfer of assets through various forms of dissolution. But the use of words such as "no assets" means that less than a total transfer, use, or any disposition of substantial amounts of the assets of the organization other than through the normal course of business, such as the sale of inventory, is also covered.

Recalling, as stated in Chapter Two, that the mission of the organization is a social contract, any change in disposition or control—especially to an organization not already mentioned in the disposition plan—gives rise to the need for a legal amendment. Since the attorney general of the state is the legal officer protecting the enforcement of this contract, invariably some notification or approval from that officer is needed—particularly if the transfer is to a party outside of those mentioned by name or by class. This is why transfers of assets of nonprofits to for-profit firms are of public interest. When they are substantial or critical they invariably call for a response from the attorney general.

Also recall that one of the characteristics of a mission is its permanence. Another is its clarity, and another the concept of approval. Accordingly, this disposition plan clearly connotes permanence in the exclusive use of the assets for the charitable purposes for which they were given to the organization in the first place. It does this by referring to contingencies such as if said organization is not alive at the time of the disposition or if the law has a successor. It further states that if none of the original intent is realizable the recommendation and approval by the state will be guiding.

> Upon dissolution and liquidation of this corporation, all assets of the corporation remaining after all liabilities and obligations of the corporation shall be paid, satisfied, and discharged, or adequate provision shall be made therefore, shall be transferred, conveyed, and distributed to _____ a 501(c)(3) or

some other distributee(s) designated by _____ which is exempt from federal income tax under the provisions of Section 501(c)(3) of the *Internal Revenue Code* of 1986 (as hereafter amended or supplemented); provided, however, that if, on the date of such proposed distribution, said distributee no longer exists or is not operated exclusively for purposes specified in, or shall not otherwise qualify under, Section 501(c)(3) of the *Internal Revenue Code* of 1986 (as _____ may hereafter be amended and supplemented) then, in such event, the assets of this corporation, upon its dissolution and liquidation, shall be transferred, conveyed, and distributed to such other nonprofit organization or organizations as may be specified in or provided for under the plan of distribution adopted by the corporation pursuant to the laws of the State of _____; but in any event, each such distributee organization shall be organized and operated exclusively for charitable or educational purposes, shall be exempt from federal income tax under the provisions of Section 501(c)(3) of the *Internal Revenue Code* of 1986 (as hereafter amended or supplemented). In no event shall the assets of this corporation, upon its dissolution and liquidation, be distributed for purposes and uses other than those set forth in Section 501(c)(3) of the *Internal Revenue Code* of 1986 (as may hereafter be amended). [*Note:* This is the author's slightly edited version of a disposition plan used by the Sisters of St. Joseph of Carondelet in mergers in the State of Minnesota from public documents in that state. It is fairly standard language.]

In addition to the dissolution plan, a change in control variably requires an action plan and an agreement between the parties. These latter two are subject to the scrutiny of the state as we described for Georgia, Ohio, and Connecticut, discussed in this chapter, and may also have to be made public. In the case of hospitals, hearings are required in several states. Here is what such a plan and agreement between the parties may cover.

The Plan

The plan of merger is analogous to a marriage announcement. It announces that two or more organizations are planning to be one. The plan is to be filed with the state. The plan gives the names of the parties to the transaction, the states in which they were incorporated, the name of the surviving corporation after the merger has taken place, the date and specific time to the minute that the merger is to take place, the tax-exempt status of the current corporations, and the tax-exempt status that the corporation will have after the merger, planned changes in the board of directors, the procedures and penalties the parties may impose on each other to terminate the plan, and the existence of a promise to do that which is necessary to effectuate the transfer.

The Merger Agreement

The "agreement" is a description of the details that the parties have decided will govern the transfer of assets and liabilities, the nature of the representation and warranties that each party will make to the other and upon which the others may rely on entering into the agreement, the consideration (amount to be paid), the covenants that cause each party to assume certain stated responsibilities that would assure that the merger will take place, the time and place of closing, the procedures for closing including what must be delivered by each party, what must be done by each party prior to and at closing, the power of the party that would have been the beneficiary of an act to waiver that requirement at closing, the way the injured party as a result of the failure to carry out this agreement may be indemnified, the time the merger will become effective, how and under what conditions the agreement will be terminated, and how the board and bylaws and surviving corporation will be reconstituted after the effective time of the merger.

In the case of a merger, there must be considerable consideration given to how the parties will integrate, how the final product would function, who will be retrained, who will head the outfit, and so on. At least two well-known hospitals in the City of New York had their merger plans fail because integration failed.

POSTMERGER TRAUMA

The hard part comes after the merger has taken place. Integration is the process through which a newly acquired activity is fitted into a cohesive whole. Sometimes this never occurs satisfactorily and the combination is dissolved. The restored units might be quite different from what was put together in the first place. But each would have all of the properties of a nonprofit organization we have discussed throughout this book.

Integration is about the meshing of cultures even though the mission might be similar. It is about making a marriage work. Integration may fail because what might have been thought to lead to economies of scale or scope did not. Integration has a better chance to succeed when postmerger planning is detailed and takes into account the interests of a variety of stakeholders or parties of interest.

THE REBIRTH

A total change in control, such as a merger between two nonprofits of a similar classification, is equivalent to a death and a rebirth. The surviving or new organization must have a dissolution plan and a new charter just as though it were starting legally from scratch (back to Part One of this book). It is reincorporated but does not, unless there are underlying changes, need to file for new exemption. As a matter of fact, the old dissolution plan, if written as the one above, may be recited in the new charter. This is so as long as the commitments remain the same.

SUMMARY AND CONCLUSION

This chapter brings our journey to a close. We have taken an organization through its birth, maturity, marriage, divorce after a merger fails, death, and rebirth. We started in Chapter One by looking at the fundamentals that must be mastered for a manager to move a nonprofit forward successfully. We have seen that the operating rules by which that manager must perform differ by type of organization, even though most of the fundamentals remain unchanged. These operating rules tell the manager how the game is to be played.

But every organization needs money. So, Part Two this book is all about money: how to increase the flow of contributions, how to apply various techniques and to attract various types of assets particularly from those who may have a substantial amount to give. But almost all nonprofits engage in some form of business income activity. These can have consequences, and successful managers learn that they must be carefully designed. Since a business is as good as the marketing, soliciting, and ability of the organization to defend its interest even at the highest levels, we ended our discussion of money-raising activities with the rules of marketing, soliciting, and lobbying.

But raising all of the money in the world would not save an organization if it cannot control costs and fraud. For this reason, this book has dedicated three chapters to cost control—ranging from budgeting to the dealing with specific costs that constitute large actual or potential portions of the liabilities of nonprofits. One of these, of course, is compensation and another is the risk of being sued.

Once a manager has successfully begun to fill the coffers of the organization, he or she better learn how to defend his or her performance, to change direction, or to reinforce the decisions that have set the organization on course. It is also critical to his or her success to know how the money is being invested, the rules of the game, the options that are available, and the good things a properly structured endowment can bring. In short, success is seeded in the ethical and efficient use of resources and the manager's ability to carry out the duties of prudence and care over these resources.

The environment that engulfs a nonprofit is not stagnant. Therefore, a successful manager maintains a record of success through constant surveillance of the relevant environment for new opportunities for programs and alliances that can contribute to his or her mission accomplishments. Such alliances can culminate in a complete restructuring of the organization. At worse, a restructuring terminates the life of the organization without traces. At best, it results in a rebirth in which the organization is transformed. Even in these processes there are rules, penalties, and liabilities. These were the subjects of this final chapter.

APPENDIX 1.1

Standards of the National Charities Information Bureau

These Standards are the result of a study in the late 1980s by a distinguished national panel. This study, which spanned two years and took hundreds of comments into account, went into full effect in 1992. NCIB believes the spirit of these Standards to be useful for all charities. However, for organizations less than three years old or with annual budgets of less than $100,000, greater flexibility in applying some of the Standards may be appropriate.

NCIB does not advise whether to give to any particular charity. Contributors are encouraged to familiarize themselves with NCIB Standards, and then decide for themselves the importance of an organization's compliance with or variation from those standards. The information and analysis published by the NCIB is furnished to assist contributors in making informed decisions and is not intended to endorse or disparage the organization.

Governance, Policy, and Program Fundamentals

1. *Board Governance:*

   The board is responsible for policy setting, fiscal guidance, and ongoing governance, and should regularly review the organization's policies, programs, and operations. The board should have

   a. an independent, volunteer membership

Source: Copyright © 1998, National Charities Information Bureau. Reprinted with permission.

    b. a minimum of five voting members

    c. an individual attendance policy

    d. specific terms of office for its officers and members

    e. in-person, face-to-face meetings, at least twice a year, evenly spaced, with a majority of voting members in attendance at each meeting

    f. no fees to members for board service, but payments may be made for costs incurred as a result of board participation

    g. no more than one paid staff person member, usually the chief staff officer, who shall not chair the board or serve as treasurer

    h. policy guidelines to avoid material conflicts of interest involving board or staff

    i. no material conflicts of interest involving board or staff

    j. a policy promoting pluralism and diversity within the organization's board, staff, and constituencies

2. *Purpose:*

The organization's purpose, approved by the board, should be formally and specifically stated.

3. *Programs:*

The organization's activities should be consistent with its statement of purpose.

4. *Information:*

Promotion, fund-raising, and public information should describe accurately the organization's identity, purpose, programs, and financial needs.

5. *Financial Support and Related Activities:*

The board is accountable for all authorized activities generating financial support on the organization's behalf:

    a. Fund-raising practices should encourage voluntary giving and should not apply unwarranted pressure.

    b. Descriptive and financial information for all substantial income and for all revenue-generating activities conducted by the organization should be disclosed on request.

    c. Basic descriptive and financial information for income derived from authorized commercial activities, involving the organization's name, which are conducted by for-profit organizations, should be available. All public promotion of such commercial activity should either include this information or indicate that it is available from the organization.

6. *Use of Funds:*

The organization's use of funds should reflect consideration of current and future needs and resources in planning for program continuity. The organization should

    a. spend at least 60 percent of annual expenses for program activities

   b. ensure that fund-raising expenses, in relation to fund-raising results, are reasonable over time
   c. have net assets available for use in the following fiscal year not usually more than twice the current year's expenses or twice the next year's budget, whichever is higher
   d. not have a persistent deficit in net current assets

Reporting and Fiscal Fundamentals

7. *Annual Reporting:*
   An annual report should be available on request, and should include
   a. an explicit narrative description of the organization's major activities, presented in the same major categories and covering the same fiscal period as the audited financial statements
   b. a list of board members
   c. audited financial statements or, at a minimum, a comprehensive financial summary that (1) identifies all revenues in significant categories, (2) reports expenses in the same program, management/general, and fund-raising categories as in the audited financial statements, and (3) reports ending net assets (When the annual report does not include the full audited financial statements, it should indicate that they are available on request.)

8. *Accountability:*
   An organization should supply on request complete financial statements that
   a. are prepared in conformity with generally accepted accounting principles (GAAP), accompanied by a report of an independent certified public accountant, and reviewed by the board; and
   b. fully disclose economic resources and obligations, including transactions with related parties and affiliated organizations, significant events affecting finances, and significant categories of income and expense; and should also supply
   c. a statement of functional allocation of expenses, in addition to such statements required by generally accepted accounting principles to be included among the financial statements
   d. consolidated or combined financial statements for a national organization operating with affiliates prepared in the foregoing manner

9. *Budget:*
   The organization should prepare a detailed annual budget consistent with the major classifications in the audited financial statements, and approved by the board.

Mathematics of Lobbying Expenditures

*L**obbying expenditures limits.* If a public charitable organization makes the election to be subject to the lobbying expenditures limits rules (instead of the substantial part of activities test), it will not lose its tax-exempt status under section 501(c)(3), unless it normally makes *lobbying expenditures* that are more than 150 percent of the *lobbying nontaxable amount* for the organization for each tax year or normally makes *grassroots expenditures* that are more than 150 percent of the *grassroots nontaxable amount* for the organization for each tax year. See *Tax on excess expenditures to influence legislation,* later in this section.

Lobbying expenditures. These are any expenditures that are made for the purpose of attempting to influence legislation, as discussed earlier under *Attempting to influence legislation.*

Grassroots expenditures. This term refers only to those lobbying expenditures that are made to influence legislation by attempting to affect the opinions of the general public or any segment thereof.

Lobbying nontaxable amount. The lobbying nontaxable amount for any organization for any tax year is the lesser of $1,000,000 or

1. 20 percent of the *exempt purpose expenditures* if the exempt purpose expenditures are not over $500,000

Source: Tax Exempt Status of Organizations, Publication 557. Washington, D.C.: Government Printing Office, Rev. May 1997, p. 38.

2. $100,000 plus 15 percent of the excess of the exempt purpose expenditures over $500,000 if the exempt purpose expenditures are over $500,000 but not over $1,000,000

3. $175,000 plus 10 percent of the excess of the exempt purpose expenditures over $1,000,000 if the exempt purpose expenditures are over $1,000,000 but not over $1,500,000, or

4. $225,000 plus 5 percent of the excess of the exempt purpose expenditures over $1,500,000 if the exempt purpose expenditures are over $1,500,000

The term *exempt purpose expenditures* means the total of the amounts paid or incurred (including depreciation and amortization, but not capital expenditures) by an organization for the tax year to accomplish its exempt purposes. In addition, it includes

1. Administrative expenses paid or incurred for the organization's exempt purposes, and

2. Amounts paid or incurred for the purpose of influencing legislation, whether or not the legislation promotes the organization's exempt purposes

Exempt purpose expenditures *do not include* amounts paid or incurred to or for

1. A separate fund-raising unit of the organization, or

2. One or more other organizations, if the amounts are paid or incurred primarily for fund-raising

APPENDIX 2.2

National Taxonomy of
Tax-Exempt Entities—Core Codes

The NTEE codes on the right are used by researchers, watchdog groups, and others as an alternative to the IRS codes that appear on the left. The alphabetic letters used in the NTEE code have the following meaning: A is for arts, culture, humanities. B is for education. C is for environmental quality, protection, beautification. D is for animal-related. E is for health—general and rehabilitative. F is for mental health, crisis intervention. G is for diseases, disorders, medical disciplines. H is for medical research. I is for crime, legal-related. J is for employment, job-related. K is for food, agriculture, nutrition. L is for housing, shelter. M is for public safety, disaster preparedness, relief. N is for recreation, sports, leisure, athletics. O is for youth employment. P is for human services—multipurpose and other. Q is for international, foreign affairs, national security. R is for civil rights, social action, advocacy. S is for community improvement, capacity building. T is for philanthropy, voluntarism, grantmaking foundations. U is for science and technology research institutes services. V is for social science research institutes services. W is for public, society benefit—multipurpose and other. X is for religion-related, spiritual development.

ACTIVITY CODE   NTEE-CC

Religious Activities

001	Church, synagogue, etc.	X20–X70
002	Association or convention of churches	X03
003	Religious order	X20–X70
004	Church auxiliary	X11–X19
005	Mission	X20–X70
006	Missionary activities	X20–X70
007	Evangelism	X20
008	Religious publishing activities	X83
029	Other religious activities	X20–X99

Schools, Colleges and Related Activities

030	School, college, trade school, etc.	B20–B60
031	Special school for the blind, handicapped, etc.	B28
032	Nursery school; Note: Day care center (use 574)	B21
033	Faculty group	B99
034	Alumni association or group	B84
035	Parent or parent-teachers association	B94
036	Fraternity or sorority; Note: Key club (use 323)	B83
037	Other student society or group	B80
038	School or college athletic association	N40
039	Scholarships for children of employees	B82
040	Scholarships (other)	B82
041	Student loans	B82, B90
042	Student housing activities	B82, B90
043	Other student aid	B80
044	Student exchange with foreign country	Q22
045	Student operated business	O53
046	Private school	B20–B50
059	Other school related activities	B80–B99

Cultural, Historical or Other Educational Activities

060	Museum, zoo, planetarium, etc.	A50–A57, D50
061	Library	B70
062	Historical site, records or reenactment	A80, A84
063	Monument	A80
064	Commemorative event (centennial, festival, pageant, etc.)	A80, A84
065	Fair	N52
088	Community theatrical group	A65
089	Singing society or group	A6B
090	Cultural performances	A60–A6E
091	Art exhibit	A40, A51
092	Literary activities	A70
093	Cultural exchanges with foreign country	Q21
094	Genealogical activities	A80
119	Other cultural or historical activities	A20–A26, A40–A99

Other Instructions and Training Activities

120	Publishing activities	A33, X83
121	Radio or television broadcasting	A32, A34, X82, X84
122	Producing films	A31, X81
123	Discussion groups, forums, panels, lectures, etc.	A20–26, A40–A99
124	Study and research (non-scientific)	Common Code 05
125	Giving information or opinion (see also Advocacy)	Common Code 02, 05
126	Apprentice training; Note: Travel tours (use 299)	J22
149	Other instruction and training	A25, A6E, J20–J30, B20–B60

Health Services and Related Activities

150	Hospital	E20–E24
151	Hospital auxiliary	E112, E122

152	Nursing or convalescent home	E91
153	Care and housing for the aged (see also 382)	E91, P75, L22, K34, K36
154	Health clinic	E30–E32
155	Rural medical facility	E30
156	Blood bank	E61
157	Cooperative hospital service organization	E192
158	Rescue and emergency service	E62, M20, M23
159	Nurses register or bureau	E039
160	Aid to the handicapped (see also 031)	P80, P82, P86, P87, E50
161	Scientific research (diseases)	H20–H99
162	Other medical research	H20–H99, U50
163	Health insurance (medical, dental, optical, etc.)	E80
164	Prepared group health plan	E80
165	Community health planning	E70
166	Mental health care	F21–F99
167	Group medical practice association	E31
168	In-faculty group practice association	E31
169	Hospital pharmacy, parking facility, food services, etc.	E192
179	Other health services	E20–E99

Scientific Research Activities

180	Contact or sponsored scientific research for industry	U20–U99
181	Scientific research for government	U20–U99
199	Other scientific research activities	U20–U99

Business and Professional Organizations

200	Business promotion	S41
201	Real estate association	S47
202	Board of trade	S40
203	Regulating business	S194
204	Promotion of fair business practices	S40

205	Professional association	Common Code 03
206	Professional association auxiliary	Common Code 11
207	Industry trade shows	S41
208	Convention displays—Testing products of public safety (use 905)	S40
209	Research, development and testing	U20–U99
210	Professional athletic league	N80
211	Underwriting municipal insurance	Y20–Y25
212	Assigned risk insurance activities	Y20–Y25
213	Tourist bureau	S30
229	Other business or professional group	Common Code 03,S41

Farming and Related Activities

230	Farming	K20
231	Farm bureau	K28
232	Agricultural group	K20
233	Horticultural group	C40
234	Farmers cooperative marketing or purchasing	K20
235	Financing crop operations	K11, K12
236	Dairy herd improvement association	K26
237	Breeders association	K26
249	Other farming and related activities	K20–K28, K99

Mutual Organizations

250	Mutual ditch, irrigation, telephone, electric company	W50, W80, 99, Y22
251	Credit union	W60
252	Reserve funds or Insurance	Y20
253	Mutual insurance company	Y23
254	Corporation organized under an Act of Congress	W20
259	Other mutual organization	Y20–Y99

Employee of Membership Benefit Organizations

260	Fraternal Beneficiary society, order, or association	Y40–Y42
261	Improvement of conditions of workers	J40
262	Association of municipal employees	J40
263	Association of employees	J40
264	Employee or member welfare association	Y20–Y40, Y99
265	Sick, accident, death, or similar benefits	Y20–Y40, Y99
266	Strike benefits	Y24
267	Unemployment benefits	Y24
268	Pension or retirement benefits	Y30–Y42
269	Vacation benefits	Y99
279	Other services or benefits to members or employees	Y20–Y40, Y99

Sports, Athletic Recreational and Social Activities

280	Country club	N50
281	Hobby club	N50
282	Dinner club	N99
283	Variety club	N99
284	Dog club	D60
285	Women's club; Note: Garden club (use 356)	N50, S81
286	Hunting or fishing club	N61
287	Swimming or tennis club	N66, N67
288	Other sports club; Note: Boys Club, Little League, etc. (use 321)	N60, N62–N66, N68–N6A
296	Community center	N31, P28, O20
297	Community recreational facilities (park, playground, etc.)	N30–N32, O20
298	Training in sports	N40
299	Travel tours	Q99
300	Amateur athletic association	N60–N6A
301	Fund-raising athletic or sports event	Common Code 11, 12

317	Other sports or athletic activities	N20–N99
318	Other recreational activities	N20–N99
319	Other social activities	N20–N99

Youth Activities

320	Boy Scouts, Girl Scouts, etc.	O40–O43
321	Boys Club, Little League, etc.	O20–O23, N63
322	FFA, FHA, 4-H club, etc.	O52
323	Key Club	O51
324	YMCA, YWCA, YMCA, etc.	P27
325	Camp	N20
326	Care and housing of children (orphanage, etc.)	P70
327	Prevention of cruelty to children	I72–I73
328	Combat juvenile delinquency	I21, O20–O31
349	Other youth organization or activities	O20–O99

Conservation, Environmental and Beautification Activities

350	Preservation of natural resources (conservation)	C30–C36
351	Combating or preventing pollution (air, water, etc.)	C20, C27, C34
352	Land acquisition for preservation	C34
353	Soil or water conservation	C30–C34, C36, K25
354	Preservation of scenic beauty	C20–C99
355	Wildlife sanctuary or refuge	D30–D34
356	Garden club	C42
379	Other conservation, environmental or beautification activities	C20–C99

Housing Activities

380	Low-income housing	L20–L25, L40
381	Low and moderate income housing	L20–L25, L40
382	Housing for the aged	L22, P75
398	Instruction and guidance on housing	L30, L80
399	Other housing activities	L20–L99

Inner City or Community Activities

400	Area development, redevelopment of renewal	S20–S32
401	Homeowners association	L50

402	Other activity aimed at combating community deterioration	S20–S32
403	Attracting new industry or retaining industry in an area	S30–S41
404	Community promotion	S20–S99
405	Loans or grants for minority businesses	S43
406	Crime prevention	I20–I33, I40, I70–I73
407	Voluntary firemen's organization or auxiliary	M24, M112, M122
408	Community service organization	S80–S82
429	Other inner city or community benefit activities	S20–S32, S80–S99

Civil Rights Activities

430	Defense of human and civil rights	R20–R99, Q70–Q71
431	Elimination of prejudice and discrimination	R30
432	Lessen neighborhood tensions	R30
449	Other civil rights activities	R20–R99

Litigation and Legal Aid Activities

460	Public interest litigation activities	I83
461	Other litigation or support of litigation	I80
462	Legal aid to indigents	I80
463	Providing bail	I40
465	Plan under IRC section 120	I118

Legislative and Political Activities

480	Propose, support, or oppose legislation	Common Code 05
481	Voter information on issues or candidates	R40
482	Voter education (mechanics of registering, voting, etc.)	R40
483	Support, oppose, or rate political candidates	R014
484	Provide facilities or services for political campaign activities	R024
509	Other legislative and political activities	Common Code 01

Advocacy/Attempt to Influence Public Opinion Concerning:

510	Firearms control	I01
511	Selective Service System	R60
512	National defense policy	Q01
513	Weapons systems	Q01
514	Government spending	W01
515	Taxes or tax exemption	W22
516	Separation of church and state	R60
517	Government aid to parochial schools	R60
518	U.S. foreign policy	Q01
519	U.S. military involvement	Q01
520	Pacifism and peace	Q01
521	Economic-political system of U.S.	W01
522	Anti-communism	R60
523	Right to work	J01
524	Zoning or rezoning	S01
525	Location of highway or transportation system	W01
526	Rights of criminal defendants	R20
527	Capital punishment	R60
528	Stricter law enforcement	I01
529	Ecology or conservation	C01
530	Protection of consumer interests	W90
531	Medical care service	E01
532	Welfare systems	P01
533	Urban renewal	S01
534	Busing student to achieve racial balance	R30
536	Use of intoxicating beverage	F01
537	Use of drugs or narcotics	F01
538	Use of tobacco	F01
539	Prohibition of erotica	R63
540	Sex education in public schools	B01
541	Population control	R61, R62
542	Birth control methods	R61, R62

| 543 | Legalized abortion | R61, R62 |
| 559 | Other matters | R99 |

Other Activities Directed to Individuals

560	Supplying money, goods or services to the poor	K30–K35, P20–P99
561	Gifts or grants to individuals (other than scholarship)	P58–P62
562	Other loans to individuals	W60
563	Marriage counseling	P46
564	Family planning	E42
565	Credit counseling and assistance	P51
566	Job training, counseling and assistance	J20–J22
567	Draft counseling	P50
568	Vocational counseling	J21
569	Referral service (social agencies)	P50
572	Rehabilitating convicts or ex-convicts	I40–I44
573	Rehabilitating alcoholics, drug abusers, compulsive gamblers, etc.	F20–F30, F50–F54, I23
574	Day care center	P33

Activities Purposes and Activities

600	Community Chest, United Way, etc.	T70
601	Booster Club	Common Code 11
602	Gifts, grants, or loans to other organizations	Common Code 11, 12
603	Non-financial services of facilities to other organizations	Common Code 19

Other Purposes and Activities

900	Cemetery or burial activities	Y50
901	Perpetual care fund (cemetery, columbarium, etc.)	Y50
902	Emergency or disaster aid fund	M20
903	Community trust or component	T70

904	Government instrumentality or agency (see also 254)	W20
905	Testing products for public safety	W90
906	Consumer interest group	W90
907	Veterans activities	W30
908	Patriotic activities	A84, W24, W30
910	Domestic organization with activities outside U.S.	Q20–Q99
911	Foreign organization	Q20–Q99
912	Title holding corporation	Common Code 11, S47
913	Prevention of cruelty to animals	D20
914	Achievement prizes or awards	W70
915	Erection or maintenance of public building or works	W40–W50, W80
916	Cafeteria, restaurant, snack bar, food services, etc.	K99, Common Code 19
917	Thrift shop, retail outlet, etc.	P29
918	Book, gift or supply store	P29
919	Advertising	Common Code 02
920	Association of employees	J40
921	Loans or credit reporting	W60
922	Endowment fund or financial services	T20–T99
923	Indians (tribes, cultures, etc.)	A23
924	Traffic or tariff bureau	W22
925	Section 501(c)(1) with 50 percent deductibility	W20
926	Government instrumentality other than section 501(c)	W20
927	Fund-raising	T20–T99, Common Code 11, 12
928	4947(a)(2) Trust	T90

930	Prepaid legal services plan exempt under IRC section 501(c)(20)	Y20
931	Withdrawal liability payment fund 990 Section 501 (k) child care organization	Y20
932	State sponsored worker's compensation reinsurance	Y25
933	501(n) Charitable risk pool	Y20
934	529 Qualified state-sponsored tuition	B82, W60
990	501(k) Child care	P33
991–999	Administrative codes	Z99
000	Uncoded	Z99

Draft Letter Awarding
Tax-Exempt Status

DRAFT   DEPARTMENT OF THE TREASURY
INTERNAL REVENUE SERVICE
WASHINGTON, D.C. 20224

Date: Employer Identification Number:

Contact Person:

Toll Free Contact Number:
LETTER.01   877-829-5500
Accounting Period Ending:

Foundation Status Classification:
509(a)(1) & 170(b)(1)(A)(vi)
Form 990 Required:
Yes

Dear Applicant:

Based on the information supplied, and assuming your operations will be as stated in your application for recognition of exemption, we have determined you are exempt from federal income tax under section 501(a) of the Internal Revenue Code as an organization described in section 501(c)(3).

We have further determined that you are not a private foundation within the meaning of section 509(a) of the Code, because you are an organization described in the section(s) indicated above.

Please notify the Ohio EP/EO Customer Service office if there is any change in your name, address, sources of support, purposes, or method of operation. If you amend your organizational document or bylaws, please send a copy of the amendment to the Ohio EP/EO Customer Service office. The mailing address for that office is Internal Revenue Service, EP/EO Customer Service, P.O. Box 2508, Cincinnati, OH 45201.

You are liable for taxes under the Federal Insurance Contributions Act (social security taxes) on remuneration of $100 or more you pay to each of your employees during a calendar year. You are not liable for the tax imposed under the Federal Unemployment Tax Act.

If you are involved in an excess benefit transaction, that transaction might be subject to the excise taxes of section 4958 of the Code. In this letter we are not determining whether any of your present or proposed arrangements would be considered an excess benefit transaction resulting in tax under section 4958. Additionally, you are not automatically exempt from other federal excise taxes.

Donors may deduct contributions to you as provided in section 170 of the Code. Bequests, legacies, devises, transfers, or gifts to you or for your use are deductible for federal estate and gift tax purposes if they meet the applicable provisions of Code sections 2055, 2106, and 2522.

Donors (including private foundations) may rely on this ruling unless the Internal Revenue Service publishes notice to the contrary. However, if you lose your 509(a) status as indicated above, donors (other than private foundations) may not rely on the classification indicated above if they were in part responsible for, or were aware of, the act that resulted in your loss of such status, or they acquired knowledge that the Internal Revenue Service had given notice that you would be removed from that classification. Private foundations may rely on the classification as long as you were not directly or indirectly controlled by them or by disqualified persons with respect to them. However, private foundations may not rely on the classification indicated above if they acquired knowledge that the Internal Revenue Service had given notice that you would be removed from that classification.

Contribution deductions are allowable to donors only to the extent that their contributions are gifts, with no consideration received. Ticket purchases and similar payments in conjunction with fund-raising events may not necessarily qualify as fully deductible contributions, depending on the circumstances. If your organization conducts fund-raising events such as benefit dinners, shows membership drives, etc., where something of value is received in return for payments, you are required to provide a written disclosure statement informing the donor of the fair market value of the specific items or services being provided.

To do this you should, in advance of the event, determine the fair market value of the benefit received and state it in your fund-raising materials such as solicitations, tickets, and receipts in such a way that the donor can determine how much is deductible and how much is not. Your disclosure statement should be made, at the latest, at the time payment is received. Subject to certain exceptions, your disclosure responsibility applies to any fund-raising circumstance where each complete payment, including the contribution portion, exceeds $75. In addition, donors must have written substantiation from the charity for any charitable contribution of $250 or more. For further details regarding these substantiation and disclosure requirements, see the enclosed copy of Publication 1771. For additional guidance in this area, see Publication 1391, Deductibility of Payments Made to Organizations Conducting Fund-Raising Events, which is available at many IRS offices or by calling 1-800-TAX-FORM (1-800-829-3678).

In the heading of this letter we have indicated whether you must file Form 990, Return of Organization Exempt from Income Tax. If "Yes" is indicated, you are required to file Form 990 only if your gross receipts each year are normally more than $25,000. If your gross receipts each year are not normally more than $25,000, we ask that you establish that you are not required to file Form 990 by completing Part I of that Form for your first year. Thereafter, you will not be required to file a return until your gross receipts exceed the $25,000 minimum. For guidance in determining if your gross receipts are "normally" not more than the $25,000 limit, see the instructions for the Form 990. If a return is required, it must be filed by the 15th day of the fifth month after the end of your annual accounting period. A penalty of $20 a day is charged when a return is filed late, unless there is reasonable cause for the delay. The maximum panalty charged cannot exceed $10,000 or 5 percent of your gross receipts for the year, whichever is less. For organizations with gross receipts exceeding $1,000,000 in any year, the penalty is $100 per day per return, unless there is reasonable cause for the delay. The maximum penalty for an organization with gross receipts exceeding $1,000,000 shall not exceed $50,000. This penalty may also be charged if a return is not complete, so please be sure your return is complete before you file it. Form 990 should be filed with the Ogden Service Center, Ogden, UT 84201-0027.

You are required to make your annual return available for public inspection for three years after the return is due. You are also required to make available a copy of your exemption application, any supporting documents, and this exemption letter. Failure to make these documents available for public inspection may subject you to a penalty of $20 per day for each day there is a failure to comply (up to a maximum of $10,000 in the case of an annual return).

You are not required to file federal income tax returns unless you are subject to the tax on unrelated business income under section 511 of the Code. If you are subject to this tax, you must file an income tax return on Form 990-T,

Exempt Organization Business Income Tax Return. In this letter we are not determining whether any of your present or proposed activities are unrelated trade or business as defined in section 513 of the Code.

Please use the employer identification number indicated in the heading of this letter on all returns you file and in all correspondence wlth the Internal Revenue Service. Because this letter could help resolve any questions about your exempt status, you should keep it in your permanent records. If you have any questions about this letter, or about filing requirements, excise employment, or other federal taxes, please contact the Ohio EP/EO Customer Service office at 877-829-5500 (a toll free number) or send correspondence to Internal Revenue Service, EP/EO Customer Service, P.O. Box 2508, Cincinnati, OH 45201.

Sincerely,

Marvin Friedlander
Chief, Exempt Organizations
Technical Branch 1

Enclosure:
  Pub. 1771

APPENDIX 6.1

Sample Conflicts of Interest Policy (Revised 5/22/97)

ARTICLE I: PURPOSE

The purpose of the conflicts of interest policy is to protect the Corporation's interest when it is contemplating entering into a transaction or arrangement that might benefit the private interest of an officer or director of the Corporation. This policy is intended to supplement but not replace any applicable state laws governing conflicts of interest applicable to nonprofit and charitable corporations.

ARTICLE II: DEFINITIONS

1. Interested Person Any director, principal officer, or member of a committee with board delegated powers who has a direct or indirect financial interest, as defined below, is an interested person. If a person is an interested person with respect to any entity in the health care

Source: Taken from the Appendix of Lawrence M. Brauer and Charles F. Kaiser, "Tax-Exempt Health Care Organizations Community Board and Conflicts of Interest Policy," in *Continuing Professional Education: Exempt Organizations* (Washington, D.C.: Department of the Treasury: Internal Revenue Service, July 1996).

system of which the Corporation is a part, he or she is an interested person with respect to all entities in the health care system.

2. Financial Interest A person has a financial interest if the person has, directly or indirectly, through business, investment, or family—

   a. an ownership or investment interest in any entity with which the Corporation has a transaction or arrangement, or

   b. a compensation arrangement with the Corporation or with any entity or individual with which the Corporation has a transaction or arrangement, or

   c. a potential ownership or investment interest in, or compensation arrangement with, any entity or individual with which the Corporation is negotiating a transaction or arrangement.

Compensation includes direct and indirect remuneration as well as gifts or favors that are substantial in nature.

A financial interest is not necessarily a conflict of interest. Under Article III, Section 2, a person who has a financial interest may have a conflict of interest only if the appropriate board of committee decides that a conflict of interest exists.

ARTICLE III: PROCEDURES

1. Duty to Disclose In connection with any actual or possible conflicts of interest, an interested person must disclose the existence of his or her financial interest and all material facts to the directors and members of committees with board delegated powers considering the proposed transaction or arrangement.

2. Determining Whether a Conflict of Interest Exists After disclosure of the financial interest and all material facts, and after any discussion with the interested person, he or she shall leave the board or committee meeting while the determination of a conflict of interest is discussed and voted upon. The remaining board or committee members shall decide if a conflict of interest exists.

3. Procedures for Addressing the Conflict of Interest

   a. An interested person may make a presentation at the board or committee meeting, but after such presentation, he/she shall leave the meeting during the discussion of, and the vote on, the transaction or arrangement that results in the conflict of interest.

   b. The chairperson of the board or committee shall, if appropriate, appoint a disinterested person or committee to investigate alternatives to the proposed transaction or arrangement.

c. After exercising due diligence, the board or committee shall determine whether the Corporation can obtain a more advantageous transaction or arrangement with reasonable efforts from a person or entity that would not give rise to a conflict of interest.

d. If a more advantageous transaction or arrangement is not reasonably attainable under circumstances that would not give rise to a conflict of interest, the board or committee shall determine by a majority vote of the disinterested directors whether the transaction or arrangement is in the Corporation's best interest and for its own benefit and whether the transaction is fair and reasonable to the Corporation and shall make its decision as to whether to enter into the transaction or arrangement in conformity with such determination.

4. Violations of the Conflicts of Interest Policy

a. If the board or committee has reasonable cause to believe that a member has failed to disclose actual or possible conflicts of interest, it shall inform the member of the basis for such belief and afford the member an opportunity to explain the alleged failure to disclose.

b. If, after hearing the response of the member and making such further investigation as may be warranted in the circumstances, the board or committee determines that the member has in fact failed to disclose an actual or possible conflict of interest, it shall take appropriate disciplinary and corrective action.

ARTICLE IV: RECORDS OF PROCEEDINGS

The minutes of the board and all committee with board-delegated powers shall contain—

1. the names of the persons who disclosed or otherwise were found to have a financial interest in connection with an actual or possible conflict of interest, the nature of the financial interest, any action taken to determine whether a conflict of interest was present, and the board's or committee's decision as to whether a conflict of interest in fact existed.

2. the names of the persons who were present for discussions and votes relating to the transaction or arrangement, the content of the discussion, including any alternatives to the proposed transaction or arrangement, and a record of any votes taken in connection therewith.

ARTICLE V: COMPENSATION COMMITTEES

1. A voting member of any committee whose jurisdiction includes compensation matters and who receives compensation, directly or indirectly, from the Corporation for services is precluded from voting on matters pertaining to that member's compensation.
2. Physicians who receive compensation, directly or indirectly, from the Corporation, whether as employees or independent contractors, are precluded from membership on any committee whose jurisdiction includes compensation matters. No physician, either individually or collectively, is prohibited from providing information to any committee regarding physician compensation.

ARTICLE VI: ANNUAL STATEMENTS

Each director, principal officer, and member of a committee with board delegated powers shall annually sign a statement which affirms that such person—

a. has received a copy of the conflicts of interest policy,
b. has read and understands the policy,
c. has agreed to comply with the policy, and
d. understands that the Corporation is a charitable organization and that in order to maintain its federal tax exemption it must engage primarily in activities which accomplish one or more of its tax-exempt purposes.

ARTICLE VII: PERIODIC REVIEWS

To ensure that the Corporation operates in a manner consistent with its charitable purposes and that it does not engage in activities that could jeopardize its status as an organization exempt from federal income tax, periodic reviews shall be conducted. The periodic reviews shall, at a minimum, include the following subjects:

a. Whether compensation arrangements and benefits are reasonable and are the result of arm's-length bargaining.
b. Whether acquisitions of physician practices and other provider services result in inurement or impermissible private benefit.

c. Whether partnership and joint venture arrangements and arrangements with management service organizations and physician hospital organizations conform to written policies, are properly recorded, reflect reasonable payments for goods and services, further the Corporation's charitable purposes, and do not result in inurement or impermissible private benefit.
d. Whether agreements to provide health care and agreements with other health care providers, employees, and third party payors further the Corporation's charitable purposes and do not result in inurement or impermissible private benefit.

ARTICLE VIII: USE OF OUTSIDE EXPERTS

In conducting the periodic reviews provided for in Article VII, the Corporation may, but need not, use outside advisors. If outside experts are used their use shall not relieve the board of its responsibility for ensuring that periodic reviews are conducted.

Restrictions Attached
to Donations Violate
Antitrust Law

A family named Peers sold land containing vermiculite to the W. R. Grace Corporation. Vermiculite is a material used in construction, fire safety, food processing, and in environmental protection. The terms of the sale included the provision that the family would receive production royalties from Grace. No production royalties were ever received by the Peers family because no production ever followed the acquisition by Grace.

Virginia Vermiculite Limited, a competing firm in the vermiculite business with a 23 percent share of the market, responded to an invitation by Grace to purchase the property it bought from the Peers. Grace, controlling some 80 percent of the market share for vermiculite, rejected the response it got from Virginia Vermiculite, which had succeeded in buying some property from the Peers.

After rejecting the response of Vermiculite, Grace gave the property as a charitable donation to Green Springs National Historic Landmark District, a not-for-profit with the mission of preserving the environment in western Virginia. Part of this mission was to prevent the mining of vermiculite in western Virginia. The donation amounted to 40 percent of the known vermiculite deposits in the United States at the time.

This donation was made in two parts. The earlier donation was made with a restrictive covenant barring the not-for-profit and its successors from mining

Source: This case description was first written by Herrington J. Bryce as editor of *Not-for-Profit Financial Strategies.* (San Diego: Harcourt Brace, January 1999), p. 7.

vermiculite on the donated property, but W. R. Grace retained the right to waive this covenant. Because a Virginia court subsequently struck down the covenant, the second portion of the donation was made without a written covenant but with the understanding that the not-for-profit would abide by the spirit of the covenant that was struck down. Grace and the not-for-profit organization saw the covenant as unnecessary because the mission of the latter was to preserve the property without mining it. Thus, the intent would have been accomplished just by the not-for-profit conducting its mission. A covenant was unnecessary.

Virginia Vermiculite, joined by the Peers family, lost some of its arguments in lower court. They took on appeal to the Fourth Circuit. Their basic argument was that the not-for-profit and Grace conspired to injure them in violation of the Sherman Anti-Trust Act. In defense of their actions, Grace and the not-for-profit argued, in part, that the latter was not subject to the Act because of its tax-exempt status.

The Fourth Circuit Court concluded that absent the donation to the nonprofit and the tacit understanding, Grace may have had to surrender mining rights to Virginia Vermiculite or be faced with a charge of improper unilateral refusal to deal after its offer to sell. And if it felt that the mission of the organization was sufficiently protecting, it would not have entered into a restrictive covenant in the first place.

The court further ruled that it is not the exempt status of the organization that is at issue, but the nature of the transaction. The Sherman Anti-Trust Act, argued the court, refers to commercial transactions by any persons. Therefore, it is the commercial nature of this activity, not the organization, that matters. Further, a number of Supreme Court decisions have supported antitrust exposure of not-for-profit organizations.

To support its view that the activity was commercial, the court pointed to the fact that the donation had an impact on the distribution of market share. As a consequence it constrained the amount of deposit that was available to Virginia Vermiculite. By so doing, it constrained supply and inflated prices of that product. In addition, the court argued that the transactions benefited the not-for-profit in a pecuniary manner. It also benefits the not-for-profit's management and those of its members who had commercial interests in mining.

Important: Donors often make gifts of property subject to certain restrictions. The important lessons from this case, aside from the implications of antitrust violations, are that such covenants cannot be used to contravene the legal obligations of the donor—and may not survive the cover offered by the mission of the organization. Beware of covenants, easements, and other restrictions attached to gifts, whether written or understood. This is the larger lesson of this case.

IRS Example of Declaration of Trust

In the first part of this chapter and in Chapter Four, it was said that a nonprofit could operate as a trust or as a corporation. Chapter Four gives an example of an acceptable charter. This appendix is an example of a trust declaration that is acceptable to the IRS.

The _____ Charitable Trust. Declaration of Trust made as of the _____ day of _____, 19____, by _____, of _____, and _____, of _____, who hereby declare and agree that they have received this day from _____, as Donor, the sum of Ten Dollars ($10) and that they will hold and manage the same, and any additions to it, in trust, as follows:

First: This trust shall be called "The _____ Charitable Trust."

Second: The trustees may receive and accept property, whether real, personal, or mixed, by way of gift, bequest, or devise, from any person, firm, trust, or corporation, to be held, administered, and disposed of in accordance with and pursuant to the provisions of this Declaration of Trust; but no gift, bequest or devise of any such property shall be received and accepted if it is conditioned or limited in such manner as to require the disposition of the income or its principal to any person or organization other than a "charitable

---

Source: Declaration of Trust, Internal Revenue Service, *Tax Exempt Status of Your Organization,* Publication 557 (Washington, D.C.: U.S. Government Printing Office, revised May 1992), pp. 15–16.

organization" or for other than "charitable purposes" within the meaning of such terms as defined in Article Third of this Declaration of Trust, or as shall in the opinion of the trustees, jeopardize the federal income tax exemption of this trust pursuant to section 501(c)(3) of the Internal Revenue Code, or the corresponding section of any future federal tax code.

Third: A. The principal and income of all property received and accepted by the trustees to be administered under this Declaration of Trust shall be held in trust by them, and the trustees may make payments or distributions from income or principal, or both, to or for the use of such charitable organizations, within the meaning of that term as defined in paragraph C, in such amounts and for such charitable purposes of the trust as the trustees shall from time to time select and determine; and the trustees may make payments or distributions from income or principal, or both, directly for such charitable purposes, within the meaning of that term as defined in paragraph D, in such amounts as the trustees shall from time to time select and determine without making use of any other charitable organization. The trustees may also make payments or distributions of all or any part of the income or principal to states, territories, or possessions of the United States, any political subdivision of any of the foregoing, or to the United States or the District of Columbia but only for charitable purposes within the meaning of that term as defined in paragraph D. Income or principal derived from contributions by corporations shall be distributed by the trustees for use solely within the United States or its possessions. No part of the net earnings of this trust shall inure or be payable to or for the benefit of any private shareholder or individual, and no substantial part of the activities of this trust shall be the carrying on of propaganda, or otherwise attempting, to influence legislation. No part of the activities of this trust shall be the participation in, or intervention in (including the publishing or distributing of statements), any political campaign on behalf of or in opposition to any candidate for public office.

B. The trust shall continue forever unless the trustees terminate it and distribute all of the principal and income, which action may be taken by the trustees in their discretion at any time. On such termination, assets shall be distributed for one or more exempt purposes within the meaning of section 501(c)(3) of the Internal Revenue Code, or the corresponding section of any future federal tax code, or shall be distributed to the federal government, or to a state or local government, for a public purpose. The donor authorizes and empowers the trustees to form and organize a nonprofit corporation limited to the uses and purposes provided for in this Declaration of Trust, such corporation to be organized under the laws of any state or under the laws of the United States as may be determined by the trustees; such corporation when organized to have power to administer and control the affairs and property and to carry out the uses, objects, and purposes of this trust. Upon the creation and organization of such corporation, the trustees are authorized and empowered to convey, transfer, and deliver to such corporation all the property and assets to which this trust may be or become entitled. The charter, bylaws, and other provisions for the organization and management of such corporation and its affairs and property shall be such as the trustees shall determine, consistent with the provisions of this paragraph.

C. In this Declaration of Trust and in any amendments to it, references to "charitable organizations" or "charitable organization" mean corporations, trusts, funds, foundations, or community chests created or organized in the United States or in any of its possessions, whether under the laws of the United States, any state or territory, the District of Columbia, or any possession of the United States, organized and operated exclusively for charitable purposes, no part of the net earnings of which inures or is payable to or for the benefit of any private shareholder or individual, and no substantial part of the activities of which is carrying on propaganda, or otherwise attempting, to influence legislation, and which do not participate in or intervene in (including the publishing or distributing of statements) any political campaign on behalf of or in opposition to any candidate for public office. It is intended that the organization described in this paragraph C shall be entitled to exemption from federal income tax under section 501(c)(3) of the Internal Revenue Code, or the corresponding section of any future federal tax code.

D. In this Declaration of Trust and in any amendments to it, the term "charitable purposes" shall be limited to and shall include only religious, charitable, scientific, literary, or educational purposes within the meaning of those terms as used in section 501(c)(3) of the Internal Revenue Code, or the corresponding section of any future federal tax code, but only such purposes as also constitute public charitable purposes under the law of trusts of the State of _____.

Fourth: This Declaration of Trust may be amended at any time or times by written instrument or instruments signed and sealed by the trustees, and acknowledged by any of the trustees, provided that no amendment shall authorize the trustees to conduct the affairs of this trust in any manner or for any purpose contrary to the provisions of section 501(c)(3) of the Internal Revenue Code, or the corresponding section of any future federal tax code. An amendment of the provisions of this Article Fourth (or any amendment to it) shall be valid only if and to the extent that such amendment further restricts the trustees' amending power. All instruments amending this Declaration of Trust shall be noted upon or kept attached to the executed original of this Declaration of Trust held by the trustees.

Fifth: Any trustee under this Declaration of Trust may, by written instrument, signed and acknowledged, resign his office. The number of trustees shall be at all times not less than two, and whenever for any reason the number is reduced to one, there shall be, and at any other time there may be, appointed one or more additional trustees. Appointments shall be made by the trustee or trustees for the time in office by written instruments signed and acknowledged. Any succeeding or additional trustee shall, upon his acceptance of the office by written instrument signed and acknowledged, have the same powers, rights and duties, and the same title to the trust estate jointly with the surviving or remaining trustee or trustees as if originally appointed.

None of the trustees shall be required to furnish any bond or surety. None of them shall be responsible or liable for the acts of omissions of any other of the trustees or of any predecessor or of a custodian, agent, depositary or counsel selected with reasonable care.

The one or more trustees, whether original or successor, for the time being in office, shall have full authority to act even though one or more vacancies may exist. A trustee may, by appropriate written instrument, delegate all or any part of his powers to another or others of the trustees for such periods and subject to such conditions as such delegating trustee may determine.

The trustees serving under this Declaration of Trust are authorized to pay to themselves amounts for reasonable expenses incurred and reasonable compensation for services rendered in the administration of this trust, but in no event shall any trustee who has made a contribution to this trust ever receive any compensation thereafter.

Sixth: In extension and not in limitation of the common law and statutory powers of trustees and other powers granted in this Declaration of Trust, the trustees shall have the following discretionary powers:

a) To invest and reinvest the principal and income of the trust in such property, real, personal, or mixed, and in such manner as they shall deem proper, and from time to time to change investments as they shall deem advisable; to invest in or retain any stocks, shares, bonds, notes, obligations, or personal or real property (including without limitation any interests in or obligations of any corporation, association, business trust, investment trust, common trust fund, or investment company) although some or all of the property so acquired or retained is of a kind or size which but for this express authority would not be considered proper and although all of the trust funds are invested in the securities of one company. No principal or income, however, shall be loaned, directly or indirectly, to any trustee or to anyone else, corporate or otherwise, who has at any time made a contribution to this trust, nor to anyone except on the basis of an adequate interest charge and with adequate security.

b) To sell, lease, or exchange any personal, mixed, or real property, at public auction or by private contract, for such consideration and on such terms as to credit or otherwise, and to make such contracts and enter into such undertakings relating to the trust property, as they consider advisable, whether or not such leases or contracts may extend beyond the duration of the trust.

c) To borrow money for such periods, at such rates of interest, and upon such terms as the trustees consider advisable, and as security for such loans to mortgage or pledge any real or personal property with or without power of sale; to acquire or hold any real or personal property, subject to any mortgage or pledge on or of property acquired or held by this trust.

d) To execute and deliver deeds, assignments, transfers, mortgages, pledges, leases, covenants, contracts, promissory notes, releases, and other instruments, sealed or unsealed, incident to any transaction in which they engage.

e) To vote, to give proxies, to participate in the reorganization, merger or consolidation of any concern, or in the sale, lease, disposition, or distribution of its assets; to join with other security holders in acting through a committee, depositary, voting trustees, or otherwise, and in this connection to delegate authority to such committee, depositary, or trustees and to deposit securities with them or transfer securities to them; to pay assessments levied on securities or to exercise subscription rights in respect of securities.

f) To employ a bank or trust company as custodian of any funds or securities and to delegate to it such powers as they deem appropriate; to hold trust property without indication of fiduciary capacity but only in the name of a registered nominee, provided the trust property is at all times identified as such on the books of the trust; to keep any or all of the trust property or funds in any place or places in the United States of America; to employ clerks, accountants, investment counsel, investment agents, and any special services, and to pay the reasonable compensation and expenses of all such services in addition to the compensation of the trustees.

Seventh: The trustees' powers are exercisable solely in the fiduciary capacity consistent with and in furtherance of the charitable purposes of this trust as specified in Article Third and not otherwise.

Eighth: In this Declaration of Trust and in any amendment to it, references to "trustees" mean the one or more trustees, whether original or successor, for the time being in office.

Ninth: Any person may rely on a copy, certified by a notary public, of the executed original of this Declaration of Trust held by the trustees, and of any of the notations on it and writings attached to it, as fully as he might rely on the original documents themselves. Any such person may rely fully on any statements of fact certified by anyone who appears from such original documents or from such certified copy to be a trustee under this Declaration of Trust. No one dealing with the trustees need inquire concerning the validity of anything the trustees purport to do. No one dealing with the trustees need see to the application of anything paid or transferred to or upon the order of the trustees of the trust.

Tenth: This Declaration of Trust is to be governed in all respects by the laws of the State of _____.

Trustee—
Trustee—

Breakeven Point

Recall that point A in Figure 9.1 represents the breakeven point where the total revenues from a business owned by the nonprofit equals the total costs. Total revenues (TR) is nothing more than the unit revenue (or average revenue brought in by a unit of product or service sold, that is, the price of that unit) multiplied by the number of units sold. If we sold 200 apples and the average price received per apple was 25 cents, the total revenues (TR) would be equal to the unit revenue (UR) or price multiplied by the quantity (Q) sold.

Total cost (TC) comprises three parts. First, there is the total fixed cost (TFC), which is the cost to the business for simply existing. It does not vary with the amount of production. Whether the business produces or not, it has to pay contractual costs such as rent and mortgages. The bankers and landlord charge for space, and once the organization signs that contract, it pays for the space regardless of how much it uses it. The cost is fixed.

Other costs are variable. They vary with the amount produced. The amount of materials and supplies used and the number of hours per worker vary with the production level. The greater the production is, the more the total variable cost (TVC). Total variable costs can therefore be divided into two parts: the quantity produced (Q) and the cost per unit produced (UC). Together, TFC + TVC make up total production cost (TC).

Accordingly, the breakeven point is where

$$TR = TC$$

or

$$UR \times Q = UC \times Q + TFC$$

If we divide both sides by Q and simplify, we get

$$UR = (TFC/Q) + UC$$

Solving for Q, we get

$$Q = TFC/(UR{-}UC)$$

This tells us that the breakeven point is equal to the total fixed cost divided by the difference between the unit revenue and the unit cost. This difference ($UR{-}UC$) is called the unit contribution, or the contribution margin.

Suppose that the nonprofit has a need for \$50,000. It decides that this must come from the operation of its business. This business has a fixed cost of \$10,000 and a unit contribution of \$2.00; that is, the difference between the average price or unit price and the average or unit cost of the item it sells is \$2.00. Each unit sold contributes \$2.00 to the total operating income of the business. By applying the following formula, it is possible to ascertain the minimum amount of units the business must produce and sell. The formula is

$$(QR) = TFC + DI/(UR{-}UC)$$

QR is the quantity required to meet the income target of the organization (\$50,000).

TFC is the total cost.

DI is desired income or income target.

$UR{-}UC$ is the unit contribution.

Accordingly,

$$QR = \$10{,}000 + (\$50{,}000/2)$$

The answer is that 30,000 units must be bought and sold to meet the organization's income target of \$50,000.

APPENDIX 10.1

Exclusions to Unrelated Business

EXCLUSION CODES

General Exceptions

01 Income from an activity that is not regularly carried on [section 512(a)(1)]

02 Income from an activity in which labor is a material income-producing factor and substantially all (at least 85 percent) of the work is performed with unpaid labor [section 513(a)(1)]

03 Section 501(c)(3) organization—Income from an activity carried on primarily for the convenience of the organization's members, students, patients, visitors, officers, or employees (hospital parking lot or museum cafeteria, for example) [section 513(a)(2)]

04 Section 501(c)(4) local association of employees organized before 5/27/69—Income from the sale of work-related clothes or equipment and items normally sold through vending machines; food dispensing facilities; or snack bars for the convenience of association members at their usual places of employment [section 513(a)(2)]

05 Income from the sale of merchandise, substantially all of which (at least 85 percent) was donated to the organization [section 513(a)(3)]

Source: U.S. Government Printing Office: Form 990.

Specific Exceptions

06 Section 501(c)(3), (4), or (5) organization conducting an agricultural or educational fair or exposition—Qualified public entertainment activity income [section 513(d)(2)]

07 Section 501(c)(3), (4), (5), or (6) organization—Qualified convention and trade show activity income [section 513(d)(3)]

08 Income from hospital services described in section (513)(e)

09 Income from noncommercial bingo games that do not violate state or local law [section 513(f)]

10 Income from games of chance conducted by an organization in North Dakota [section 311 of the Deficit Reduction Act of 1984, as amended]

11 Section 501(c)(12) organization—Qualified pole rental income [section 513(g)]

12 Income from the distribution of low-cost articles in connection with the solicitation of charitable contributions [section 513(h)]

13 Income from the exchange or rental of membership or donor list with an organization eligible to receive charitable contributions by a section 501(c)(3) organization; by a war veterans' organization; or an auxiliary unit or society of, or trust or foundation for, a war veterans' post or organization [section 513(h)]

Modifications and Exclusions

14 Dividends, interest, or payments with respect to securities loans, and annuities excluded by section 512(b)(1)

15 Royalty income excluded by section 512(b)(2)

16 Real property rental income that does not depend on the income or profits derived by the person leasing the property and is excluded by section 512(b)(3)

17 Rent from personal property leased with real property and incidental (10 percent or less) in relation to the combined income from the real and personal property [section 512(b)(3)]

18 Proceeds from the sale of investments and other noninventory property [capital gains excluded by section 512(b)(5)]

19 Income (gains) from the lapse or termination of options to buy or sell securities [section 512(b)(5)]

20 Income from research for the United States; its agencies or instrumentalities; or any state or political subdivision [section 512(b)(7)]

21 Income from research conducted by a college, university, or hospital [section 512(b)(8)]

22 Income from research conducted by an organization whose primary activity is conducting fundamental research, the results of which are freely available to the general public [section 512(b)(9)]

23 Income from services provided under license issued by a federal regulatory agency and conducted by a religious order or school operated by a religious order, but only if the trade or business has been carried on by the organization since before May 27, 1959 [section 512(b)(15)]

Foreign Organizations

24 Foreign organizations only—Income from a trade or business NOT conducted in the United States and NOT derived from United States sources (patrons) [section 512(a)(2)]

Social Clubs and VEBAs

25 Section 501(c)(7), (9), (17), or (20) organization—Nonexempt function income set aside for a charitable, etc., purpose specified in section 170(c)(4) [section 512(a)(3)(B)(I)]

26 Section 501(c)(7), (9), (17), or (20) organization—Proceeds from the sale of exempt function property that was or will be timely reinvested in similar property [section 512(a)(3)(D)]

27 Section 501(c)(9), (17), or (20) organization—Nonexempt function income set aside for the payment of life, sick, accident, or other benefits [section 512(a)(3)(B)(ii)]

Veterans' Organizations

28 Section 501(c)(19) organization—Payments for life, sick, accident, or health insurance for members or their dependents that are set aside for the payment of such insurance benefits or for a charitable, etc., purpose specified in section 170(c)(4) [section 512(a)(4)]

29 Section 501(c)(19) organization—Income from an insurance set-aside (see code 28 above) that is set aside for payment of insurance benefits or for a charitable, etc., purpose specified in section 170(c)(4) [Regs. 1.512(a)–4(b)(2)]

Debt-Financed Income

30 Income exempt from debt-financed (section 514) provisions because at least 85 percent of the use of the property is for the organization's exempt purposes (*Note:* This code is only for income from the 15 percent or less nonexempt purpose use.) [section 514(b)(1)(A)]

31 Gross income from mortgaged property used in research activities described in section 512(b)(7), (8), or (9) [section 514(b)(1)(C)]

32 Gross income from mortgaged property used in any activity described in section 513(a)(1), (2), or (3) [section 514(b)(1)(D)]

33 Income from mortgaged property (neighborhood land) acquired for exempt purpose use within ten years [section 514(b)(3)]

34 Income from mortgaged property acquired by bequest or devise [applies to income received within ten years from the date of acquisition) (section 514(c)(2)(B)]

35 Income from mortgaged property acquired by gift where the mortgage was placed on the property more than five years previously and the property was held by the donor for more than five years [applies to income received within ten years from the date of gift (section 514(c)(2)(B)]

36 Income from property received in return for the obligation to pay an annuity described in section 514(c)(5)

37 Income from mortgaged property that provides housing to low and moderate income persons, to the extent the mortgage is insured by the Federal Housing Administration [section 514(c)(6)] [*Note:* In many cases, this would be exempt function income reportable in column (e). It would not be so in the case of a section 501(c)(5) or (6) organization, for example, that acquired the housing as an investment or as a charitable activity.]

38 Income from mortgaged real property owned by a school described in section 170(b)(1)(A)(ii); a section 509(a)(3) affiliated support organization of such a school; a section 501(c)(25) organization, or by a partnership in which any of the above organizations owns an interest if the requirements of section 514(c)(9)(B)(vi) are met [section 514(c)(9)]

Special Rules

39 Section 501(c)(5) organization—Farm income used to finance the operation and maintenance of a retirement home, hospital, or similar facility operated by the organization for its members on property adjacent to the farm land [section 1951(b)(8)(B) of Public Law 94–455]

Trade or Business

40 Gross income from an unrelated activity that is regularly carried on but, in light of continuous losses sustained over a number of tax periods, cannot be regarded as being conducted with the motive to make a profit (not a trade or business)

APPENDIX 11.1

Unified Registration
Statement

The National Association of Attorneys General and the National Association of State Charities Officials have put together the following unified registration statement called the "Standardized Registration for Nonprofit Organizations Under State Charitable Solicitation Laws" (Exhibit A.11.1). It is accepted by nearly all states requiring nonprofits to register for solicitation purposes. This 1998 version of the form does not replace the annual financial reporting that states may require. It also does not replace the specific additional requirements that each state may impose from time to time. It is reproduced here to give the manager an idea of kinds of information request that cut across state lines.

Exhibit A.11.1 Unified Registration Statement (URS) for Charitable Organizations.

☐ **Initial registration** ☐ **Renewal/Update**

This URS covers the reporting year which ended (day/month/year)_____

Filer EIN _____

State _____ State ID _____

1. Organization's legal name_____

   If changed since prior filings, previous name used _____

   All other name(s) used _____

2 (A). Street address _____

   City _____ County _____

   State _____ Zip Code _____

   (B). Mailing address (if different)

   City _____ County _____

   State _____ Zip Code _____

3. Telephone number(s)_____ Fax number(s) _____

   E-mail _____ Web site _____

4. Names, addresses (Street & P.O.), telephone numbers of other offices/chapters/branches/affiliates (attach list).

5. Date incorporated _____ State of incorporation _____
   Fiscal year end: day/month _____

6. If not incorporated, type of organization, state and date established _____

   _____

7. Has organization or any of its officers, directors, employees or fund raisers:

   A. Been enjoined or otherwise prohibited by a government agency/court
      from soliciting?   Yes ☐   No ☐

   B. Had its registration been denied or revoked?   Yes ☐   No ☐

   C. Been the subject of a proceeding regarding any solicitation or
      registration?   Yes ☐   No ☐

   D. Entered into a voluntary agreement of compliance with any government
      agency or in a case before a court or administrative agency?
      Yes ☐   No ☐

   E. Applied for registration or exemption from registration (but not yet
      completed or obtained)?   Yes ☐   No ☐

   F. Registered with or obtained exemption from any state or agency?
      Yes ☐   No ☐

G. Solicited funds in any state?   Yes ☐   No ☐

If "yes" to 7A, B, C, D, E, *attach explanation.*

If "yes" to 7F & G, *attach list* of states where registered, exempted or where it solicited, including registering agency, dates of registration, registration numbers, any other names under which the organization was/is registered, and the dates and type (mail, telephone, door to door, special events, etc.) of the solicitation conducted.

8. Has the organization applied for or been granted IRS tax exempt status?
   Yes ☐   No ☐

   If yes, date of application _____ OR date of determination letter _____.
   If granted, exempt under 501(c) _____. Are contributions to the organization tax deductible?   Yes ☐   No ☐

9. Has tax exempt status ever been denied, revoked or modified?
   Yes ☐   No ☐

10. Indicate all methods of solicitations:
    Mail ☐   Telephone ☐   Personal Contact ☐   Radio/TV Appeals ☐
    Special Events ☐   Newspaper/magazine ads ☐   Other(s) ☐
    (specify) _____

11. List the NTEE code(s) that best describes your organization ____, ____, ____

12. Describe the purposes and programs of the organization and those for which funds are solicited (*attach separate sheet if necessary*).

    _____
    _____
    _____
    _____
    _____

13. List the names, titles, addresses (Street & P. O.), and telephone numbers of officers, directors, trustees, and the principal salaried executives of organization (*attach separate sheet*).

14. (A) (1). Are any of the organization's officers, directors, trustees or employees related by blood, marriage, or adoption to: (i) any other officer, director, trustee or employee OR (ii) any officer, agent, or employee of any fundraising professional firm under contract to the organization OR (iii) any officer, agent, or employee of a supplier or vendor firm providing goods or services to the organization? Yes ☐   No ☐

    (2). Does the organization or any of its officers, directors, employees, or anyone holding a financial interest in the organization have a financial interest in a business described in (ii) or (iii) above OR

serve as an officer, director, partner or employee of a business
described in (ii) or (iii) above?   Yes ☐   No ☐
(If yes to any part of 14A, *attach sheet* which specifies the
relationship and provides the names, businesses, and addresses of
the related parties.)

(B). Have any of the organization's officers, directors, or principal executives
been convicted of a misdemeanor or felony? (*If yes, attach a complete
explanation.*)   Yes ☐   No ☐

15. *Attach separate sheet listing names and addresses (street & P.O.)
for all below:*

Individual(s) responsible for
custody of funds.

Individual(s) responsible for
distribution of funds.

Individual(s) responsible for
fund raising.

Individual(s) responsible for custody
of financial records.

Individual(s) authorized to sign
checks.

Bank(s) in which registrant's funds
are deposited (*include account number
and bank phone number*).

16. Name, address (Street & P.O.), and telephone number of accountant/auditor.

Name _____

Address_____

City _____ State _____ Zip Code _____ Telephone _____

Method of accounting _____

17. Name, address (Street & P.O.), and telephone number of person authorized to
receive service of process. *This is a state-specific item. See instructions.*

Name _____

Address _____

City _____ State _____ Zip Code _____ Telephone _____

18. **(A)**. Does the organization receive financial support from other non-profit
organizations (foundations, public charities, combined campaigns, etc.)?
Yes ☐   No ☐

(B). Does the organization share revenue or governance with any other
non-profit organization?   Yes ☐   No ☐

(C). Does any other person or organization own a 10% or greater interest in
your organization OR does your organization own a 10% or greater
interest in any other organization?   Yes ☐   No ☐

(If "yes" to A, B or C, *attach an explanation* including name of person or
organization, address, relationship to your organization, and type of
organization.)

19. Does the organization use volunteers to solicit directly?   Yes ☐   No ☐

Does the organization use professionals to solicit directly?   Yes ☐   No ☐

20. If your organization contracts with or otherwise engages the services of any outside fundraising professional (such as a "professional fundraiser," "paid solicitor," "fund raising counsel," or "commercial co-venturer"), *attach list* including their names, addresses (street & P.O.), telephone numbers, and location of offices used by them to perform work on behalf of your organization. Each entry *must include* a simple statement of services provided, description of compensation arrangement, dates of contract, date of campaign/event, whether the professional solicits on your behalf, and whether the professional at any time has custody or control of donations.

21. Amount paid to PFR/PS/FRC during previous year: $ _____

22. (A). Contributions in previous year: $ _____

(B). Fundraising cost in previous year: $ _____

(C). Management & general costs in previous year: $ _____

(D). Fundraising costs as a percentage of funds raised: _____

(E). Fundraising costs plus management & general costs as a percentage of funds raised: _____

Under penalty of perjury, we certify that the above information and the information contained in any attachments is true, correct, and complete.

Sworn to before me on (or signed on)_____, 19_____

_____

Notary public (if required)

_____	_____
Name (printed)	Name (printed)
_____	_____
Name (signature)	Name (signature)
_____	_____
Title (printed)	Title (printed)

Consult the state-by-state appendix to the URS to determine whether supporting documents, supplementary state forms or fees must accompany this form. Before submitting your registration, *make sure you have attached or included everything required by each state to the respective copy of the URS.*

Attachments may be prepared as one continuous document or as separate pages for each item requiring elaboration. In either case, please number the response to correspond with the URS item number.

APPENDIX 12.1

Key Concepts in Federal Contracting and Glossary of Common Financial Terms Found in Such Contracts

This appendix begins with a discussion of key principles in Federal contacting, which is followed by a glossary of terms used in Federal contracts.

KEY CONCEPTS IN FEDERAL CONTRACT MANAGEMENT

The Uniform Administrative Requirements for Grants and Agreements with Institutions of Higher Education, Hospitals, and Other Non-Profit Organizations (OMB Circular A-110) as issued on August 29, 1997 lays out key concepts that are consistent across Federal agencies when contracting with nonprofit organizations.Circular A-110 states that the organization must keep complete up-to-date records showing all costs and the documentation to support each, show unit costs when possible, develop procedures and exercise effective control over the use of program assets. Records must be kept for three years after the termination of a program. Furthermore, an awarding agency can impose the frequency and form of reporting it requires. They may also set specific milestones: key dates and accomplishments and to require explanations for why milestones are not met. Performance bonds (insurance) and property insurance may also be required as well as a commitment to considering minority and female firms when subcontracting portions of the Federal contract. A-110 also makes other provisions that are discussed below.

CONFLICT OF INTEREST

No Federal employee can participate in the awarding, administration or selection of a contractor if that employee has a relationship with the contractor. That relationship may be through the family of the employee, business or other associates of the employee. Nominal and unsolicited gifts to such employees by organization may be limited by specific agency rules.

CASH ADVANCES

Where electronic transfer is available, monthly advances on an automatic scheduled basis is possible. Advances will occur close to the period that actual payment of the expense by the organization must be made. Advances, where it is evident that the organization does not have the working capital, is possible. In general, advances that are in the form of reimbursement for expenses paid is preferred. Advances would not usually be denied unless the organization is delinquent on a debt to the United States or if the organization has failed to meet the terms of the contract—including under performance and failure to keep adequate records.

Advances must be kept in a secure interest-bearing account unless the depository requires an unusually large deposit before interest is paid or the interest that would be earned is less than $250 or the organization receives less than $120,000 from the Federal government per year.

COST SHARING

All contributions including those from a third party may be used in cost sharing arrangements, but the same contributions cannot be used in more than one Federal matching program, they must be verifiable, are necessary and reasonable for the accomplishment of the contract and were approved by the Federal agency. Federal contract money from one program cannot be used as a match for another Federal program, but indirect costs that were not recovered may be used with the agency's approval as a matching contribution.

Matching contributions of property must be their fair market value or the value as certified in the books of the organization prior to the contribution. The value of volunteer services is equal to the compensation (including fringes) of the same skills hired by the organization. If the organization does not hire such persons, then value is compensation an equivalent person would receive in the surrounding market.

When the donated property is land or equipment the value that is used to assess the organization's contribution depends upon where the project contemplated the acquisition of the land or equipment. If acquisition is the objective, then, the total fair market value of the equipment or land is used. If acquisition is not the objective, then, the value is the rental value or the depreciation. Rental value is used for donated space not intended to be permanently acquired.

PROGRAM INCOME

Program income can be used to finance objectives that are consistent with the contract, to fund the non-Federal portion of the contract, or be used to reduce the Federal cost of the program. When the Federal contract does not specify the use of program income, then, it is to be used to reduce the Federal cost of the program. Unless provided for, the organization has no obligation to the Federal government for program income earned after the end of the project. This may include income from patents, royalties, copyrights and sales.

BUDGET DEVIATIONS

Deviations from the approved contract budget must be reported. In particular, reduction in the time allotted by key personnel—defined as absence for more than three months or a 25 percent reduction—in time must be reported. The subcontracting of part of the contract unless previously provided for in the budget must also get approval. The budget may also be revised to include cost 90 days before the contract actually began and for a one-year extension after it is ended.

TITLE OF REAL PROPERTY

Unless provided otherwise, title to real property acquired through the contract remains with the organization as long as is needed. But the organization cannot sell, lease or pledge the property without the approval of the Federal government. When the property is no longer needed for the contract, the Federal government may allow the organization to retain the property or it may require to transfer the title. Property which is owned by the Federal government (not just acquired through the contract by the organization) remains under title of the government and a regular inventory of such properties may be asked for by the agency. However, at the end of the contract, the agency has the option of giving title to the organization as "Federally exempt property."

EQUIPMENT

Title of equipment acquired with the use of Federal funds remains with the organization. When the equipment is not be used for the project under which it was acquired, it may be used for other projects funded by the agency for which it was acquired or any other Federal agency. The organization is prohibited from leasing the property or charging fees for it to others that are less than the commercial rates. It is also not allowed to sell or pledge the property without permission.

At the end of the contract, the organization may be given the equipment (if less than $5000) or purchase or be instructed to transfer it at the agency's expense or to sell it. If the latter, a small commission may be earned by the organization.

SUPPLIES AND EXPENDABLE PROPERTY

The organization retains title to supplies and expendable property acquired to satisfy the contract. But upon termination, the Federal government must be paid if the fair market value of the total supplies bought through the contract and still in existence is at least $5000—assuming that the organization elects to keep the residual supplies. Supplies cannot be used by others outside of the organization without attaching a commercial use rate.

INTANGIBLE PERSONAL PROPERTY

The organization may copyright or patent its results emanating from the contract. However, the Federal government retains the right to royalty-free use of these results and may transfer this free use to others. These uses cover recording, publication, distribution, reproduction, and so on.

GLOSSARY

Circular A-110 is also useful because it contains a glossary of terms that the nonprofit manager will often see in Federal contracts. This is a compilation of definitions found in OMB Circulars A-122 and A-110 published by the Office of Management and Budget, Washington, D.C. Definitions marked with an asterisk are taken from Circular A-122. All other definitions are drawn from Circular A-110.

Accrued expenditures: The charges incurred by the recipient during a given period requiring the provision of funds for goods and other tangible property received; services performed by: employees, contractors, sub-recipients and other payees; and other amounts becoming owed under programs for which no current services or performance is required.

Accrued income: The sum earnings during a given period from services performed by the recipient, and goods and other tangible property delivered to purchasers; and amounts becoming owed to the recipient for which no current services or performance is required by the recipient.

Acquisition cost of equipment: The net invoice price of the equipment, including: the cost of modifications, attachments, accessories, or auxiliary apparatus necessary to make the property usable for the purpose for which it was acquired. Other charges, such as the cost of installation, transportation, taxes, duty or protective in-transit insurance, shall be included or excluded from the unit acquisition cost in accordance with the recipient's regular accounting practices.

Advance: A payable made by Treasury check or other appropriate payment mechanism to a recipient upon its result either before outlays are made by the recipient or through the use of predetermined payment schedules.

Award: Financial assistance that provides support or stimulation to accomplish a public purpose. Awards include grants and other agreements in the form of money or property in lieu of money, by the Federal government to an eligible recipient. The term does not include: technical assistance, which provides services instead of money; other assistance in the form of loans, loan guarantees, interest subsidies, or insurance; direct payments of any kind to individuals; and, contracts which are required to be entered into and administered under procurement laws and regulations.

Cash contributions: The recipient's cash outlay, including the outlay of money contributed to the recipient by third parties.

Closeout: The process by which a Federal awarding agency determines that all applicable administrative actions and all required work of the award have been completed by the recipient and Federal awarding agency.

Cognizant agency*: The Federal agency responsible for negotiating and approving indirect cost rates for a nonprofit organization on behalf of all Federal agencies.

Contract: A procurement contract under an award or sub-award, and a procurement sub-contract under a recipient's or sub-recipients contract.

Cost objective*: A function, organizational subdivision, contract, grant, or other work unit for which cost data are desired and for which provision is made to accumulate and measure the cost of processes, projects, jobs and capitalized projects.

Cost sharing or matching: That portion of project or program costs not borne by the Federal Government.

Date of completion: The date on which all work under an award is completed or the date on the award document, or any supplement or amendment thereto, on which Federal sponsorship ends.

Direct allocation method: Some nonprofit organizations treat all costs as direct costs except the general administration and general expenses. These organizations generally separate their costs into three basic categories: (1) general administration and general expenses, (2) fund raising, and (3) other direct functions (including projects performed under Federal awards.) Joint costs, such as depreciation, rental costs, operation and maintenance of facilities, telephone expenses, and the like are prorated individually as direct costs to each category and to each award, or other activity using a base most appropriate to the particular cost being prorated.

Disallowed costs: Those charges to an award that the Federal awarding agency determines to be unallowable, in accordance with the applicable Federal cost principles or other terms and conditions contained in the award.

Equipment: Tangible non-expendable personal property including exempt property charged directly to the award having a useful life of more than one year and an acquisition cost of $5,000 or more per unit. However, consistent with recipient policy, lower limits may be established.

Excess property: Tangible personal property acquired in whole or in part with Federal funds, where the Federal awarding agency has statutory authority to vest title in the recipient without further obligation to the Federal Government. An example of exempt property authority is contained in the Federal Grant and Cooperative Agreement Act (31 U.S.C. 6306), for property acquired under an award to conduct basic or applied research by a nonprofit institution of higher education or nonprofit organization whose principal purpose is conducting scientific research.

Federal awarding agency: The Federal agency that provides an award to the recipient.

Federal funds authorized: The total amount of Federal funds obligated by the Federal Government for use by the recipient. This amount may include any authorized carryover of unobligated funds from prior funding periods when permitted by agency regulations or agency implementing instructions.

Federal share of real property, equipment, or supplies: Percentage of the property's acquisition costs and any improvement expenditures paid with Federal funds.

Final rate*: An indirect cost rate applicable to a specified past period which is based on the actual costs of the period. A final rate is not subject to adjustment.

Fixed rate*: An indirect cost rate which has the same characteristics as a predetermined rate, except that the difference between the estimated costs and the actual costs of the period covered by the rate is carried forward as an adjustment to the rate computation of a subsequent period.

Funding period: The period of time when Federal funding is available for obligation by the recipient.

Indirect cost*: Those that have been incurred for common or joint objectives and cannot be readily identified with a particular final cost objective.

Indirect cost proposal*: The documentation prepared by an organization to substantiate its claim for the reimbursement of indirect costs. This proposal provides the basis for the review and negotiation leading to the establishment of an organization's indirect cost rate.

Intangible property and debt instruments: Is but is not limited to trademarks, copyrights, patents, and patent applications and such property as loans, notes and other debt instruments, lease agreements, stock and other instruments of property ownership, whether considered tangible or intangible.

Multiple allocation base method*: (1) Where an organization's indirect costs benefit its major functions in varying degrees, such costs shall be accumulated into separate cost groupings. Each grouping shall then be allocated individually to benefiting functions by means of a base, which best measures the relative benefits. (2) The groupings shall be established so as to permit the allocation of each grouping on the basis of benefits provided to the major functions. Each grouping should constitute a pool of expenses that are of like character in terms of the functions they benefit and in terms of the allocation base which best measures the relative benefits provided to each function. The number of separate groupings should be held within practical limits, taking into consideration the materiality of the amounts involved and the degree of precision desired.

Obligations: The amounts of orders placed, contracts and grants awarded, services received and similar transactions during a given period that require payment by the recipient during the same or a future period.

Outlays or expenditures: Charges made to the project or program. They may be reported on a cash or accrual basis. For reports prepared on a cash basis, outlays are the sum of cash disbursements for direct charges for goods and services, the amount of indirect expense charged, the value of third party in-kind contributions applied and the amount of cash advances and payments made to sub-recipients. For reports prepared on an accrual basis, outlays are the sum of cash disbursements for direct charges for goods and services, the amount of indirect expense incurred, the value of in-kind contributions applied, and the net increase (or decrease) in the amounts owed by the recipient for goods and other property received, for services performed by employees, contractors, sub-recipients and other payees and other amounts becoming owed under programs for which no current services or performance are required.

Personal property: Property of any kind except real property. It may be tangible, having physical existence, or intangible, having no physical existence, such as copyrights, patents, or securities.

Predetermined rate*: An indirect cost rate, applicable to a specified current or future period, usually the organization's fiscal year. The rate is based on an estimate of the costs to be incurred during the period. A predetermined rate is not subject to adjustment.

Prior approval: Written approval by an authorized official evidencing prior consent.

Program income: Gross income earned by the recipient that is directly generated by a supported activity or earned as a result of the award. Program income includes, but is not limited to, income from fees for services performed, the use or rental of real or personal property acquired under Federally funded projects, the sale of commodities or items fabricated under an award, license fees and royalties on patents and copyrights, and interest on loans made with award funds. Interest earned on advances of Federal funds is not program income. Except as otherwise provided in Federal awarding agency regulations or the terms and conditions of the award, program income does not include the receipt of principal on loans, rebates, credits, discounts, etc., or interest earned on any of them.

Project costs: All allowable costs, as set forth in the applicable Federal cost principles, incurred by a recipient and the value of the contributions made by third parties in accomplishing the objectives of the award during the project period.

Project period: The period established in the award document during which Federal sponsorship begins and ends.

Property: Real property, equipment, intangible property and debt instruments (unless otherwise stated.).

Provisional rate or billing rate*: A temporary indirect cost rate applicable to a specified period which is used for funding, interim reimbursement, and reporting indirect costs on awards pending the establishment of a final rate for the period.

Real property: Land, including land improvements, structures and appurtenances thereto, but excludes movable machinery and equipment.

Recipient: An organization receiving financial assistance directly from Federal awarding agencies to carry out a project or program. The term includes public and private institutions of higher education, public and private hospitals, and other quasi-public and private non-profit organizations such as, but not limited to, community action agencies, research institutes, educational associations, and health centers. The term may include commercial organizations, foreign or international organizations (such as agencies of the United Nations) which are recipients, sub-recipients, or contractors or subcontractors of recipients or sub-recipients at the discretion of the Federal-awarding agency. The term does not include government-owned contractor-operated facilities or research centers providing continued support for mission-oriented, large-scale programs that are government owned or controlled, or are designated as Federally funded research and development centers.

Research and development: All research activities, both basic and applied, and all development activities that are supported at universities, colleges, and other nonprofit institutions. "Research" is defined as a systematic, study directed toward fuller scientific knowledge or understanding of the subject studied. "Development" is the systematic use of knowledge and understanding gained from research directed toward the production of useful materials, devices, systems, or methods, including design and development of prototypes and processes. The term research also includes activities involving the training of individuals in research techniques where such activities utilize the same facilities as other research and development activities and where such activities are not included in the instruction function.

Simplified allocation method*: Where an organization's major functions benefit from its indirect costs to approximately the same degree the allocation of indirect costs may be accomplished by (a) separating the organization's total costs for the base period as either direct or indirect, and (b) dividing the total allowable indirect costs (net of applicable credits) by an equitable distribution base. The result of this process is an indirect cost rate that is used to distribute indirect costs to individual awards. The rate should be expressed as the percentage, which the total amount of allowable indirect costs bears to the base selected. This method should also be used where an organization has only one major function encompassing a number of individual projects or activities, and may be used where the level of Federal awards to an organization is relatively small.

Small awards: A grant or cooperative agreement not exceeding the small purchase threshold fixed at 41 U.S.C. 403 (11) (currently $25,000).

Sub-award: An award of financial assistance in the form of money, or property in lieu of money made under an award by a recipient to an eligible sub-recipient or by a sub-recipient to a lower tier sub-recipient. The term includes financial assistance when provided by any legal agreement, even if the agreement is called a contract, but does not include procurement of goods and services nor does it include any form of assistance which is excluded from the definition of "award."

Sub-recipient: The legal entity to which a sub-award is made and which is accountable to the recipient for the use of the funds provided. The term may include foreign or international organizations (such as agencies of the United Nations) at the discretion of the Federal-awarding agency.

Supplies: All personal property excluding equipment, intangible property, and debt instruments as defined in this section, and inventions of a contractor conceived or first actually reduced to practice in the performance of work under a funding agreement ("subject inventions"), as defined in 37 CFR part 401, "Rights to Inventions Made by Nonprofit Organizations and Small Business Firms Under Government Grants, Contracts, and Cooperative Agreements."

Suspension: An action by a Federal awarding agency that temporarily withdraws Federal sponsorship under an award, pending corrective action by the recipient or pending a decision to terminate the award by the Federal awarding agency. Suspension of an award is a separate action from suspension under Federal agency regulations implementing E.O.s 12549 and 12689, "Debarment and Suspension."

Termination: The cancellation of Federal sponsorship, in whole or in part, under an agreement at any time prior to the date of completion.

Third party in-kind contributions: The value of non-cash contributions provided by non-Federal third parties. Third party in-kind contributions may be in the form of real property, equipment, supplies and other expendable property, and the value of goods and services directly benefiting and specifically identifiable to the project or program.

Unliquidated obligation, for financial reports prepared on a cash basis: The amount of obligations incurred by the recipient that has not been paid. For reports prepared on an accrued expenditure basis, they represent the amount of obligations incurred by the recipient for which an outlay has not been recorded.

Unobligated balance: The portion of the funds authorized by the Federal awarding agency that has not been obligated by the recipient and is determined by deducting the cumulative obligations form the cumulative funds authorized.

Unrecovered indirect cost: The difference between the amount awarded and the amount, which could have been awarded under the recipient's approved, negotiated indirect cost rate.

Working capital advance: A procedure where by funds are advanced to the recipient to cover its estimated disbursement needs for a given initial period.

APPENDIX 12.2

Risks of Cost Denial

A major risk that any organization that contracts to do work for the federal government faces is that certain costs will not be honored. OMB Circular A-122, "Cost Principles for Nonprofit Organizations," explains how certain costs will be treated. I summarize these below beginning with a statement of the general principles that determine all cost recognition by the federal government.

The cost must be reasonable relative to the job, it must conform to government regulations on costs, must be applied consistently and uniformly across government and others, be documented, not be included in meeting cost-sharing requirements of any other government contract, and it must conform to generally accepted accounting principles. These principles are basic to billing the federal government. Table 14 gives specific costs and a brief statement of how they are likely to be treated according to Circular A-122.

Costs Item	Allowable Costs
Advertising	For the recruitment, disposal of surplus, and procurement of goods or services.
Bad debt	Not allowable.

Source: The text has been abbreviated from Office of Management and Budget, Circular A-122, "Costs Principles for Nonprofit Organizations," as reissued in June 1997.

Bonding costs	If required by the organization in general or the project in particular.
Communication	For telephone, mail, telegrams and the like.
Compensation	If reasonable and consistent for government and others. This includes incentives and fringe benefits. Insurance not covered if organization is beneficiary. Salaries must be amount actually incurred and signed by employee or supervisor for the periods past.
Contingency reserves	Amounts set aside for contingencies not allowable.
Contributions	Donations to other organizations not allowable.
Depreciation and use allowances	Allowed but must exclude cost of land, any portion of costs of building or equipment borne by or donated by government or any portion of costs of building or equipment contributed by or for the organization as part of a matching requirement.
Donations	Services donated to the organization itself are not allowable, but the fair market value of services donated to accomplish the specific government project may be included. Donation of space is not allowable.
Employee morale and welfare	Allowable but any fee charged must be credited against cost.
Entertainment	Not allowable.
Equipment and capital expenditures	Capital expenditures for building, equipment and improvements may be allowable with prior approval and may have to be treated as indirect cost.
Fines and penalties	Not allowable.
Fringe benefits	Allowable as part of compensation.

Idle facilities and capacity	Not allowable except to meet fluctuations in workloads or were necessary when project started.
Insurance and indemnification	Costs of insurance to protect government interest, as part of compensation are allowable. Indemnification of organization by government limited to agreement in contract.
Interest	On debt (other than from the organization's endowment) incurred to acquire facility in fulfillment of contract allowable but will depend upon size of debt and will be reduced by any interest earned on funds during the interim between debt proceeds and actual expenditures.
Labor relations	Allowable.
Lobbying	Not allowable.
Losses on other contracts	Not allowable.
Maintenance and repairs	Allowable to the extent that it does not add to value or life of building.
Materials and supplies	Allowable but price must be reduced for discounts or rebates.
Meetings and conferences	Allowable either as direct cost to project or to conduct the general administration of the organization.
Memberships, subscriptions, professional activities	Allowable.
Organizing, i.e., incorporating	Not allowable.
Overtime	Allowable only with approval unless lower costs to government would result or for emergencies or for administrative purposes.
Page charges in journals	Allowed.
Participant support	These costs when not related to employees are allowable only with prior approval. Cover training, symposia, conferences.

Patents	May not be allowable if government cannot get royalty-free use or title.
Pensions	See fringe and compensation.
Plant security	Allowable if necessary to comply with government security requirements.
Pre contract award	Allowable if approved but must be of the type that would be allowed after the contract.
Professional services	Allowable but not when associated with anti-trust or patent. Infringement defense.
Profits or losses on property	Generally not allowable on sale of depreciated property.
Public information service	Allowable but as direct cost to project that is seeking involvement or dissemination to general public.
Rearrangement and alteration	Allowable if normal or specifically for project. May need prior approval if specifically for project. Restoration Allowable to the extent to restore facilities to conditions immediately preceding award and to account for fair wear.
Recruiting	Allowable and may include costs of travel, education and headhunter.
Relocation	Allowable but must be reasonable and associated with a written policy. Move must benefit organization. May include costs of relocating family, closing costs incident to the disposition of former home, continuing costs of holding that home. Fees associating with acquiring new home or losses from sale of old home or mortgage payments on that home are not allowable.

Rental	Allowable. Under certain circumstances may be limited to the costs if organization had own the property.
Royalties	Allowed when necessary for performance of contract. When royalty is paid to the organization, reasonableness is necessary.
Severance Pay	Allowable but on a case-by-case basis.
Specialized services	Allowable—sometimes as direct and sometimes as indirect costs.
Taxes	Allowable but must be reduced by refunds or credits.
Termination costs	Allowable if retention would cause losses. Settlement fees and unexpired leases allowed. With later, organization must try to reduce or avoid and must subtract any residual value.
Training and education	Allowable whether or not training is by organization. May vary by whether education is full or part-time.
Transportation	Allowable. Includes freight, cartage, postage.
Travel	Allowable but the difference between first-class and less than that class will not be allowed unless not available. Includes lodging, subsistence, transportation. Foreign travel may have to receive prior approval.

Accounting for Gifts and Contributions

Here are eleven basic rules for accounting for gifts and contributions.

1. FASB Statement 116 requires that a transfer of cash or other financial assets from a donor be recorded as unrestricted support when received free of any donor-set restrictions, after the conditions of these restrictions are substantially met or if there is no remote possibility whatever that such conditions will not be met. Otherwise, the transfer to the organization should be recorded as restricted. The restriction may be temporary or permanent.

2. FASB Statement 117 requires that all accounts be recorded in the statement of financial position as unrestricted, permanently restricted, or temporarily restricted. It further requires that changes in these net assets be recorded in the statement of activities. It does not prohibit the organization from using other means of categorizing funds for its own purposes. Under any of the three major categories, the organization may have subcategories; that is, gifts permanently restricted by donors for building maintenance. Board restrictions are treated as unrestricted. The crucial restriction under 117 is the donor

Source: Herrington J. Bryce, *Not-for-Profit Financial Strategies,* a newsletter published by Harcourt Brace Professional Publishers.

restriction—a requirement for the passage of a specific time or occurrence of an event without which the donor is free of his or her promise to contribute or is entitled to a return of the gift.

3. A promise to give is treated as contribution revenue and receivable if the promise is unconditional, if the condition is substantially met or has no remote chance of not being met. Before a promise can be recognized for accounting purposes, however, there must be some reproducible evidence of it. A promise, of course, may be restricted (temporarily or permanently) or unrestricted.

4. A conditional promise to give is not recognized. An unconditional promise to give is recorded at present net realizable value (gross value of the gift is based on the date it is expected to be received by the organization minus an allowance for uncollectible portions). An appreciation in the value of the property before it is received is not recognized but a decline is. The discount rate used should be a risk-free rate and not the rate at which the donor or donee borrows. The discount is recorded as a reduction from contributions receivable and may be placed in the notes.

5. In-kind gifts must be recorded at fair market value adjusted, for example, for quantity discounts. Worthless gifts do not have to be recognized.

6. Contributed services are recognized if they enhance the value of a non-monetary asset, or are rendered by a specialist such as a lawyer, accountant, appraiser, or teacher and if the organization would otherwise have had to purchase that service. The service is recorded at fair market value.

7. Donations of utilities such as electricity are recognized when given but expensed as used.

8. Donations of long-lived assets are recognized when given but are capitalized.

9. Donations of split-interest gifts such as an annuity or remainder and lead trusts are treated in two portions and depend upon whether a third party is the trustee of the gift. Under the latter situation, the gift may have to be first recorded as an intent to give. If there is no third party, the portion of the gift going to the not-for-profit will be treated as revenue or gain and recorded as an investment (if that is what it is) and the second part is treated as a liability to the recipient—normally a noncharity.

10. Transfers received by one entity for another entity in which it is tied by economic interests (a foundation for its parents) are recorded by the

first entity as a contribution and by the second as a claim against the assets of the first.

11. Transfers to one entity on behalf of another (to which it is not tied) are recorded by the first as a liability to the second and recorded by the second as a receivable from the first—unless the first has the power to deny or vary the transfer to the second. See the exposure draft referred to below.

See FASB Statements No. 116, 117, and the exposure draft "Transfers of Assets Involving a Not-for-Profit Organization that Raises or Holds Contributions for Others."

NOTES

Chapter One

1. Ronald R. Sims and John G. Veres III. *Keys to Employee Success in Coming Decades.* (Westport, CT: Quorum Books, 1999), p. 1.

2. Regina Herzingler. "Can Public Trust in Nonprofits and Governments Be Restored?" *Harvard Business Review,* March–April 1996, 97–107.

3. American Institute of Certified Public Accountants. SAS 47. *Audit Risk and Materiality in Conducting an Audit.* (Westport, CT, 1994).

4. Ronald R. Sims. *Ethics and Organizational Decision Making: A Call for Renewal.* (Westport, CT: Quorum Books, 1994), pp. 189–209.

5. See Herrington J. Bryce. "Trustees vs. Scoundrels." *Director's Monthly.* (Washington, D.C.: National Association of Corporate Directors, July 1995), p. 9; "Many Ask: What Are the Duties of Trusteeship?" *Museum Trusteeship,* 6(4), (Washington, D.C., September 1992), p. 1.

Chapter Two

1. *Church of the Chosen People v. U.S.,* U.S.D.C. Minn. Civil 4:81–311, 10/18 82, 82–2 U.S.T.C., Section 9646.

2. This is the author's extraction from the Canadian Supreme Court's decision in the case, *Vancouver Society of Immigrant and Visible Minority Women* v. *Minister of National Revenue and others,* File 25359, January 28, 1998. The numbers in parentheses give the page source of specific quotations or near quotations.

Chapter Four

1. Revenue Letter 9047001.

2. Note that the income test for private operating foundations requires the lesser of the adjusted net income or minimum investment income. The distribution requirement for private foundations is that the greater of the two be distributed.

3. Summarized by the author from the Ontario Law Reform Commission, Law on Charities, *Report on the Law on Charities*. (Ontario, Canada: Queen's Printer for Ontario, 1998).

Chapter Five

1. *American Society of Association Executives Operating Ratio Report*. (Washington, D.C.: American Society of Association Executives, 1998).

2. This discussion is distilled by the author from the Associations Incorporation Act of 1985 of South Australia.

Chapter Six

1. IRS Private Letter 8948034.

2. Stewart P. Hoover, "Nonprofit Corporations and Maryland's Director and Officer Liability Statute: A Study of the Mechanics of Maryland's Statutory Corporate Law," *University of Baltimore Law Review, 18,* no. 2 (Winter 1989), 384–402.

3. Stewart P. Hoover, "Nonprofit Corporations and Maryland's Director and Officer Liability Statute: A Study of the Mechanics of Maryland's Statutory Corporate Law," *University of Baltimore Law Review, 18,* no. 2 (Winter 1989), 384–402; and James J. Hanks, Jr., and Larry P. Scriggins, "Let Stockholders Decide: The Origins of the Maryland Director and Officer Liability Statute of 1988," *University of Baltimore Law Review, 18,* no. 2 (Winter 1989), 235–253.

4. Julie J. Bisceglia, "Practical Aspects of Director's and Officers' Liability Insurance—Allocating Legal Fees and the Duty to Defend," *UCLA Law Review, 322,* no. 3 (Feb. 1985), pp. 690–718.

5. Michael Gawel, "Directors and Officers Indemnification Insurance: What Is Being Offered?" *Journal of the American Society of CLU, 39,* no. 6 (Nov. 1985), 92–101.

6. *Chronicle of Higher Education, The Washington Post, The Wall Street Journal* are among the newspapers telling about the Barnes during the 1990s—often several times.

7. Blenda Wilson, in *Reports,* Association of Governing Boards of Universities and Colleges, Jan.–Feb. 1990, p. 2.

Chapter Seven

1. The 1986 tax reform allows only taxpayers who itemize deductions to deduct charitable contributions. The literature showing a close and strong correlation between the deductibility of a gift and giving is extensive. It includes Charles T. Clotfelter, *Federal Tax Policy and Charitable Giving.* (Chicago: University of Chicago Press, 1985); Martin Feldstein and Charles Clotfelter, "Tax Incentives and Charitable Contributions in the United States," *Journal of Public Economics, 5* (1976), 1–26; Charles T. Clotfelter and E. Eugene Steuerle, "Charitable Contributions," in Henry Aaron and Joseph Pechman, *How Taxes Affect Economic Behavior.* (Washington, D.C.: Brookings Institution, 1981); Michael Taussig, "Economic Aspects of the Personal Income Tax Treatment of Charitable Contributions," *National Tax Journal, 20,* no. 1 (March 1967), 1–19.

2. On the relationship between taxation and the estate tax, see Thomas Barthold and Robert Plotnick, "Estate Taxation and Other Determinants of Charitable Bequests," *National Tax Journal, 38,* no. 2 (June 1984), 225–236; Michael J. Boskin, "Estate Taxation and Charitable Bequests," *Commission on Private Philanthropy and Public Need.* (Washington, D.C.: U.S. Treasury, 1977), pp. 1453–1483; Martin S. Feldstein, "Charitable Bequests, Estate Taxation, and Intergenerational Wealth Transfer," *Commission on Private Philanthropy and Public Need.* (Washington, D.C.: U.S. Treasury, 1977), pp. 1485–1497.

3. For a review of the literature on this topic, see Melvin M. Mark and R. Lance Shotland, "Increasing Charitable Contributions: An Experimental Evaluation of the American Cancer Society's Recommended Solicitation Procedures," *Journal of Voluntary Action Research, 12,* no. 3 (Apr.–June 1983), 8–21.

4. J. L. Freedman and S. C. Fraser, "Compliance Without Pressure: The Foot in the Door Technique," *Journal of Personality and Social Psychology, 31* (1975), 206–215.

5. R. B. Cialdini and others, "Reciprocal Concessions Procedure for Inducing Compliance: The Door-in-the-Face Technique," *Journal of Personality and Social Psychology, 31* (1975), 206–215.

6. C. Wagner and L. Wheeler, "Model, Need, and Cost Effects in Helping Behavior," *Journal of Personality and Social Psychology, 12* (1969), 111–116; and J. H. Bryan and M. A. Test, "Models and Helping: Naturalistic Studies in Aiding Behavior," *Journal of Personality and Social Psychology, 6* (1967), 400–407.

7. R. B. Cialdini and D. A. Schroeder, "Increasing Contributions by Legitimizing Paltry Contributions," *Journal of Personality and Social Psychology, 34* (1976), 599–604.

8. See Mark and Shotland, "Increasing Charitable Contributions: An Experimental Evaluation of the American Cancer Society's Recommended Solicitation Procedures," *Journal of Voluntary Action Research, 12,* no. 3 (Apr.–June 1983), 11.

9. James N. Morgan, Richard F. Dye, and Judith H. Hybels, "Results from Two National Surveys of Philanthropic Activity," *Research Papers: Commission on Philanthropy and Public Needs, 1* (Washington, D.C.: U.S. Treasury, 1977), 157–324, especially Table 17.

10. James N. Morgan, Richard F. Dye, and Judith H. Hybels, "Results from Two National Surveys of Philanthropic Activity," *Research Papers: Commission on Philanthropy and Public Needs, 1* (Washington, D.C.: U.S. Treasury, 1977), p. 201.

11. Charles T. Clotfelter and E. Eugene Steuerle, "Charitable Contributions," in Henry Aaron and Joseph Pechman, *How Taxes Affect Economic Behavior.* (Washington, D.C.: Brookings Institution, 1981).

12. R. Palmer Baker, Jr., and J. Edward Schillingburg, "Corporate Charitable Contributions," *Research Papers: Commission on Philanthropy and Public Needs, 3* (Washington, D.C.: U.S. Treasury, 1977), 1853–1905.

13. Alfred C. Neal, "A More Rational Basis for Nonprofit Activities," *Conference Board Record, 5* (Jan. 1968), 5–7.

14. Richard Eells, "A Philosophy for Corporate Giving," *Conference Board Record, 5* (Jan. 1968), 14–17.

15. W. J. Baumol, "Enlightened Self-interest and Corporate Philanthropy," *Foundations, Private Giving and Public Policy: Report and Recommendations of the Commission on Foundations and Private Philanthropies.* (Chicago: University of Chicago Press, 1971), pp. 22–75.

16. James F. Harris and Anne Klepper, "Corporate Philanthropic Public Service Activities," *Research Papers: Commission on Philanthropy and Public Needs, Vol. 3* (Washington, D.C.: U.S. Treasury, 1977), pp. 1741–1788.

17. For a review of these, see Bette Ann Stead, "Corporate Giving: A Look at the Arts," *Journal of Business Ethics, 4,* no. 3 (1985), 215–222; and Frank Koch, "A Primer on Corporate Philosophy," *Business and Society Review, 38* (1980), 48–52.

18. Congressional Research Service, "Charitable Contributions: Pros and Cons of Deductibility." (Washington, D.C.: Government Printing Office, 1990).

19. The Combined Federal Campaign, *Employee Benefits Review.* (Aug. 1990), pp. 1–3. No author.

20. *Venni* v. *Commissioner,* Tax Court Memo 1984–17, 1/10/84.

21. *Davis* v. *Commissioner,* 81 Tax Court No. 49, 10/26/83.

22. *Magin* v. *Commissioner,* Tax Court Memo 1982–383, 7/7/82.

23. The value of the gift is the difference between the exercise price and the fair market value of the property at the time the option is exercised.

24. *Wall Street Journal,* Oct. 12, 1988, p. 1.

25. See the discussion of the attribution rule in Chapter Four.

26. A donation could not be made of the legs of the horse while the owner keeps the body. The property may be made up of a single item or many items.

27. The value of the easement is the difference between the market price before the easement and the price after the easement. The easement tends to reduce the price of the property by restricting its use and market.

28. Properties such as this are best passed on by creating a trust. As we shall see in Chapter Eight, these rules are aimed at preserving the property for the person with the remainder interest.

29. *Tax Notes,* May 1, 1989, p. 554. Revenue Ruling 63–252.

30. Revenue Ruling 84–132, 1984–1 Cumulative Bulletin.

31. Revenue Ruling 67–246.

32. *Kenneth Allen and Barbara Allen* v. *Commissioner,* Tax Court, No. 22877–84, Sept. 5, 1989.

33. *Joel H. Goldstein and Elain P. Goldstein* v. *Commissioner,* Tax Court Report No. 89, p. 535.

34. The principal on the debt is deductible as a gift, but the interest is not because the interest is otherwise deductible as other interest payments are.

35. Peter H. Karlin, "Appraiser's Responsibility for Determining Fair Market Value," *Columbia Journal of Law and the Arts, 13,* no. 2 (Winter 1989), pp. 185–220.

36. Peter H. Karlin, "Appraiser's Responsibility for Determining Fair Market Value," *Columbia Journal of Law and the Arts, 13,* no. 2 (Winter 1989), pp. 185–220.

37. Allen W. Kaftinow, T. C. Memo 1986–396.

38. The current penalty is 30 percent of the true tax liability.

39. Depreciation is a deductible allowance for the use of capital in production of income. Excess depreciation is the difference between a constant sum taken every year and one that assumes that the rate of use of capital per year is largest in the first years.

40. It is true that most times capital gains are not taxable to nonprofits. However, this example is not unlikely if the gift is to a private foundation holding it as an investment, if the property is acquired by debt as that concept is defined in Chapter Ten, and if the property is part of an inventory. Any of these could lead to the results stated.

41. Long-term capital gain property must be held for twelve or more months. Current law divides holding periods less than twelve, twelve to eighteen months, five years.

42. Internal Revenue Letter 9037001.

43. *William Thornton* v. *Commissioner,* No. 89–70147, July 24, 1990.

44. *Alexander Weintrob* v. *Commissioner,* T.C. Memo 1990, p. 513.

45. Adjusted gross income is essentially all one's income except such items as workmen's compensation, insurance proceeds, individual retirement account contributions, and certain expenses, such as moving expenses.

46. "Large" simply means sufficient to affect the classification of the nonprofit. The number of dollars that may be large for one organization may be small for another. See Chapter Three.

47. The author's principal source for Canadian tax information is *Gifts and Income Tax,* P113(E), Rev. 98 1920, published by Revenue Canada.

Chapter Eight

1. *American Bar Endowment* v. *U.S.*, 56 AFTR 2d 85–5005 (5–10–85), aff'g and rev'g, in part, 53 AFTR 2d 84–942. The Claims Court also concluded that the income derived by the American Bar Association was not taxable to them; that is, it was not unrelated business income. But on April 28, 1986, the Supreme Court ruled that this was an unrelated business and was taxable. (*Supreme Court of the United States, United States* v. *American Bar Endowment,* No. 85–599, April 28, 1986.)

2. The laws on income, estate, and gift taxes state that if the creator of a trust has any incidence of ownership in the property that is in the trust, that person is deemed to derive economic benefits from it and therefore must pay both income and estate taxes on the earnings and value of the property. This rule, as we shall see, is relaxed in the case of charitable remainder trusts.

3. There are some differences in the treatment of irrevocable and revocable trusts at the time of death. If, for example, a trust is revocable and becomes irrevocable at the time of death through the estate, then a "reasonable" period is granted to transform the trust to a charitable one. The basic point to keep in mind is that a revocable transfer, even though a trust, is not a gift.

4. The reader should see the discussion in Chapter Seven for more on the treatment of real property and other partial gifts.

5. Paul Taylor, "Hughes Settlement," *Washington Post,* Thursday, August 30, 1984, p. C18.

6. See the Ellsworth B. Warner Estate, file 15–81–1118, in the office of the Register of Wills, Chester County Courthouse, Westchester, Pennsylvania.

7. Associated Press story appearing in *Washington Post,* February 8, 1986, page A2.

8. A "reasonable period" is that period required for the trustees to perform the ordinary duties of the trust. This includes the collection of assets, the payment of debt, the payment of taxes, and the determination of the rights of the subsequent beneficiaries.

9. Chapter Seven discusses capital gains and charitable contributions and organizations.

10. Normally, a property is valued on the date of death. An alternate date is six months after that period or anytime within the first six months that the property is first distributed. If the value of the property is affected by the mere lapse of time, such as a savings account or an annuity because it increases in value over time, then the property is valued as of the time of death.

11. Loans from the policy to purchase income-producing assets will lead to an unrelated business income tax because the assets would have been acquired through debt. *Mose & Garrison Sisken Memorial Foundation, Inc.* v. *U.S.*, 55 AFTR 2d 85–1024, (12–4–84). See also Chapter Ten of this book. Loans taken within the first seven years of a policy can create an income-tax liability. Check with your tax advisor before taking loans in the first seven years of the contract.

12. We say immediately or within a few years because with a term policy one pays every year as long as the term lasts. One could conceivably pay every year for seventy years or more, in which case some single premiums or universal life policies would have afforded greater leverage.

13. See J. Barry McGannon, "The Endowment Builders of Saint Louis University," *Fund Raising Management,* January 1988, p. 24.

14. I am grateful to Barrett Caron for the example.

15. This strategy, which I have concocted, may be less simple from a tax perspective than it appears. A tax attorney should check the following: the unrelated business income tax, exchange of value treatment of insurance contracts, and bargain sale implications.

16. General Consul's Memorandum (GEM) 39826.

Chapter Nine

1. Herrington J. Bryce, "Profitability of HMOs: Does Non-Profit Status Make a Difference," *Health Policy,* Vol. 28 (1994), pp. 197–210.

2. For a review of the literature on this subject, see John P. Persons, John J. Osborn, Jr., and Charles F. Feldman, "Criteria for Exemption under Section 501(c)(3)," *Research Papers: Commission on Philanthropy and Public Needs, 4* (Washington, D.C.: U.S. Treasury, 1979), pp. 1909–2075.

3. John P. Persons, John J. Osborn, Jr., and Charles F. Feldman, "Criteria for Exemption under Section 501(c)(3)," *Research Papers: Commission on Philanthropy and Public Needs, 4* (Washington, D.C.: U.S. Treasury, 1979), pp. 1909–2075.

4. Revenue Ruling 74–587, 1974–2, Cumulative Bulletin 162, and Revenue Ruling 81–284, 1981–2, Cumulative Bulletin 230.

5. General Consul's Memorandum, 39047, 1/2/83.

6. Revenue Ruling 76–94, 1976–1, Cumulative Bulletin 171.

7. Revenue Ruling 81–62, 1981–1, Cumulative Bulletin 355.

8. *Fraternal Medical Services Incorporated* v. *Commissioner,* Tax Court Memorandum, 84, 644 (12–20–84).

9. *Black's Dictionary of Law,* 5th ed. (St. Paul, MN: West Publishing Company, 1979), p. 212.

10. *Fraternal Medical Specialist Services, Inc.* v. *Commissioner,* Tax Court Memorandum, 84, 644 (12–20–84).

11. *Church in Boston* v. *Commissioner,* 71 Tax Court Memo 102, 106 (1978).

12. *Better Business Bureau* v. *United States,* 326 U.S. 279 (34 after 5) (1945). This is a seminal case.

13. *Trinidad* v. *Sagrada Orden,* 263 U.S. 578, 581, 44 S. Ct. 204, 205, 68 L. Ed. 458 (1924).

14. Revenue Ruling, 73–104, 1973–1, Cumulative Bulletin.

15. *American College of Physicians* v. *United States,* Appeal No. 84–715, Sept. 17, 1984.

16. Revenues Ruling 73–105, 1973–1, Cumulative Bulletin 264. See Alan J. Yanowitz and Elizabeth A. Purcell, "IRS's Recent Approaches to Retail Sales by Exempt Organizations: Analyzing Standards," *Journal of Taxation, 59,* no. 4 (Oct. 1983), 250–255, for a comparison.

17. See Persons et al., Research Papers, for history and citations of congressional debate. At least one economist argues that the law is unfair because it tends to encourage nonprofits to stick to related businesses. The consequence of this is that for-profit industries that are most likely to be a related business for nonprofits must contend with competition from nonprofits, whereas other sectors less likely to be a related business do not face the same intervention and competition from non-profits. Competition is healthy for the economy. Susan Rose-Ackerman, "Unfair Competition and Corporate Income Taxation," *Stanford Law Review, 34,* no. 36 (1982), 1017–1039.

18. *Piety Inc.* v. *Commissioner,* 82 T.C. No. 16, 1/26/84.

19. *Church of Scientology of California* v. *Commissioner,* U.S. Tax Court Docket, 3352–78.

20. Society of Costa Rica Collectors, T.C.M. 1984–648, 12/13/84.

21. Annual salaries and benefits data for foundations can be obtained from the Council of Foundations and from the Society of Association Executives, both of Washington, D.C.

22. Alan Piper, *Philanthropy in an Age of Transition.* (New York: The Foundation Center, 1984), p. 23.

23. Technically, one could make a gift to a for-profit corporation, but this is not a normal source of revenues for such corporations.

24. Nonprofits cannot be shareholders in Subchapter S corporations, which are corporations with special tax advantages. We are therefore referring to a regular corporation.

25. Economic or normal profits are the percentage, over full cost, that represents a return to capital when the capital market is in equilibrium, that is, when no lender wishes to shift funds to some other user. For-profit firms in highly competitive markets that are new and developing often use a price that is so low that potential competitors are kept out because they would not be able to make a profit or pay the interest on the funds they would have to borrow to enter the business. Contrary to popular opinion, a for-profit firm does not always charge the highest price possible.

26. Goodwill is the amount paid for assets that is above the value of the asset. Goodwill reflects a number of intangibles, such as the existence of a clientele, good location, and a good reputation. A seller of a business that has a large clientele would ask more for that business than if the business had no clients at all.

27. When we refer to benefits and present value in this section, we are talking about a net concept. The expected operating costs each year are deducted from the expected operating revenues, and we find the present value of this net. In the income statement, it is represented by the income or revenues from operation.

28. Charles A. Berry and Edward B. Roberts, "Entering New Businesses," *Sloan Management Review, 26,* no. 3 (Spring 1985), 3–15.

29. Wherever there is a controversy, there are several sides to the same story. Rather than list all the articles and books that have come out, each of which is an advocate (even discussed as an academic treatise) of one position or the other, I recommend reading the hearings of the U.S. House of Representatives, Subcommittee on Oversight of the Committee on Ways and Means, 1987. The testimony of then Deputy Assistant Secretary (Tax Policy) O. Donald Chapoton is particularly good because it provides a rich factual background.

30. Private Letter Ruling 955003.

Chapter Ten

1. These numbers are calculated from the 1989 annual reports of these organizations.

2. *NCAA* v. *Commissioner,* no. 89, 9005 (10th Circuit 9/20/90).

3. Revenue Letters 9629030 and 9630031.

4. Revenue Letter 9629002.

5. Revenue Letter 9046039.

6. April 28, 1986, No. 1986–17, page 9.

7. "Not-for-profit" does not necessarily imply a charitable or related business, just that there is no motive for a profit, for example, a hobby.

8. *West Virginia State Medical Association* v. *Commissioner,* T.C. 3746–86, 9/20/88, and *North Ridge Country Club* v. *Commissioner,* T.C. 20651–82, 9/15/87.

9. *Living Faith* v. *Commissioner,* T.C. Memo 1990–484.

10. Supreme Court of the United States, *United States* v. *American College of Physicians,* No. 84–1737, April 22, 1986, p. 2.

11. *U.S.* v. *City of Spokane,* No. 90–35118 (9th Circuit, Oct. 31, 1990).

12. Fundamental research is distinguished from applied or commercial research. The latter is done to assist others to be profitable, and the results need not be published within a reasonable time.

13. GCM 39825.

14. TAM 8445005, GCM 39825 and Sec. 1.512(b)–1(c)(5) of the Code.

Chapter Eleven

1. The operative word is deductible. Even in exchanges involving property of like kind, such as real estate, there is no deductibility. Such exchanges, called 1035 exchanges, are not taxable.

2. Whether these taxes are assessed depends on the transaction being classified as an unrelated or related business income. See Chapter Ten.

3. These rules are explained in Revenue Procedures 90–21.

4. IRS Private Letter Ruling, 9004030, February 5, 1990.

5. Leon E. Wynter, "Edley of United Negro College Fund to Retire after 17 Years in Top Post." *Wall Street Journal*, Aug. 1, 1990, p. B4.

6. Emmett D. Carson, *The Charitable Appeals Fact Book: How Blacks and Whites Respond to Different Types of Fund-raising Efforts* (Lanham, MD: University Press of America, 1989).

7. Ann Bubnic's research on physicians as discussed in "Doctors Are Not Stingy, A New Survey Shows." *Nonprofit Times.* (May 1988), p. 3.

8. Lyle E. Schaller, "Megachurch." *Christianity Today*, May 5, 1990, pp. 20–24.

9. Wade Lambert and Wayne E. Green, "Law." *Wall Street Journal*, Mar. 8, 1990, B8.

10. Based on Internal Revenue Letter 9044071.

11. Based on Internal Revenue Letter 9023003.

12. Internal Revenue Letter 8828011.

Chapter Twelve

1. Some levels of efficiency are required by law. Day-care centers, hospitals, and housing providers are all subject to legal regulations that affect their productivity. Housing providers, for example, must meet housing codes; hospitals and day-care centers must meet health and zoning codes.

2. See *Federal Register*, 45(132), July 8, 1980, p. A6025, for federal regulations concerning overhead specifically for nonprofits.

3. See citation in the Suggested Readings section.

4. It is possible to consider a membership center a revenue or profit center as well because it generates revenues and because it is hoped that its revenues are greater than its costs so that it generates an excess for the organization. The issue being discussed, however, is not what the center is called, but how its costs are treated.

5. *Rensselaer Polytechnic Institute* v. *Commissioner*, Docket k#7024–79, 79 Tax Court #60, 12/1/82.

6. Revenue Ruling 79–18 and Revenue Ruling 72–124.

Chapter Thirteen

1. Disability tax liabilities depend on who pays the premiums and the extent to which the payments of disability income may be construed as regular salary payments. If they can be construed as regular salary payments, they are neither exempt nor eligible for tax credit but are taxable as regular income.

2. The requirements are more lenient when the disability is blindness.

3. Death benefits for any single death that do not exceed a total of $5,000 are exempt from income taxes by the recipients.

4. The requirements for conversion may be more difficult if the separation is due to the demise of the organization.

5. Consider the tax effect. When an organization pays the contribution, it is not taxable to the employee as income. However, if the employee receives the same amount as payment, not only will it be taxed as income, but the after-tax income, being smaller, will buy less insurance.

6. Survivors who are themselves recipients of Social Security retirement benefits may elect between receiving their check or the check of the deceased spouse, but two checks cannot be received.

7. Basically, both the event that caused the injury and the injury itself must be accidental.

8. See Section 13–10 of the Public Health Service Act of 1973, and Section 42 of the Code of Federal Regulations, Part 110–801.

9. There are several variations of benefit definitions; for example, it might be the average salary earned in the final ten, five, or three years of the worker's tenure. The years may or may not have to be consecutive. There are numerous variations.

10. The factors that are placed in the actuarial equation to determine the amount that must be contributed include the defined benefit, the annual valuation of the pension fund, the expected mortality rate, the withdrawal rate, and the expected interest earnings.

11. There are SIMPLE plans, which we discuss in this chapter, that permit the employer to make deposits into the IRA accounts held by the employee.

12. Actually, there is a strict mathematical rule stating that 70 percent of the workers (excluding those previously mentioned) must be eligible and, if only 70 percent are eligible, then 80 percent must benefit.

13. The IRS disallows vesting schedules that are too restrictive. Variations from the schedules discussed should be attempted with extreme caution.

14. An organization may give a worker a five-year period during which he or she may be away from paid employment with the organization. But at the end of that period, the worker either buys back into the system and becomes a participating employee in the plan, or all previous credits earned toward vesting or eligibility may be forfeited. Once the employee reenters the plan, he or she may recoup one year of eligibility for every one year worked.

15. It is important that this process be understood. The plan must be the employer's, not the employee's. Even though the contributions come from the employee's pay, the transfer of funds must be made by the employer in accordance with a written agreement. The employee cannot first receive pay and then give money to the employer to place in the fund. This would constitute constructive receipt, and the contribution would be taxed as income to the employee.

16. The actual amount that can be contributed depends on the election of one of three formulas by the employee. There was an upper limit, however, of the lesser of 25 percent of income or $30,000. This limit has been changed to $9,500 by the U.S. Congress.

17. Prior to January 1, 1985, the employee could choose among cash, nontaxable and taxable benefits, and property. Now the employee must choose between cash and nontaxable benefits.

18. Revenue Ruling 69–383, 69–2 Cumulative Bulletin 113, General Counsel Memorandum 38283, Internal Revenue Service, Feb. 15, 1980, and prior to that General Counsel Memorandum 35638, Jan. 28, 1974. For a brief history of the IRS position on these plans, see Edward J. Schnee and Walter A. Robbins, "Profit-Sharing Plans and Tax-Exempt Organizations—A New Benefit for All." *Taxes—The Tax Magazine, 62*(4) (April 1984), 220–223.

19. See General Counsel Memorandum, 35638.

20. Edward J. Schnee and Walter A. Robbins, "Profit-Sharing Plans and Tax-Exempt Organizations," pp. 220–223 (see note 18).

21. For a comparison of 403(b) and 401(k) properties, see Labh S. Hira, "Profit-Sharing Plans for Nonprofit Entities." *Taxes—The Tax Magazine, 62*(10) (Oct. 1984), 679–683. See also Robert J. Angell and Joseph E. Johnson, "403(b) Loans: A Money Machine." *Journal of the American Society of CLU, 39*(1) (1985), 56–61.

22. 1989 *Annual Report,* Boys Clubs (now Boys and Girls Clubs) of America, p. 29.

Chapter Fourteen

1. *The Citation, 60*(3), Nov. 15, 1990, p. 84.

2. *The Citation, 60*(7), Jan. 15, 1990, p. 84.

3. *The Citation, 60*(7), Jan. 15, 1990.

4. Kelly W. Bhirdo, "The Liability and Responsibility of Institutions of Higher Education for the On-Campus Victimization of Students." *Journal of College and University Law, 16* (Summer 1989), 119–135.

5. Fernand N. Dutile, "Higher Education and the Courts: 1988 in Review." *Journal of College and University Law, 16*(2) (Fall 1989), 201–285.

6. Fernand N. Dutile, "Higher Education and the Courts: 1988 in Review." *Journal of College and University Law, 16*(2) (Fall 1989), 201–285.

7. Susan J. Curry, "Hazing and the Rush." *Journal of College and University Law, 16*(1) (Summer 1989), 93–118.

8. Terri S. Hall, "Liability for Transfusion-Borne Diseases." *Journal of Product Liability, 12*(1,2) (1989), 25–44.

9. Ronald Sullivan, "Liability Waiver Barred at NYU Dental Clinic." *New York Times,* Dec. 30, 1990, p. 27.

10. Nan Morris, "State Art and Artifacts—Indemnity: A Solution Without a Problem." *Comment: Hasting Communications and Entertainment Law Journal, 12*(3) (Spring 1990), 413–422.

Chapter Fifteen

1. The reader is referred to the references in accounting at the end of this text for alternative treatments of the financial statements of nonprofit organizations.

2. Bonds are bought usually at a discount or premium. At maturity the full face value of the bond is paid. During the period between purchase and maturity, the difference between the full face value and the amount paid for the bond is amortized, that is, paid in increments.

3. We refer to the "first-in, first-out" and "last-in, last-out" methods of valuing inventory.

4. The reader may look at a standard accounting text for ratio measures of profitability.

5. Although for-profits do not generally receive gifts and contributions, this does not mean that they cannot receive them or be deemed to have received them. But no deduction is allowed. For our purposes, however, it is safe to ignore gifts and contributions to corporations or to their shareholders in the case of closely held corporations.

6. The source of this discussion is the American Institute of Certified Public Accountants, *Audits of Certain Nonprofit Organizations.* (New York: The Institute, 1981), pp. 53–54.

Chapter Sixteen

1. Susan Kenny Stevens, "Loan Fund Eases Temporary Financial Binds." *Giving Forum,* July 1990, p. 7.

2. Gregory H. Eden, "Tax-Exempt Leasing for Colleges and Universities." Richard E. Anderson and Joel W. Meyerson (eds.), *Financing Higher Education: Strategies after Tax Reform.* (San Francisco: Jossey-Bass, 1987), pp. 41–52.

3. United States Catholic Conference, *Reports on Examinations of Financial Statements and Additional Information,* 1983 and 1984. (Washington, D.C.: The Conference, April 19, 1985), p. 6.

4. American Red Cross, *Annual Report 1989,* p. 31.

5. National Urban League, Inc., *Annual Report,* 1989, p. 41.

6. Camp Fire Boys and Girls, *Annual Report,* 1988–89, p. 32.

7. Private Letter Ruling, 8910001.

Chapter Seventeen

1. U.S.C.A., 9th #88–15490, February 27, 1990.

2. Beaufort B. Longest, Jr., "Interorganizational Linkages in the Health Sector," *Health Care Management Review.* (Winter 1990), p. 18.

3. There is no pretense that some sectors of the nonprofit world have barriers to entry. Schools, hospitals, and day-care centers must meet zoning and licensing requirements, for example.

4. These are Sherman antitrust laws that are referred to in other chapters of this book, especially Chapter Nineteen.

5. Recall that each of these circles represents a maximum frontier. Each represents a point superior to the receding circle and can only be reached by the combination of policies indicated. The situation is analogous to production frontiers in economic theory of production; those frontiers are technically circles. The "prisoner's dilemma" is usually presented in a matrix. The intent in this chapter is not to present a discussion of the dilemma, but to use the principle rather than a theoretical discussion of it.

6. See Richard O. Mason and Ian I. Mitroff, *Challenging Strategic Planning Assumptions.* (New York: Wiley, 1981).

7. The Academy for Contemporary Problems, now the Academy for State and Local Governments, was owned and operated on behalf of the Council of State and Local Governments, International City Management Association, National Association of Counties, National Conference of State Legislatures, National League of Cities, and the U.S. Conference of Mayors.

Chapter Eighteen

1. *Goodwill Industries Annual Report,* 1989, p. 3.

2. YWCA, Public Policy 1988–1989, pp. 8–9.

3. The reader will recognize two strains of thought: The first is the direct identification of specific functions, as in Table 2.2, and the second is the theoretical, which is the essence of the discussion that follows.

4. Henry B. Hansmann, "Reforming Nonprofit Corporation Law." *University of Pennsylvania Law Review, 129*(3) (Jan. 1981), 397–623.

5. Ira Mark Ellmann, "Another Theory of Nonprofit Corporation." *Michigan Law Review, 80*(5) (Apr. 1982), 999–1050.

6. See Tibor Scitovsky, "The Place of Economic Welfare in Human Welfare." *Quarterly Review of Economics and Business, 13*(3) (Autumn 1973), 7–19; M. V. Pauly, "Cores and Clubs." *Public Choice, 9* (Fall 1970), 53–55; Y. K. Ng, "The Economic Theory of Clubs: Pareto Optimality Conditions." *Economica, 40*(159) (Aug. 1973), 291–298; Martin McGuire, "Private Good Clubs and Public Good Clubs: Economic Models of Group Formation." *Swedish Journal of Economics, 74* (1972), 84–99.

7. Revenue Ruling 69-144, 1969-2, Cumulative Bulletin 115.

8. Revenue Ruling 67-138, 1967-1, Cumulative Bulletin 129.

9. Reg. Section 1.501(c)(3)-1(d)(3).

10. Sue Shellenbarger, "Stimulating a Pocket of Appalachia with Venture Funds." *Wall Street Journal*, Sept. 15, 1989, p. B2.

11. *Munsell Color Foundation, Inc.* v. *U.S.* (DC, Md; 1973), 33 AFTR2d 74-339.

12. Revenue Ruling 71-506, 1971-2, Cumulative Bulletin 233.

13. Revenue Ruling 55-656, 1955-2, Cumulative Bulletin 262.

14. Revenue Ruling 78-69, 1978-1, Cumulative Bulletin 156.

15. Revenue Ruling 68-71, 1968-1, Cumulative Bulletin 249.

16. Revenue Ruling 69-441, 1969-2, Cumulative Bulletin 115.

17. Other terms for externalities are indirect effect, neighborhood effect, and spillover.

18. Revenue Ruling 74-194, 1974-1, Cumulative Bulletin 129.

19. Of course, a fee could also be charged. More is said about fees in Chapters Five and Ten.

20. Revenue Ruling 76-205, 1976, Cumulative Bulletin 154.

21. Revenue Ruling 76-204, 1976-1, Cumulative Bulletin 152.

22. Virginia Professional Standards Review Foundation 79-1, United States Tax Court No. 9167.

23. Revenue Ruling 54-296, 1954-2, Cumulative Bulletin 59.

24. Revenue Ruling 70-186, 1970-1, Cumulative Bulletin 128.

25. Horst Rittle, "Systems Analysis of the First and Second Generations." In Pierre LaConte, J. Gibson, and A. Rapport (eds.), *Human Energy Factors in Urban Planning*. (New York: Martinus Nijhoff Publishers, 1982), pp. 35–52.

26. Horst Rittle, "Systems Analysis of the First and Second Generations." In Pierre LaConte, J. Gibson, and A. Rapport (eds.), *Human Energy Factors in Urban Planning*. (New York: Martinus Nijhoff Publishers, 1982), pp. 35–52.

27. Herbert A. Simon, "Theories of Decision Making in Economics." *American Economic Review, 49*(3) (June 1959), 253–283; and *Models of Man*. (New York: Wiley, 1957).

28. The Deficit Reduction Act of 1984 placed some limitations on these transactions. The limitations are largely on the private partner. See David Warren, "Leases and Service Contracts with Tax-Exempt Entities after the DRA." *Tax Advisor*. (April 1985), pp. 239–134.

29. Kendyl K. Monroe, "Collaboration Between Tax-Exempt Research Organizations and Commercial Enterprises—Federal Income Tax Limitations," *Taxes—The Tax Magazine, 62*(5) (May 1984), 297–316.

30. IRS Revenue Letter, 9045015.

31. General Counsel Memorandum 39005 and Alan J. Yanowitz, "Using the Investment Partnership as a Charitable Activity: A Means/Ends Analysis." *Journal of Taxation, 60*(4) (April 1984), 214–218.

32. *Plumstead Theatre Society* v. *Commissioner,* 74 Tax Court 1324, 1980.

33. IRS Letter Ruling 8201072.

34. For a discussion of these principles, see Michael Schell, "The Participation of Charities in Limited Partnerships." *Yale Law Review, 93* (1984), 1330–63, and Louise A. Howells, "Community Development under Section 501(c)(3) of the Internal Revenue Code: The Charity in Economic Development." *Taxes—The Tax Magazine, 62*(2) (Feb. 1984), 83–93.

35. *Copyright Clearance Center* v. *Commissioner,* T.C., 793–810 (1982).

Chapter Nineteen

1. U.S. Rockford Memorial Corporation, CA 7, No. 1, 89–1900.

2. Transcript of case cited in text, p. 21.

3. *World Wildlife Fund, 1989 Report,* p. 65.

4. *The John F. Kennedy Center for the Performing Arts and National Symphony Orchestra, 1988–89 Annual Report,* p. 7.

5. IRS Letter Ruling 8913051, Jan. 4, 1989.

6. IRS Letter Ruling 8920021, Feb. 14, 1989.

7. IRS Letter Ruling #9010073.

8. IRS Letter Ruling #8952076, Oct. 5, 1989.

9. IRS Revenue Letter 9005068, Nov. 9, 1989.

10. Private Letter Ruling, 9043028.

SUGGESTED READINGS

American Association of Fund-Raising Counsel, Inc., *Giving in U.S.A.* (New York: American Association of Fund-Raising Counsel, issued annually).

American Institute of Certified Public Accountants, *Accounting Principles and Reporting Practices for Certain Nonprofit Organizations* (New York: The Institute, 1978).

American Institute of Certified Public Accountants, *Audit of Certain Nonprofit Organizations* (New York: The Institute, 1981).

American Institute of Certified Public Accountants (AICPA), *Accounting and Audit Guide for Health Care Organizations* (May 1, 1997).

American Institute of Certified Public Accountants, Statement of Position 98-2.

American Institute of Certified Public Accountants, *Tax Planning Tips* (New York: AICPA, produced annually).

Anthony, Robert N., Young, David W. *Management Control in Nonprofit Organizations*, 6th ed. (Boston: Irwin, McGraw-Hill, 1998).

Baker, Johnathan B. "The Antitrust Analysis of Hospital Mergers and the Transformation of the Hospital Industry." *Law and Contemporary Problems, 51,* no. 2 (Spring 1988), 93–164.

Baughman, James. *Trustees, Trusteeships and the Public Good* (New York: Quorum Books, 1987).

Bell, J., Snyder, H., Tien, C., and Silas, J. "The Prescription of Charitable Health Care Assets." *Health Affairs, 16,* 1997, 125–130.

Bergman, Jed, Bowen, I. William G., Nygen, Thomas I. *Managing Change in the Nonprofit Sector* (San Francisco: Jossey-Bass, 1995).

Better Business Bureau of Washington, D.C. v. United States, 326 U.S. 279, 283 (1945).

Blum, Steven. "Tax-Free Exchanges of Appreciated Art." *Columbia Journal of Law and the Arts, 14*(4), 557–570.

Bookman, Mark. *Protecting Your Organization's Tax-Exempt Status* (San Francisco: Jossey-Bass, 1991).

Boris, Elizabeth, and Mosher-Williams, Rachel. "Nonprofit Advocacy Organizations: Assessing the Definitions, Classifications, and Data." *Nonprofit and Voluntary Sector Quarterly, 27*(4), December 1998, 488–506.

Bowen, William G. *Inside the Boardroom: Governance by Directors and Trustees* (New York: Wiley, 1994).

Bowen, William G. "When a Business Leader Joins a Nonprofit Board." *Harvard Business Review,* September–October, 1996.

Bradshaw, P., Murray, V., and Wolpin, Julian. "Do Nonprofit Boards Make a Difference?" *Nonprofit and Voluntary Sector Quarterly, 21,* 1992, 227–249.

Brauer, Lawrence M., and Kaiser, Charles F. "Tax-Exempt Health Care Organizations Community Board and Conflicts of Interest Policy." In *Continuing Professional Education: Exempt Organizations* (Department of the Treasury: Internal Revenue Service, July 1996).

Bryce, Herrington J. "The Corporate Director on the Nonprofit Board: A Guide to Nonprofit Service." *Director's Monthly,* Apr. 1988.

Bryce, Herrington J. "Tired of Complicated Retirement Plans?" *Not-for-Profit Financial Strategies, 13*(6), June 1998, p. 3.

Bryce, Herrington J. "Make the Most of Gifts of Appreciated Stocks." *Not-for-Profit Financial Strategies,* July 1998, p. 8. Bryce, Herrington J. "10 Nonprofit Board Guidelines." *Director's Monthly,* July–Aug. 1988.

Bryce, Herrington J. "Is Your NPO at Risk for Fraud?" *Not-for-Profit Financial Strategies, 2*(9), September 1998, p. 1.

Bryce, Herrington J. "Planning for New Rules on Allocating Joint Costs." *Not-for-Profit Financial Strategies, 2*(9), September 1998, p. 1.

Bryce, Herrington J. "Single Audit Update." *Not-for-Profit Financial Strategies, 3*(10), November 1998, p. 3.

Bryce, Herrington J. "Should You File as a Lobbyist?" *Not-for-Profit Financial Strategies, 3*(10), November 1998, p. 5.

Bryce, Herrington J. "Accounting for Gifts and Contributions." *Not-for-Profit Financial Strategies, 10*(12), December 1998.

Bryce, Herrington J. "Joint Ventures: Teaming Up with For-Profits." *Nonprofit World, 7*(1), January/February 1989, 11–13.

Bryce, Herrington J. "Measuring the Liquidity of Life Insurance Companies." *Journal of the American Society of CLU and ChFC,* January 1994, 58–62.

Bryce, Herrington J. "Profitability of HMOs: Does Non-profit Status Make a Difference?" *Health Policy, 28,* 1994, 197–210.

Bryce, Herrington J. "A Fiduciary Road Map." *Nonprofit Times,* May 1995, p. 45.

Bryce, Herrington J. *The Nonprofit's Boards Role in Establishing Financial Policies* (Washington, D.C.: National Center for Nonprofit Boards, 1996).

Bryson, John M. *Strategic Planning for Public and Nonprofit Organizations* (San Francisco: Jossey-Bass, 1995).

Butler, P. "State Policy Issues in Nonprofit Conversions." *Health Affairs, 16,* 1997, 69–84.

Buzbee, William W., and Dineen, Patricia M. "How to Deal with Gifts of Contaminated Real Estate." *The Philanthropy Monthly, 24*(2), March 1991, 6–14.

Chait, R. P., and Taylor, B. E. "Charting the Territory of Nonprofit Boards." *Harvard Business Review,* Jan.–Feb. 1989, no. 1, pp. 44–139.

Conger, Jay A., Finegold, David, and Lawler, Edward E. III. "Appraising Boardroom Performance." *Harvard Business Review, 76*(1), February 1998, 136–148.

Cress, William P., and Pettijohn, James. "A Survey of Budget-Related Planning and Control Policies and Procedures." *Journal of Accounting Education, 3*(2), Fall 1985, 61–80.

deSmit, J., and Rade, N. L. "Rational and Non-Rational Planning." *Long-Range Planning, 13*(2), 1980, 82–101.

Dewees, Seth. "Healthcare Organizations and 501(c)(3) Uncertainty in the Post-Geisinger World." *Health Matrix: Journal of Law-Medicine, 7,* Summer 1997, 351–380.

Distelhorst, Garis. "When Associations Become Entrepreneurs." *Association Management,* February 1985, pp. 109–111.

Douglas, James, *Why Charity?* (Beverly Hills: Sage Publications, 1983).

Drucker, Peter F. "What Business Can Learn from Nonprofits." *Harvard Business Review,* July–Aug. 1989, no. 4, 88–94.

Duca, Diane. *Nonprofit Boards: Roles, Responsibilities and Performance* (New York: Wiley, 1996).

Dzamba, Andrew. *Retirement Plans for Not-for-Profit Organizations* (San Diego: Harcourt Brace, 1998).

Feldstein, Martin (ed.). *The Economics of Art Museums* (Chicago, Illinois: University of Chicago Press, 1991).

Financial Accounting Standards Board, *Accounting for Contributions Received and Contributions Made and Capitalization of Works of Art, Historical Treasures, and Similar Assets.* Exposure Draft, No. 096–B, October 31, 1990.

Foster, Mary, Becker, Howard, Terrano, Richard. *1999 Miller Not-for-Profit Reporting* (Orlando: Harcourt Brace & Company, 1998).

Foundation & Corporate Giving (Rockville, MD: The Taft Group, annually).

The Foundation Center (Annual Survey of Compensation).

Fry, Robert P. *Nonprofit Investment Policies* (New York: John Wiley, 1997).

Geisinger Health Plan v. *Commissioner,* 985, F 2d, 1210 (3rd Cir. 1993), 62 TCM 1656 (1991).

Giving and Volunteering in the United States (Washington, D.C.: The Independent Sector, issued every two years).

Glenn, Richard W., and Glenn, A. S. Vol. 70 TCM (CCH), pp. 453–458.

Golensky, M. "The Board-Executive Relationship in Nonprofit Organizations: Partnership or Power Struggle?" *Nonprofit Management and Leadership, 4*(2), 1993, 177–192.

Green, J. C., and Griesinger, D. W. "Board Performance and Organizational Effectiveness in Nonprofit Social Service Organizations." *Nonprofit Management and Leadership, 6,* 1996, 381–402.

Greiner, Larry E. "Evolution and Revolution as Organizations Grow." *Harvard Business Review,* May–June 1998, *76*(3), pp. 51–155.

Gronbjerg, Kirsten. *Understanding Nonprofit Funding: Managing Revenues in Social Services and Community Development Organizations* (San Francisco: Jossey-Bass, 1993).

Harlan, S. L., and Saidel, J. R. "Board Members' Influence on the Government-Nonprofit Relationship." *Nonprofit Management and Leadership, 5*(1), 1994, 173–196.

Hausmann, Henry B. "Why Do Universities Have Endowments?" *Journal of Legal Studies, 19,* 1990, pp. 3–42.

Herzlinger, Regina E. "Effective Oversight." *Harvard Business Review,* July/August 1994.

Herzlinger, Regina E. "Measuring the Financial Performance of Nonprofit Organizations: Solutions Manual." Harvard Business School, N9–197–111, May 19, 1997.

Herzlinger, Regina E. "Measuring the Financial Performance of Nonprofit Organizations: Text and Cases." Harvard Business School, N9–197–111, May 19, 1997.

Herzingler, R. E., and Krasker, W. S. "Who Profits from Nonprofits." *Harvard Business Review, 87*(10), 1987, 93–106.

Herzlinger, Regina, and Nitterhouse, D. *Financial Accounting and Managerial Control for Nonprofit Organizations* (Cincinnati: South-Western, 1994).

Hilgenkamp, Ramona K. "Identify the Nonprofit." *Harvard Business School,* 9–195–215, Rev. March 15, 1996.

Hodgkinson, Virginia A., Weitzman, M. S., Crutchfield, E. A., Heffron, A. J., and Kirsch, A. D. *Giving and Volunteering in the United States: Findings from a National Survey* (annual edition). (Washington, D.C.: Independent Sector).

Hodgkinson, Virginia A., Weitzman, Murray S., Toppe, Christopher M., and Noga, Stephen M. *Nonprofit Almanac 1992–1993: Dimensions of the Independent Sector* (San Francisco: Jossey-Bass, 1992).

Hollis, S. "Strategic and Economic Factors in the Hospital Conversion Process." *Health Affairs, 16,* 1997, 131–143.

Hopkins, Bruce R. *The Tax Law of Charitable Giving* (New York: Wiley, 1993).

Horwritz, Paul J. "Scientology in Court: A Comparative Analysis and Some Thoughts on Selected Issues in Law and Religion." *De Paul Law Review, 47*(1), Fall 1997, 85–154.

Houle, Cyril. *Governing Boards* (San Francisco: Jossey-Bass, 1989).

Housing Pioneers v. *Commissioner,* 65 TCM (CCH), 2191, (1993), (9th Cir., 1995).

Internal Revenue Bulletin 1989–37, September 11, 1989, p. 4.

Internal Revenue Code, Sections 4943, 6056.

Internal Revenue Letter, #9516040.

Internal Revenue Regulation 601, 201(n)(b).

Internal Revenue Service, Department of the Treasury, *Charitable Contributions,* Publication 526 (Washington, D.C.: U.S. Government Printing Office).

Internal Revenue Service, Department of the Treasury, *Determining the Value of Donated Property,* Publication 561, rev. November (Washington, D.C.: U.S. Government Printing Office).

Internal Revenue Service, Department of the Treasury, *Federal Estate and Gift Taxes,* Publication 448, rev. September 1989 (Washington, D.C.: U.S. Government Printing Office, 1989).

Internal Revenue Service, U.S. Department of the Treasury, *Instructions for Form 990.*

Internal Revenue Service, U.S. Department of the Treasury, *Pension and Annuity Income,* Publication 575, Revised January 1991.

Internal Revenue Service, U.S. Department of the Treasury. *Tax Exempt Status for Your Organization,* Publication 557. Revised. May 1997.

Internal Revenue Service, Department of Treasury, *Tax Information for Private Foundations and Foundation Managers,* Publication 578, rev. January 1989 (Washington, D.C.: U.S. Government Printing Office).

Internal Revenue Service, Department of the Treasury, *Tax Information on Corporations,* Publication 542, rev. November (Washington, D.C.: U.S. Government Printing Office).

Internal Revenue Service, U.S. Department of the Treasury, *Tax on Unrelated Business Income of the Tax Exempt Organization,* Publication 598, Revised November 1987.

Internal Revenue Service, U.S. Department of the Treasury, *Tax Sheltered Annuity Programs for Employees of Public Schools and Certain Tax-Exempt Organizations,* Revised December.

Internal Revenue Service, U.S. Department of the Treasury, *U.S. Corporation Income Tax Package,* Package 1120.

Internal Revenue Service, Publication 535.

Internal Revenue Service, Publication 1391: *Deductibility of Payments Made to Charities Conducting Fund-Raising Events.*

Jackson, Anthony. "Exclusion of Diocesan Liability for Negligence of Parish Priest." *University of Cincinnati Law Review, 58*(1), 323–339.

Jackson, Douglas, and Thomas, Holland. "Measuring the Effectiveness of Nonprofit Boards." *Nonprofit and Voluntary Sector Quarterly, 27*(2), June 1998, 159–182.

Johnson, Edward A., and Weeks, Kent M. "To Save a College: Independent College Trustees and Decisions on Financial Exigency, Endowment Use, and Closure." *Journal of College and University Law, 12*(4) Spring 1986, 455–486.

Jones, Tonia Peoles. "Constitutional Law—Religious Freedom—Forced Disclosure of Church Records Pursuant to State Nonprofit Corporation Statute Prohibited." *University of Arkansas Law Review, 12*(1), 1989–90, 75–97.

Kahn, Jeffrey. "Organization's Liability for Tools of Volunteers." *University of Pennsylvania Law Review,* 1985, 1433–1452.

Kearns, Kevin. *Managing for Accountability* (San Francisco: Jossey-Bass, 1998).

Kotler, Neil, and Kotler, Philip. *Museum Strategy and Marketing* (San Francisco: Jossey-Bass, 1998).

Kotler, Philip, and Anderson, Alan. *Strategic Marketing for Non-Profit Organizations* (Englewood Cliffs, N.J.: Prentice Hall, 1996).

Kramer, Ralph M. *Voluntary Agencies in the Welfare State* (Berkeley, Calif.: University of California Press, 1981).

Kurtz, Daniel L. *Board Liability* (Mt. Kisco, N.Y.: Moyer Bell Limited, 1988).

Lajoux, Alexandra Reed. *The Art of M&A Integration* (New York: McGraw-Hill, 1998).

Letts, Christine, Ryan, William P., and Grossman, Allen. (New York: Wiley, 1998).

Lientz, Bennet P., and Rea, Kathryn P. *Strategic Systems Planning and Management* (San Diego: Harcourt Brace, 1998).

Light, Paul, *Sustaining Innovation* (San Francisco: Jossey-Bass, 1998).

McMahon, T. "Fair Value? The Conversion of Non-profit HMOs." *University of San Francisco Law Review, 30,* 1996, pp. 355–394.

Massy, William F. *Endowment Perspectives, Policies, and Management.* (Washington, D.C.: National Association of College and University Business Officers, 1990).

National Health Council. *Accounting and Financial Reporting for Voluntary Health and Welfare Organizations* (New York: National Health Council, 1988).

Nelsen, William C. "Incentive-Based Management for Nonprofit Organizations." *Nonprofit Management and Leadership, 2*(1), Fall 1991, 59–69.

The Nonprofit Times (annual survey of compensation of nonprofit managers).

The NSFRE Fund-Raising Dictionary (New York: Wiley, Inc.).

Office of Management and Budget (OMB) Circular A–133.

Omnibus Budget Reconciliation Act of 1987, particularly sections 6113, 6711, and 6710.

O'Neill, Michael. "Philanthropic Dimensions of Mutual Benefit Organizations." *Nonprofit and Voluntary Sector Quarterly, 23*(1), 199.

Peterson, Donald J., and Massengill, Douglas. "The Negligent Hiring Doctrine: A Growing Dilemma for Employees." *Employee Relations Law Journal, 15*(3), Winter 1989/90, 419–432.

Philanthropy Monthly, Survey of State Laws Regulating Charitable Solicitation. New Melford, Connecticut, 1991 update.

Razek, Joseph R., and Price, Shirley H. "Gain Control of Your Organization's Finances: Budgetary Control Reports." *The Nonprofit World, 7*(1), January–February 1989, 29–33.

Reed, Stanley, and Lajoux, Alexandra. *The Art of M&A* (Burr Ridge, Ill.: Irwin Professional Publishing, 1995).

Revenue Procedure 90–21 in *Internal Revenue Bulletin,* No. 1990–8, Feb. 20, 1990, p. 20.

Revenue Procedure 90–27, 1990–1, Cumulative Bulletin 514.

Revenue Procedure 98–19 to Section 501(c)(3).

Revenue Ruling 81–43, 1981–43, 1981–1, Cumulative Bulletin 350.

Revenue Ruling 98–15, *Internal Revenue Bulletin,* 1998–12, March 23, 1998.

Rittle, Horst. "Systems Analysis of the First and Second Generations" and "Structure and Usefulness of Planning Information Systems." In Pierre LaConte, J. Gibson, and A. Rapport (eds.), *Human Energy Factors in Urban Planning* (New York: Martinus Nijhoff Publishers, 1982, pp. 35–52, 53–64.)

Rose-Ackerman, Susan. "Unfair Competition and Corporate Income Taxation." *Stanford Law Review, 34*(5) (May 1982), 1017–1039.

Rubin, Helena C. "Nonprofit Hospitals and the Federal Tax Exemption: A Fresh Prescription." *Health Matrix Journal of Medicine, 7,* Summer 1997, 321–426.

Rulppel, Warren. *Not-for-Profit Organization Audits* (San Diego: Harcourt Brace, 1998).

Salamon, Lester M. "Foundations as Investment Managers: Part I: The Process." *Nonprofit Management and Leadership, 3*(2), Winter 1992, 117–137.

Salamon, Lester M. "Foundations as Investment Managers: Part II: The Performance." *Nonprofit Management and Leadership, 3*(3), Spring 1993.

Salcoski, Carol J. "Looking a Gift Stock in the Mouth." *Michigan Law Review, 88*(3) Dec. 1989, 604–634.

Schervish, P. G., and Havens, J. J. "Embarking on a Republic of Benevolence? New Survey Findings on Charitable Giving." *Nonprofit and Voluntary Sector Quarterly, 27*(2), 1998, 237–242.

Schmolha, Leo L., "Income Taxation of Charitable Remainder Trusts and Decedents' Estates: Sixty-Six Years of Astigmatism." *Tax Law Review, 40*(1), Fall 1984, 1–350.

Sharpe, Robert, *Planning Giving Simplified: The Gift, the Giver, and the Gift Planner* (New York: Wiley, Inc.)

Sims, Joe. "A New Approach to the Analysis of Hospital Mergers." *Antitrust Law Journal, 64,* 1996.

Sims, Ronald R. *Reinventing Training and Development* (Westport, Conn.: Quorum, 1998).

Singer, Mark, and Yankey, John. "Organizational Metamorphosis: A Study of Eighteen Nonprofit Mergers, Acquisitions, Consolidations." *Nonprofit Management and Leadership, 1,* Summer 1991, 357–369.

Smith, D. H. "The Rest of the Nonprofit Sector: Grassroots Associations as the Dark Matter Ignored in Prevailing Flat Earth Maps of the Sector." *Nonprofit and Voluntary Sector Quarterly, 26*(2), 1997, 114–131.

The Society for Nonprofit Organizations. *Nonprofit World.* (Annual Survey of compensation of nonprofit managers).

Steinberg, Richard. "Economic Perspectives on the Regulation of Charitable Solicitation." *Case Western Reserve University Law Review, 39*(3), 1988–89, 775–797.

Steiner, George A. *Strategic Planning* (New York: Free Press, 1979).

Taylor, Barbara E., Chait, Richard P., and Holland, Thomas P. "The New Work of the Nonprofit Board." *Harvard Business Review,* September–October, 1996.

Tremper, Charles Robert. "Compensation for Harm from Charitable Activity." *Cornell Law Review, 76*(2), January 1991, 401–475.

United Way. *Accounting and Financial Reporting: A Guide for United Ways and Not-for-Profit Human Service Organizations* (Alexandria, Virginia, 1989).

United States v. *Carilion Health System and Community Hospital of Roanoke Valley,* U.S. District Court of Western District of Virginia, Roanoke Division, 2/18/89.

U.S. Department of Labor, *Employer Centers and Child Care Liability Insurance* (Washington, D.C.: U.S. Government Printing Office, Dec. 1989).

U.S. Supreme Court, *Robert L. Hernandez* v. *Commissioner,* No. 87–963.

Veres, John C., and Sims, Ronald R. *Human Resource Management and the American with Disabilities Act* (Westport, Conn., Quorum, 1995).

Veres, Joseph A. "Using Pooled Income Funds to Pass ITC and Depreciation Through to Life-Income Donors." *Journal of Taxation, 61*(1), July 1984, 28–33.

Virtue, Juliet. "Tort Liabilities for California Public Facilities." *Santa Clara Law Review, 29*(2), Spring 1989, 459–487.

Wellington, Ralph C., and Camisa, Vance G. "The Trade Association of Product Safety Standards: Of Good Samaritans and Liability." *Wayne Law Review, 35*(1), Fall 1988, 37–61.

White, Douglas E. *The Art of Planned Giving* (New York: Wiley, 1995).

Wilkins, Aaron, and Jacobson, Peter. "Fiduciary Responsibilities in Nonprofit Health Care Conversions." *Health Care Management Review, 23*(1), 1998, 77–90.

Willis, Robert T. "Prudent Investor Rule Gives Trustees New Guidelines." *Estate Planning,* November 1992.

Young, Dennis. *If Not for Profit, For What* (San Francisco: Lexington Books, 1983).

Zander, Alvin. *Making Boards Effective: The Dynamics of Nonprofit Governance* (San Francisco: Jossey-Bass, 1993).

INDEX